by
NAOKI URASAWA
STORY by
HOKUSEI KATSUSHIKA, TAKASHI NAGASAKI

2

by
## NAOKI URASAWA
STORY by
## HOKUSEI KATSUSHIKA, TAKASHI NAGASAKI

# MASTER
# KEATON

# CONTENTS

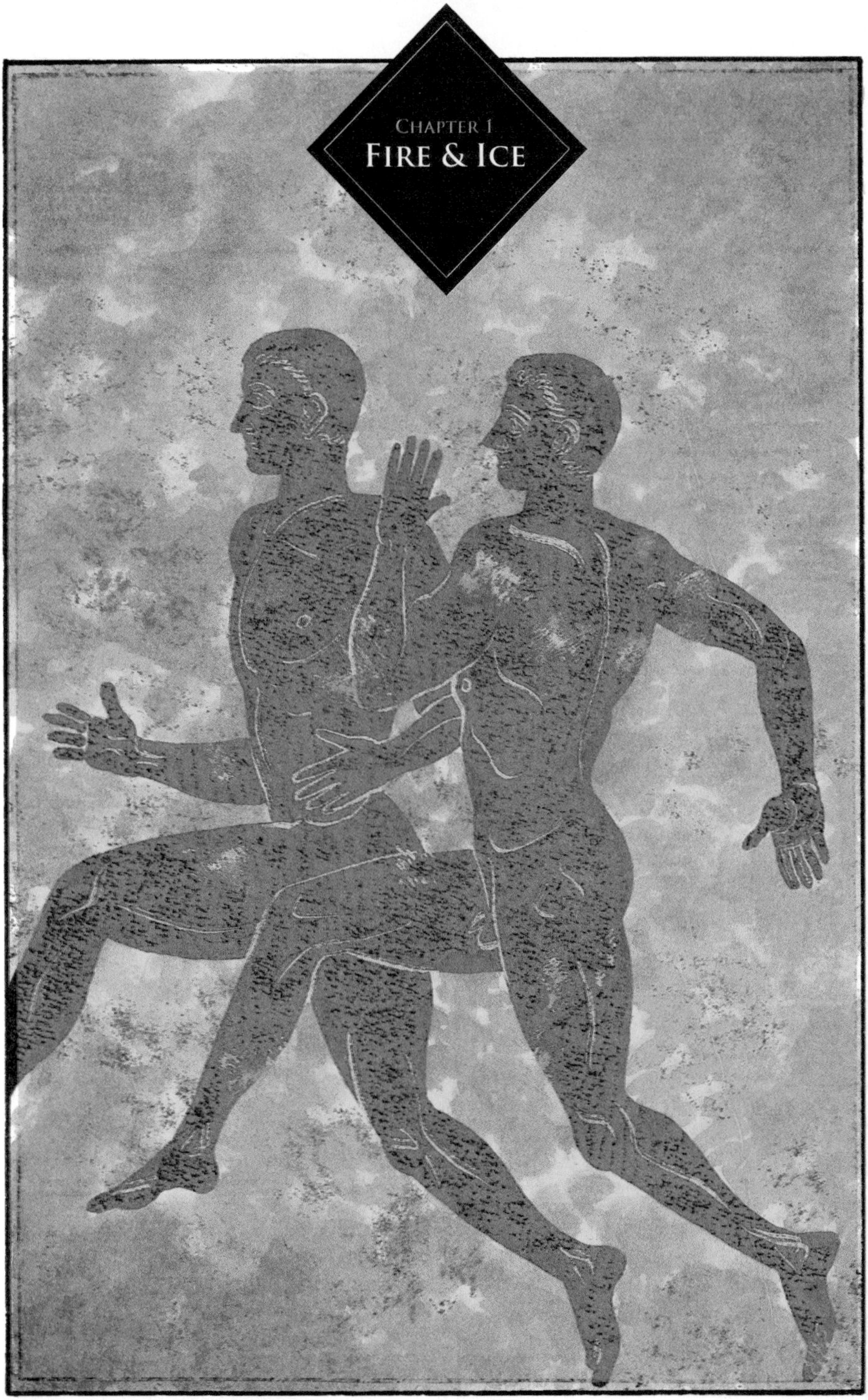
CHAPTER 1
FIRE & ICE

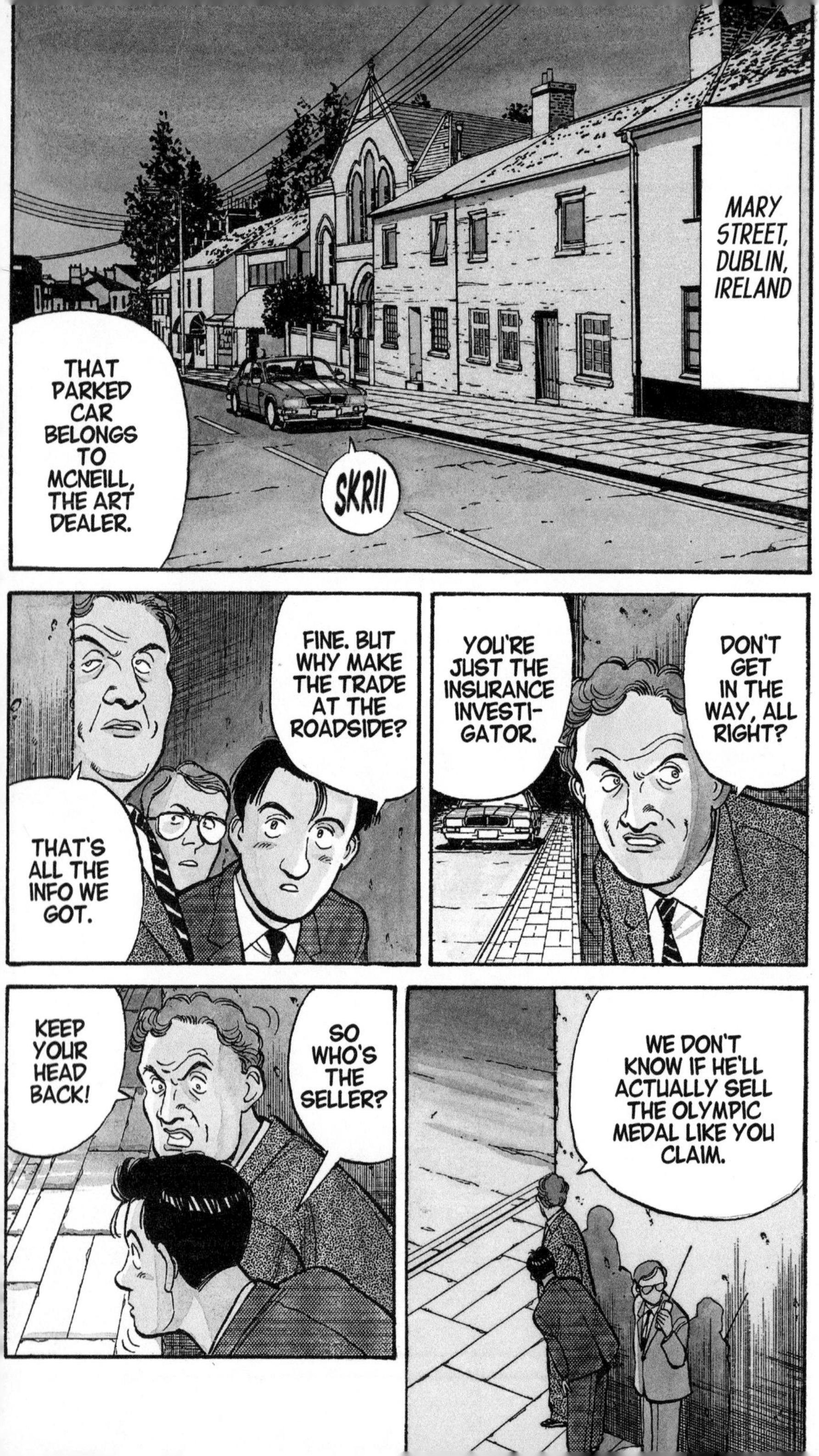
MARY STREET, DUBLIN, IRELAND
THAT PARKED CAR BELONGS TO MCNEILL, THE ART DEALER.
SKRII
DON'T GET IN THE WAY, ALL RIGHT?
YOU'RE JUST THE INSURANCE INVESTI- GATOR.
FINE. BUT WHY MAKE THE TRADE AT THE ROADSIDE?
THAT'S ALL THE INFO WE GOT.
WE DON'T KNOW IF HE'LL ACTUALLY SELL THE OLYMPIC MEDAL LIKE YOU CLAIM.
SO WHO'S THE SELLER?
KEEP YOUR HEAD BACK!

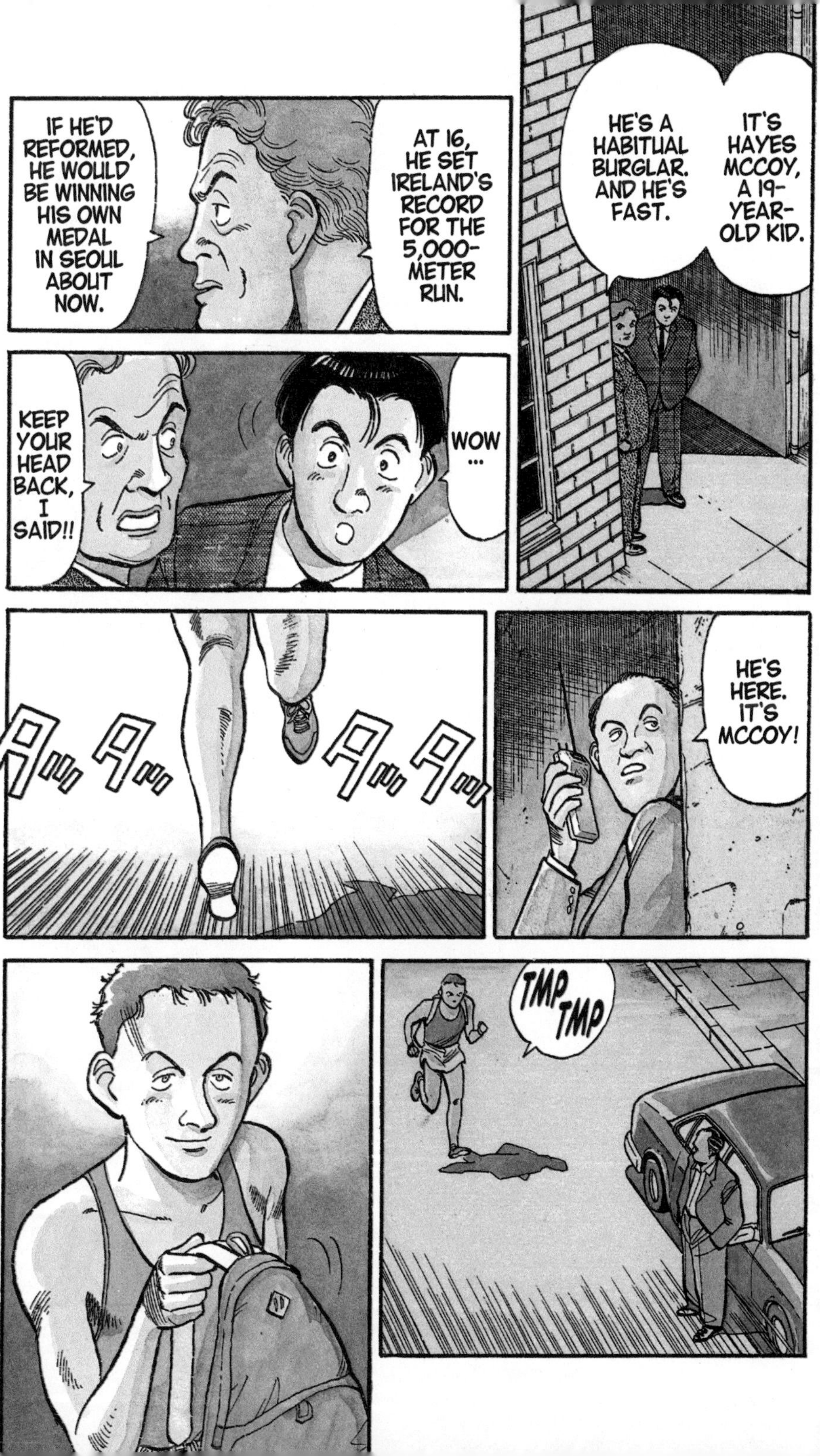
IT'S HAYES MCCOY, A 19-YEAR-OLD KID.
HE'S A HABITUAL BURGLAR. AND HE'S FAST.
AT 16, HE SET IRELAND'S RECORD FOR THE 5,000-METER RUN.
IF HE'D REFORMED, HE WOULD BE WINNING HIS OWN MEDAL IN SEOUL ABOUT NOW.
WOW ...
KEEP YOUR HEAD BACK, I SAID!!
HE'S HERE. IT'S MCCOY!
タッタッ
タッタッ
TMP TMP

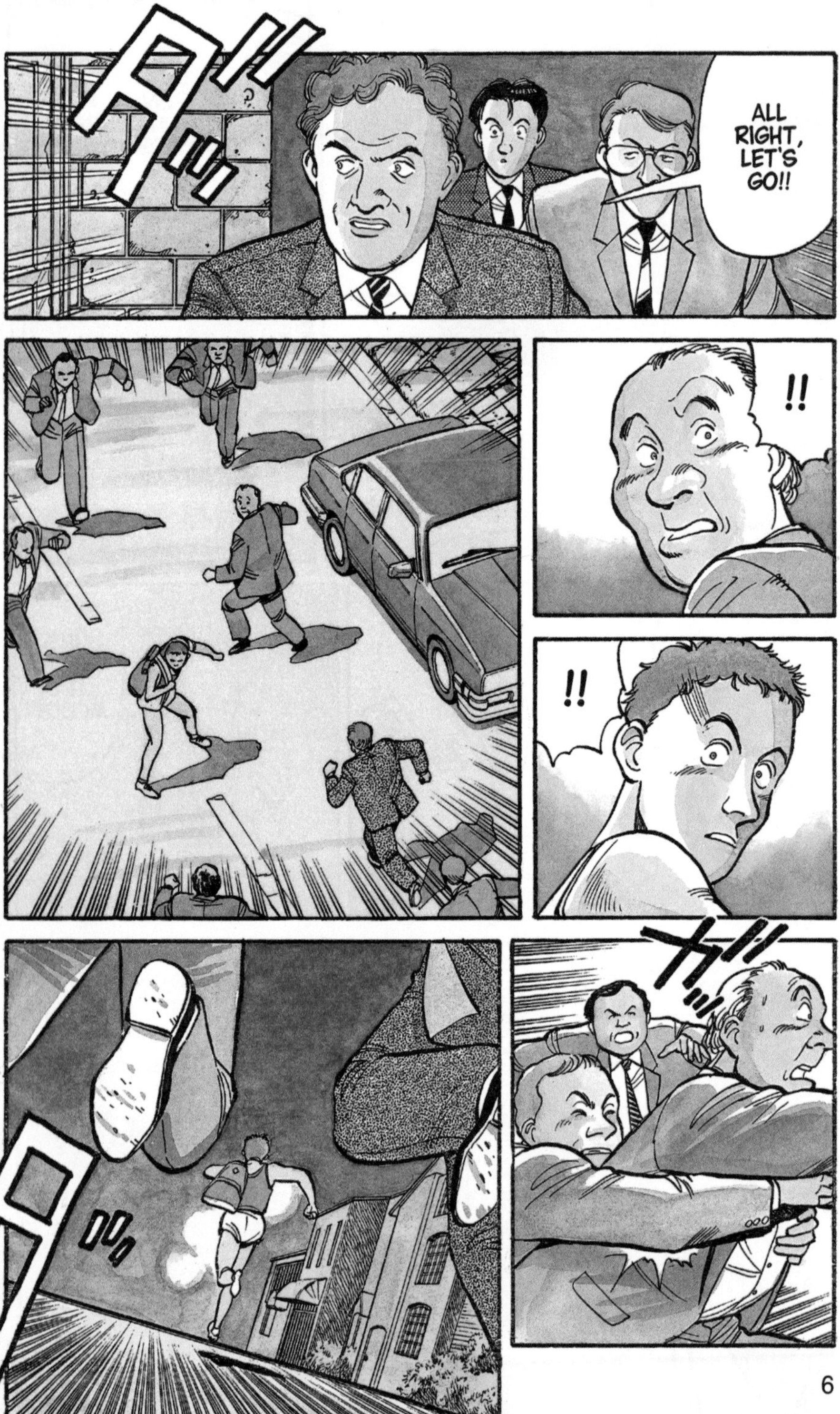
ALL RIGHT, LET'S GO!!
!!
!!

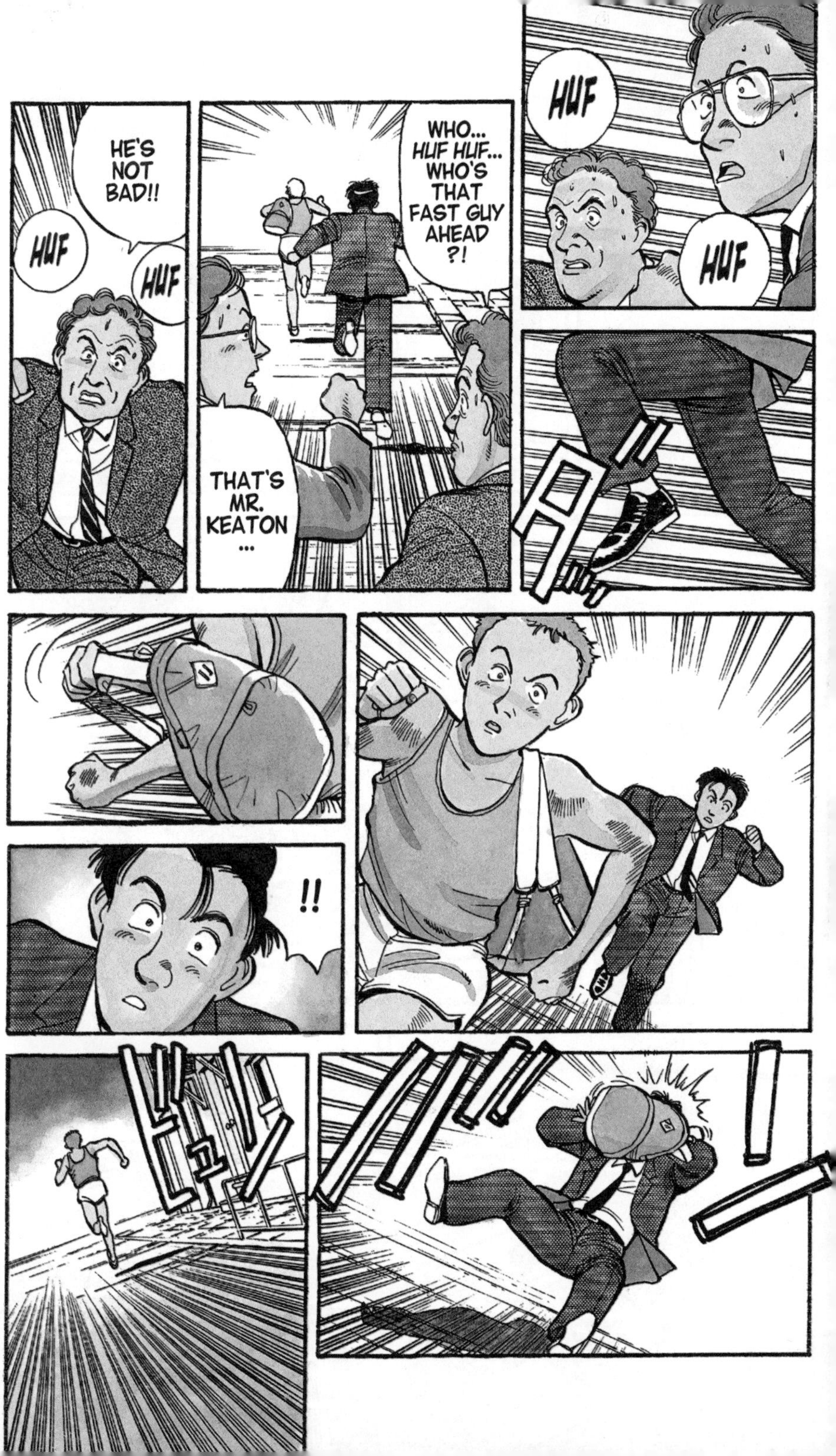
HUF
HUF
WHO... HUF HUF... WHO'S THAT FAST GUY AHEAD ?!
THAT'S MR. KEATON ...
HE'S NOT BAD!!
HUF
HUF
!!

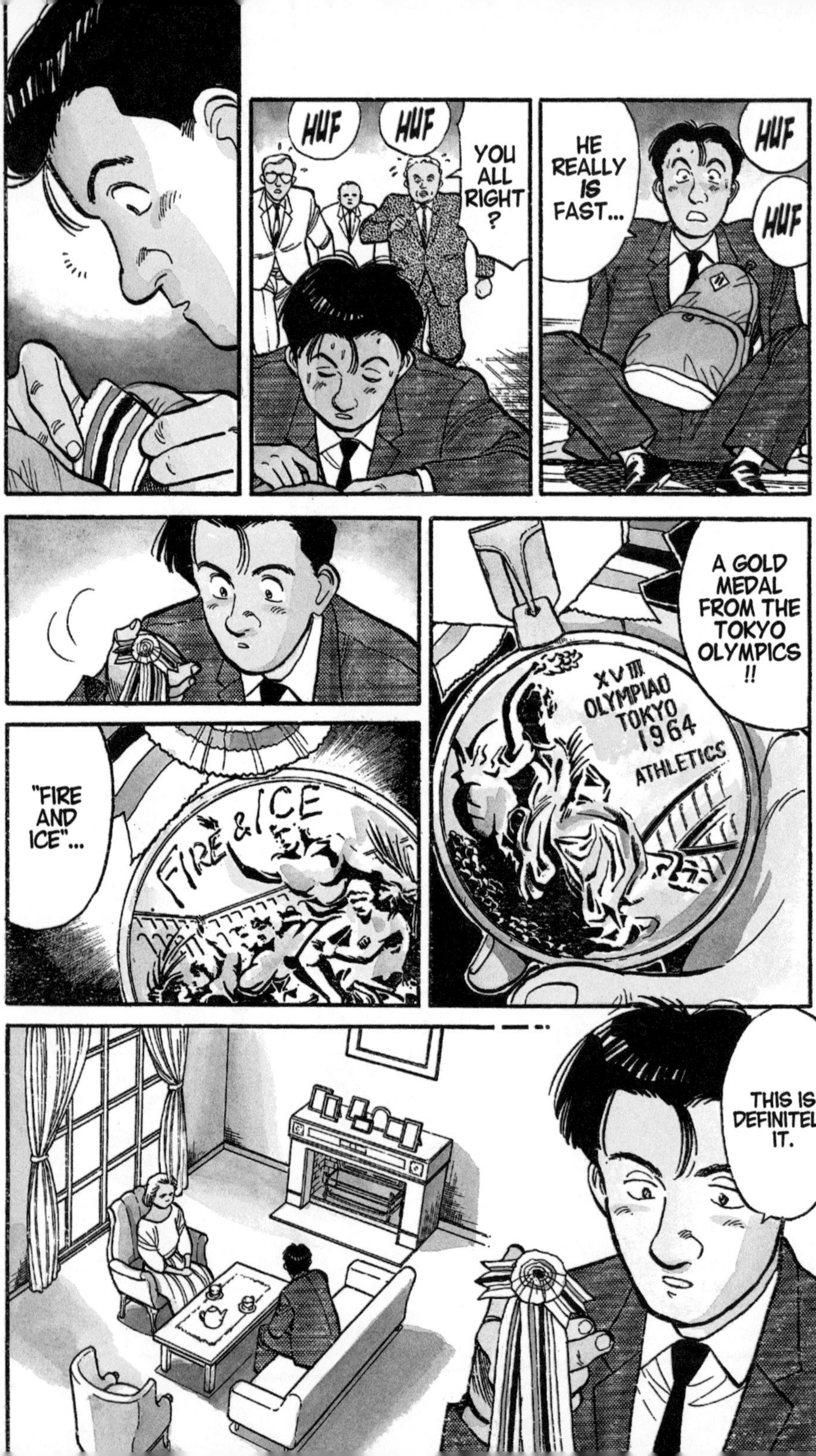
HE REALLY IS FAST...
HUF
HUF
HUF
HUF
YOU ALL RIGHT?
A GOLD MEDAL FROM THE TOKYO OLYMPICS !!
XVIII OLYMPIAO TOKYO 1964
ATHLETICS
"FIRE AND ICE"...
FIRE & ICE
THIS IS DEFINITELY IT.

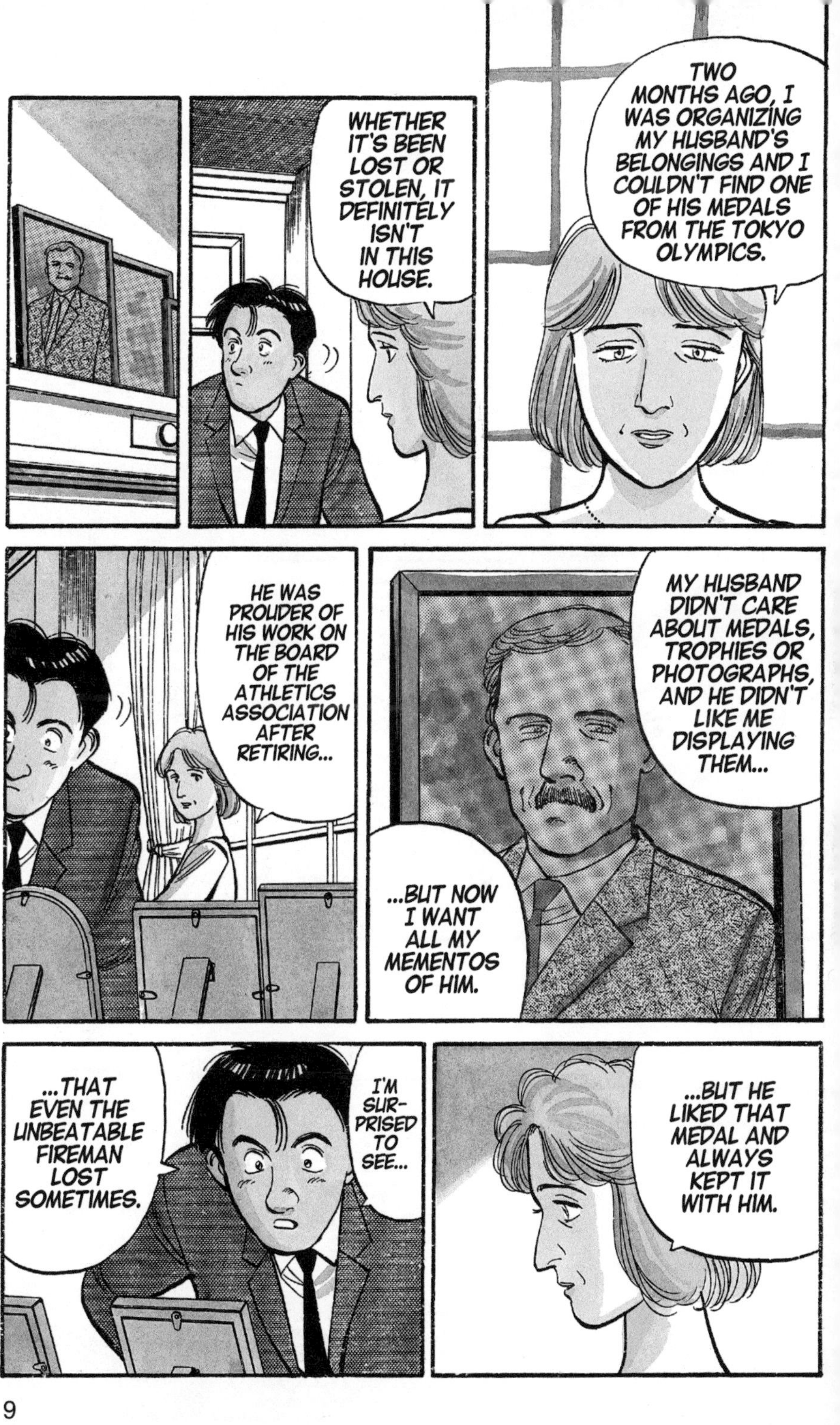
TWO MONTHS AGO, I WAS ORGANIZING MY HUSBAND'S BELONGINGS AND I COULDN'T FIND ONE OF HIS MEDALS FROM THE TOKYO OLYMPICS.
WHETHER IT'S BEEN LOST OR STOLEN, IT DEFINITELY ISN'T IN THIS HOUSE.
MY HUSBAND DIDN'T CARE ABOUT MEDALS, TROPHIES OR PHOTOGRAPHS, AND HE DIDN'T LIKE ME DISPLAYING THEM...
...BUT NOW I WANT ALL MY MEMENTOS OF HIM.
HE WAS PROUDER OF HIS WORK ON THE BOARD OF THE ATHLETICS ASSOCIATION AFTER RETIRING...
...BUT HE LIKED THAT MEDAL AND ALWAYS KEPT IT WITH HIM.
I'M SUR-PRISED TO SEE...
...THAT EVEN THE UNBEATABLE FIREMAN LOST SOMETIMES.

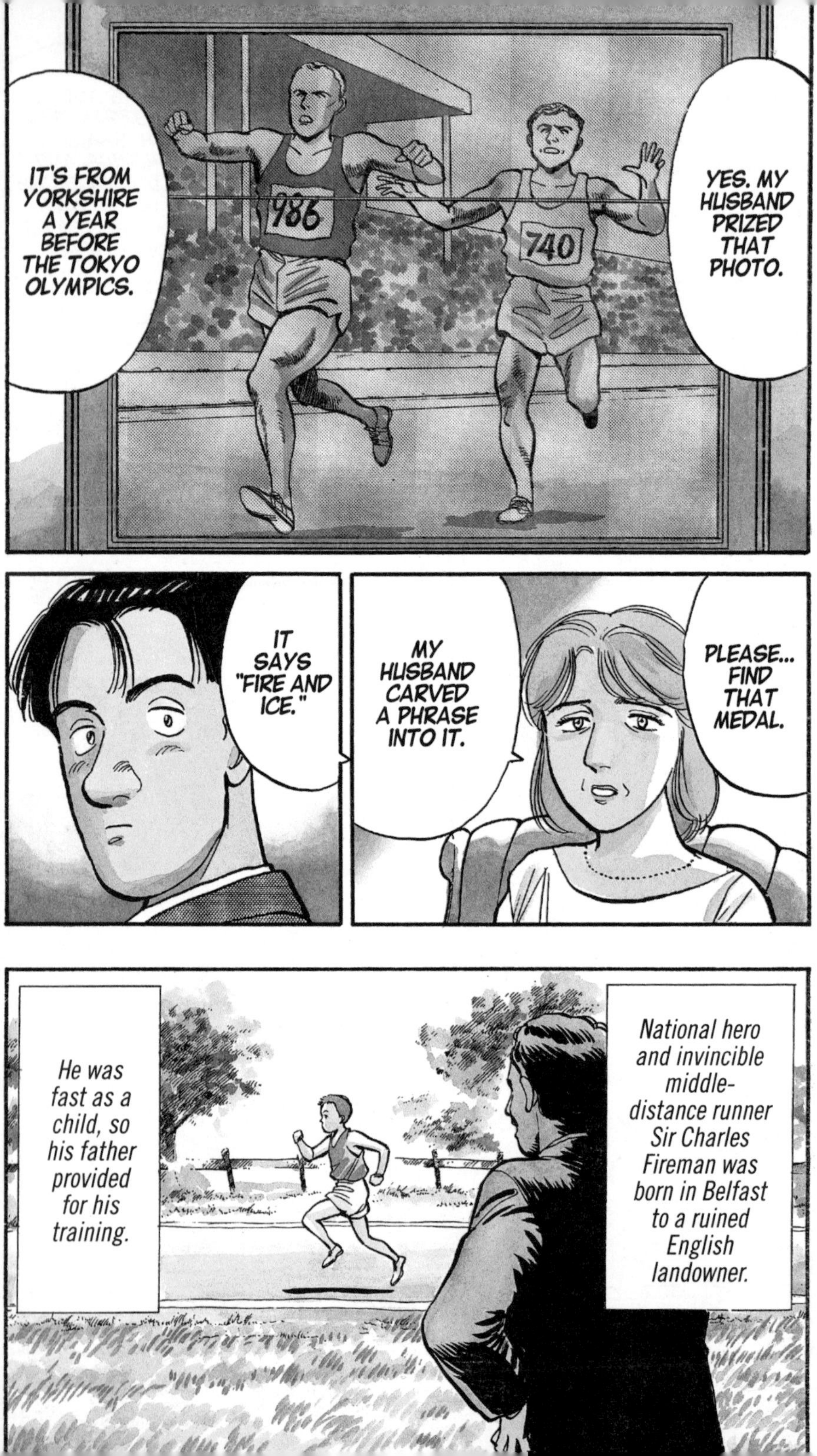
YES. MY HUSBAND PRIZED THAT PHOTO.
740
986
IT'S FROM YORKSHIRE A YEAR BEFORE THE TOKYO OLYMPICS.
PLEASE... FIND THAT MEDAL.
MY HUSBAND CARVED A PHRASE INTO IT.
IT SAYS "FIRE AND ICE."
National hero and invincible middle-distance runner Sir Charles Fireman was born in Belfast to a ruined English landowner.
He was fast as a child, so his father provided for his training.

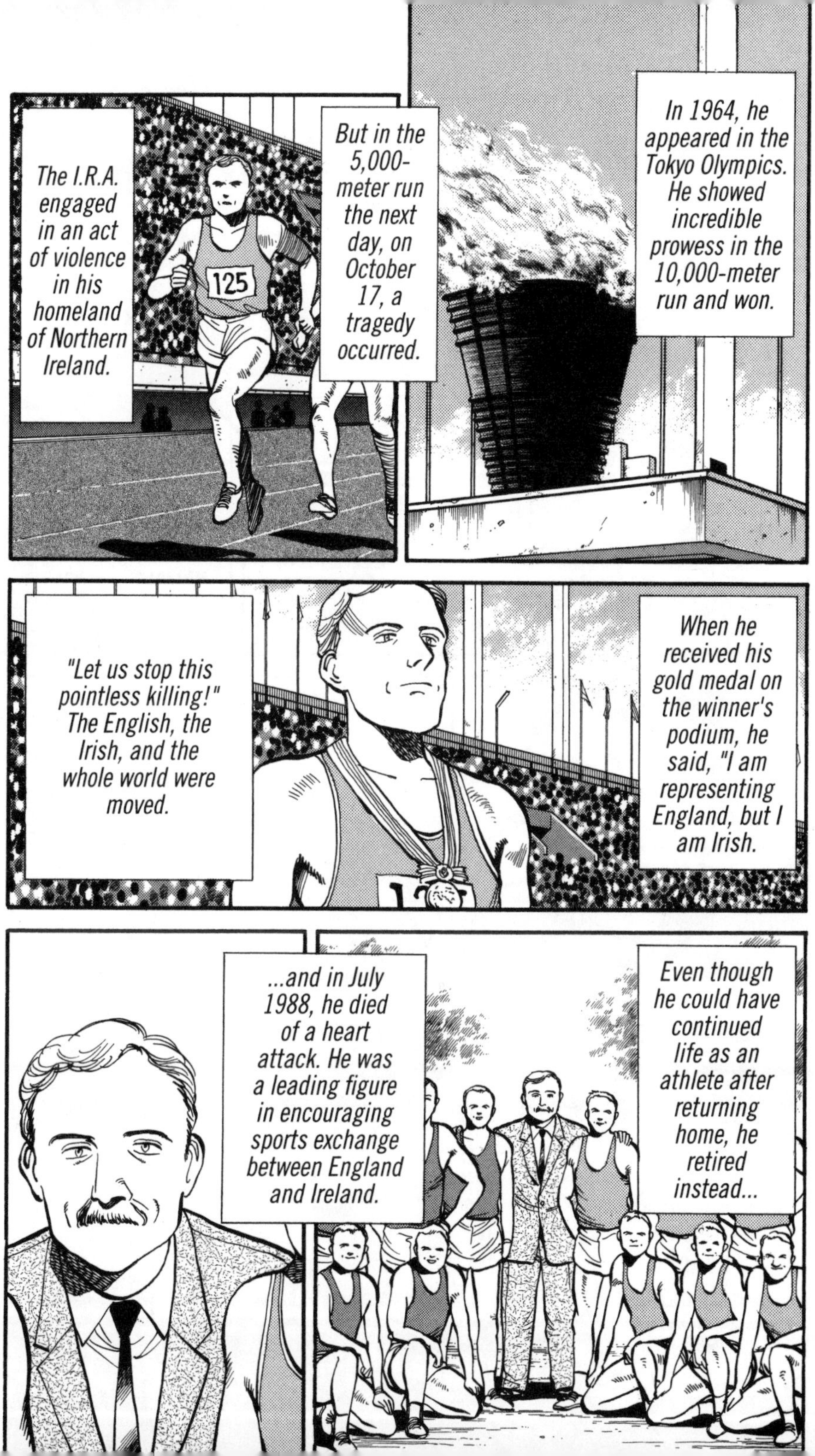
In 1964, he appeared in the Tokyo Olympics. He showed incredible prowess in the 10,000-meter run and won.
But in the 5,000-meter run the next day, on October 17, a tragedy occurred.
The I.R.A. engaged in an act of violence in his homeland of Northern Ireland.
125
When he received his gold medal on the winner's podium, he said, "I am representing England, but I am Irish.
"Let us stop this pointless killing!" The English, the Irish, and the whole world were moved.
Even though he could have continued life as an athlete after returning home, he retired instead...
...and in July 1988, he died of a heart attack. He was a leading figure in encouraging sports exchange between England and Ireland.

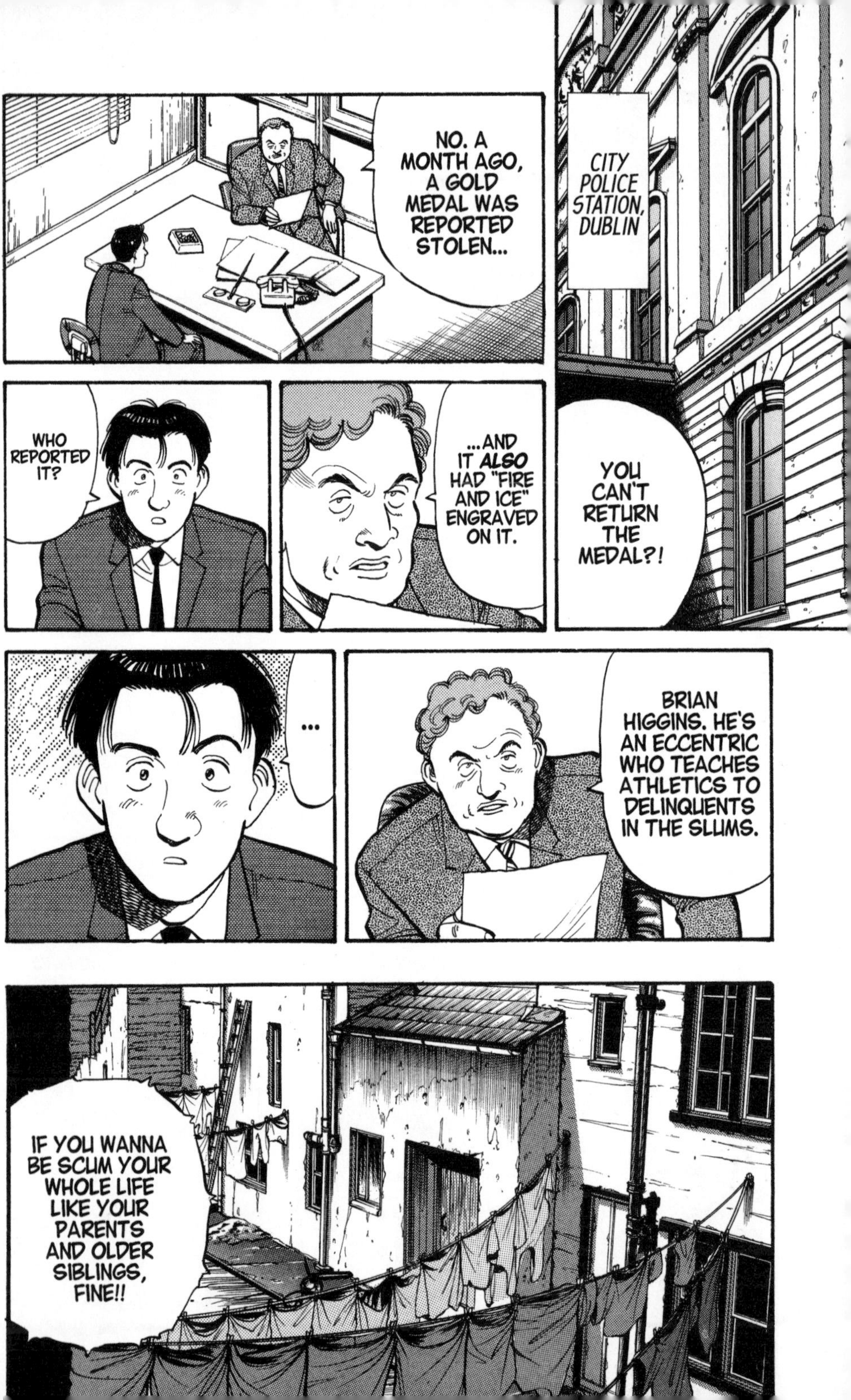
CITY POLICE STATION, DUBLIN
YOU CAN'T RETURN THE MEDAL?!
NO. A MONTH AGO, A GOLD MEDAL WAS REPORTED STOLEN...
...AND IT **ALSO** HAD "FIRE AND ICE" ENGRAVED ON IT.
WHO REPORTED IT?
BRIAN HIGGINS. HE'S AN ECCENTRIC WHO TEACHES ATHLETICS TO DELINQUENTS IN THE SLUMS.
...
IF YOU WANNA BE SCUM YOUR WHOLE LIFE LIKE YOUR PARENTS AND OLDER SIBLINGS, FINE!!

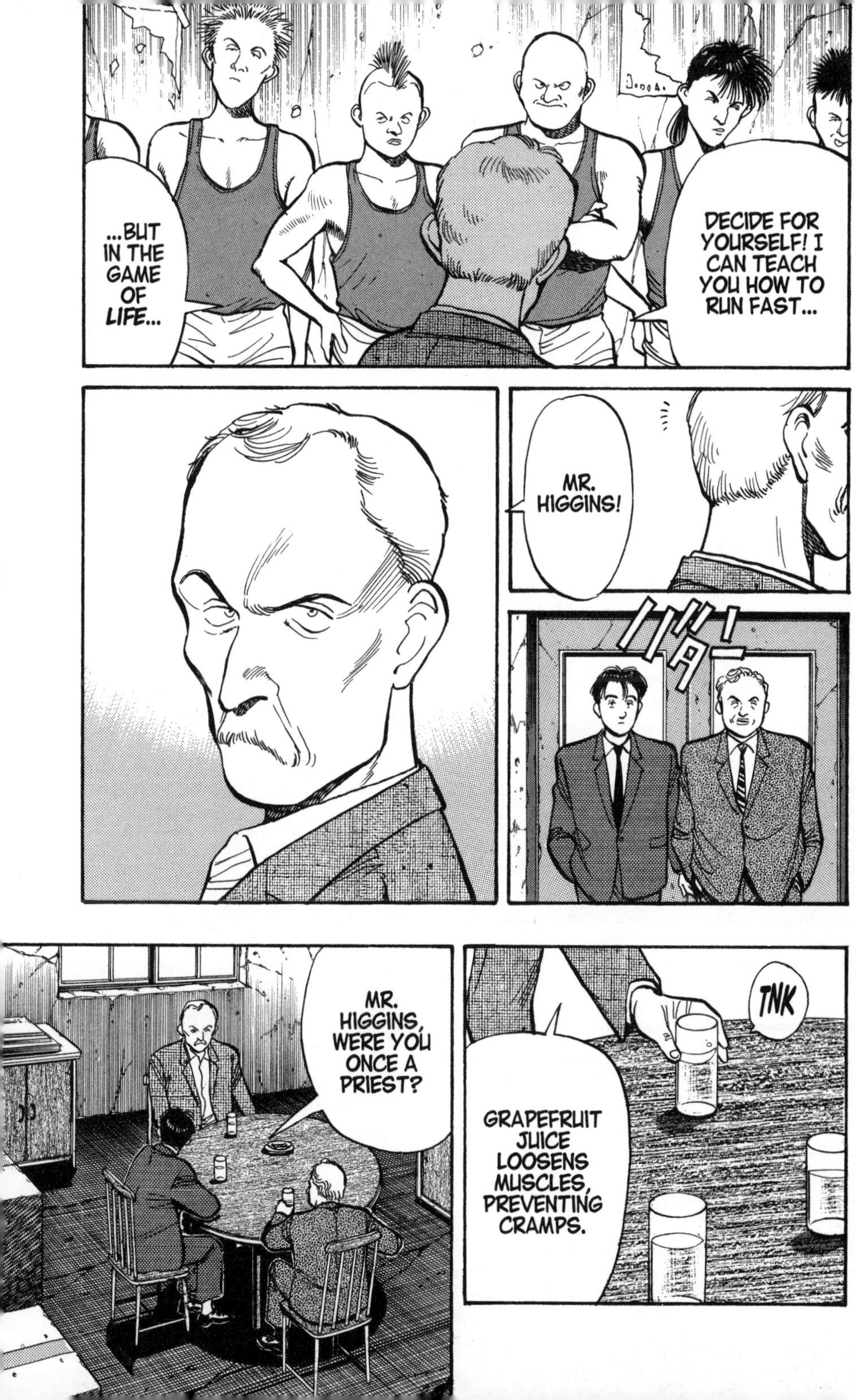
DECIDE FOR YOURSELF! I CAN TEACH YOU HOW TO RUN FAST...
...BUT IN THE GAME OF LIFE...
MR. HIGGINS!
TNK
GRAPEFRUIT JUICE LOOSENS MUSCLES, PREVENTING CRAMPS.
MR. HIGGINS, WERE YOU ONCE A PRIEST?

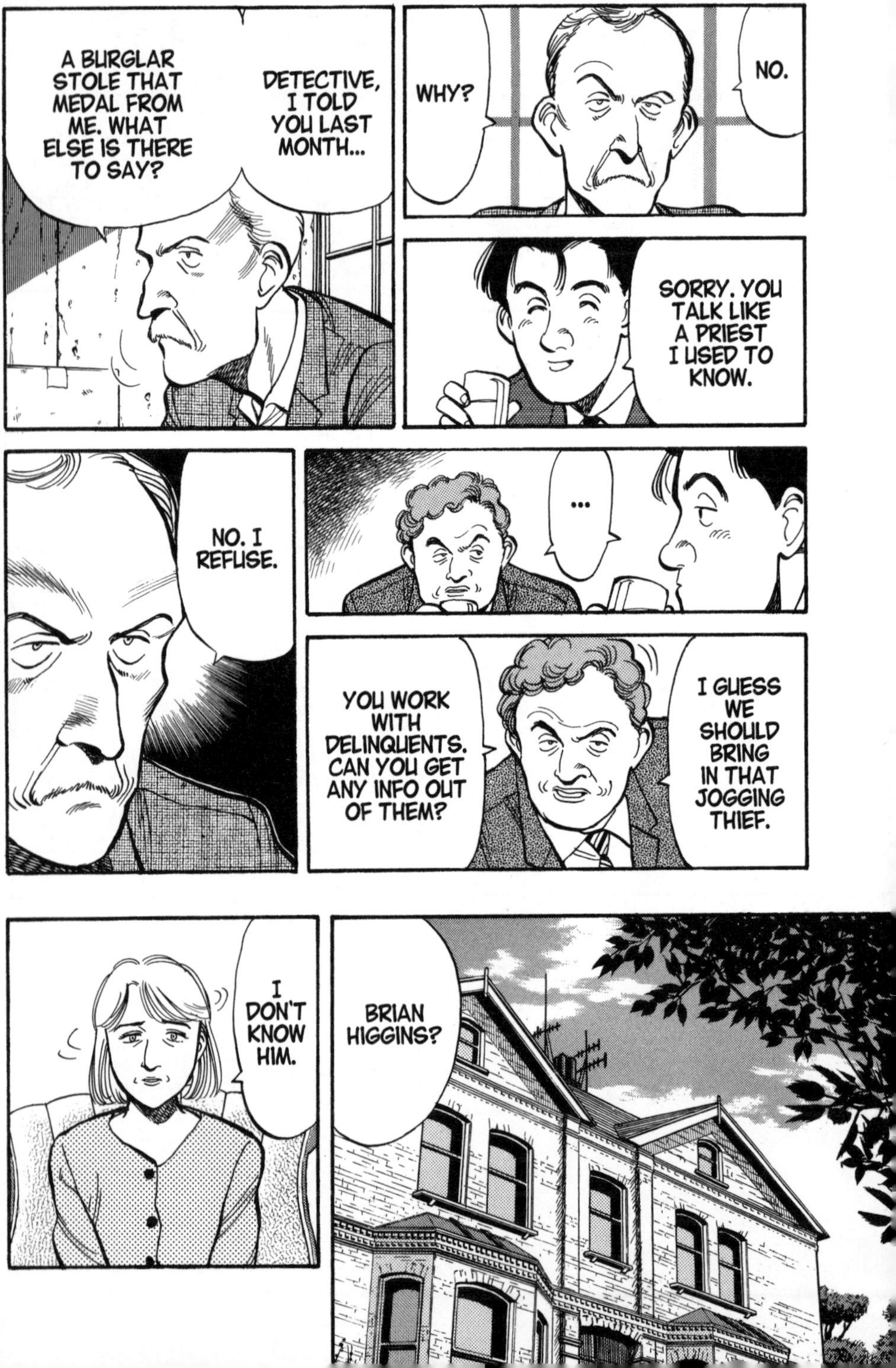
NO.
WHY?
SORRY. YOU TALK LIKE A PRIEST I USED TO KNOW.
DETECTIVE, I TOLD YOU LAST MONTH...
A BURGLAR STOLE THAT MEDAL FROM ME. WHAT ELSE IS THERE TO SAY?
...
I GUESS WE SHOULD BRING IN THAT JOGGING THIEF.
YOU WORK WITH DELINQUENTS. CAN YOU GET ANY INFO OUT OF THEM?
NO. I REFUSE.
BRIAN HIGGINS?
I DON'T KNOW HIM.

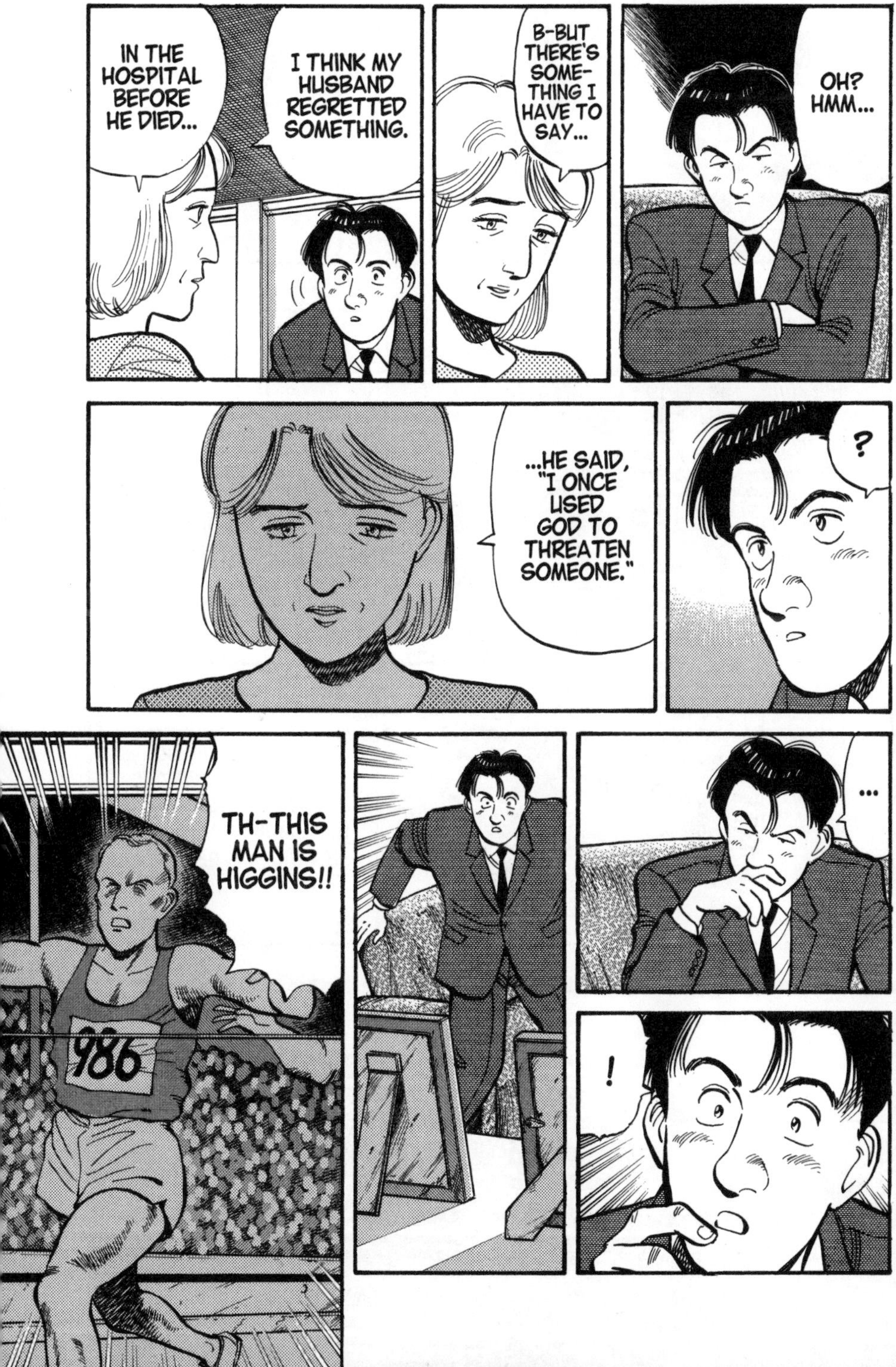
OH? HMM...
B-BUT THERE'S SOME-THING I HAVE TO SAY...
I THINK MY HUSBAND REGRETTED SOMETHING.
IN THE HOSPITAL BEFORE HE DIED...
?
...HE SAID, "I ONCE USED GOD TO THREATEN SOMEONE."
...
!
TH-THIS MAN IS HIGGINS!!
986

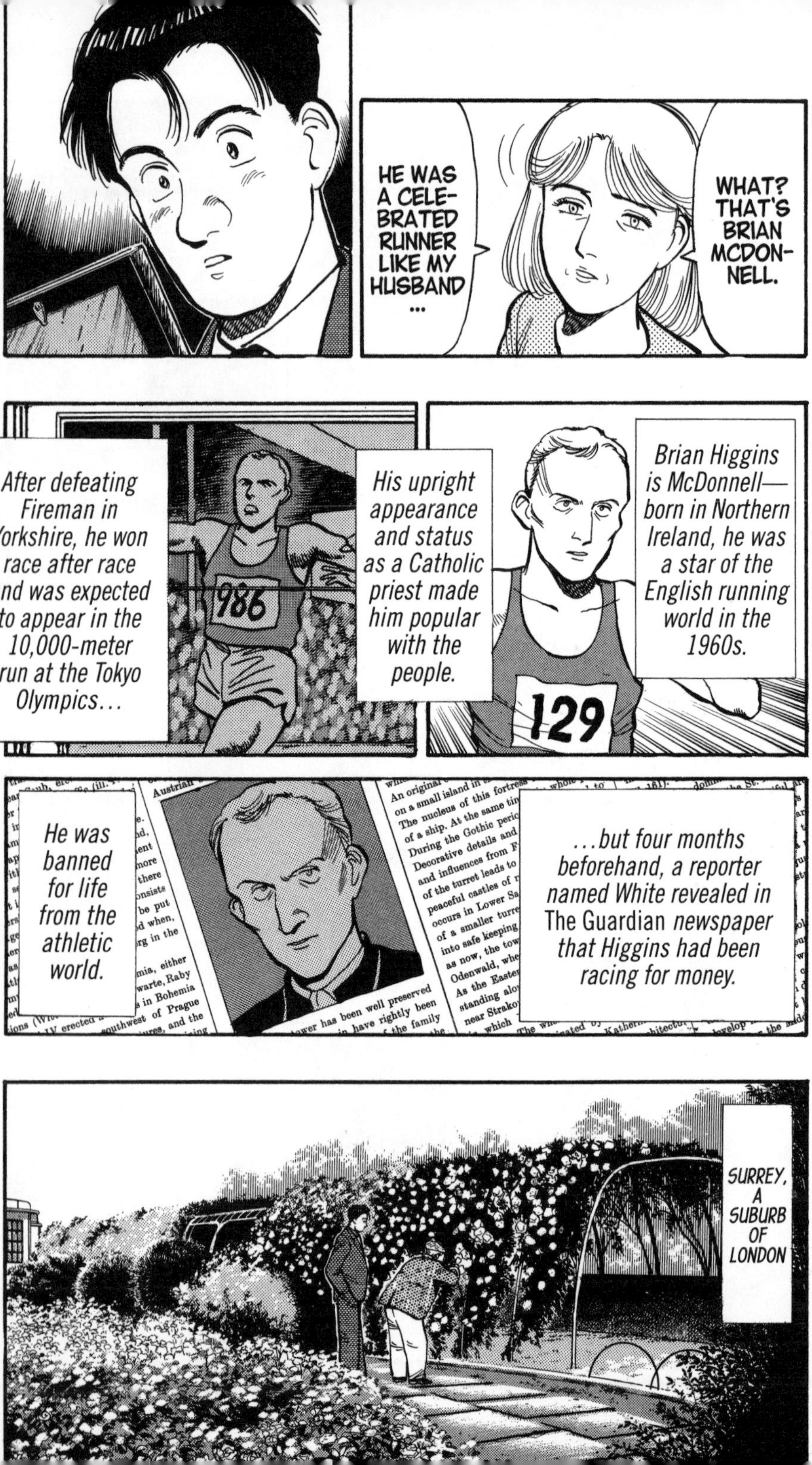

WHAT? THAT'S BRIAN MCDONNELL.
HE WAS A CELEBRATED RUNNER LIKE MY HUSBAND...
Brian Higgins is McDonnell—born in Northern Ireland, he was a star of the English running world in the 1960s.
His upright appearance and status as a Catholic priest made him popular with the people.
After defeating Fireman in Yorkshire, he won race after race and was expected to appear in the 10,000-meter run at the Tokyo Olympics...
...but four months beforehand, a reporter named White revealed in The Guardian newspaper that Higgins had been racing for money.
He was banned for life from the athletic world.
SURREY, A SUBURB OF LONDON

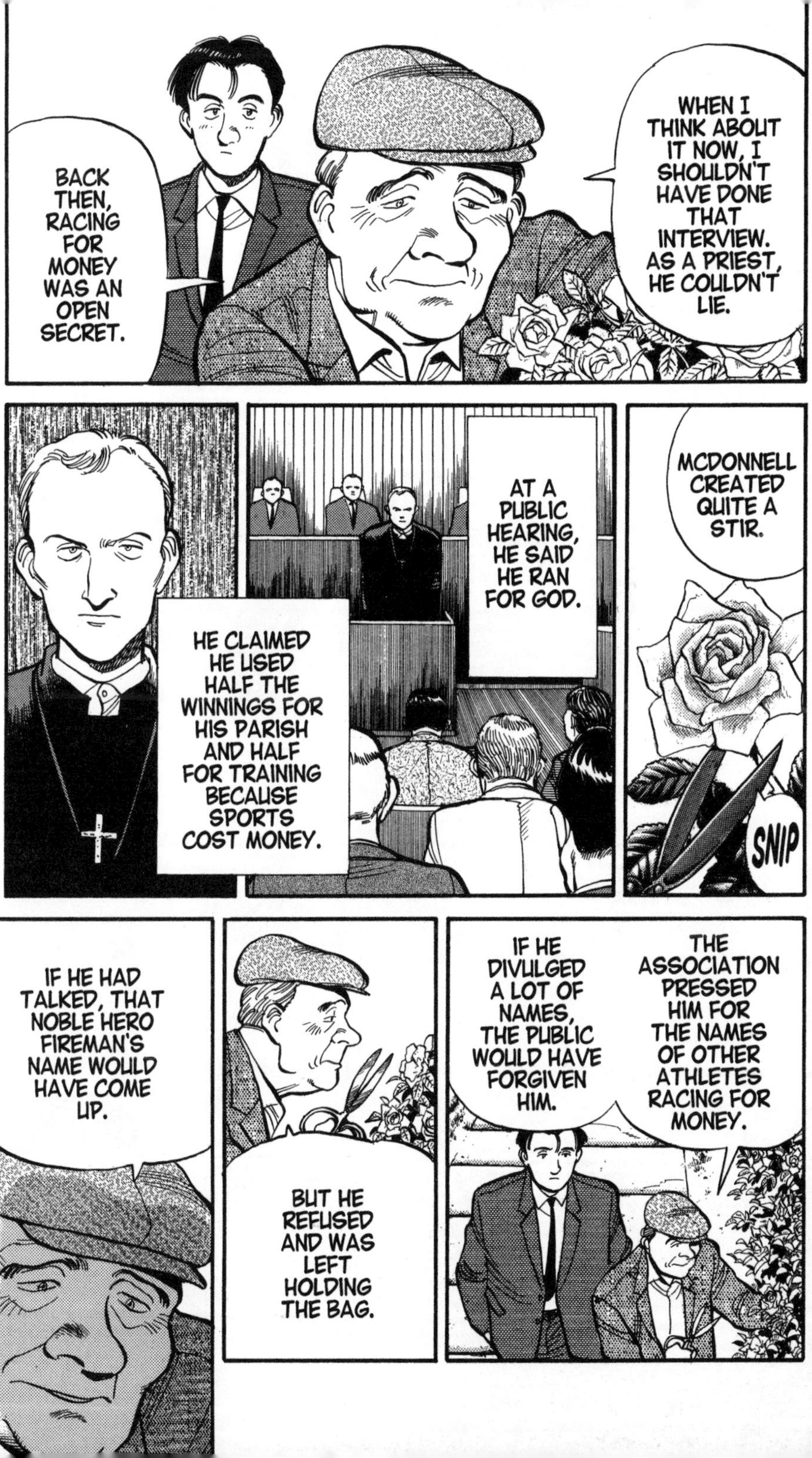
WHEN I THINK ABOUT IT NOW, I SHOULDN'T HAVE DONE THAT INTERVIEW. AS A PRIEST, HE COULDN'T LIE.
BACK THEN, RACING FOR MONEY WAS AN OPEN SECRET.
MCDONNELL CREATED QUITE A STIR.
SNIP
AT A PUBLIC HEARING, HE SAID HE RAN FOR GOD.
HE CLAIMED HE USED HALF THE WINNINGS FOR HIS PARISH AND HALF FOR TRAINING BECAUSE SPORTS COST MONEY.
THE ASSOCIATION PRESSED HIM FOR THE NAMES OF OTHER ATHLETES RACING FOR MONEY.
IF HE DIVULGED A LOT OF NAMES, THE PUBLIC WOULD HAVE FORGIVEN HIM.
BUT HE REFUSED AND WAS LEFT HOLDING THE BAG.
IF HE HAD TALKED, THAT NOBLE HERO FIREMAN'S NAME WOULD HAVE COME UP.

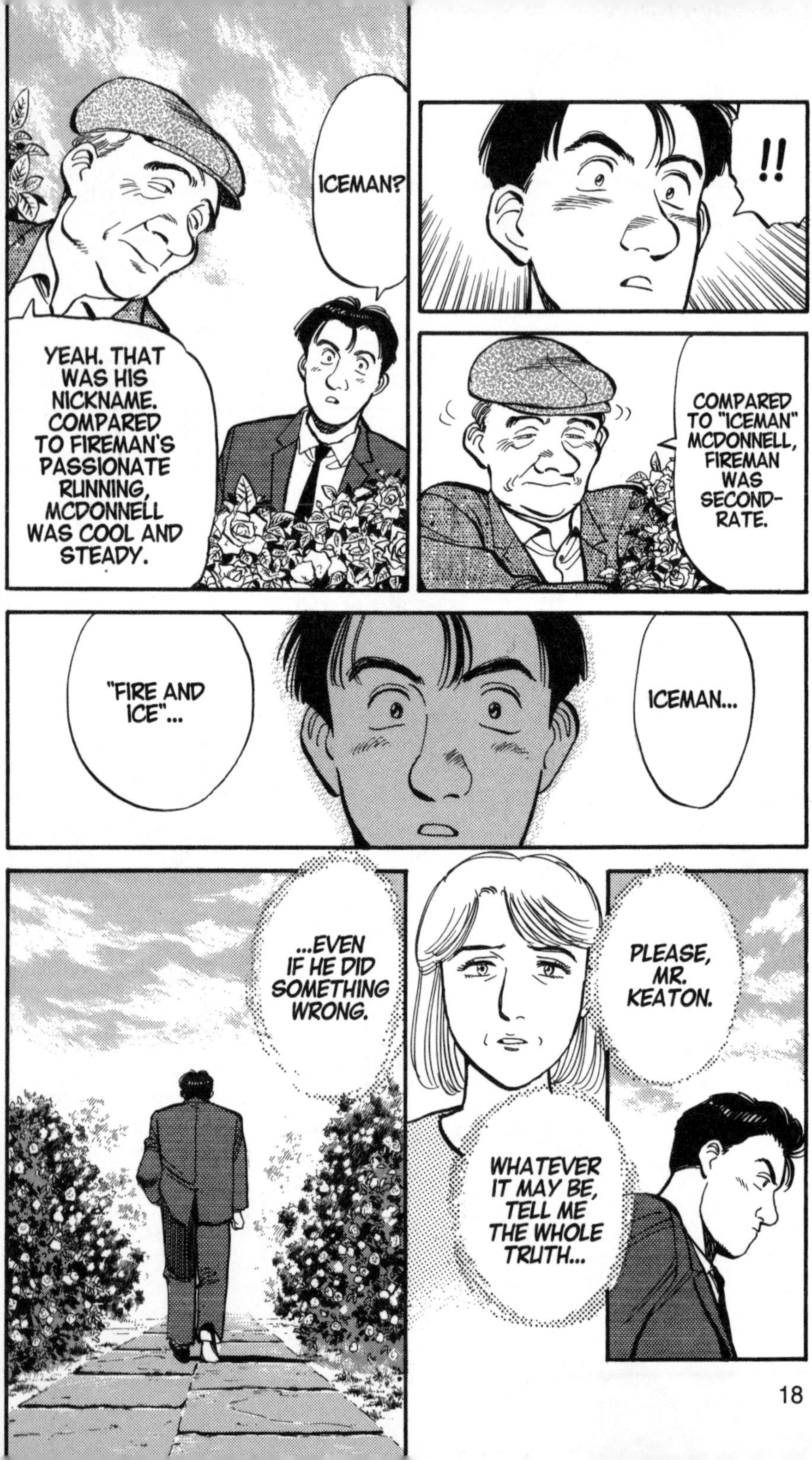
!!
COMPARED TO "ICEMAN" MCDONNELL, FIREMAN WAS SECOND-RATE.
ICEMAN?
YEAH. THAT WAS HIS NICKNAME. COMPARED TO FIREMAN'S PASSIONATE RUNNING, MCDONNELL WAS COOL AND STEADY.
ICEMAN...
"FIRE AND ICE"...
PLEASE, MR. KEATON.
WHATEVER IT MAY BE, TELL ME THE WHOLE TRUTH...
...EVEN IF HE DID SOMETHING WRONG.

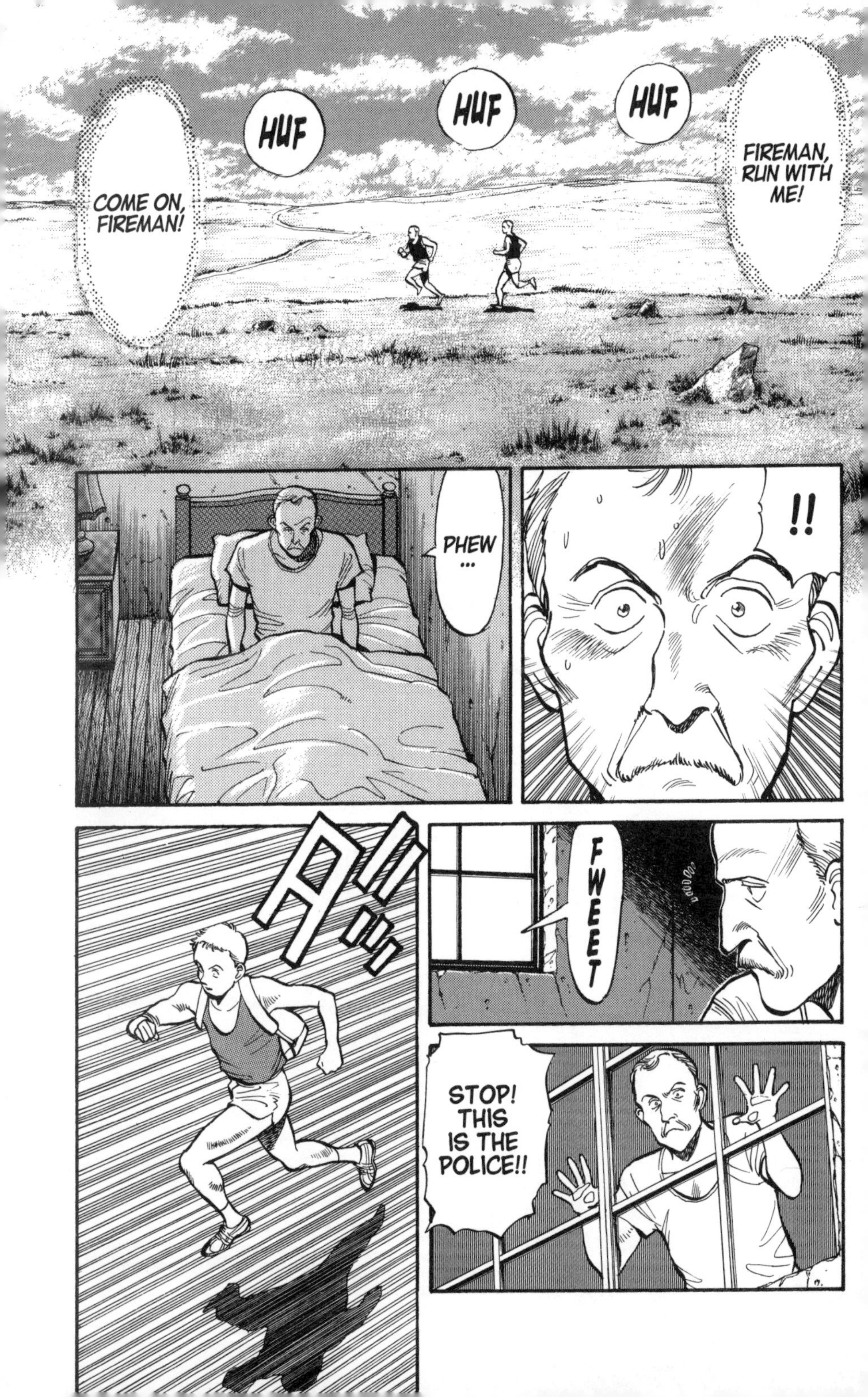
FIREMAN, RUN WITH ME!
HUF
HUF
HUF
COME ON, FIREMAN!
!!
PHEW ...
FWEET
STOP! THIS IS THE POLICE!!

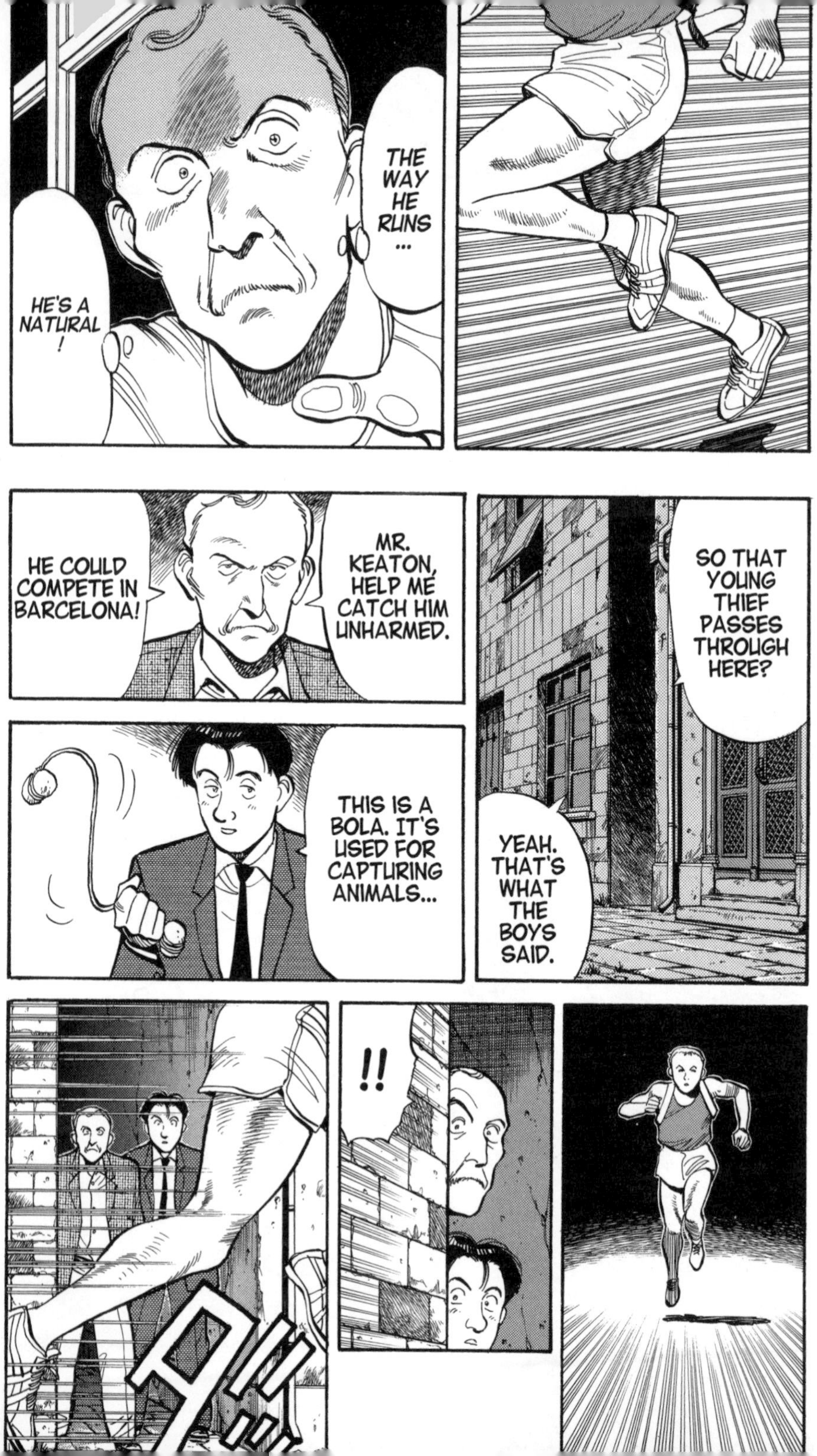
THE WAY HE RUNS...
HE'S A NATURAL!
SO THAT YOUNG THIEF PASSES THROUGH HERE?
YEAH. THAT'S WHAT THE BOYS SAID.
MR. KEATON, HELP ME CATCH HIM UNHARMED.
HE COULD COMPETE IN BARCELONA!
THIS IS A BOLA. IT'S USED FOR CAPTURING ANIMALS...
!!

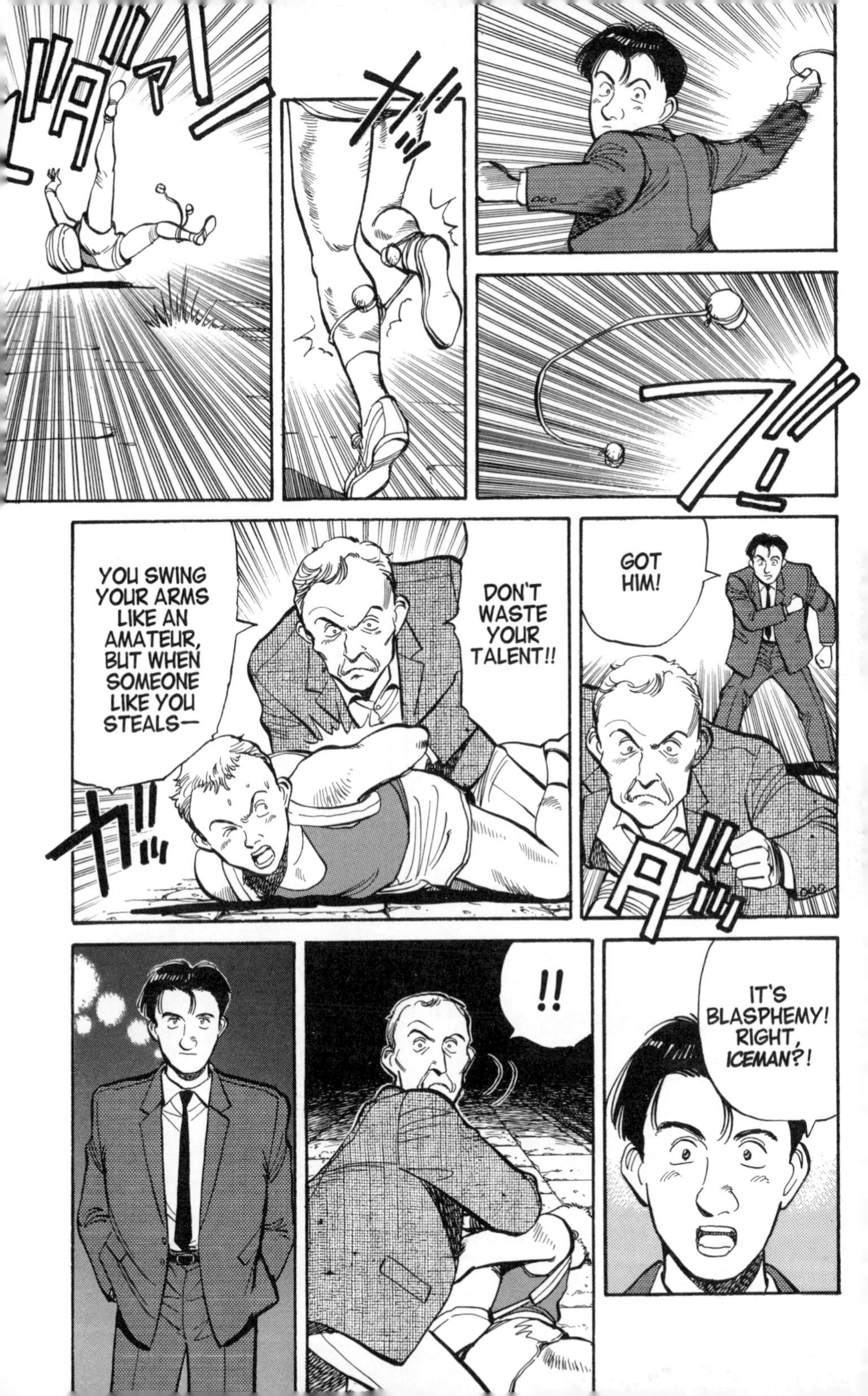
GOT HIM!
DON'T WASTE YOUR TALENT!!
YOU SWING YOUR ARMS LIKE AN AMATEUR, BUT WHEN SOMEONE LIKE YOU STEALS—
IT'S BLASPHEMY! RIGHT, ICEMAN?!
!!

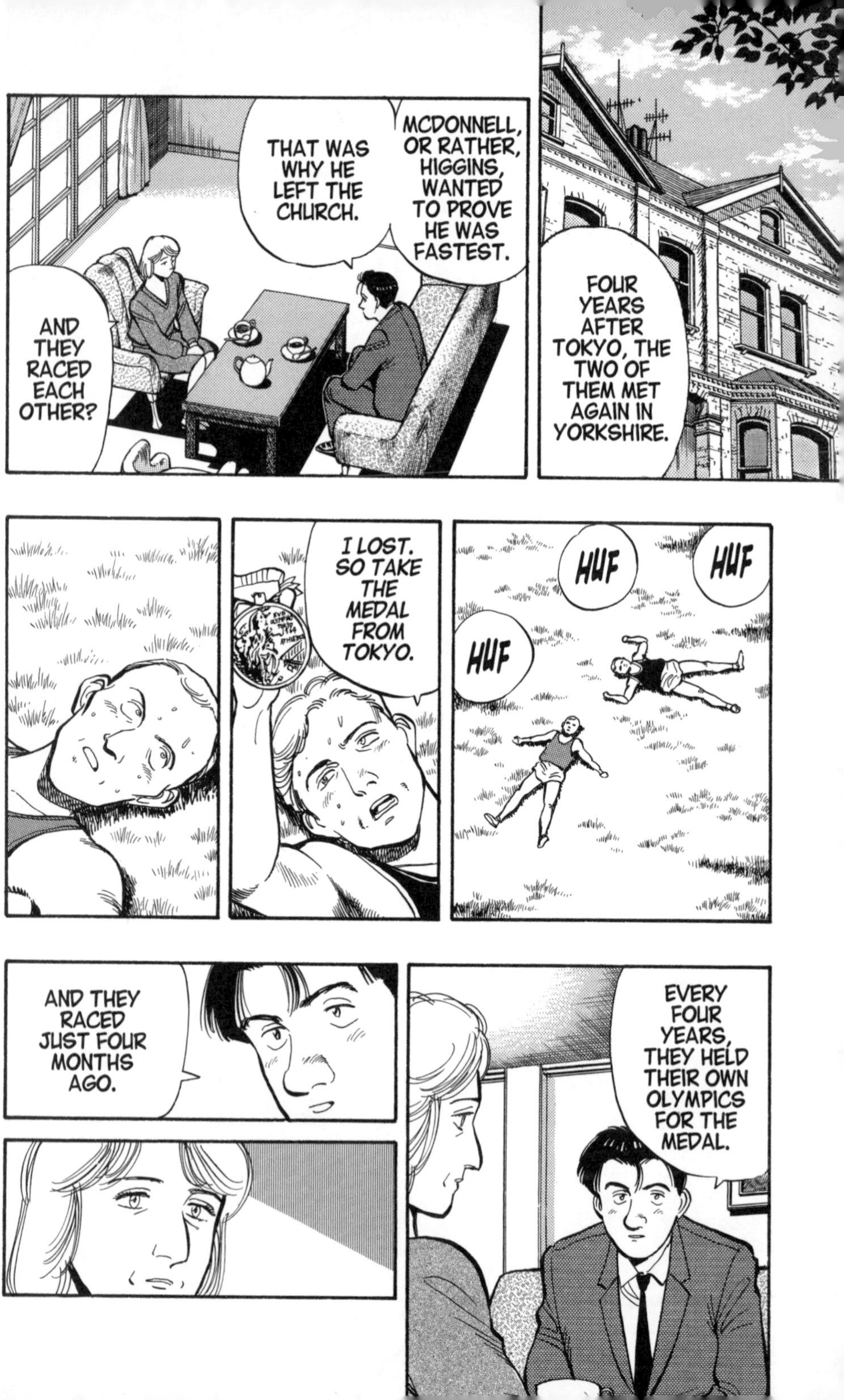
FOUR YEARS AFTER TOKYO, THE TWO OF THEM MET AGAIN IN YORKSHIRE.
MCDONNELL, OR RATHER, HIGGINS, WANTED TO PROVE HE WAS FASTEST.
THAT WAS WHY HE LEFT THE CHURCH.
AND THEY RACED EACH OTHER?
HUF
HUF
HUF
I LOST. SO TAKE THE MEDAL FROM TOKYO.
EVERY FOUR YEARS, THEY HELD THEIR OWN OLYMPICS FOR THE MEDAL.
AND THEY RACED JUST FOUR MONTHS AGO.

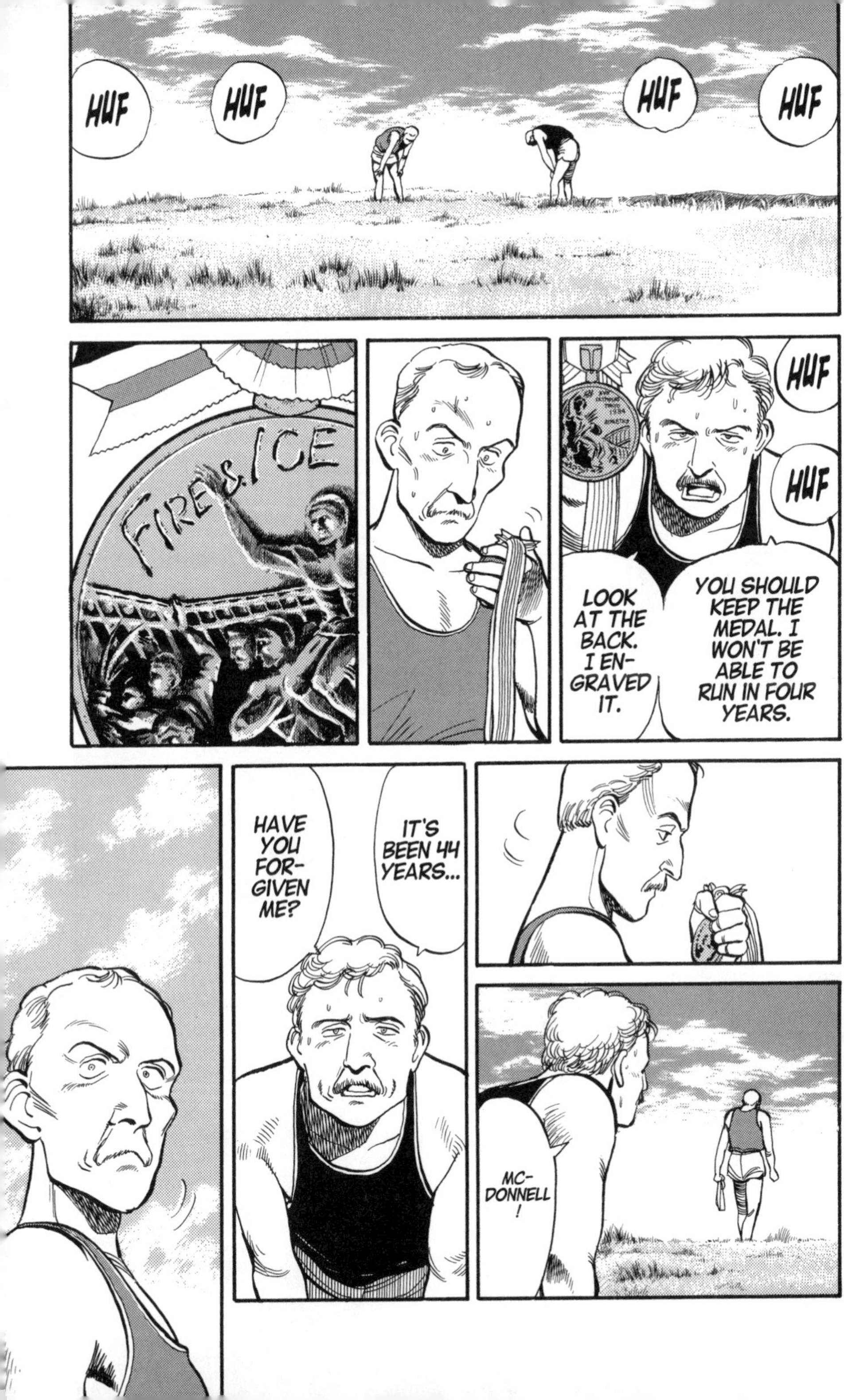
HUF
HUF
HUF
HUF
HUF
HUF
YOU SHOULD KEEP THE MEDAL. I WON'T BE ABLE TO RUN IN FOUR YEARS.
LOOK AT THE BACK. I EN-GRAVED IT.
FIRE & ICE
MC-DONNELL!
IT'S BEEN 44 YEARS...
HAVE YOU FOR-GIVEN ME?

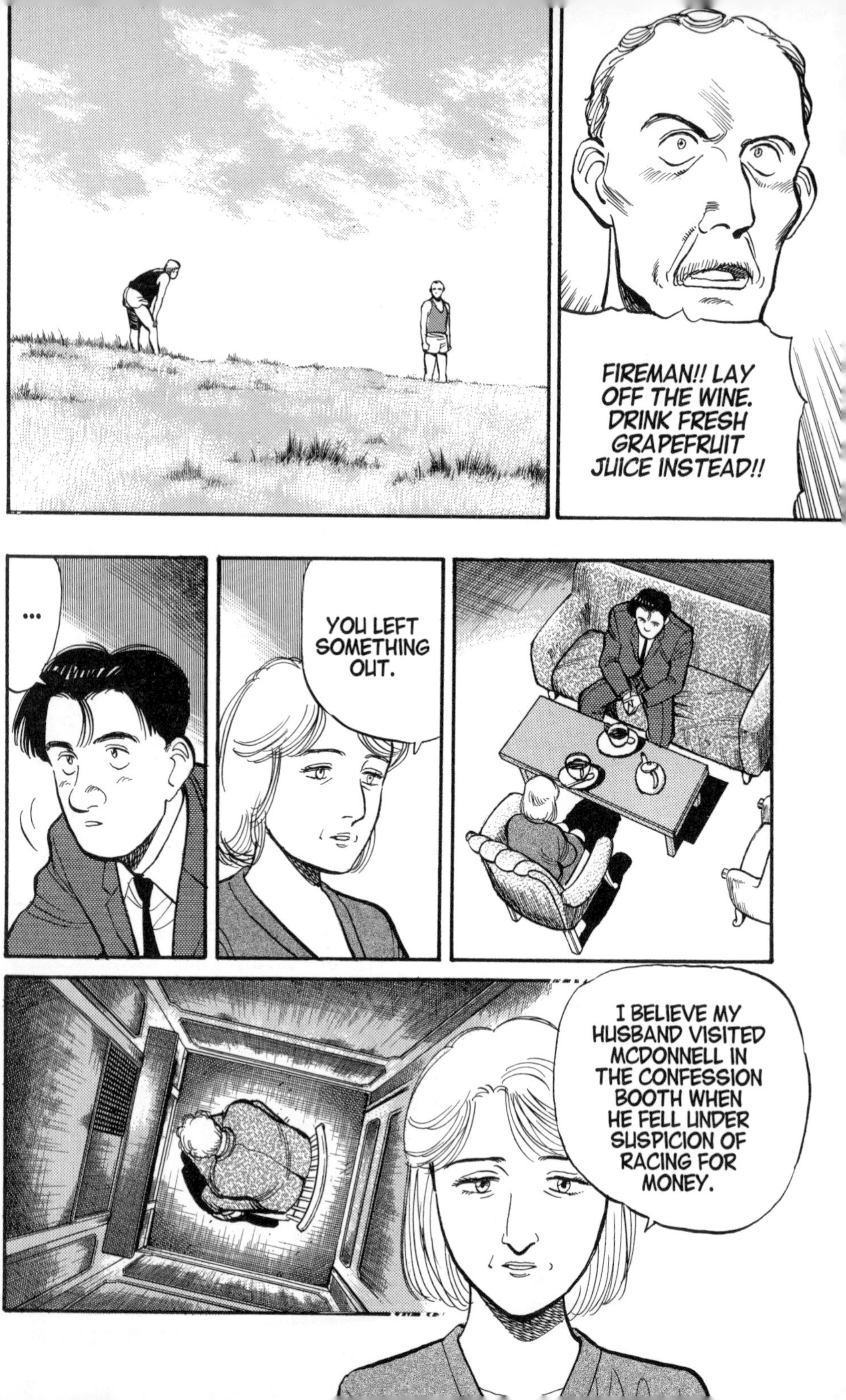
FIREMAN!! LAY OFF THE WINE. DRINK FRESH GRAPEFRUIT JUICE INSTEAD!!
YOU LEFT SOMETHING OUT.
...
I BELIEVE MY HUSBAND VISITED MCDONNELL IN THE CONFESSION BOOTH WHEN HE FELL UNDER SUSPICION OF RACING FOR MONEY.

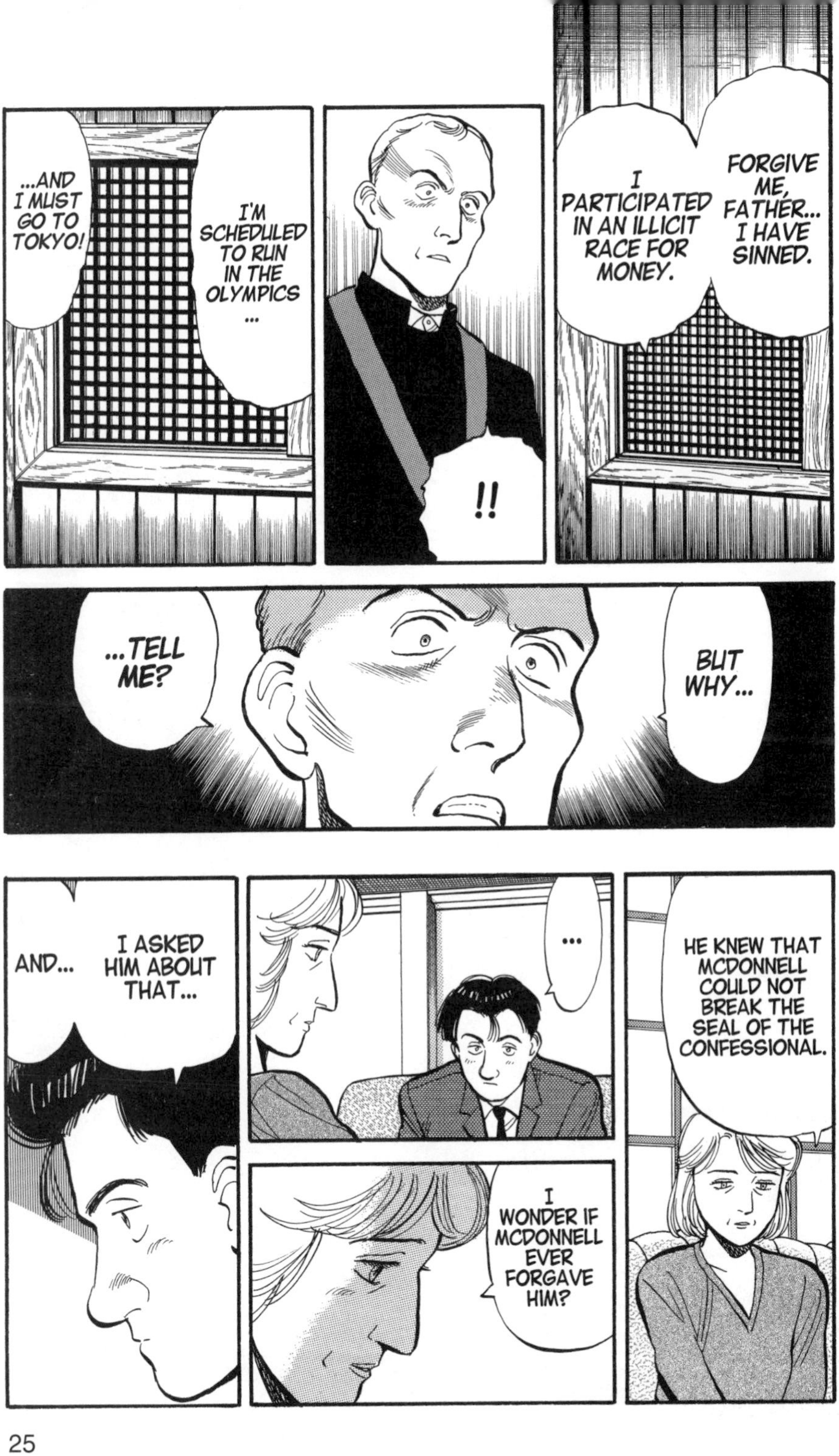
FORGIVE ME, FATHER... I HAVE SINNED.
I PARTICIPATED IN AN ILLICIT RACE FOR MONEY.
!!
I'M SCHEDULED TO RUN IN THE OLYMPICS ...
...AND I MUST GO TO TOKYO!
BUT WHY...
...TELL ME?
HE KNEW THAT MCDONNELL COULD NOT BREAK THE SEAL OF THE CONFESSIONAL.
...
I WONDER IF MCDONNELL EVER FORGAVE HIM?
I ASKED HIM ABOUT THAT...
AND...

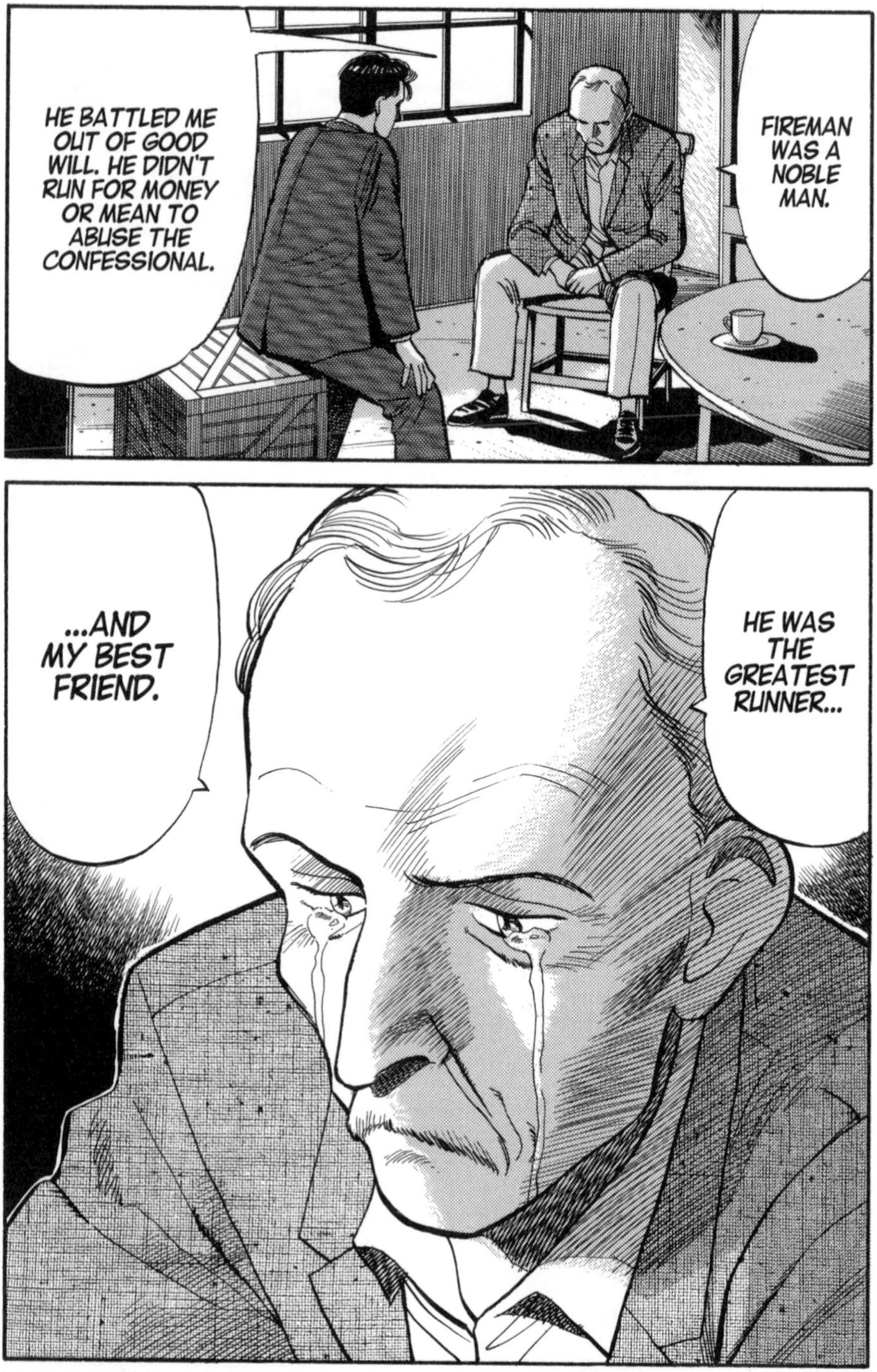
FIREMAN WAS A NOBLE MAN.
HE BATTLED ME OUT OF GOOD WILL. HE DIDN'T RUN FOR MONEY OR MEAN TO ABUSE THE CONFESSIONAL.
HE WAS THE GREATEST RUNNER...
...AND MY BEST FRIEND.

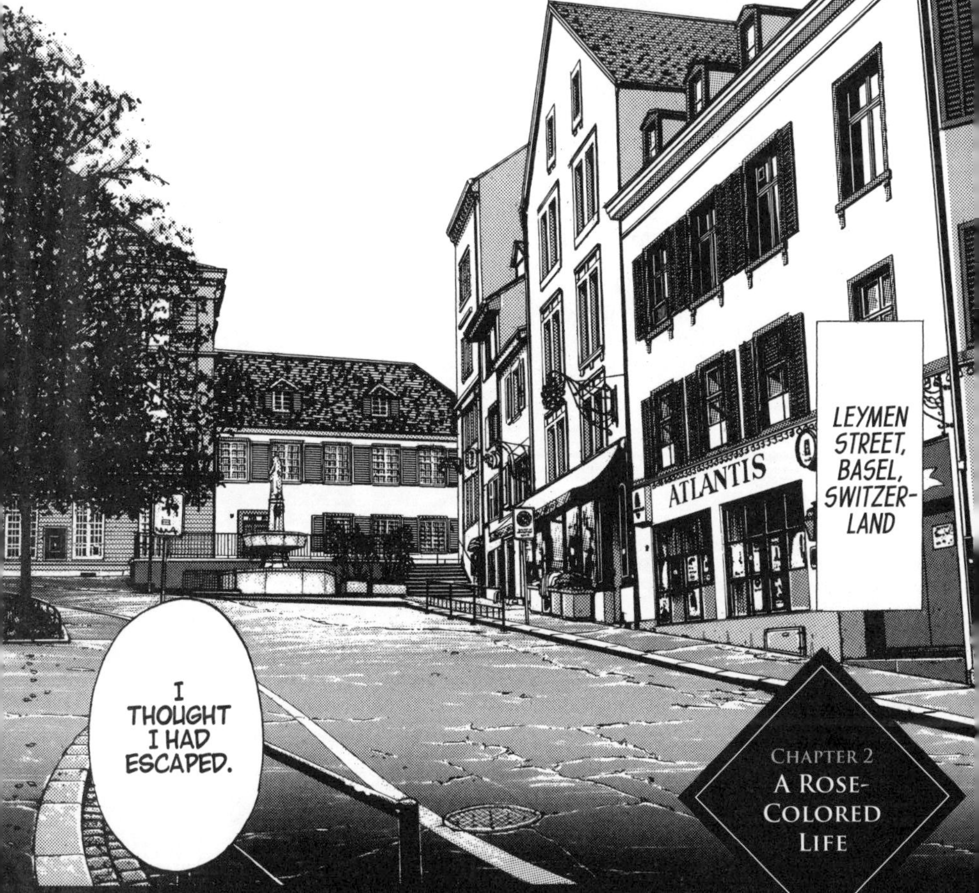
LEYMEN STREET, BASEL, SWITZERLAND
ATLANTIS
Chapter 2
A Rose-Colored Life
I THOUGHT I HAD ESCAPED.

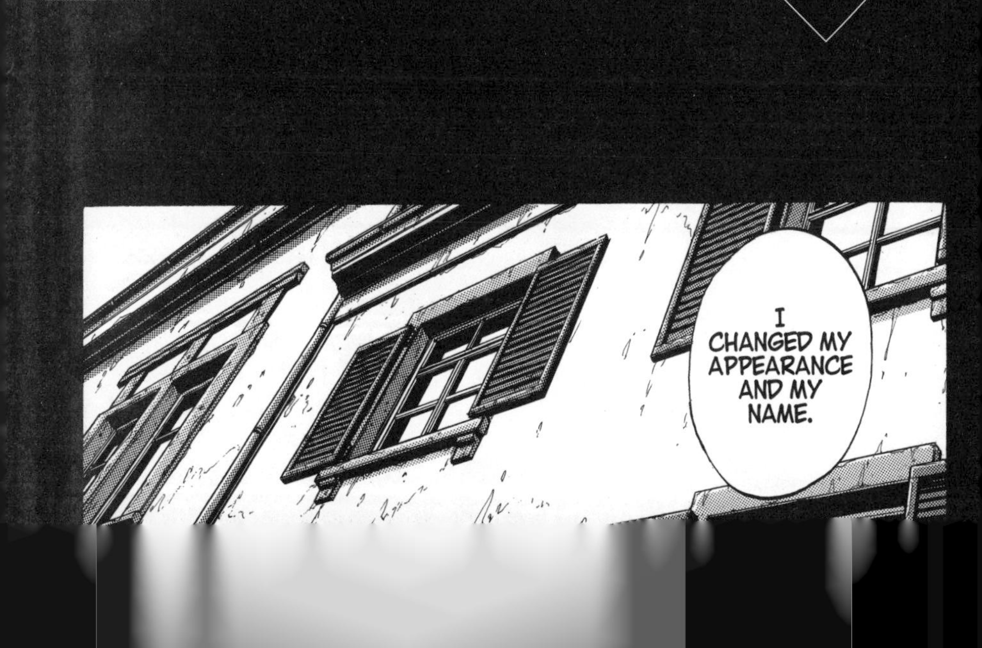
I CHANGED MY APPEARANCE AND MY NAME.

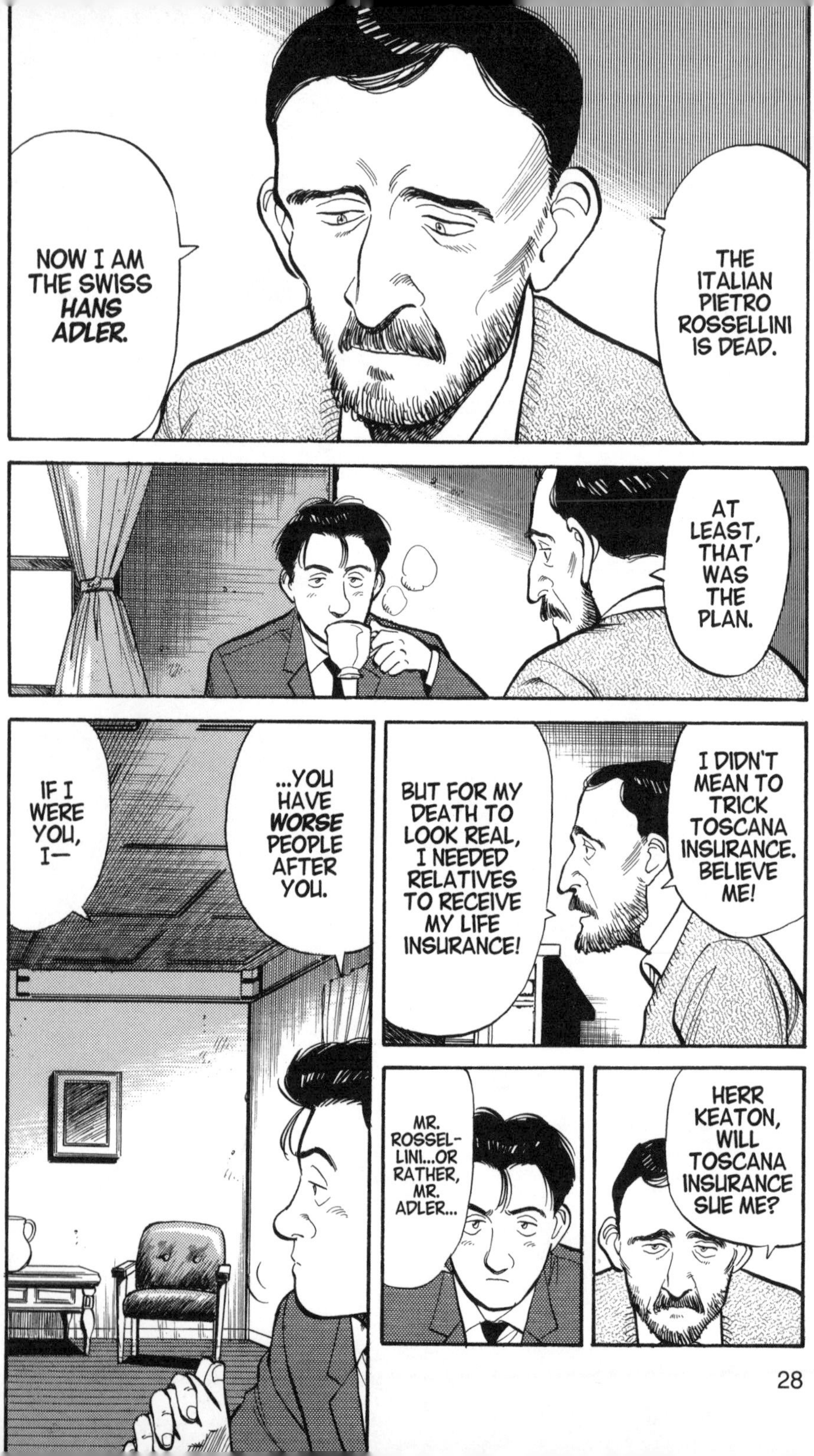
THE ITALIAN PIETRO ROSSELLINI IS DEAD.
NOW I AM THE SWISS **HANS ADLER.**
AT LEAST, THAT WAS THE PLAN.
I DIDN'T MEAN TO TRICK TOSCANA INSURANCE. BELIEVE ME!
BUT FOR MY DEATH TO LOOK REAL, I NEEDED RELATIVES TO RECEIVE MY LIFE INSURANCE!
HERR KEATON, WILL TOSCANA INSURANCE SUE ME?
MR. ROSSEL-LINI...OR RATHER, MR. ADLER...
...YOU HAVE **WORSE** PEOPLE AFTER YOU.
IF I WERE YOU, I—

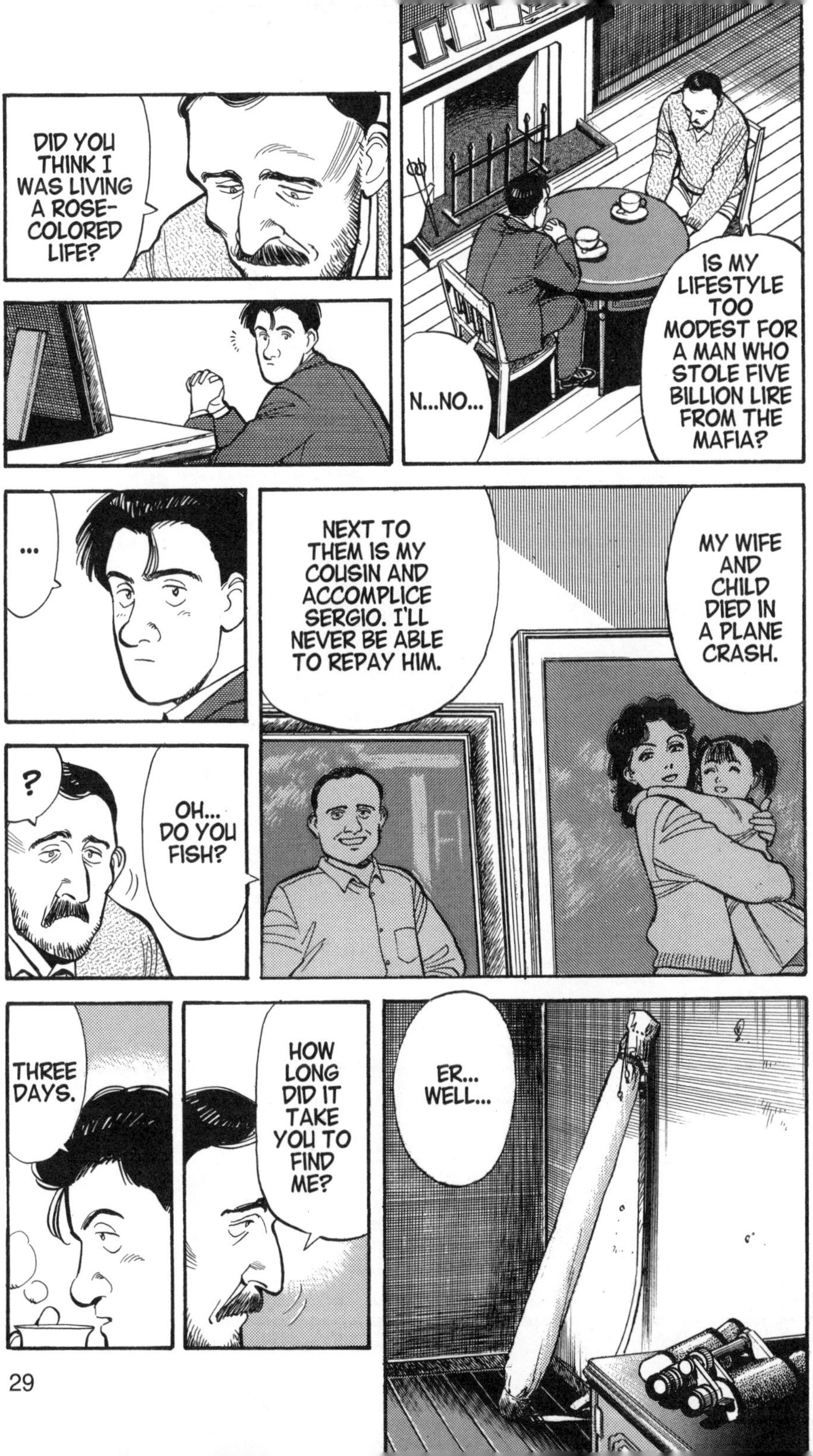
IS MY LIFESTYLE TOO MODEST FOR A MAN WHO STOLE FIVE BILLION LIRE FROM THE MAFIA?
N...NO...
DID YOU THINK I WAS LIVING A ROSE-COLORED LIFE?
MY WIFE AND CHILD DIED IN A PLANE CRASH.
NEXT TO THEM IS MY COUSIN AND ACCOMPLICE SERGIO. I'LL NEVER BE ABLE TO REPAY HIM.
...
OH... DO YOU FISH?
?
ER... WELL...
HOW LONG DID IT TAKE YOU TO FIND ME?
THREE DAYS.

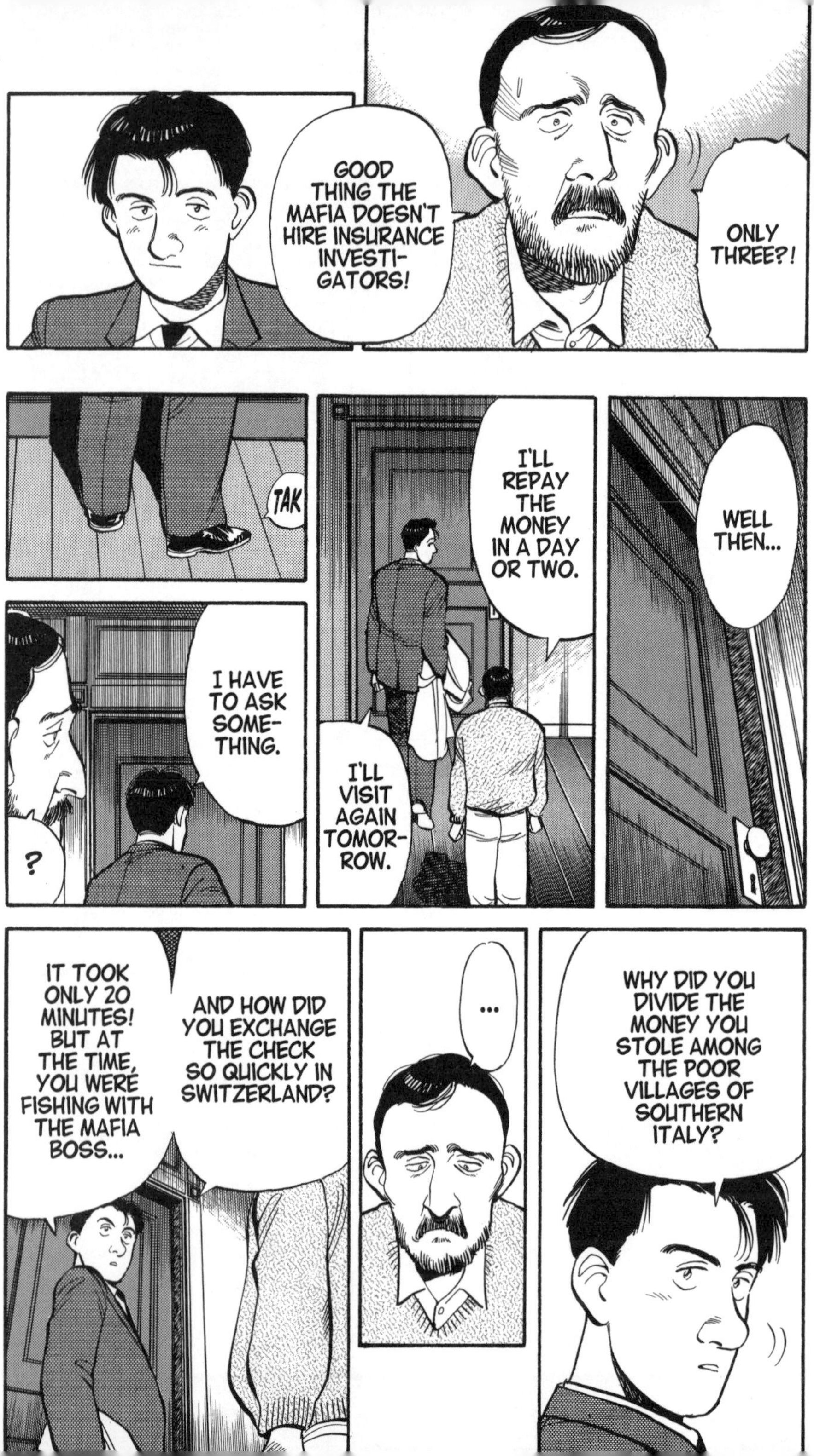
ONLY THREE?!
GOOD THING THE MAFIA DOESN'T HIRE INSURANCE INVESTI-GATORS!
WELL THEN...
I'LL REPAY THE MONEY IN A DAY OR TWO.
I'LL VISIT AGAIN TOMOR-ROW.
TAK
I HAVE TO ASK SOME-THING.
?
WHY DID YOU DIVIDE THE MONEY YOU STOLE AMONG THE POOR VILLAGES OF SOUTHERN ITALY?
...
AND HOW DID YOU EXCHANGE THE CHECK SO QUICKLY IN SWITZERLAND?
IT TOOK ONLY 20 MINUTES! BUT AT THE TIME, YOU WERE FISHING WITH THE MAFIA BOSS...

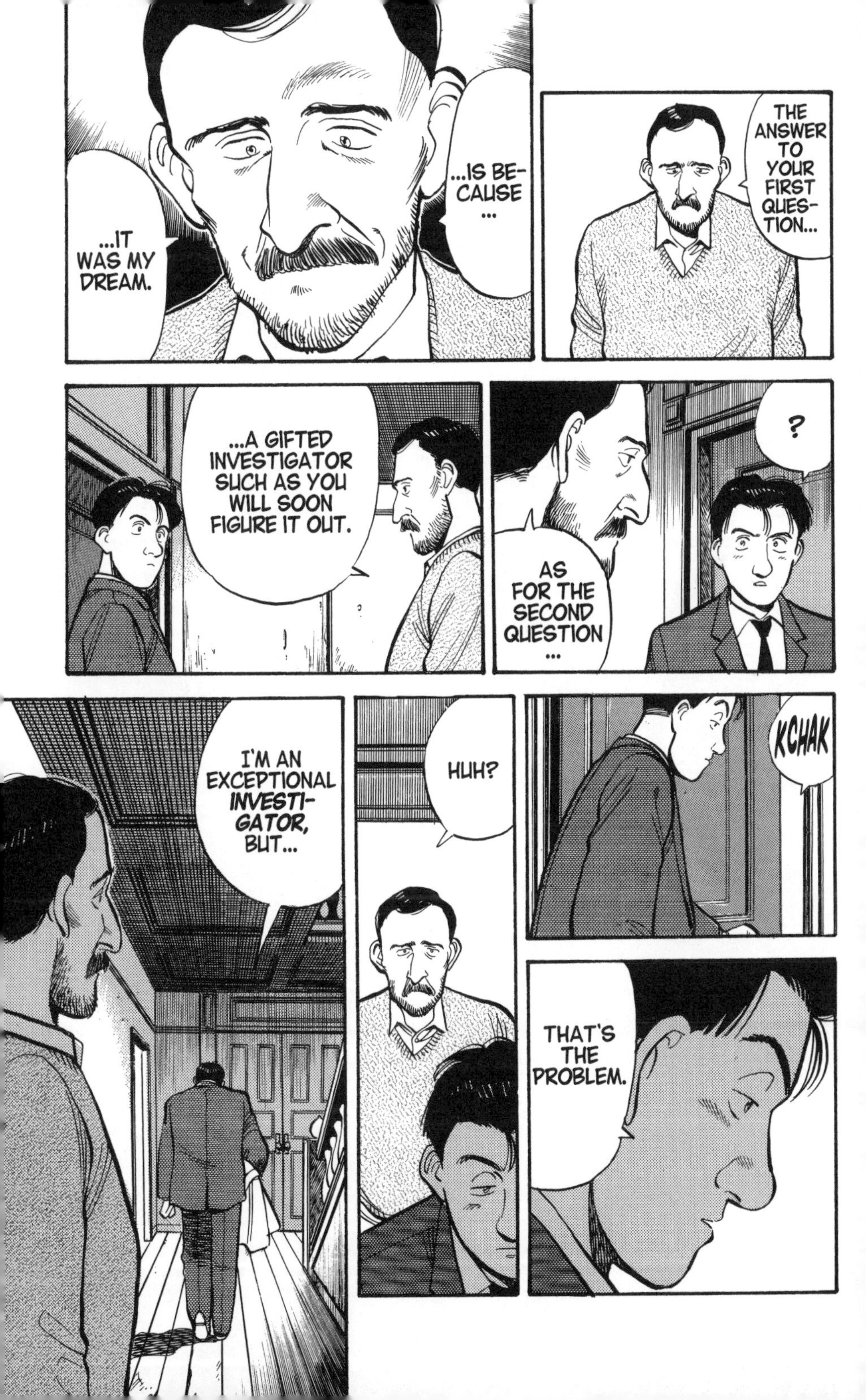
THE ANSWER TO YOUR FIRST QUESTION...
...IS BE-CAUSE...
...IT WAS MY DREAM.
?
AS FOR THE SECOND QUESTION...
...A GIFTED INVESTIGATOR SUCH AS YOU WILL SOON FIGURE IT OUT.
KCHAK
THAT'S THE PROBLEM.
HUH?
I'M AN EXCEPTIONAL **INVESTIGATOR,** BUT...

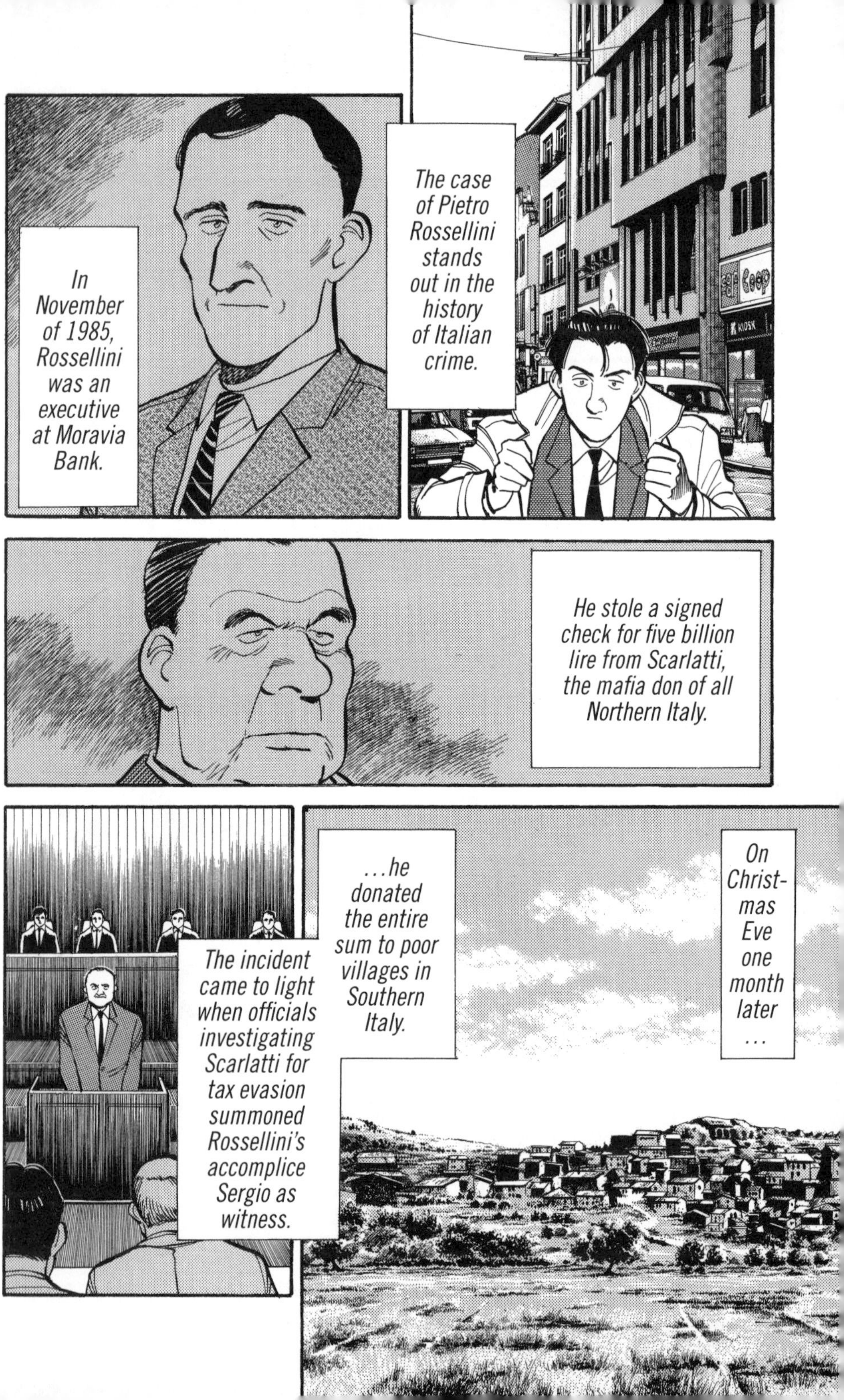
The case of Pietro Rossellini stands out in the history of Italian crime.
KIOSK
In November of 1985, Rossellini was an executive at Moravia Bank.
He stole a signed check for five billion lire from Scarlatti, the mafia don of all Northern Italy.
On Christmas Eve one month later . . .
. . .he donated the entire sum to poor villages in Southern Italy.
The incident came to light when officials investigating Scarlatti for tax evasion summoned Rossellini's accomplice Sergio as witness.

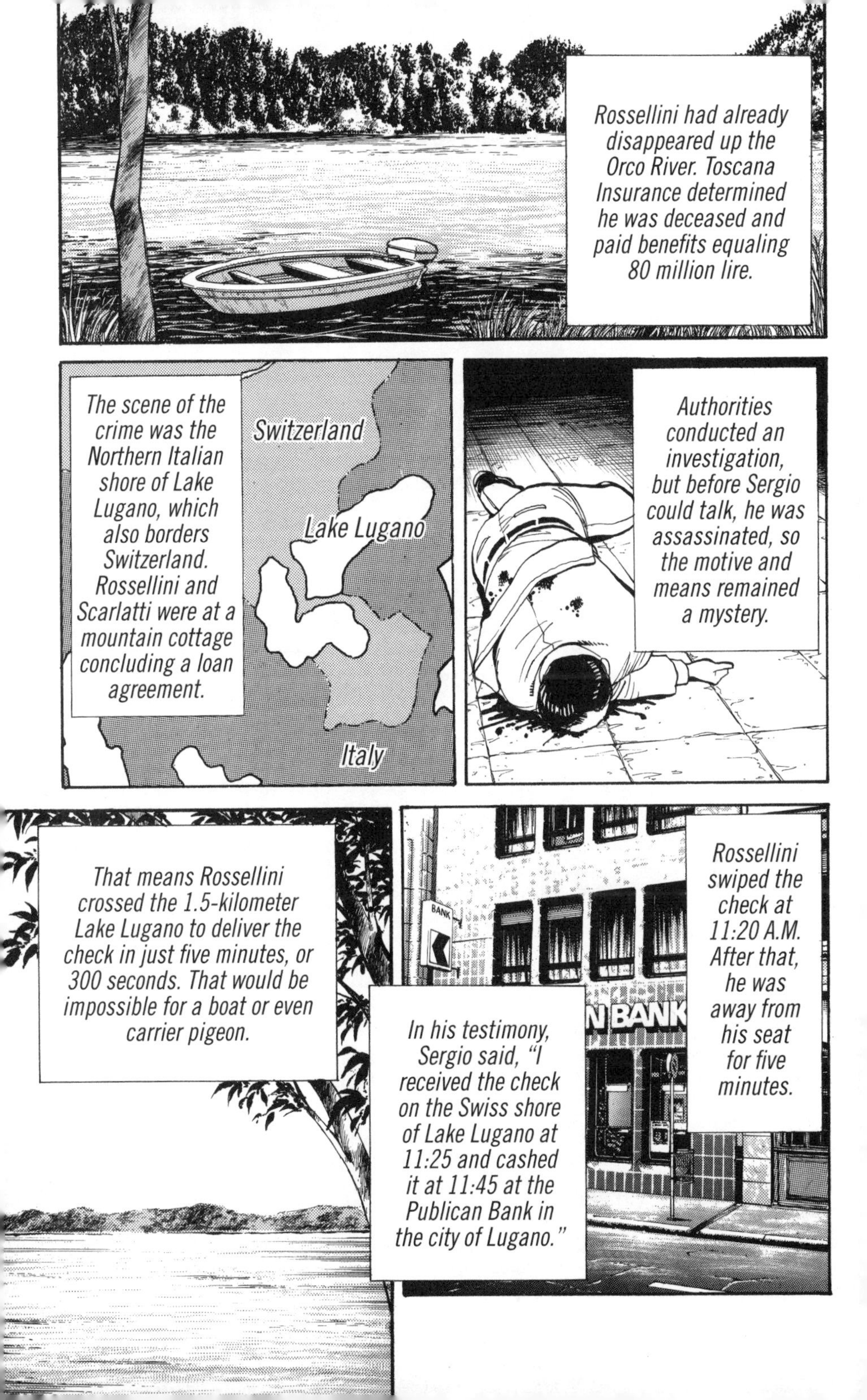
Rossellini had already disappeared up the Orco River. Toscana Insurance determined he was deceased and paid benefits equaling 80 million lire.
Authorities conducted an investigation, but before Sergio could talk, he was assassinated, so the motive and means remained a mystery.
The scene of the crime was the Northern Italian shore of Lake Lugano, which also borders Switzerland. Rossellini and Scarlatti were at a mountain cottage concluding a loan agreement.
Switzerland
Lake Lugano
Italy
Rossellini swiped the check at 11:20 A.M. After that, he was away from his seat for five minutes.
BANK
N BANK
In his testimony, Sergio said, "I received the check on the Swiss shore of Lake Lugano at 11:25 and cashed it at 11:45 at the Publican Bank in the city of Lugano."
That means Rossellini crossed the 1.5-kilometer Lake Lugano to deliver the check in just five minutes, or 300 seconds. That would be impossible for a boat or even carrier pigeon.

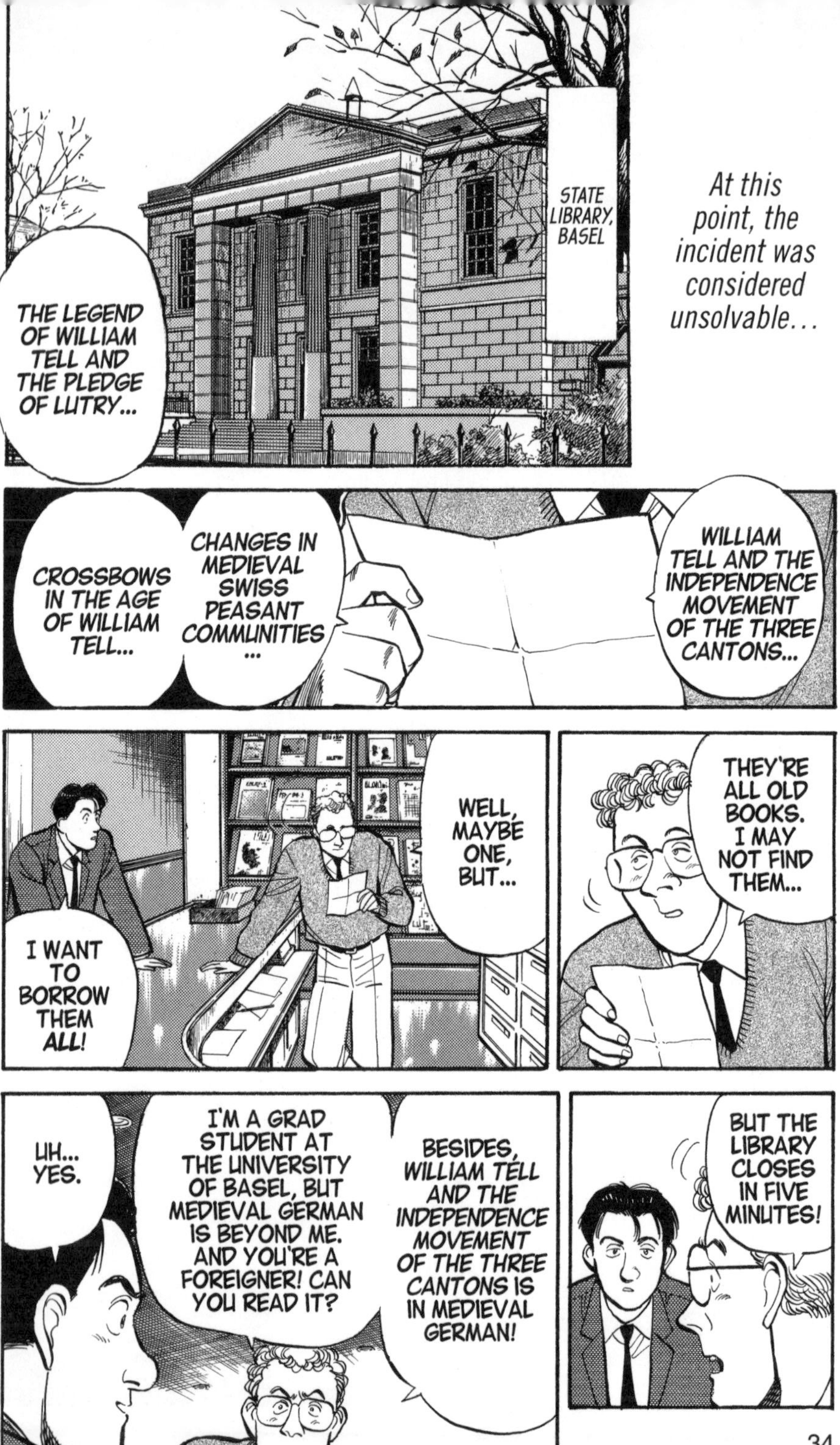
At this point, the incident was considered unsolvable...
STATE LIBRARY, BASEL
THE LEGEND OF WILLIAM TELL AND THE PLEDGE OF LUTRY...
WILLIAM TELL AND THE INDEPENDENCE MOVEMENT OF THE THREE CANTONS...
CHANGES IN MEDIEVAL SWISS PEASANT COMMUNITIES ...
CROSSBOWS IN THE AGE OF WILLIAM TELL...
THEY'RE ALL OLD BOOKS. I MAY NOT FIND THEM...
WELL, MAYBE ONE, BUT...
I WANT TO BORROW THEM ALL!
BUT THE LIBRARY CLOSES IN FIVE MINUTES!
BESIDES, WILLIAM TELL AND THE INDEPENDENCE MOVEMENT OF THE THREE CANTONS IS IN MEDIEVAL GERMAN!
I'M A GRAD STUDENT AT THE UNIVERSITY OF BASEL, BUT MEDIEVAL GERMAN IS BEYOND ME. AND YOU'RE A FOREIGNER! CAN YOU READ IT?
UH... YES.

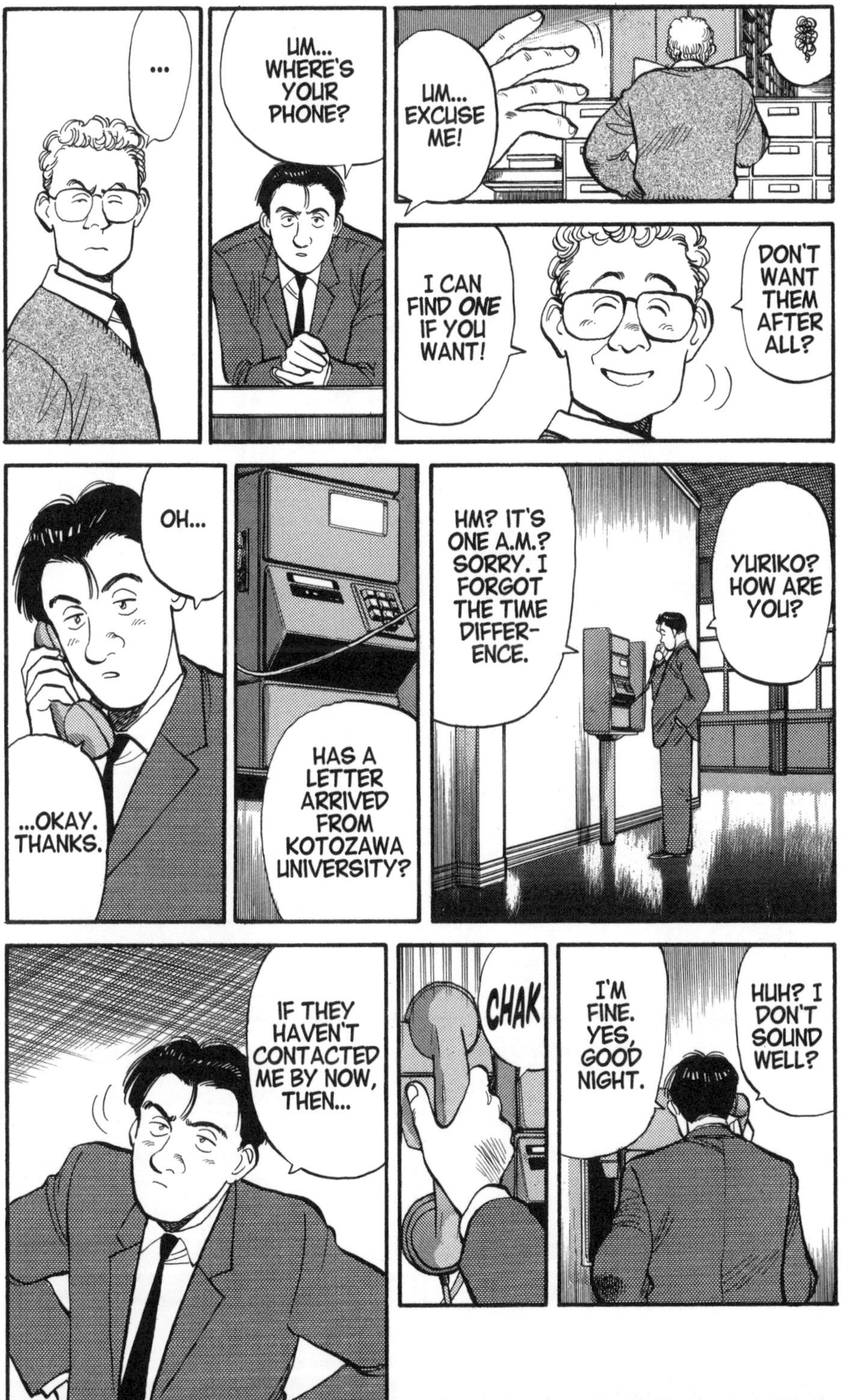
UM... EXCUSE ME!
DON'T WANT THEM AFTER ALL?
I CAN FIND ONE IF YOU WANT!
UM... WHERE'S YOUR PHONE?
...
YURIKO? HOW ARE YOU?
HM? IT'S ONE A.M.? SORRY. I FORGOT THE TIME DIFFERENCE.
HAS A LETTER ARRIVED FROM KOTOZAWA UNIVERSITY?
OH...
...OKAY. THANKS.
HUH? I DON'T SOUND WELL?
I'M FINE. YES, GOOD NIGHT.
CHAK
IF THEY HAVEN'T CONTACTED ME BY NOW, THEN...

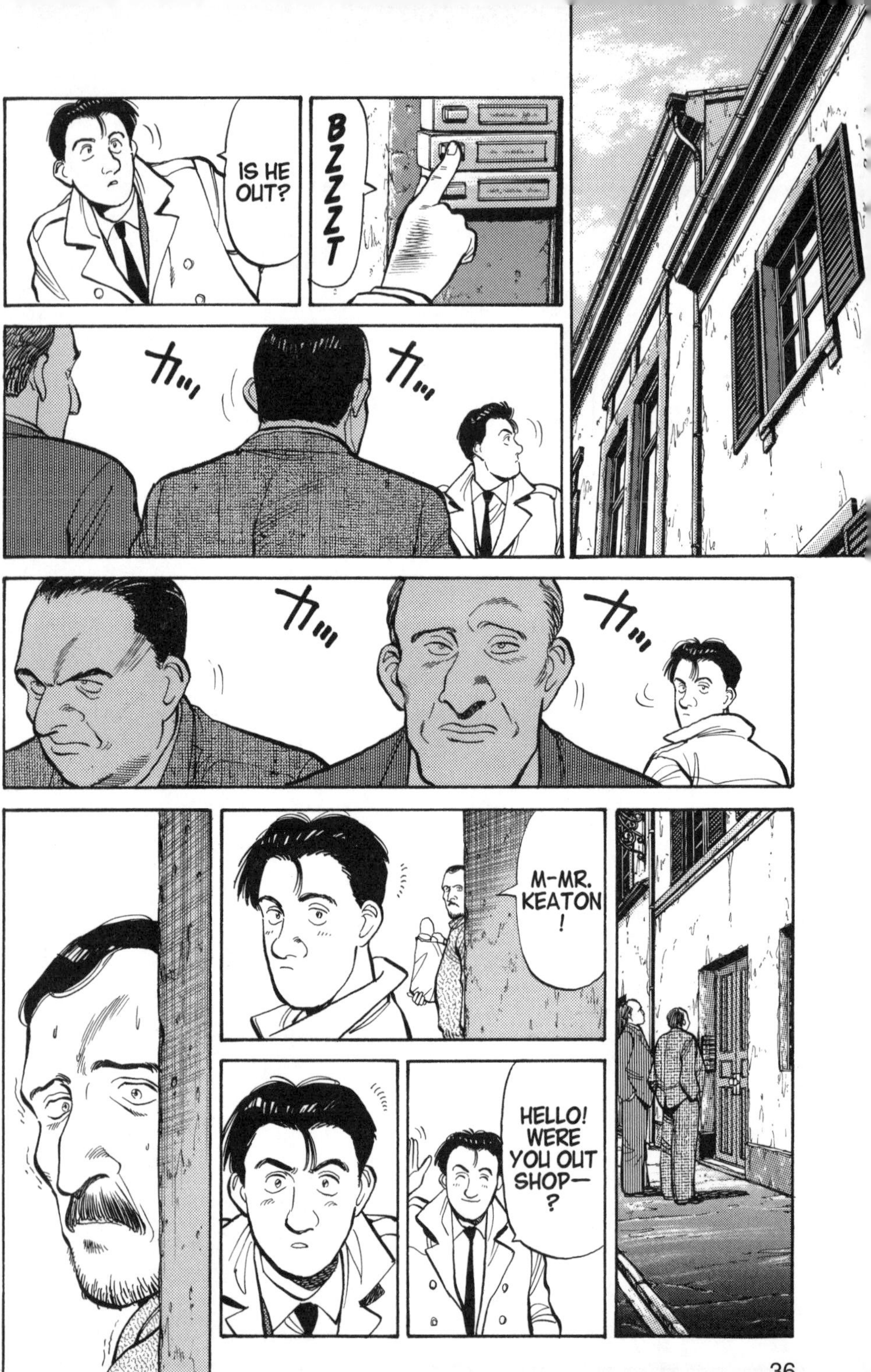
BZZZT
IS HE OUT?
カッ
カッ
カッ
カッ
M-MR. KEATON!
HELLO! WERE YOU OUT SHOP—?

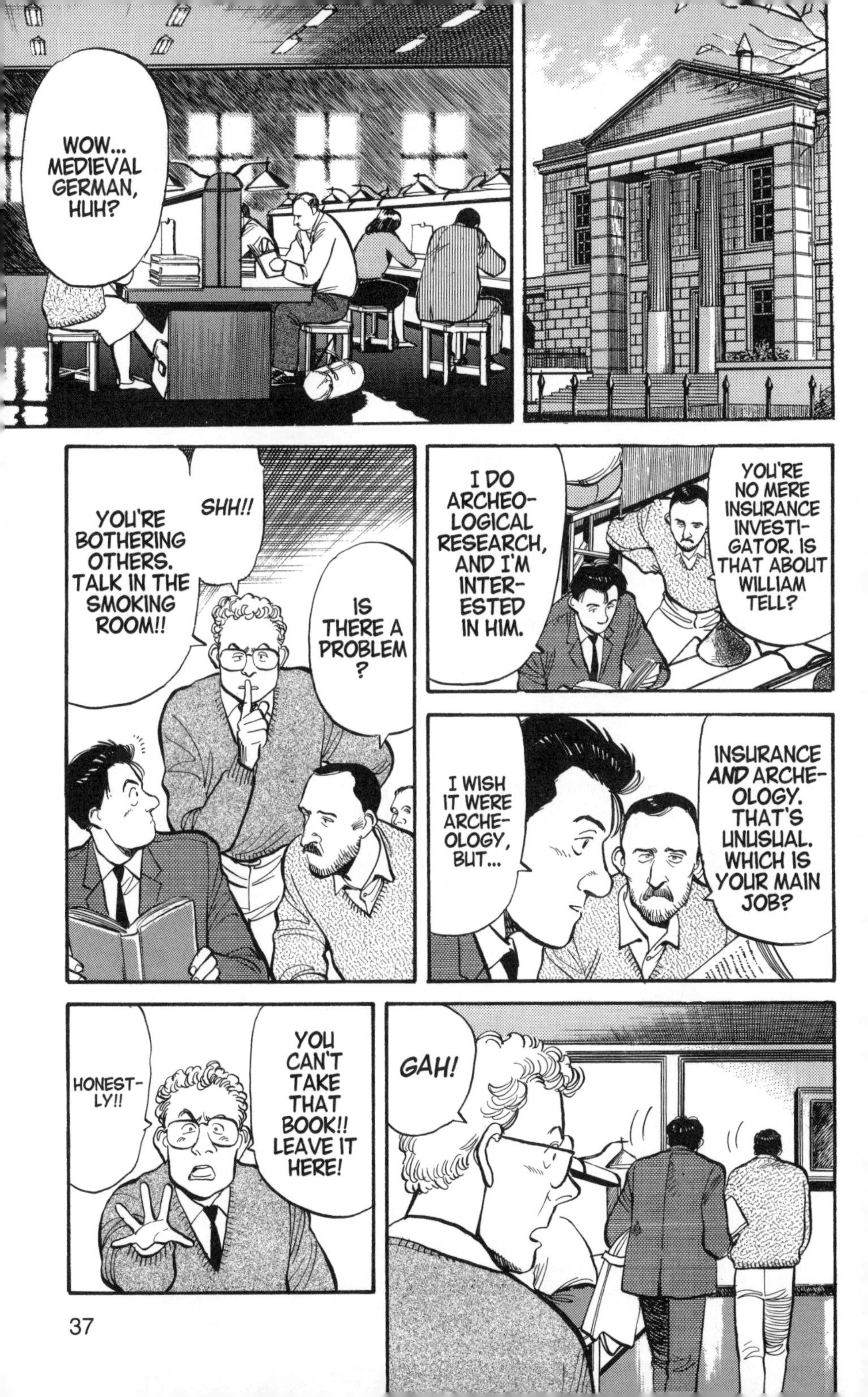
WOW... MEDIEVAL GERMAN, HUH?
YOU'RE NO MERE INSURANCE INVESTIGATOR. IS THAT ABOUT WILLIAM TELL?
I DO ARCHEOLOGICAL RESEARCH, AND I'M INTERESTED IN HIM.
INSURANCE AND ARCHEOLOGY. THAT'S UNUSUAL. WHICH IS YOUR MAIN JOB?
I WISH IT WERE ARCHEOLOGY, BUT...
IS THERE A PROBLEM?
SHH!!
YOU'RE BOTHERING OTHERS. TALK IN THE SMOKING ROOM!!
GAH!
YOU CAN'T TAKE THAT BOOK!! LEAVE IT HERE!
HONESTLY!!

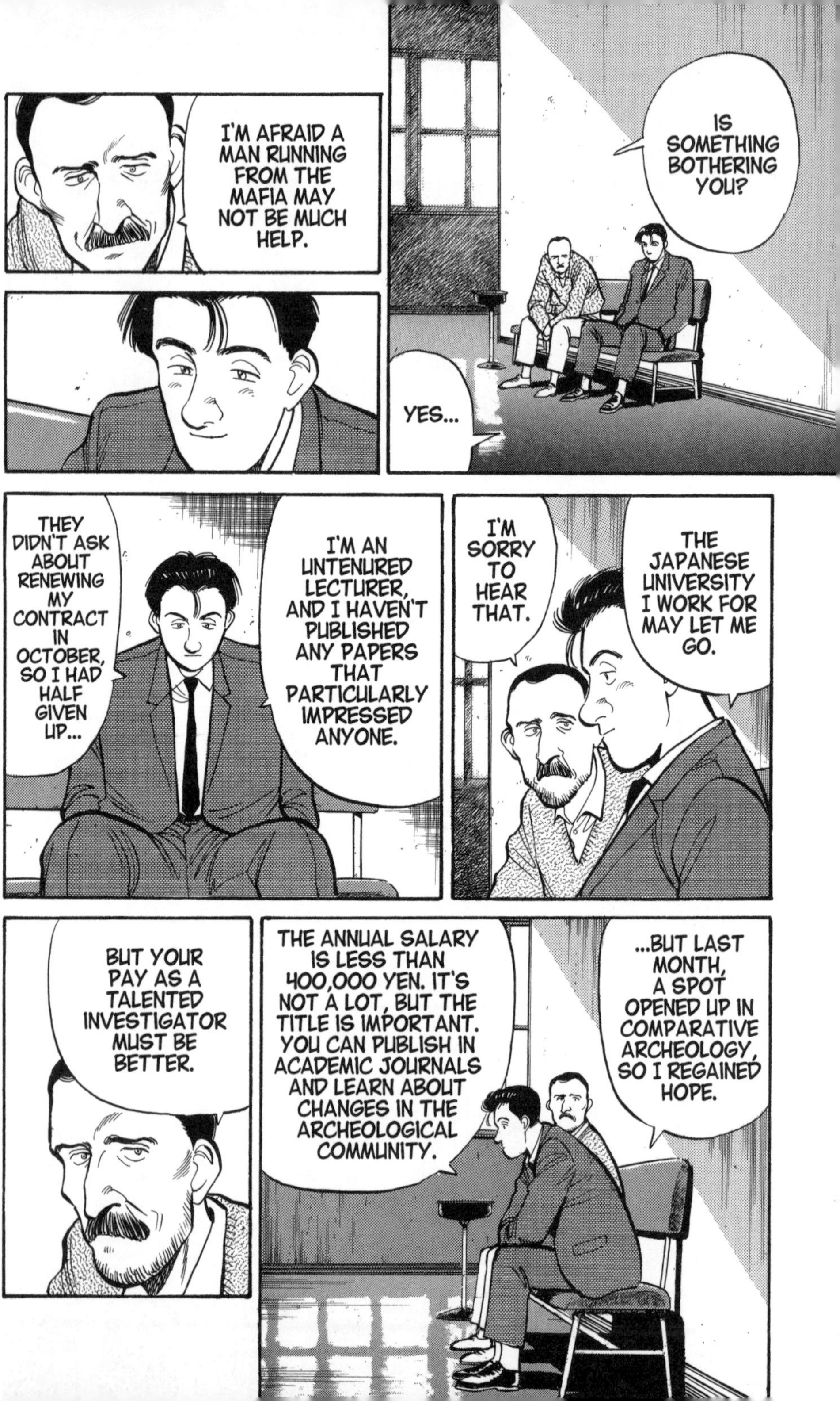
IS SOMETHING BOTHERING YOU?
YES...
I'M AFRAID A MAN RUNNING FROM THE MAFIA MAY NOT BE MUCH HELP.
THE JAPANESE UNIVERSITY I WORK FOR MAY LET ME GO.
I'M SORRY TO HEAR THAT.
I'M AN UNTENURED LECTURER, AND I HAVEN'T PUBLISHED ANY PAPERS THAT PARTICULARLY IMPRESSED ANYONE.
THEY DIDN'T ASK ABOUT RENEWING MY CONTRACT IN OCTOBER, SO I HAD HALF GIVEN UP...
...BUT LAST MONTH, A SPOT OPENED UP IN COMPARATIVE ARCHEOLOGY, SO I REGAINED HOPE.
THE ANNUAL SALARY IS LESS THAN 400,000 YEN. IT'S NOT A LOT, BUT THE TITLE IS IMPORTANT. YOU CAN PUBLISH IN ACADEMIC JOURNALS AND LEARN ABOUT CHANGES IN THE ARCHEOLOGICAL COMMUNITY.
BUT YOUR PAY AS A TALENTED INVESTIGATOR MUST BE BETTER.

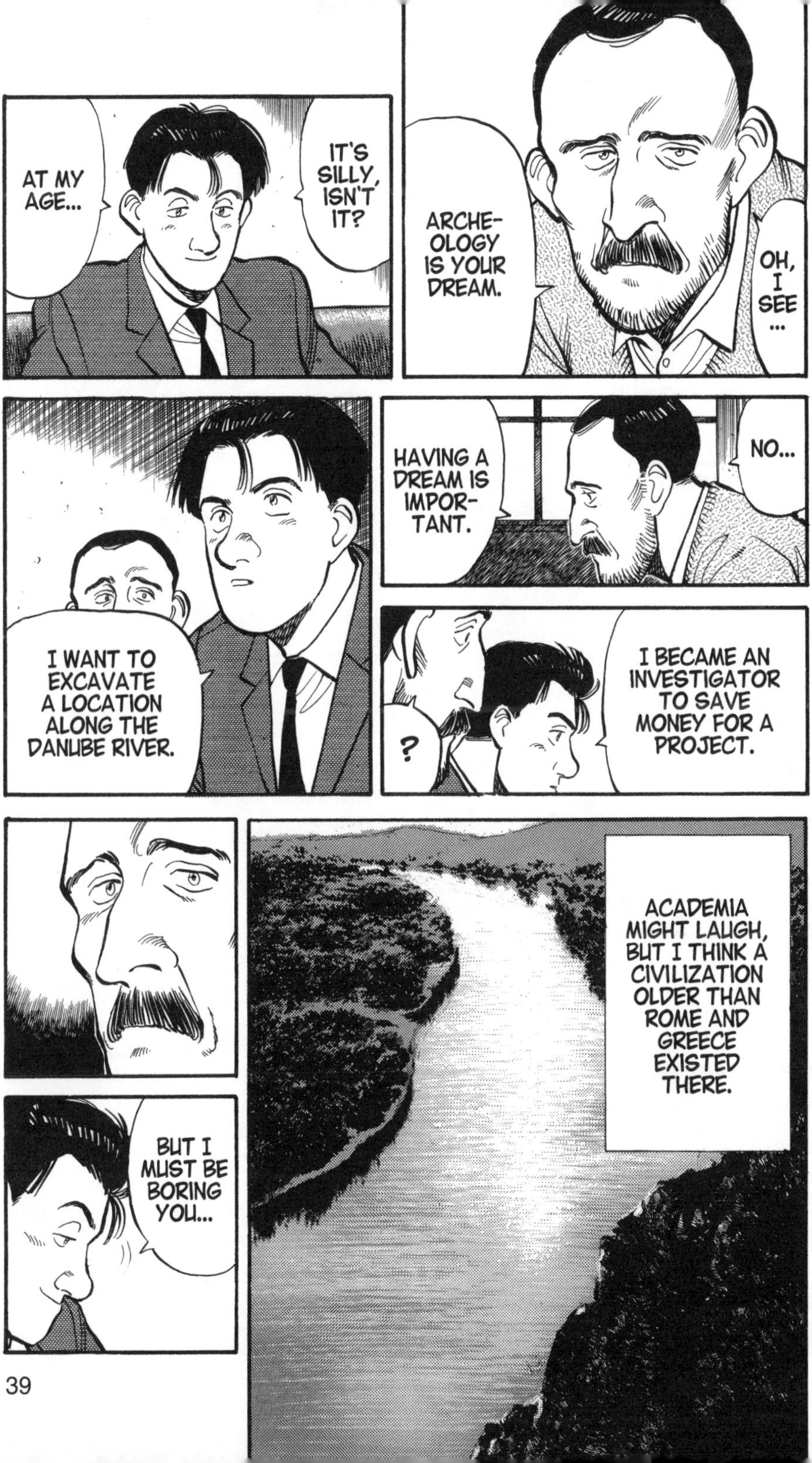
OH, I SEE...
ARCHE-OLOGY IS YOUR DREAM.
IT'S SILLY, ISN'T IT?
AT MY AGE...
NO...
HAVING A DREAM IS IMPOR-TANT.
I BECAME AN INVESTIGATOR TO SAVE MONEY FOR A PROJECT.
?
I WANT TO EXCAVATE A LOCATION ALONG THE DANUBE RIVER.
ACADEMIA MIGHT LAUGH, BUT I THINK A CIVILIZATION OLDER THAN ROME AND GREECE EXISTED THERE.
BUT I MUST BE BORING YOU...

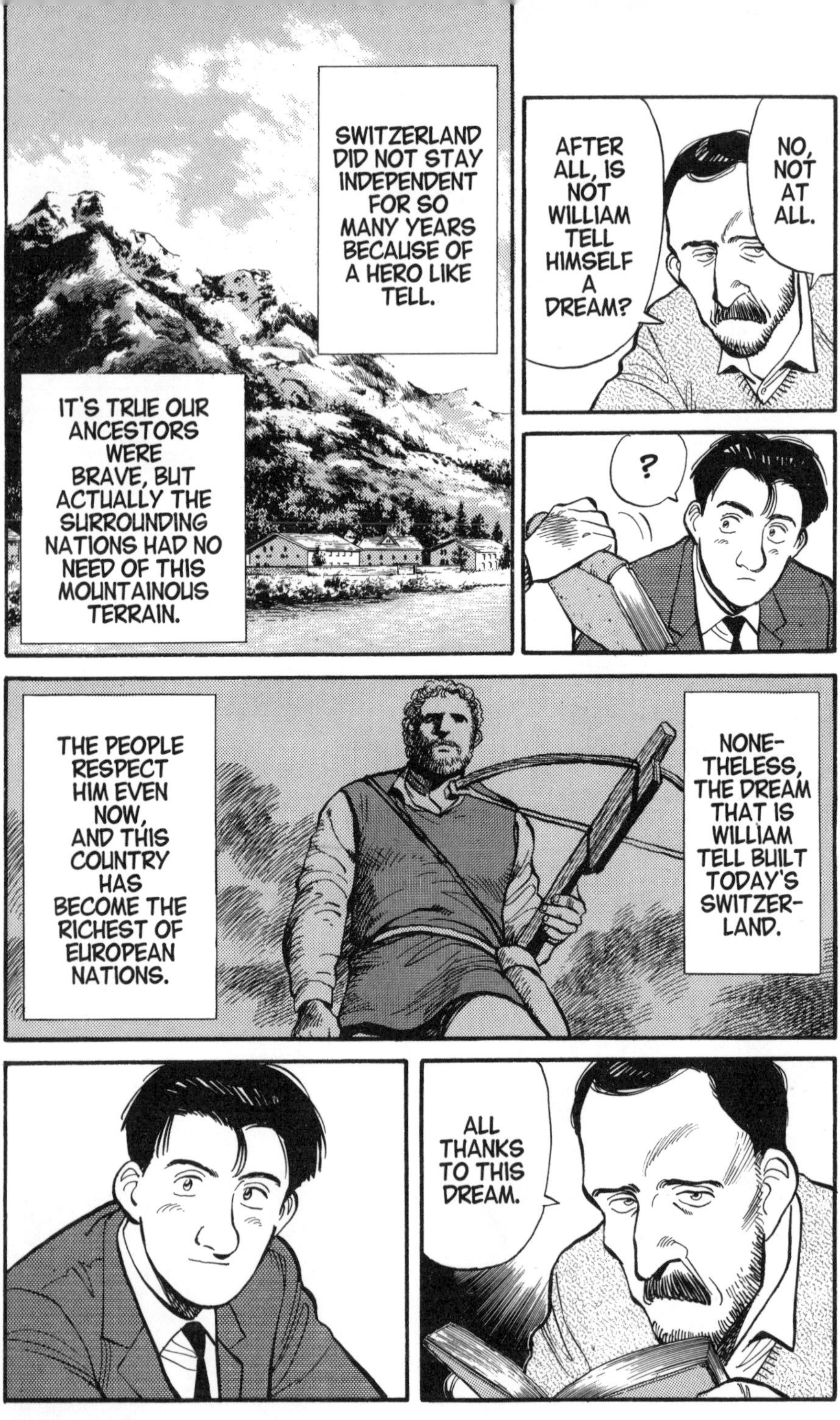
NO, NOT AT ALL.
AFTER ALL, IS NOT WILLIAM TELL HIMSELF A DREAM?
?
SWITZERLAND DID NOT STAY INDEPENDENT FOR SO MANY YEARS BECAUSE OF A HERO LIKE TELL.
IT'S TRUE OUR ANCESTORS WERE BRAVE, BUT ACTUALLY THE SURROUNDING NATIONS HAD NO NEED OF THIS MOUNTAINOUS TERRAIN.
NONE-THELESS, THE DREAM THAT IS WILLIAM TELL BUILT TODAY'S SWITZER-LAND.
THE PEOPLE RESPECT HIM EVEN NOW, AND THIS COUNTRY HAS BECOME THE RICHEST OF EUROPEAN NATIONS.
ALL THANKS TO THIS DREAM.

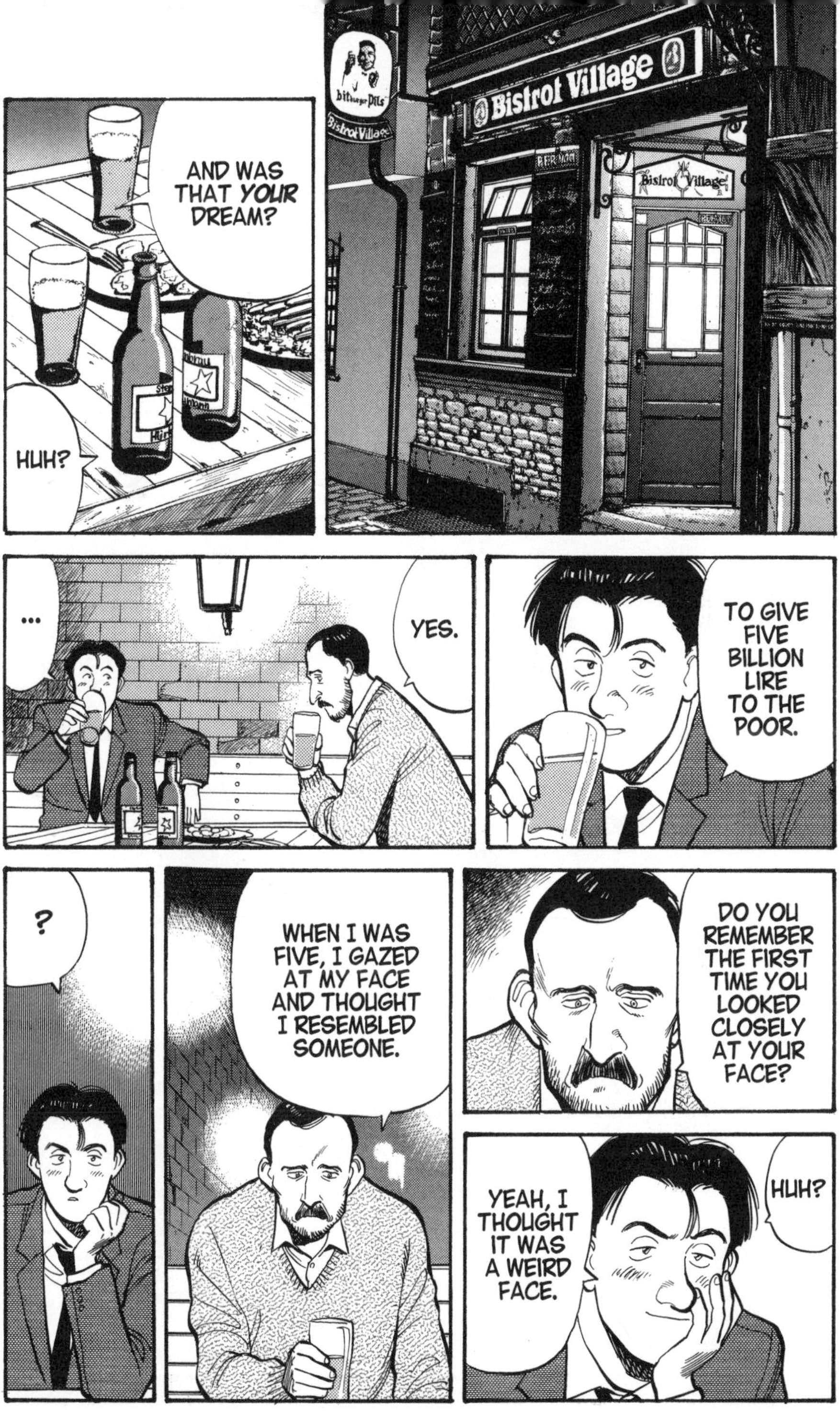

Bistrot Village
AND WAS THAT YOUR DREAM?
HUH?
TO GIVE FIVE BILLION LIRE TO THE POOR.
YES.
...
DO YOU REMEMBER THE FIRST TIME YOU LOOKED CLOSELY AT YOUR FACE?
HUH?
YEAH, I THOUGHT IT WAS A WEIRD FACE.
WHEN I WAS FIVE, I GAZED AT MY FACE AND THOUGHT I RESEMBLED SOMEONE.
?

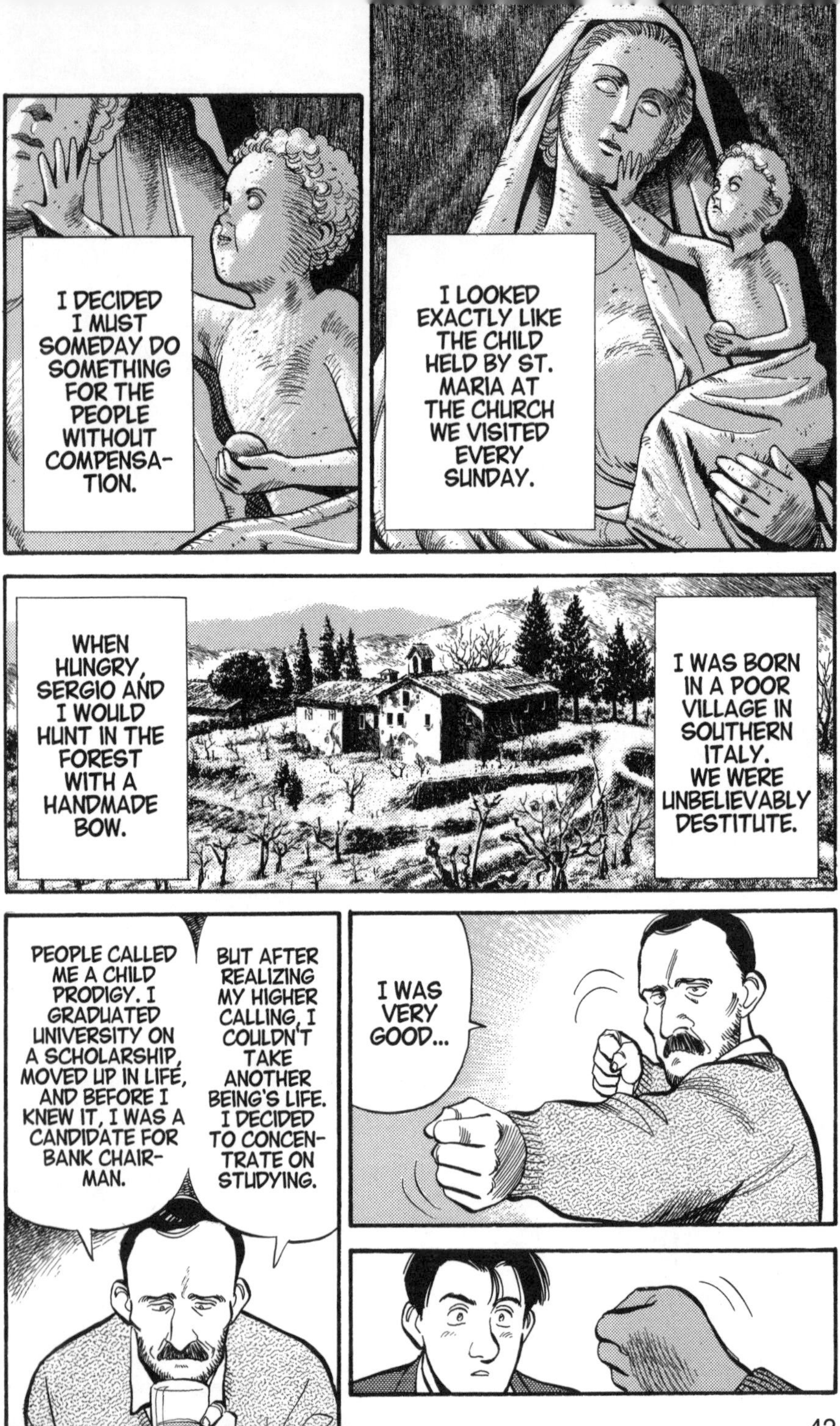
I LOOKED EXACTLY LIKE THE CHILD HELD BY ST. MARIA AT THE CHURCH WE VISITED EVERY SUNDAY.
I DECIDED I MUST SOMEDAY DO SOMETHING FOR THE PEOPLE WITHOUT COMPENSA- TION.
I WAS BORN IN A POOR VILLAGE IN SOUTHERN ITALY. WE WERE UNBELIEVABLY DESTITUTE.
WHEN HUNGRY, SERGIO AND I WOULD HUNT IN THE FOREST WITH A HANDMADE BOW.
I WAS VERY GOOD...
BUT AFTER REALIZING MY HIGHER CALLING, I COULDN'T TAKE ANOTHER BEING'S LIFE. I DECIDED TO CONCEN- TRATE ON STUDYING.
PEOPLE CALLED ME A CHILD PRODIGY. I GRADUATED UNIVERSITY ON A SCHOLARSHIP, MOVED UP IN LIFE, AND BEFORE I KNEW IT, I WAS A CANDIDATE FOR BANK CHAIR- MAN.

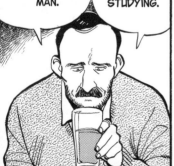

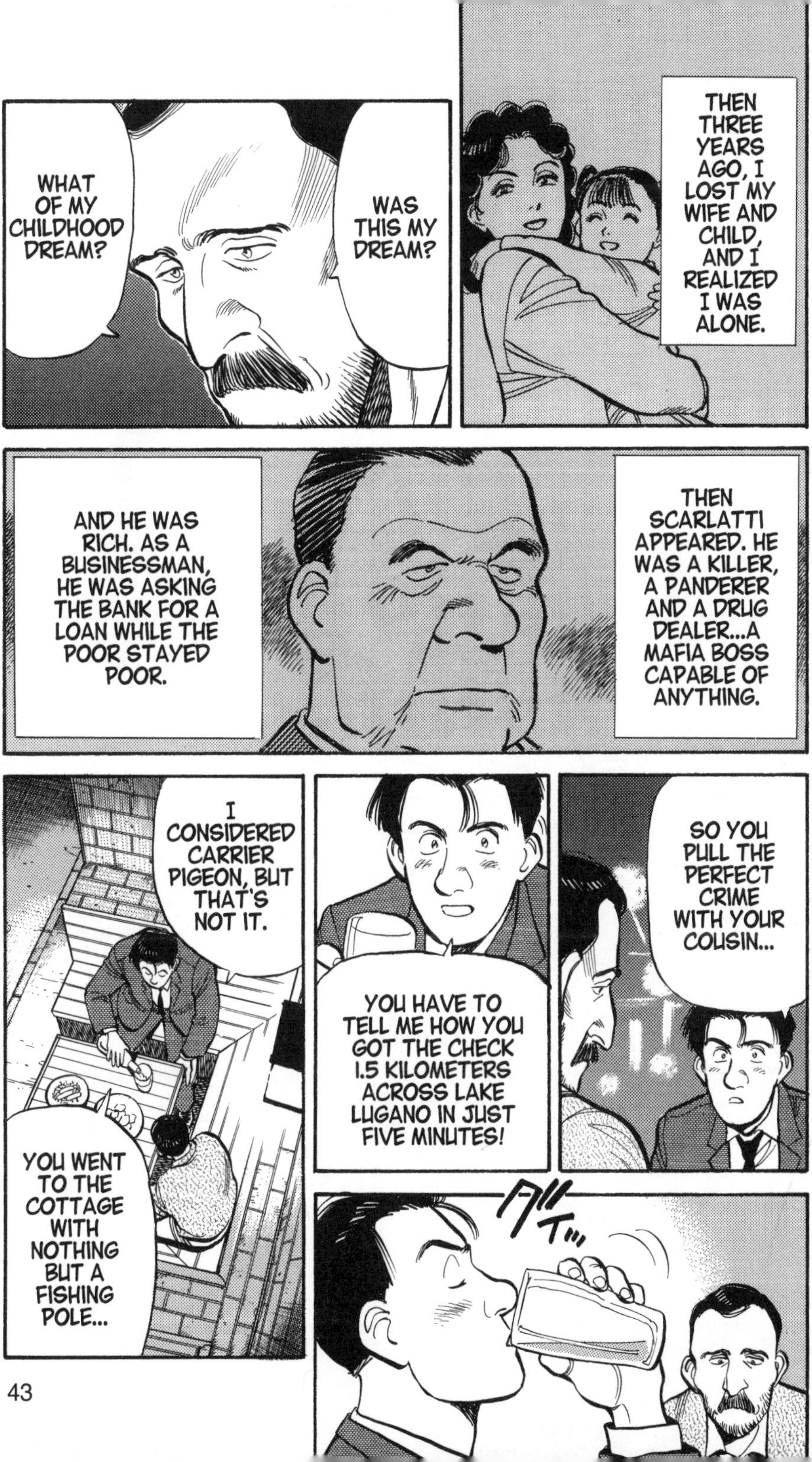
THEN THREE YEARS AGO, I LOST MY WIFE AND CHILD, AND I REALIZED I WAS ALONE.
WAS THIS MY DREAM?
WHAT OF MY CHILDHOOD DREAM?
THEN SCARLATTI APPEARED. HE WAS A KILLER, A PANDERER AND A DRUG DEALER...A MAFIA BOSS CAPABLE OF ANYTHING.
AND HE WAS RICH. AS A BUSINESSMAN, HE WAS ASKING THE BANK FOR A LOAN WHILE THE POOR STAYED POOR.
SO YOU PULL THE PERFECT CRIME WITH YOUR COUSIN...
YOU HAVE TO TELL ME HOW YOU GOT THE CHECK 1.5 KILOMETERS ACROSS LAKE LUGANO IN JUST FIVE MINUTES!
I CONSIDERED CARRIER PIGEON, BUT THAT'S NOT IT.
YOU WENT TO THE COTTAGE WITH NOTHING BUT A FISHING POLE...

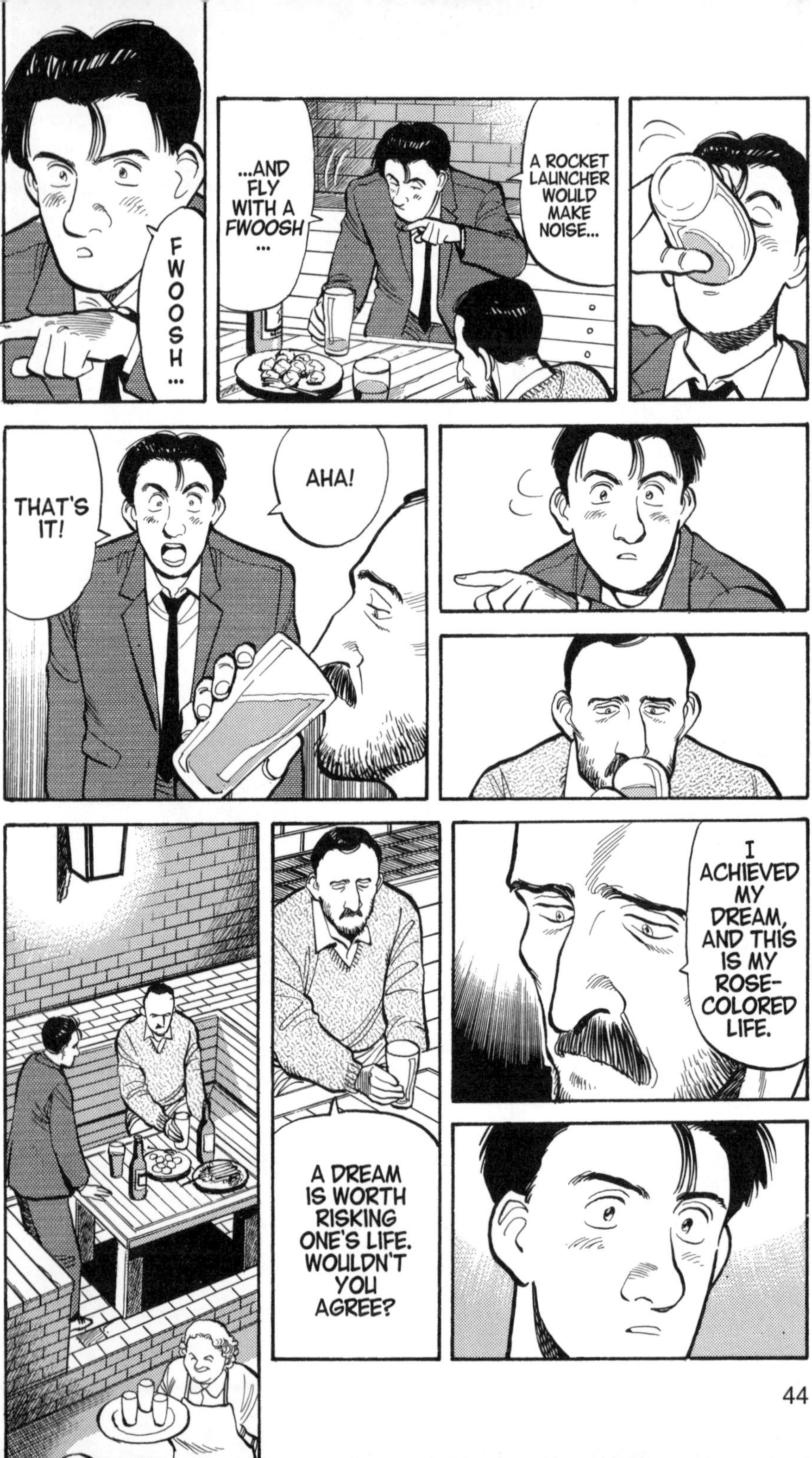
A ROCKET LAUNCHER WOULD MAKE NOISE...
...AND FLY WITH A FWOOSH...
FWOOSH...
AHA!
THAT'S IT!
I ACHIEVED MY DREAM, AND THIS IS MY ROSE-COLORED LIFE.
A DREAM IS WORTH RISKING ONE'S LIFE. WOULDN'T YOU AGREE?

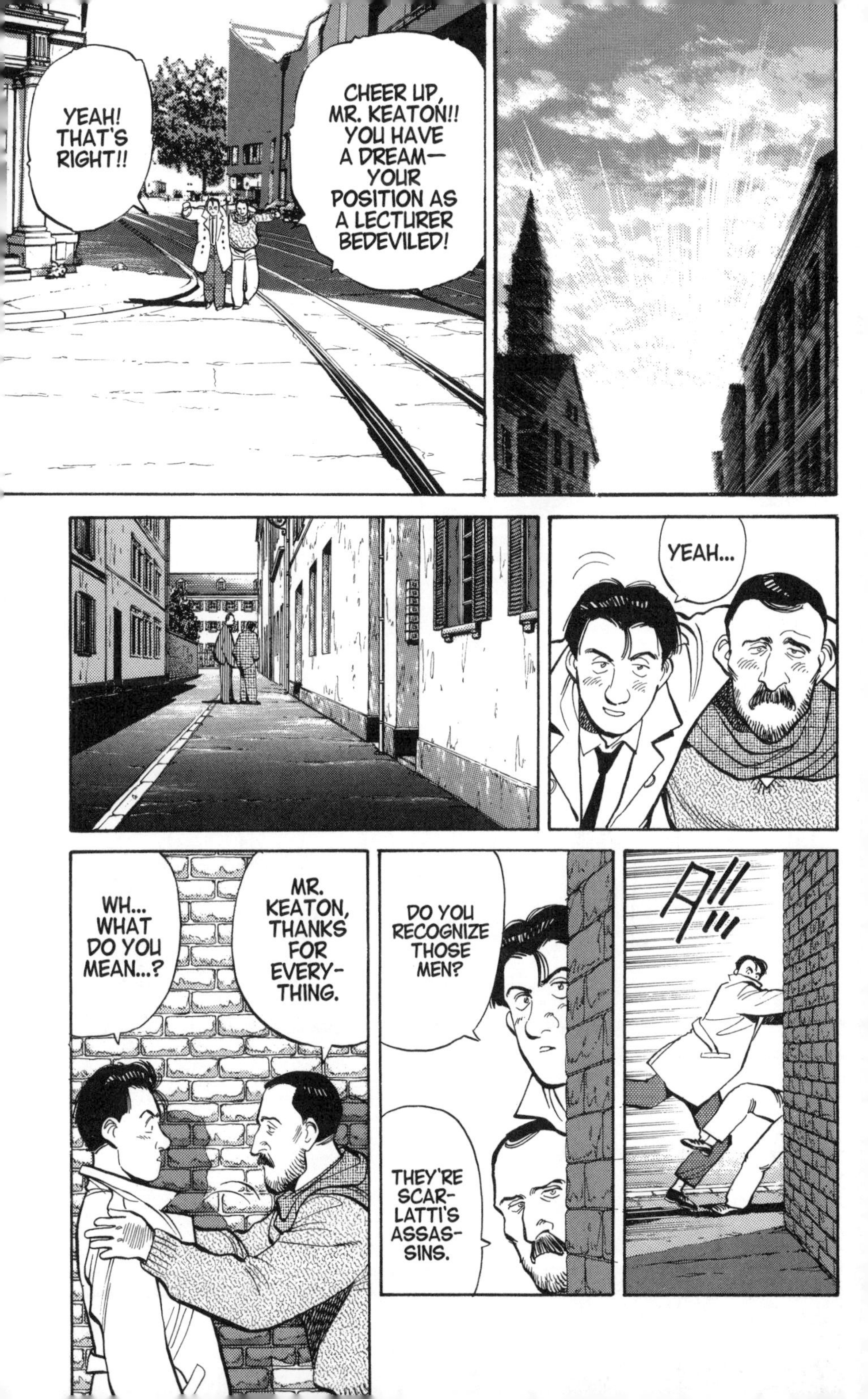
CHEER UP, MR. KEATON!! YOU HAVE A DREAM—YOUR POSITION AS A LECTURER BEDEVILED!
YEAH! THAT'S RIGHT!!
YEAH...
DO YOU RECOGNIZE THOSE MEN?
THEY'RE SCAR-LATTI'S ASSAS-SINS.
MR. KEATON, THANKS FOR EVERY-THING.
WH... WHAT DO YOU MEAN...?

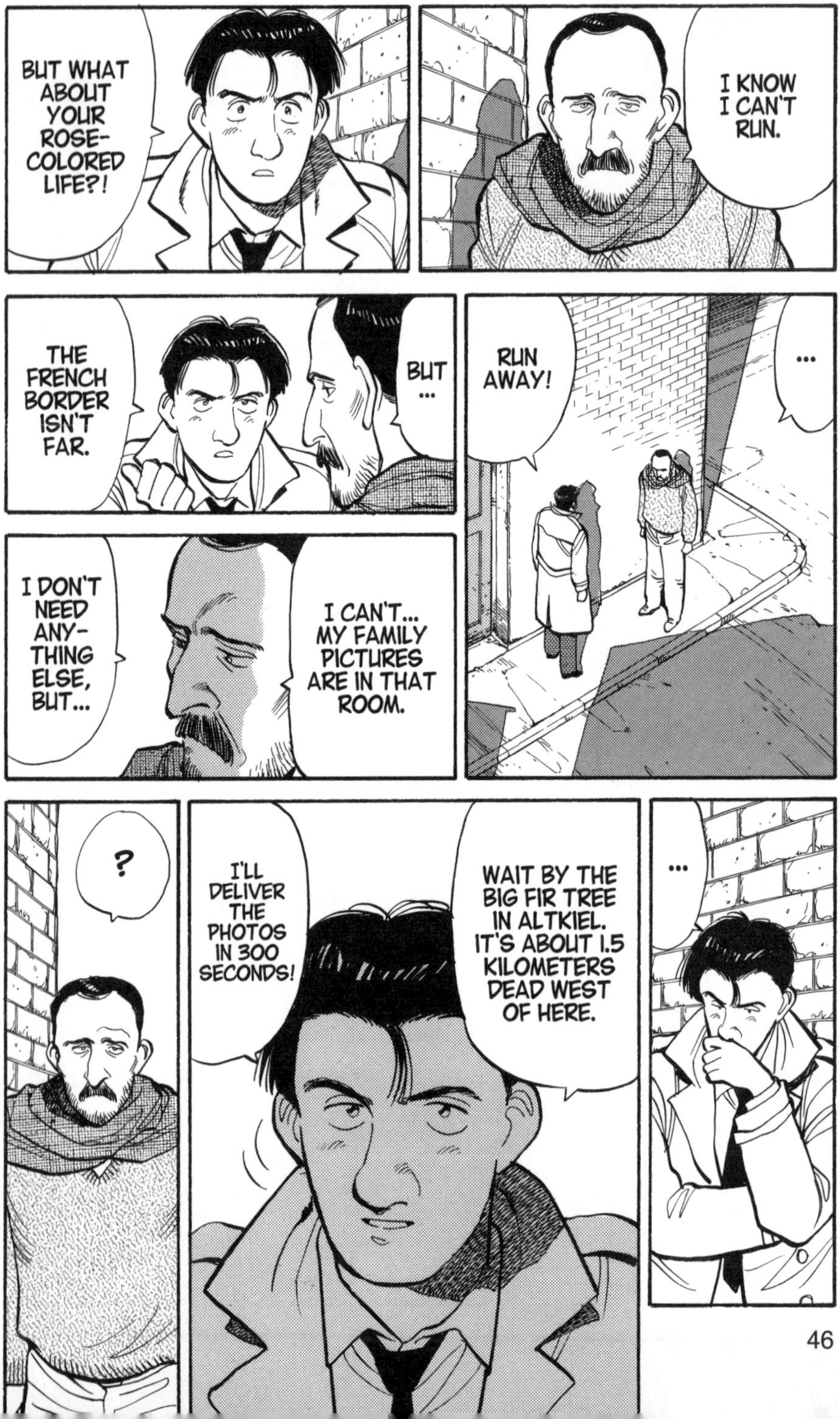
I KNOW I CAN'T RUN.
BUT WHAT ABOUT YOUR ROSE-COLORED LIFE?!
...
RUN AWAY!
BUT ...
THE FRENCH BORDER ISN'T FAR.
I CAN'T... MY FAMILY PICTURES ARE IN THAT ROOM.
I DON'T NEED ANYTHING ELSE, BUT...
...
WAIT BY THE BIG FIR TREE IN ALTKIEL. IT'S ABOUT 1.5 KILOMETERS DEAD WEST OF HERE.
I'LL DELIVER THE PHOTOS IN 300 SECONDS!
?

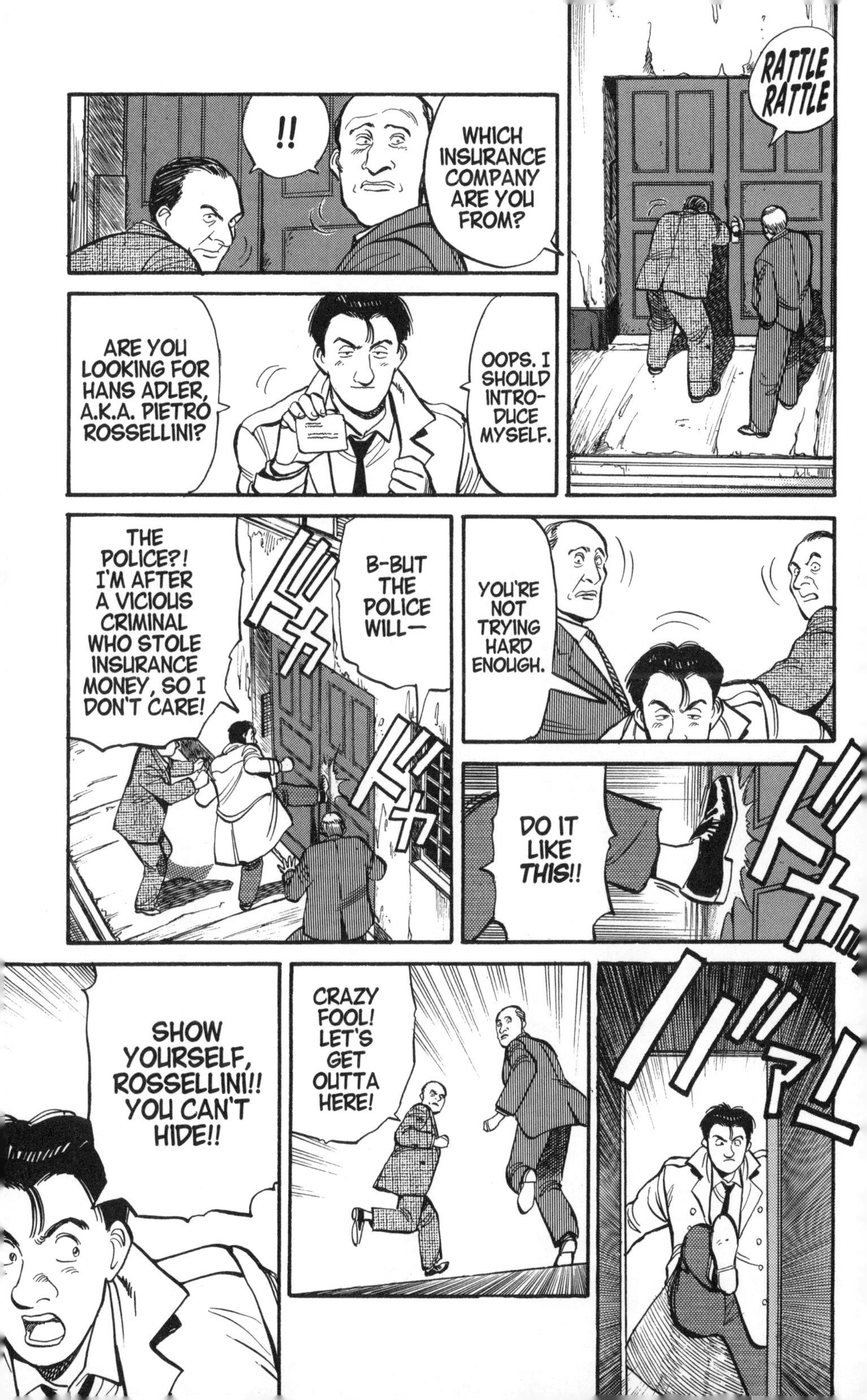
RATTLE RATTLE
WHICH INSURANCE COMPANY ARE YOU FROM?
!!
OOPS. I SHOULD INTRO-DUCE MYSELF.
ARE YOU LOOKING FOR HANS ADLER, A.K.A. PIETRO ROSSELLINI?
YOU'RE NOT TRYING HARD ENOUGH.
DO IT LIKE THIS!!
ドカッ
B-BUT THE POLICE WILL—
ドカ
THE POLICE?! I'M AFTER A VICIOUS CRIMINAL WHO STOLE INSURANCE MONEY, SO I DON'T CARE!
ドカ
CRAZY FOOL! LET'S GET OUTTA HERE!
SHOW YOURSELF, ROSSELLINI!! YOU CAN'T HIDE!!

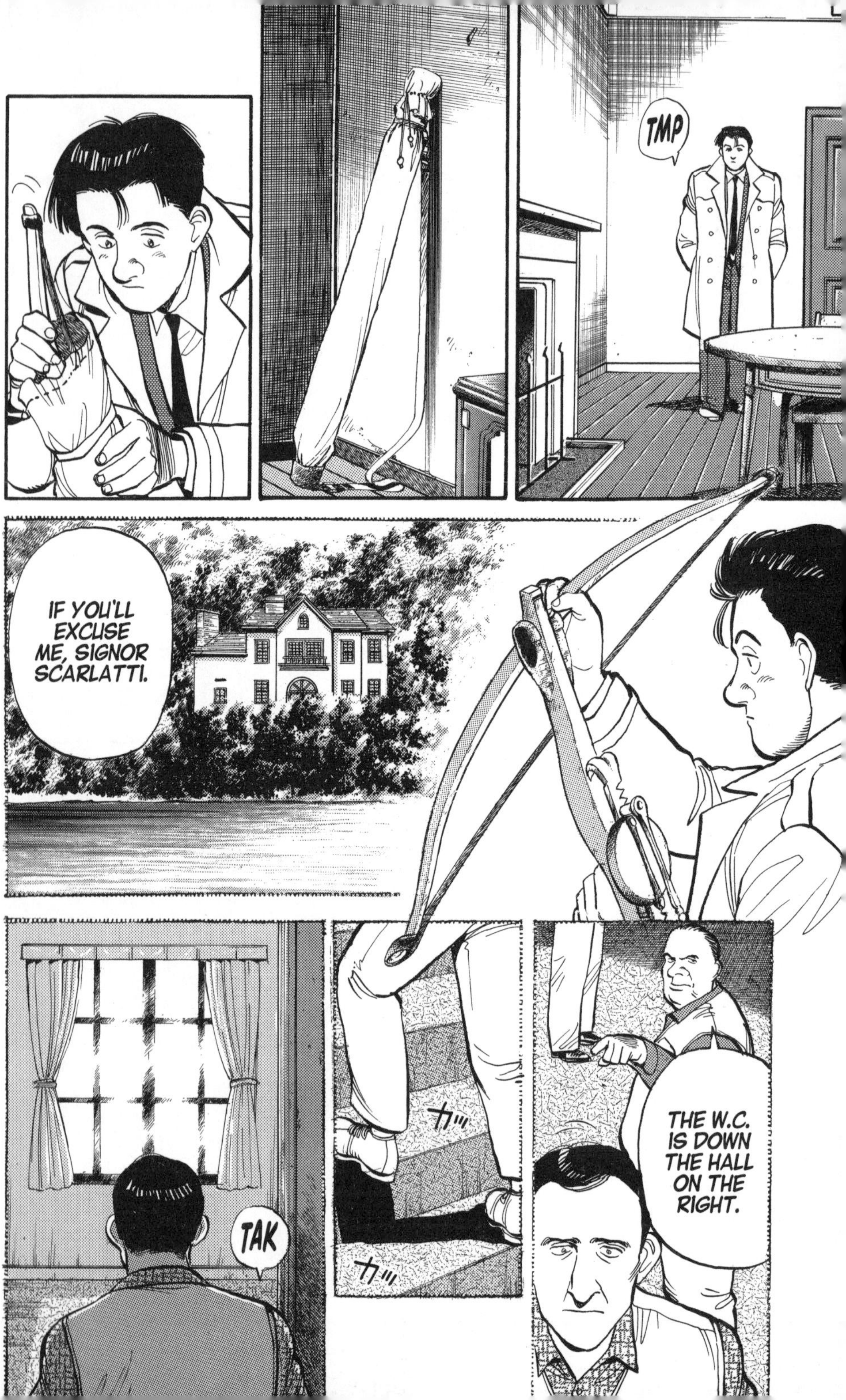
TMP
IF YOU'LL EXCUSE ME, SIGNOR SCARLATTI.
THE W.C. IS DOWN THE HALL ON THE RIGHT.
TAK

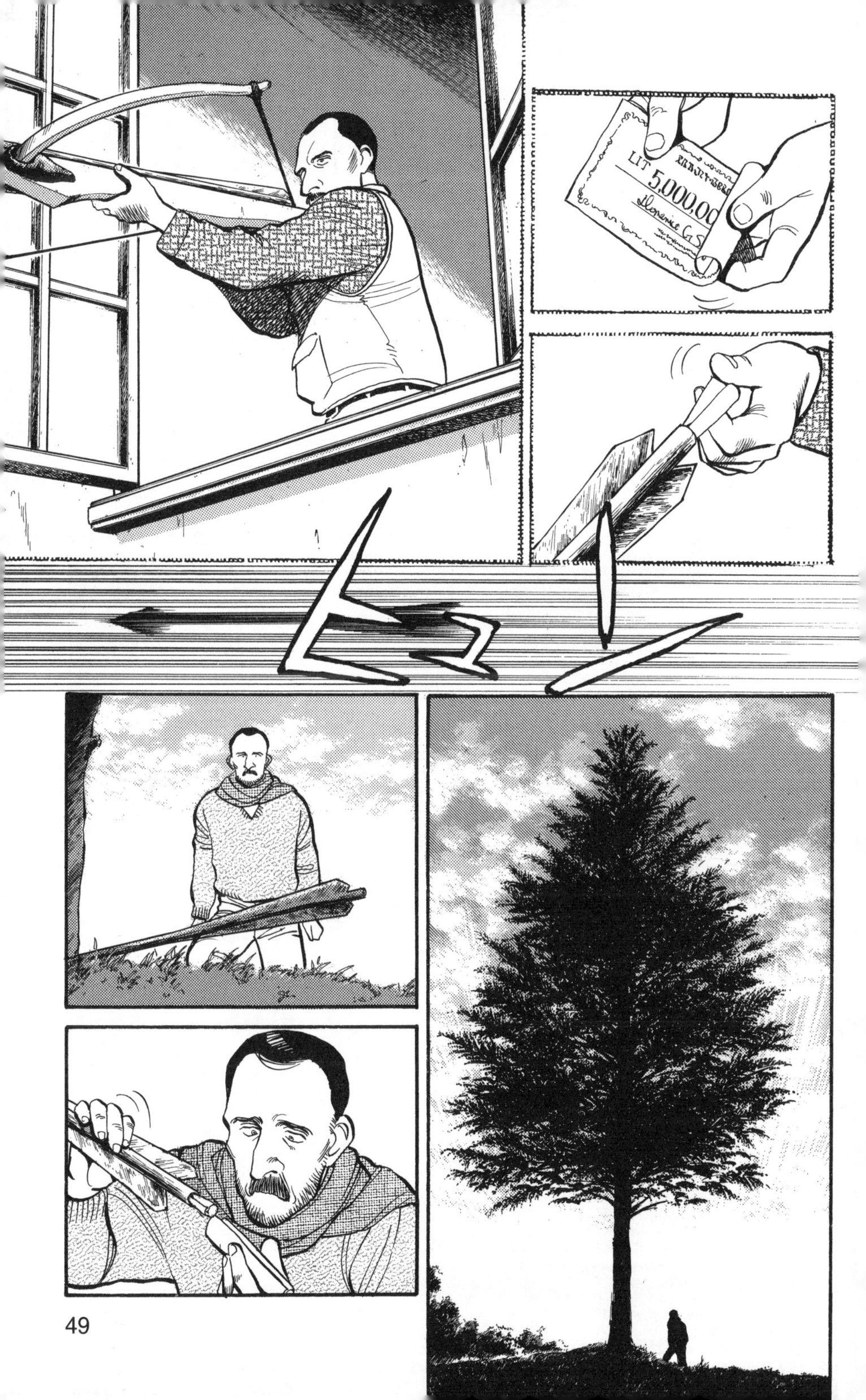
LIT 5,000,00
ヒュン

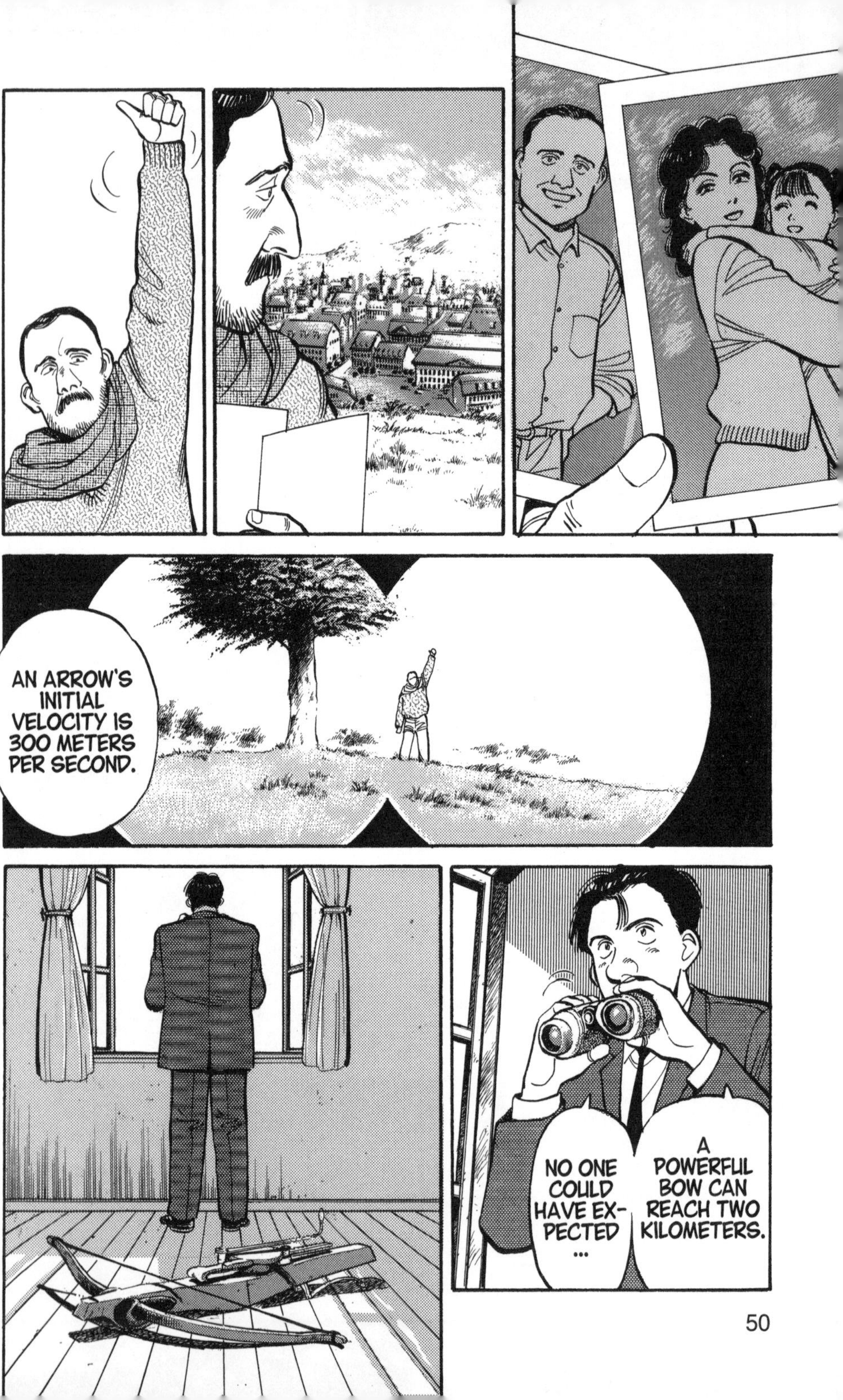
AN ARROW'S INITIAL VELOCITY IS 300 METERS PER SECOND.
A POWERFUL BOW CAN REACH TWO KILOMETERS.
NO ONE COULD HAVE EX-PECTED ...

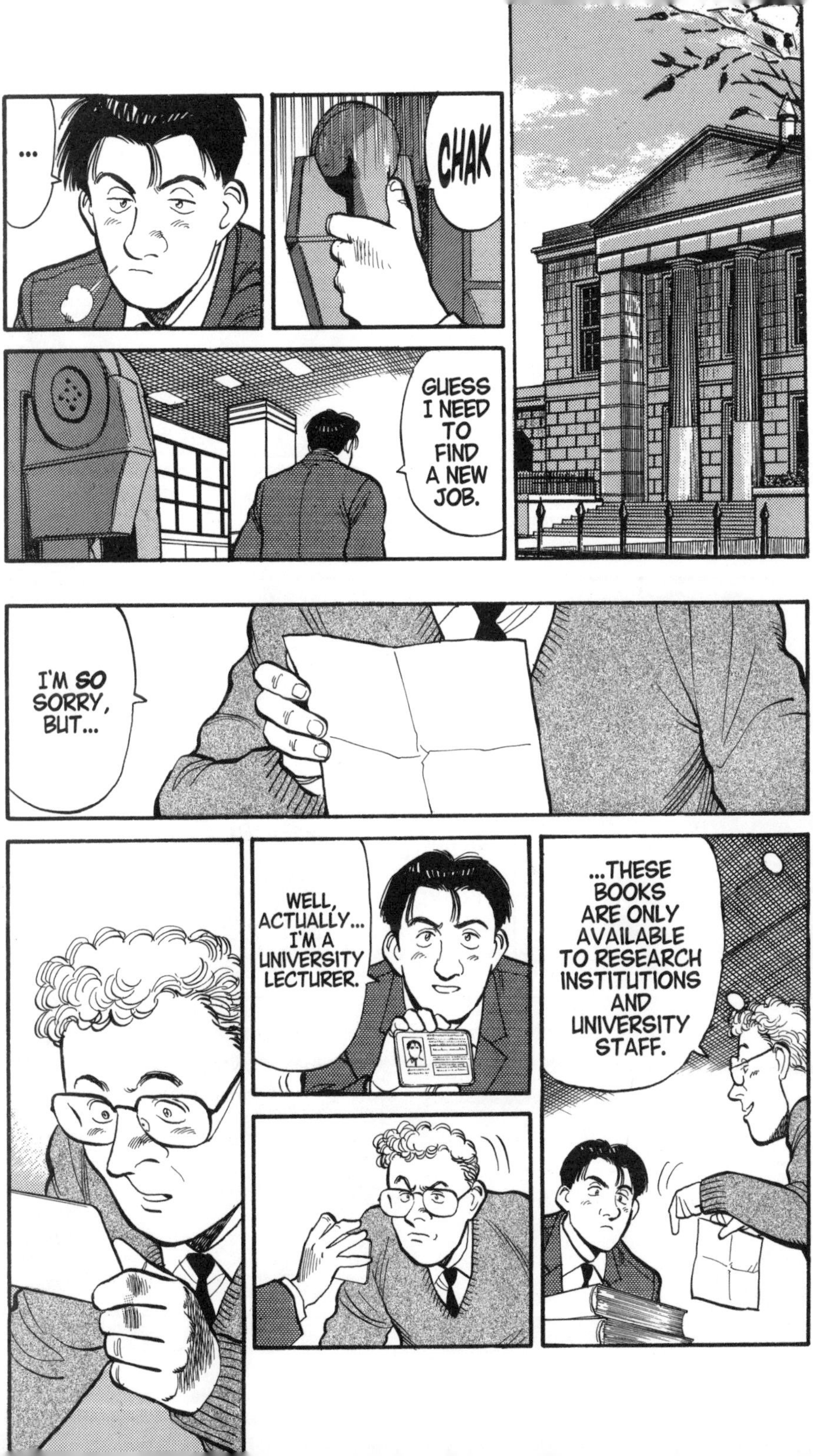
CHAK
...
GUESS I NEED TO FIND A NEW JOB.
I'M SO SORRY, BUT...
...THESE BOOKS ARE ONLY AVAILABLE TO RESEARCH INSTITUTIONS AND UNIVERSITY STAFF.
WELL, ACTUALLY... I'M A UNIVERSITY LECTURER.

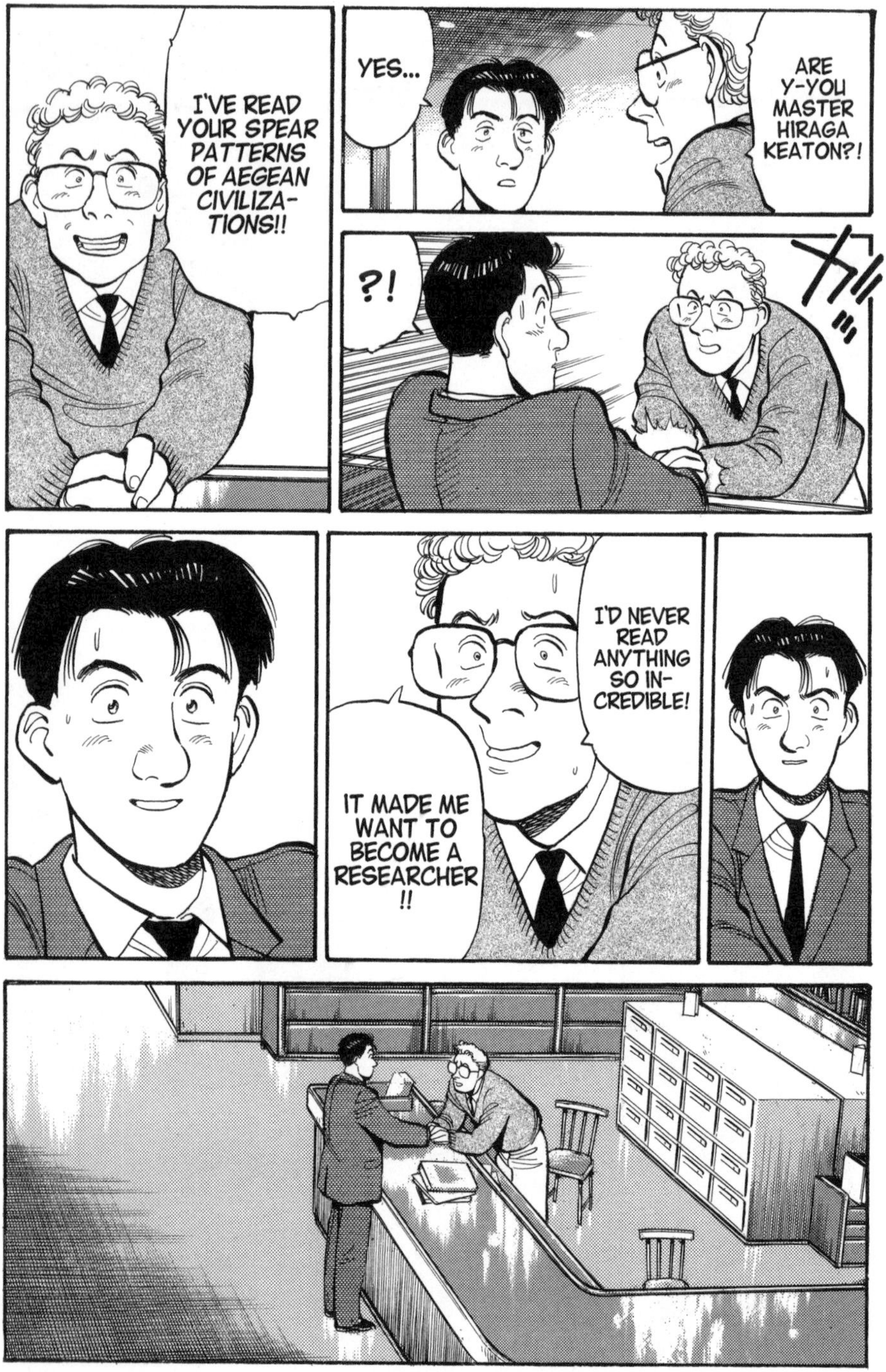
ARE Y-YOU MASTER HIRAGA KEATON?!
YES...
?!
I'VE READ YOUR SPEAR PATTERNS OF AEGEAN CIVILIZA-TIONS!!
I'D NEVER READ ANYTHING SO IN-CREDIBLE!
IT MADE ME WANT TO BECOME A RESEARCHER!!

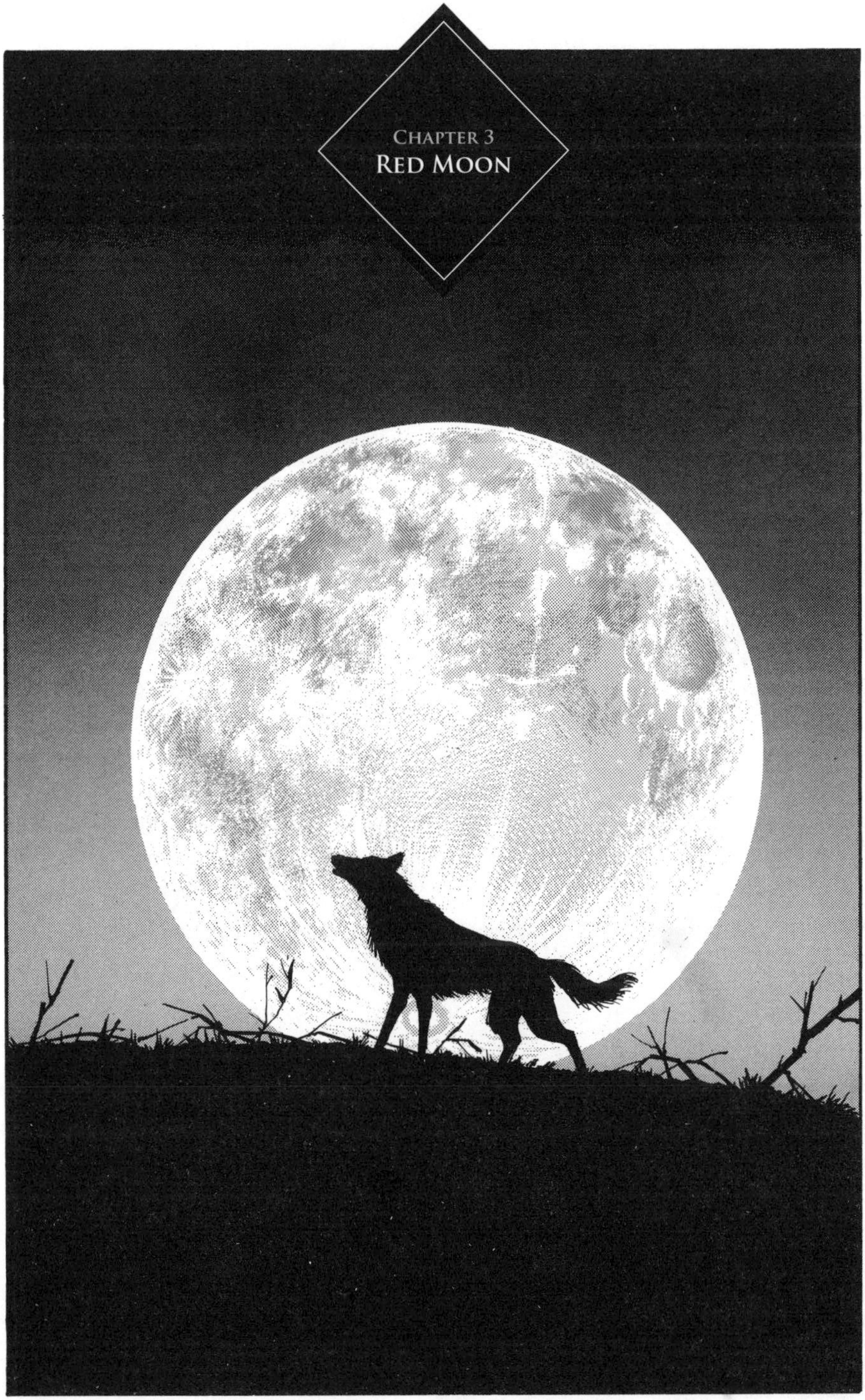
CHAPTER 3
RED MOON

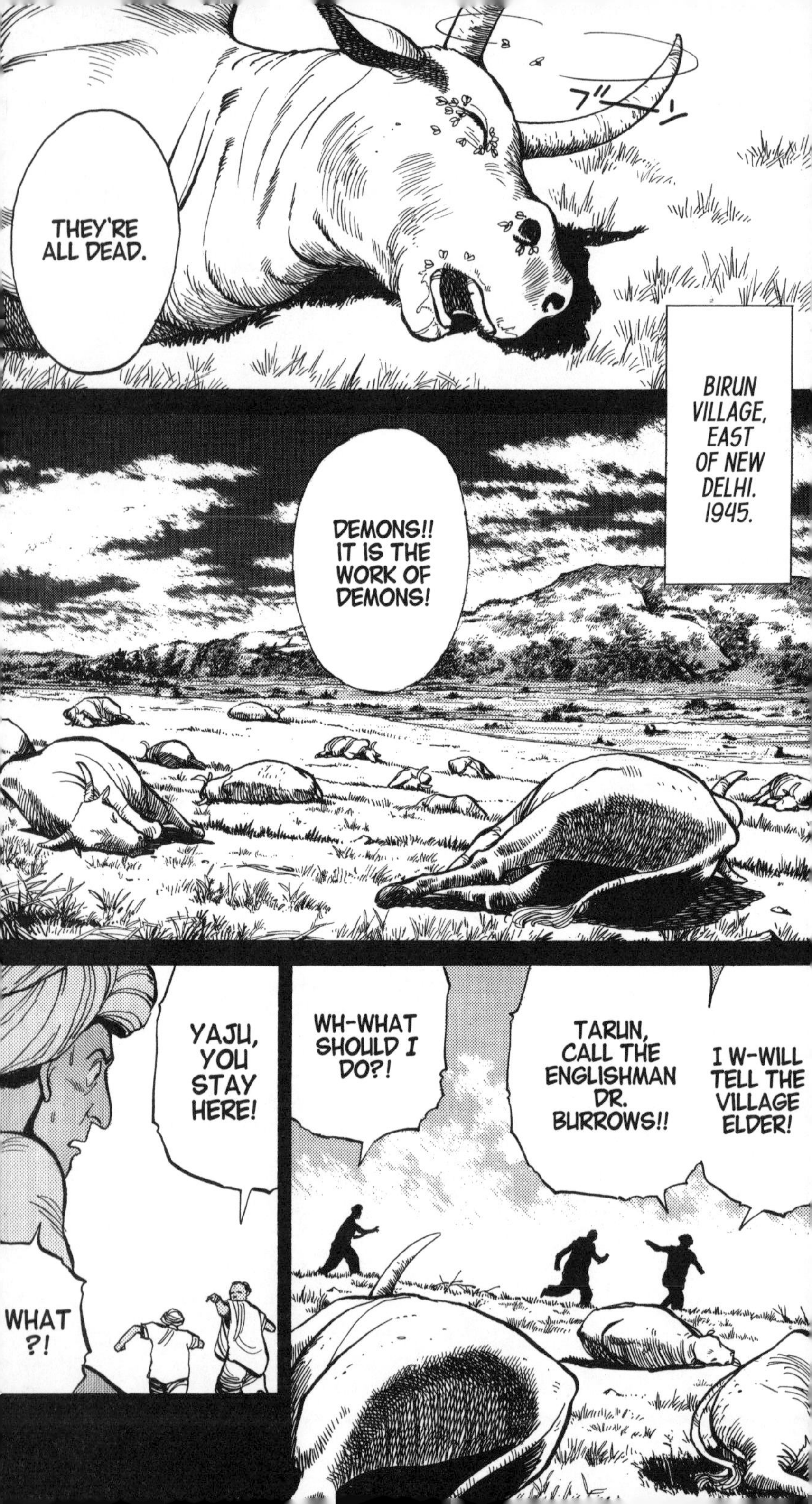
THEY'RE ALL DEAD.
BIRUN VILLAGE, EAST OF NEW DELHI. 1945.
DEMONS!! IT IS THE WORK OF DEMONS!
I W-WILL TELL THE VILLAGE ELDER!
TARUN, CALL THE ENGLISHMAN DR. BURROWS!!
WH-WHAT SHOULD I DO?!
YAJU, YOU STAY HERE!
WHAT?!

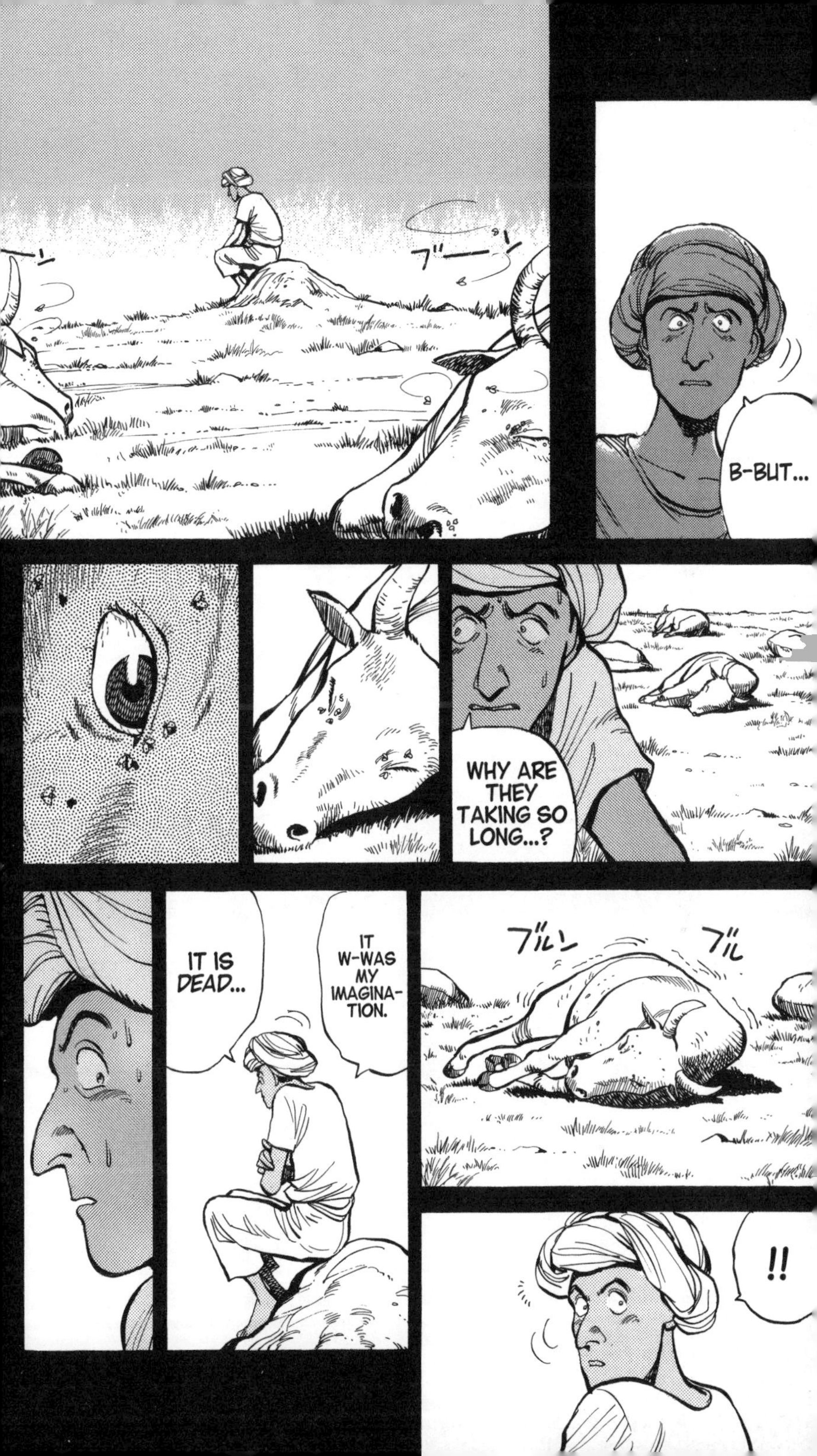
B-BUT...
ブーン
WHY ARE THEY TAKING SO LONG...?
ブルン
ブル
!!
IT W-WAS MY IMAGINATION.
IT IS DEAD...

WH...
WHA...
WHAAAAAA!!

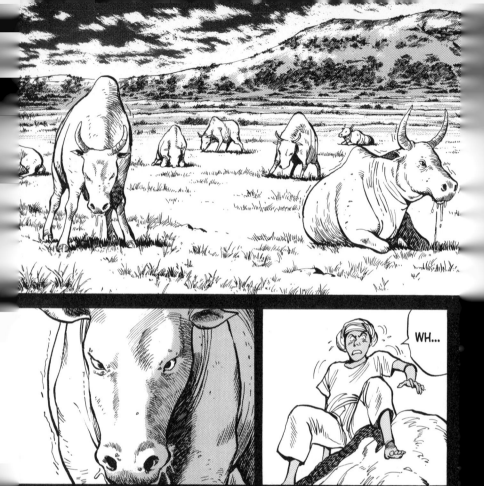

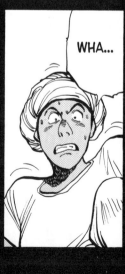

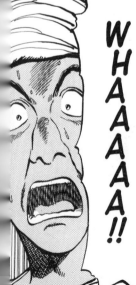

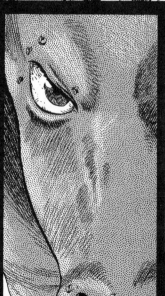

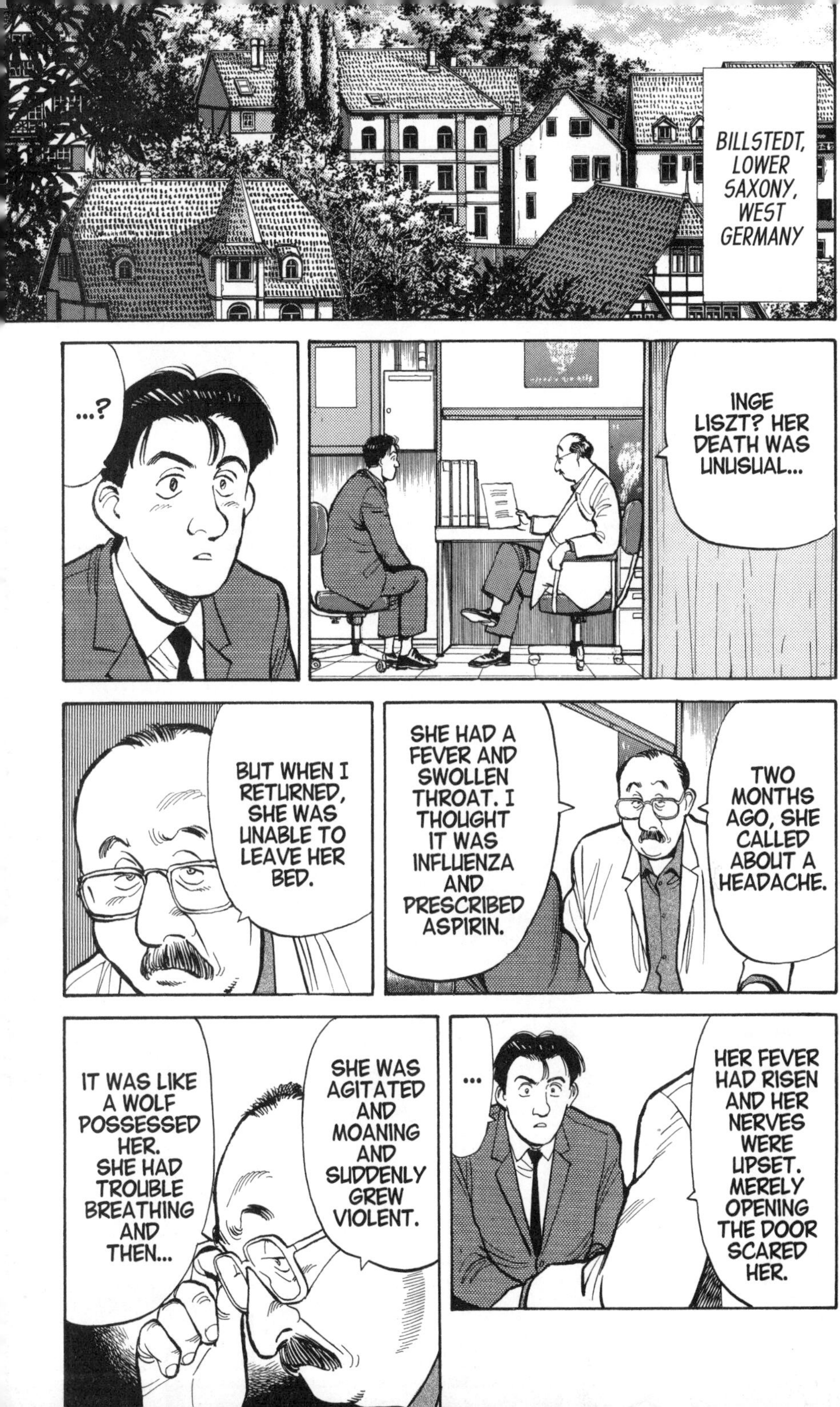
BILLSTEDT, LOWER SAXONY, WEST GERMANY
INGE LISZT? HER DEATH WAS UNUSUAL...
...?
TWO MONTHS AGO, SHE CALLED ABOUT A HEADACHE.
SHE HAD A FEVER AND SWOLLEN THROAT. I THOUGHT IT WAS INFLUENZA AND PRESCRIBED ASPIRIN.
BUT WHEN I RETURNED, SHE WAS UNABLE TO LEAVE HER BED.
HER FEVER HAD RISEN AND HER NERVES WERE UPSET. MERELY OPENING THE DOOR SCARED HER.
...
SHE WAS AGITATED AND MOANING AND SUDDENLY GREW VIOLENT.
IT WAS LIKE A WOLF POSSESSED HER. SHE HAD TROUBLE BREATHING AND THEN...

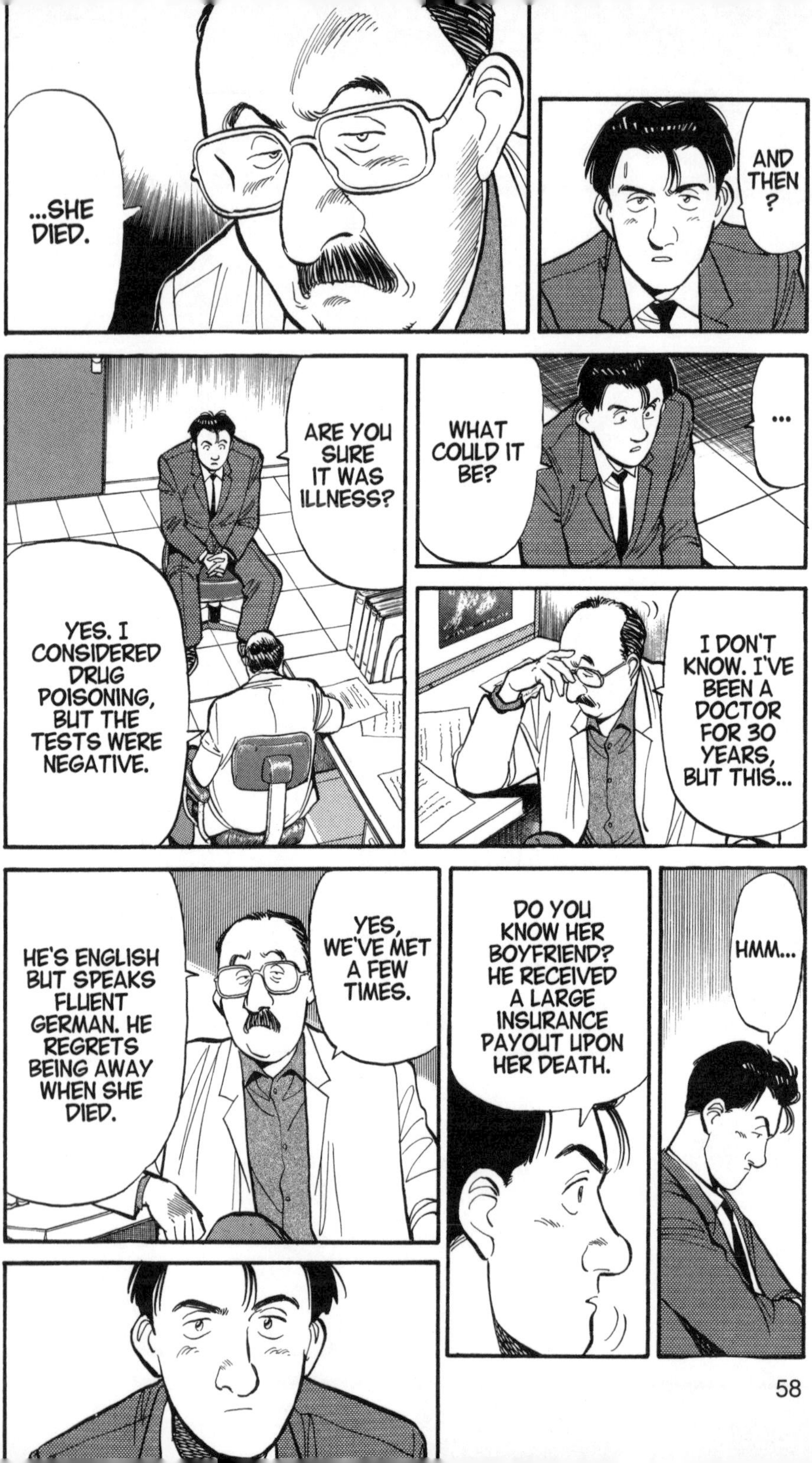
AND THEN?
...SHE DIED.
...
WHAT COULD IT BE?
I DON'T KNOW. I'VE BEEN A DOCTOR FOR 30 YEARS, BUT THIS...
ARE YOU SURE IT WAS ILLNESS?
YES. I CONSIDERED DRUG POISONING, BUT THE TESTS WERE NEGATIVE.
HMM...
DO YOU KNOW HER BOYFRIEND? HE RECEIVED A LARGE INSURANCE PAYOUT UPON HER DEATH.
YES, WE'VE MET A FEW TIMES.
HE'S ENGLISH BUT SPEAKS FLUENT GERMAN. HE REGRETS BEING AWAY WHEN SHE DIED.

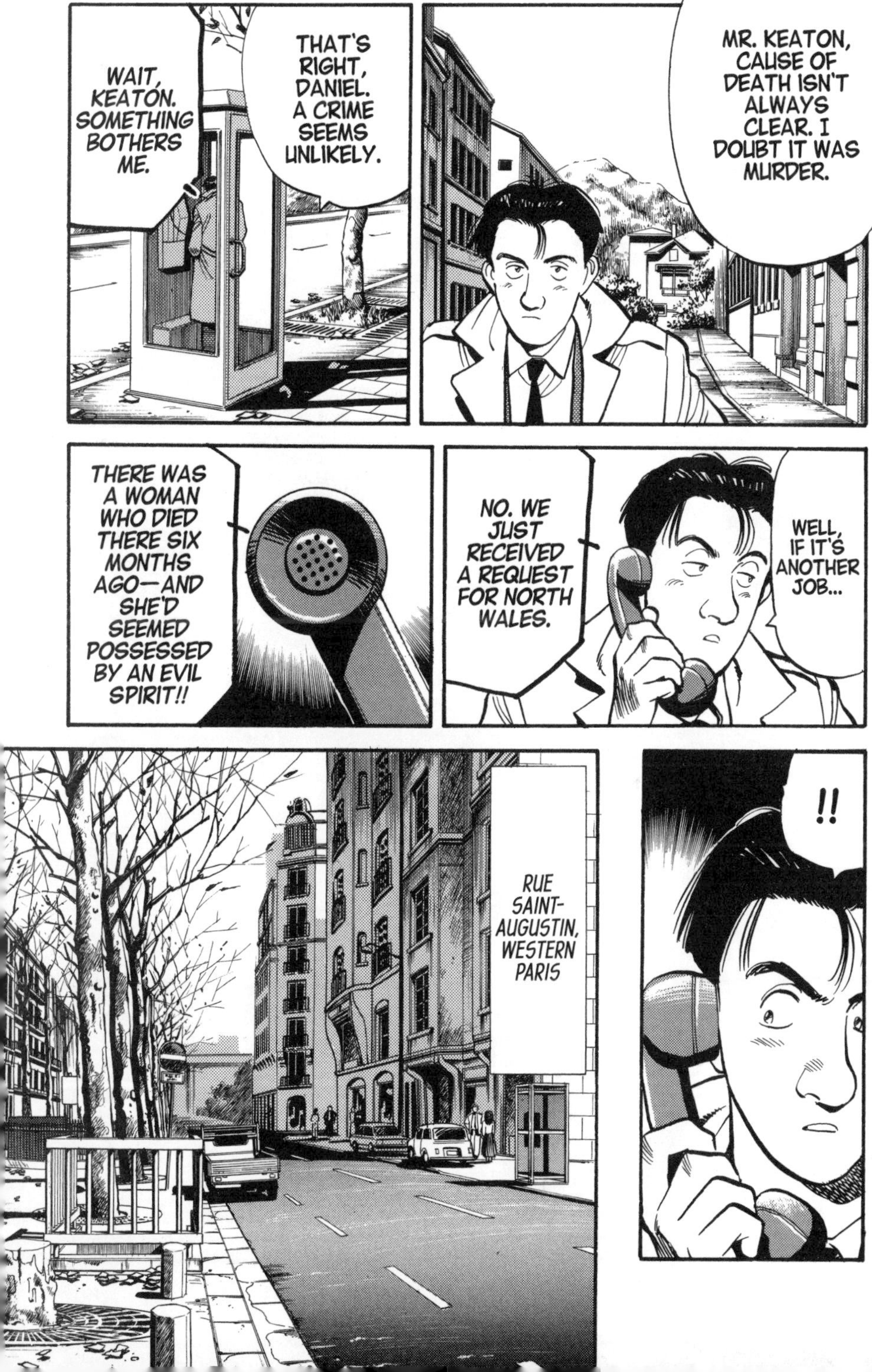
MR. KEATON, CAUSE OF DEATH ISN'T ALWAYS CLEAR. I DOUBT IT WAS MURDER.
THAT'S RIGHT, DANIEL. A CRIME SEEMS UNLIKELY.
WAIT, KEATON. SOMETHING BOTHERS ME.
WELL, IF IT'S ANOTHER JOB...
NO. WE JUST RECEIVED A REQUEST FOR NORTH WALES.
THERE WAS A WOMAN WHO DIED THERE SIX MONTHS AGO—AND SHE'D SEEMED POSSESSED BY AN EVIL SPIRIT!!
!!
RUE SAINT-AUGUSTIN, WESTERN PARIS

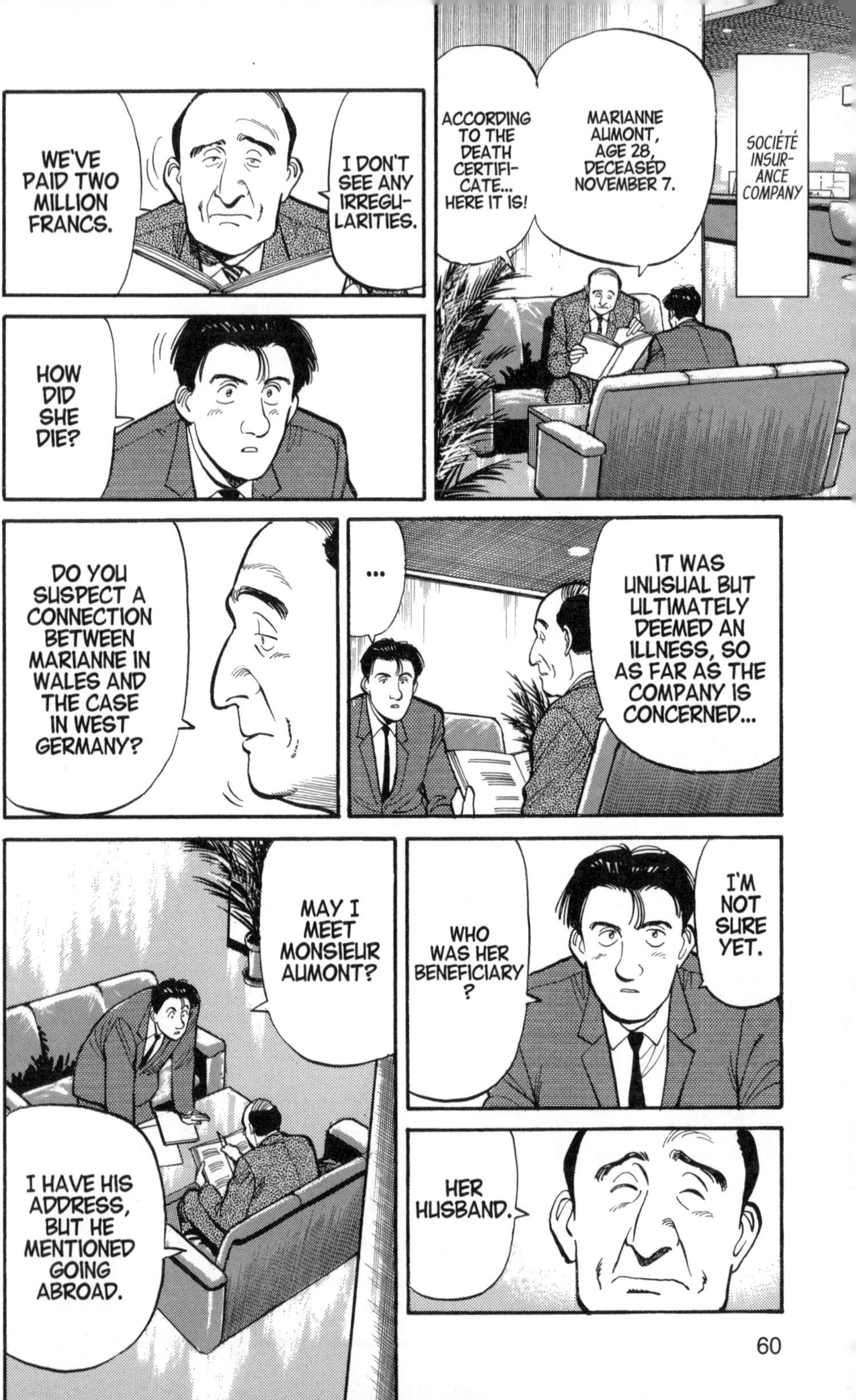

SOCIÉTÉ INSURANCE COMPANY
MARIANNE AUMONT, AGE 28, DECEASED NOVEMBER 7.
ACCORDING TO THE DEATH CERTIFICATE... HERE IT IS!
I DON'T SEE ANY IRREGULARITIES.
WE'VE PAID TWO MILLION FRANCS.
HOW DID SHE DIE?
IT WAS UNUSUAL BUT ULTIMATELY DEEMED AN ILLNESS, SO AS FAR AS THE COMPANY IS CONCERNED...
...
DO YOU SUSPECT A CONNECTION BETWEEN MARIANNE IN WALES AND THE CASE IN WEST GERMANY?
I'M NOT SURE YET.
WHO WAS HER BENEFICIARY?
HER HUSBAND.
MAY I MEET MONSIEUR AUMONT?
I HAVE HIS ADDRESS, BUT HE MENTIONED GOING ABROAD.

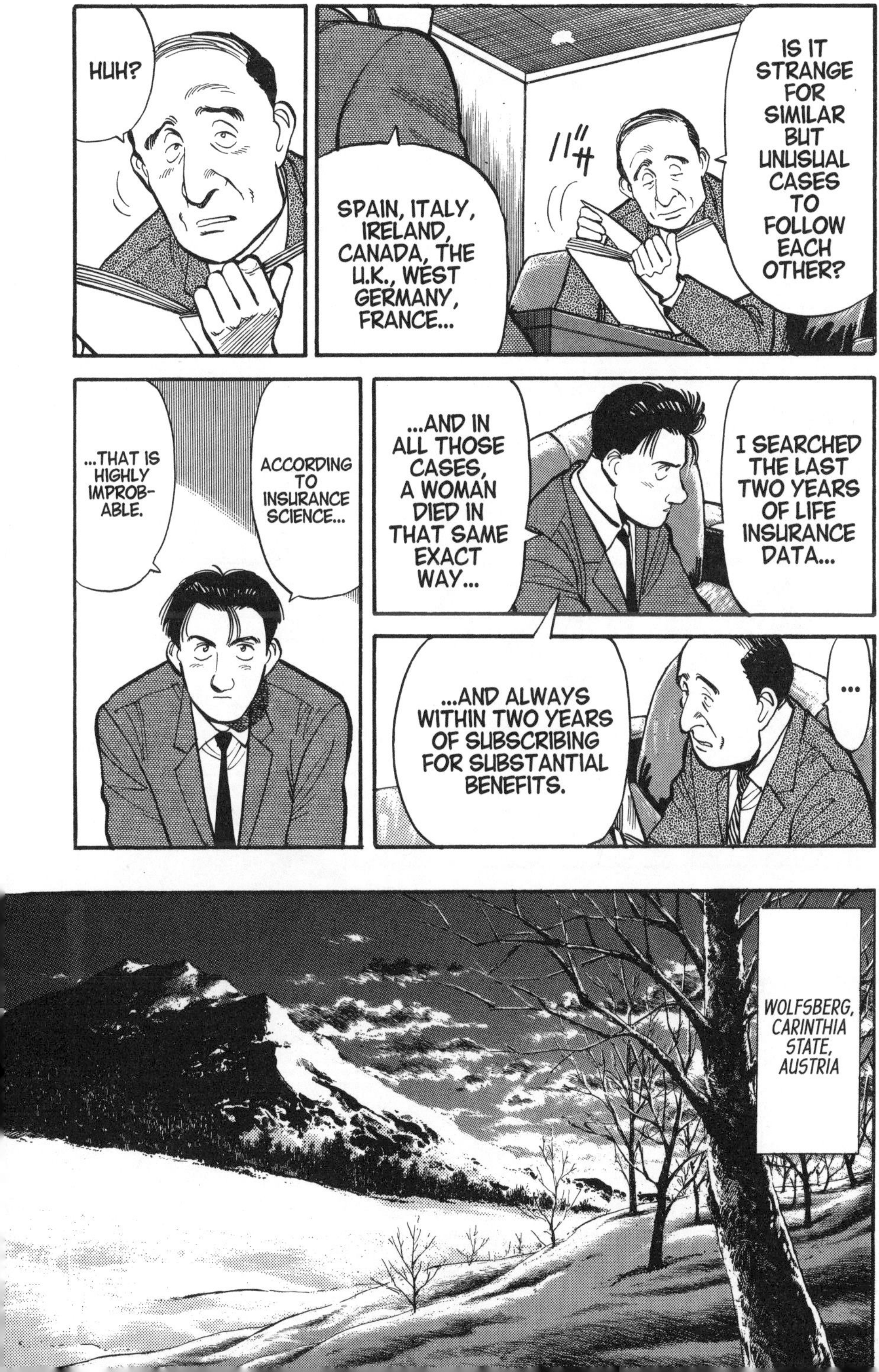
IS IT STRANGE FOR SIMILAR BUT UNUSUAL CASES TO FOLLOW EACH OTHER?
SPAIN, ITALY, IRELAND, CANADA, THE U.K., WEST GERMANY, FRANCE...
HUH?
I SEARCHED THE LAST TWO YEARS OF LIFE INSURANCE DATA...
...AND IN ALL THOSE CASES, A WOMAN DIED IN THAT SAME EXACT WAY...
...
...AND ALWAYS WITHIN TWO YEARS OF SUBSCRIBING FOR SUBSTANTIAL BENEFITS.
ACCORDING TO INSURANCE SCIENCE...
...THAT IS HIGHLY IMPROB-ABLE.
WOLFSBERG, CARINTHIA STATE, AUSTRIA

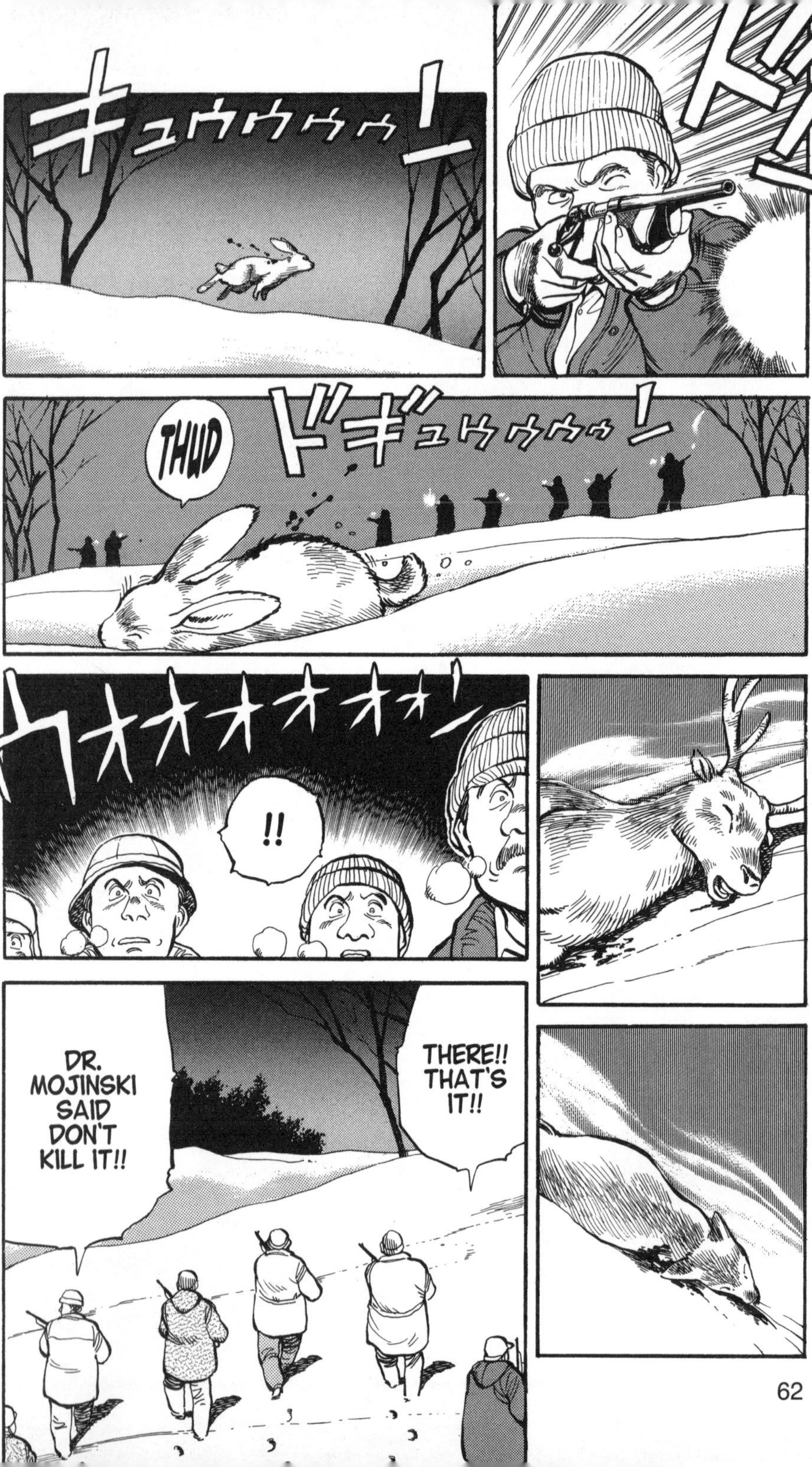
ドン!
キュウウウゥ!
THUD
ドギュウウウゥ!
ウオオオオオオン
!!
THERE!! THAT'S IT!!
DR. MOJINSKI SAID DON'T KILL IT!!

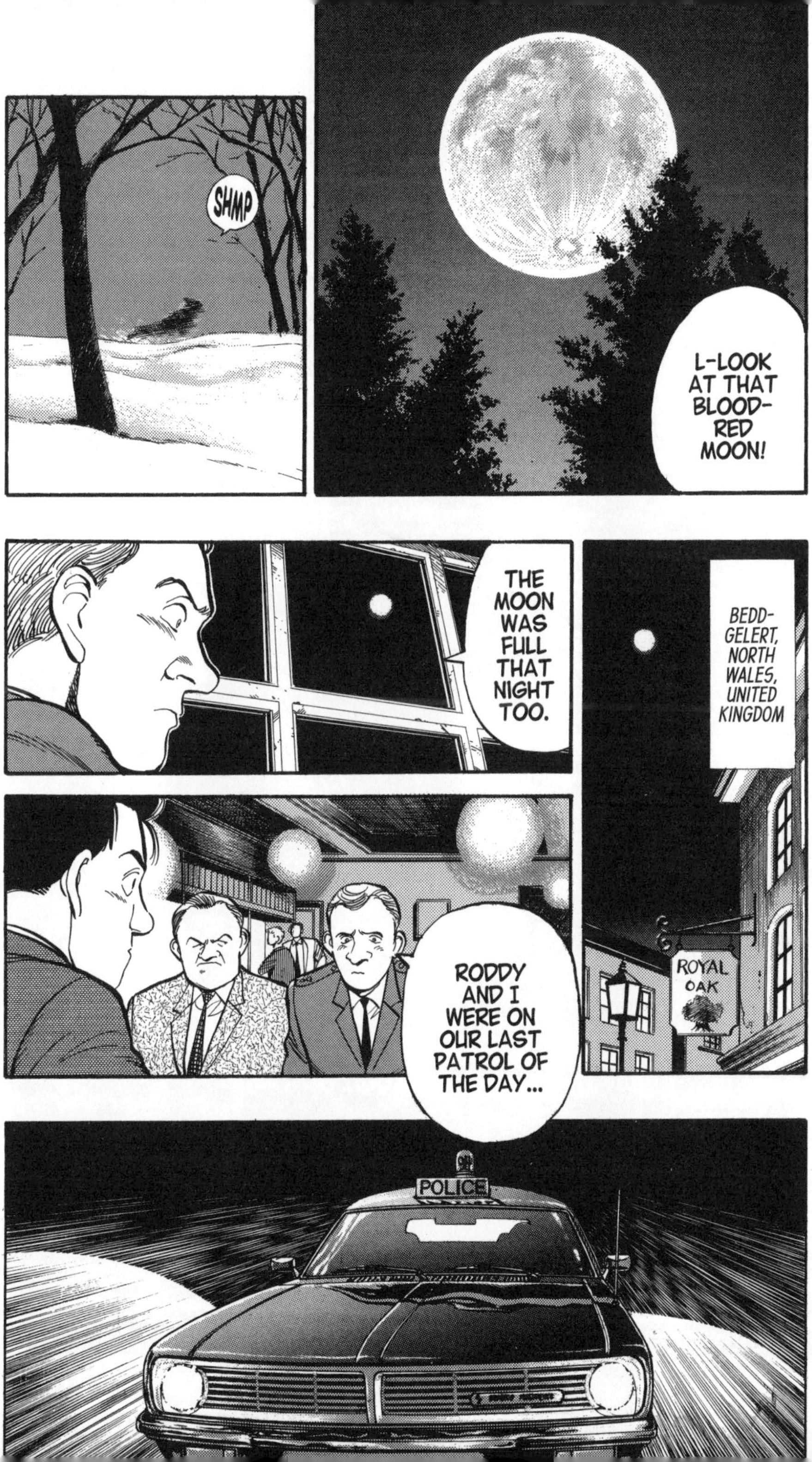
L-LOOK AT THAT BLOOD-RED MOON!
SHMP
BEDD-GELERT, NORTH WALES, UNITED KINGDOM
ROYAL OAK
THE MOON WAS FULL THAT NIGHT TOO.
RODDY AND I WERE ON OUR LAST PATROL OF THE DAY...
POLICE

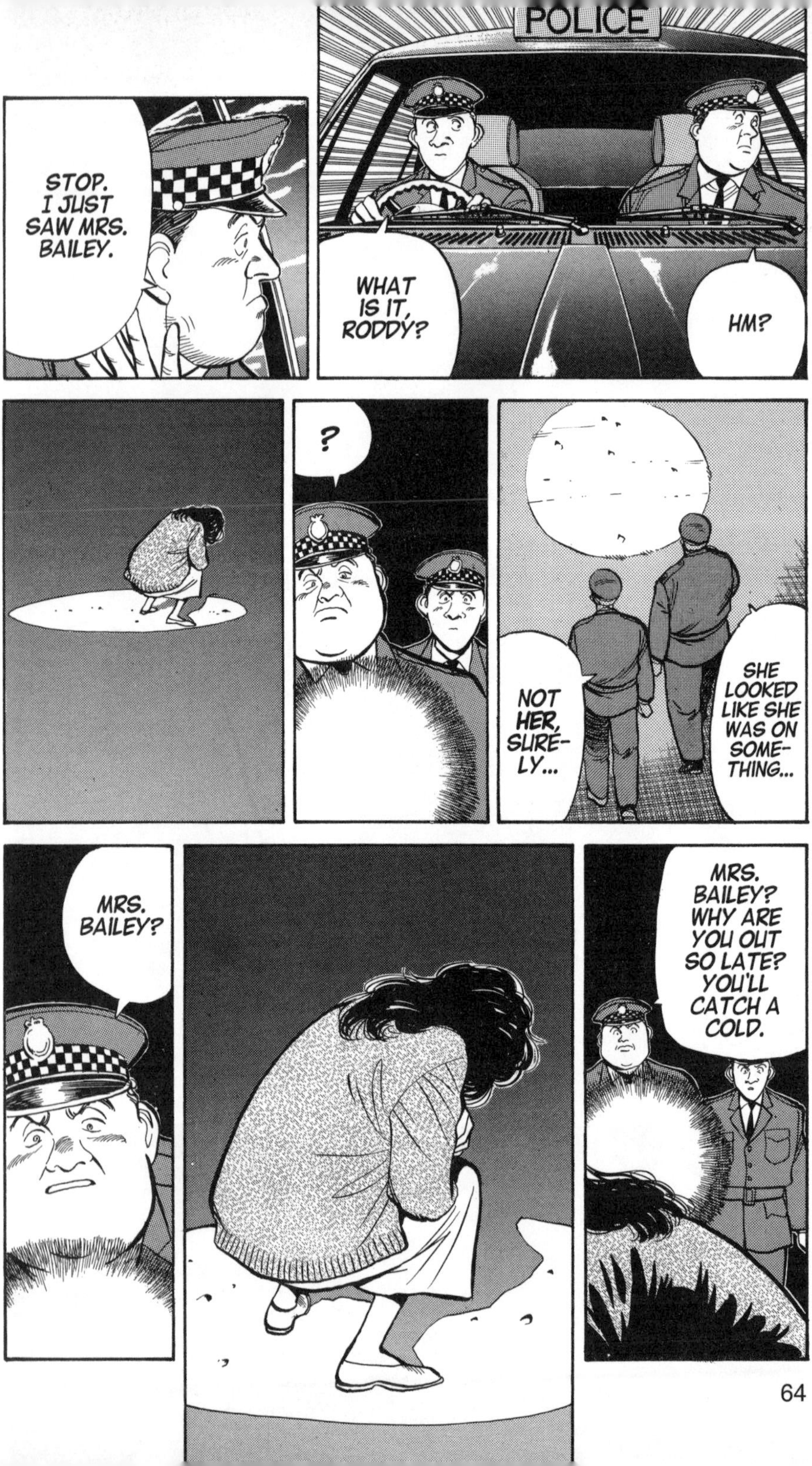
POLICE
HM?
WHAT IS IT, RODDY?
STOP. I JUST SAW MRS. BAILEY.
SHE LOOKED LIKE SHE WAS ON SOME-THING...
NOT HER, SURE-LY...
?
MRS. BAILEY? WHY ARE YOU OUT SO LATE? YOU'LL CATCH A COLD.
MRS. BAILEY?

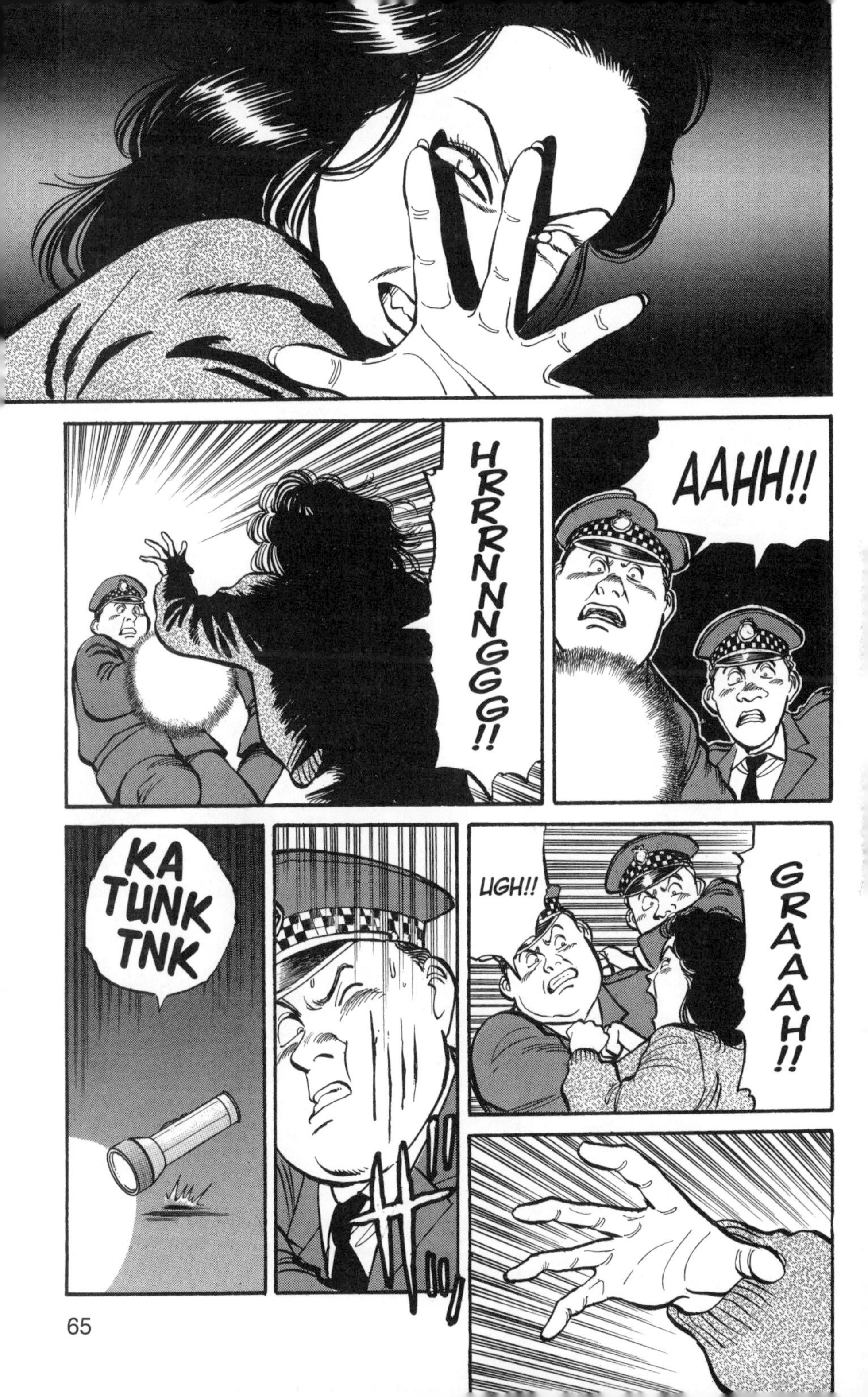
AAHH!!
HRRRNNNGGG!!
GRAAAH!!
UGH!!
KA TUNK TNK

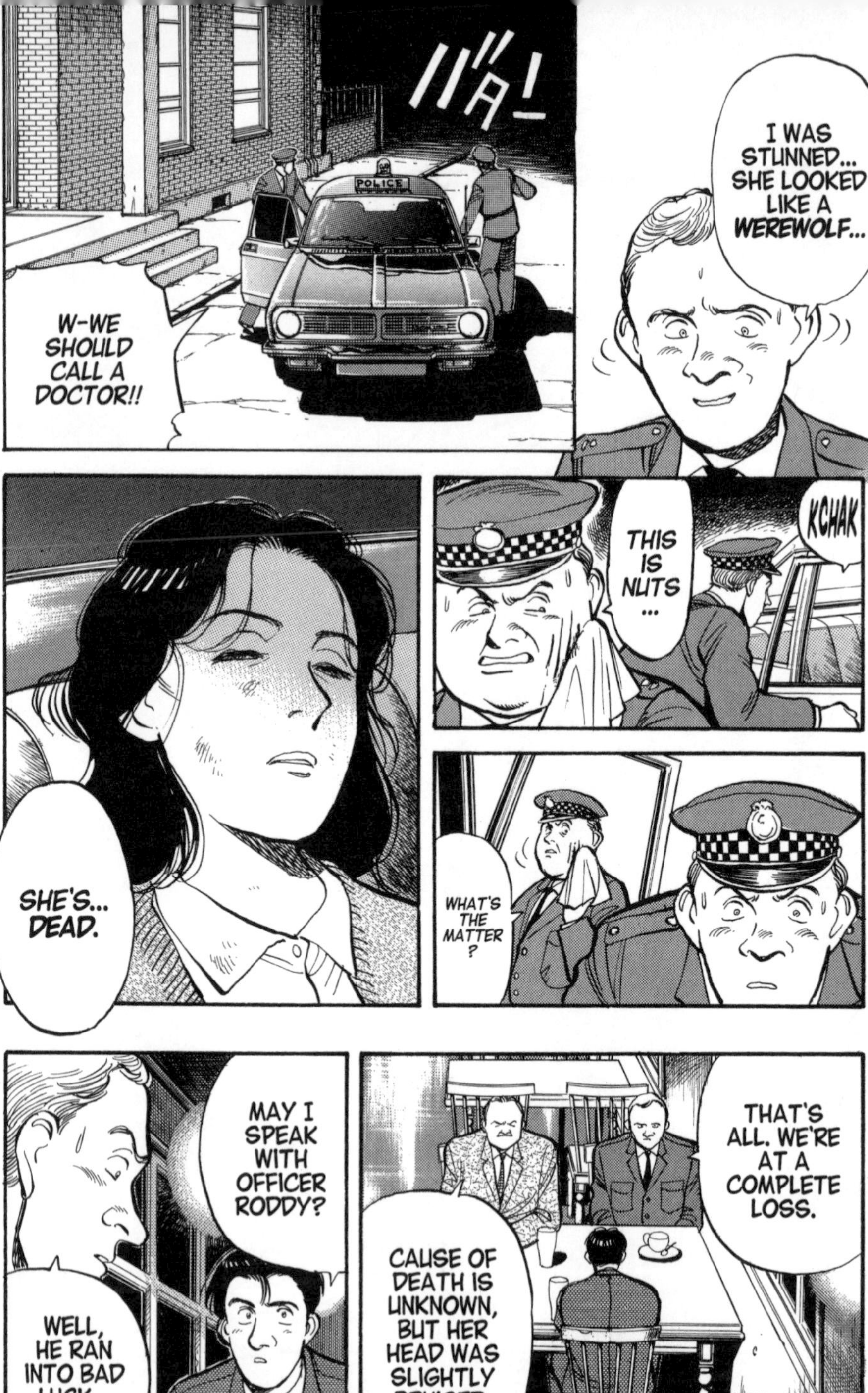

I WAS STUNNED... SHE LOOKED LIKE A WEREWOLF...
W-WE SHOULD CALL A DOCTOR!!
POLICE
KCHAK
THIS IS NUTS...
WHAT'S THE MATTER?
SHE'S... DEAD.
THAT'S ALL. WE'RE AT A COMPLETE LOSS.
CAUSE OF DEATH IS UNKNOWN, BUT HER HEAD WAS SLIGHTLY BRUISED.
MAY I SPEAK WITH OFFICER RODDY?
WELL, HE RAN INTO BAD LUCK...

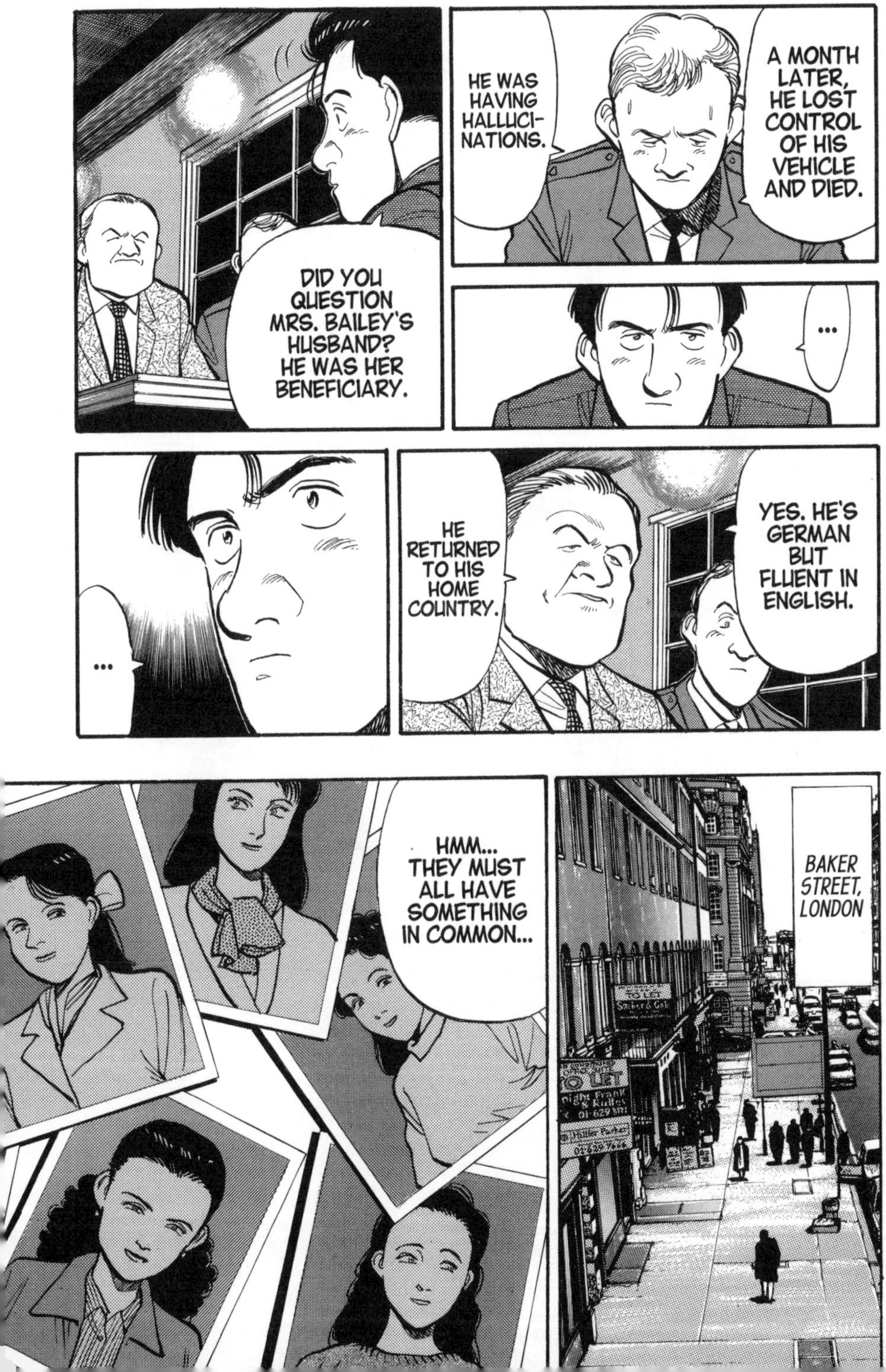
A MONTH LATER, HE LOST CONTROL OF HIS VEHICLE AND DIED.
HE WAS HAVING HALLUCI-NATIONS.
...
DID YOU QUESTION MRS. BAILEY'S HUSBAND? HE WAS HER BENEFICIARY.
YES. HE'S GERMAN BUT FLUENT IN ENGLISH.
HE RETURNED TO HIS HOME COUNTRY.
...
BAKER STREET, LONDON
HMM... THEY MUST ALL HAVE SOMETHING IN COMMON...

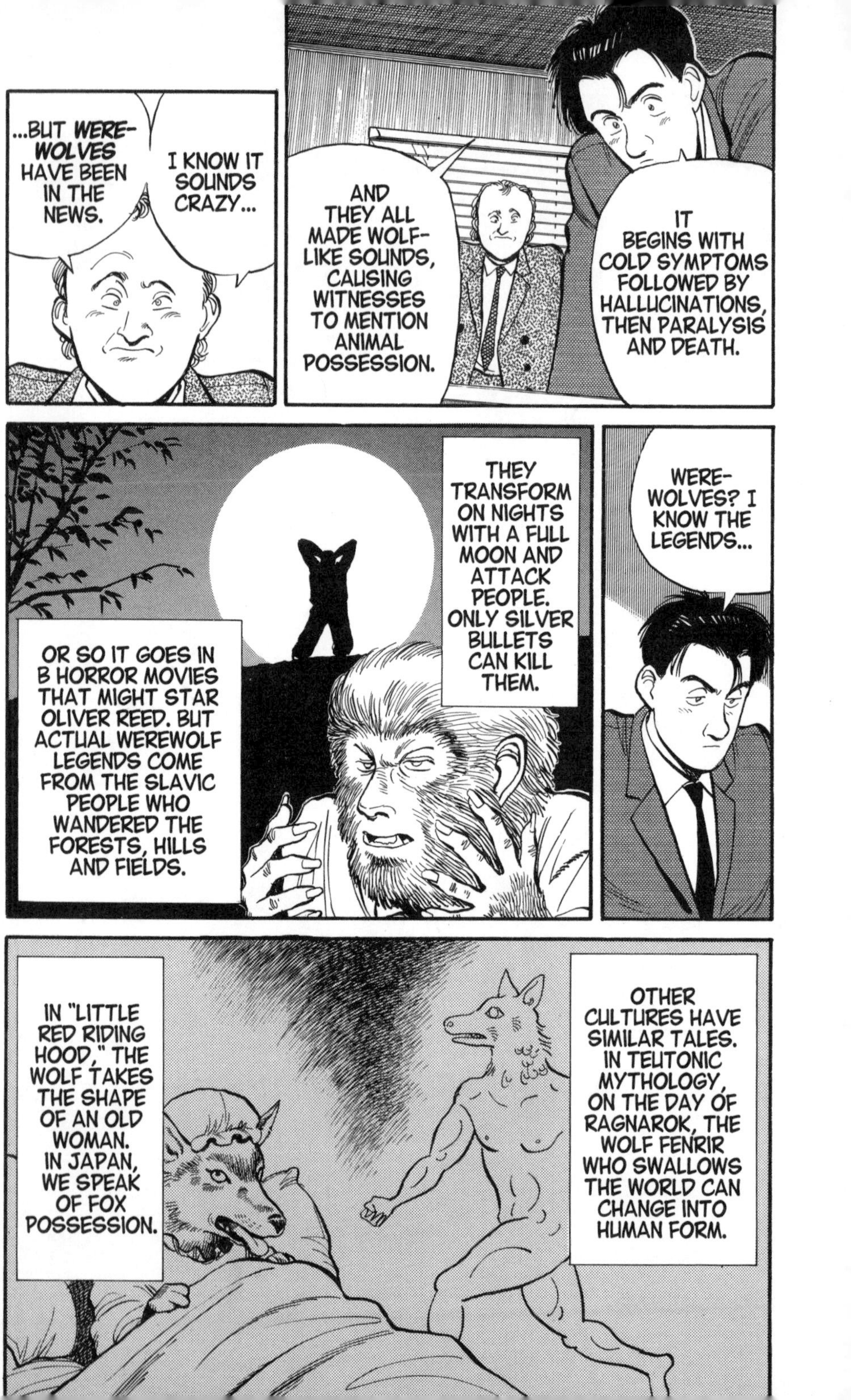
IT BEGINS WITH COLD SYMPTOMS FOLLOWED BY HALLUCINATIONS, THEN PARALYSIS AND DEATH.
AND THEY ALL MADE WOLF-LIKE SOUNDS, CAUSING WITNESSES TO MENTION ANIMAL POSSESSION.
I KNOW IT SOUNDS CRAZY...
...BUT *WEREWOLVES* HAVE BEEN IN THE NEWS.
WEREWOLVES? I KNOW THE LEGENDS...
THEY TRANSFORM ON NIGHTS WITH A FULL MOON AND ATTACK PEOPLE. ONLY SILVER BULLETS CAN KILL THEM.
OR SO IT GOES IN B HORROR MOVIES THAT MIGHT STAR OLIVER REED. BUT ACTUAL WEREWOLF LEGENDS COME FROM THE SLAVIC PEOPLE WHO WANDERED THE FORESTS, HILLS AND FIELDS.
OTHER CULTURES HAVE SIMILAR TALES. IN TEUTONIC MYTHOLOGY, ON THE DAY OF RAGNAROK, THE WOLF FENRIR WHO SWALLOWS THE WORLD CAN CHANGE INTO HUMAN FORM.
IN "LITTLE RED RIDING HOOD," THE WOLF TAKES THE SHAPE OF AN OLD WOMAN. IN JAPAN, WE SPEAK OF FOX POSSESSION.

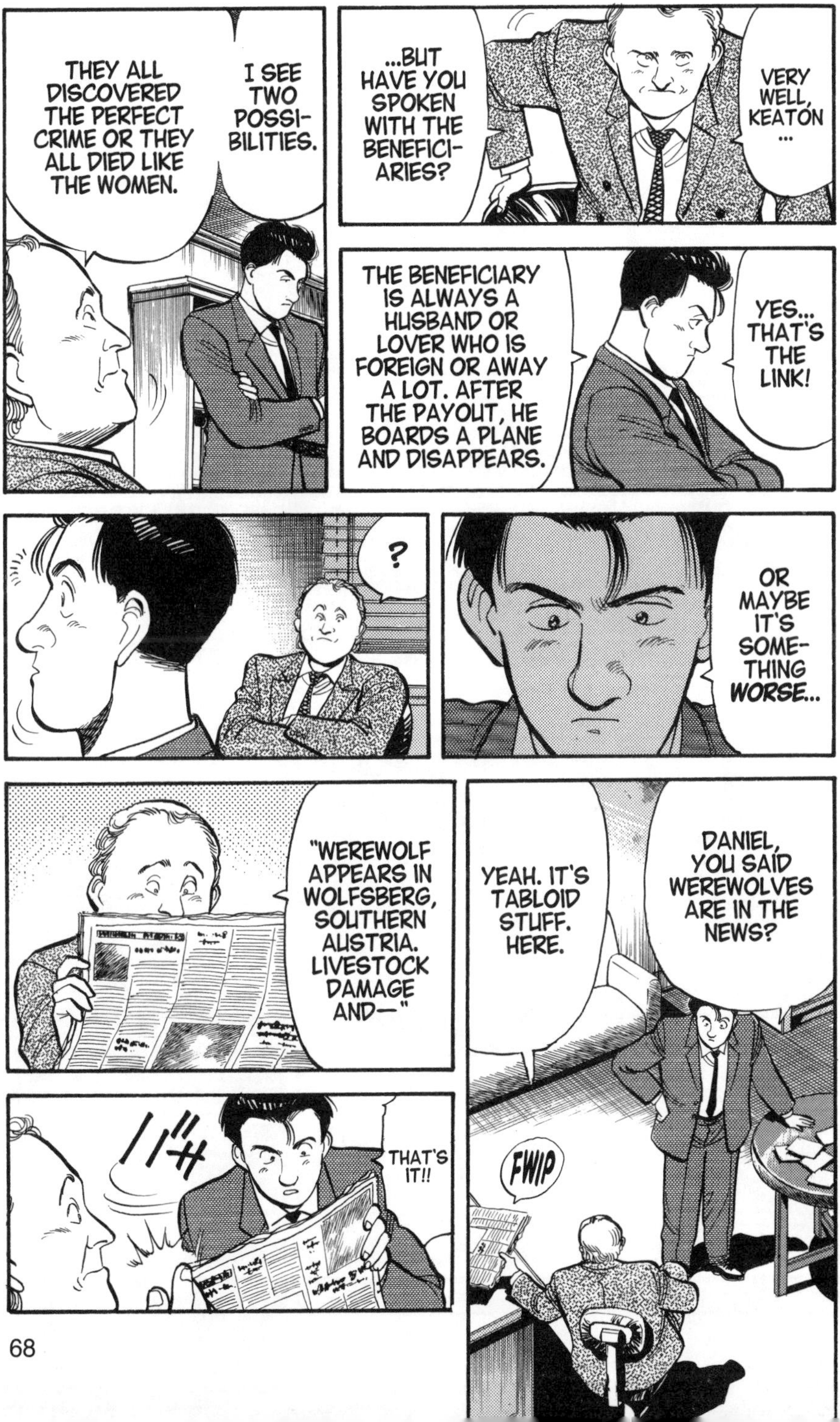
VERY WELL, KEATON...
...BUT HAVE YOU SPOKEN WITH THE BENEFICIARIES?
YES... THAT'S THE LINK!
THE BENEFICIARY IS ALWAYS A HUSBAND OR LOVER WHO IS FOREIGN OR AWAY A LOT. AFTER THE PAYOUT, HE BOARDS A PLANE AND DISAPPEARS.
I SEE TWO POSSIBILITIES.
THEY ALL DISCOVERED THE PERFECT CRIME OR THEY ALL DIED LIKE THE WOMEN.
OR MAYBE IT'S SOMETHING ***WORSE***...
?
DANIEL, YOU SAID WEREWOLVES ARE IN THE NEWS?
YEAH. IT'S TABLOID STUFF. HERE.
FWIP
"WEREWOLF APPEARS IN WOLFSBERG, SOUTHERN AUSTRIA. LIVESTOCK DAMAGE AND—"
THAT'S IT!!

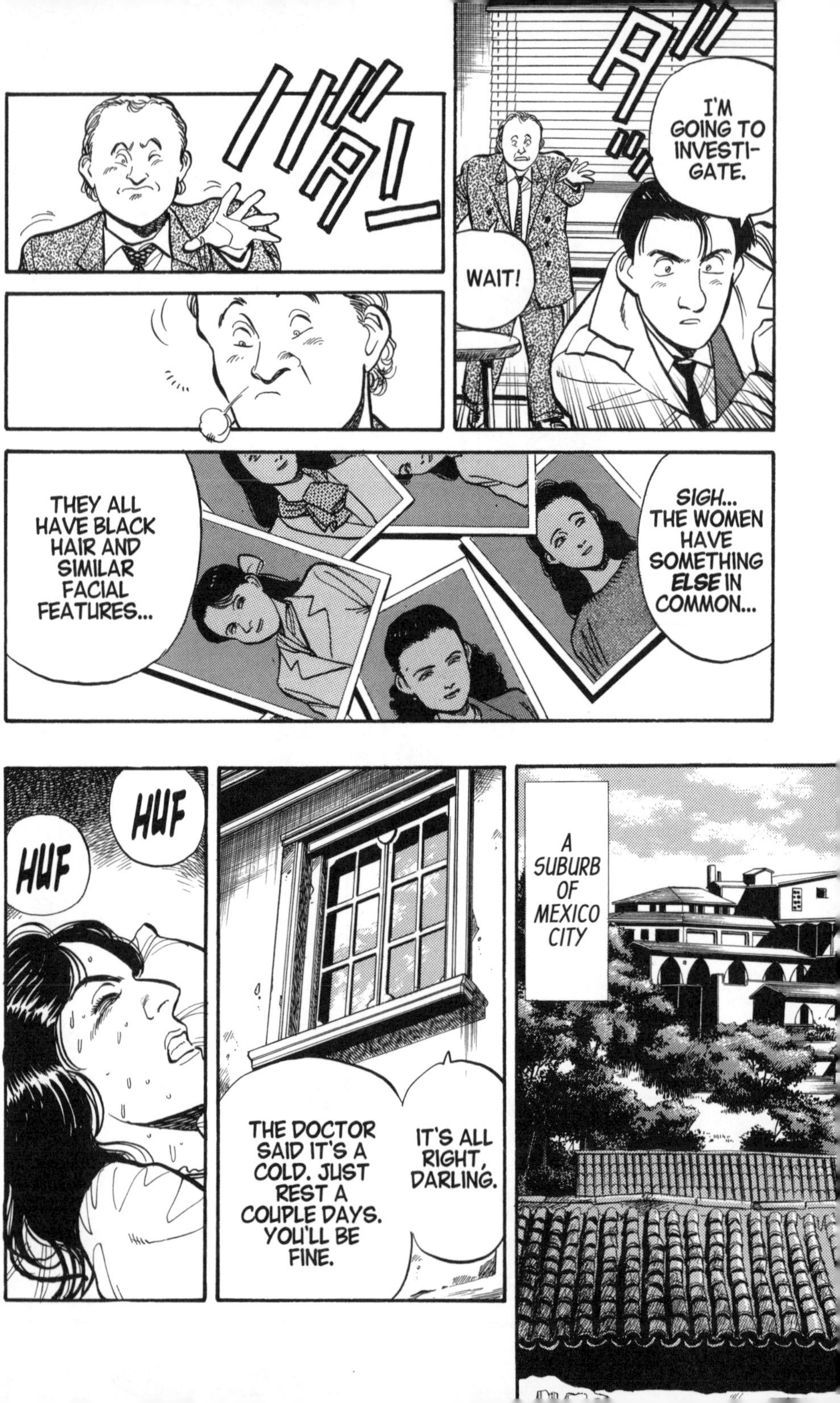
I'M GOING TO INVESTIGATE.
WAIT!
SIGH... THE WOMEN HAVE SOMETHING ELSE IN COMMON...
THEY ALL HAVE BLACK HAIR AND SIMILAR FACIAL FEATURES...
A SUBURB OF MEXICO CITY
IT'S ALL RIGHT, DARLING.
THE DOCTOR SAID IT'S A COLD. JUST REST A COUPLE DAYS. YOU'LL BE FINE.
HUF
HUF

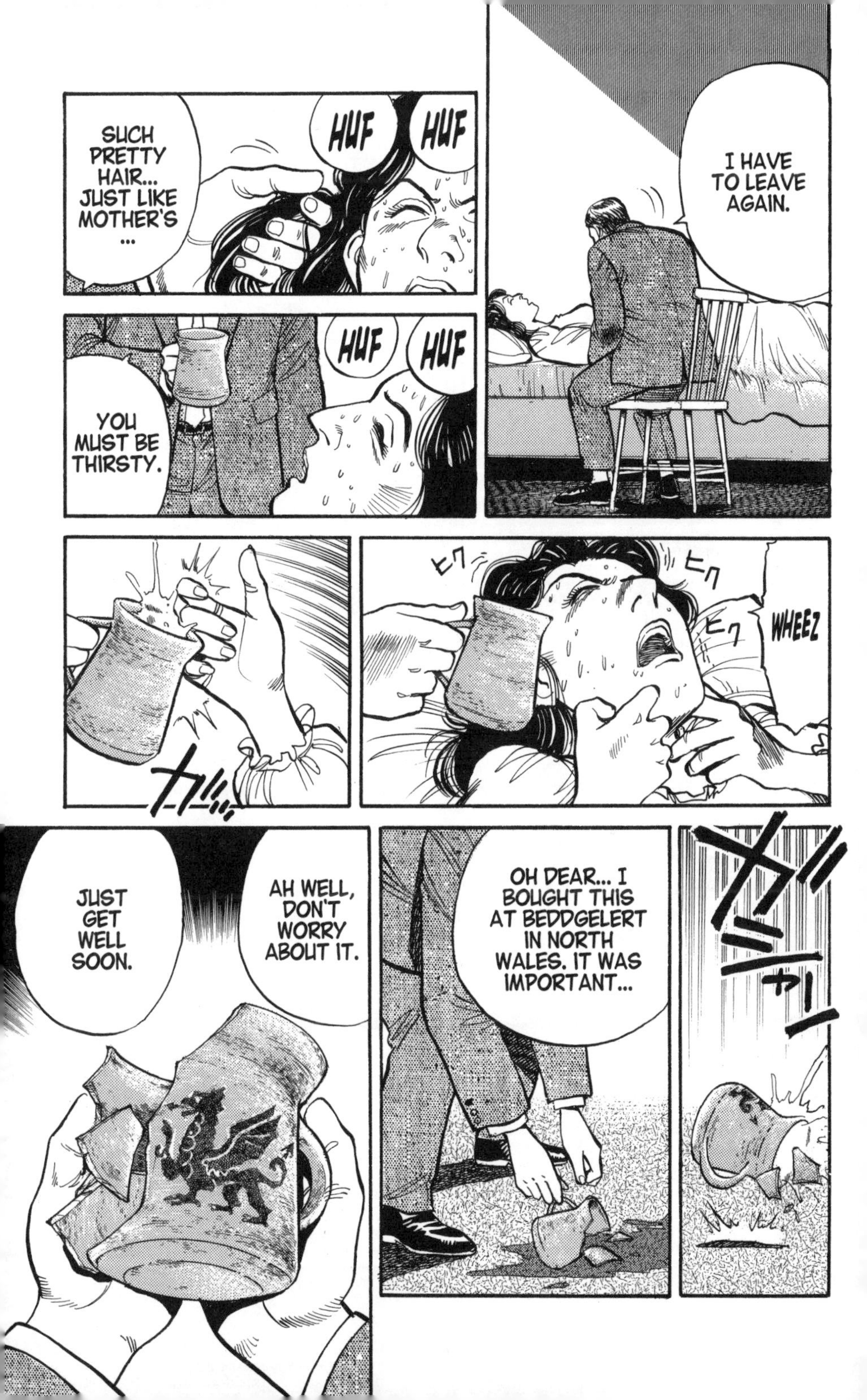

I HAVE TO LEAVE AGAIN.
HUF
HUF
SUCH PRETTY HAIR... JUST LIKE MOTHER'S ...
HUF
HUF
YOU MUST BE THIRSTY.
WHEEZ
ヒク
ヒク
ヒク
カッ
ガシャーン
OH DEAR... I BOUGHT THIS AT BEDDGELERT IN NORTH WALES. IT WAS IMPORTANT...
AH WELL, DON'T WORRY ABOUT IT.
JUST GET WELL SOON.

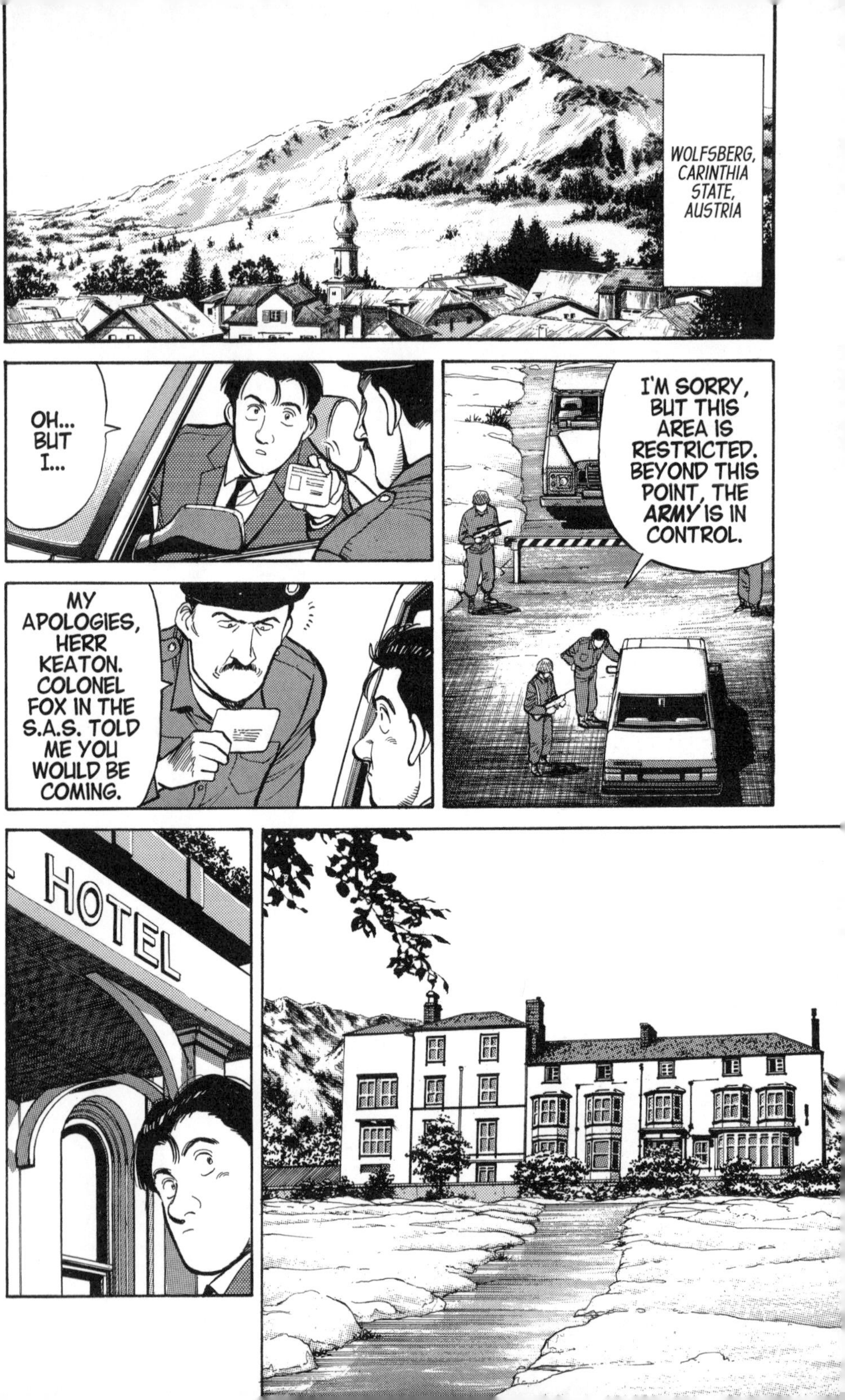
WOLFSBERG, CARINTHIA STATE, AUSTRIA
I'M SORRY, BUT THIS AREA IS RESTRICTED. BEYOND THIS POINT, THE ARMY IS IN CONTROL.
OH... BUT I...
MY APOLOGIES, HERR KEATON. COLONEL FOX IN THE S.A.S. TOLD ME YOU WOULD BE COMING.
HOTEL

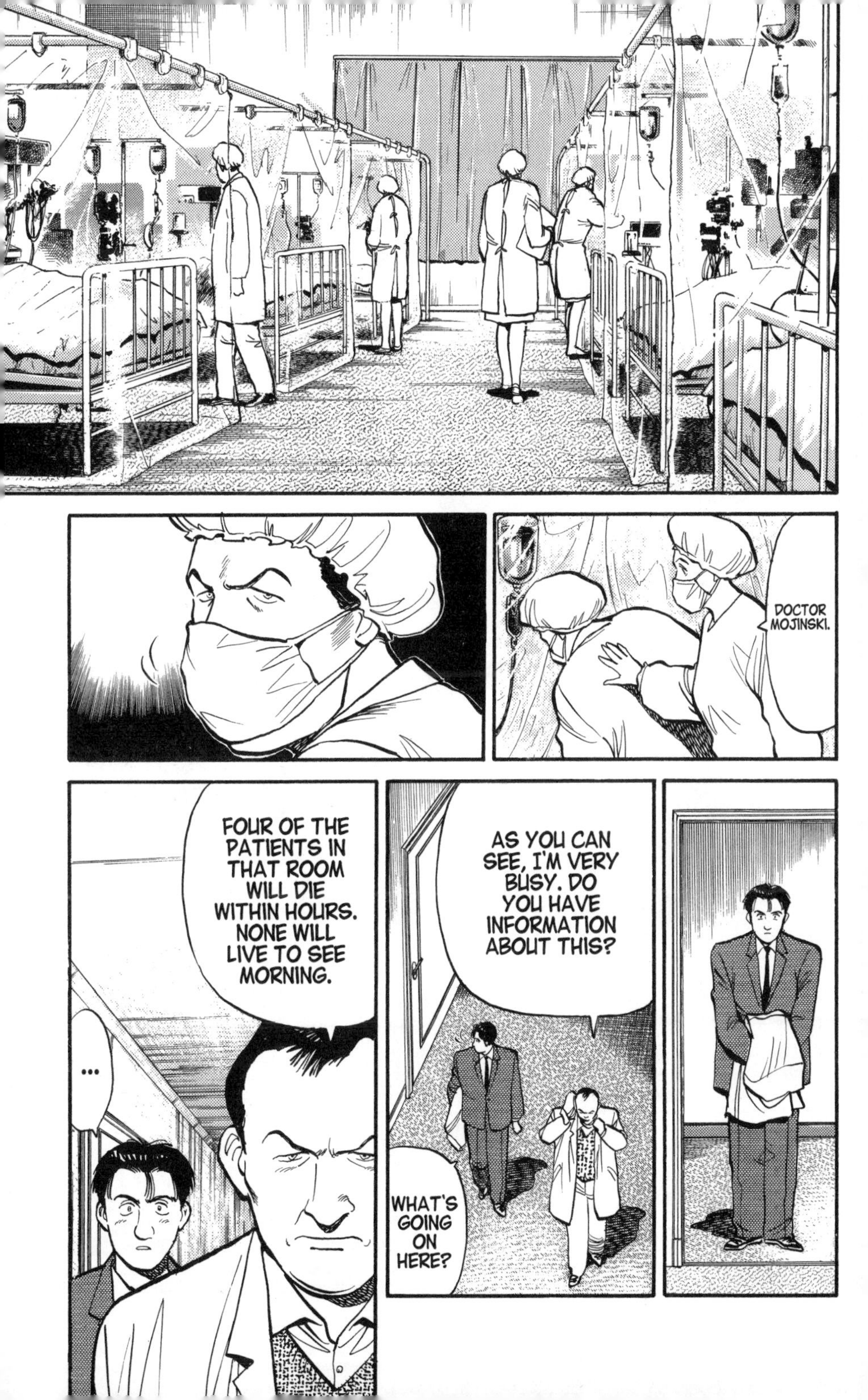
DOCTOR MOJINSKI.
AS YOU CAN SEE, I'M VERY BUSY. DO YOU HAVE INFORMATION ABOUT THIS?
WHAT'S GOING ON HERE?
FOUR OF THE PATIENTS IN THAT ROOM WILL DIE WITHIN HOURS. NONE WILL LIVE TO SEE MORNING.
...

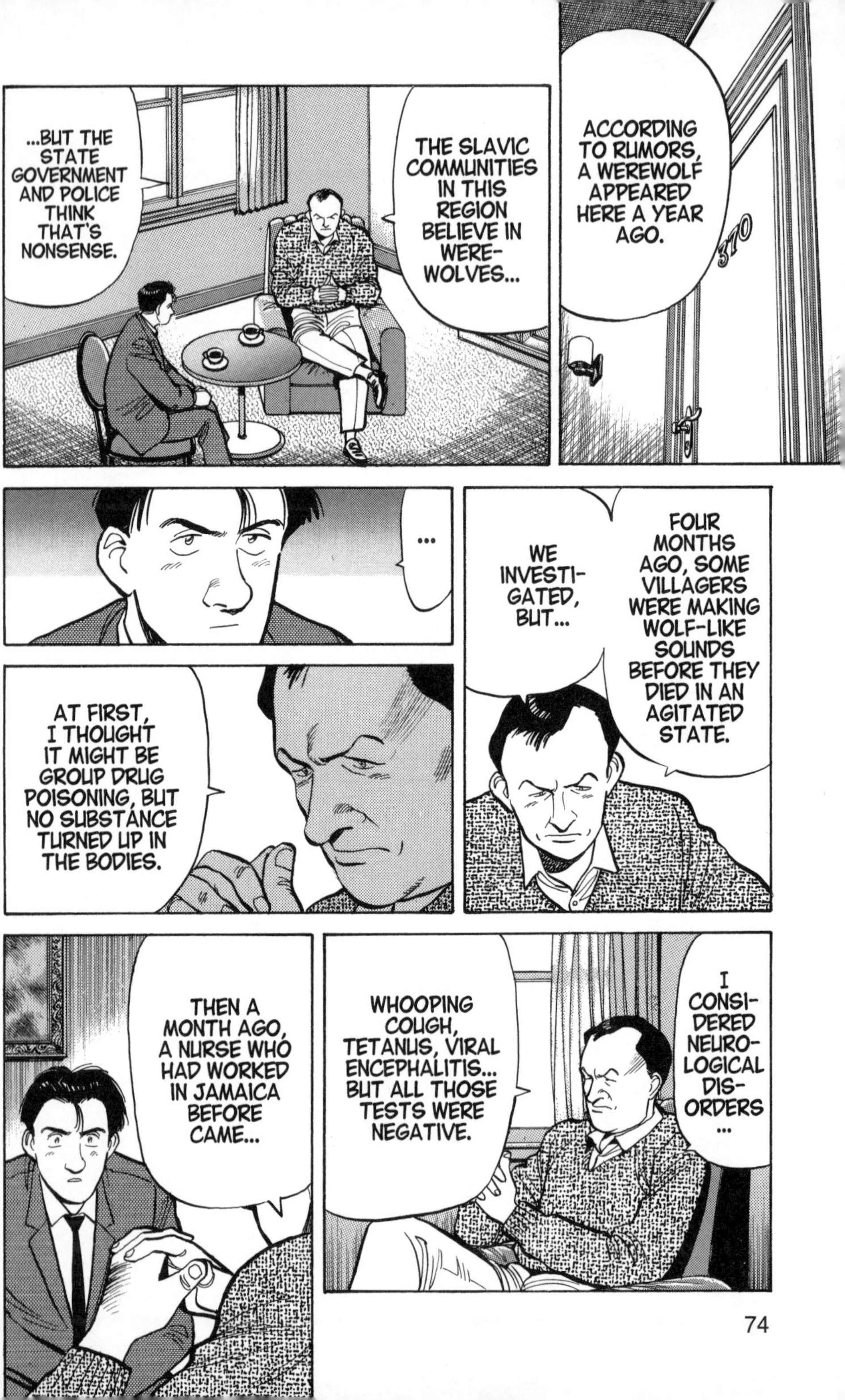
ACCORDING TO RUMORS, A WEREWOLF APPEARED HERE A YEAR AGO.
370
THE SLAVIC COMMUNITIES IN THIS REGION BELIEVE IN WERE-WOLVES...
...BUT THE STATE GOVERNMENT AND POLICE THINK THAT'S NONSENSE.
FOUR MONTHS AGO, SOME VILLAGERS WERE MAKING WOLF-LIKE SOUNDS BEFORE THEY DIED IN AN AGITATED STATE.
WE INVESTI-GATED, BUT...
...
AT FIRST, I THOUGHT IT MIGHT BE GROUP DRUG POISONING, BUT NO SUBSTANCE TURNED UP IN THE BODIES.
I CONSI-DERED NEURO-LOGICAL DIS-ORDERS...
WHOOPING COUGH, TETANUS, VIRAL ENCEPHALITIS... BUT ALL THOSE TESTS WERE NEGATIVE.
THEN A MONTH AGO, A NURSE WHO HAD WORKED IN JAMAICA BEFORE CAME...

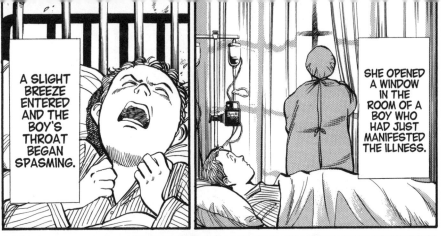

SHE OPENED A WINDOW IN THE ROOM OF A BOY WHO HAD JUST MANIFESTED THE ILLNESS.
A SLIGHT BREEZE ENTERED AND THE BOY'S THROAT BEGAN SPASMING.
!!
?
SHE HAD SEEN THE SAME THING IN JAMAICA.
ABOUT THAT TIME, A CHANGE OCCURRED IN THE VILLAGE DOGS AS WELL AS IN THE CATS, LIVESTOCK, AND WILD ANIMALS IN THE FOREST.
THEY GREW FEROCIOUS AND ATTACKED PEOPLE.
IF ONLY THOSE SIGNS HAD APPEARED ***BEFORE*** THEY SHOWED UP IN HUMANS...
WE EXAMINED THE DECEASED PATIENTS' BRAIN CELLS WITH A MICRO-SCOPE...
...AND FINALLY FOUND IT.
?!

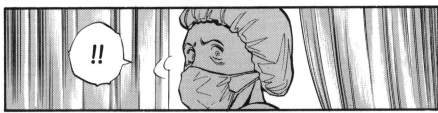

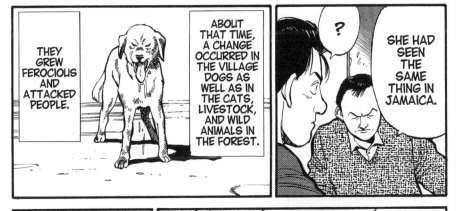

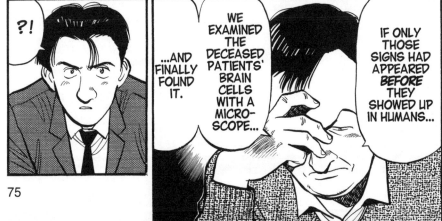

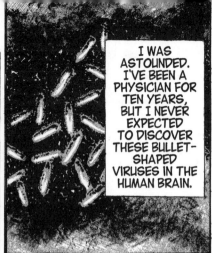

I WAS ASTOUNDED. I'VE BEEN A PHYSICIAN FOR TEN YEARS, BUT I NEVER EXPECTED TO DISCOVER THESE BULLET-SHAPED VIRUSES IN THE HUMAN BRAIN.
?!
WE SCOURED THE AREA FOR A WEREWOLF—THE *HUMAN* ORIGIN OF THE DISEASE.
AND SHE WAS ALIVE.
SHE?
YES. THE DISEASE CAUSES NERVE TISSUE ABNORMALITIES, RESULTING IN A DESIRE FOR DARK AND A FEAR OF THE LIGHT. EVEN THE LIGHT OF A FULL MOON CAN CAUSE DISCOMFORT. THE PAIN CAUSES VICTIMS TO WANDER AIMLESSLY—JUST AS IN WEREWOLF LEGENDS!
IS IT INFECTIOUS?
YES, USUALLY VIA A BODILY FLUID THROUGH AN OPEN WOUND.
HOWEVER, IT ISN'T AIRBORNE.
COULD SOMEONE INTENTIONALLY TRANSMIT THE PATHOGEN?
?

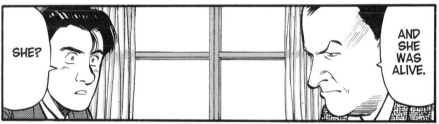

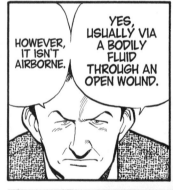

I SUSPECT A *CRIME*.
WELL... I DID WONDER WHY IT SHOWED UP IN HUMANS BEFORE ANIMALS...
...AND THAT WOULD EXPLAIN IT...
DID THE WOMAN SAY ANYTHING?
NO. SHE'S IN A COMA.
A COMA? SHE'S ALIVE?!
YES. THE VIRUS AFFECTS EVERYONE DIFFERENTLY. SOME PATIENTS LIVE LONGER.
HER HUSBAND IS HERE NOW SAYING GOOD-BYE.
HER HUSBAND?!
204

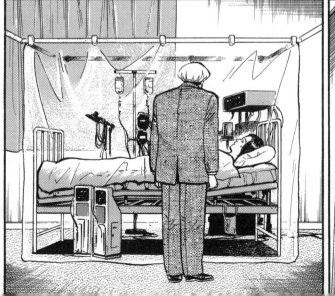

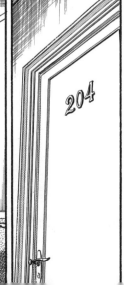

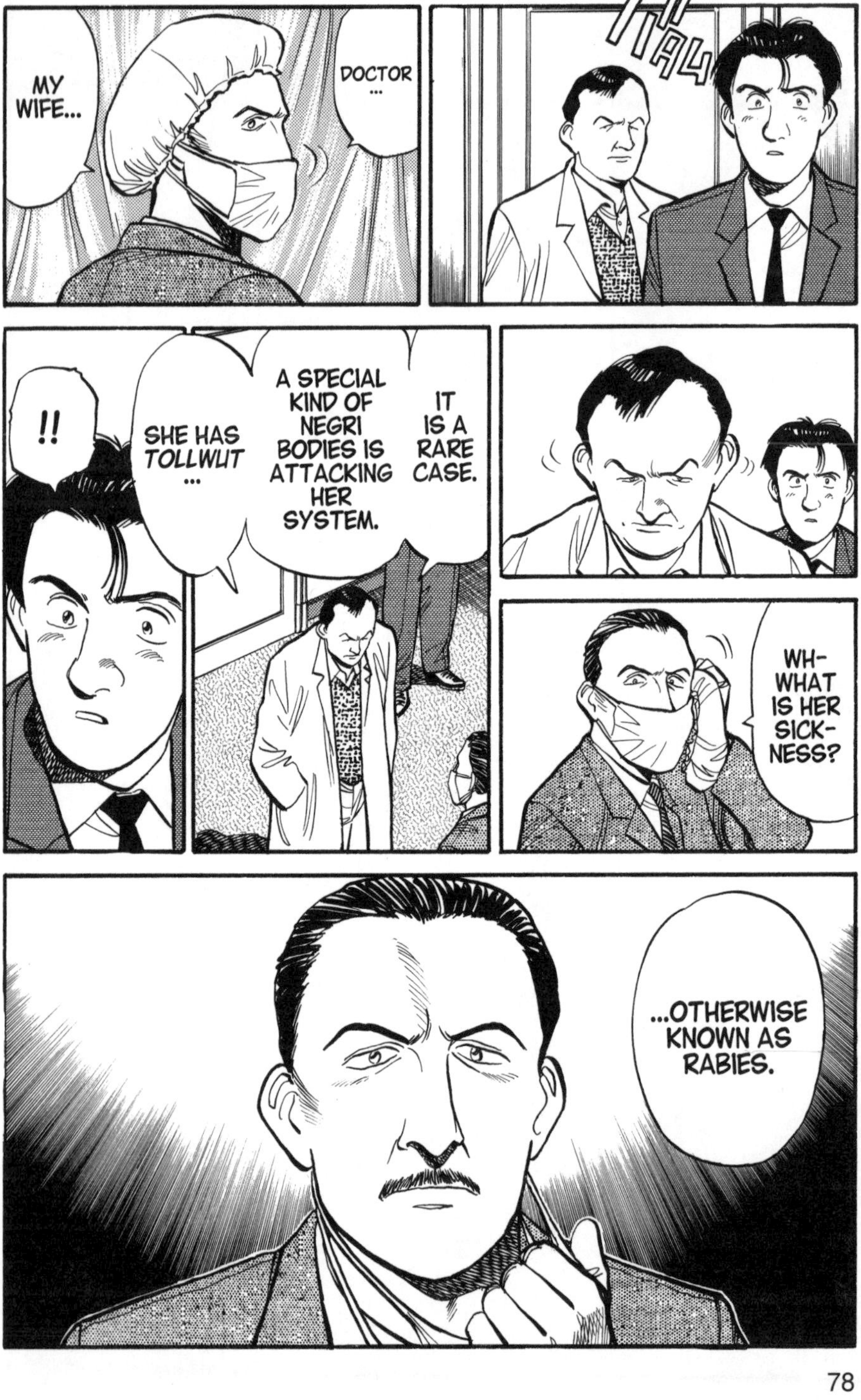
DOCTOR ...
MY WIFE...
WH- WHAT IS HER SICKNESS?
IT IS A RARE CASE.
A SPECIAL KIND OF NEGRI BODIES IS ATTACKING HER SYSTEM.
SHE HAS *TOLLWUT* ...
!!
...OTHERWISE KNOWN AS RABIES.

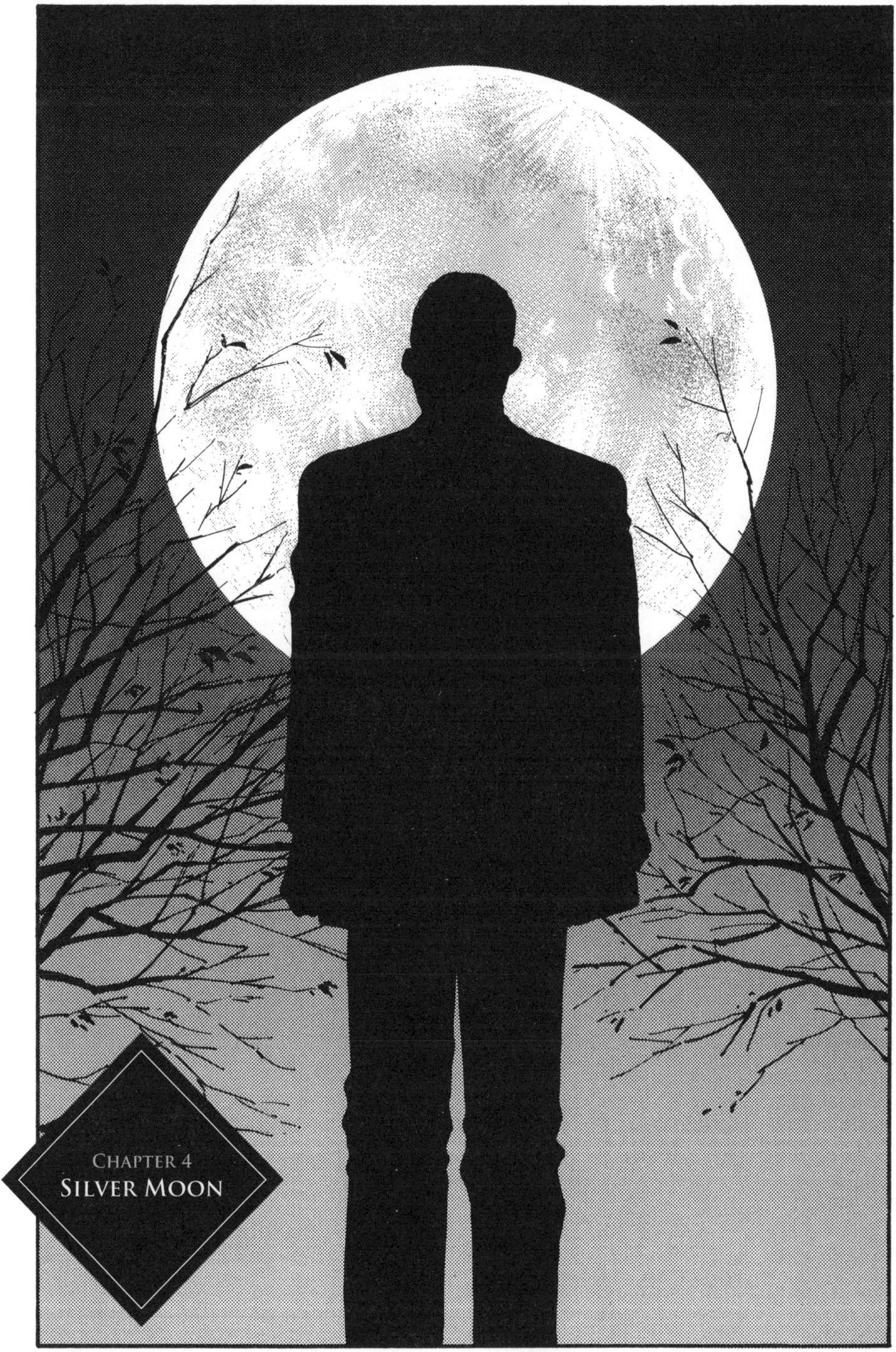
CHAPTER 4
SILVER MOON

WOLFSBERG,
CARINTHIA
STATE,
AUSTRIA

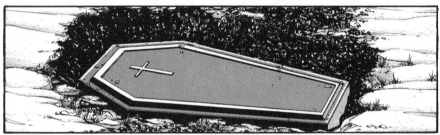

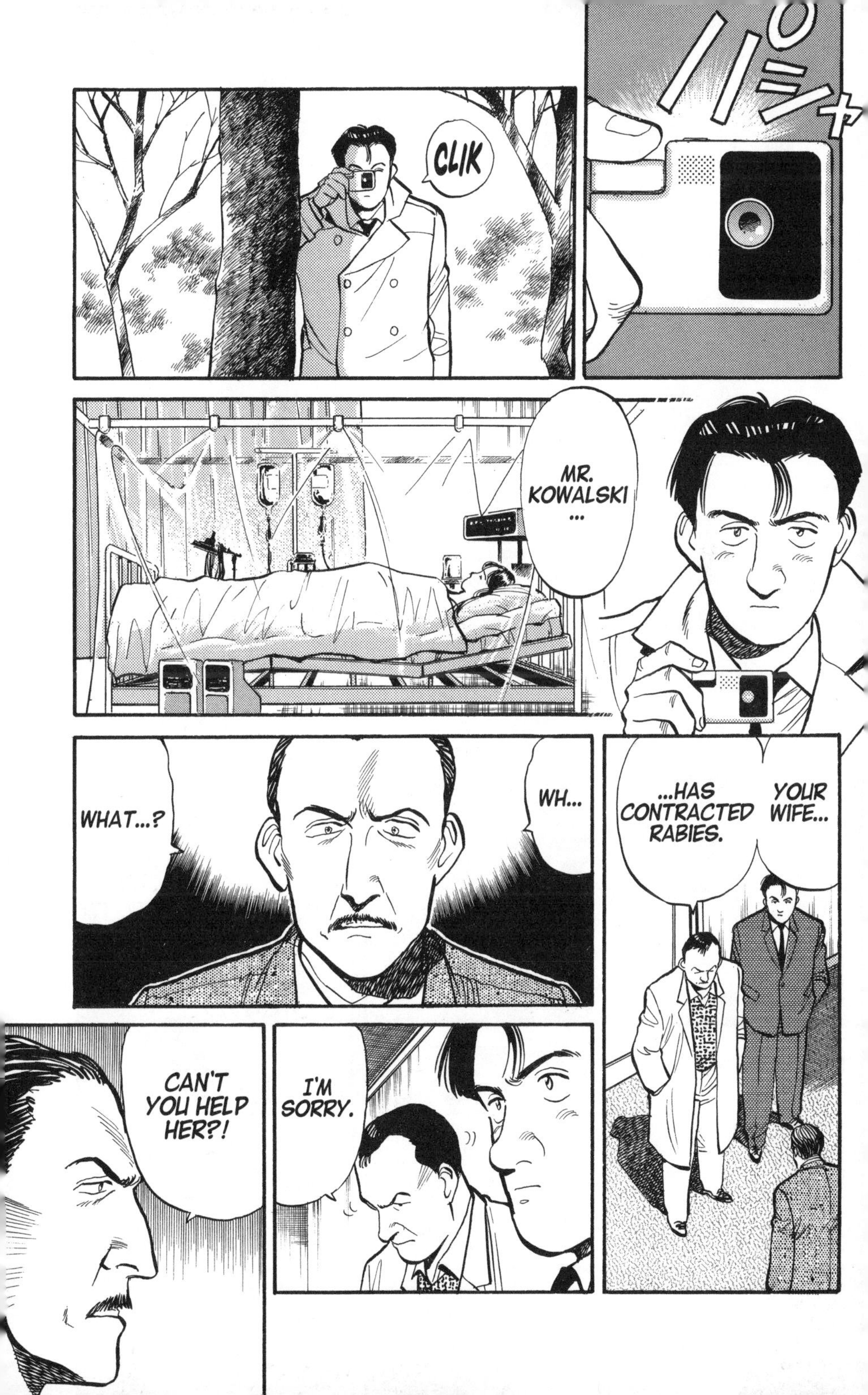
パシャ
CLIK
MR. KOWALSKI ...
YOUR WIFE...
...HAS CONTRACTED RABIES.
WH...
WHAT...?
I'M SORRY.
CAN'T YOU HELP HER?!

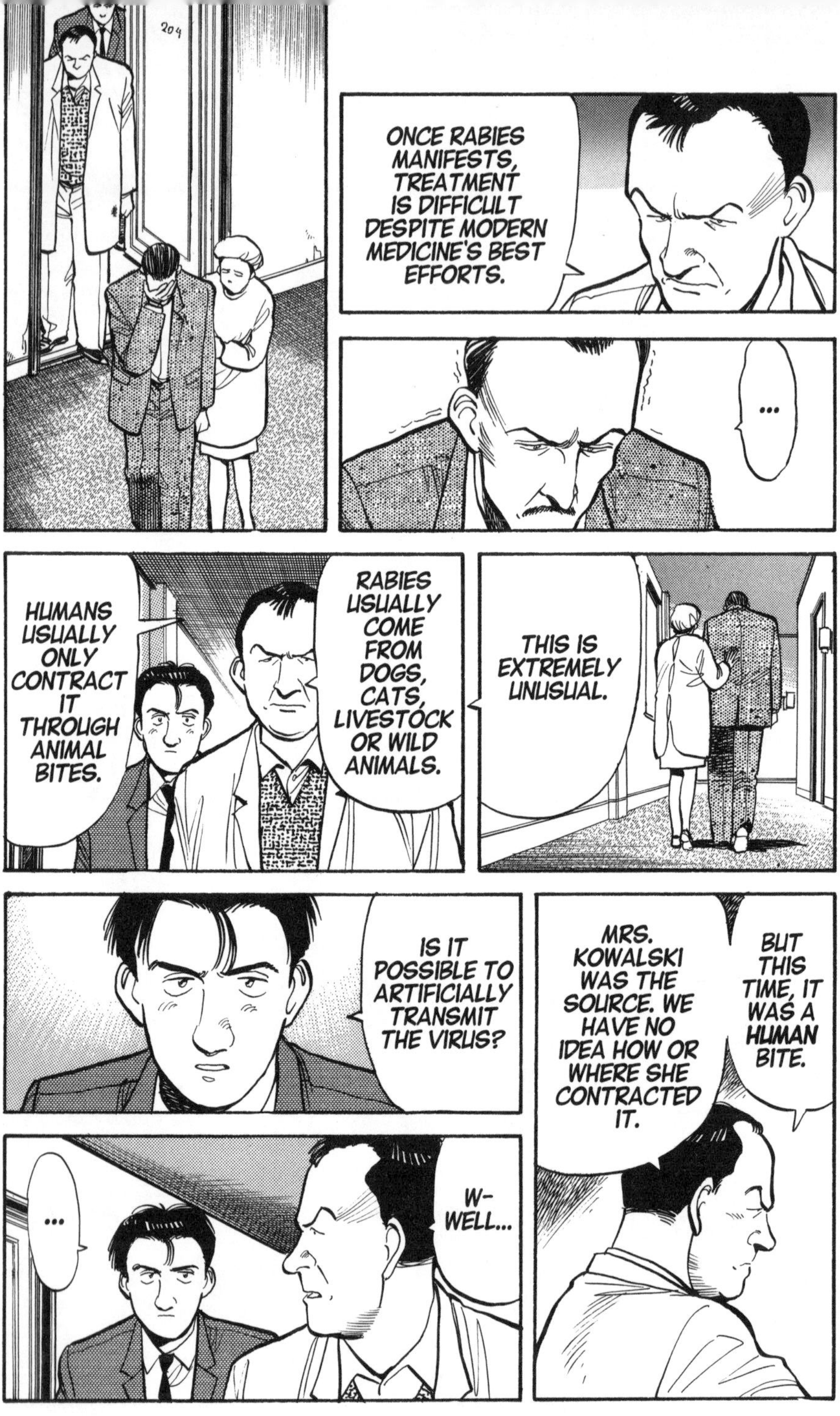
ONCE RABIES MANIFESTS, TREATMENT IS DIFFICULT DESPITE MODERN MEDICINE'S BEST EFFORTS.
...
204
THIS IS EXTREMELY UNUSUAL.
RABIES USUALLY COME FROM DOGS, CATS, LIVESTOCK OR WILD ANIMALS.
HUMANS USUALLY ONLY CONTRACT IT THROUGH ANIMAL BITES.
BUT THIS TIME, IT WAS A HUMAN BITE.
MRS. KOWALSKI WAS THE SOURCE. WE HAVE NO IDEA HOW OR WHERE SHE CONTRACTED IT.
IS IT POSSIBLE TO ARTIFICIALLY TRANSMIT THE VIRUS?
W-WELL...
...

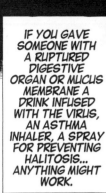

IT WOULD BE EASY TO INSERT INTO THE BODY.
YOU COULD EXPOSE A WOUND TO A VIRAL CULTURE. A MERE SCRATCH BY A PATIENT WOULD SUFFICE.
IF YOU GAVE SOMEONE WITH A RUPTURED DIGESTIVE ORGAN OR MUCUS MEMBRANE A DRINK INFUSED WITH THE VIRUS, AN ASTHMA INHALER, A SPRAY FOR PREVENTING HALITOSIS... ANYTHING MIGHT WORK.
HAS ANYONE BESIDE MR. KOWALSKI VISITED?
THE VILLAGE PRIEST HAS BEEN HERE...
...BUT HER HUSBAND COULD TELL YOU MORE THAN—
NO, I'M INTERESTED IN MR. KOWALSKI.
?!
FOR TWO YEARS, WOMEN AROUND THE WORLD HAVE BEEN DYING IN STRANGE BUT SIMILAR CIRCUMSTANCES.
DO YOU THINK A BROKER IS SELLING THE VIRUS TO WOULD-BE MURDERERS?

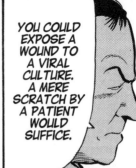

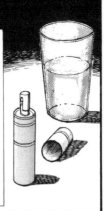

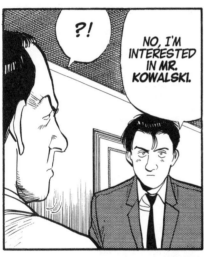

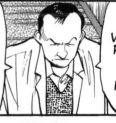

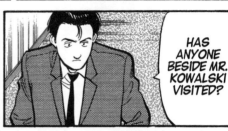

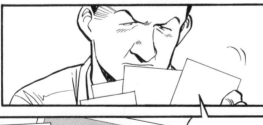

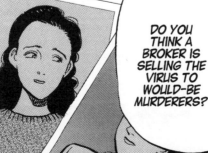

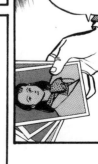

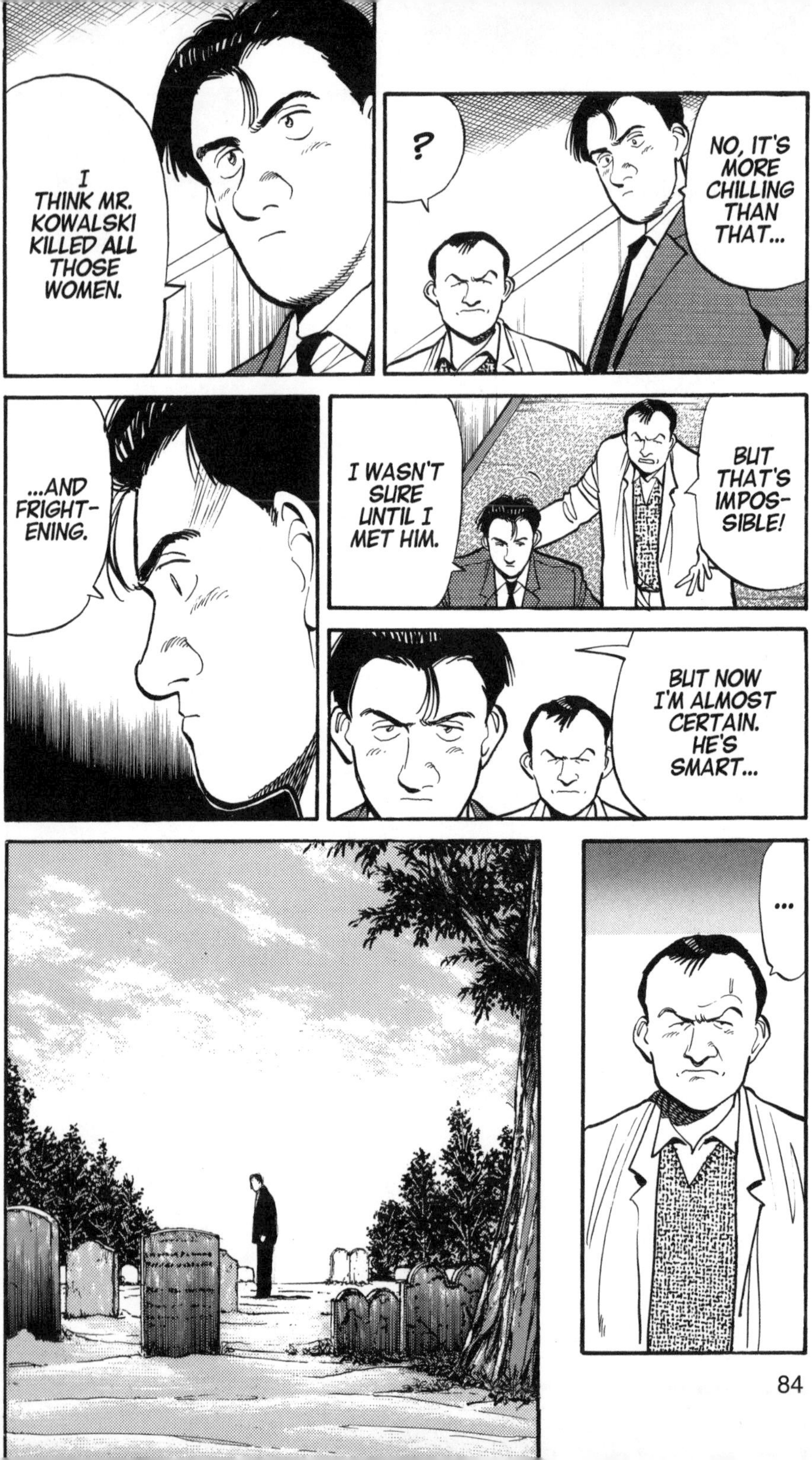
NO, IT'S MORE CHILLING THAN THAT...
?
I THINK MR. KOWALSKI KILLED ALL THOSE WOMEN.
BUT THAT'S IMPOSSIBLE!
I WASN'T SURE UNTIL I MET HIM.
BUT NOW I'M ALMOST CERTAIN. HE'S SMART...
...AND FRIGHTENING.
...

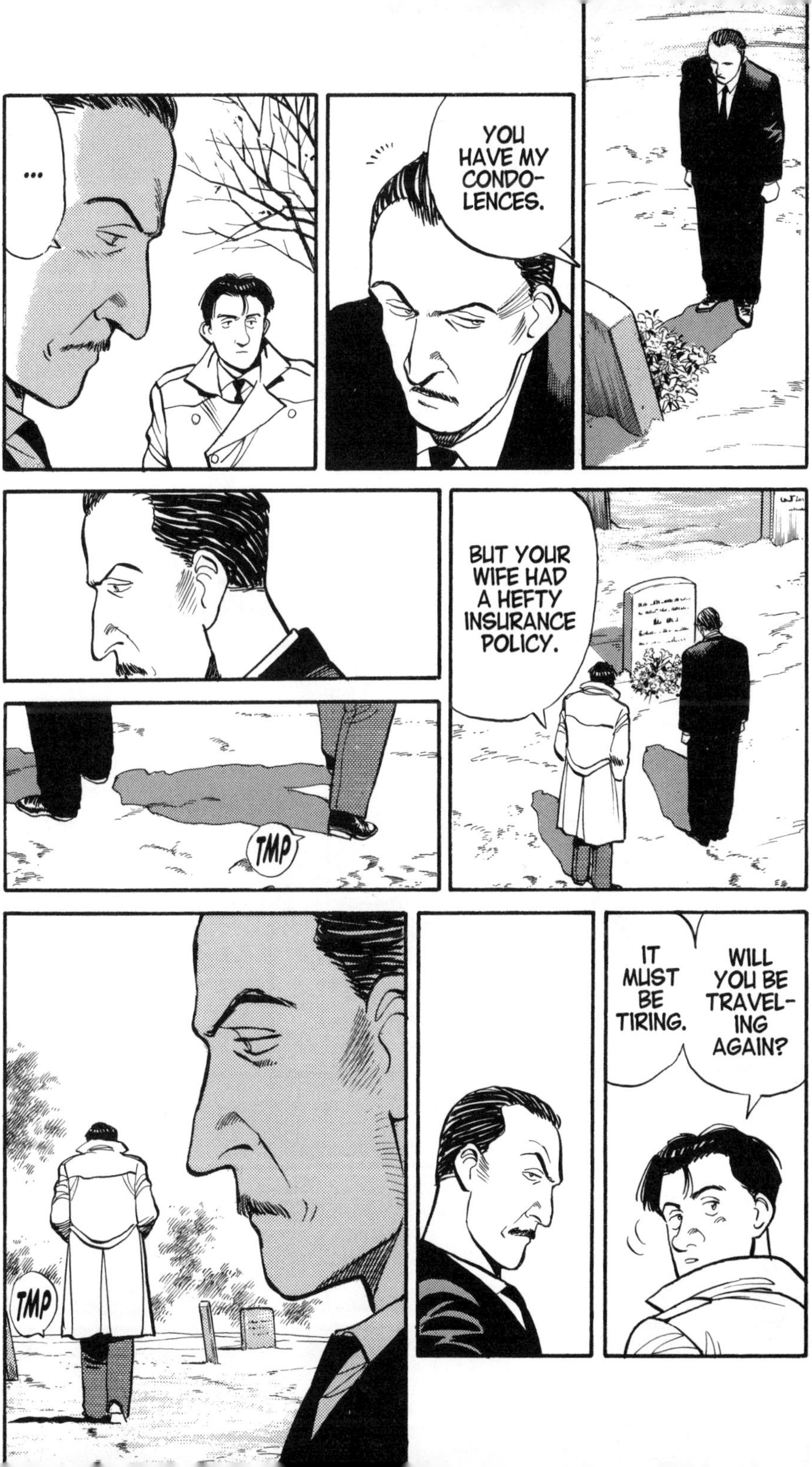
YOU HAVE MY CONDOLENCES.
...
BUT YOUR WIFE HAD A HEFTY INSURANCE POLICY.
TMP
WILL YOU BE TRAVEL-ING AGAIN?
IT MUST BE TIRING.
TMP

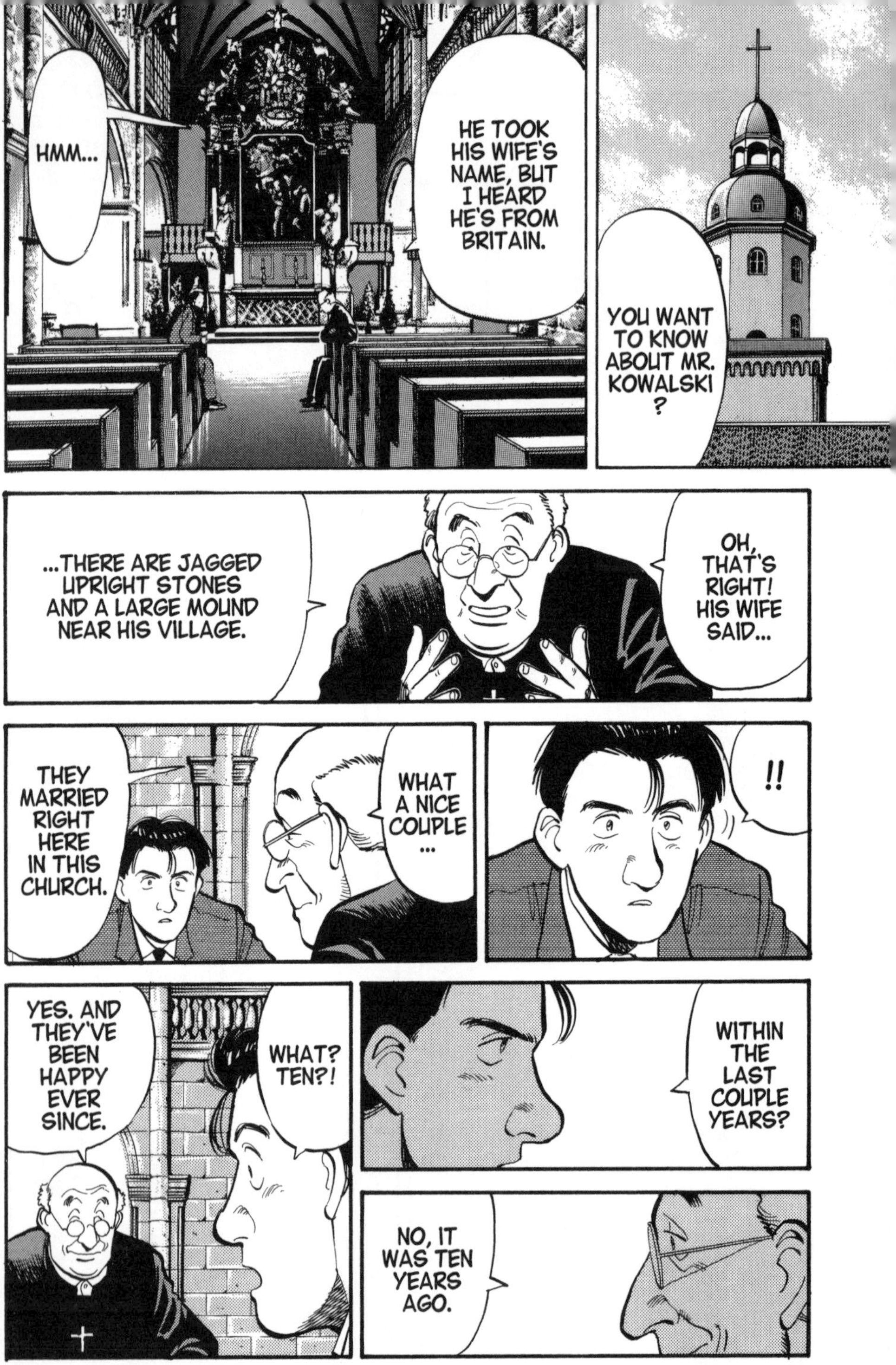
YOU WANT TO KNOW ABOUT MR. KOWALSKI?
HE TOOK HIS WIFE'S NAME, BUT I HEARD HE'S FROM BRITAIN.
HMM...
OH, THAT'S RIGHT! HIS WIFE SAID...
...THERE ARE JAGGED UPRIGHT STONES AND A LARGE MOUND NEAR HIS VILLAGE.
!!
WHAT A NICE COUPLE...
THEY MARRIED RIGHT HERE IN THIS CHURCH.
WITHIN THE LAST COUPLE YEARS?
NO, IT WAS TEN YEARS AGO.
WHAT? TEN?!
YES. AND THEY'VE BEEN HAPPY EVER SINCE.

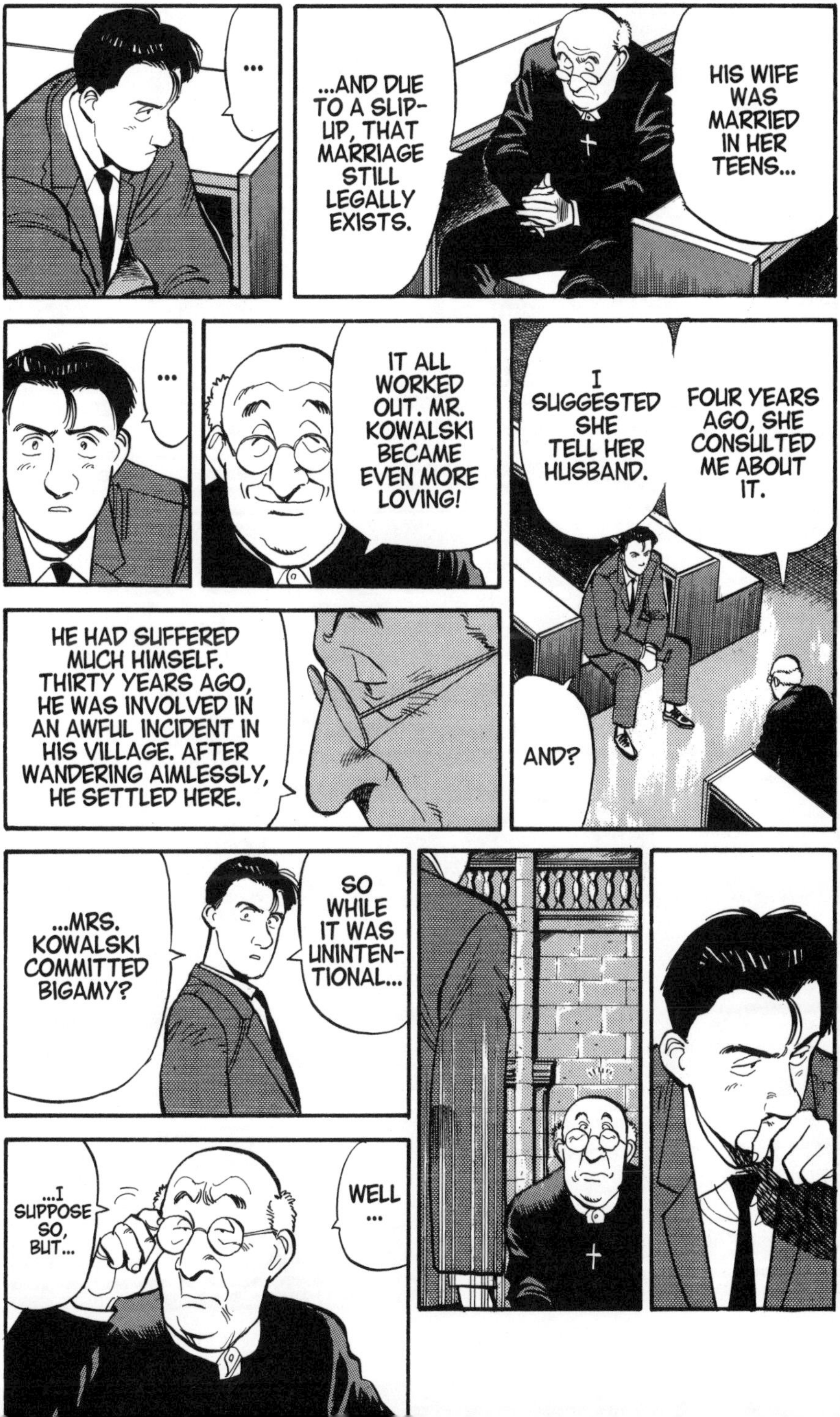
HIS WIFE WAS MARRIED IN HER TEENS...
...AND DUE TO A SLIP-UP, THAT MARRIAGE STILL LEGALLY EXISTS.
...
FOUR YEARS AGO, SHE CONSULTED ME ABOUT IT.
I SUGGESTED SHE TELL HER HUSBAND.
AND?
IT ALL WORKED OUT. MR. KOWALSKI BECAME EVEN MORE LOVING!
...
HE HAD SUFFERED MUCH HIMSELF. THIRTY YEARS AGO, HE WAS INVOLVED IN AN AWFUL INCIDENT IN HIS VILLAGE. AFTER WANDERING AIMLESSLY, HE SETTLED HERE.
SO WHILE IT WAS UNINTENTIONAL...
...MRS. KOWALSKI COMMITTED BIGAMY?
WELL...
...I SUPPOSE SO, BUT...

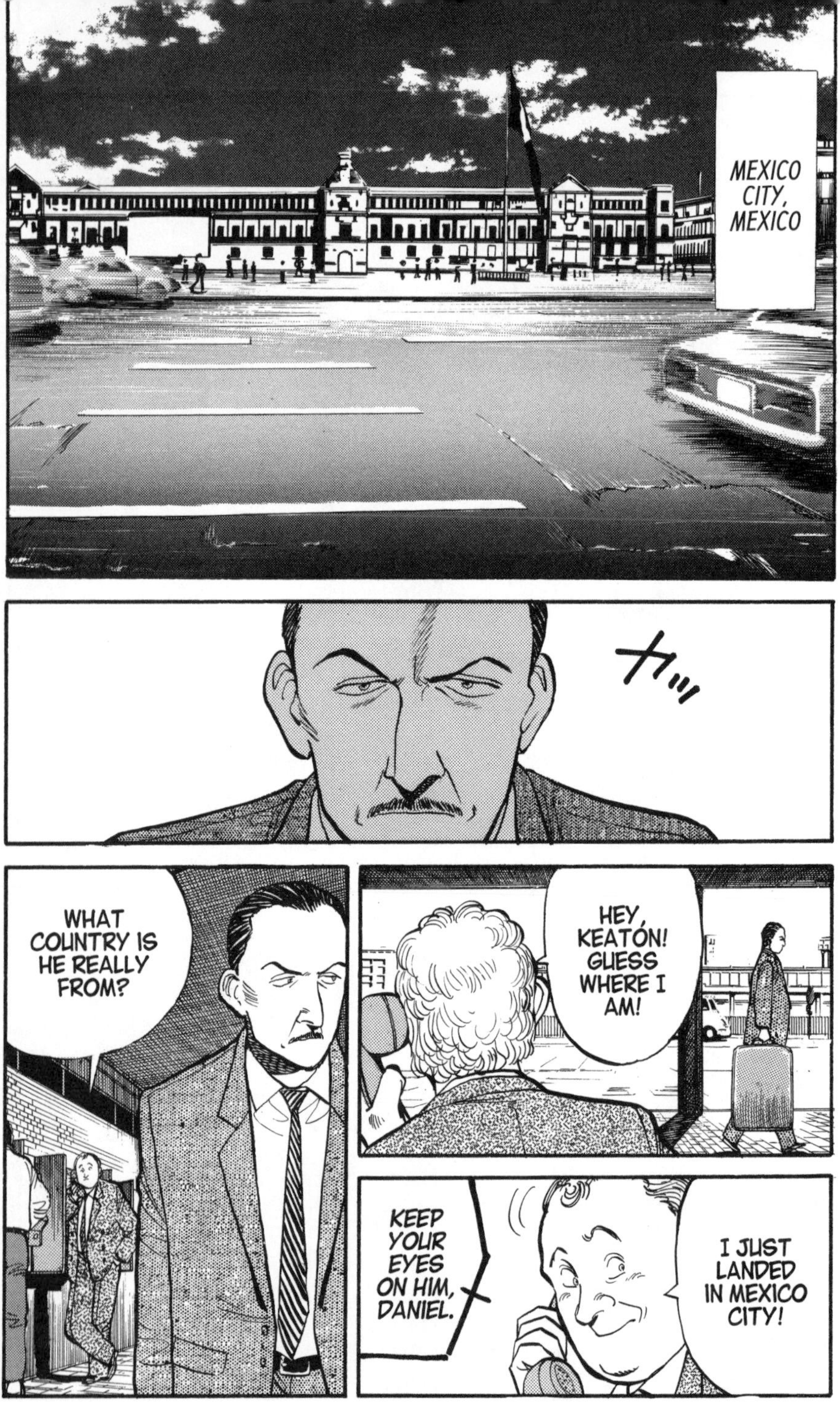
MEXICO CITY, MEXICO
カッ
HEY, KEATÓN! GUESS WHERE I AM!
I JUST LANDED IN MEXICO CITY!
KEEP YOUR EYES ON HIM, DANIEL.
WHAT COUNTRY IS HE REALLY FROM?

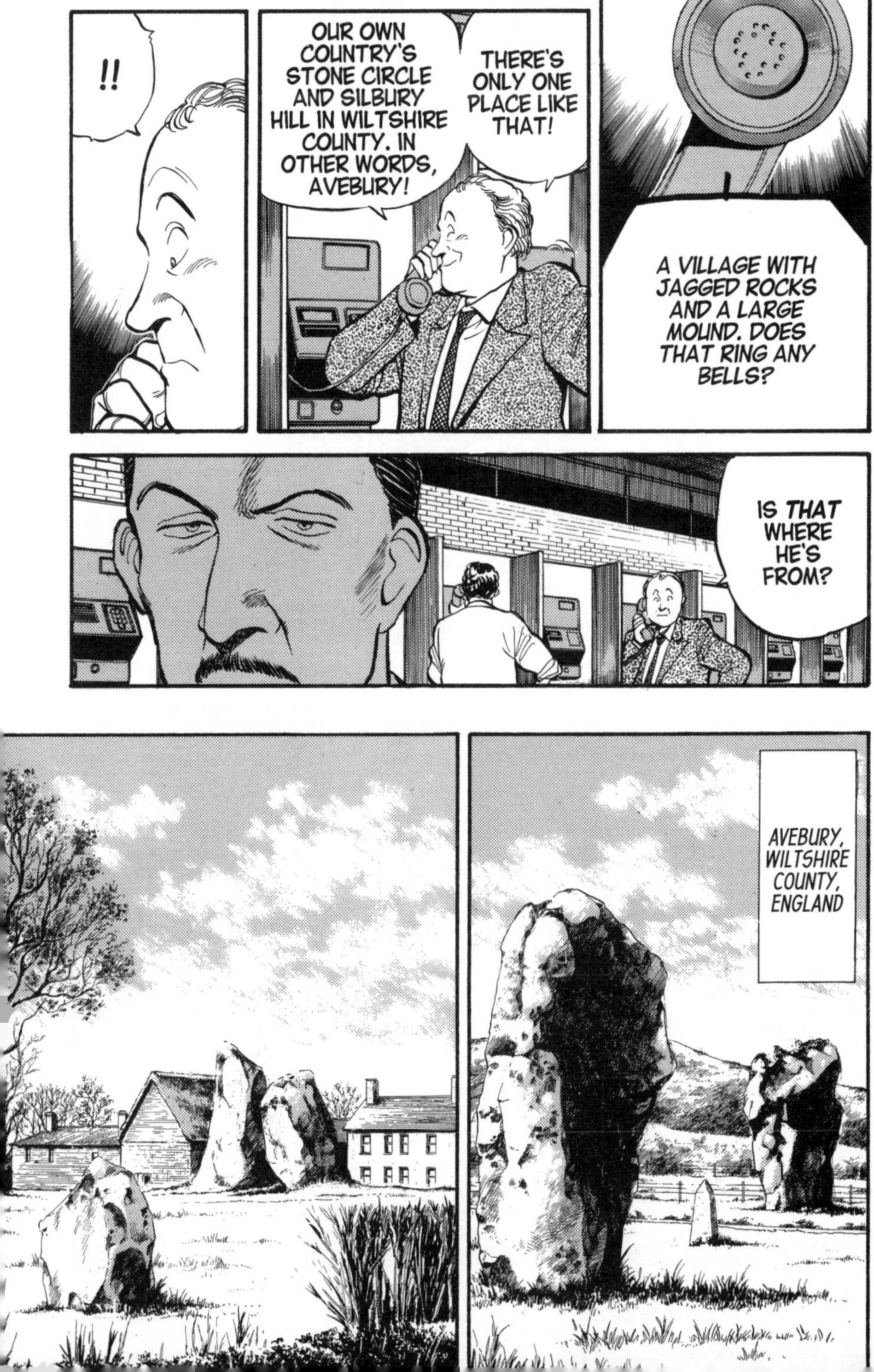
A VILLAGE WITH JAGGED ROCKS AND A LARGE MOUND. DOES THAT RING ANY BELLS?
THERE'S ONLY ONE PLACE LIKE THAT!
OUR OWN COUNTRY'S STONE CIRCLE AND SILBURY HILL IN WILTSHIRE COUNTY. IN OTHER WORDS, AVEBURY!
!!
IS THAT WHERE HE'S FROM?
AVEBURY, WILTSHIRE COUNTY, ENGLAND

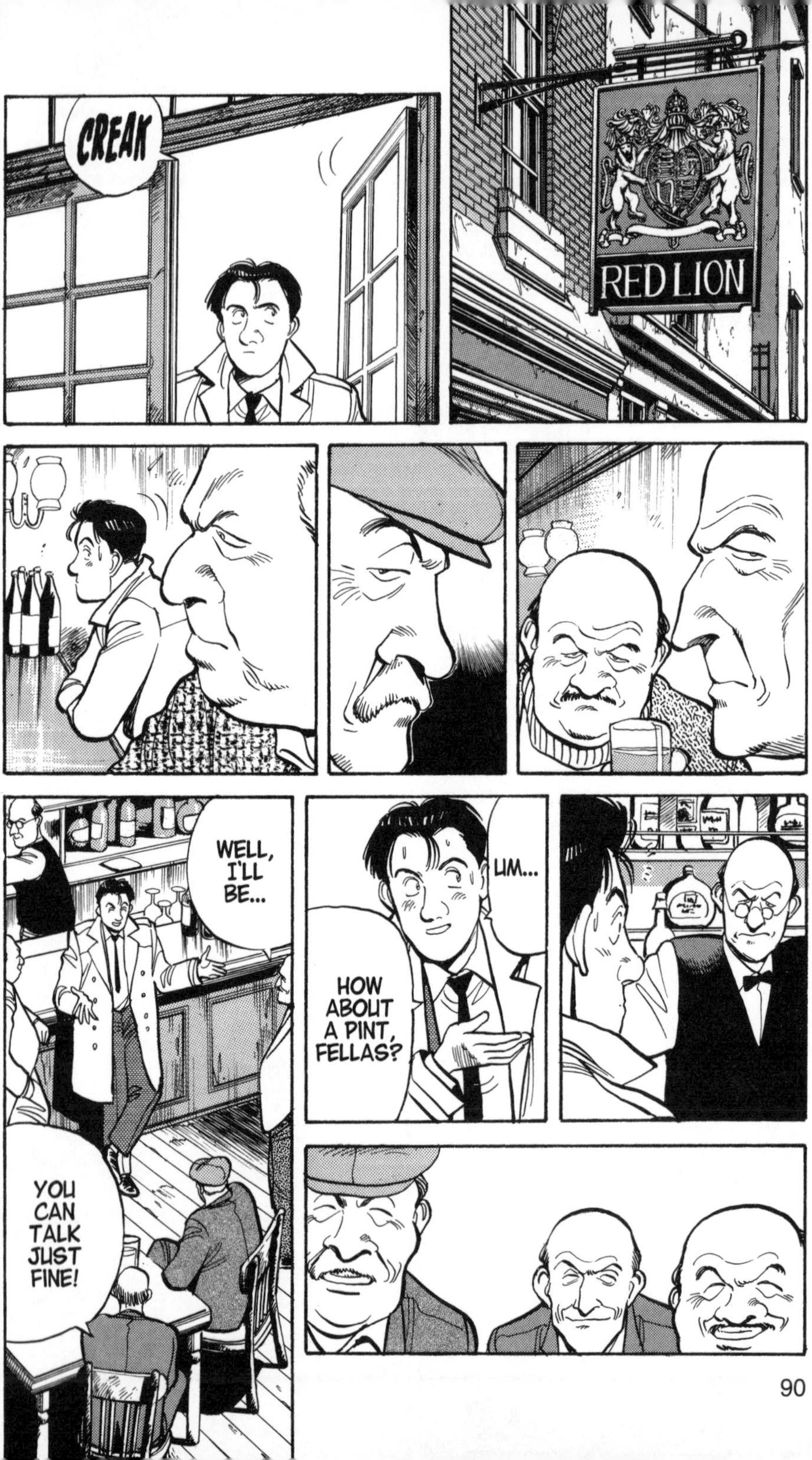
RED LION
CREAK
UM...
HOW ABOUT A PINT, FELLAS?
WELL, I'LL BE...
YOU CAN TALK JUST FINE!

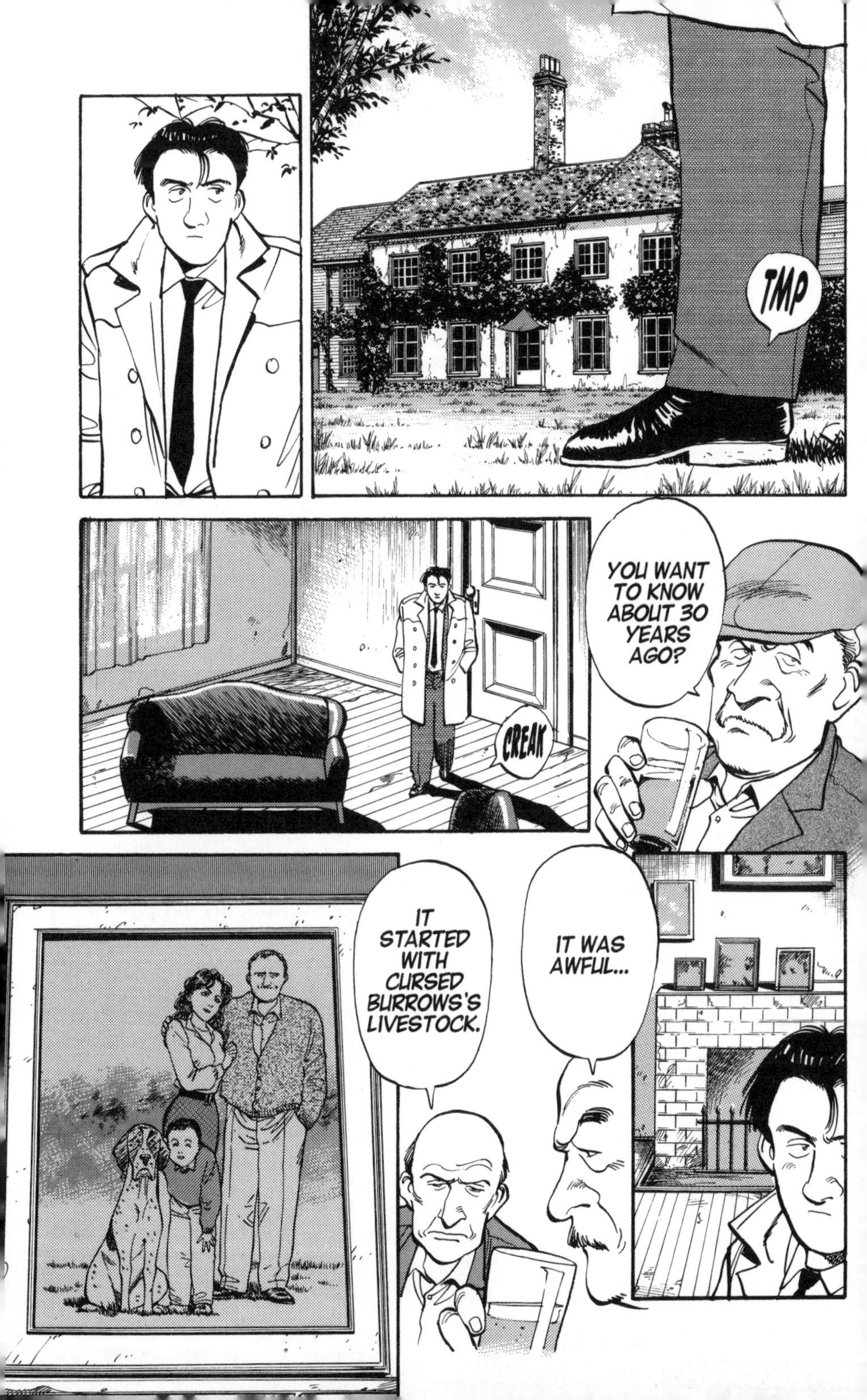
TMP
YOU WANT TO KNOW ABOUT 30 YEARS AGO?
CREAK
IT WAS AWFUL...
IT STARTED WITH CURSED BURROWS'S LIVESTOCK.

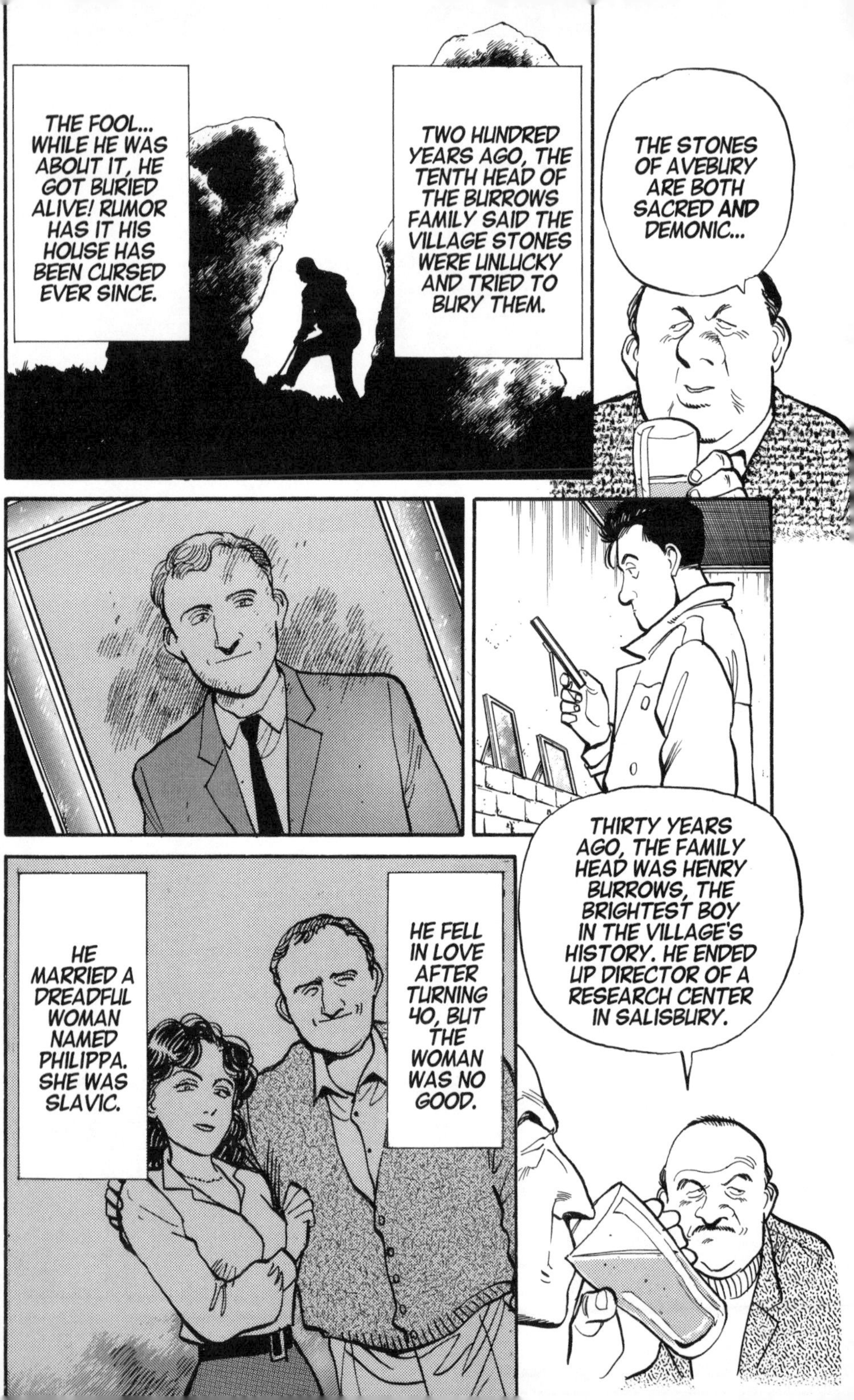
THE STONES OF AVEBURY ARE BOTH SACRED AND DEMONIC...
TWO HUNDRED YEARS AGO, THE TENTH HEAD OF THE BURROWS FAMILY SAID THE VILLAGE STONES WERE UNLUCKY AND TRIED TO BURY THEM.
THE FOOL... WHILE HE WAS ABOUT IT, HE GOT BURIED ALIVE! RUMOR HAS IT HIS HOUSE HAS BEEN CURSED EVER SINCE.
THIRTY YEARS AGO, THE FAMILY HEAD WAS HENRY BURROWS, THE BRIGHTEST BOY IN THE VILLAGE'S HISTORY. HE ENDED UP DIRECTOR OF A RESEARCH CENTER IN SALISBURY.
HE FELL IN LOVE AFTER TURNING 40, BUT THE WOMAN WAS NO GOOD.
HE MARRIED A DREADFUL WOMAN NAMED PHILIPPA. SHE WAS SLAVIC.

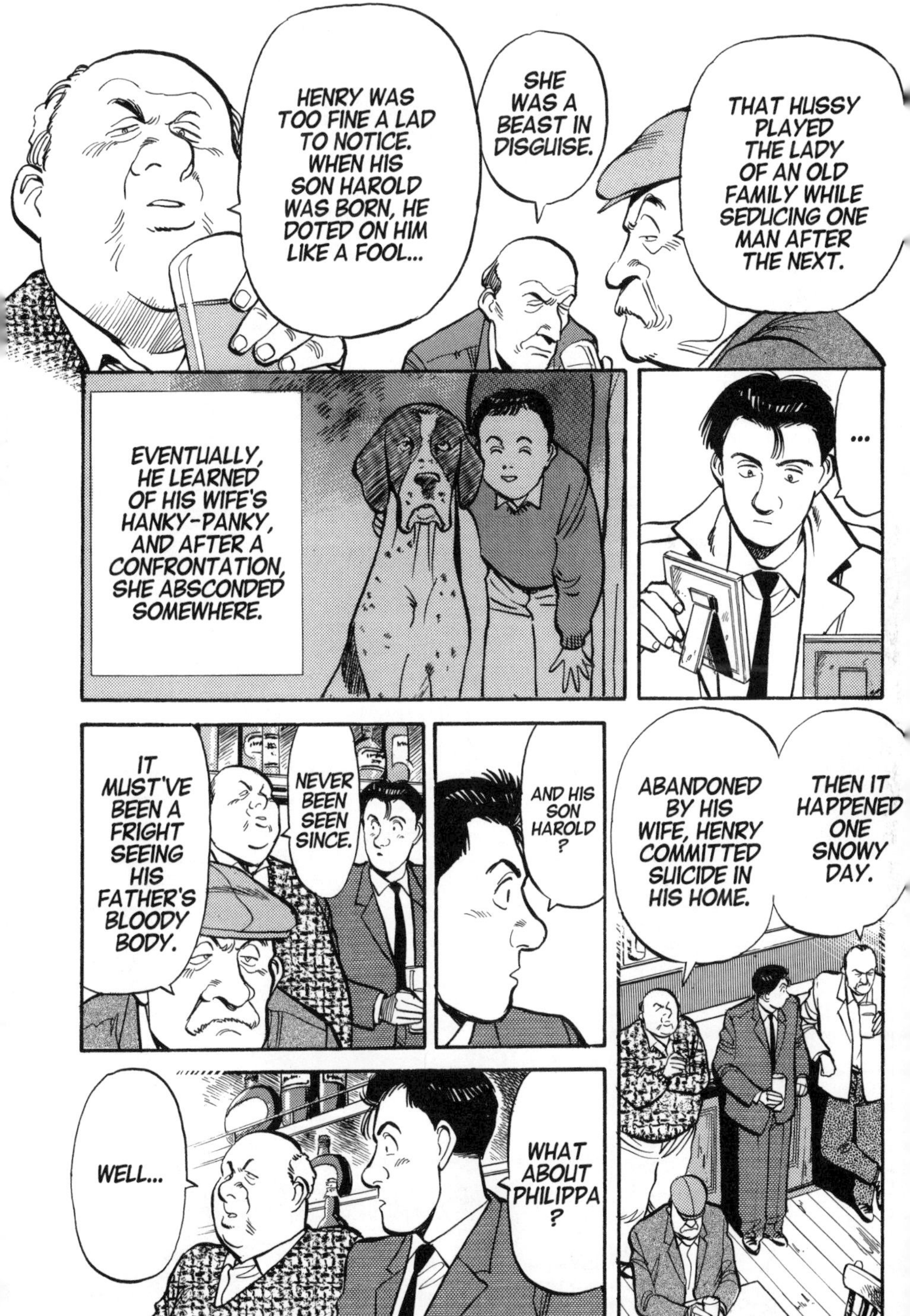
THAT HUSSY PLAYED THE LADY OF AN OLD FAMILY WHILE SEDUCING ONE MAN AFTER THE NEXT.
SHE WAS A BEAST IN DISGUISE.
HENRY WAS TOO FINE A LAD TO NOTICE. WHEN HIS SON HAROLD WAS BORN, HE DOTED ON HIM LIKE A FOOL...
...
EVENTUALLY, HE LEARNED OF HIS WIFE'S HANKY-PANKY, AND AFTER A CONFRONTATION, SHE ABSCONDED SOMEWHERE.
THEN IT HAPPENED ONE SNOWY DAY.
ABANDONED BY HIS WIFE, HENRY COMMITTED SUICIDE IN HIS HOME.
AND HIS SON HAROLD?
NEVER BEEN SEEN SINCE.
IT MUST'VE BEEN A FRIGHT SEEING HIS FATHER'S BLOODY BODY.
WHAT ABOUT PHILIPPA?
WELL...

...AS FOR HER...

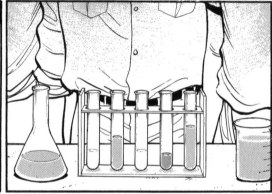

MNCH MNCH

YOUR GUESS WAS SPOT-ON.

YEAH... KEATON?

MEXICO CITY

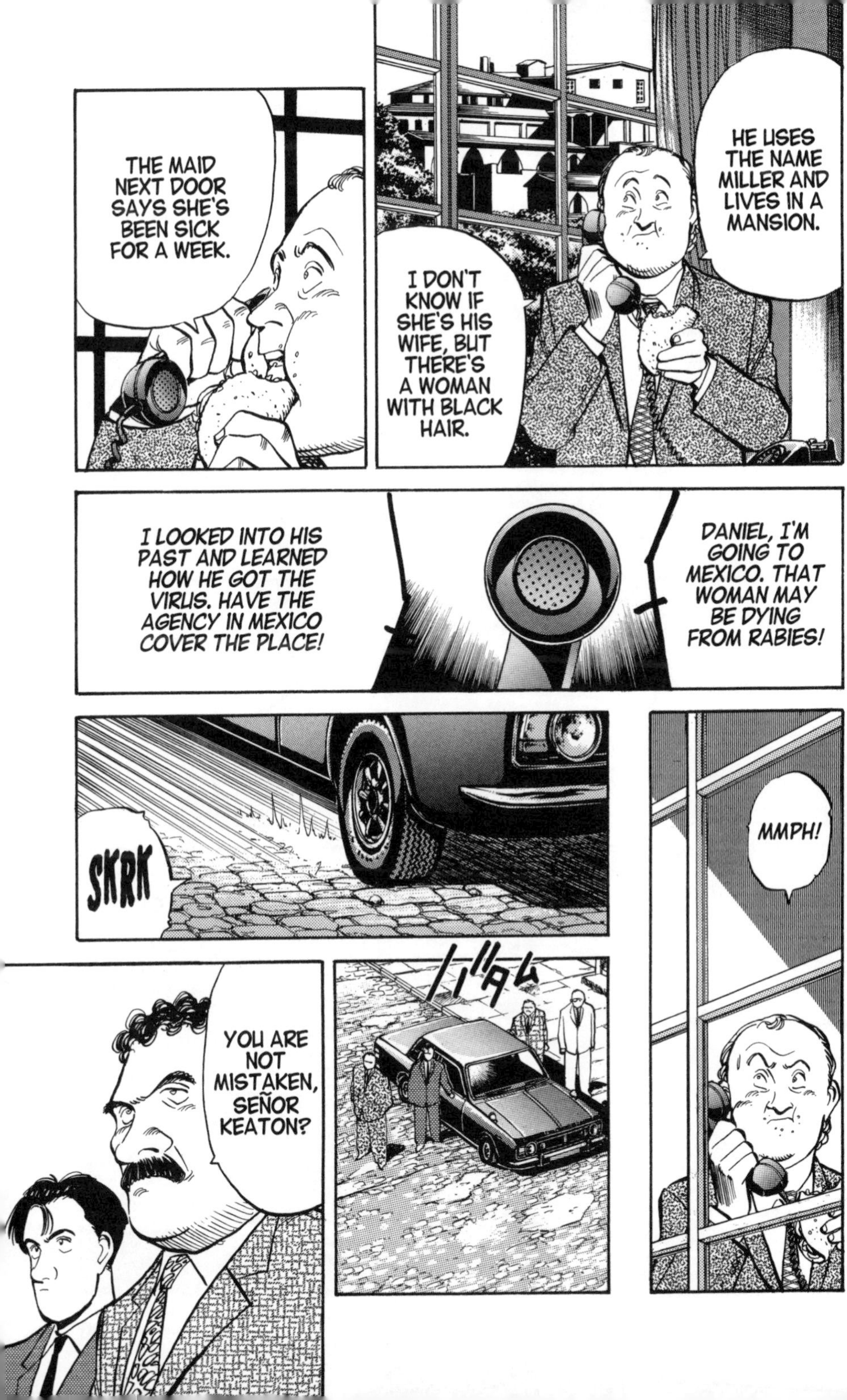
HE USES THE NAME MILLER AND LIVES IN A MANSION.
I DON'T KNOW IF SHE'S HIS WIFE, BUT THERE'S A WOMAN WITH BLACK HAIR.
THE MAID NEXT DOOR SAYS SHE'S BEEN SICK FOR A WEEK.
DANIEL, I'M GOING TO MEXICO. THAT WOMAN MAY BE DYING FROM RABIES!
I LOOKED INTO HIS PAST AND LEARNED HOW HE GOT THE VIRUS. HAVE THE AGENCY IN MEXICO COVER THE PLACE!
MMPH!
SKRK
バタム
YOU ARE NOT MISTAKEN, SEÑOR KEATON?

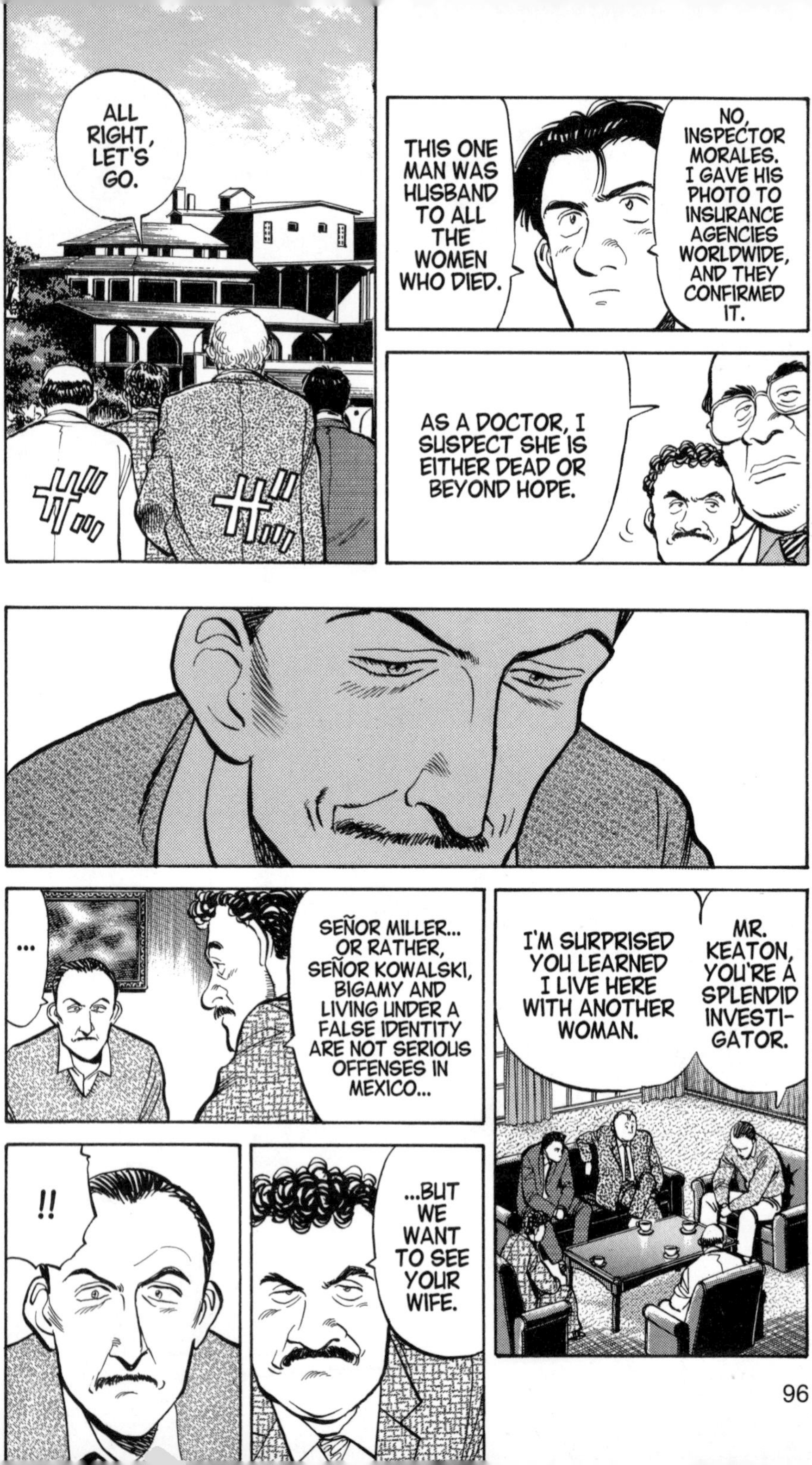
NO, INSPECTOR MORALES. I GAVE HIS PHOTO TO INSURANCE AGENCIES WORLDWIDE, AND THEY CONFIRMED IT.
THIS ONE MAN WAS HUSBAND TO ALL THE WOMEN WHO DIED.
AS A DOCTOR, I SUSPECT SHE IS EITHER DEAD OR BEYOND HOPE.
ALL RIGHT, LET'S GO.
MR. KEATON, YOU'RE A SPLENDID INVESTI-GATOR.
I'M SURPRISED YOU LEARNED I LIVE HERE WITH ANOTHER WOMAN.
SEÑOR MILLER... OR RATHER, SEÑOR KOWALSKI, BIGAMY AND LIVING UNDER A FALSE IDENTITY ARE NOT SERIOUS OFFENSES IN MEXICO...
...
...BUT WE WANT TO SEE YOUR WIFE.
!!

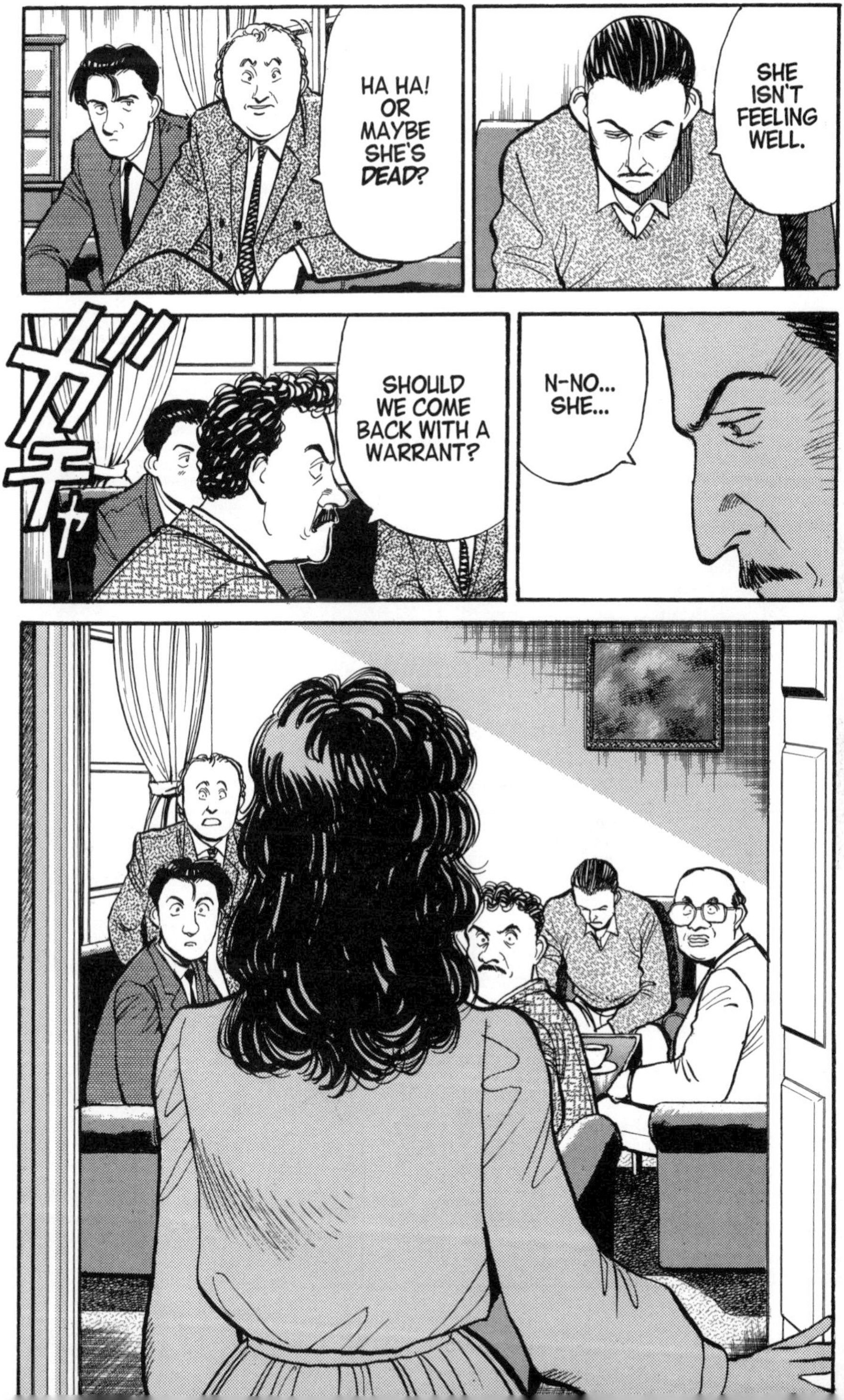
SHE ISN'T FEELING WELL.
HA HA! OR MAYBE SHE'S DEAD?
N-NO... SHE...
SHOULD WE COME BACK WITH A WARRANT?
ガチャ

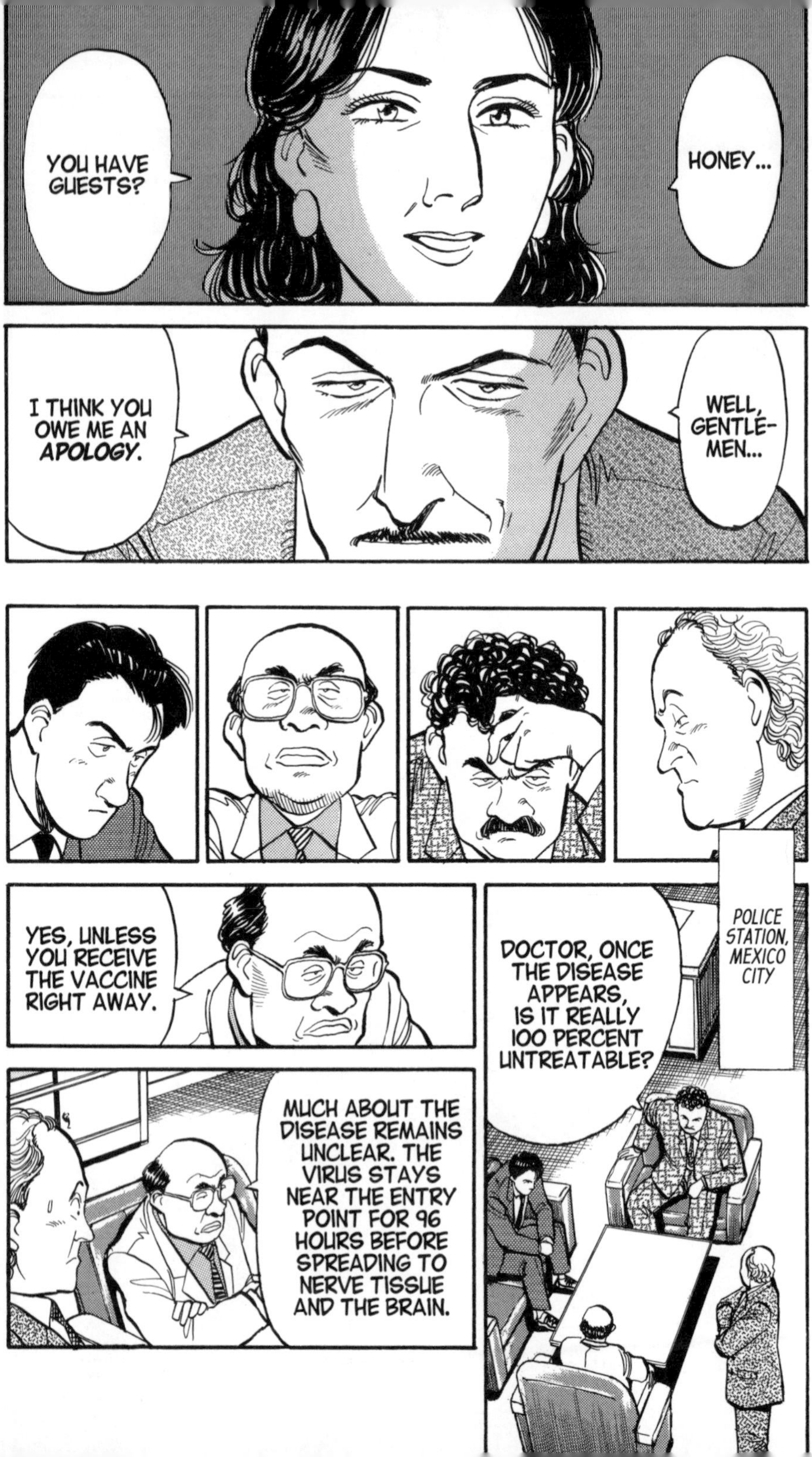
HONEY...
YOU HAVE GUESTS?
WELL, GENTLE-MEN...
I THINK YOU OWE ME AN *APOLOGY*.
POLICE STATION, MEXICO CITY
DOCTOR, ONCE THE DISEASE APPEARS, IS IT REALLY 100 PERCENT UNTREATABLE?
YES, UNLESS YOU RECEIVE THE VACCINE RIGHT AWAY.
MUCH ABOUT THE DISEASE REMAINS UNCLEAR. THE VIRUS STAYS NEAR THE ENTRY POINT FOR 96 HOURS BEFORE SPREADING TO NERVE TISSUE AND THE BRAIN.

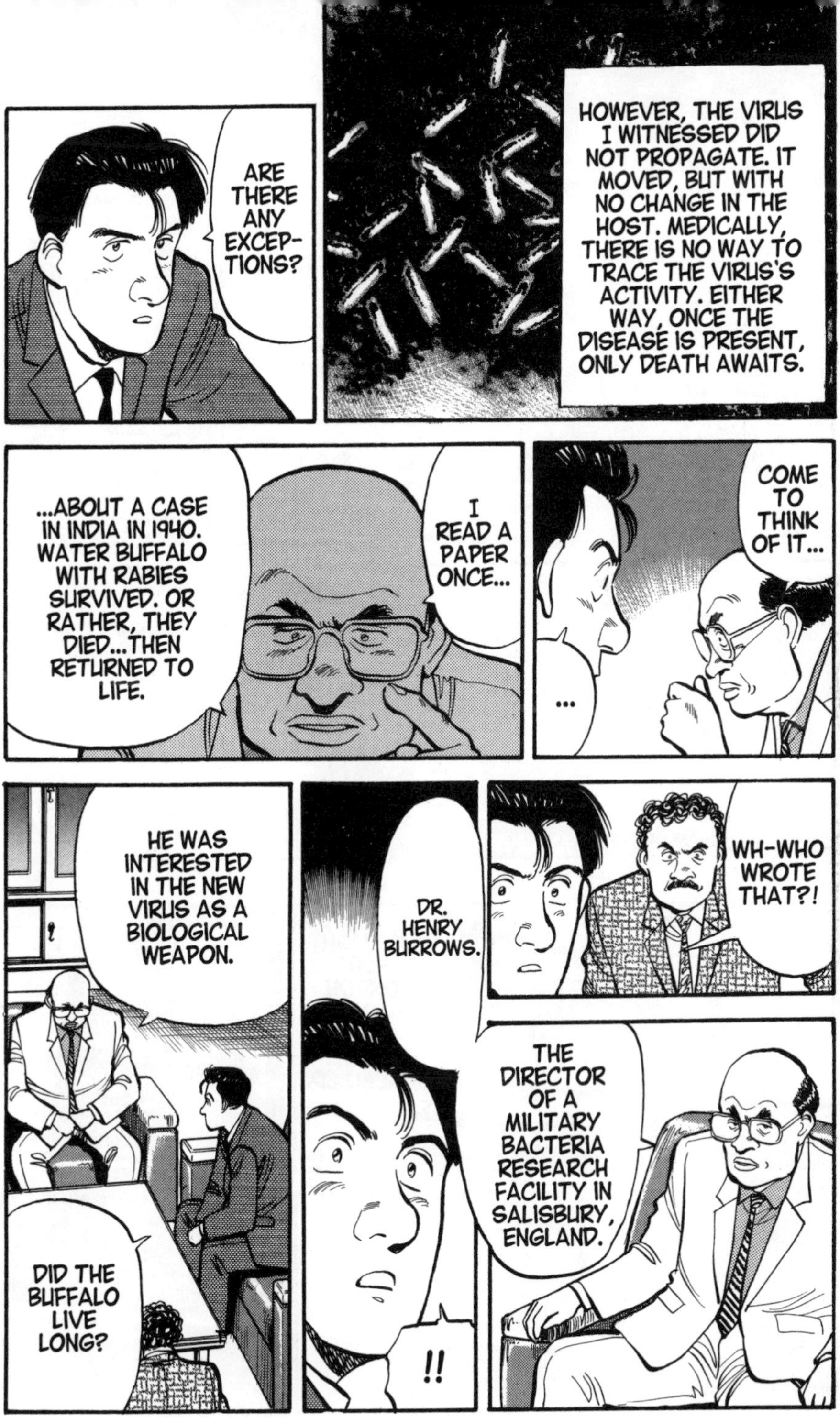
HOWEVER, THE VIRUS I WITNESSED DID NOT PROPAGATE. IT MOVED, BUT WITH NO CHANGE IN THE HOST. MEDICALLY, THERE IS NO WAY TO TRACE THE VIRUS'S ACTIVITY. EITHER WAY, ONCE THE DISEASE IS PRESENT, ONLY DEATH AWAITS.
ARE THERE ANY EXCEPTIONS?
COME TO THINK OF IT...
...
I READ A PAPER ONCE...
...ABOUT A CASE IN INDIA IN 1940. WATER BUFFALO WITH RABIES SURVIVED. OR RATHER, THEY DIED...THEN RETURNED TO LIFE.
WH-WHO WROTE THAT?!
THE DIRECTOR OF A MILITARY BACTERIA RESEARCH FACILITY IN SALISBURY, ENGLAND.
DR. HENRY BURROWS.
!!
HE WAS INTERESTED IN THE NEW VIRUS AS A BIOLOGICAL WEAPON.
DID THE BUFFALO LIVE LONG?

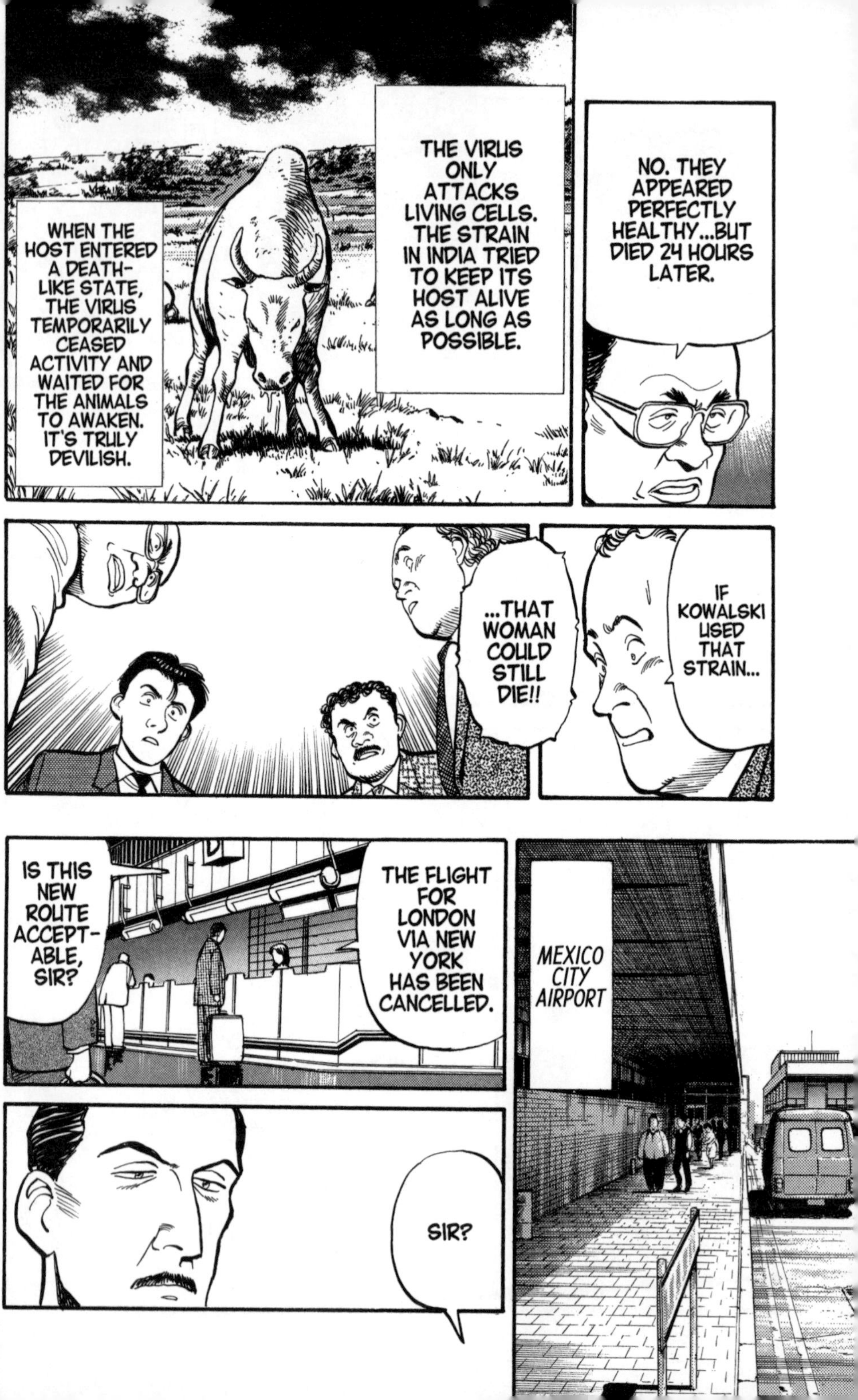
NO. THEY APPEARED PERFECTLY HEALTHY...BUT DIED 24 HOURS LATER.
THE VIRUS ONLY ATTACKS LIVING CELLS. THE STRAIN IN INDIA TRIED TO KEEP ITS HOST ALIVE AS LONG AS POSSIBLE.
WHEN THE HOST ENTERED A DEATH-LIKE STATE, THE VIRUS TEMPORARILY CEASED ACTIVITY AND WAITED FOR THE ANIMALS TO AWAKEN. IT'S TRULY DEVILISH.
IF KOWALSKI USED THAT STRAIN...
...THAT WOMAN COULD STILL DIE!!
MEXICO CITY AIRPORT
THE FLIGHT FOR LONDON VIA NEW YORK HAS BEEN CANCELLED.
IS THIS NEW ROUTE ACCEPT-ABLE, SIR?
SIR?

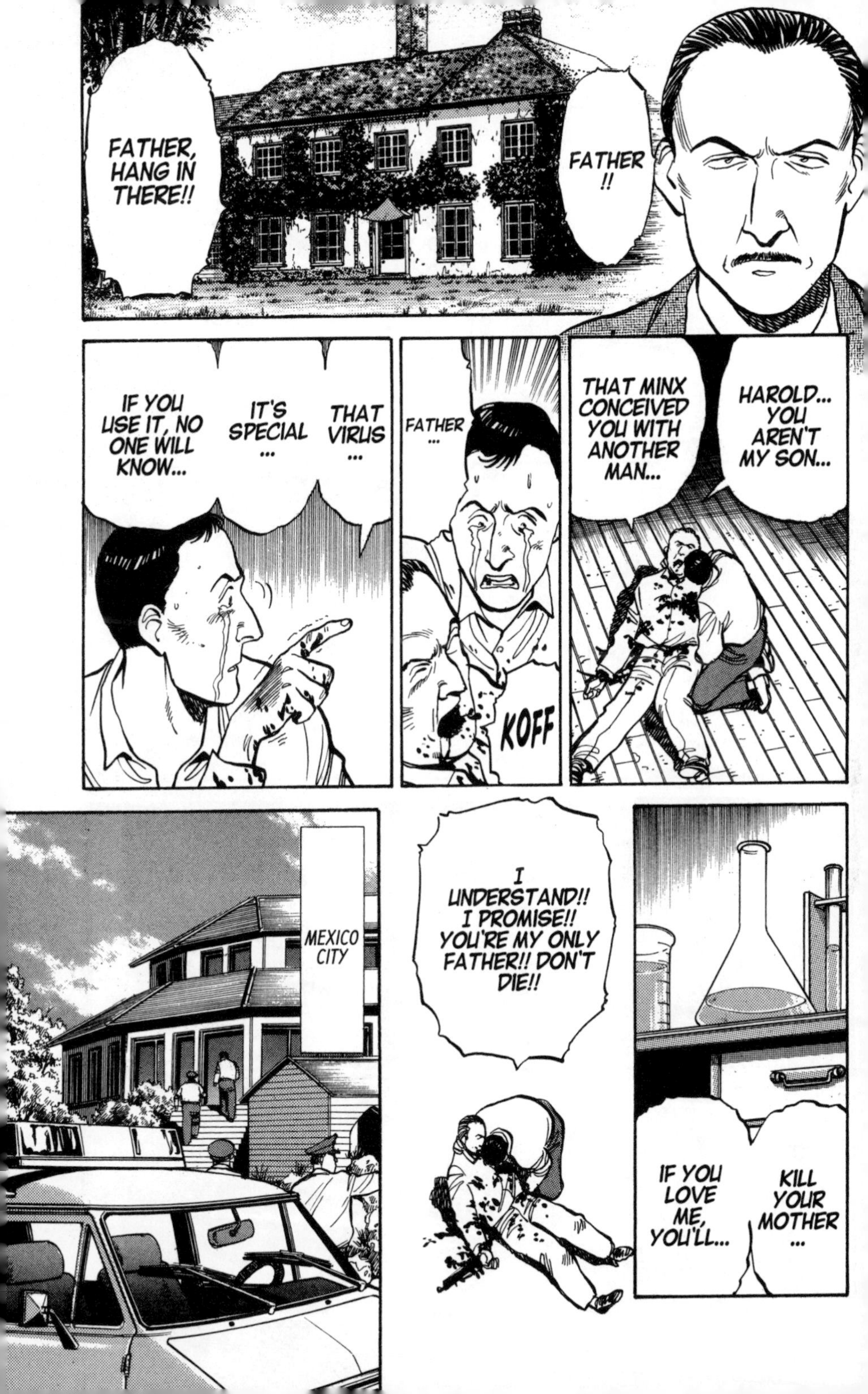
FATHER !!
FATHER, HANG IN THERE!!
HAROLD... YOU AREN'T MY SON...
THAT MINX CONCEIVED YOU WITH ANOTHER MAN...
FATHER...
KOFF
THAT VIRUS...
IT'S SPECIAL...
IF YOU USE IT, NO ONE WILL KNOW...
KILL YOUR MOTHER...
IF YOU LOVE ME, YOU'LL...
I UNDERSTAND!! I PROMISE!! YOU'RE MY ONLY FATHER!! DON'T DIE!!
MEXICO CITY

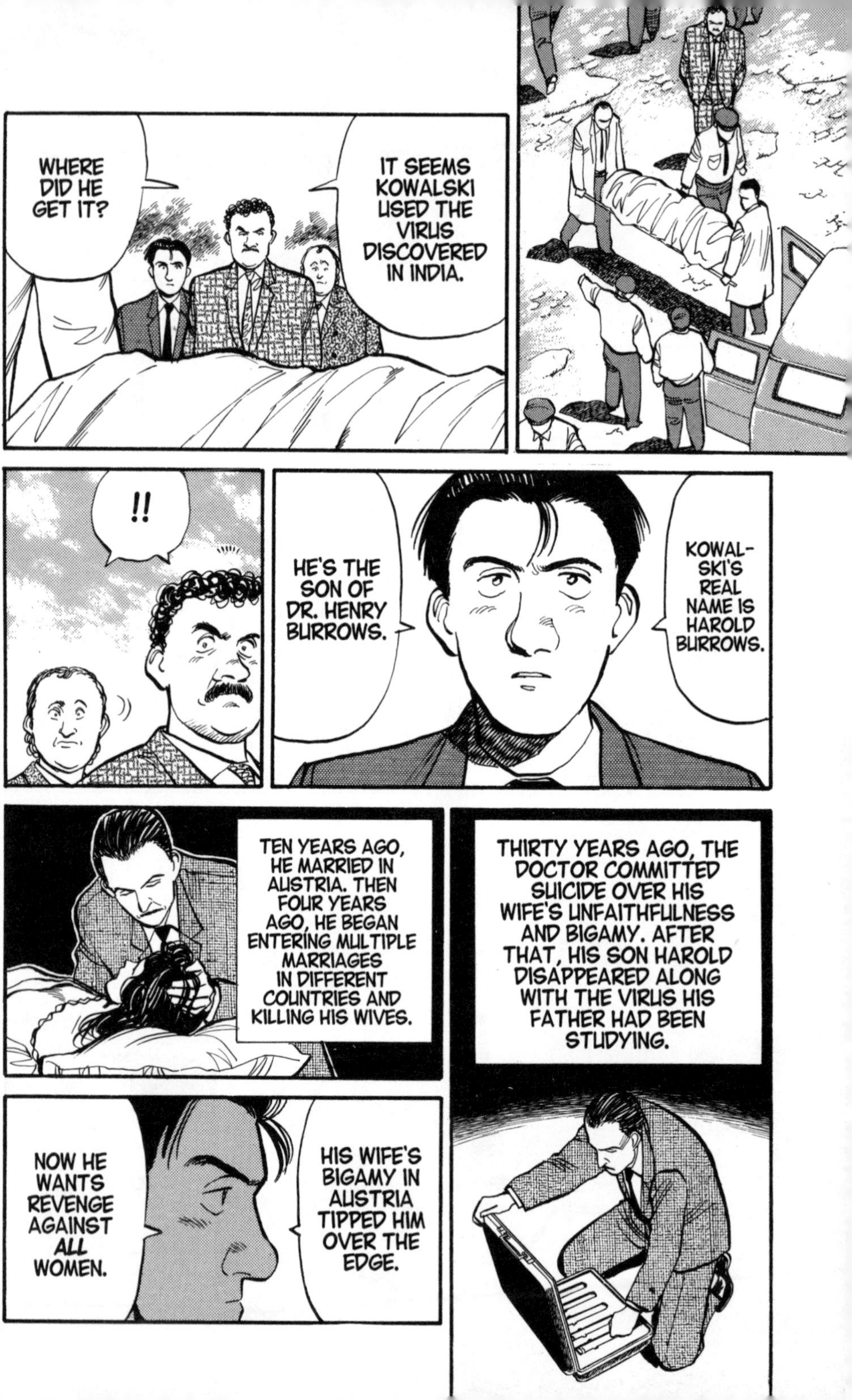
IT SEEMS KOWALSKI USED THE VIRUS DISCOVERED IN INDIA.
WHERE DID HE GET IT?
KOWAL-SKI'S REAL NAME IS HAROLD BURROWS.
HE'S THE SON OF DR. HENRY BURROWS.
!!
THIRTY YEARS AGO, THE DOCTOR COMMITTED SUICIDE OVER HIS WIFE'S UNFAITHFULNESS AND BIGAMY. AFTER THAT, HIS SON HAROLD DISAPPEARED ALONG WITH THE VIRUS HIS FATHER HAD BEEN STUDYING.
TEN YEARS AGO, HE MARRIED IN AUSTRIA. THEN FOUR YEARS AGO, HE BEGAN ENTERING MULTIPLE MARRIAGES IN DIFFERENT COUNTRIES AND KILLING HIS WIVES.
HIS WIFE'S BIGAMY IN AUSTRIA TIPPED HIM OVER THE EDGE.
NOW HE WANTS REVENGE AGAINST ALL WOMEN.

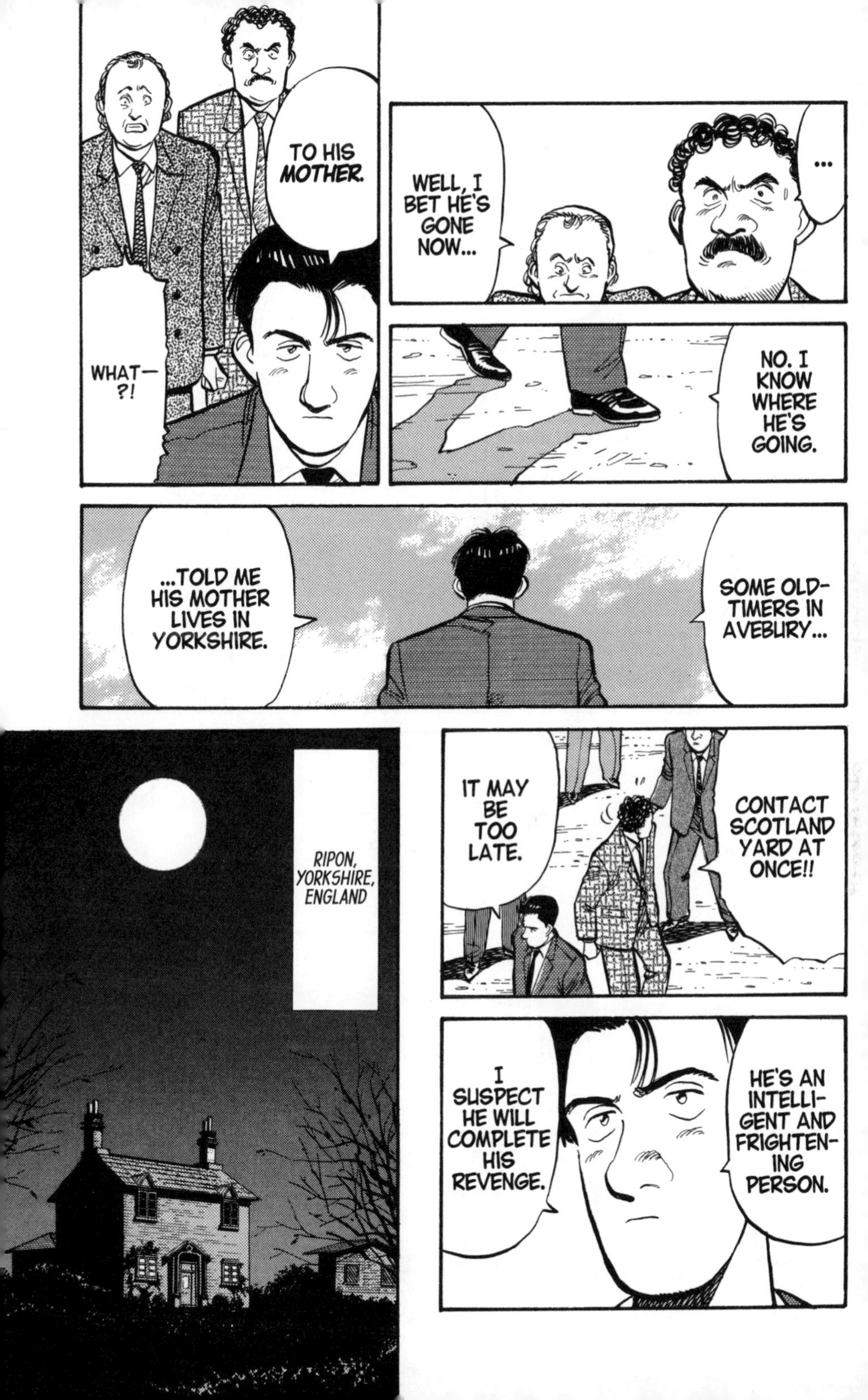
...
WELL, I BET HE'S GONE NOW...
NO. I KNOW WHERE HE'S GOING.
TO HIS *MOTHER.*
WHAT—?!
SOME OLD-TIMERS IN AVEBURY...
...TOLD ME HIS MOTHER LIVES IN YORKSHIRE.
CONTACT SCOTLAND YARD AT ONCE!!
IT MAY BE TOO LATE.
HE'S AN INTELLIGENT AND FRIGHTENING PERSON.
I SUSPECT HE WILL COMPLETE HIS REVENGE.
*RIPON, YORKSHIRE, ENGLAND*

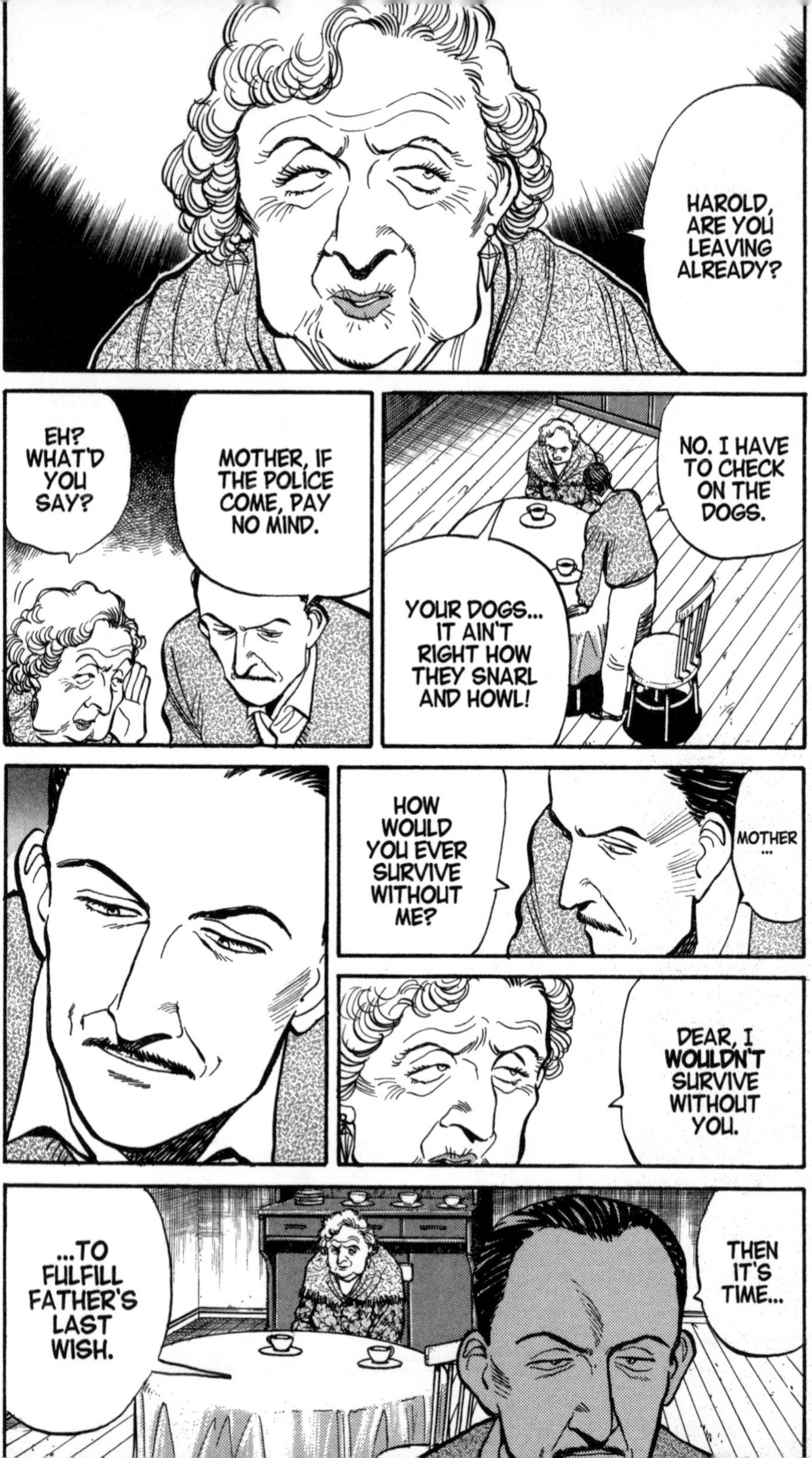
HAROLD, ARE YOU LEAVING ALREADY?
NO. I HAVE TO CHECK ON THE DOGS.
YOUR DOGS... IT AIN'T RIGHT HOW THEY SNARL AND HOWL!
MOTHER, IF THE POLICE COME, PAY NO MIND.
EH? WHAT'D YOU SAY?
MOTHER...
HOW WOULD YOU EVER SURVIVE WITHOUT ME?
DEAR, I WOULDN'T SURVIVE WITHOUT YOU.
THEN IT'S TIME...
...TO FULFILL FATHER'S LAST WISH.

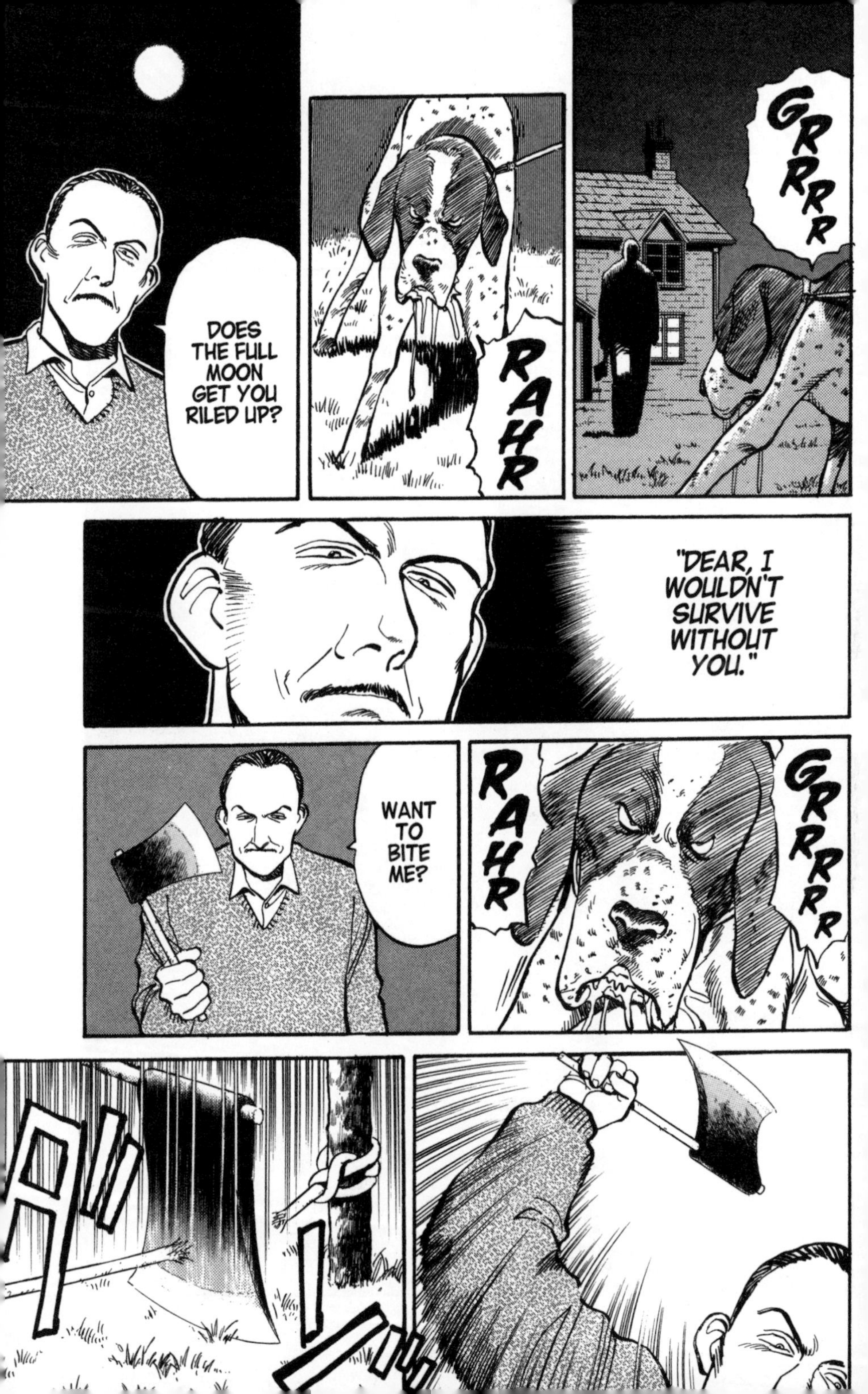
GRRRR
RAHR
DOES THE FULL MOON GET YOU RILED UP?
"DEAR, I WOULDN'T SURVIVE WITHOUT YOU."
GRRRRR
RAHR
WANT TO BITE ME?

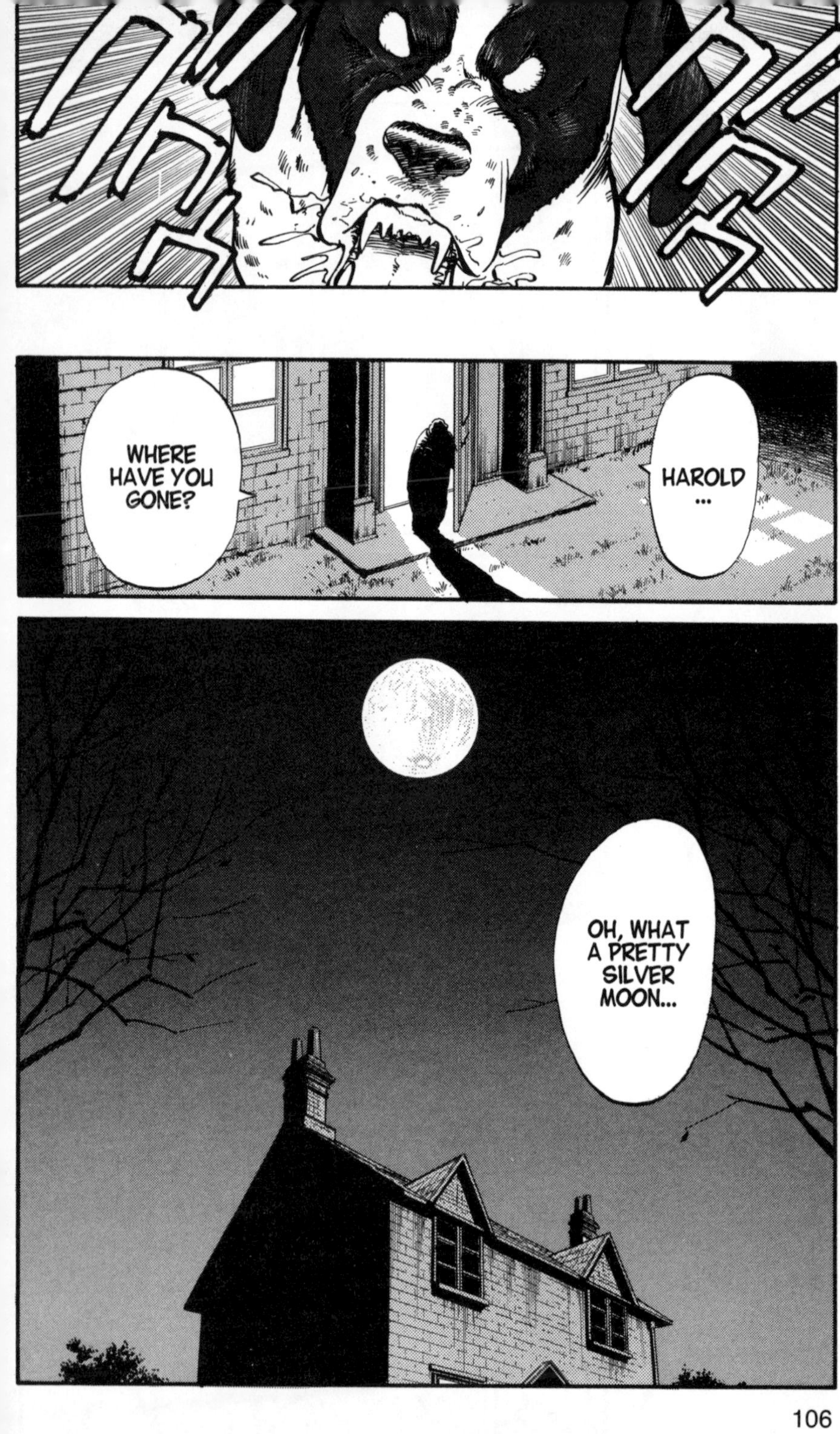
HAROLD ...
WHERE HAVE YOU GONE?
OH, WHAT A PRETTY SILVER MOON...

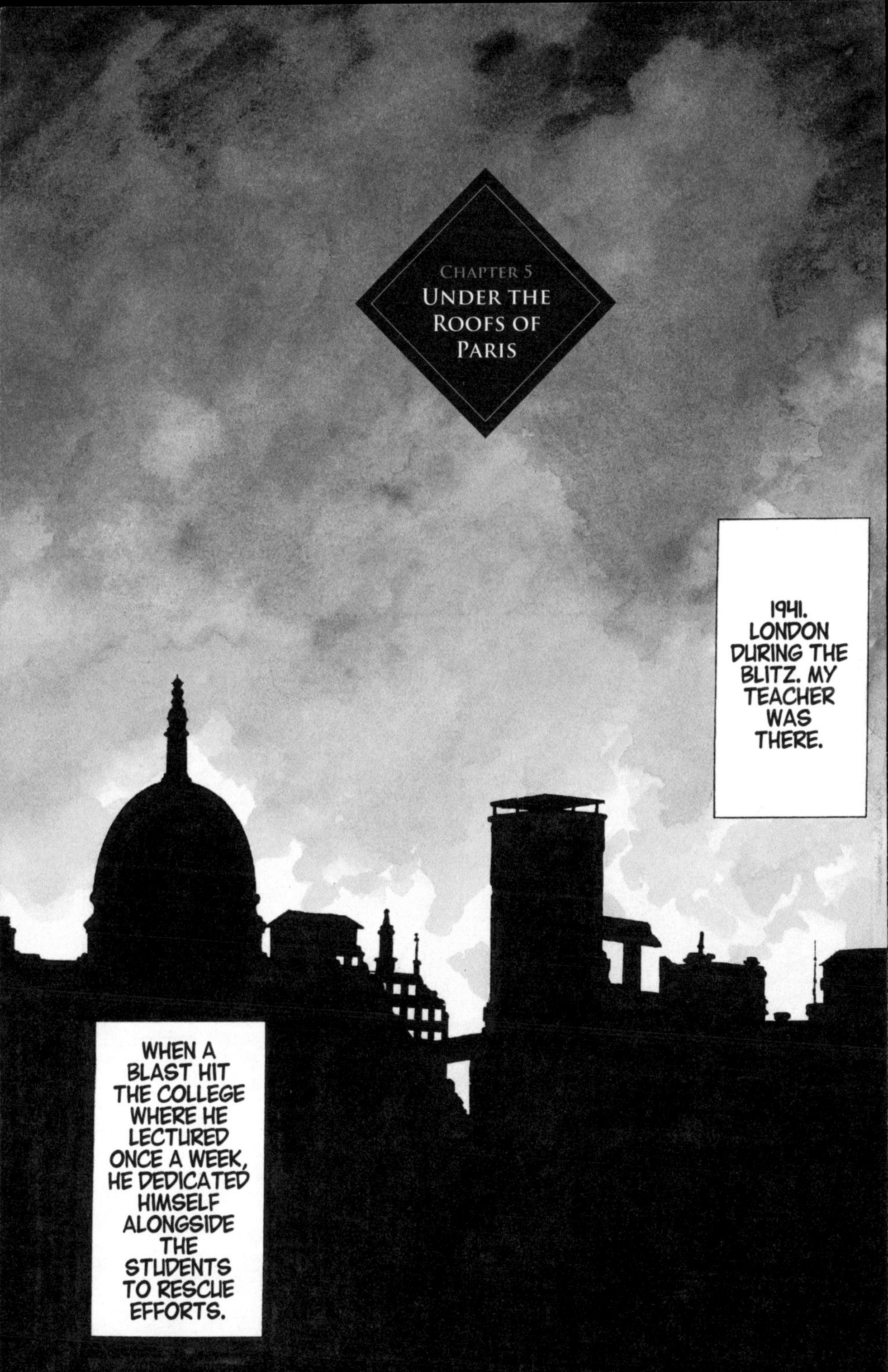
CHAPTER 5
UNDER THE ROOFS OF PARIS
1941. LONDON DURING THE BLITZ. MY TEACHER WAS THERE.
WHEN A BLAST HIT THE COLLEGE WHERE HE LECTURED ONCE A WEEK, HE DEDICATED HIMSELF ALONGSIDE THE STUDENTS TO RESCUE EFFORTS.

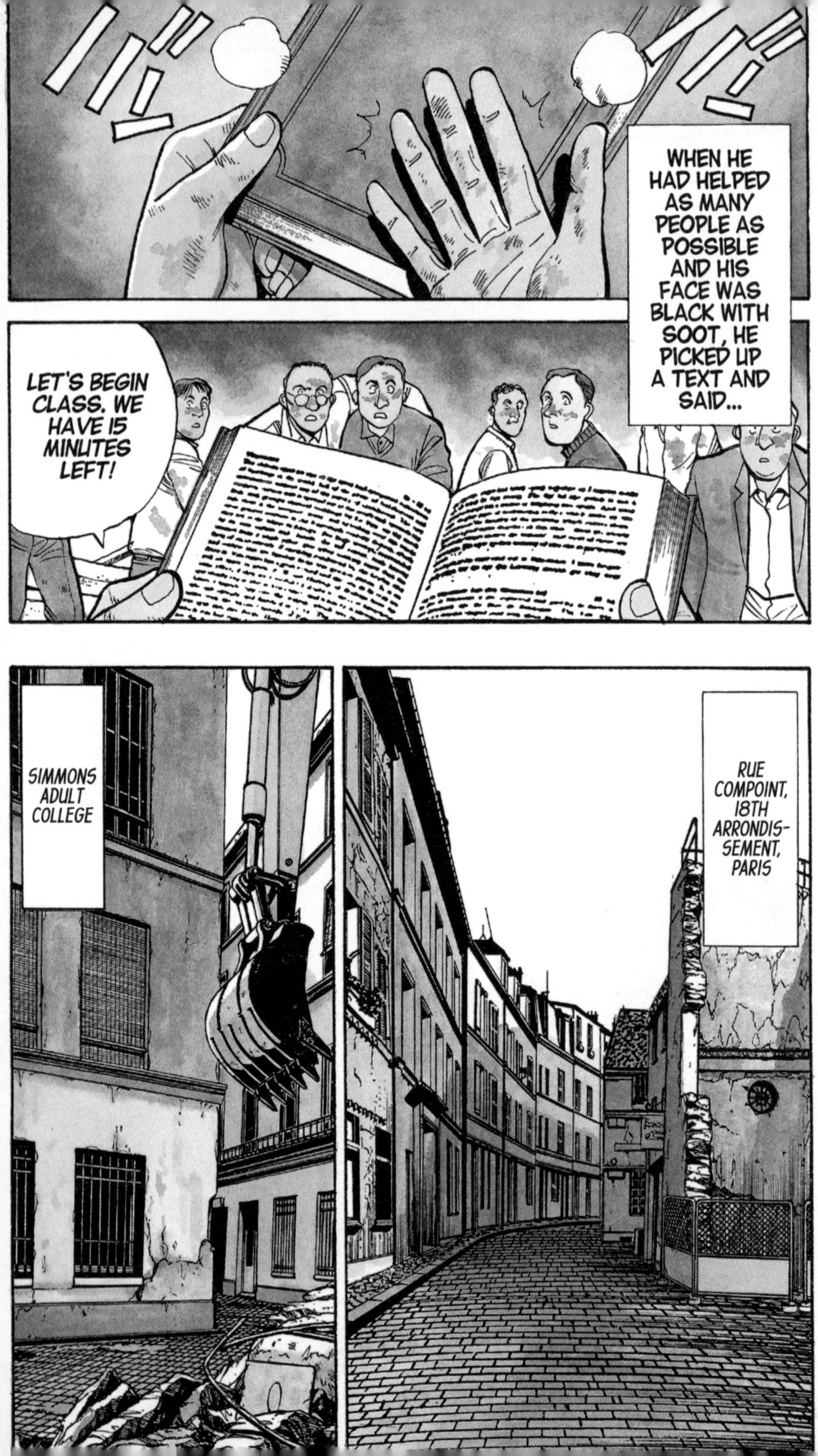
WHEN HE HAD HELPED AS MANY PEOPLE AS POSSIBLE AND HIS FACE WAS BLACK WITH SOOT, HE PICKED UP A TEXT AND SAID...
LET'S BEGIN CLASS. WE HAVE 15 MINUTES LEFT!
RUE COMPOINT, 18TH ARRONDIS-SEMENT, PARIS
SIMMONS ADULT COLLEGE

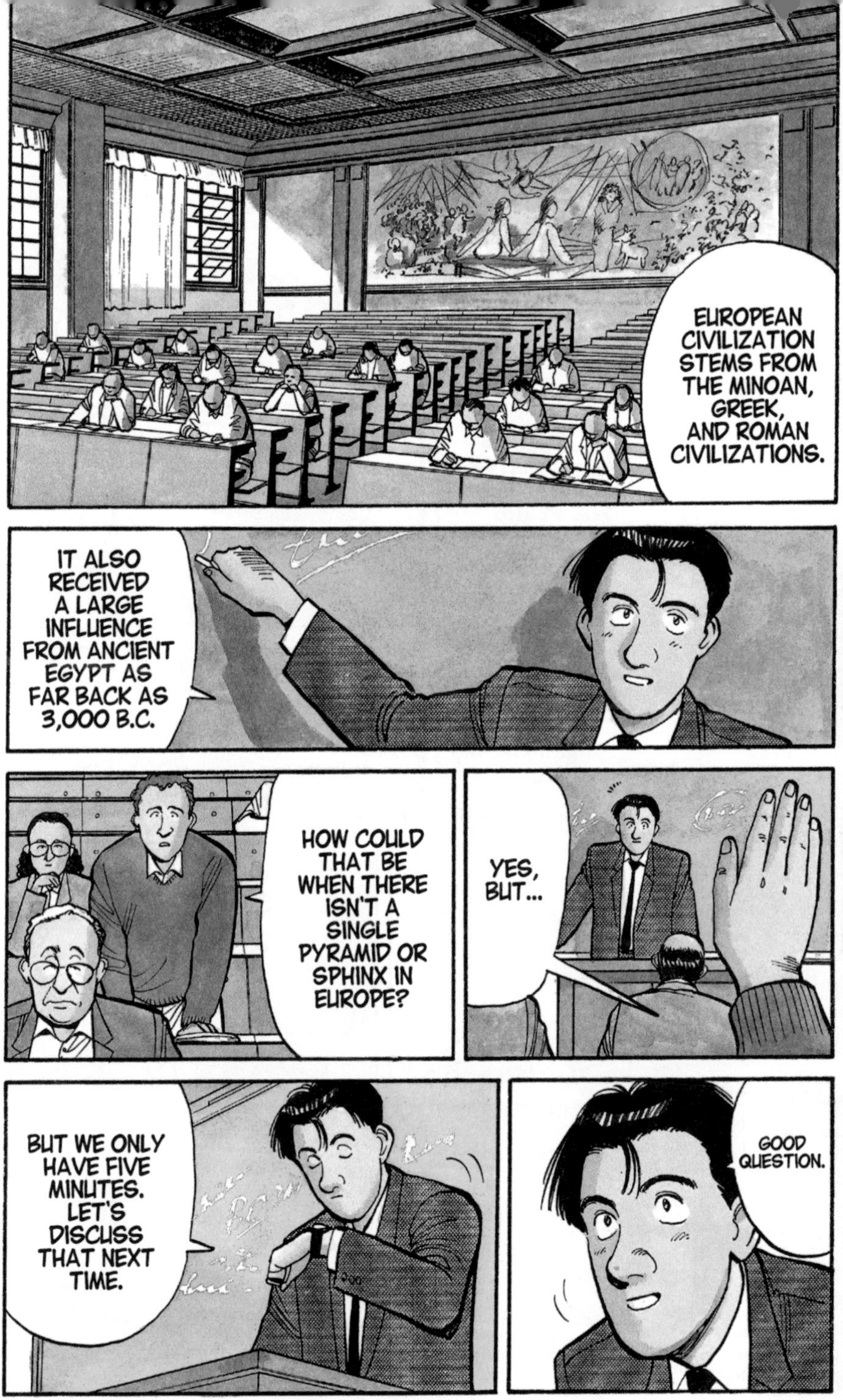
EUROPEAN CIVILIZATION STEMS FROM THE MINOAN, GREEK, AND ROMAN CIVILIZATIONS.
IT ALSO RECEIVED A LARGE INFLUENCE FROM ANCIENT EGYPT AS FAR BACK AS 3,000 B.C.
YES, BUT...
HOW COULD THAT BE WHEN THERE ISN'T A SINGLE PYRAMID OR SPHINX IN EUROPE?
GOOD QUESTION.
BUT WE ONLY HAVE FIVE MINUTES. LET'S DISCUSS THAT NEXT TIME.

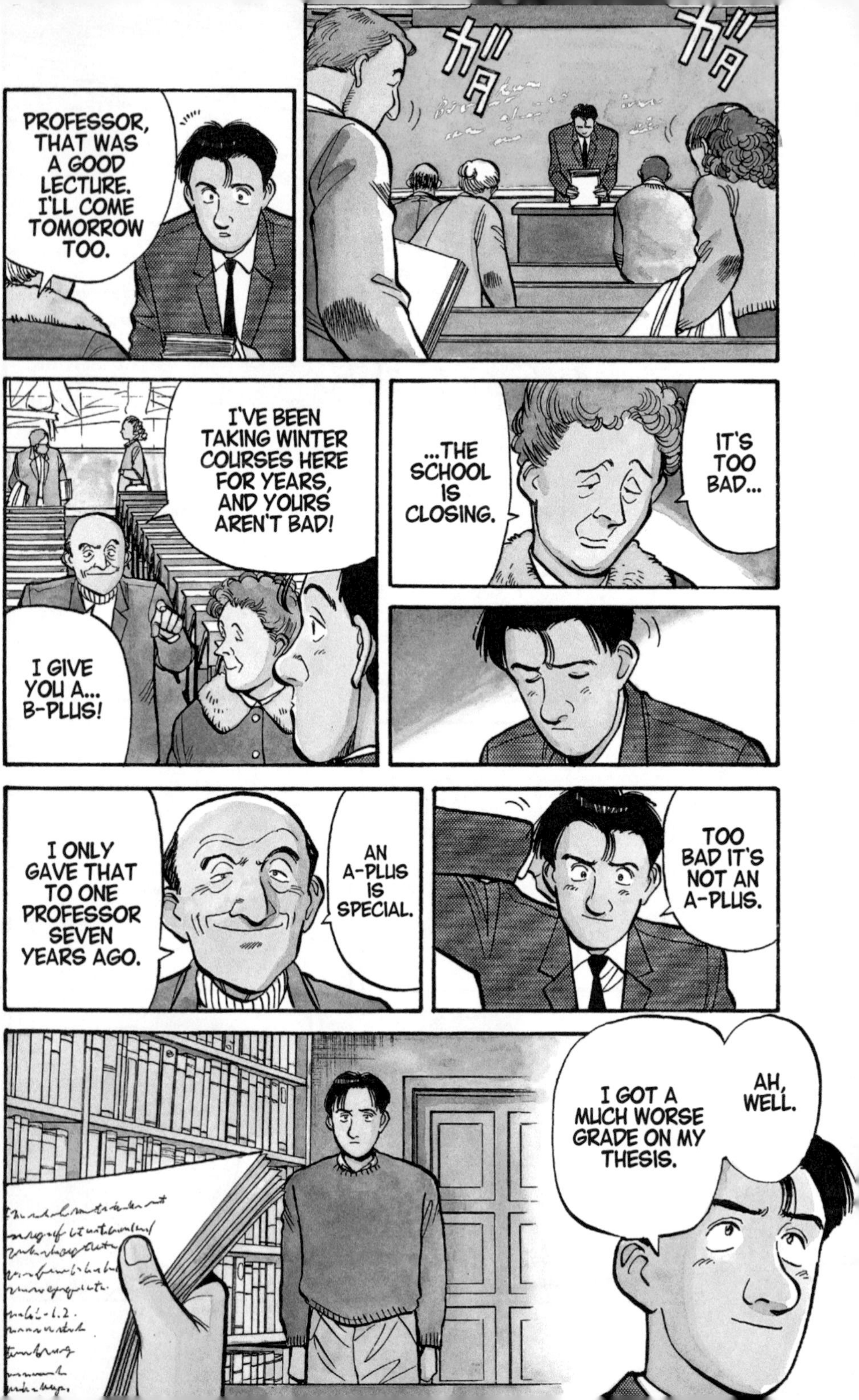
ガタ
ガタ
PROFESSOR, THAT WAS A GOOD LECTURE. I'LL COME TOMORROW TOO.
IT'S TOO BAD...
...THE SCHOOL IS CLOSING.
I'VE BEEN TAKING WINTER COURSES HERE FOR YEARS, AND YOURS AREN'T BAD!
I GIVE YOU A... B-PLUS!
TOO BAD IT'S NOT AN A-PLUS.
AN A-PLUS IS SPECIAL.
I ONLY GAVE THAT TO ONE PROFESSOR SEVEN YEARS AGO.
AH, WELL.
I GOT A MUCH WORSE GRADE ON MY THESIS.

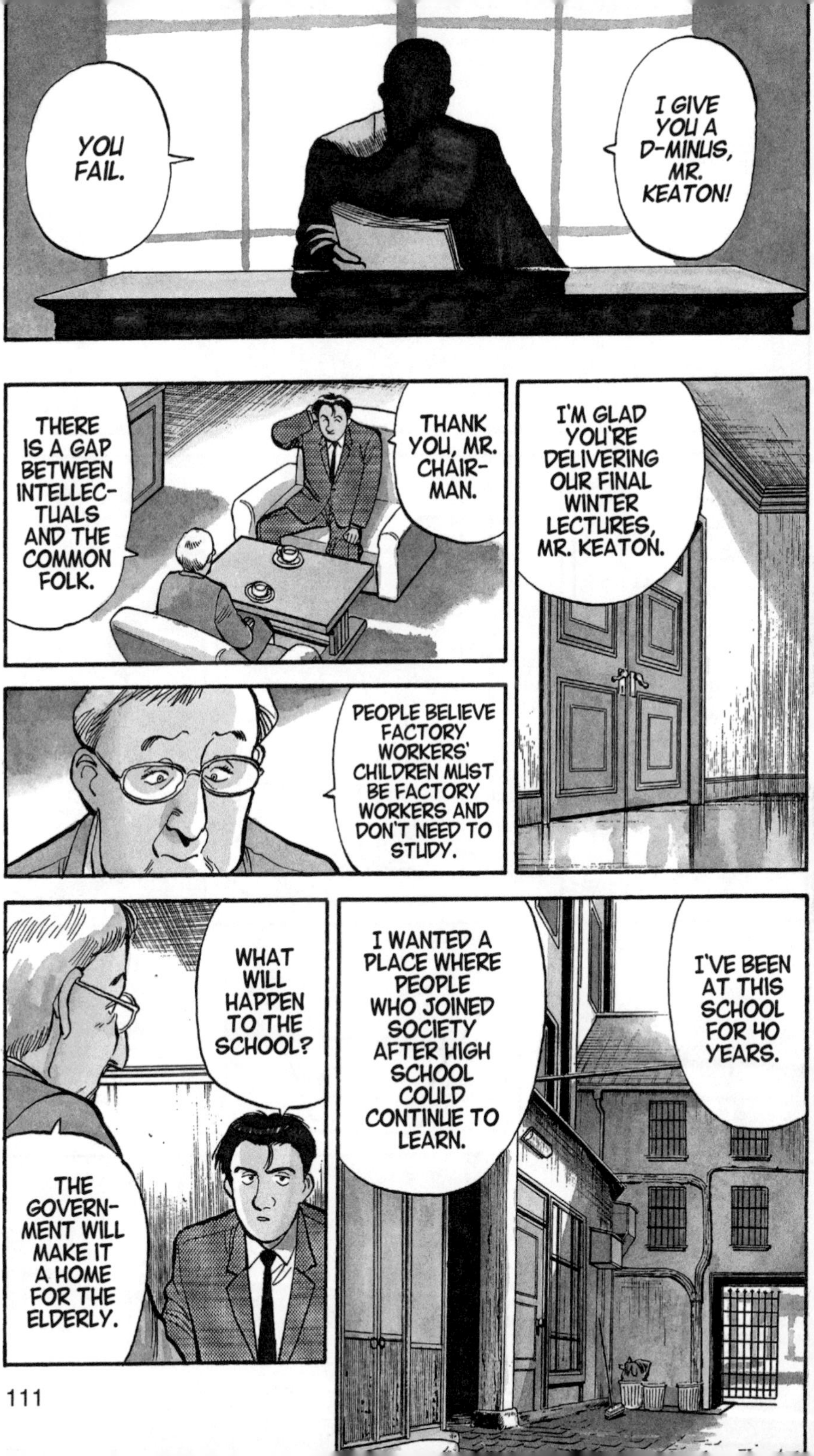
I GIVE YOU A D-MINUS, MR. KEATON!
YOU FAIL.
I'M GLAD YOU'RE DELIVERING OUR FINAL WINTER LECTURES, MR. KEATON.
THANK YOU, MR. CHAIRMAN.
THERE IS A GAP BETWEEN INTELLECTUALS AND THE COMMON FOLK.
PEOPLE BELIEVE FACTORY WORKERS' CHILDREN MUST BE FACTORY WORKERS AND DON'T NEED TO STUDY.
I'VE BEEN AT THIS SCHOOL FOR 40 YEARS.
I WANTED A PLACE WHERE PEOPLE WHO JOINED SOCIETY AFTER HIGH SCHOOL COULD CONTINUE TO LEARN.
WHAT WILL HAPPEN TO THE SCHOOL?
THE GOVERNMENT WILL MAKE IT A HOME FOR THE ELDERLY.

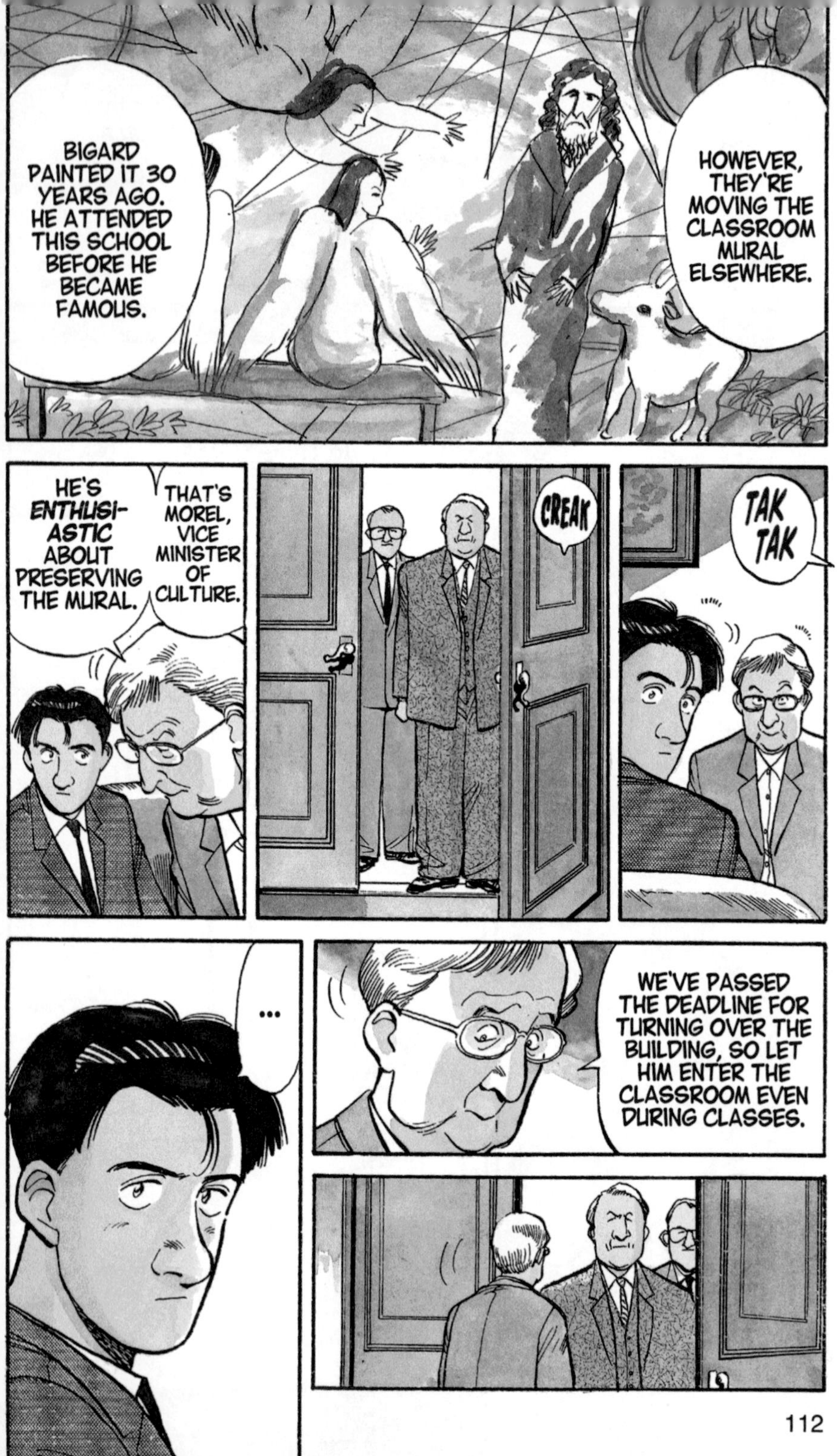
BIGARD PAINTED IT 30 YEARS AGO. HE ATTENDED THIS SCHOOL BEFORE HE BECAME FAMOUS.
HOWEVER, THEY'RE MOVING THE CLASSROOM MURAL ELSEWHERE.
TAK TAK
CREAK
THAT'S MOREL, VICE MINISTER OF CULTURE.
HE'S *ENTHUSIASTIC* ABOUT PRESERVING THE MURAL.
WE'VE PASSED THE DEADLINE FOR TURNING OVER THE BUILDING, SO LET HIM ENTER THE CLASSROOM EVEN DURING CLASSES.
...

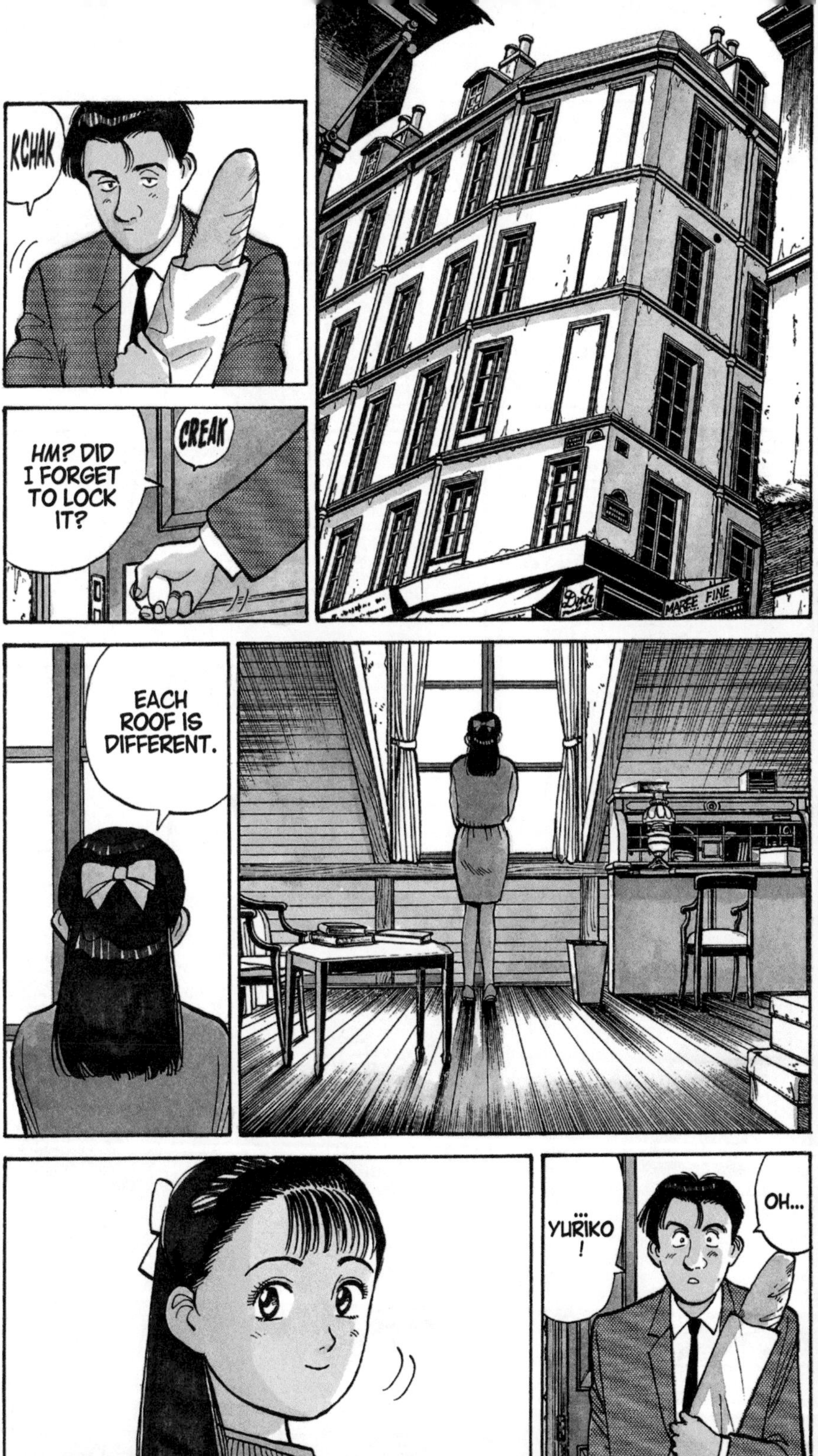
KCHAK
CREAK
HM? DID I FORGET TO LOCK IT?
EACH ROOF IS DIFFERENT.
OH...
...YURIKO!

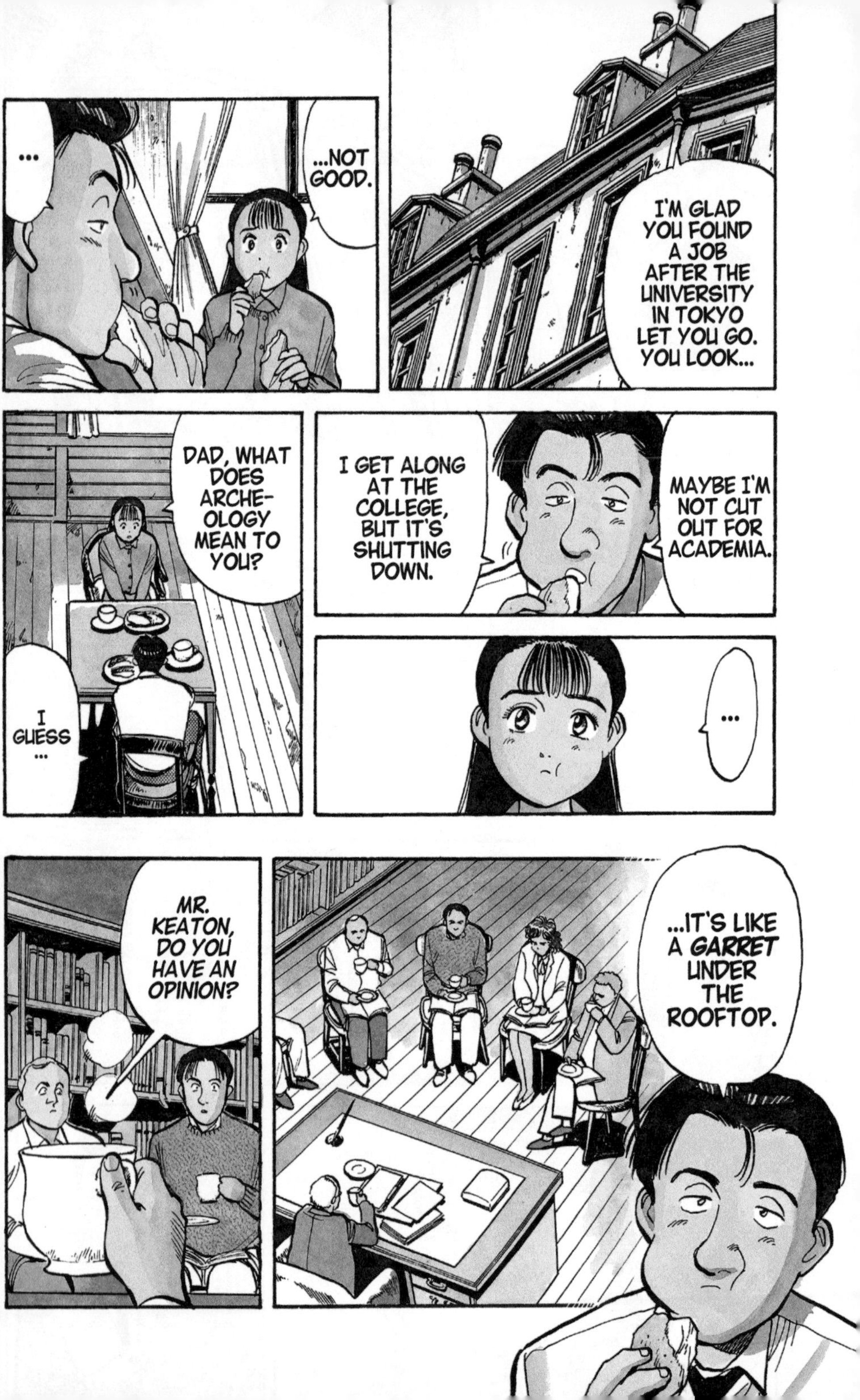
I'M GLAD YOU FOUND A JOB AFTER THE UNIVERSITY IN TOKYO LET YOU GO. YOU LOOK...
...NOT GOOD.
...
MAYBE I'M NOT CUT OUT FOR ACADEMIA.
I GET ALONG AT THE COLLEGE, BUT IT'S SHUTTING DOWN.
...
DAD, WHAT DOES ARCHE-OLOGY MEAN TO YOU?
I GUESS...
...IT'S LIKE A GARRET UNDER THE ROOFTOP.
MR. KEATON, DO YOU HAVE AN OPINION?

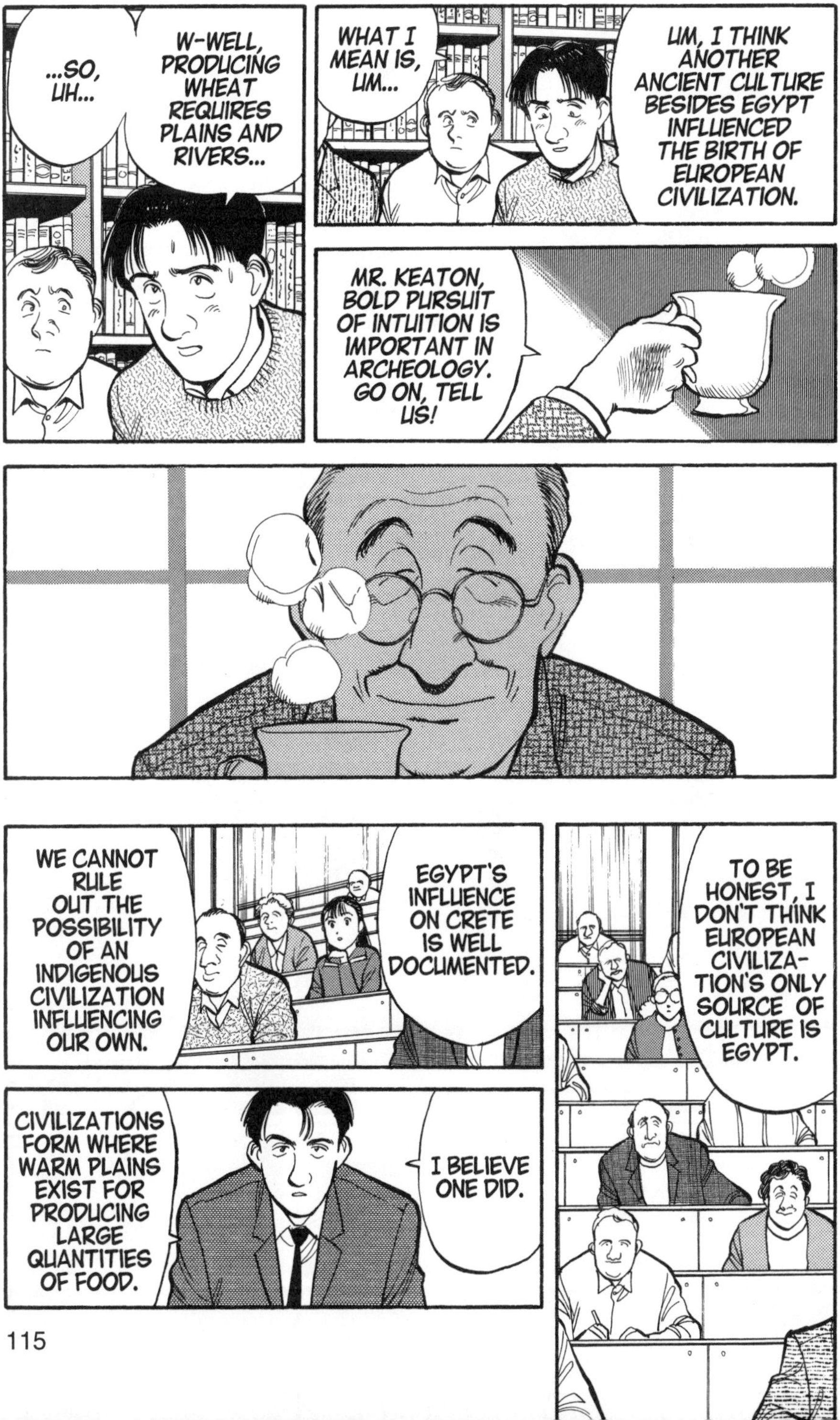
UM, I THINK ANOTHER ANCIENT CULTURE BESIDES EGYPT INFLUENCED THE BIRTH OF EUROPEAN CIVILIZATION.
WHAT I MEAN IS, UM...
MR. KEATON, BOLD PURSUIT OF INTUITION IS IMPORTANT IN ARCHEOLOGY. GO ON, TELL US!
W-WELL, PRODUCING WHEAT REQUIRES PLAINS AND RIVERS...
...SO, UH...
TO BE HONEST, I DON'T THINK EUROPEAN CIVILIZA-TION'S ONLY SOURCE OF CULTURE IS EGYPT.
EGYPT'S INFLUENCE ON CRETE IS WELL DOCUMENTED.
WE CANNOT RULE OUT THE POSSIBILITY OF AN INDIGENOUS CIVILIZATION INFLUENCING OUR OWN.
I BELIEVE ONE DID.
CIVILIZATIONS FORM WHERE WARM PLAINS EXIST FOR PRODUCING LARGE QUANTITIES OF FOOD.

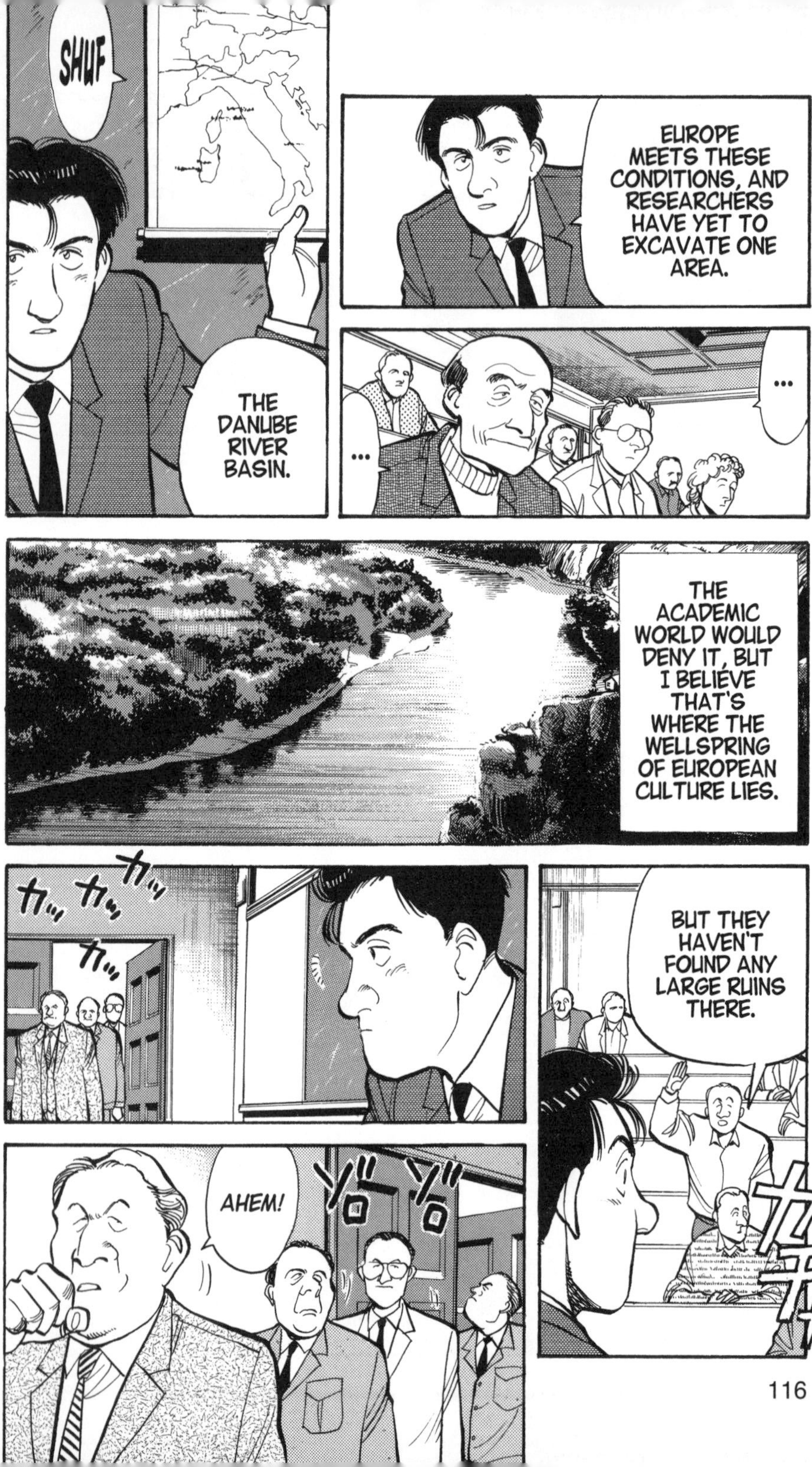

EUROPE MEETS THESE CONDITIONS, AND RESEARCHERS HAVE YET TO EXCAVATE ONE AREA.
...
...
SHUF
THE DANUBE RIVER BASIN.
THE ACADEMIC WORLD WOULD DENY IT, BUT I BELIEVE THAT'S WHERE THE WELLSPRING OF EUROPEAN CULTURE LIES.
BUT THEY HAVEN'T FOUND ANY LARGE RUINS THERE.
ガチャ
カッ カッ カッ カッ
AHEM!
ゾロ ゾロ

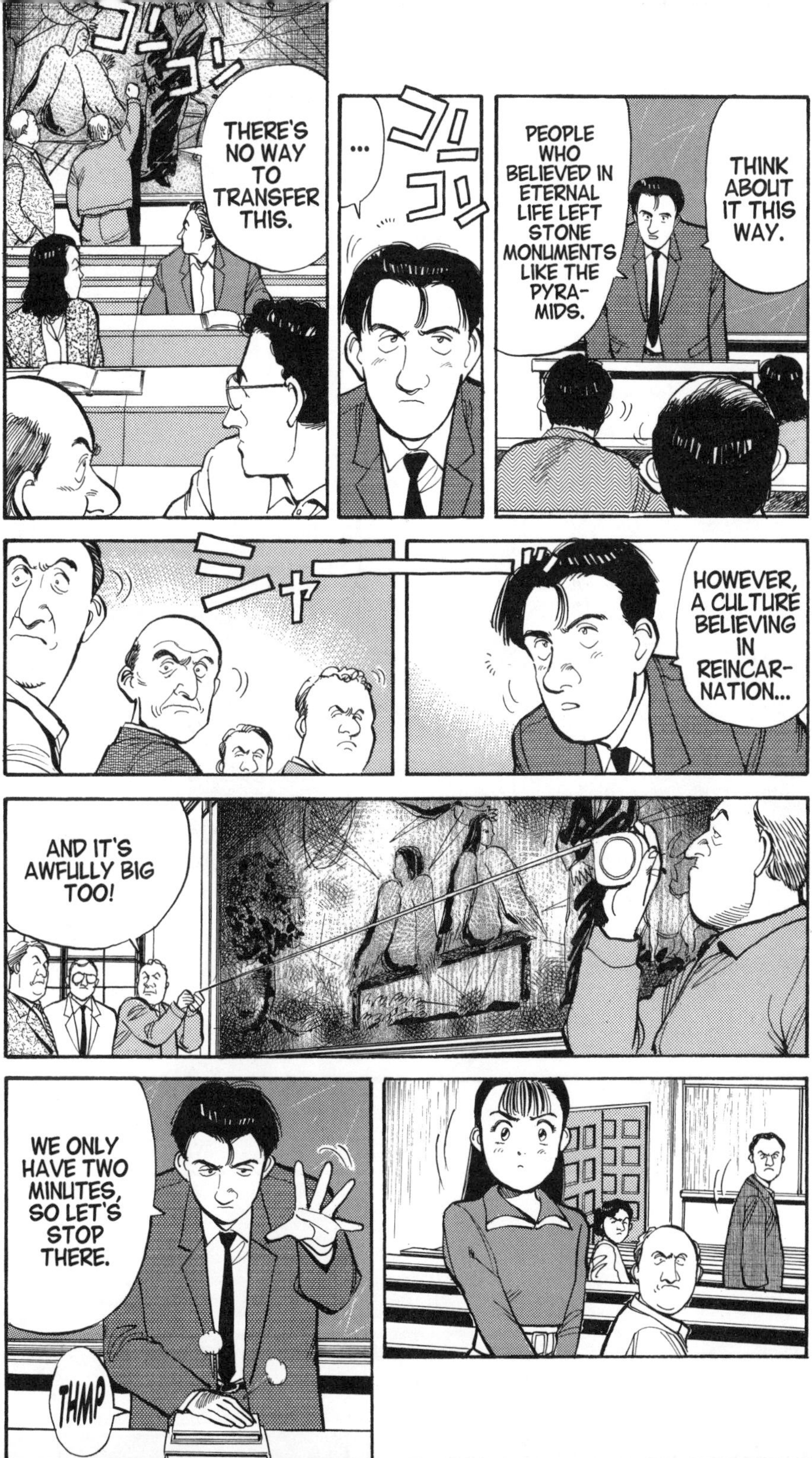
THINK ABOUT IT THIS WAY.
PEOPLE WHO BELIEVED IN ETERNAL LIFE LEFT STONE MONUMENTS LIKE THE PYRAMIDS.
...
THERE'S NO WAY TO TRANSFER THIS.
HOWEVER, A CULTURE BELIEVING IN REINCARNATION...
AND IT'S AWFULLY BIG TOO!
WE ONLY HAVE TWO MINUTES, SO LET'S STOP THERE.
THMP

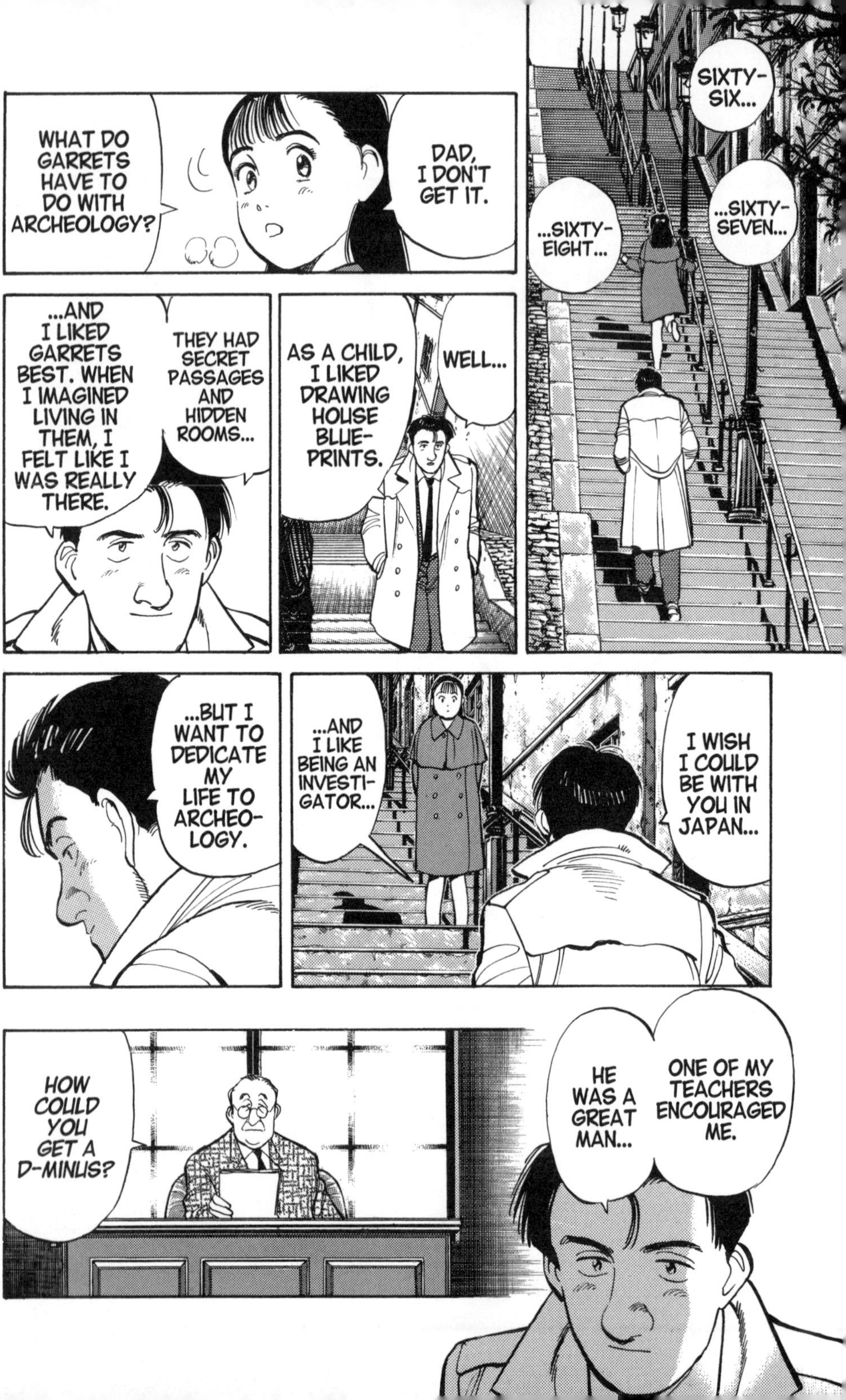
SIXTY-SIX...
...SIXTY-SEVEN...
...SIXTY-EIGHT...
DAD, I DON'T GET IT.
WHAT DO GARRETS HAVE TO DO WITH ARCHEOLOGY?
WELL...
AS A CHILD, I LIKED DRAWING HOUSE BLUEPRINTS.
THEY HAD SECRET PASSAGES AND HIDDEN ROOMS...
...AND I LIKED GARRETS BEST. WHEN I IMAGINED LIVING IN THEM, I FELT LIKE I WAS REALLY THERE.
I WISH I COULD BE WITH YOU IN JAPAN...
...AND I LIKE BEING AN INVESTIGATOR...
...BUT I WANT TO DEDICATE MY LIFE TO ARCHEOLOGY.
ONE OF MY TEACHERS ENCOURAGED ME.
HE WAS A GREAT MAN...
HOW COULD YOU GET A D-MINUS?

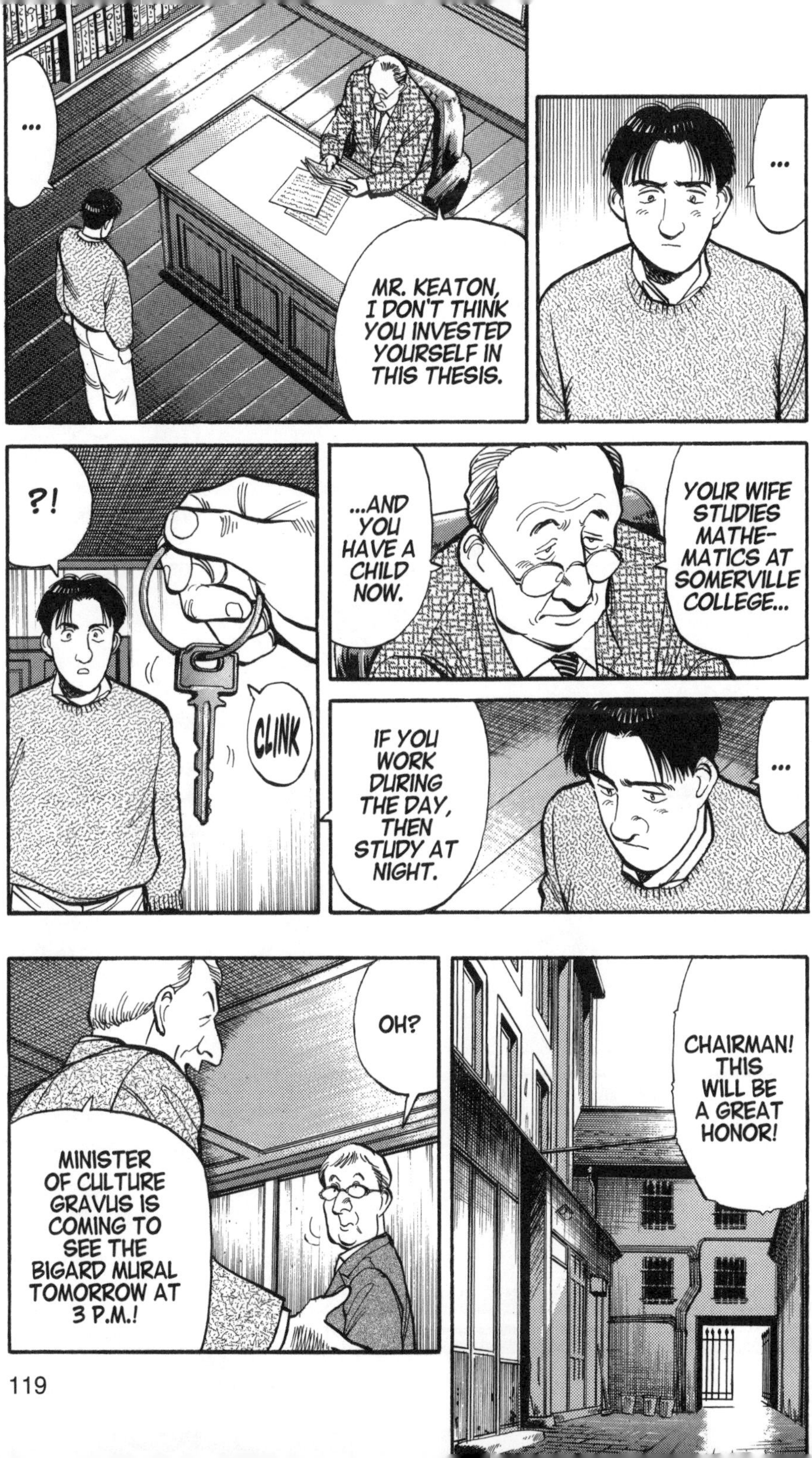
...
MR. KEATON, I DON'T THINK YOU INVESTED YOURSELF IN THIS THESIS.
...
YOUR WIFE STUDIES MATHE-MATICS AT SOMERVILLE COLLEGE...
...AND YOU HAVE A CHILD NOW.
...
IF YOU WORK DURING THE DAY, THEN STUDY AT NIGHT.
?!
CLINK
CHAIRMAN! THIS WILL BE A GREAT HONOR!
OH?
MINISTER OF CULTURE GRAVUS IS COMING TO SEE THE BIGARD MURAL TOMORROW AT 3 P.M.!

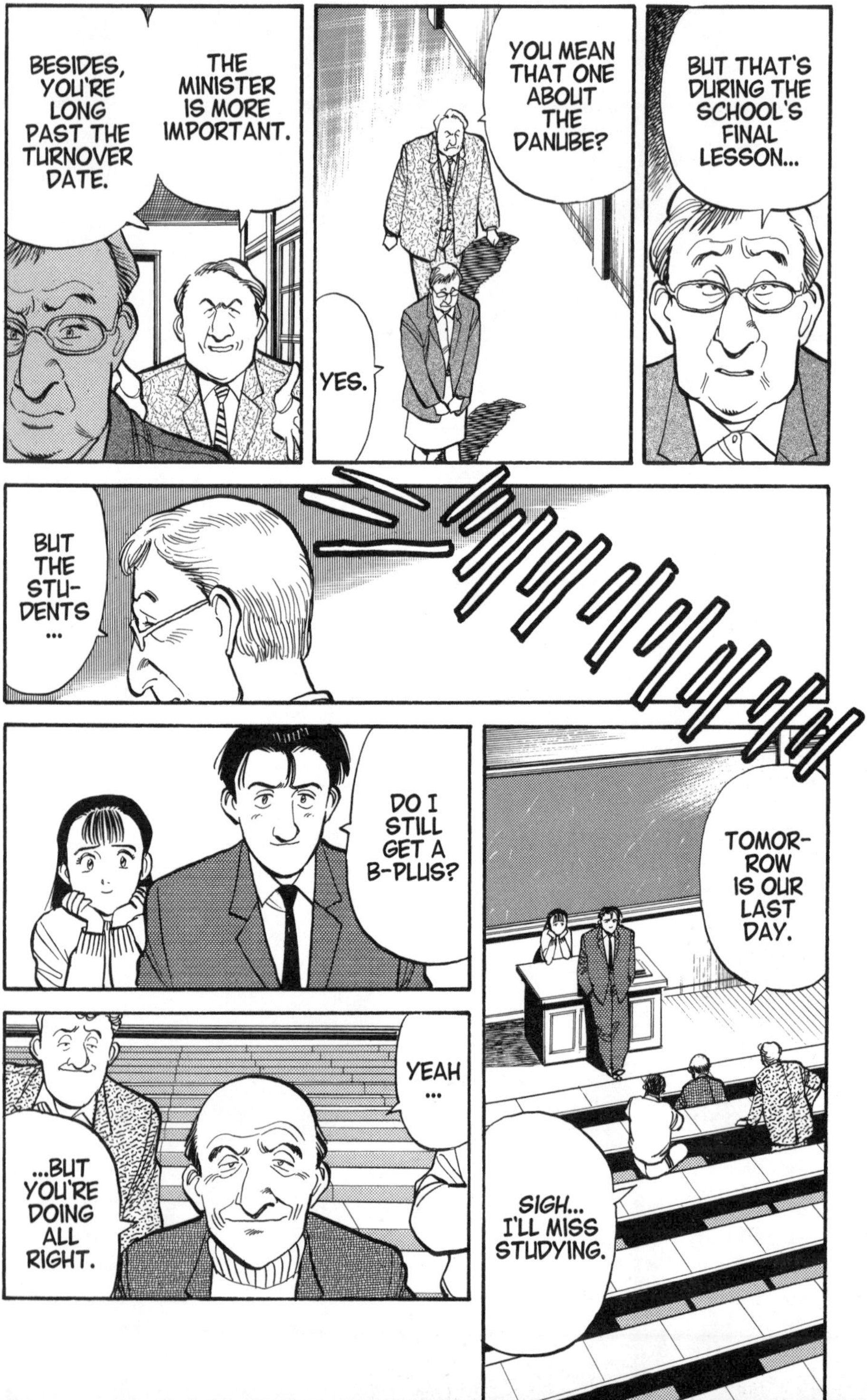
BUT THAT'S DURING THE SCHOOL'S FINAL LESSON...
YOU MEAN THAT ONE ABOUT THE DANUBE?
YES.
THE MINISTER IS MORE IMPORTANT.
BESIDES, YOU'RE LONG PAST THE TURNOVER DATE.
BUT THE STU-DENTS...
TOMOR-ROW IS OUR LAST DAY.
SIGH... I'LL MISS STUDYING.
DO I STILL GET A B-PLUS?
YEAH...
...BUT YOU'RE DOING ALL RIGHT.

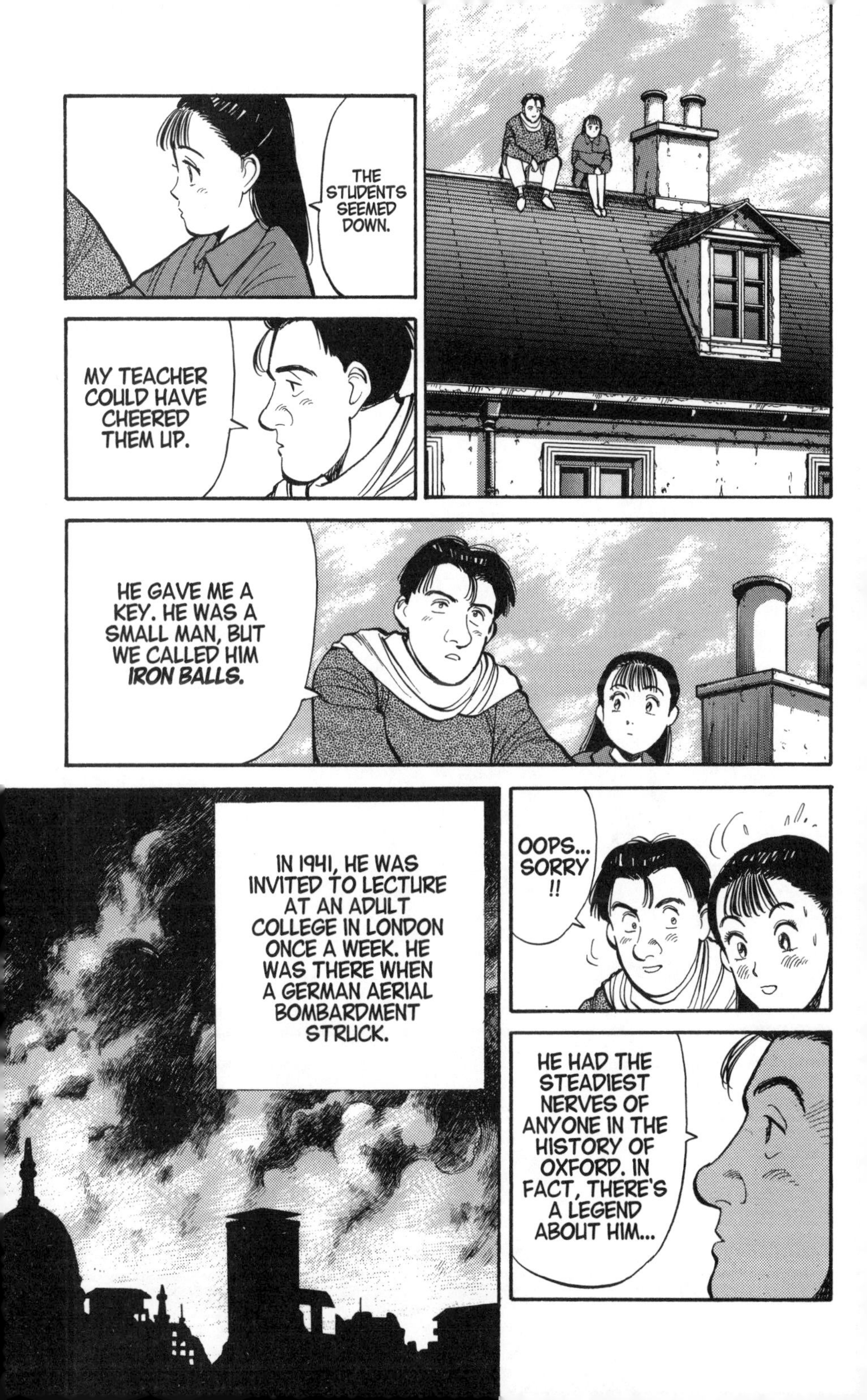
THE STUDENTS SEEMED DOWN.
MY TEACHER COULD HAVE CHEERED THEM UP.
HE GAVE ME A KEY. HE WAS A SMALL MAN, BUT WE CALLED HIM IRON BALLS.
OOPS... SORRY !!
HE HAD THE STEADIEST NERVES OF ANYONE IN THE HISTORY OF OXFORD. IN FACT, THERE'S A LEGEND ABOUT HIM...
IN 1941, HE WAS INVITED TO LECTURE AT AN ADULT COLLEGE IN LONDON ONCE A WEEK. HE WAS THERE WHEN A GERMAN AERIAL BOMBARDMENT STRUCK.

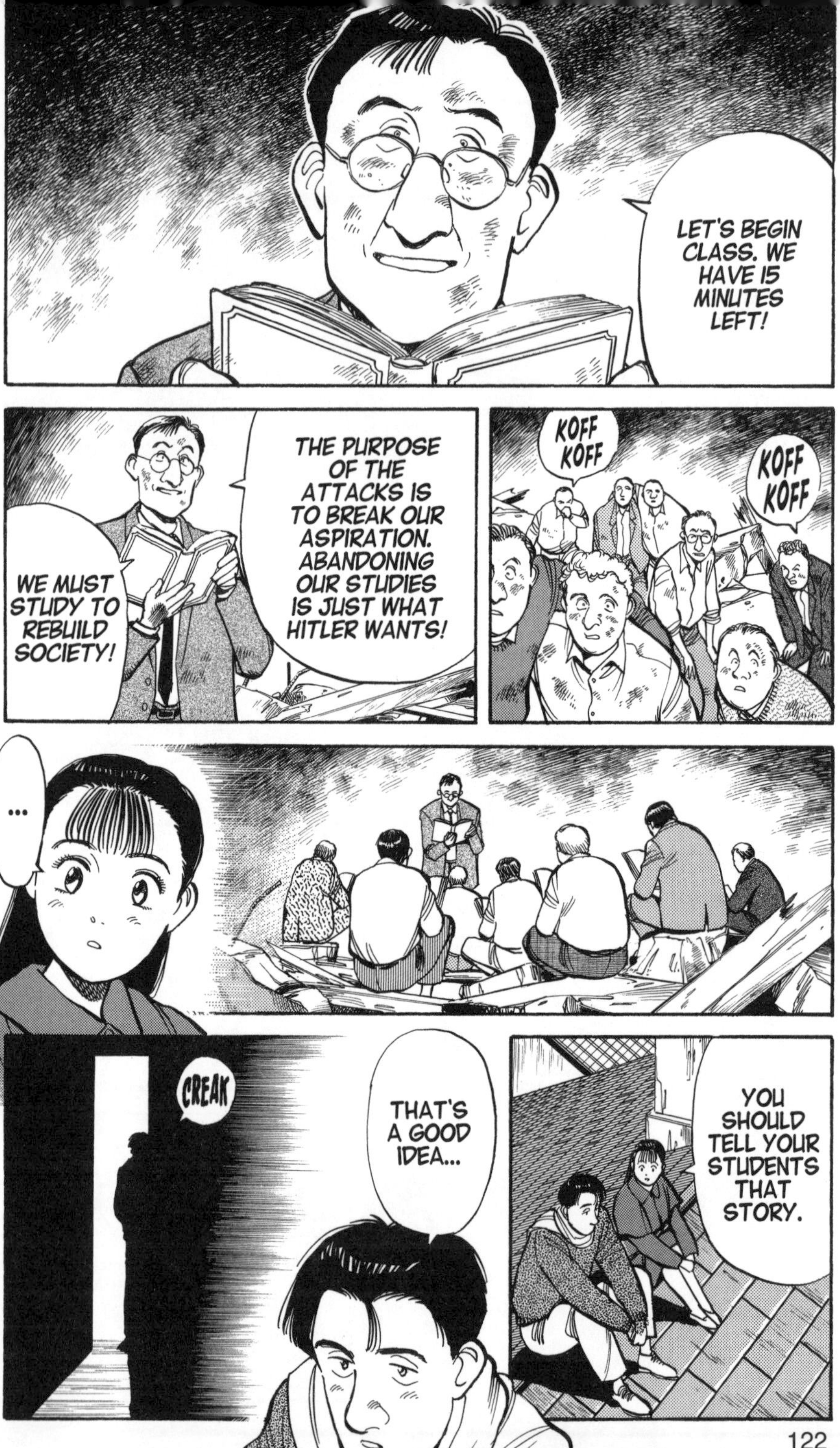
LET'S BEGIN CLASS. WE HAVE 15 MINUTES LEFT!
KOFF KOFF
KOFF KOFF
THE PURPOSE OF THE ATTACKS IS TO BREAK OUR ASPIRATION. ABANDONING OUR STUDIES IS JUST WHAT HITLER WANTS!
WE MUST STUDY TO REBUILD SOCIETY!
...
YOU SHOULD TELL YOUR STUDENTS THAT STORY.
THAT'S A GOOD IDEA...
CREAK

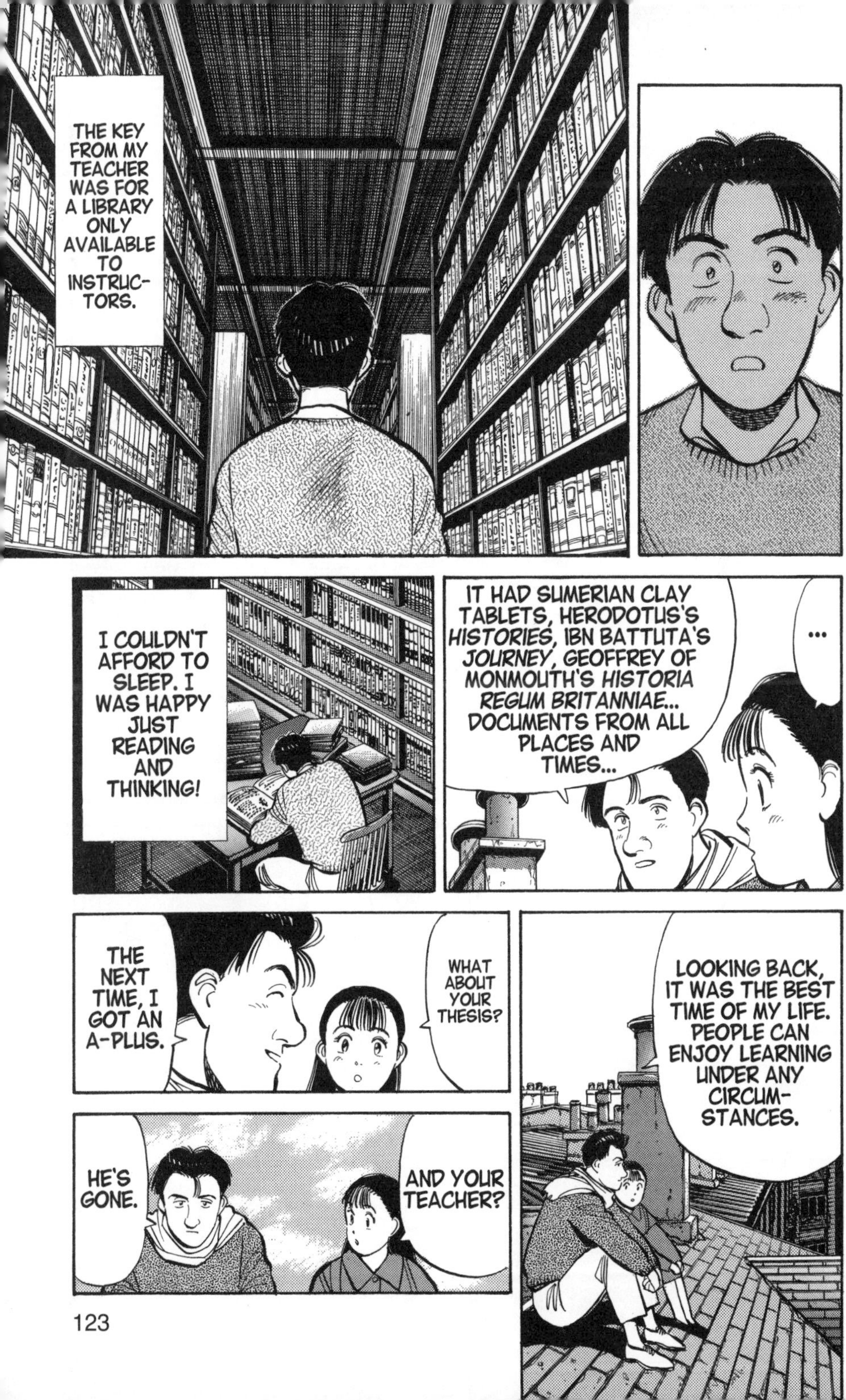
THE KEY FROM MY TEACHER WAS FOR A LIBRARY ONLY AVAILABLE TO INSTRUC-TORS.
...
IT HAD SUMERIAN CLAY TABLETS, HERODOTUS'S *HISTORIES*, IBN BATTUTA'S *JOURNEY*, GEOFFREY OF MONMOUTH'S *HISTORIA REGUM BRITANNIAE*... DOCUMENTS FROM ALL PLACES AND TIMES...
I COULDN'T AFFORD TO SLEEP. I WAS HAPPY JUST READING AND THINKING!
LOOKING BACK, IT WAS THE BEST TIME OF MY LIFE. PEOPLE CAN ENJOY LEARNING UNDER ANY CIRCUM-STANCES.
WHAT ABOUT YOUR THESIS?
THE NEXT TIME, I GOT AN A-PLUS.
AND YOUR TEACHER?
HE'S GONE.

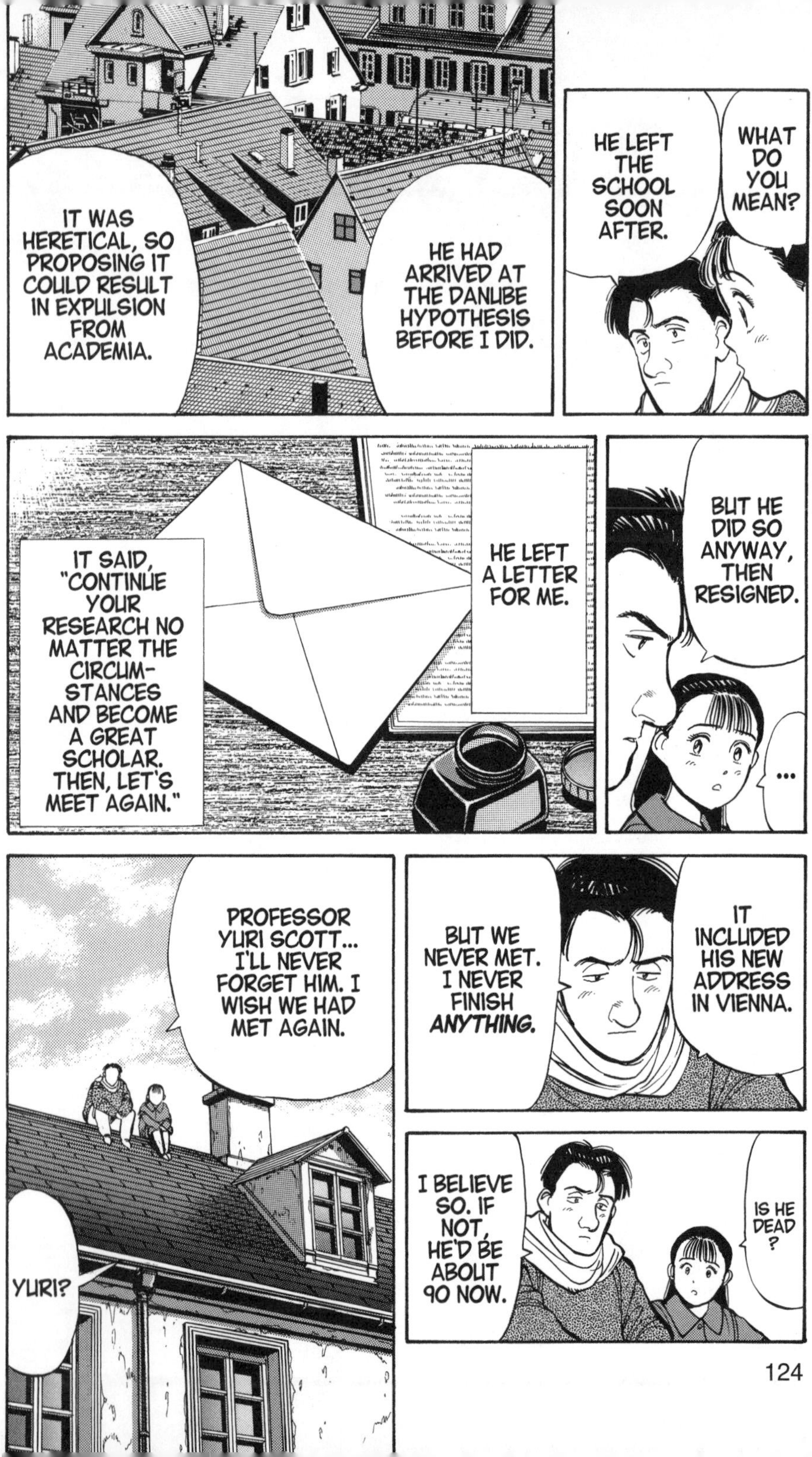
WHAT DO YOU MEAN?
HE LEFT THE SCHOOL SOON AFTER.
HE HAD ARRIVED AT THE DANUBE HYPOTHESIS BEFORE I DID.
IT WAS HERETICAL, SO PROPOSING IT COULD RESULT IN EXPULSION FROM ACADEMIA.
BUT HE DID SO ANYWAY, THEN RESIGNED.
...
HE LEFT A LETTER FOR ME.
IT SAID, "CONTINUE YOUR RESEARCH NO MATTER THE CIRCUM-STANCES AND BECOME A GREAT SCHOLAR. THEN, LET'S MEET AGAIN."
IT INCLUDED HIS NEW ADDRESS IN VIENNA.
BUT WE NEVER MET. I NEVER FINISH *ANYTHING.*
IS HE DEAD?
I BELIEVE SO. IF NOT, HE'D BE ABOUT 90 NOW.
PROFESSOR YURI SCOTT... I'LL NEVER FORGET HIM. I WISH WE HAD MET AGAIN.
YURI?

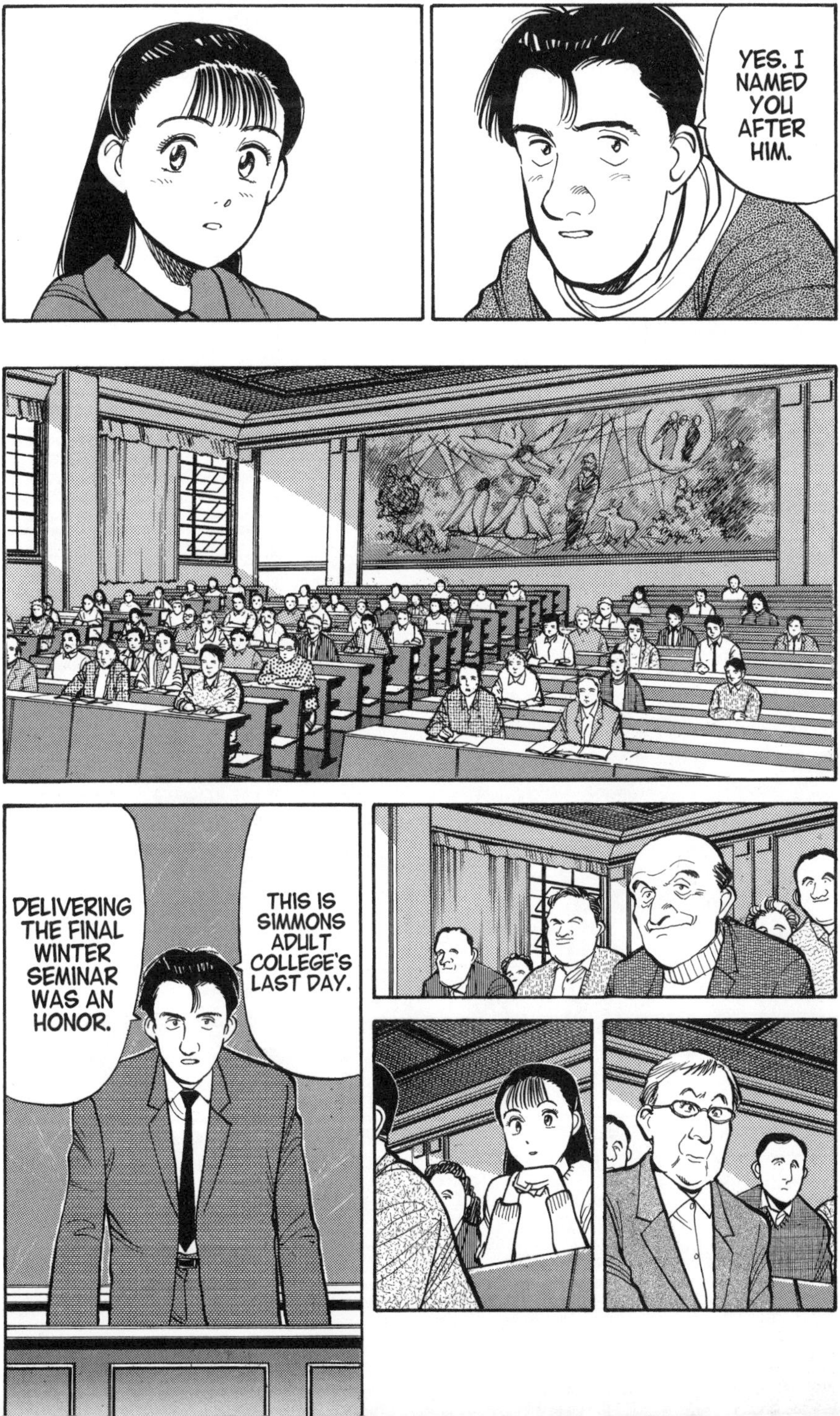
YES. I NAMED YOU AFTER HIM.
THIS IS SIMMONS ADULT COLLEGE'S LAST DAY.
DELIVERING THE FINAL WINTER SEMINAR WAS AN HONOR.

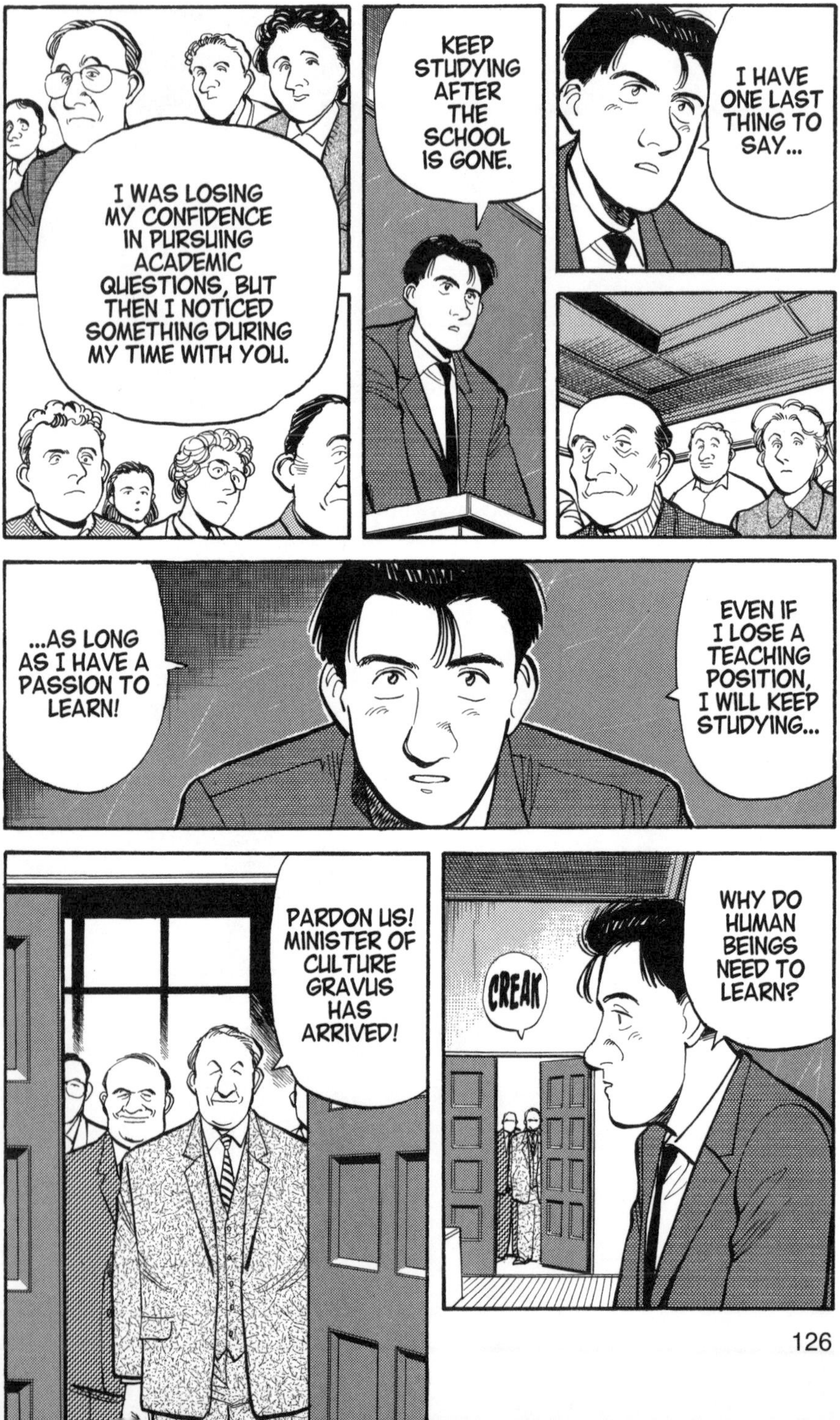
I HAVE ONE LAST THING TO SAY...
KEEP STUDYING AFTER THE SCHOOL IS GONE.
I WAS LOSING MY CONFIDENCE IN PURSUING ACADEMIC QUESTIONS, BUT THEN I NOTICED SOMETHING DURING MY TIME WITH YOU.
EVEN IF I LOSE A TEACHING POSITION, I WILL KEEP STUDYING...
...AS LONG AS I HAVE A PASSION TO LEARN!
WHY DO HUMAN BEINGS NEED TO LEARN?
CREAK
PARDON US! MINISTER OF CULTURE GRAVUS HAS ARRIVED!

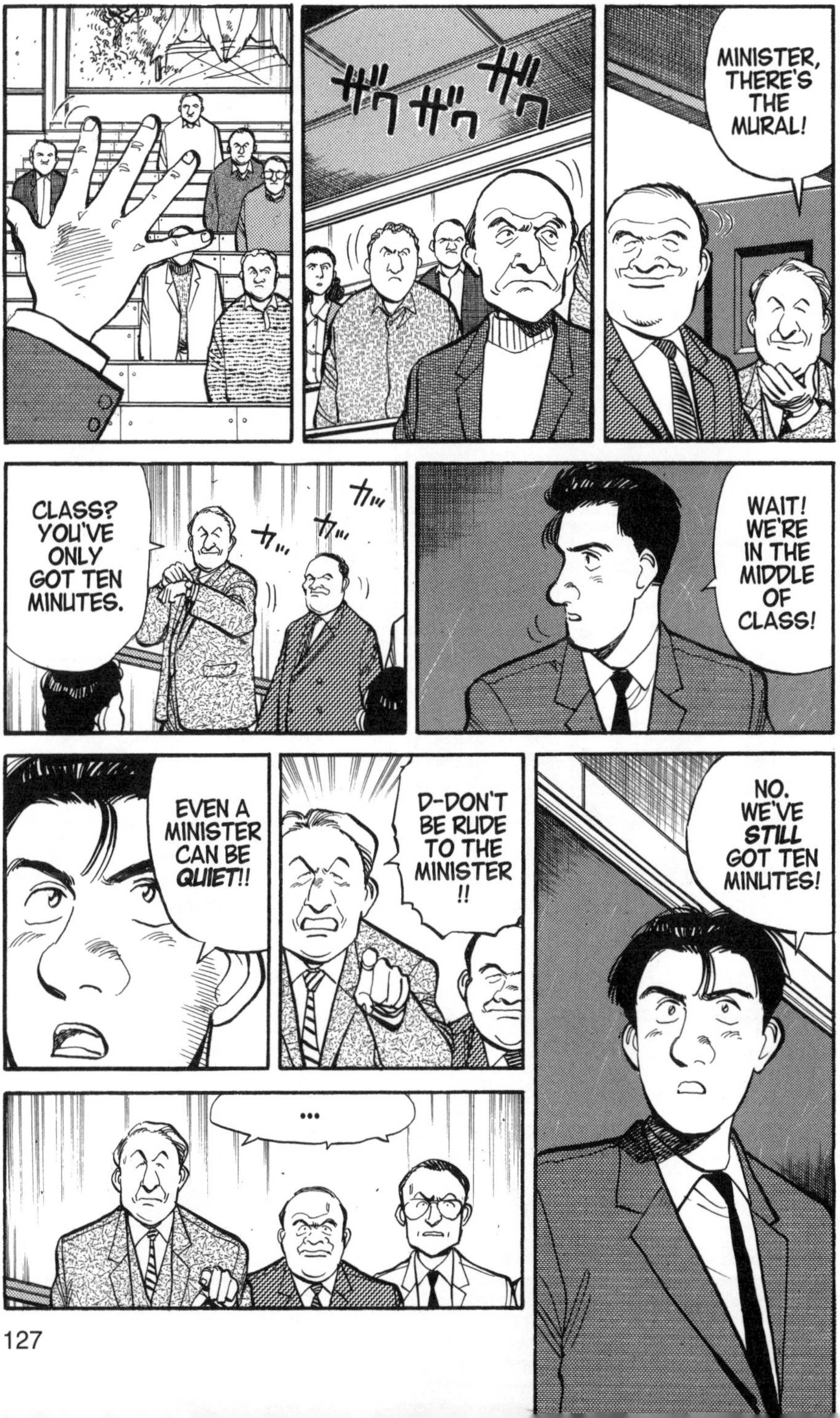
MINISTER, THERE'S THE MURAL!
ザク ザク ザク
WAIT! WE'RE IN THE MIDDLE OF CLASS!
カッ カッ カッ
CLASS? YOU'VE ONLY GOT TEN MINUTES.
NO. WE'VE *STILL* GOT TEN MINUTES!
D-DON'T BE RUDE TO THE MINISTER !!
EVEN A MINISTER CAN BE *QUIET*!!
...

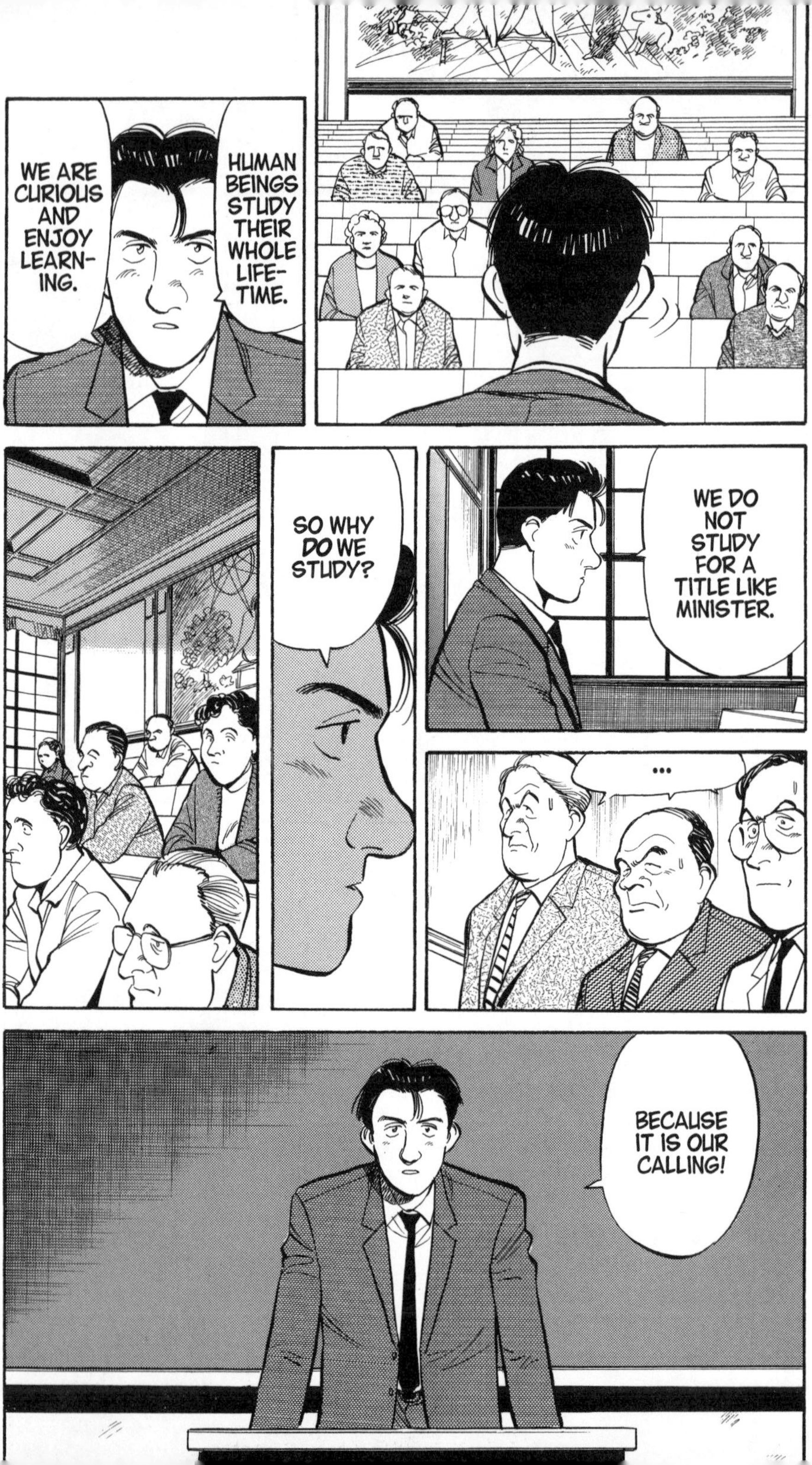
HUMAN BEINGS STUDY THEIR WHOLE LIFETIME.
WE ARE CURIOUS AND ENJOY LEARNING.
WE DO NOT STUDY FOR A TITLE LIKE MINISTER.
...
SO WHY *DO* WE STUDY?
BECAUSE IT IS OUR CALLING!

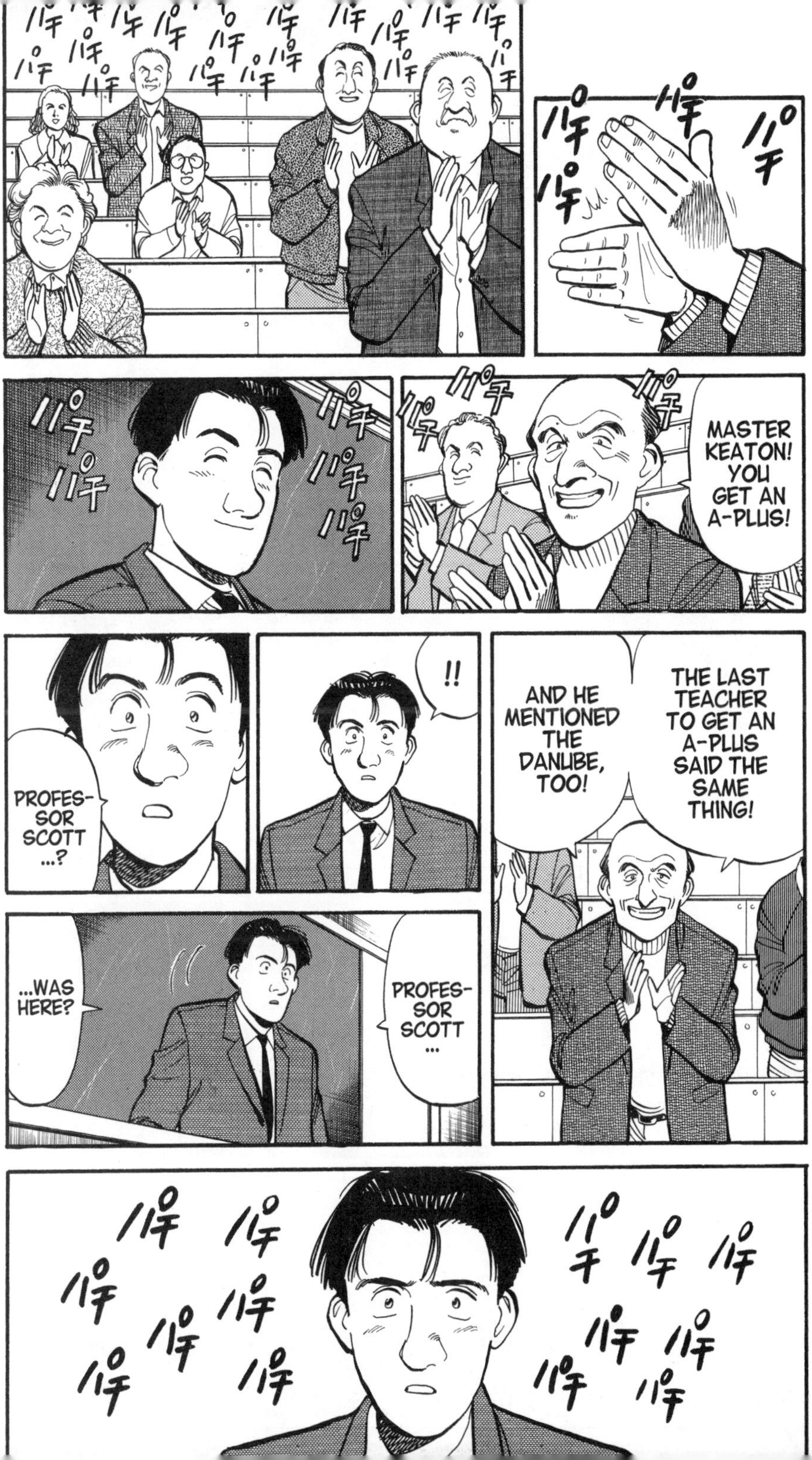
パチ パチ パチ パチ
パチ パチ パチ パチ
MASTER KEATON! YOU GET AN A-PLUS!
パチ パチ パチ パチ
THE LAST TEACHER TO GET AN A-PLUS SAID THE SAME THING!
AND HE MENTIONED THE DANUBE, TOO!
!!
PROFES-SOR SCOTT ...?
PROFES-SOR SCOTT ...
...WAS HERE?
パチ パチ パチ パチ パチ パチ
パチ パチ パチ パチ パチ パチ パチ

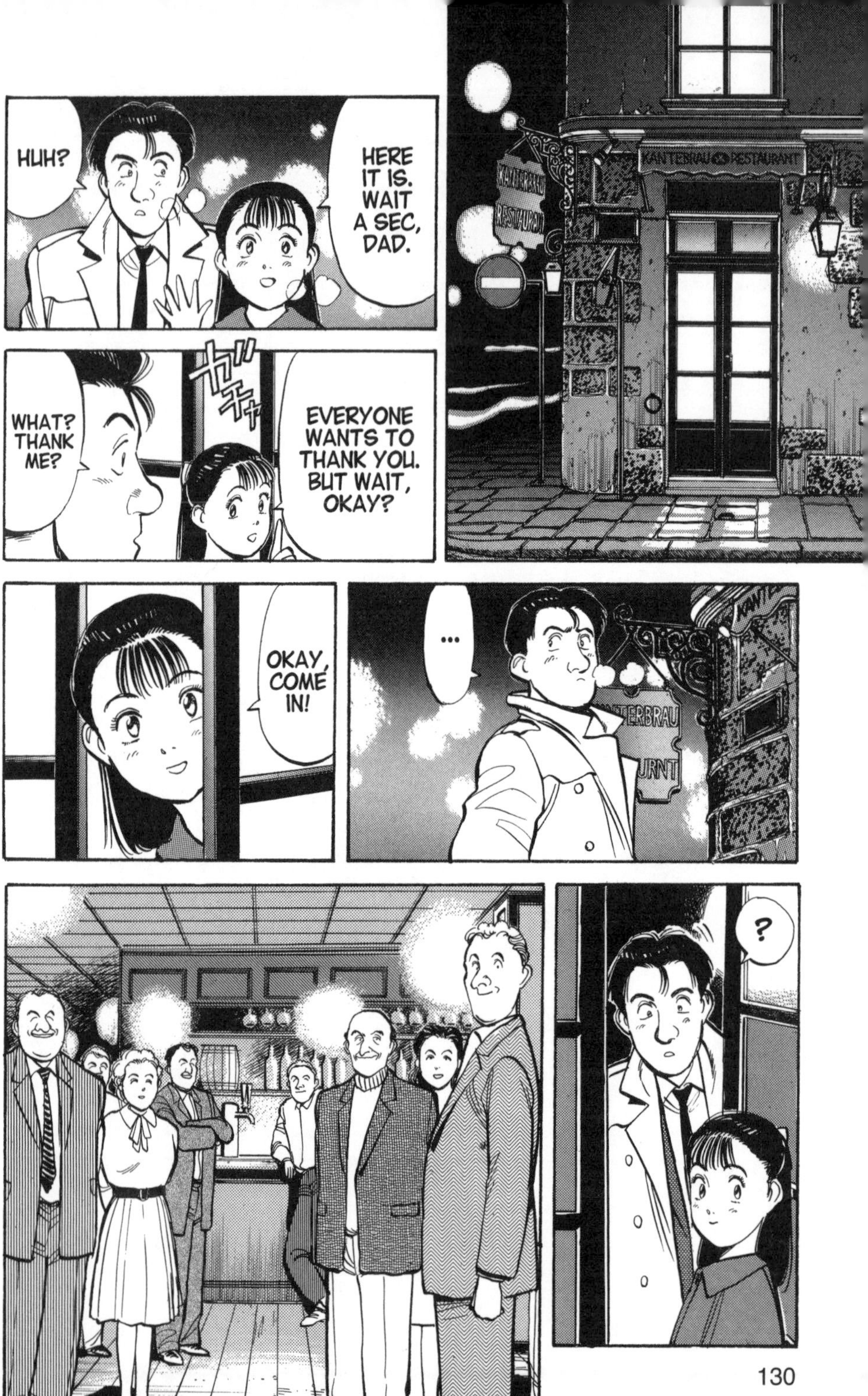
KANTERBRAU RESTAURANT
HERE IT IS. WAIT A SEC, DAD.
HUH?
ガチャ
EVERYONE WANTS TO THANK YOU. BUT WAIT, OKAY?
WHAT? THANK ME?
...
OKAY, COME IN!
?

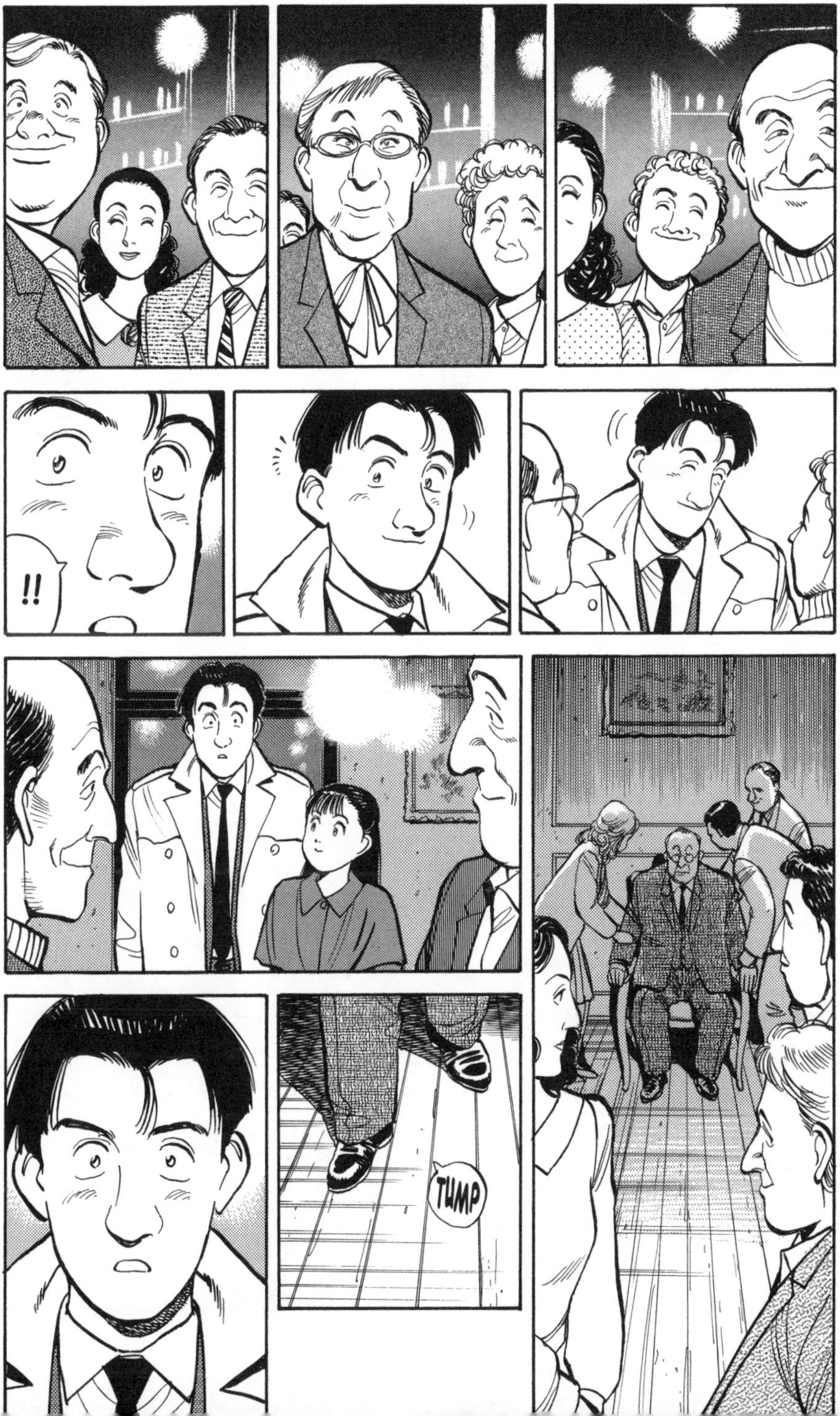
!!
TUMP

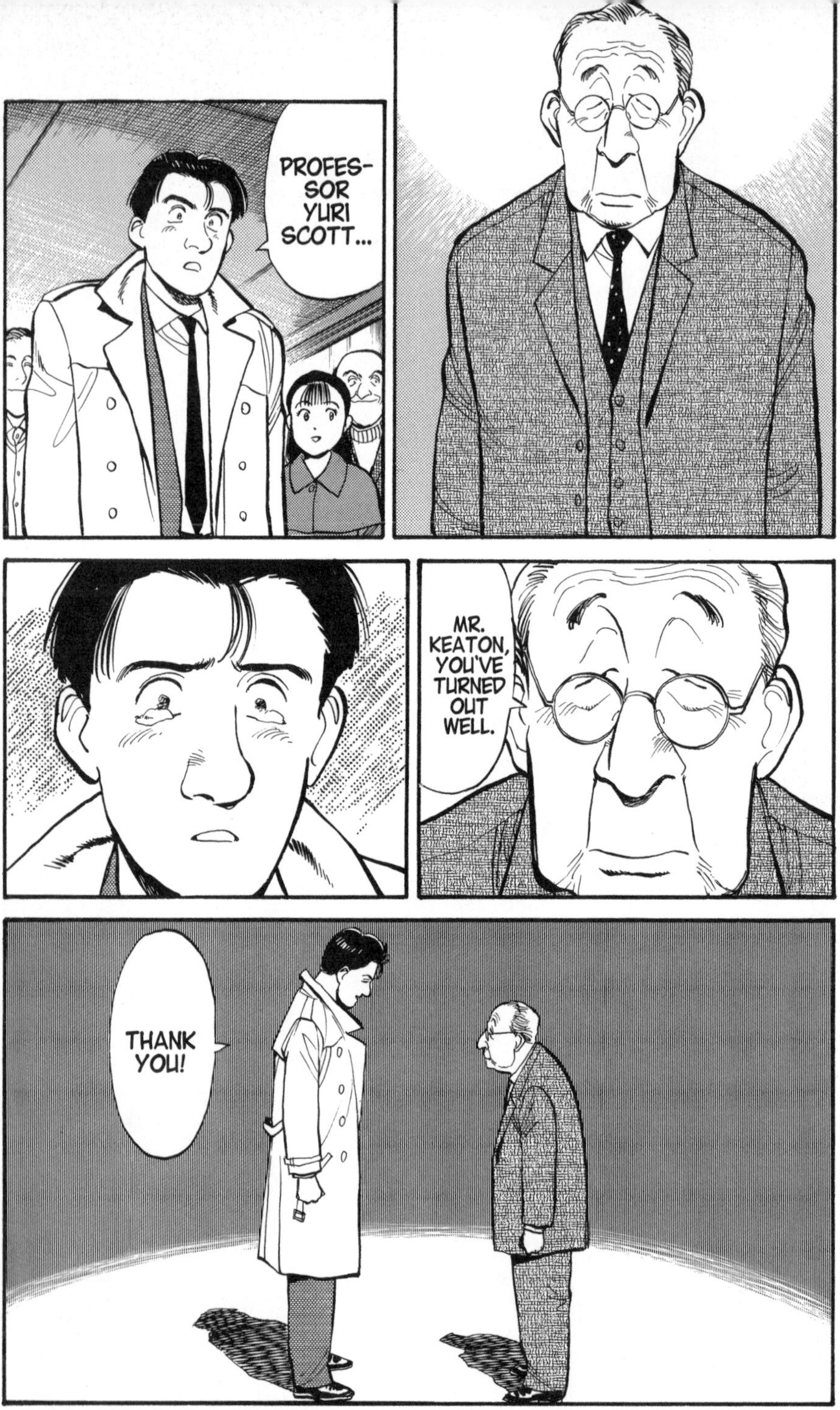
PROFES-SOR YURI SCOTT...
MR. KEATON, YOU'VE TURNED OUT WELL.
THANK YOU!

Chapter 6

# Little Big Man

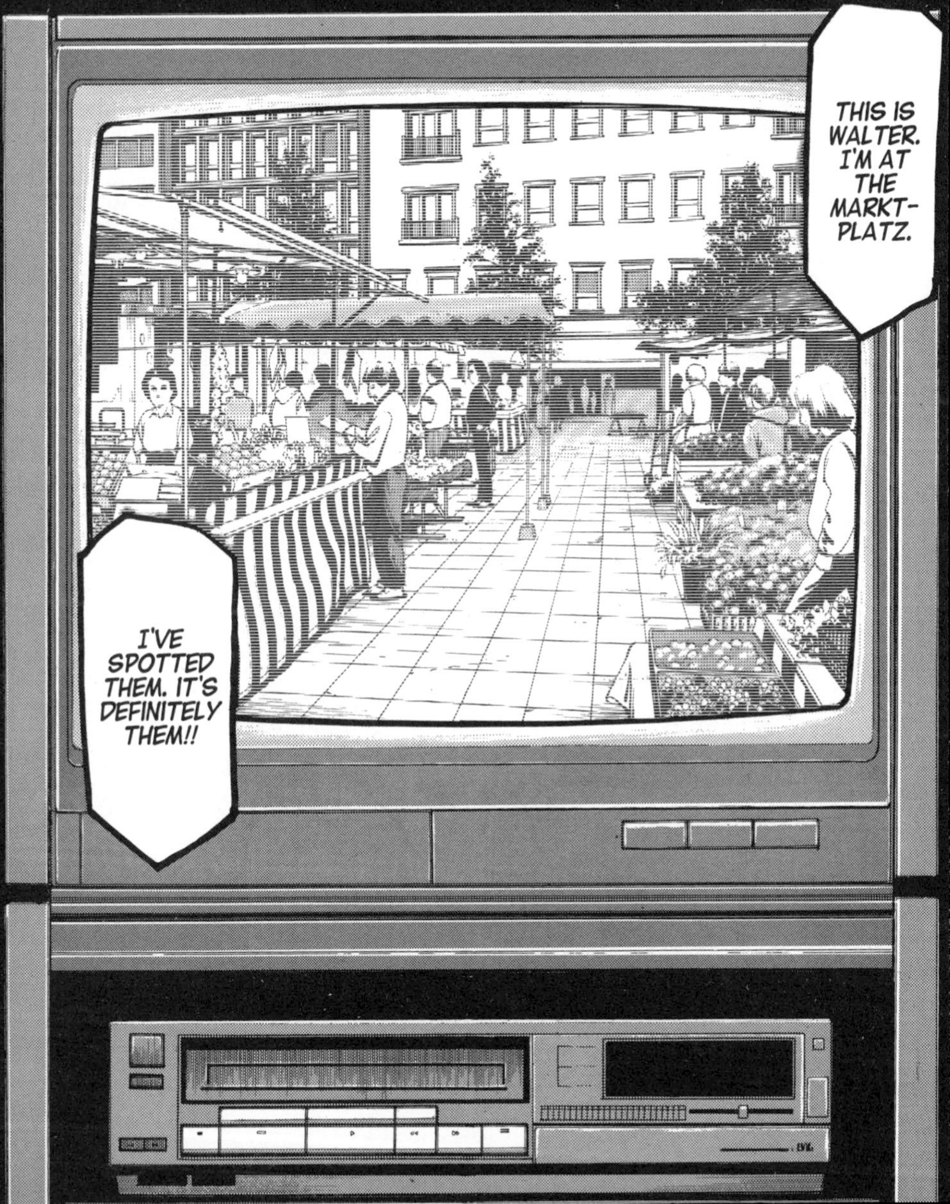
THIS IS WALTER. I'M AT THE MARKT-PLATZ.
I'VE SPOTTED THEM. IT'S DEFINITELY THEM!!

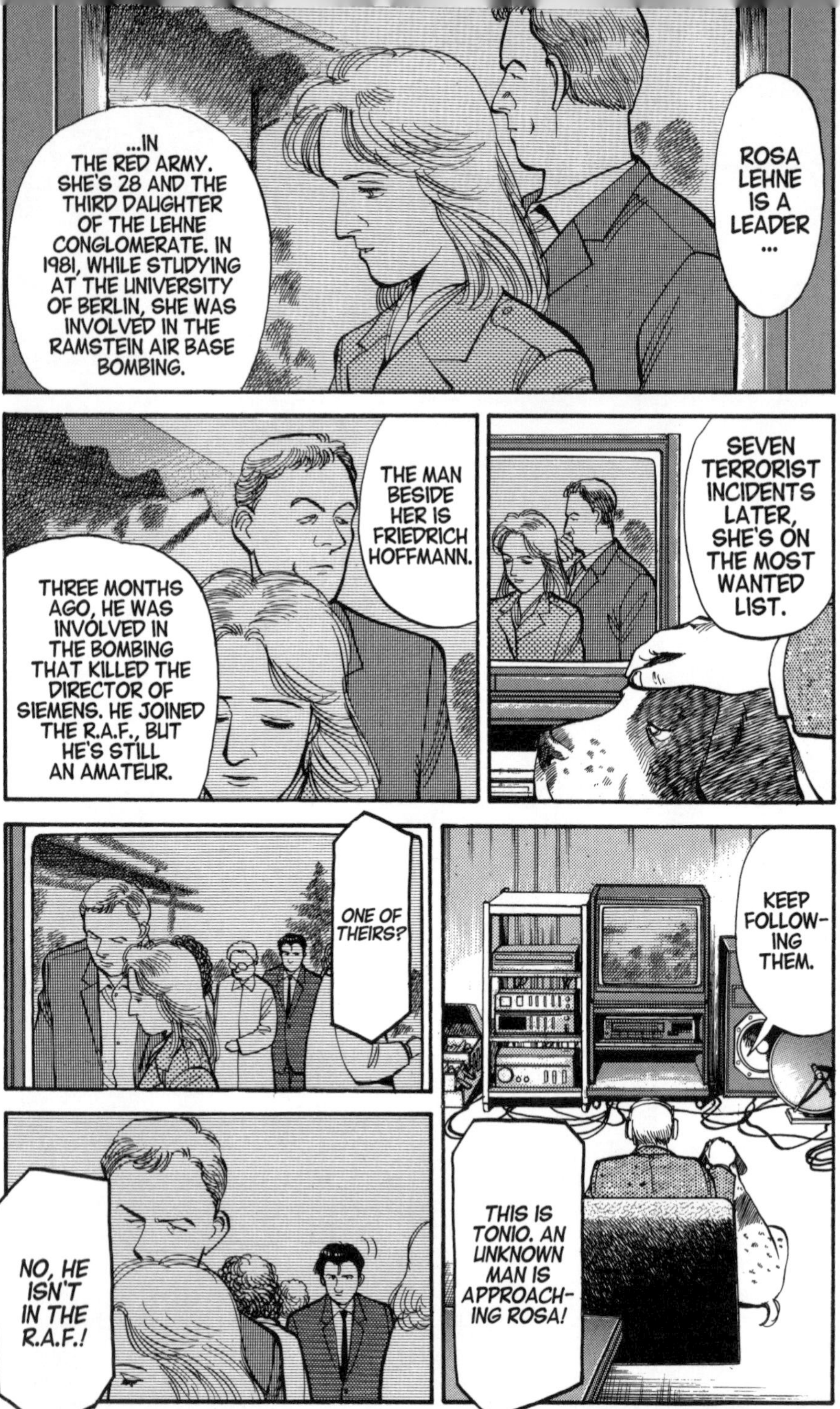
ROSA LEHNE IS A LEADER ...
...IN THE RED ARMY. SHE'S 28 AND THE THIRD DAUGHTER OF THE LEHNE CONGLOMERATE. IN 1981, WHILE STUDYING AT THE UNIVERSITY OF BERLIN, SHE WAS INVOLVED IN THE RAMSTEIN AIR BASE BOMBING.
SEVEN TERRORIST INCIDENTS LATER, SHE'S ON THE MOST WANTED LIST.
THE MAN BESIDE HER IS FRIEDRICH HOFFMANN.
THREE MONTHS AGO, HE WAS INVOLVED IN THE BOMBING THAT KILLED THE DIRECTOR OF SIEMENS. HE JOINED THE R.A.F., BUT HE'S STILL AN AMATEUR.
KEEP FOLLOWING THEM.
THIS IS TONIO. AN UNKNOWN MAN IS APPROACHING ROSA!
ONE OF THEIRS?
NO, HE ISN'T IN THE R.A.F.!

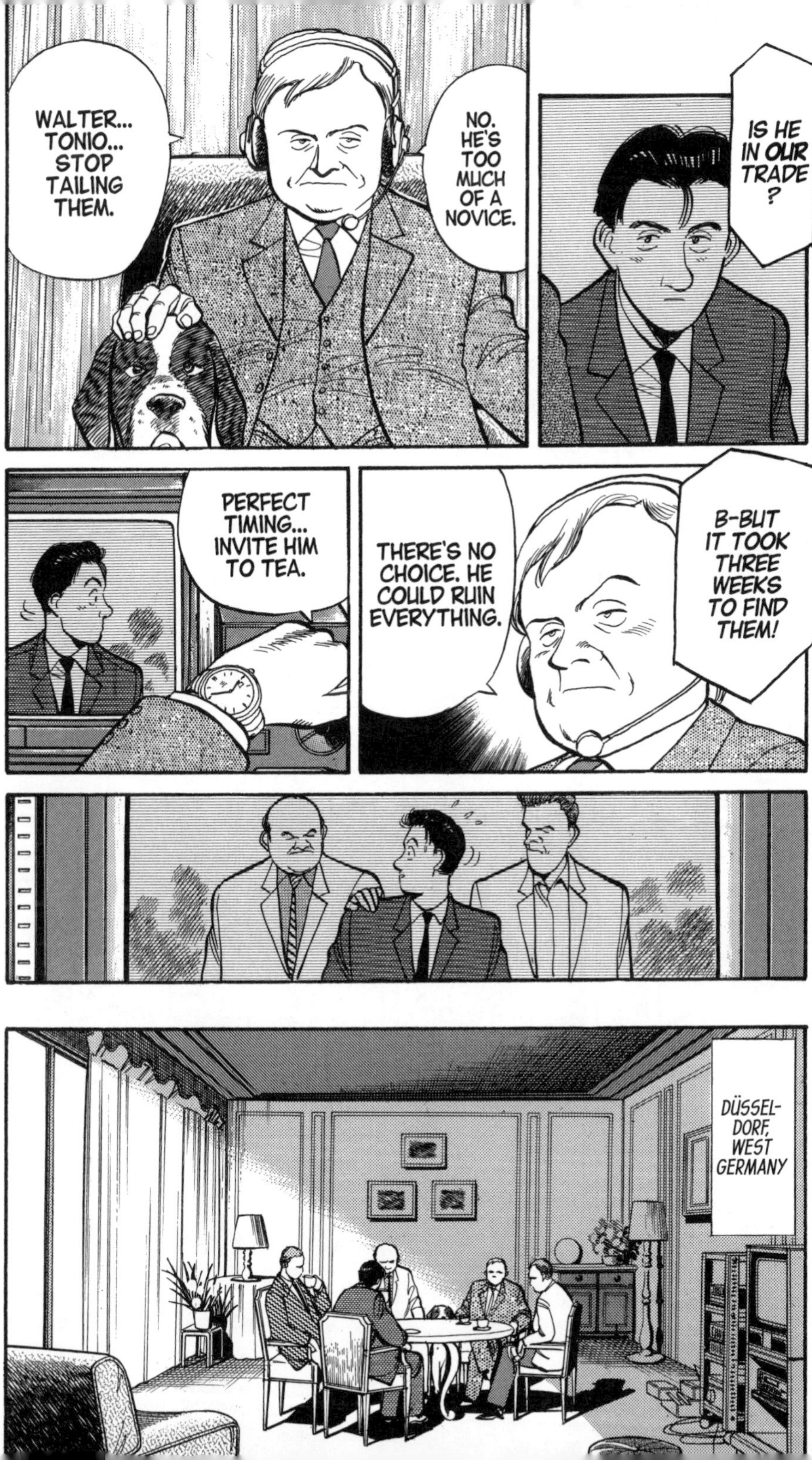
IS HE IN OUR TRADE?
NO. HE'S TOO MUCH OF A NOVICE.
WALTER... TONIO... STOP TAILING THEM.
B-BUT IT TOOK THREE WEEKS TO FIND THEM!
THERE'S NO CHOICE. HE COULD RUIN EVERYTHING.
PERFECT TIMING... INVITE HIM TO TEA.
DÜSSEL-DORF, WEST GERMANY

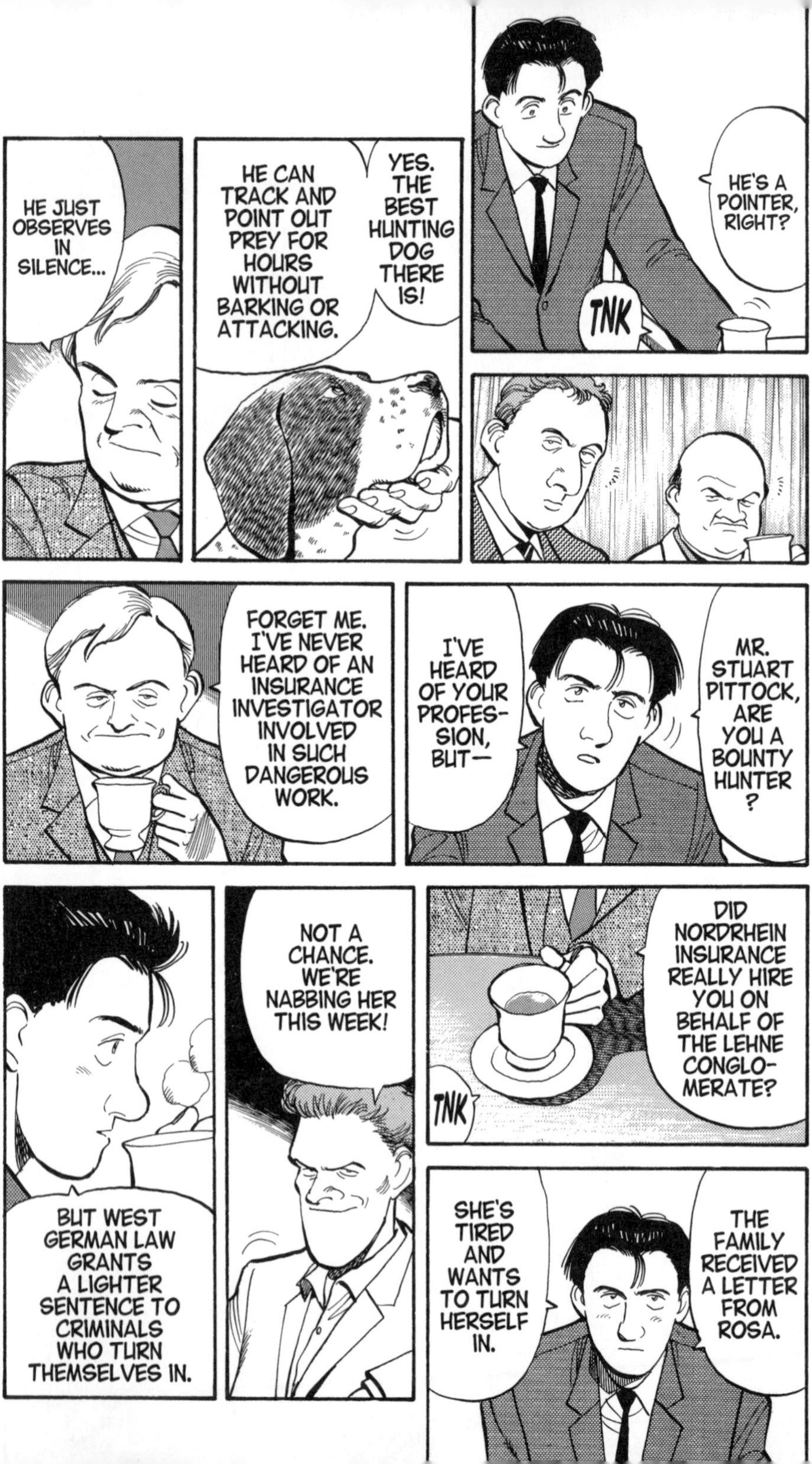
HE'S A POINTER, RIGHT?
TNK
YES. THE BEST HUNTING DOG THERE IS!
HE CAN TRACK AND POINT OUT PREY FOR HOURS WITHOUT BARKING OR ATTACKING.
HE JUST OBSERVES IN SILENCE...
MR. STUART PITTOCK, ARE YOU A BOUNTY HUNTER?
I'VE HEARD OF YOUR PROFES-SION, BUT—
FORGET ME. I'VE NEVER HEARD OF AN INSURANCE INVESTIGATOR INVOLVED IN SUCH DANGEROUS WORK.
DID NORDRHEIN INSURANCE REALLY HIRE YOU ON BEHALF OF THE LEHNE CONGLO-MERATE?
TNK
THE FAMILY RECEIVED A LETTER FROM ROSA.
SHE'S TIRED AND WANTS TO TURN HERSELF IN.
NOT A CHANCE. WE'RE NABBING HER THIS WEEK!
BUT WEST GERMAN LAW GRANTS A LIGHTER SENTENCE TO CRIMINALS WHO TURN THEMSELVES IN.

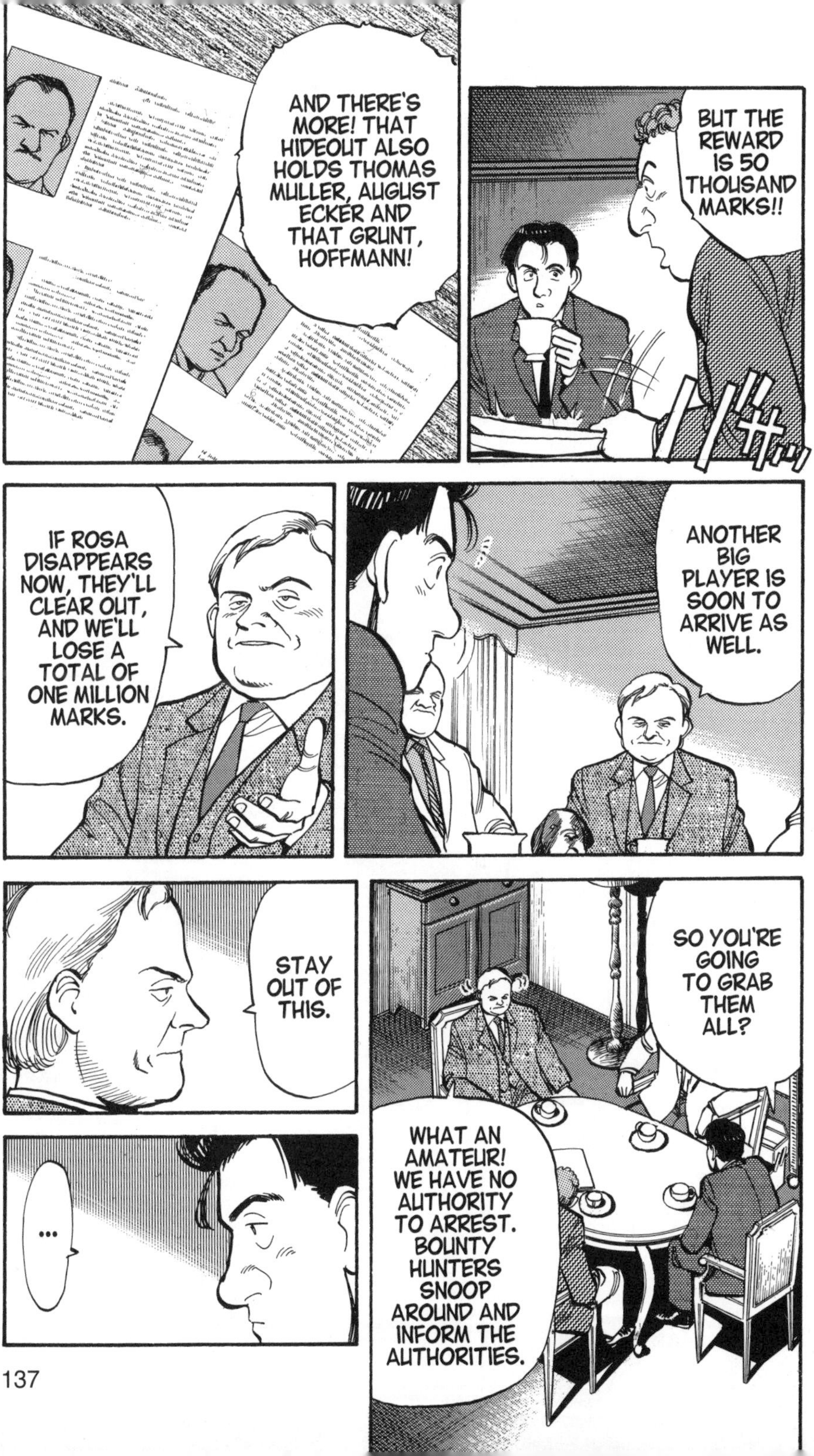
BUT THE REWARD IS 50 THOUSAND MARKS!!
AND THERE'S MORE! THAT HIDEOUT ALSO HOLDS THOMAS MULLER, AUGUST ECKER AND THAT GRUNT, HOFFMANN!
ANOTHER BIG PLAYER IS SOON TO ARRIVE AS WELL.
IF ROSA DISAPPEARS NOW, THEY'LL CLEAR OUT, AND WE'LL LOSE A TOTAL OF ONE MILLION MARKS.
SO YOU'RE GOING TO GRAB THEM ALL?
WHAT AN AMATEUR! WE HAVE NO AUTHORITY TO ARREST. BOUNTY HUNTERS SNOOP AROUND AND INFORM THE AUTHORITIES.
STAY OUT OF THIS.
...

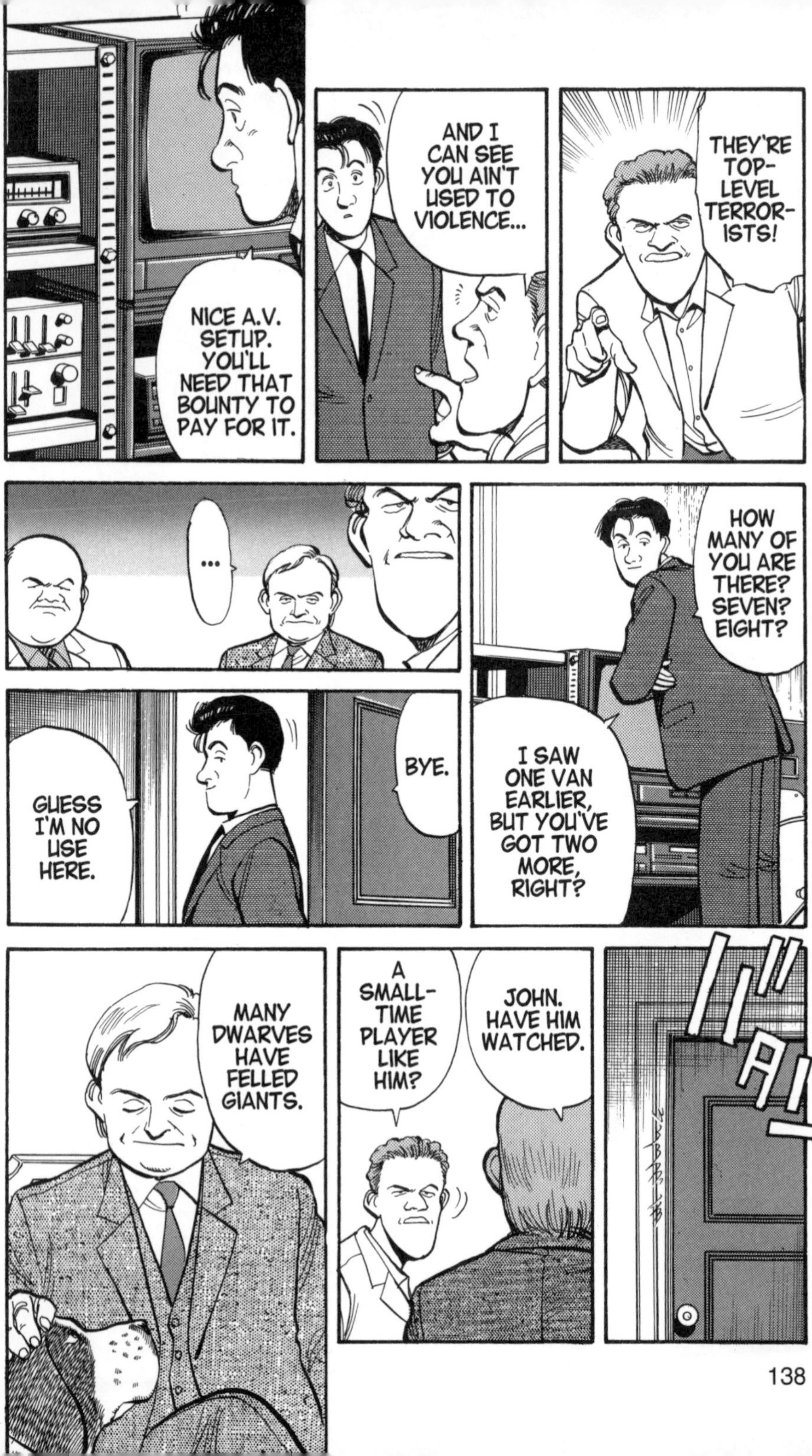
THEY'RE TOP-LEVEL TERRORISTS!
AND I CAN SEE YOU AIN'T USED TO VIOLENCE...
NICE A.V. SETUP. YOU'LL NEED THAT BOUNTY TO PAY FOR IT.
HOW MANY OF YOU ARE THERE? SEVEN? EIGHT?
I SAW ONE VAN EARLIER, BUT YOU'VE GOT TWO MORE, RIGHT?
...
BYE.
GUESS I'M NO USE HERE.
JOHN. HAVE HIM WATCHED.
A SMALL-TIME PLAYER LIKE HIM?
MANY DWARVES HAVE FELLED GIANTS.

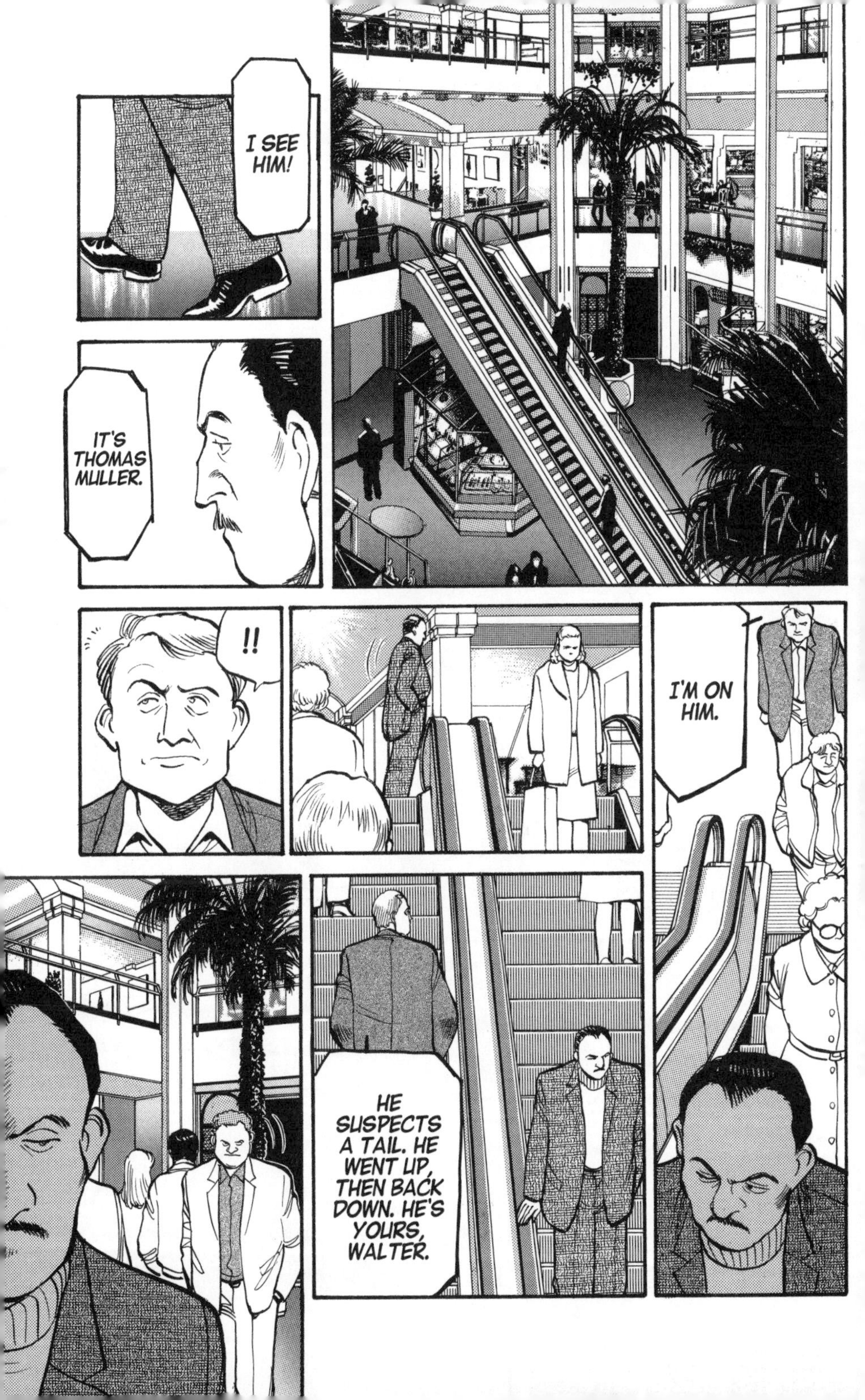
I SEE HIM!
IT'S THOMAS MULLER.
I'M ON HIM.
!!
HE SUSPECTS A TAIL. HE WENT UP, THEN BACK DOWN. HE'S YOURS, WALTER.

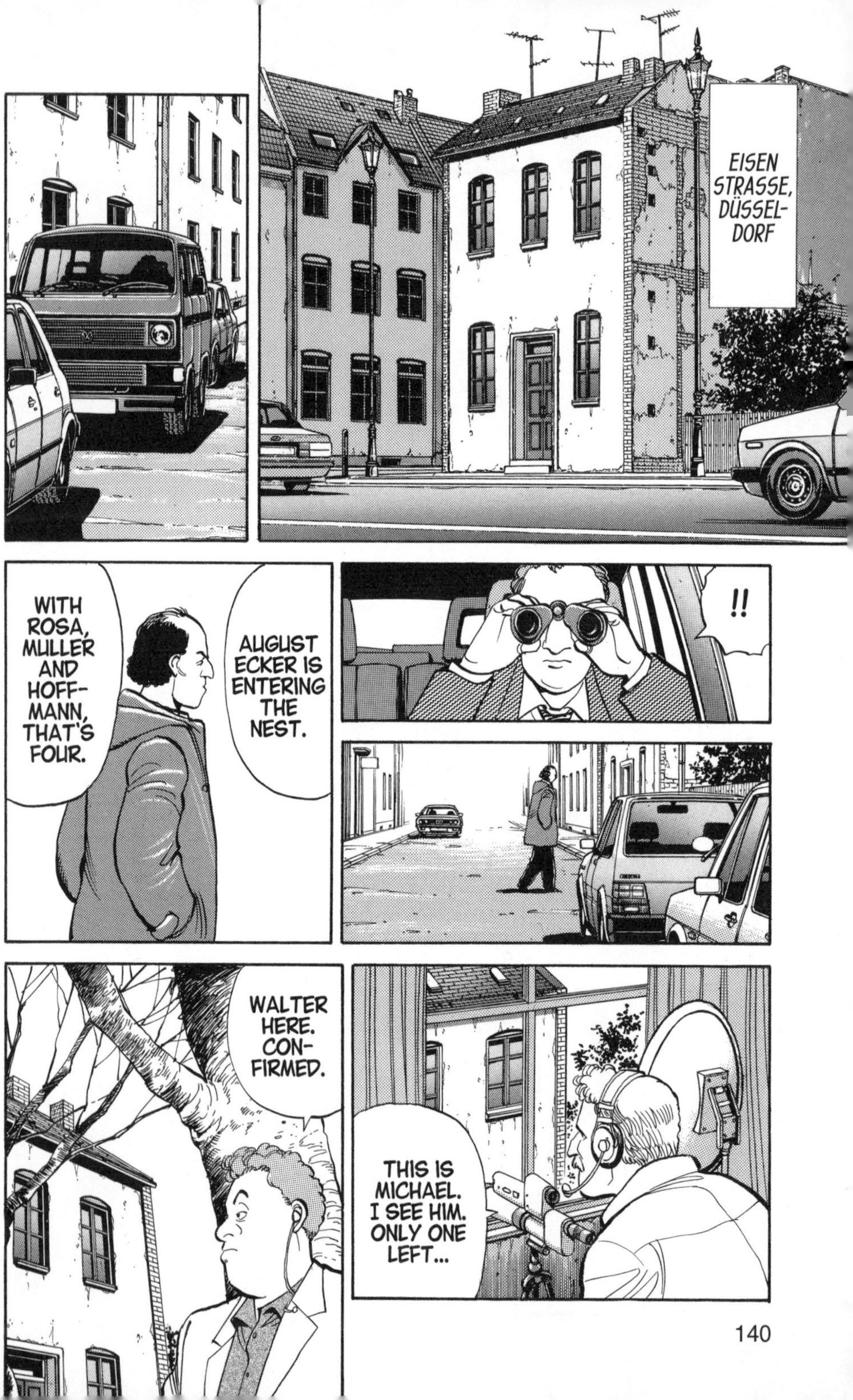
EISEN STRASSE, DÜSSELDORF
!!
AUGUST ECKER IS ENTERING THE NEST.
WITH ROSA, MULLER AND HOFFMANN, THAT'S FOUR.
THIS IS MICHAEL. I SEE HIM. ONLY ONE LEFT...
WALTER HERE. CONFIRMED.

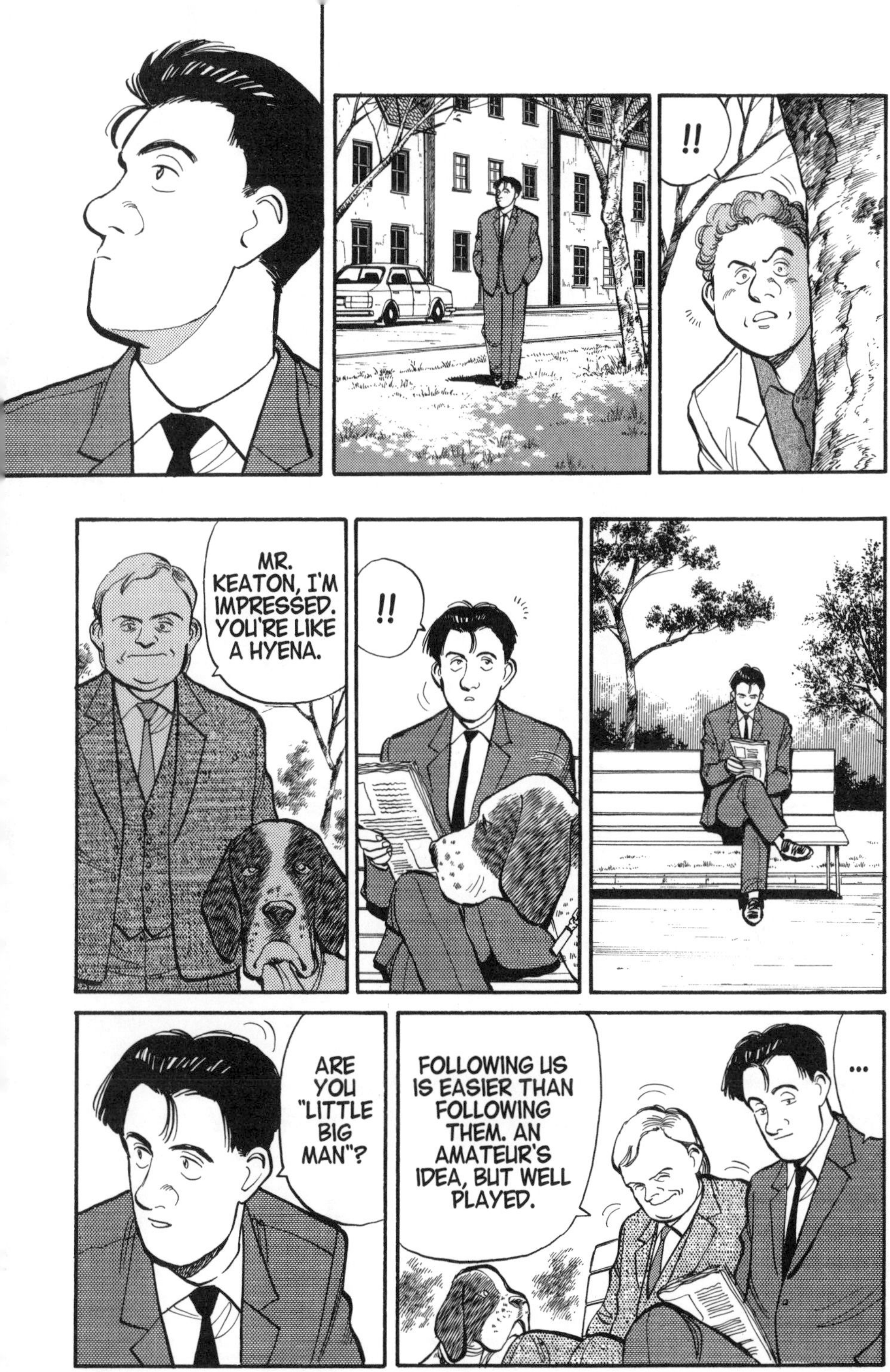
!!
!!
MR. KEATON, I'M IMPRESSED. YOU'RE LIKE A HYENA.
...
FOLLOWING US IS EASIER THAN FOLLOWING THEM. AN AMATEUR'S IDEA, BUT WELL PLAYED.
ARE YOU "LITTLE BIG MAN"?

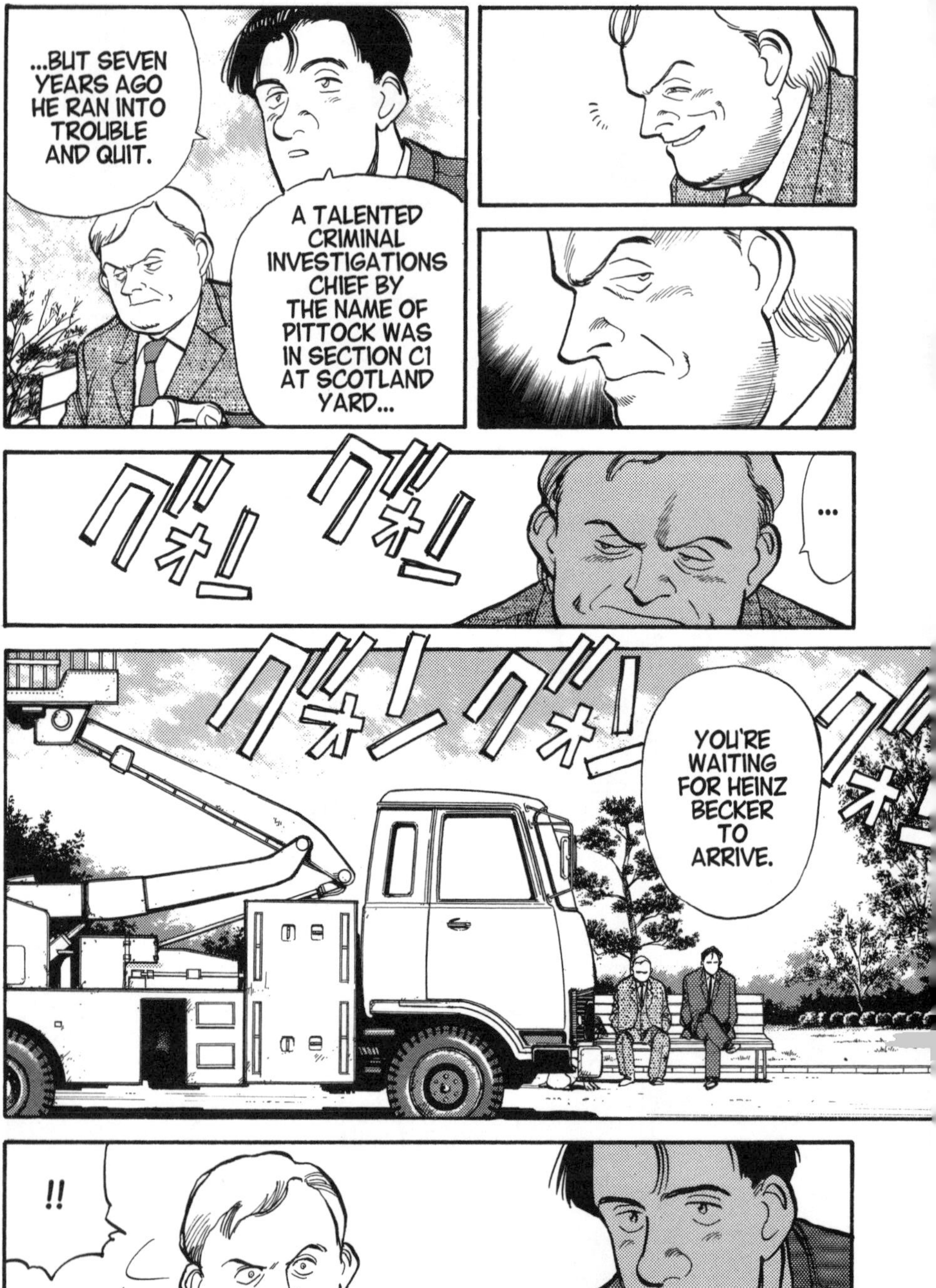
A TALENTED CRIMINAL INVESTIGATIONS CHIEF BY THE NAME OF PITTOCK WAS IN SECTION C1 AT SCOTLAND YARD...
...BUT SEVEN YEARS AGO HE RAN INTO TROUBLE AND QUIT.
...
グォン
グォン
グォン
YOU'RE WAITING FOR HEINZ BECKER TO ARRIVE.
グォン
グォン
!!

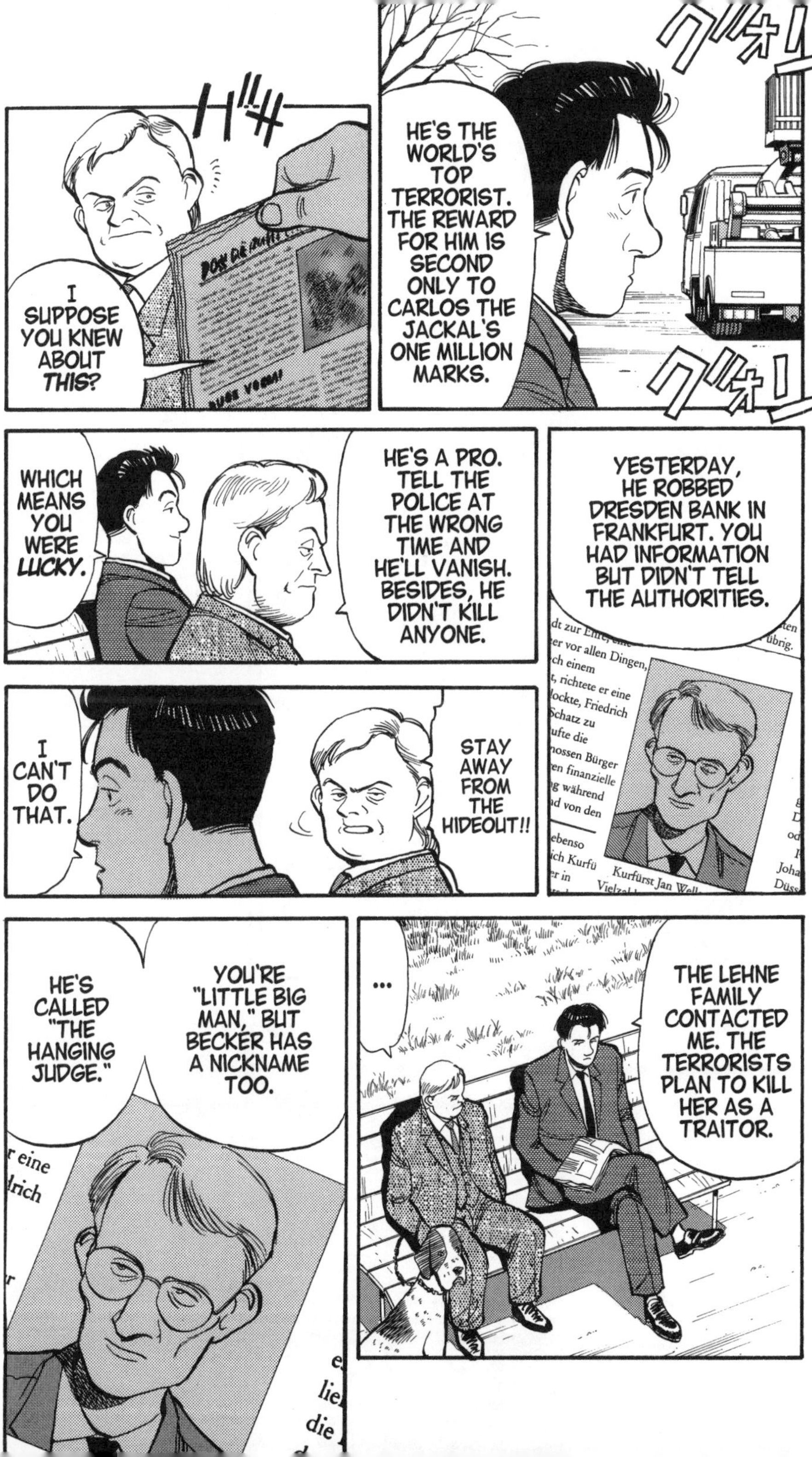
HE'S THE WORLD'S TOP TERRORIST. THE REWARD FOR HIM IS SECOND ONLY TO CARLOS THE JACKAL'S ONE MILLION MARKS.
I SUPPOSE YOU KNEW ABOUT THIS?
YESTERDAY, HE ROBBED DRESDEN BANK IN FRANKFURT. YOU HAD INFORMATION BUT DIDN'T TELL THE AUTHORITIES.
HE'S A PRO. TELL THE POLICE AT THE WRONG TIME AND HE'LL VANISH. BESIDES, HE DIDN'T KILL ANYONE.
WHICH MEANS YOU WERE LUCKY.
STAY AWAY FROM THE HIDEOUT!!
I CAN'T DO THAT.
THE LEHNE FAMILY CONTACTED ME. THE TERRORISTS PLAN TO KILL HER AS A TRAITOR.
...
YOU'RE "LITTLE BIG MAN," BUT BECKER HAS A NICKNAME TOO.
HE'S CALLED "THE HANGING JUDGE."

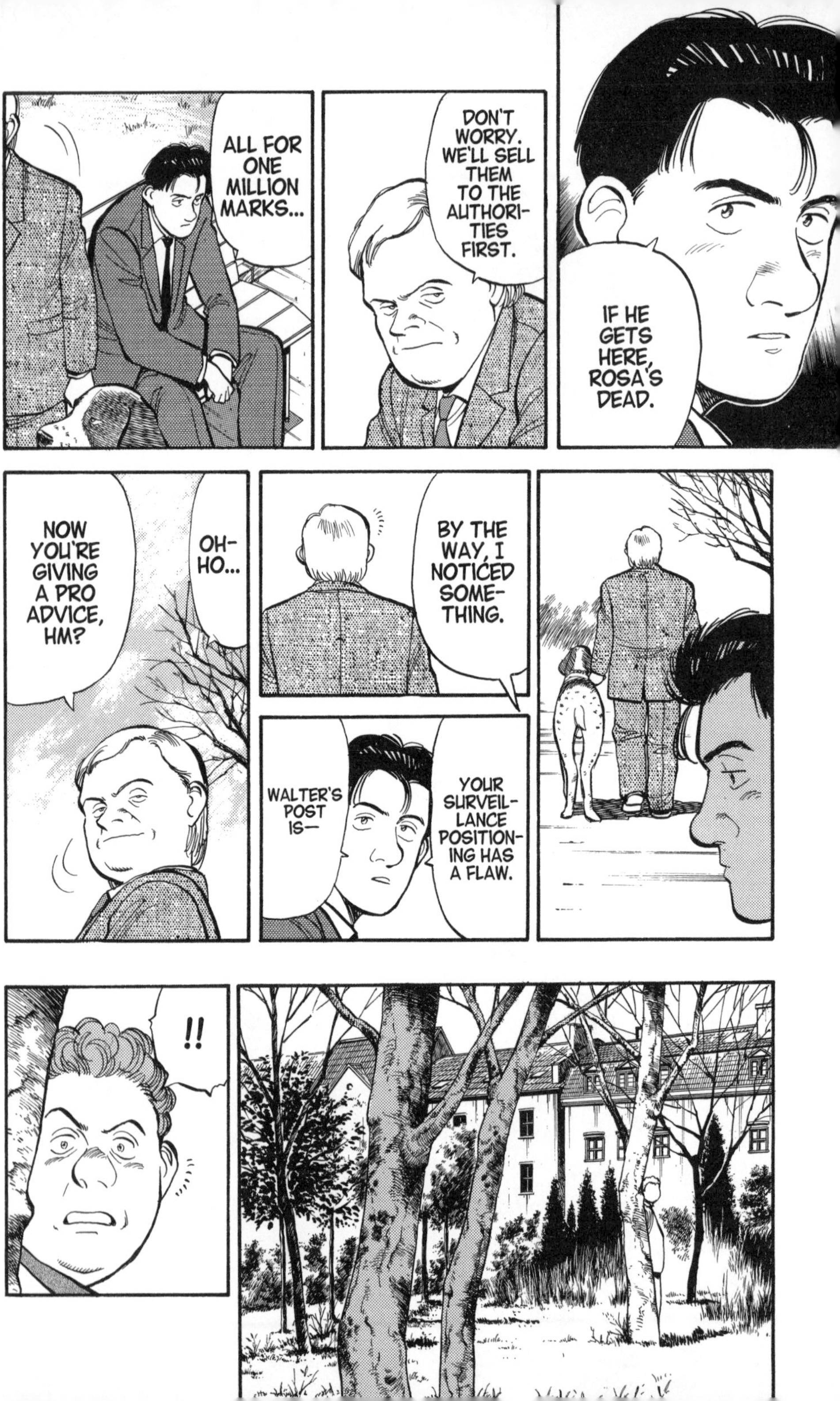
IF HE GETS HERE, ROSA'S DEAD.
DON'T WORRY. WE'LL SELL THEM TO THE AUTHORITIES FIRST.
ALL FOR ONE MILLION MARKS...
BY THE WAY, I NOTICED SOMETHING.
YOUR SURVEILLANCE POSITIONING HAS A FLAW.
WALTER'S POST IS—
OH-HO...
NOW YOU'RE GIVING A PRO ADVICE, HM?
!!

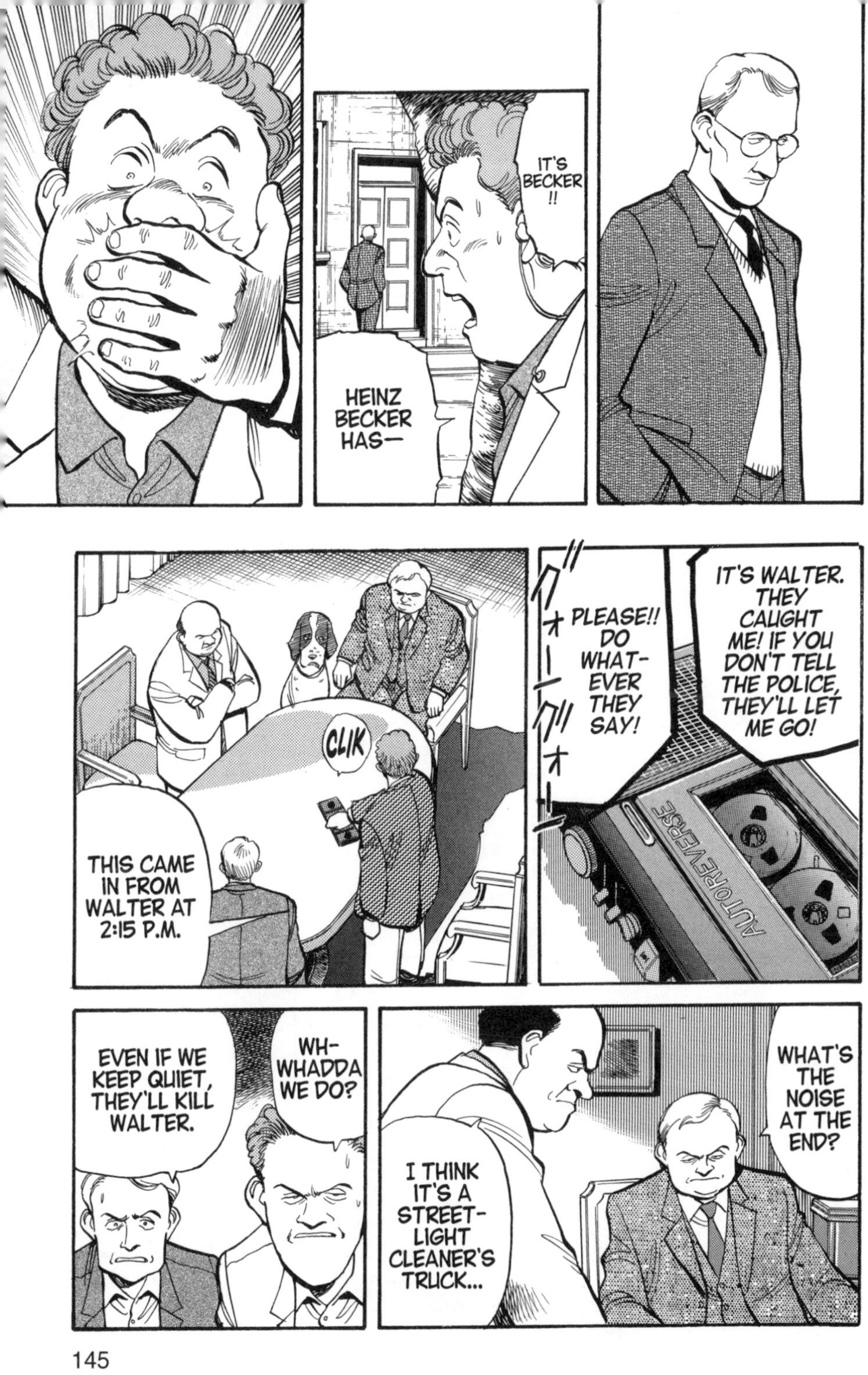
IT'S BECKER!!
HEINZ BECKER HAS—
IT'S WALTER. THEY CAUGHT ME! IF YOU DON'T TELL THE POLICE, THEY'LL LET ME GO!
PLEASE!! DO WHAT-EVER THEY SAY!
グォーーグォーー
AUTOREVERSE
CLIK
THIS CAME IN FROM WALTER AT 2:15 P.M.
WHAT'S THE NOISE AT THE END?
I THINK IT'S A STREET-LIGHT CLEANER'S TRUCK...
WH-WHADDA WE DO?
EVEN IF WE KEEP QUIET, THEY'LL KILL WALTER.

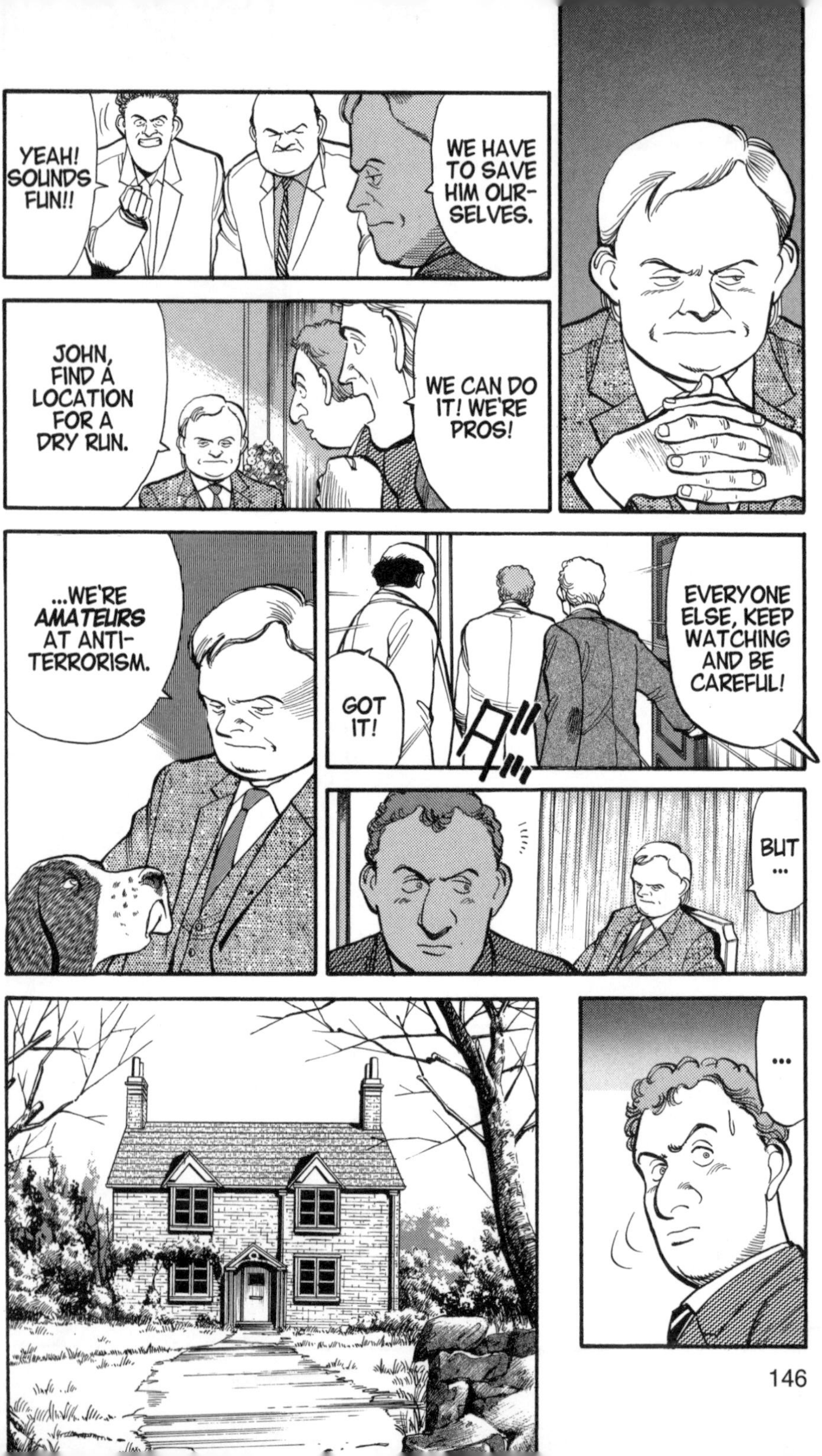

WE HAVE TO SAVE HIM OURSELVES.
YEAH! SOUNDS FUN!!
WE CAN DO IT! WE'RE PROS!
JOHN, FIND A LOCATION FOR A DRY RUN.
EVERYONE ELSE, KEEP WATCHING AND BE CAREFUL!
GOT IT!
BUT...
...WE'RE *AMATEURS* AT ANTI-TERRORISM.
...

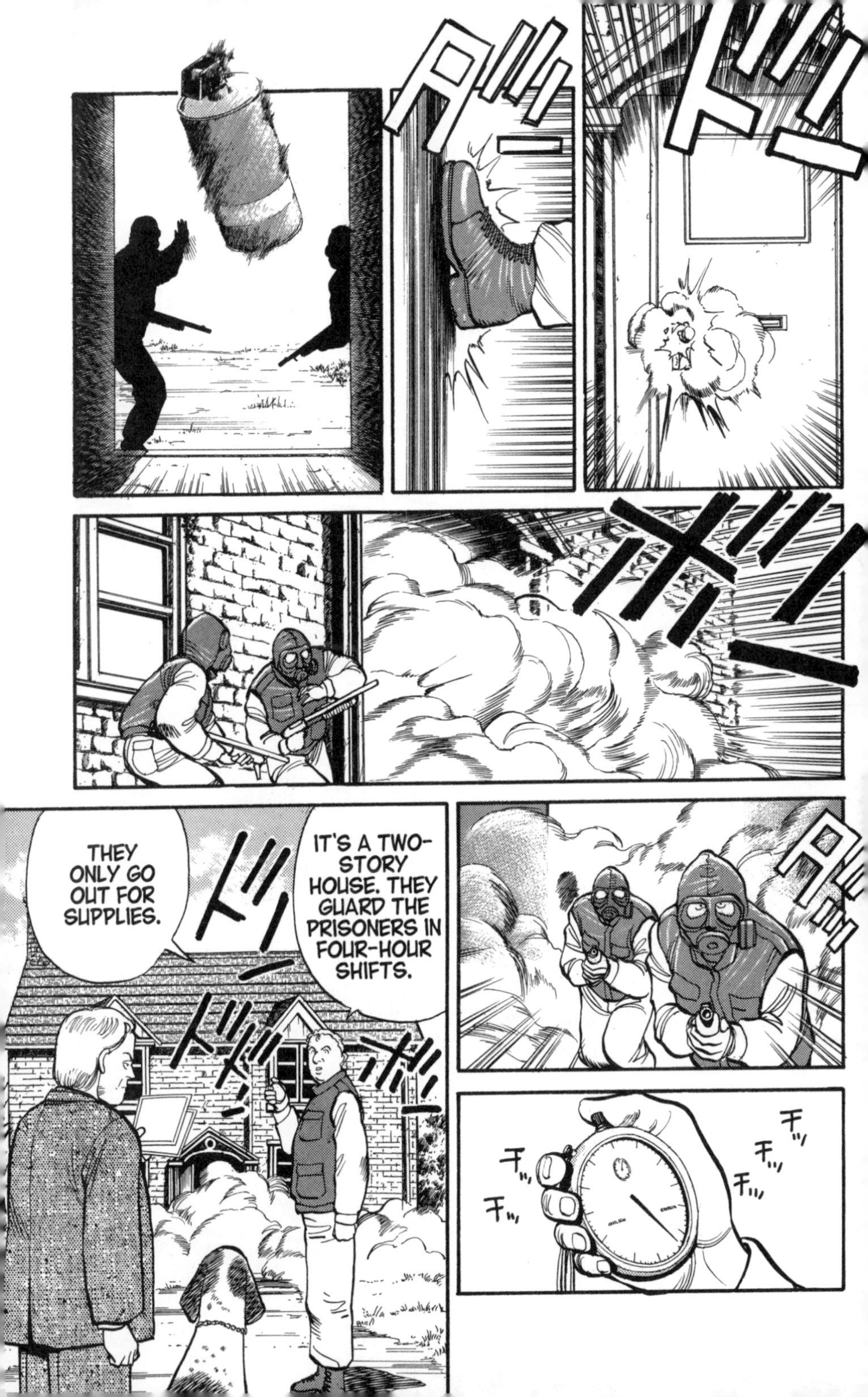
IT'S A TWO-STORY HOUSE. THEY GUARD THE PRISONERS IN FOUR-HOUR SHIFTS.
THEY ONLY GO OUT FOR SUPPLIES.

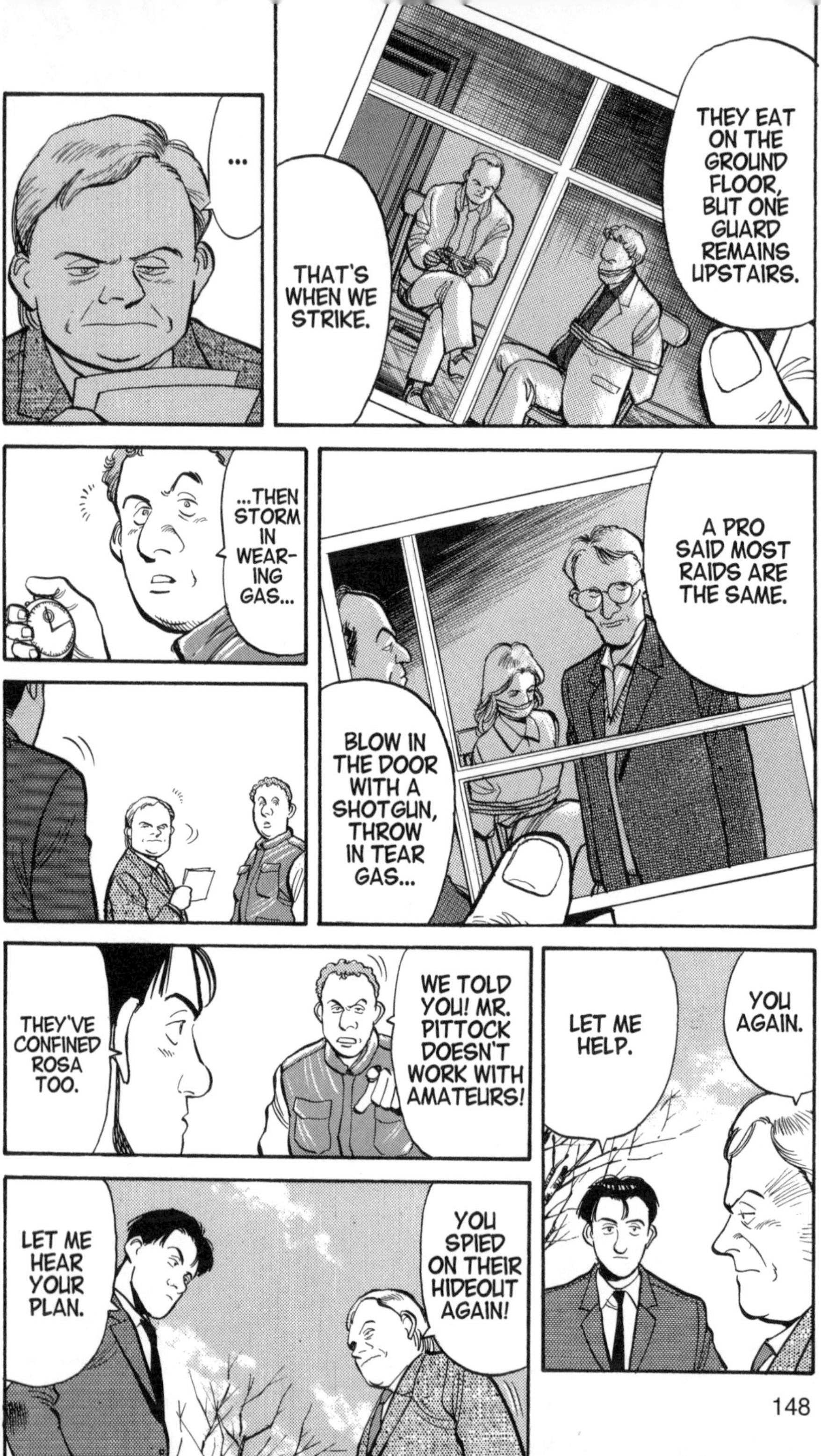
THEY EAT ON THE GROUND FLOOR, BUT ONE GUARD REMAINS UPSTAIRS.
THAT'S WHEN WE STRIKE.
...
A PRO SAID MOST RAIDS ARE THE SAME.
BLOW IN THE DOOR WITH A SHOTGUN, THROW IN TEAR GAS...
...THEN STORM IN WEAR-ING GAS...
YOU AGAIN.
LET ME HELP.
WE TOLD YOU! MR. PITTOCK DOESN'T WORK WITH AMATEURS!
THEY'VE CONFINED ROSA TOO.
YOU SPIED ON THEIR HIDEOUT AGAIN!
LET ME HEAR YOUR PLAN.

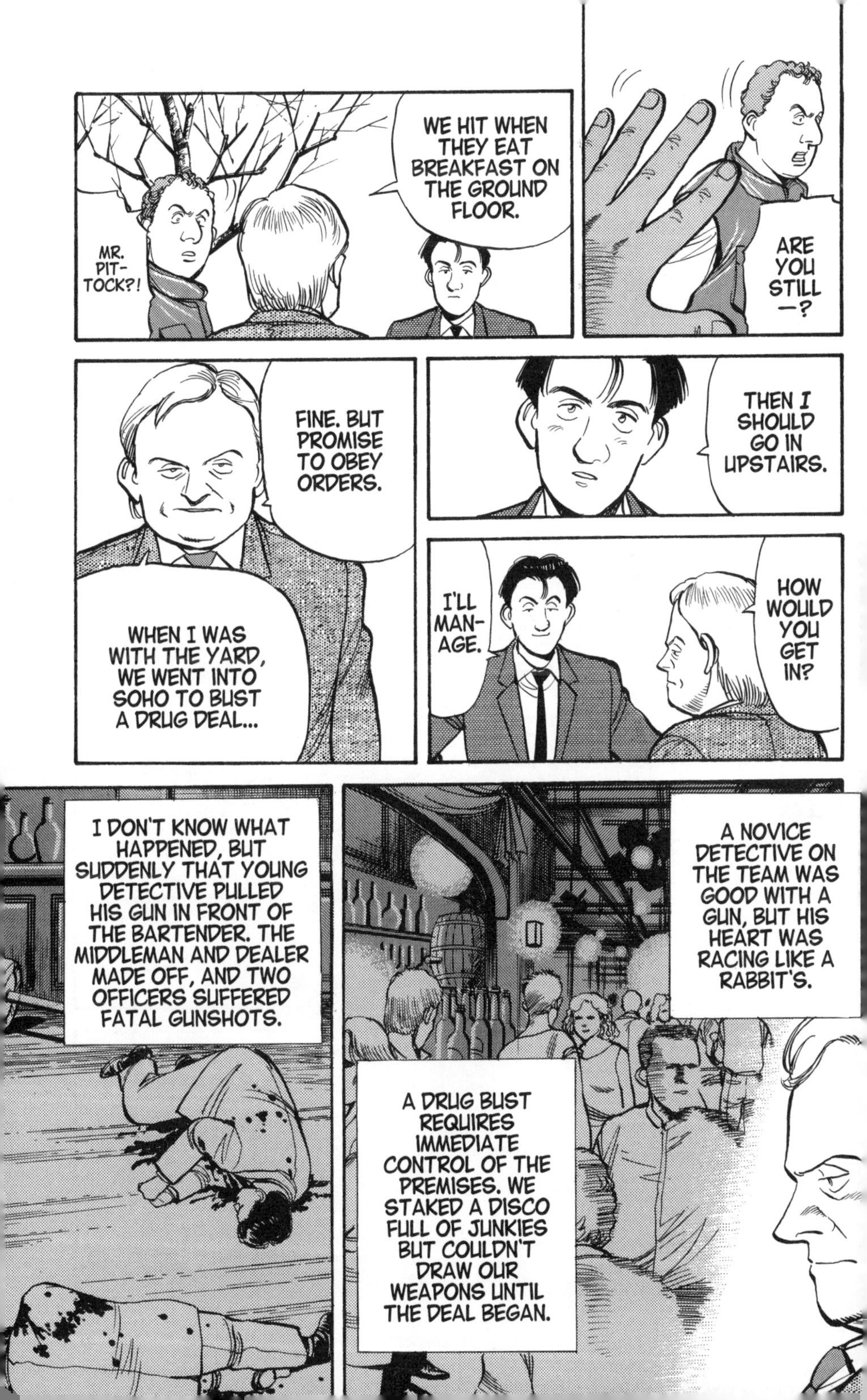
ARE YOU STILL—?
WE HIT WHEN THEY EAT BREAKFAST ON THE GROUND FLOOR.
MR. PIT-TOCK?!
THEN I SHOULD GO IN UPSTAIRS.
HOW WOULD YOU GET IN?
I'LL MAN-AGE.
FINE. BUT PROMISE TO OBEY ORDERS.
WHEN I WAS WITH THE YARD, WE WENT INTO SOHO TO BUST A DRUG DEAL...
A NOVICE DETECTIVE ON THE TEAM WAS GOOD WITH A GUN, BUT HIS HEART WAS RACING LIKE A RABBIT'S.
A DRUG BUST REQUIRES IMMEDIATE CONTROL OF THE PREMISES. WE STAKED A DISCO FULL OF JUNKIES BUT COULDN'T DRAW OUR WEAPONS UNTIL THE DEAL BEGAN.
I DON'T KNOW WHAT HAPPENED, BUT SUDDENLY THAT YOUNG DETECTIVE PULLED HIS GUN IN FRONT OF THE BARTENDER. THE MIDDLEMAN AND DEALER MADE OFF, AND TWO OFFICERS SUFFERED FATAL GUNSHOTS.

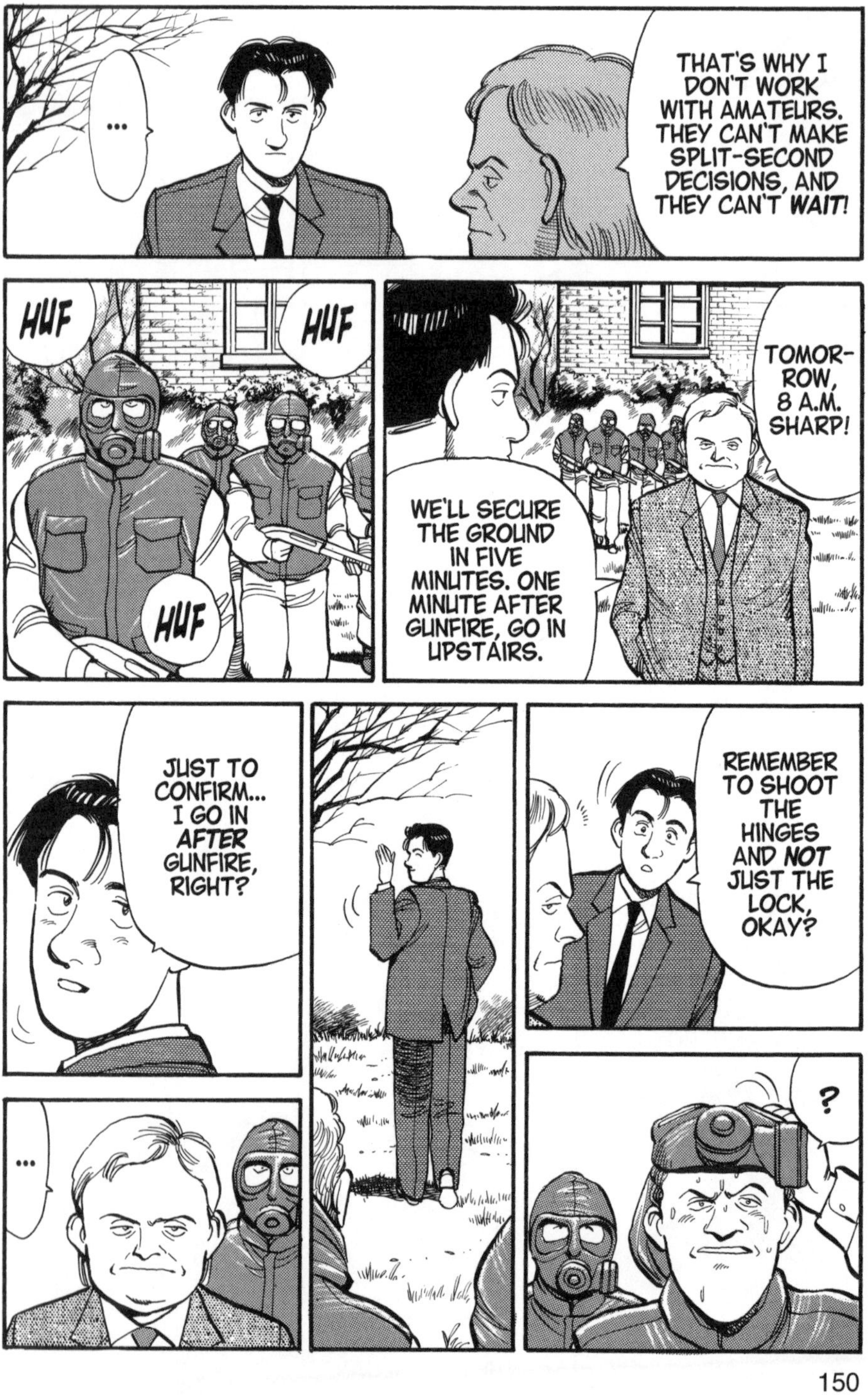
THAT'S WHY I DON'T WORK WITH AMATEURS. THEY CAN'T MAKE SPLIT-SECOND DECISIONS, AND THEY CAN'T WAIT!
...
TOMOR-ROW, 8 A.M. SHARP!
WE'LL SECURE THE GROUND IN FIVE MINUTES. ONE MINUTE AFTER GUNFIRE, GO IN UPSTAIRS.
HUF
HUF
HUF
REMEMBER TO SHOOT THE HINGES AND NOT JUST THE LOCK, OKAY?
?
JUST TO CONFIRM... I GO IN AFTER GUNFIRE, RIGHT?
...

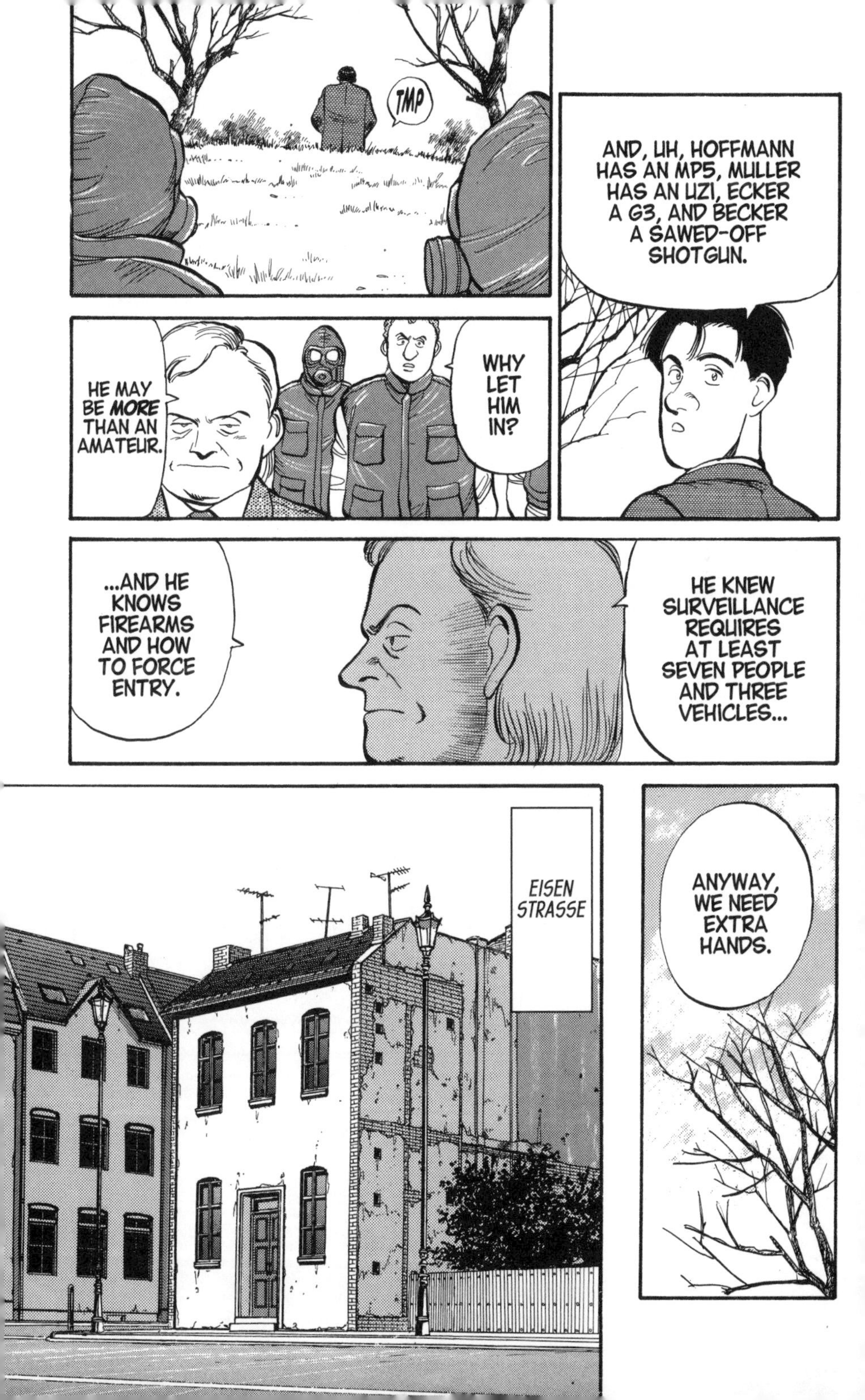
AND, UH, HOFFMANN HAS AN MP5, MULLER HAS AN UZI, ECKER A G3, AND BECKER A SAWED-OFF SHOTGUN.
TMP
WHY LET HIM IN?
HE MAY BE ***MORE*** THAN AN AMATEUR.
HE KNEW SURVEILLANCE REQUIRES AT LEAST SEVEN PEOPLE AND THREE VEHICLES...
...AND HE KNOWS FIREARMS AND HOW TO FORCE ENTRY.
ANYWAY, WE NEED EXTRA HANDS.
EISEN STRASSE

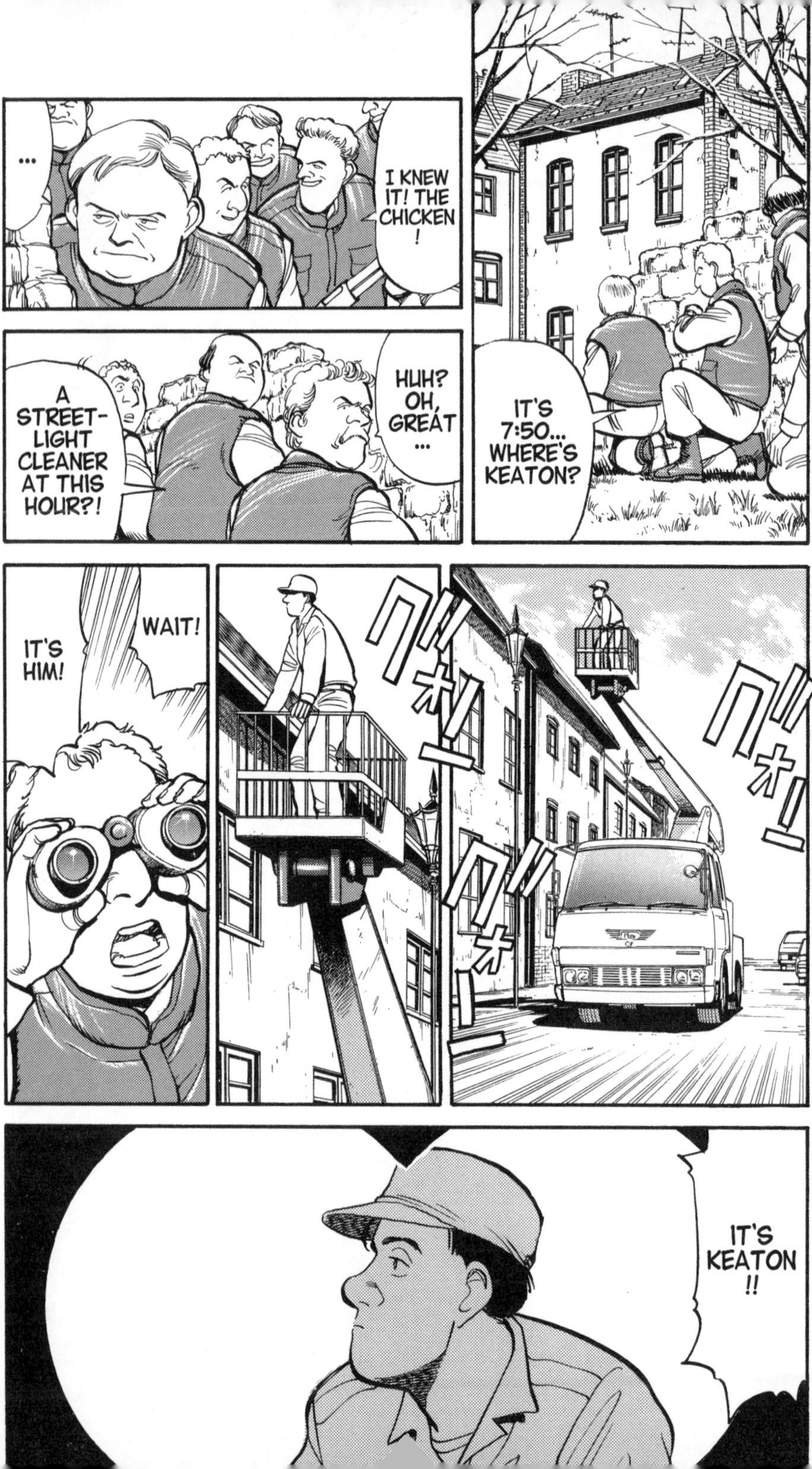
IT'S 7:50... WHERE'S KEATON?
I KNEW IT! THE CHICKEN!
...
HUH? OH, GREAT...
A STREET-LIGHT CLEANER AT THIS HOUR?!
WAIT!
IT'S HIM!
IT'S KEATON!!

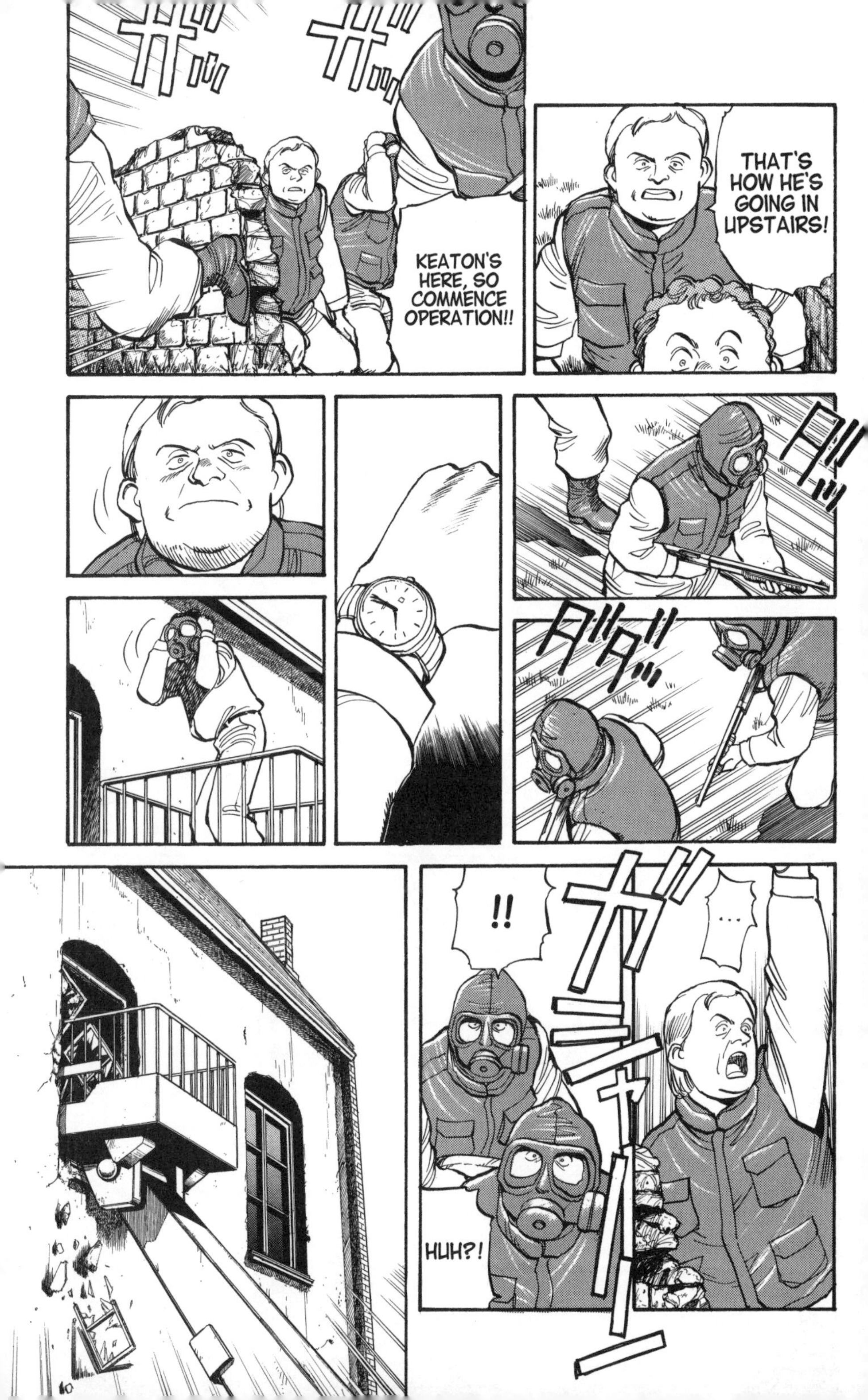
THAT'S HOW HE'S GOING IN UPSTAIRS!
KEATON'S HERE, SO COMMENCE OPERATION!!
...
!!
HUH?!

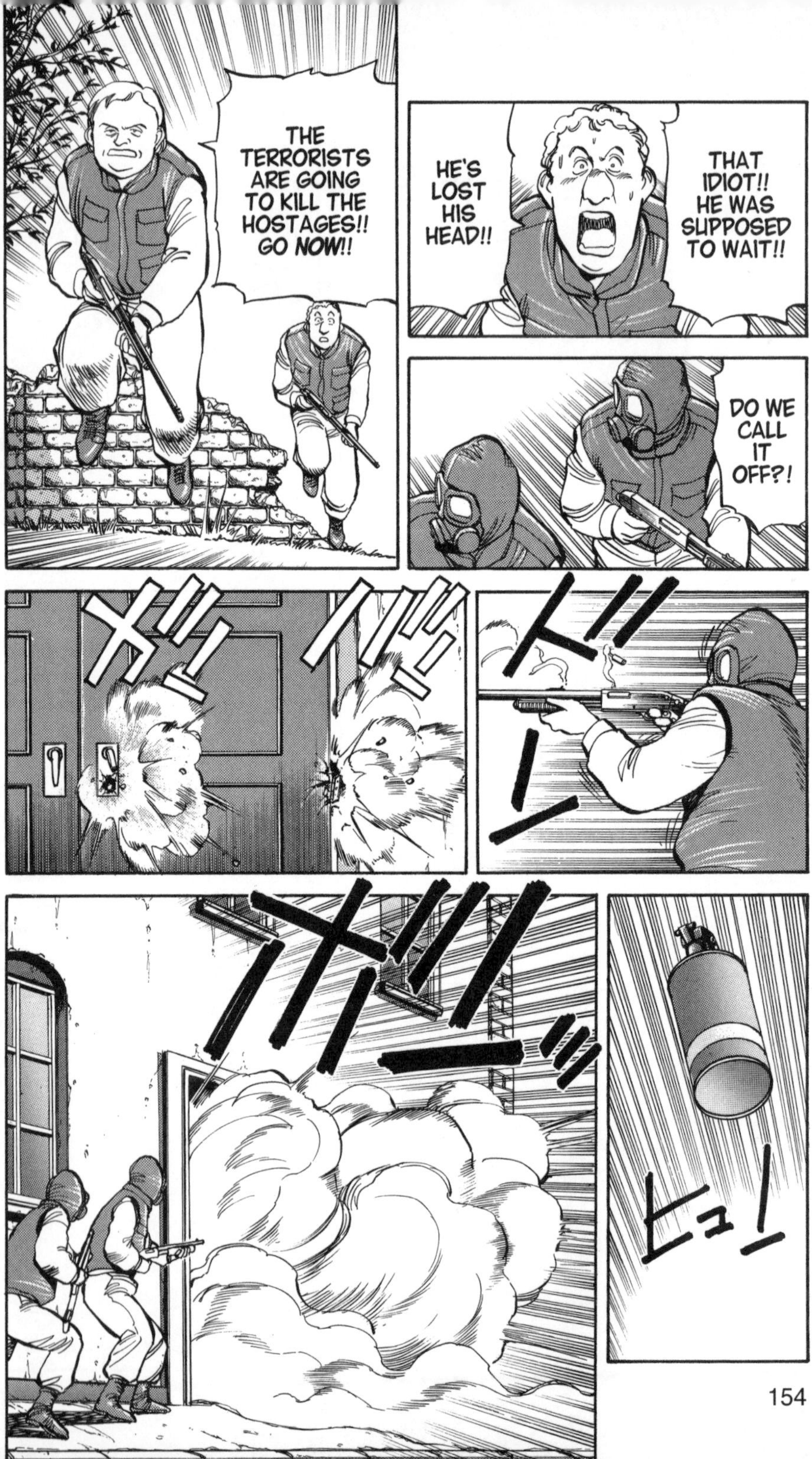

THAT IDIOT!! HE WAS SUPPOSED TO WAIT!!
HE'S LOST HIS HEAD!!
DO WE CALL IT OFF?!
THE TERRORISTS ARE GOING TO KILL THE HOSTAGES!! GO NOW!!

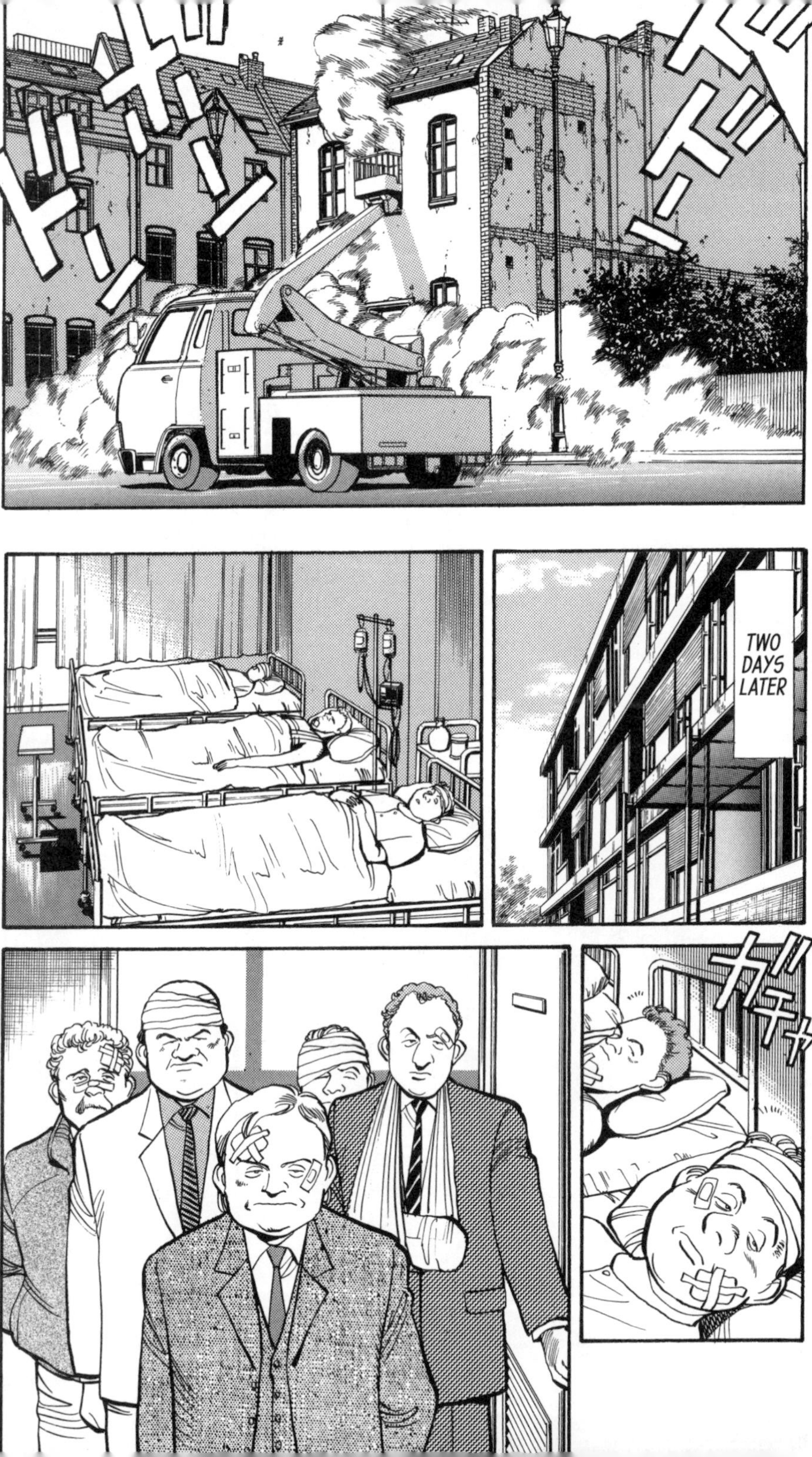
TWO DAYS LATER
ガチャ

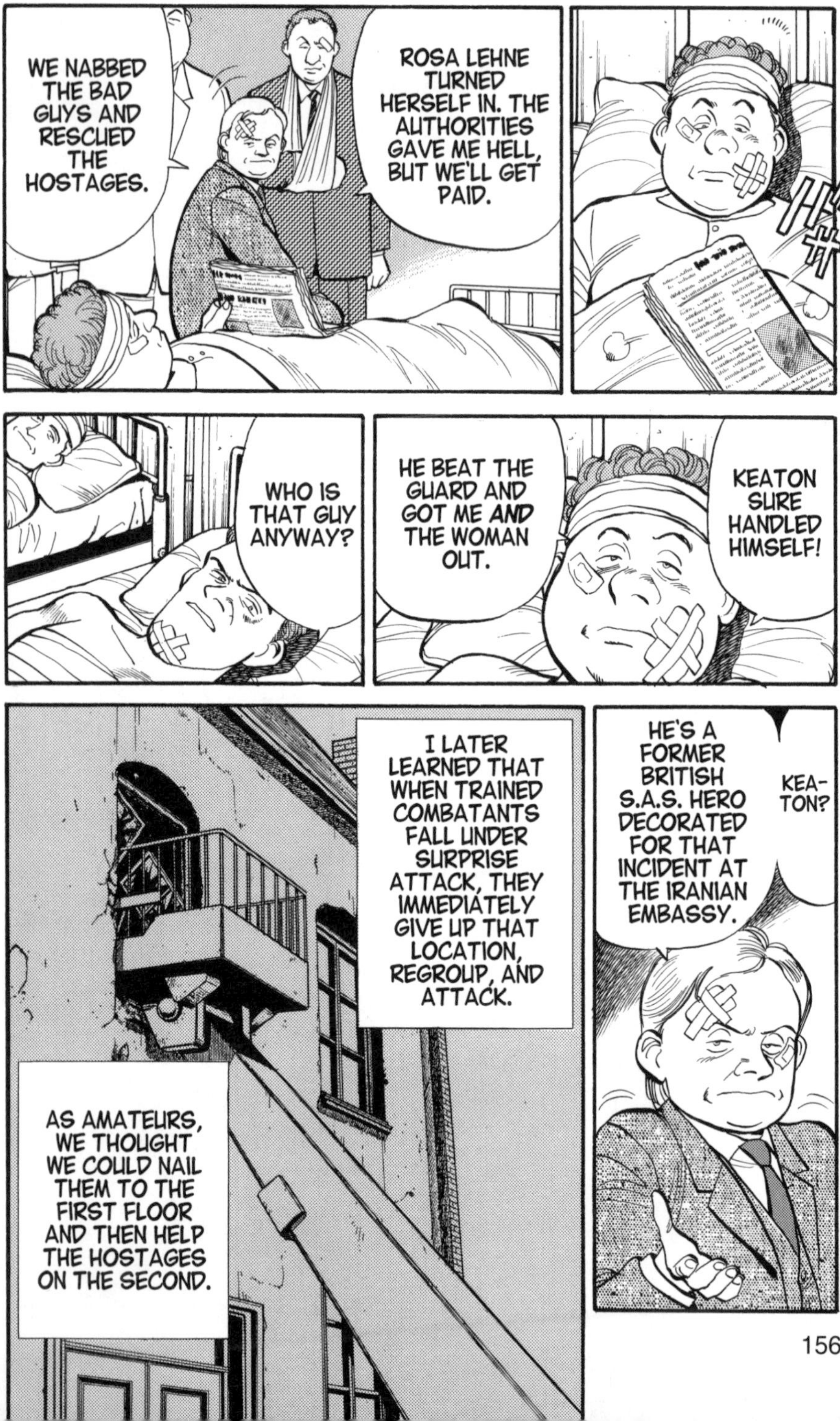
ROSA LEHNE TURNED HERSELF IN. THE AUTHORITIES GAVE ME HELL, BUT WE'LL GET PAID.
WE NABBED THE BAD GUYS AND RESCUED THE HOSTAGES.
KEATON SURE HANDLED HIMSELF!
HE BEAT THE GUARD AND GOT ME AND THE WOMAN OUT.
WHO IS THAT GUY ANYWAY?
KEA-TON?
HE'S A FORMER BRITISH S.A.S. HERO DECORATED FOR THAT INCIDENT AT THE IRANIAN EMBASSY.
I LATER LEARNED THAT WHEN TRAINED COMBATANTS FALL UNDER SURPRISE ATTACK, THEY IMMEDIATELY GIVE UP THAT LOCATION, REGROUP, AND ATTACK.
AS AMATEURS, WE THOUGHT WE COULD NAIL THEM TO THE FIRST FLOOR AND THEN HELP THE HOSTAGES ON THE SECOND.

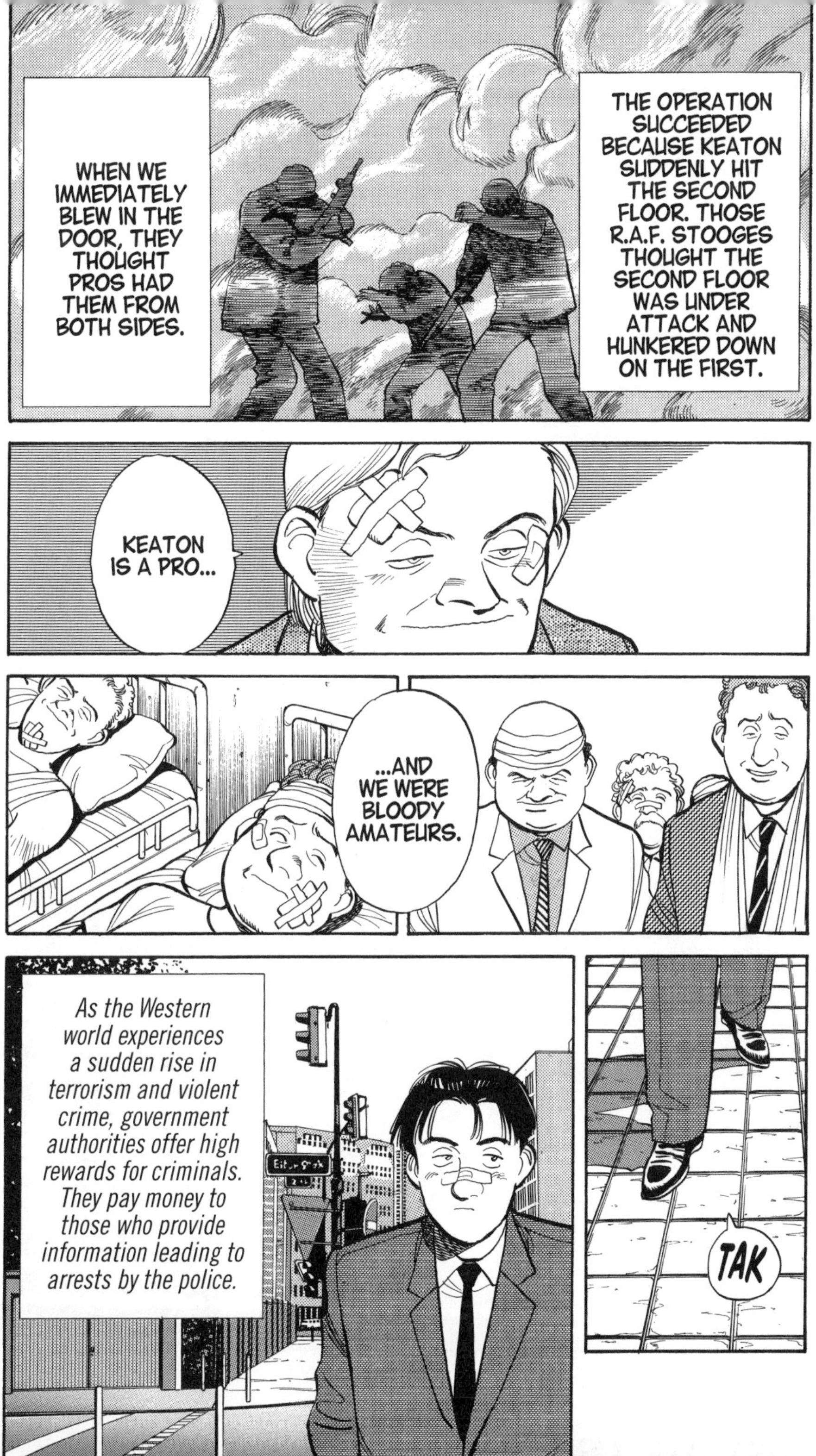
THE OPERATION SUCCEEDED BECAUSE KEATON SUDDENLY HIT THE SECOND FLOOR. THOSE R.A.F. STOOGES THOUGHT THE SECOND FLOOR WAS UNDER ATTACK AND HUNKERED DOWN ON THE FIRST.
WHEN WE IMMEDIATELY BLEW IN THE DOOR, THEY THOUGHT PROS HAD THEM FROM BOTH SIDES.
KEATON IS A PRO...
...AND WE WERE BLOODY AMATEURS.
TAK
As the Western world experiences a sudden rise in terrorism and violent crime, government authorities offer high rewards for criminals. They pay money to those who provide information leading to arrests by the police.

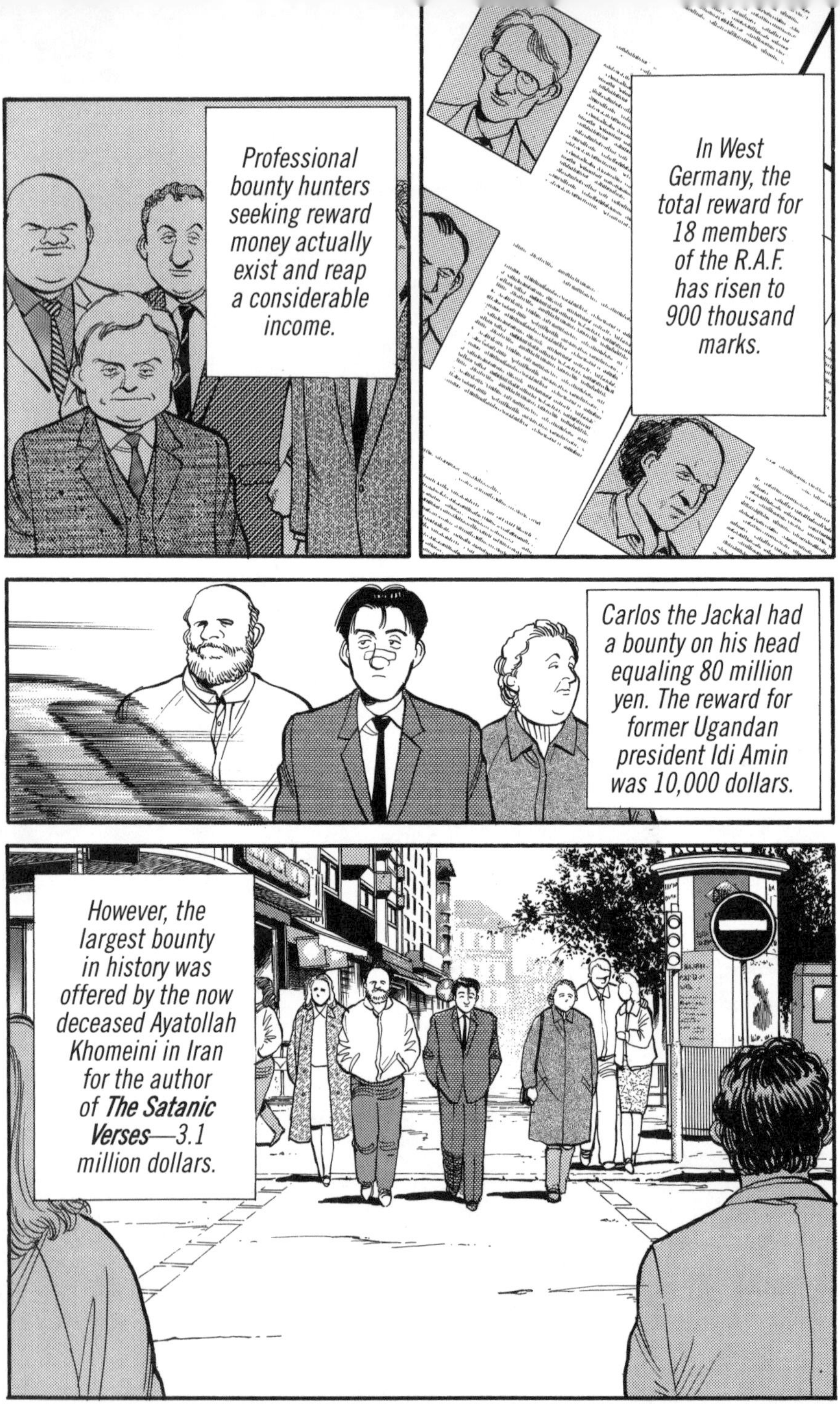
In West Germany, the total reward for 18 members of the R.A.F. has risen to 900 thousand marks.
Professional bounty hunters seeking reward money actually exist and reap a considerable income.
Carlos the Jackal had a bounty on his head equaling 80 million yen. The reward for former Ugandan president Idi Amin was 10,000 dollars.
However, the largest bounty in history was offered by the now deceased Ayatollah Khomeini in Iran for the author of **The Satanic Verses**—3.1 million dollars.

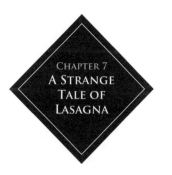

# Chapter 7
# A Strange Tale of Lasagna

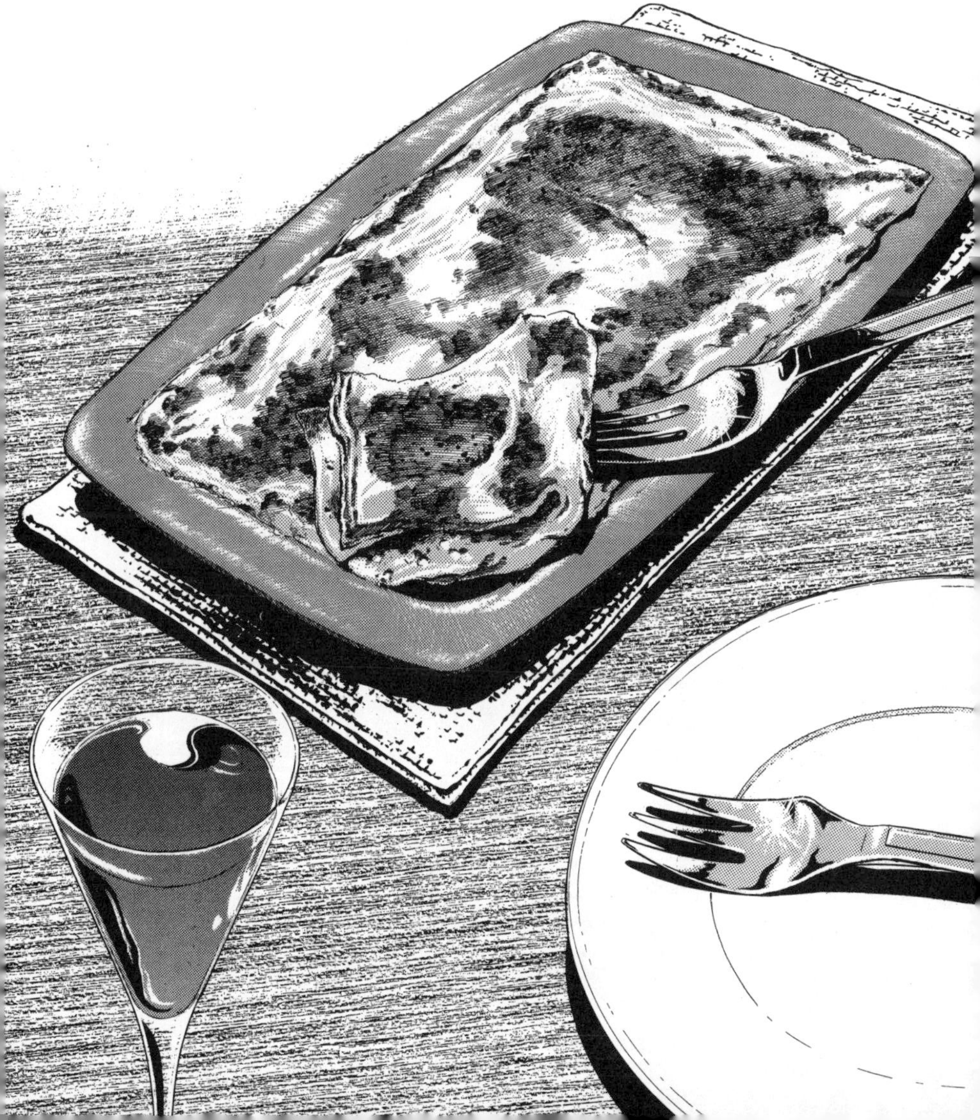

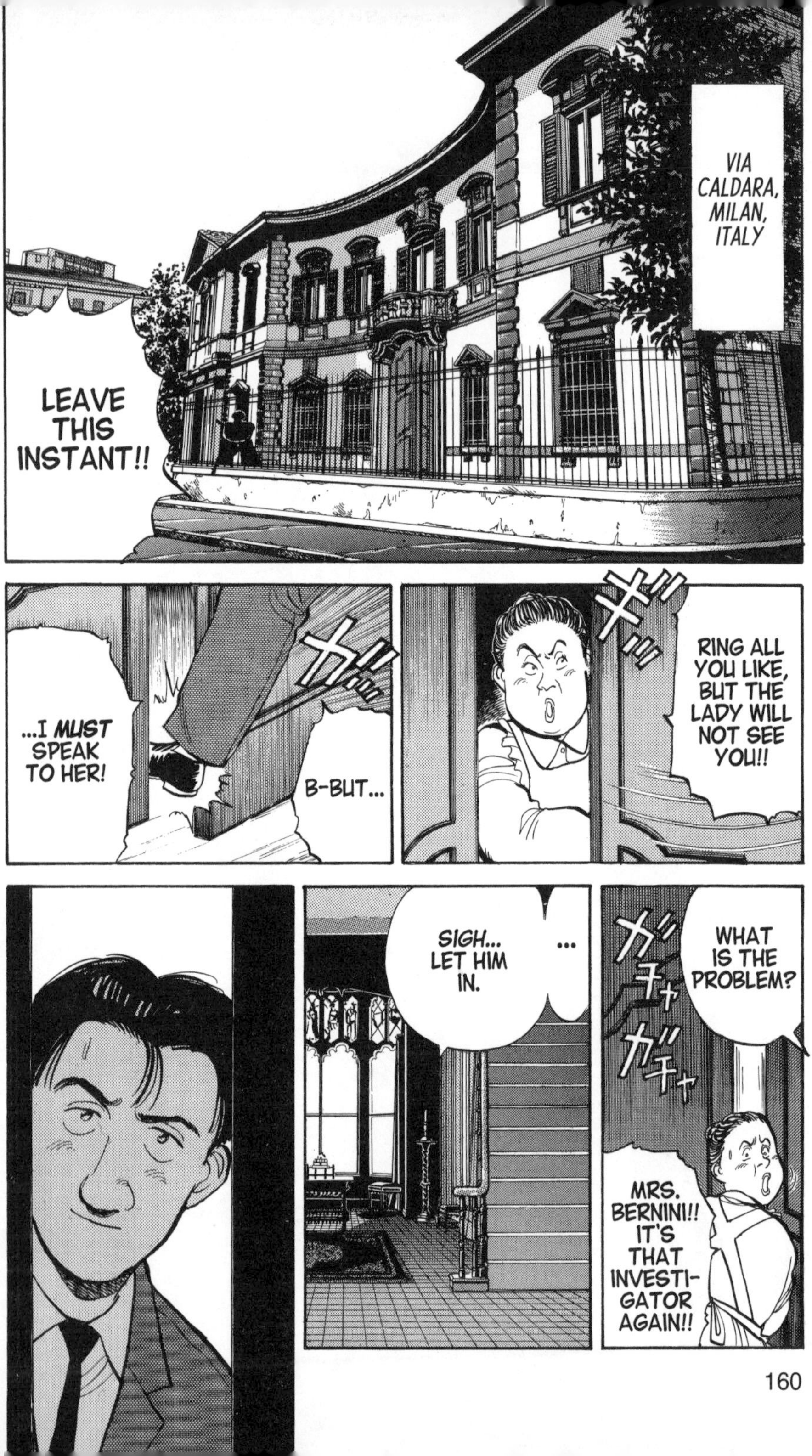
VIA CALDARA, MILAN, ITALY
LEAVE THIS INSTANT!!
RING ALL YOU LIKE, BUT THE LADY WILL NOT SEE YOU!!
...I MUST SPEAK TO HER!
B-BUT...
WHAT IS THE PROBLEM?
MRS. BERNINI!! IT'S THAT INVESTIGATOR AGAIN!!
...
SIGH... LET HIM IN.

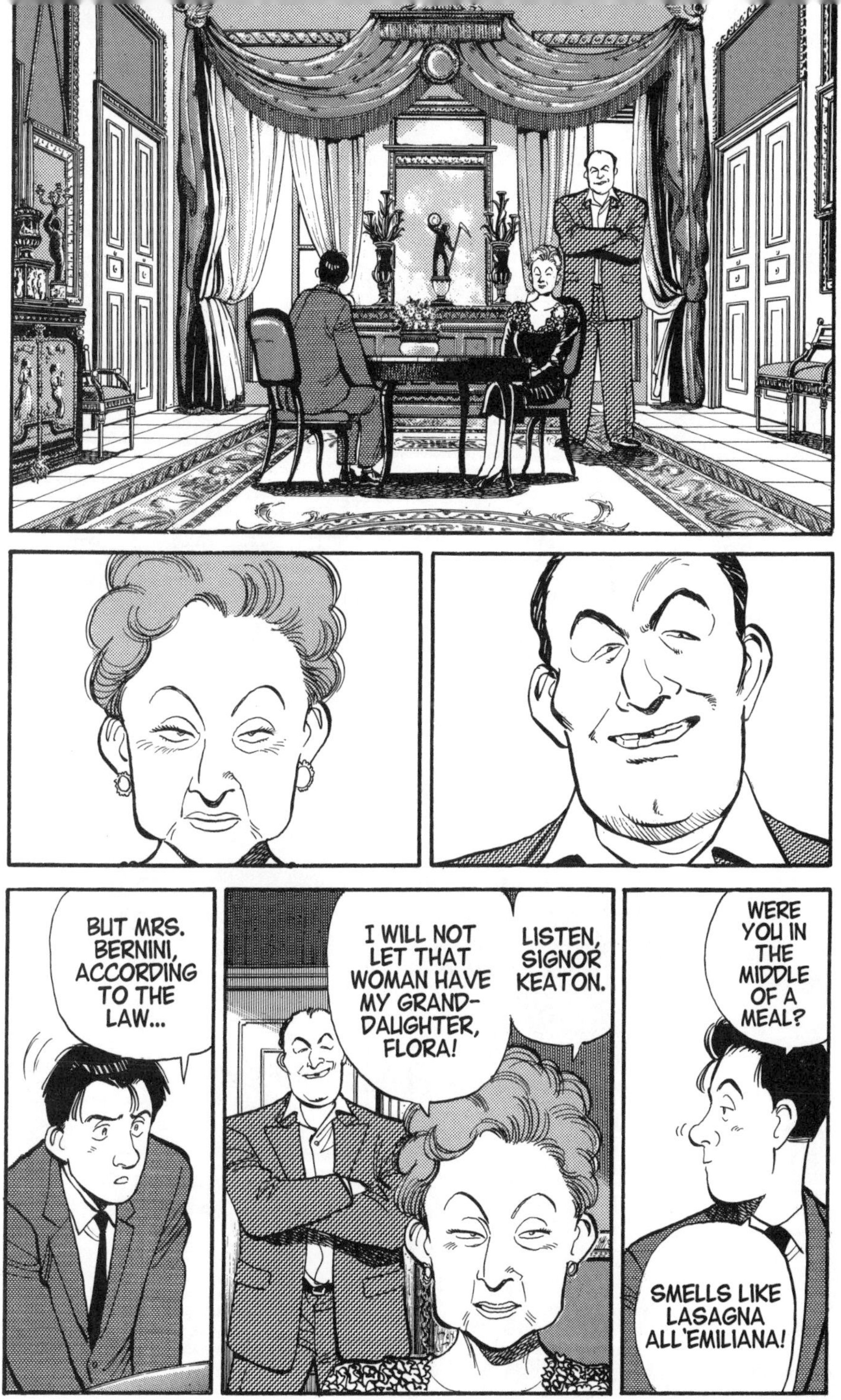
WERE YOU IN THE MIDDLE OF A MEAL?
SMELLS LIKE LASAGNA ALL'EMILIANA!
LISTEN, SIGNOR KEATON.
I WILL NOT LET THAT WOMAN HAVE MY GRAND-DAUGHTER, FLORA!
BUT MRS. BERNINI, ACCORDING TO THE LAW...

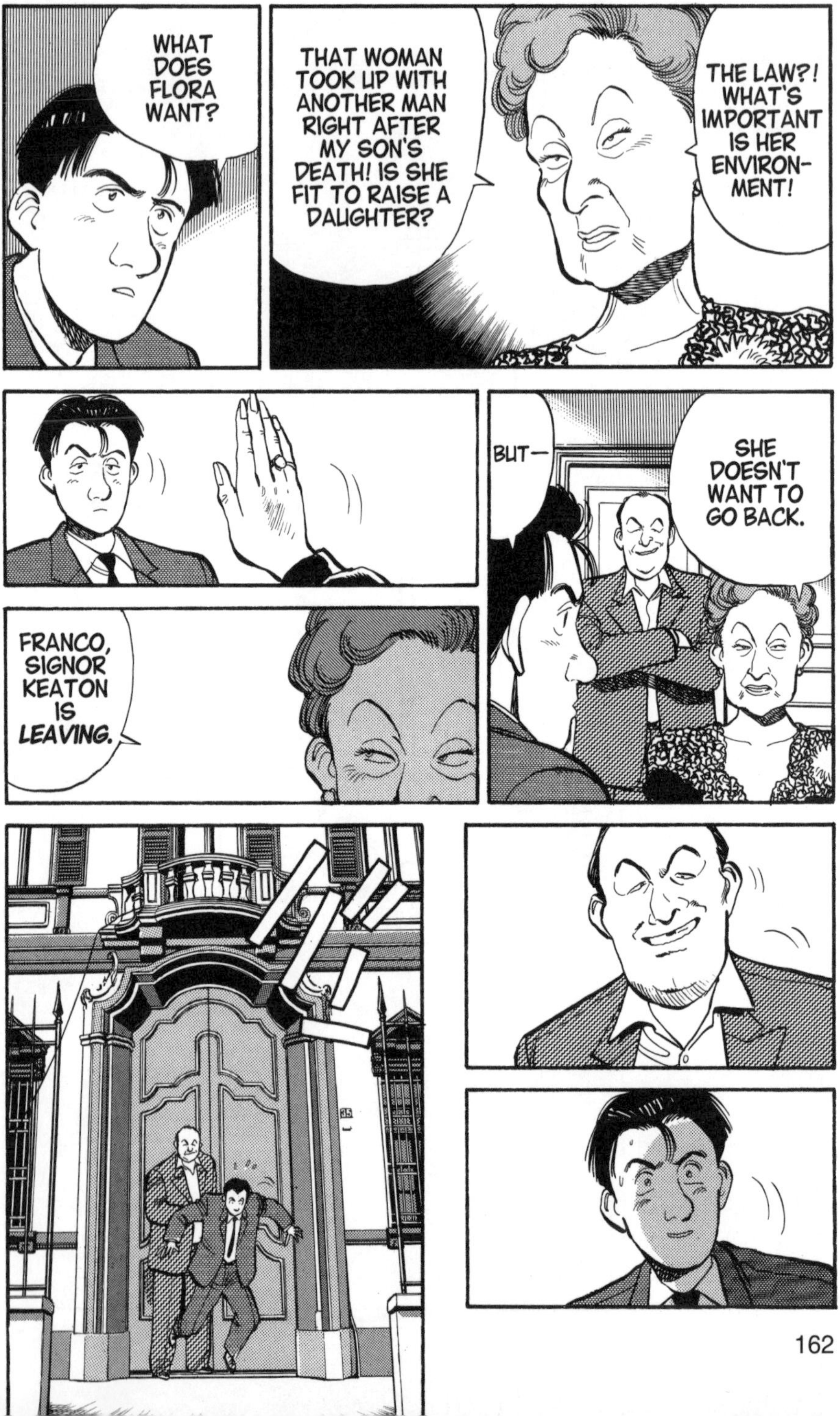
THE LAW?! WHAT'S IMPORTANT IS HER ENVIRONMENT!
THAT WOMAN TOOK UP WITH ANOTHER MAN RIGHT AFTER MY SON'S DEATH! IS SHE FIT TO RAISE A DAUGHTER?
WHAT DOES FLORA WANT?
SHE DOESN'T WANT TO GO BACK.
BUT—
FRANCO, SIGNOR KEATON IS *LEAVING.*

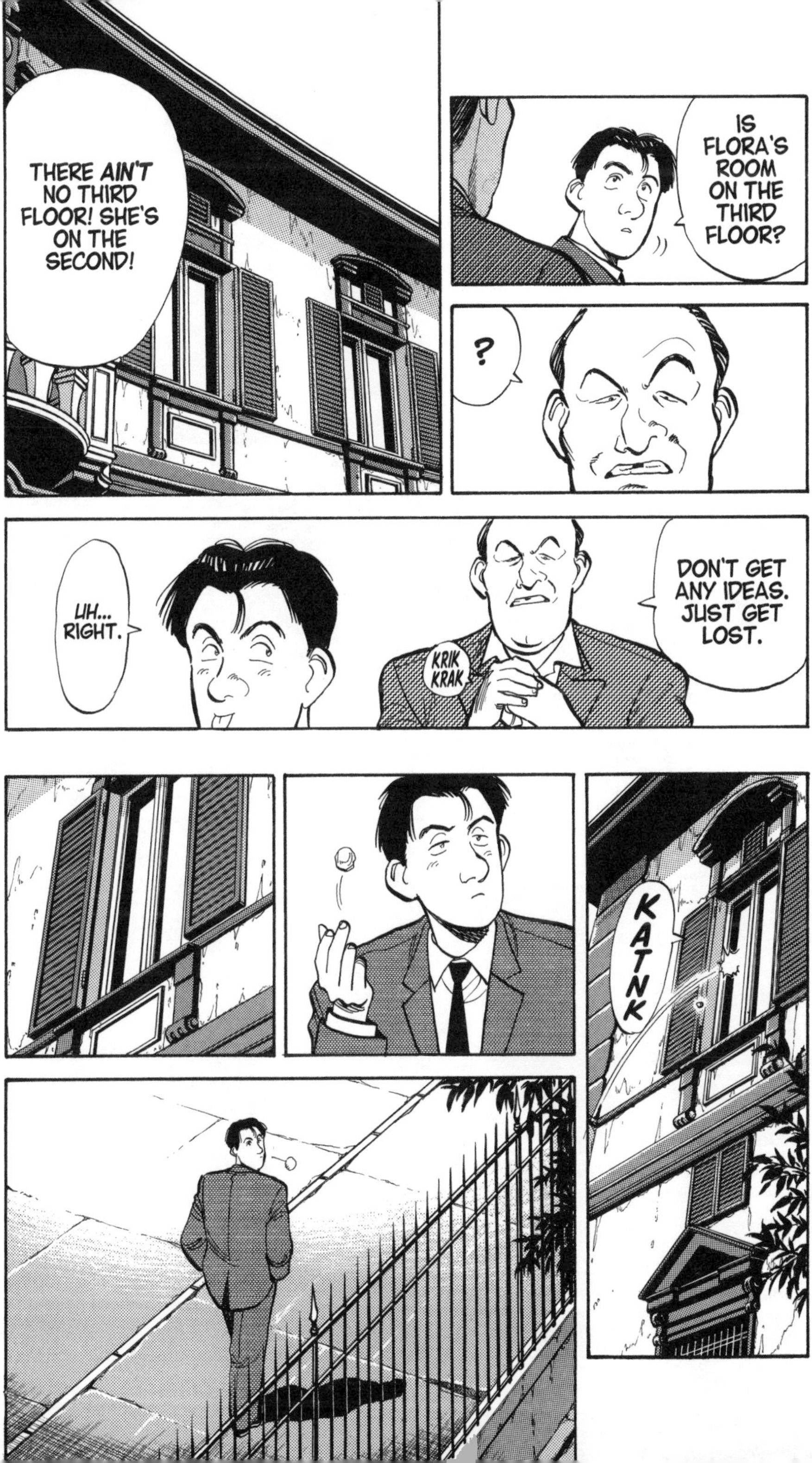
IS FLORA'S ROOM ON THE THIRD FLOOR?
?
THERE AIN'T NO THIRD FLOOR! SHE'S ON THE SECOND!
DON'T GET ANY IDEAS. JUST GET LOST.
KRIK KRAK
UH... RIGHT.
KATNK

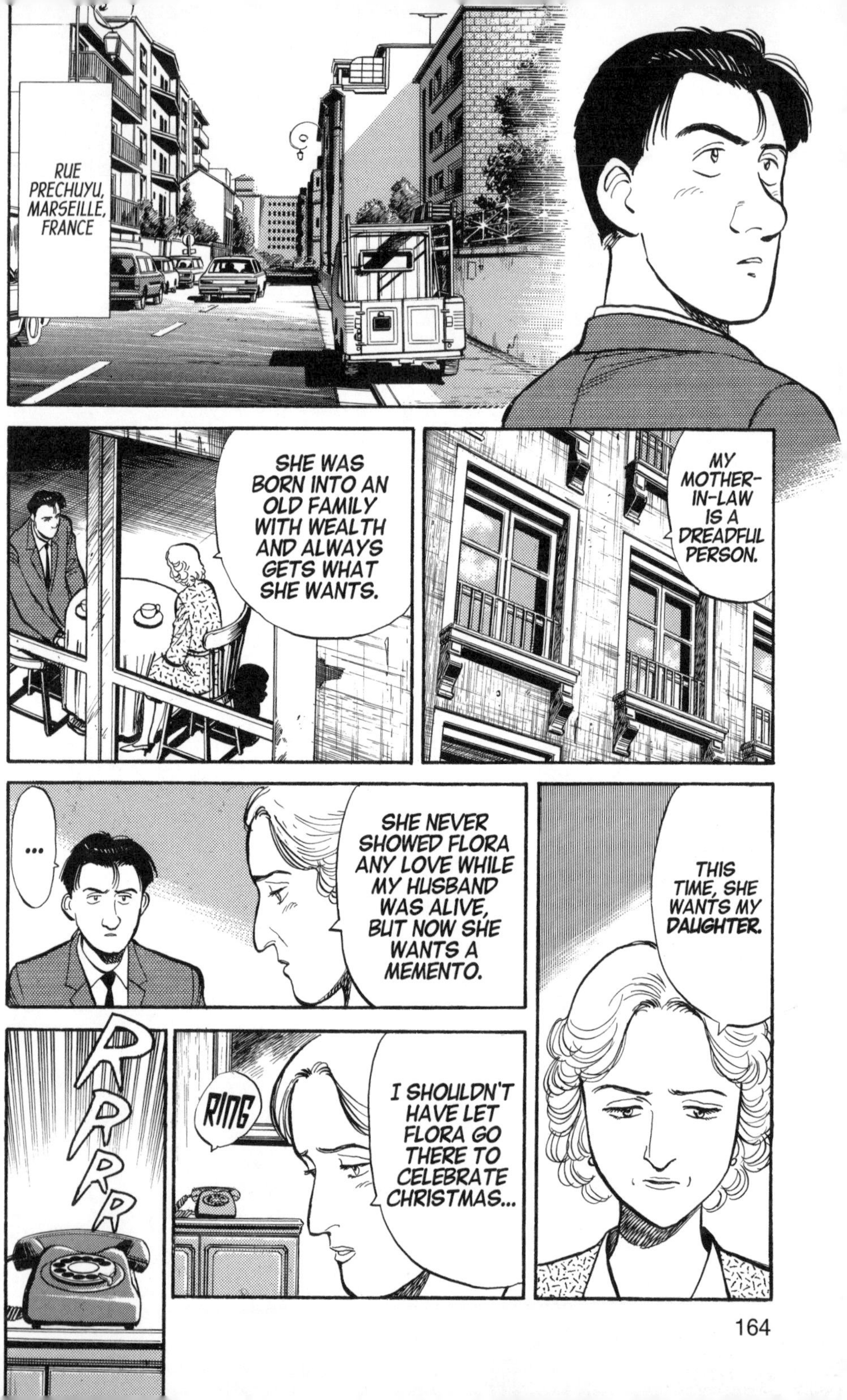
RUE PRECHUYU, MARSEILLE, FRANCE
MY MOTHER-IN-LAW IS A DREADFUL PERSON.
SHE WAS BORN INTO AN OLD FAMILY WITH WEALTH AND ALWAYS GETS WHAT SHE WANTS.
THIS TIME, SHE WANTS MY DAUGHTER.
SHE NEVER SHOWED FLORA ANY LOVE WHILE MY HUSBAND WAS ALIVE, BUT NOW SHE WANTS A MEMENTO.
...
I SHOULDN'T HAVE LET FLORA GO THERE TO CELEBRATE CHRISTMAS...
RING
RRRRR

Y-YES. BUT ALAN, YOU AND I...

...

HELLO?

...

I'M SORRY...

KCHAK

!!

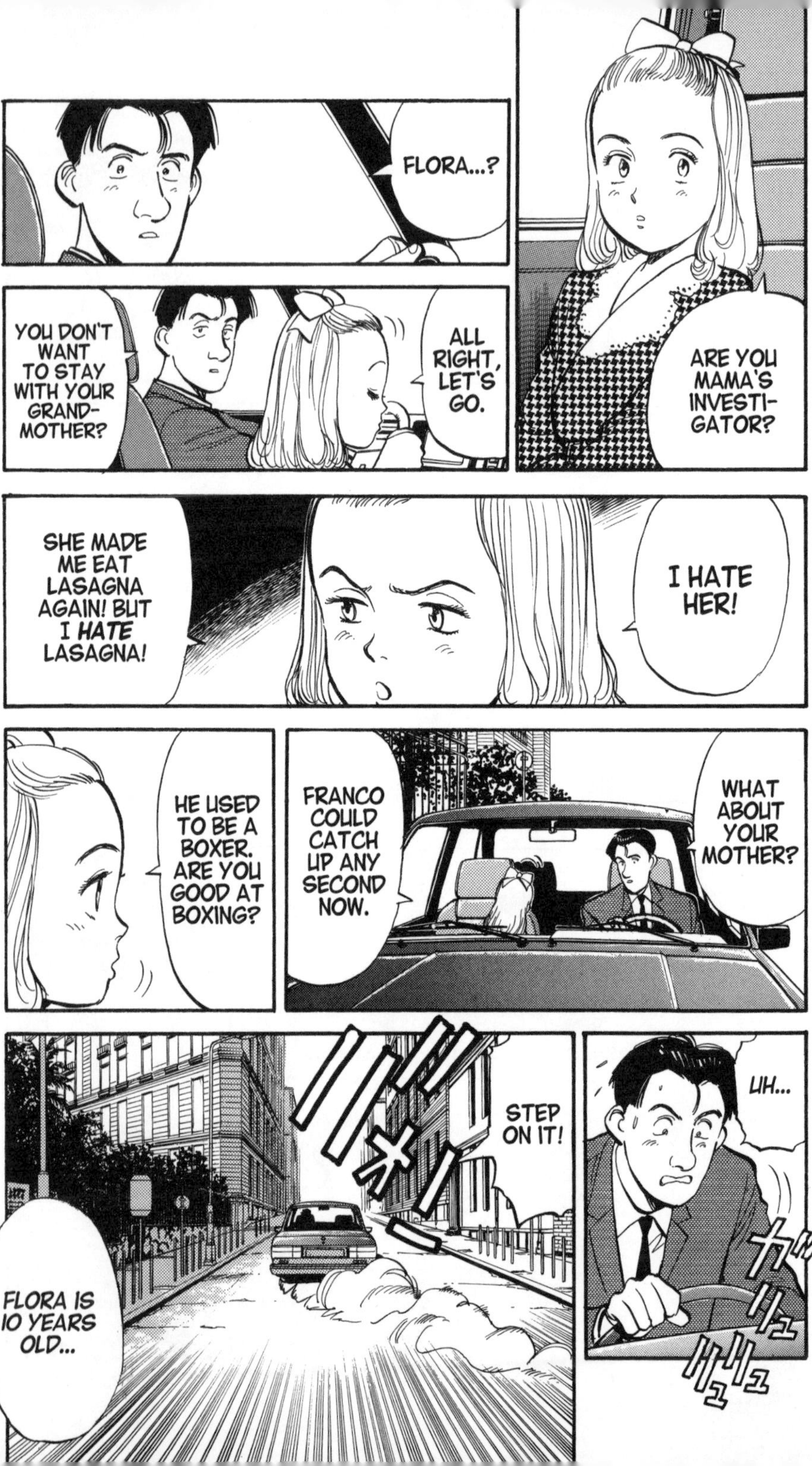
ARE YOU MAMA'S INVESTI-GATOR?
FLORA...?
ALL RIGHT, LET'S GO.
YOU DON'T WANT TO STAY WITH YOUR GRAND-MOTHER?
I HATE HER!
SHE MADE ME EAT LASAGNA AGAIN! BUT I *HATE* LASAGNA!
WHAT ABOUT YOUR MOTHER?
FRANCO COULD CATCH UP ANY SECOND NOW.
HE USED TO BE A BOXER. ARE YOU GOOD AT BOXING?
UH...
STEP ON IT!
FLORA IS 10 YEARS OLD...

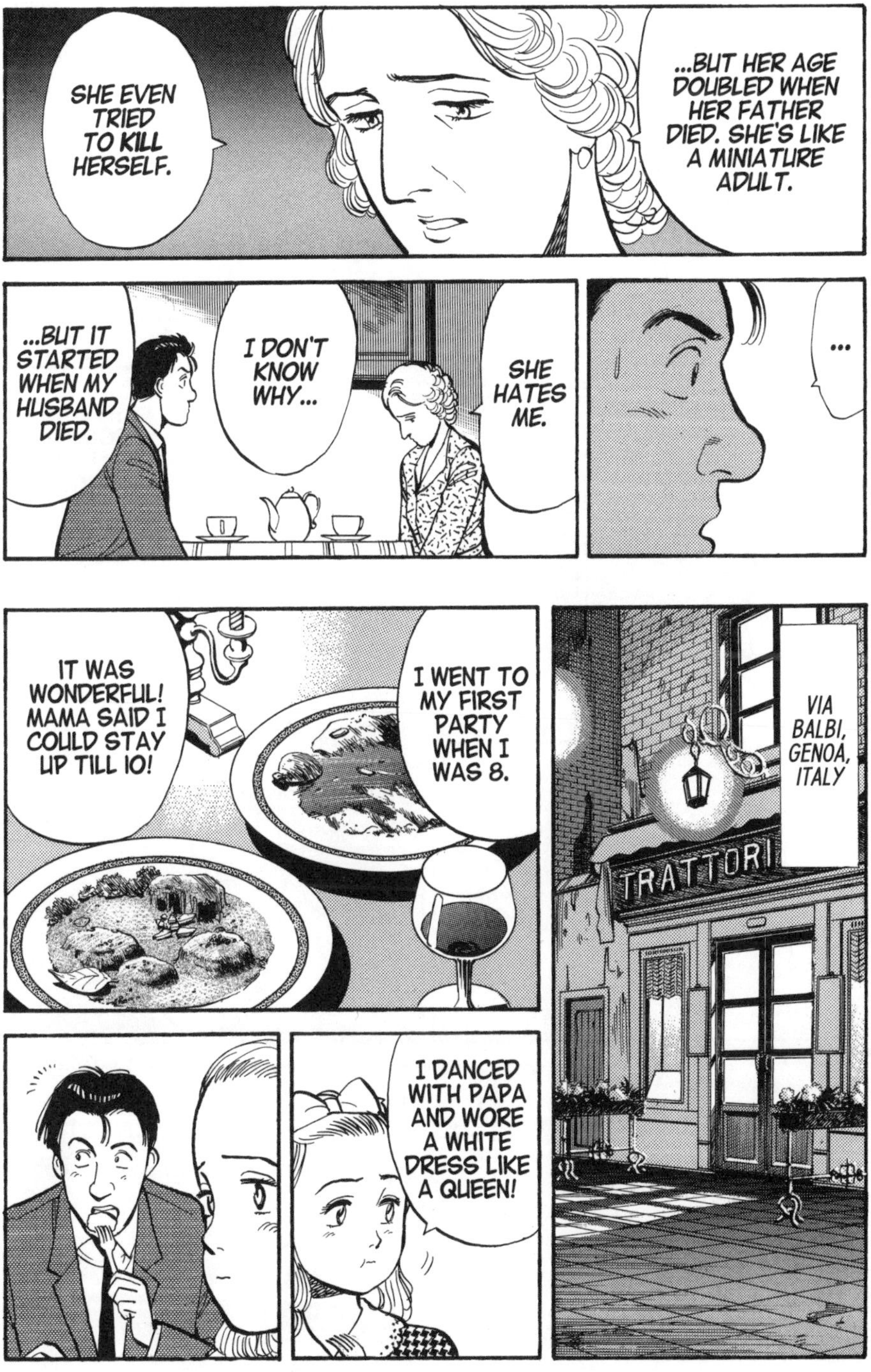
...BUT HER AGE DOUBLED WHEN HER FATHER DIED. SHE'S LIKE A MINIATURE ADULT.
SHE EVEN TRIED TO KILL HERSELF.
...
SHE HATES ME.
I DON'T KNOW WHY...
...BUT IT STARTED WHEN MY HUSBAND DIED.
VIA BALBI, GENOA, ITALY
TRATTORI
I WENT TO MY FIRST PARTY WHEN I WAS 8.
IT WAS WONDERFUL! MAMA SAID I COULD STAY UP TILL 10!
I DANCED WITH PAPA AND WORE A WHITE DRESS LIKE A QUEEN!

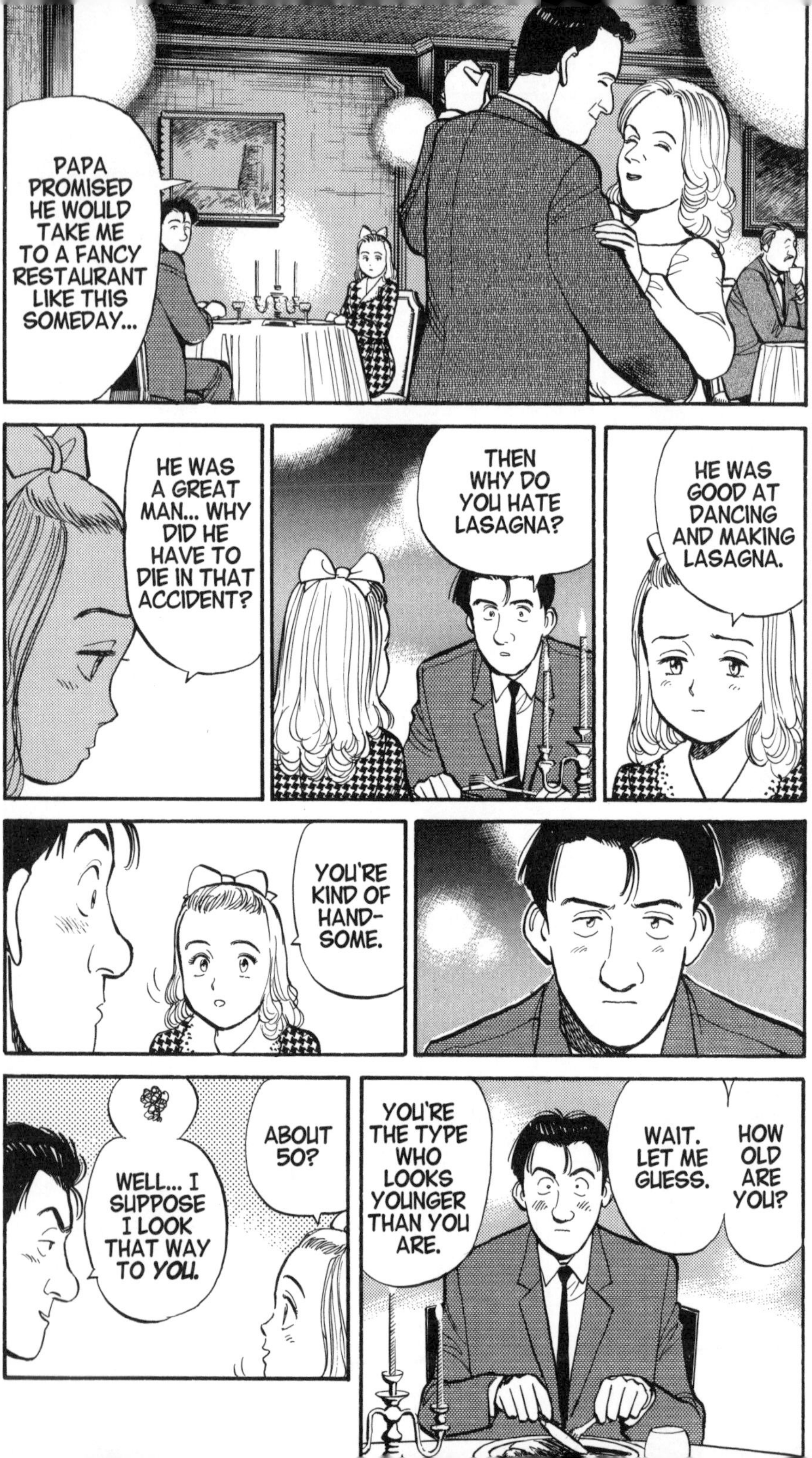
PAPA PROMISED HE WOULD TAKE ME TO A FANCY RESTAURANT LIKE THIS SOMEDAY...
HE WAS GOOD AT DANCING AND MAKING LASAGNA.
THEN WHY DO YOU HATE LASAGNA?
HE WAS A GREAT MAN... WHY DID HE HAVE TO DIE IN THAT ACCIDENT?
YOU'RE KIND OF HANDSOME.
HOW OLD ARE YOU?
WAIT. LET ME GUESS.
YOU'RE THE TYPE WHO LOOKS YOUNGER THAN YOU ARE.
ABOUT 50?
WELL... I SUPPOSE I LOOK THAT WAY TO YOU.

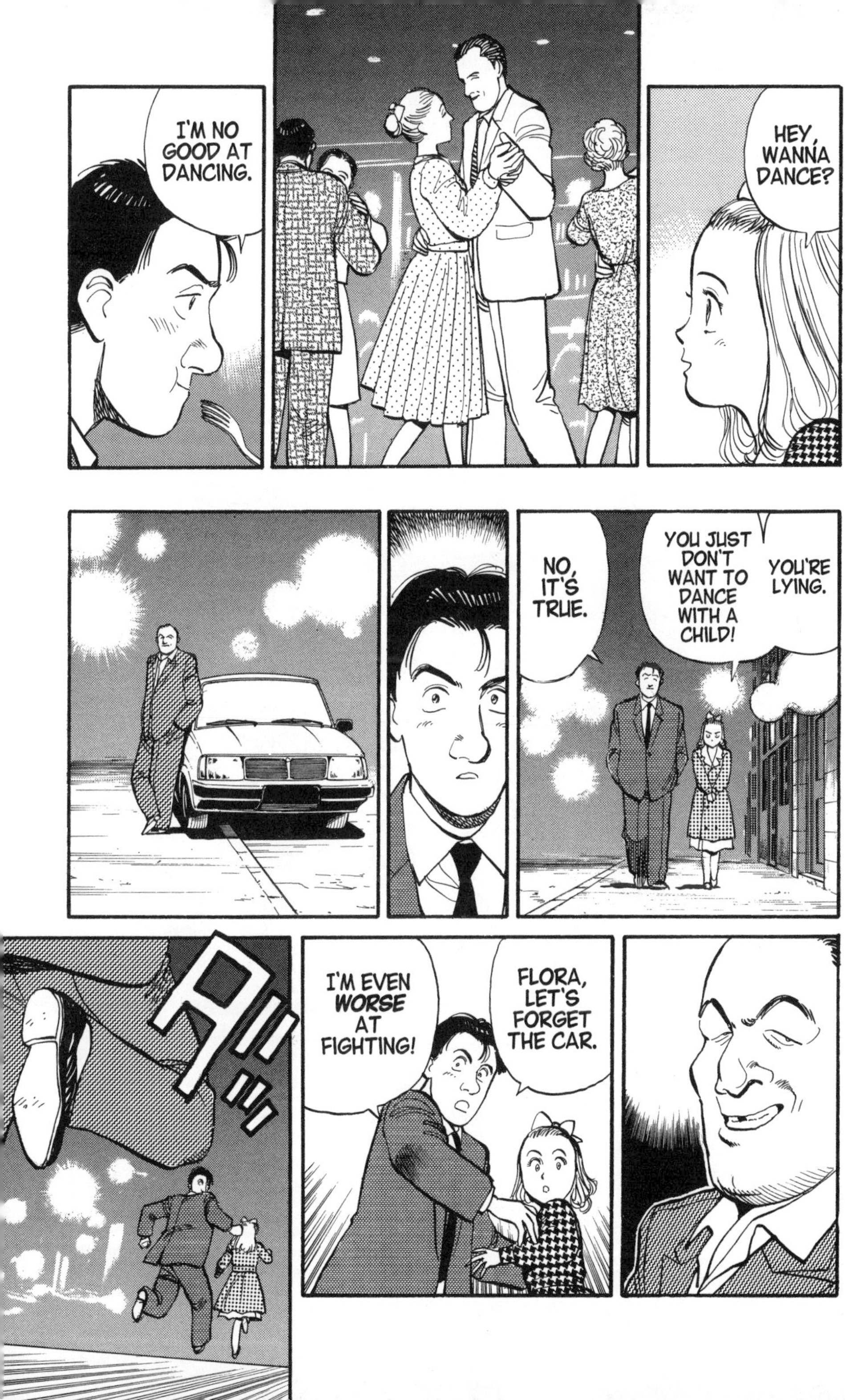
HEY, WANNA DANCE?
I'M NO GOOD AT DANCING.
YOU'RE LYING.
YOU JUST DON'T WANT TO DANCE WITH A CHILD!
NO, IT'S TRUE.
FLORA, LET'S FORGET THE CAR.
I'M EVEN **WORSE** AT FIGHTING!
ダッ

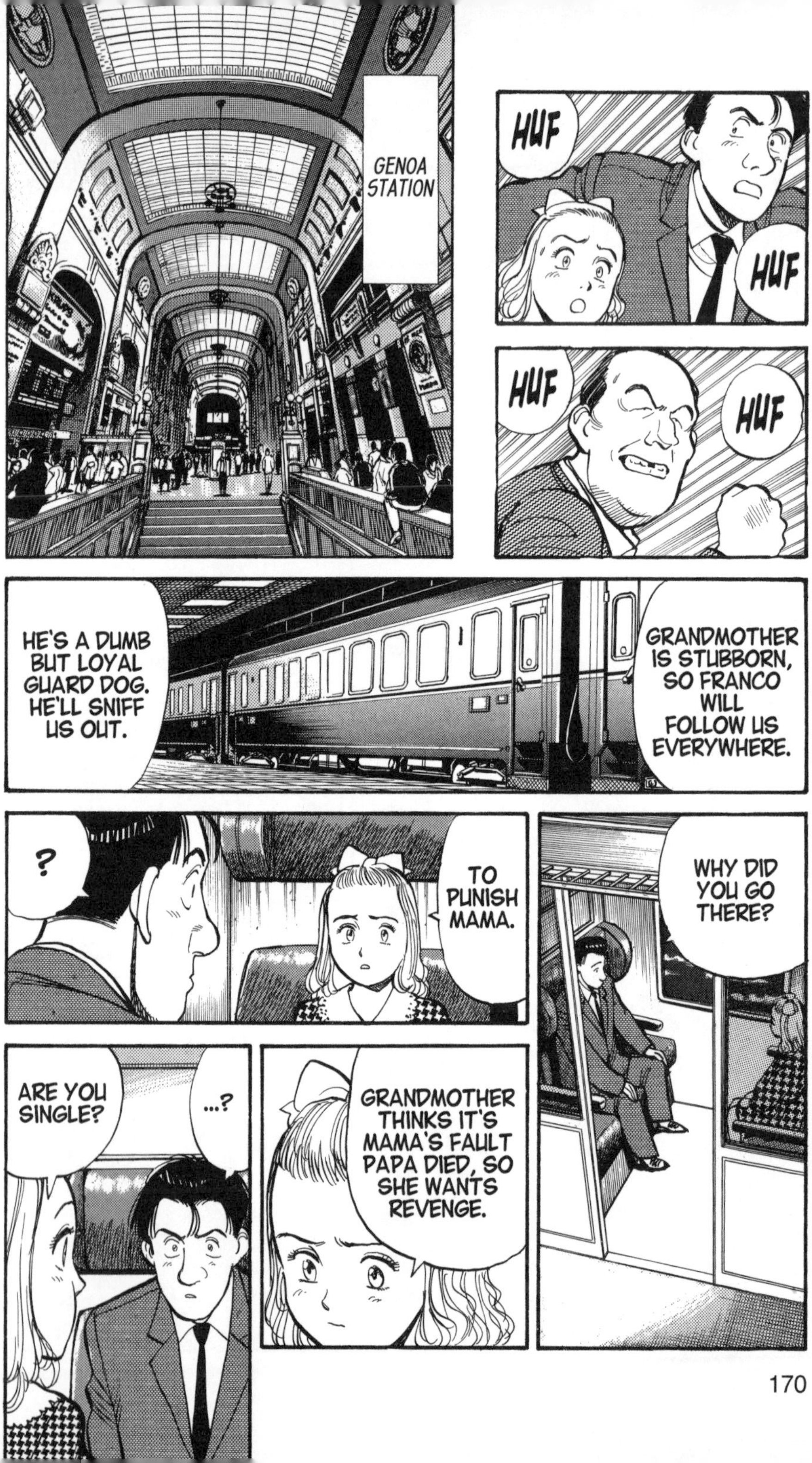
HUF
HUF
HUF
HUF
GENOA STATION
GRANDMOTHER IS STUBBORN, SO FRANCO WILL FOLLOW US EVERYWHERE.
HE'S A DUMB BUT LOYAL GUARD DOG. HE'LL SNIFF US OUT.
WHY DID YOU GO THERE?
TO PUNISH MAMA.
?
GRANDMOTHER THINKS IT'S MAMA'S FAULT PAPA DIED, SO SHE WANTS REVENGE.
...?
ARE YOU SINGLE?

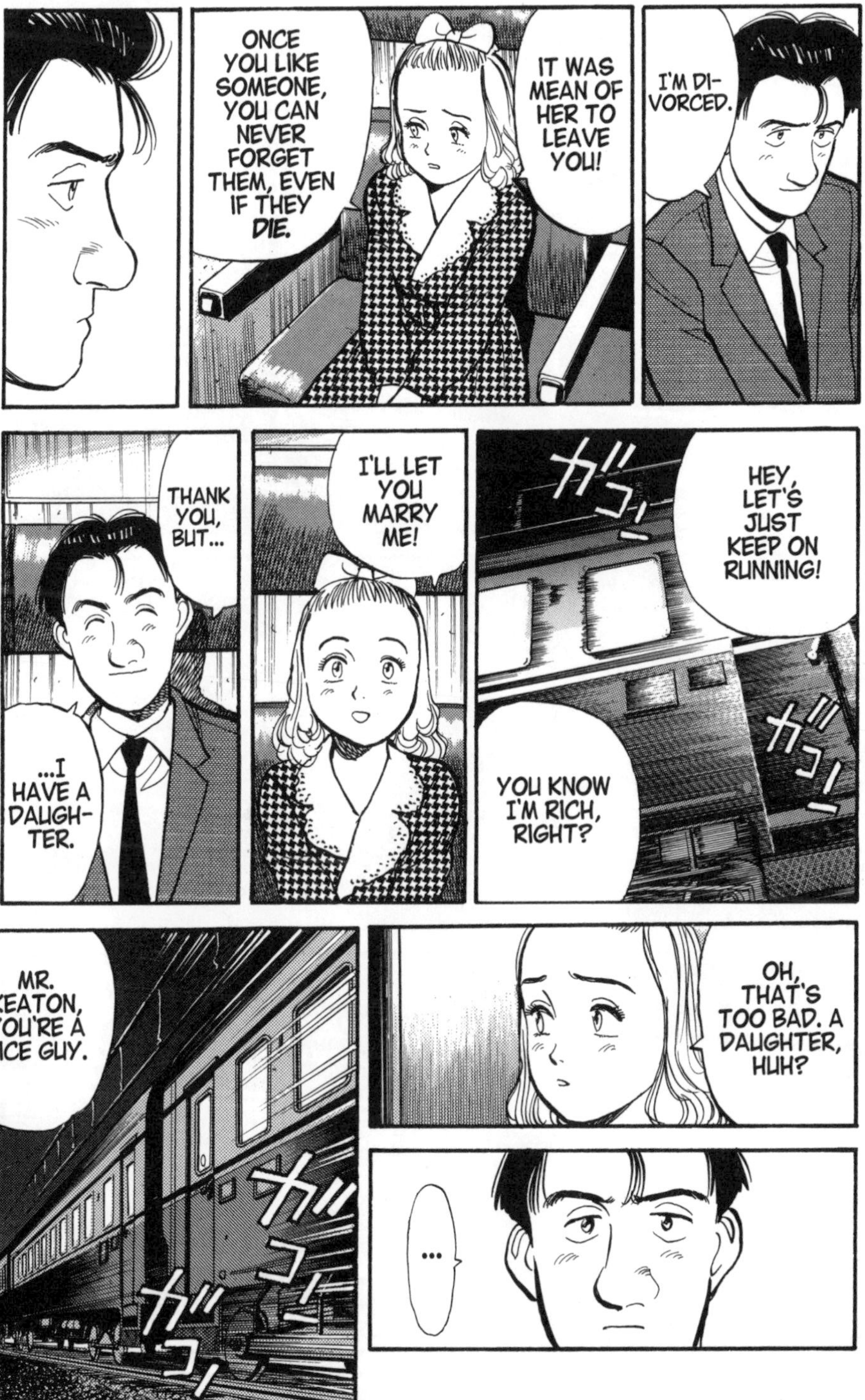
I'M DI-VORCED.
IT WAS MEAN OF HER TO LEAVE YOU!
ONCE YOU LIKE SOMEONE, YOU CAN NEVER FORGET THEM, EVEN IF THEY DIE.
HEY, LET'S JUST KEEP ON RUNNING!
YOU KNOW I'M RICH, RIGHT?
I'LL LET YOU MARRY ME!
THANK YOU, BUT...
...I HAVE A DAUGHTER.
OH, THAT'S TOO BAD. A DAUGHTER, HUH?
...
MR. KEATON, YOU'RE A NICE GUY.

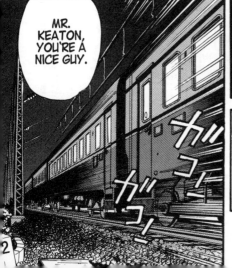

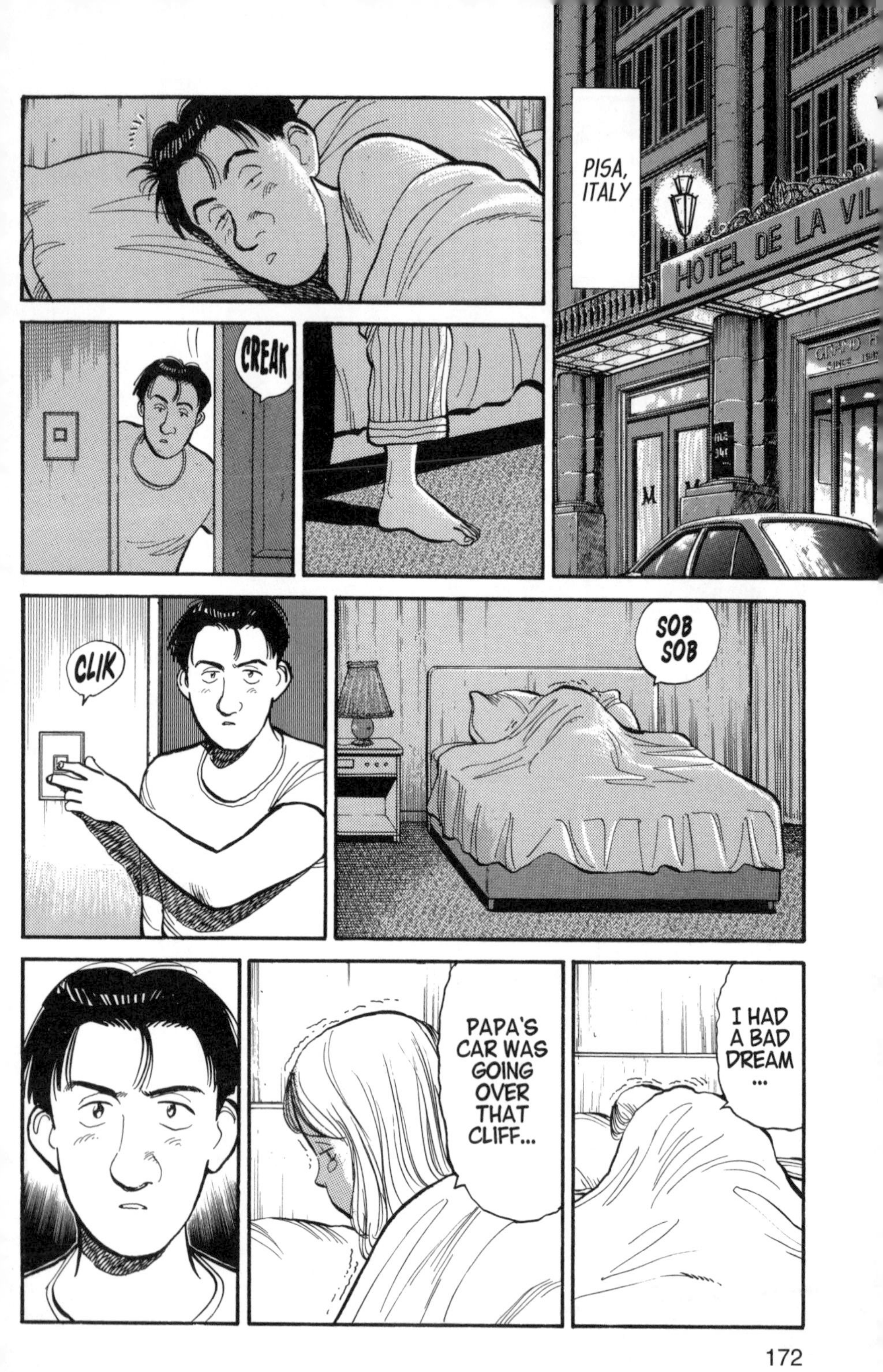
PISA, ITALY
CREAK
SOB SOB
CLIK
I HAD A BAD DREAM ...
PAPA'S CAR WAS GOING OVER THAT CLIFF...

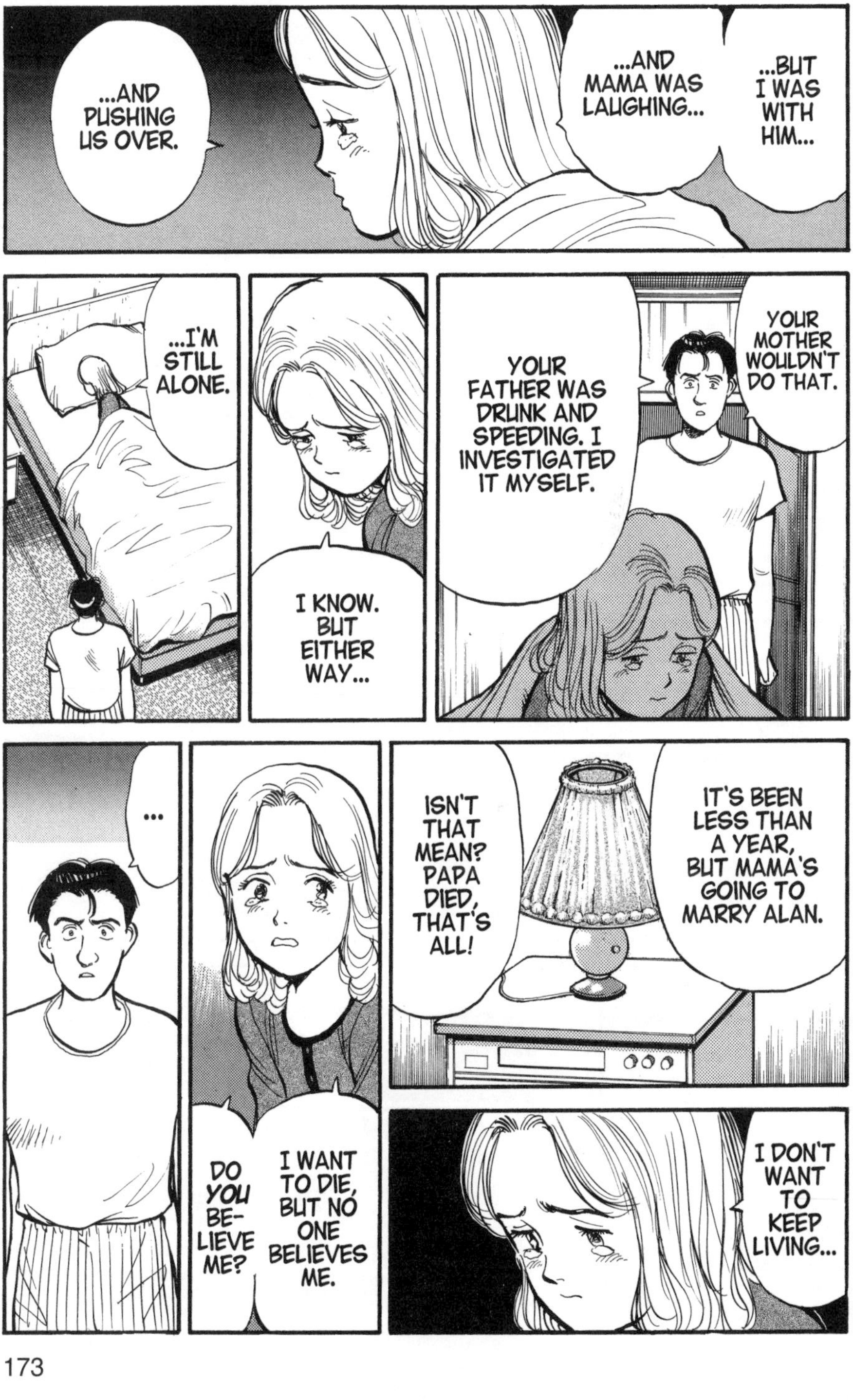
...BUT I WAS WITH HIM...
...AND MAMA WAS LAUGHING...
...AND PUSHING US OVER.
YOUR MOTHER WOULDN'T DO THAT.
YOUR FATHER WAS DRUNK AND SPEEDING. I INVESTIGATED IT MYSELF.
I KNOW. BUT EITHER WAY...
...I'M STILL ALONE.
IT'S BEEN LESS THAN A YEAR, BUT MAMA'S GOING TO MARRY ALAN.
ISN'T THAT MEAN? PAPA DIED, THAT'S ALL!
I DON'T WANT TO KEEP LIVING...
I WANT TO DIE, BUT NO ONE BELIEVES ME.
DO *YOU* BE-LIEVE ME?
...

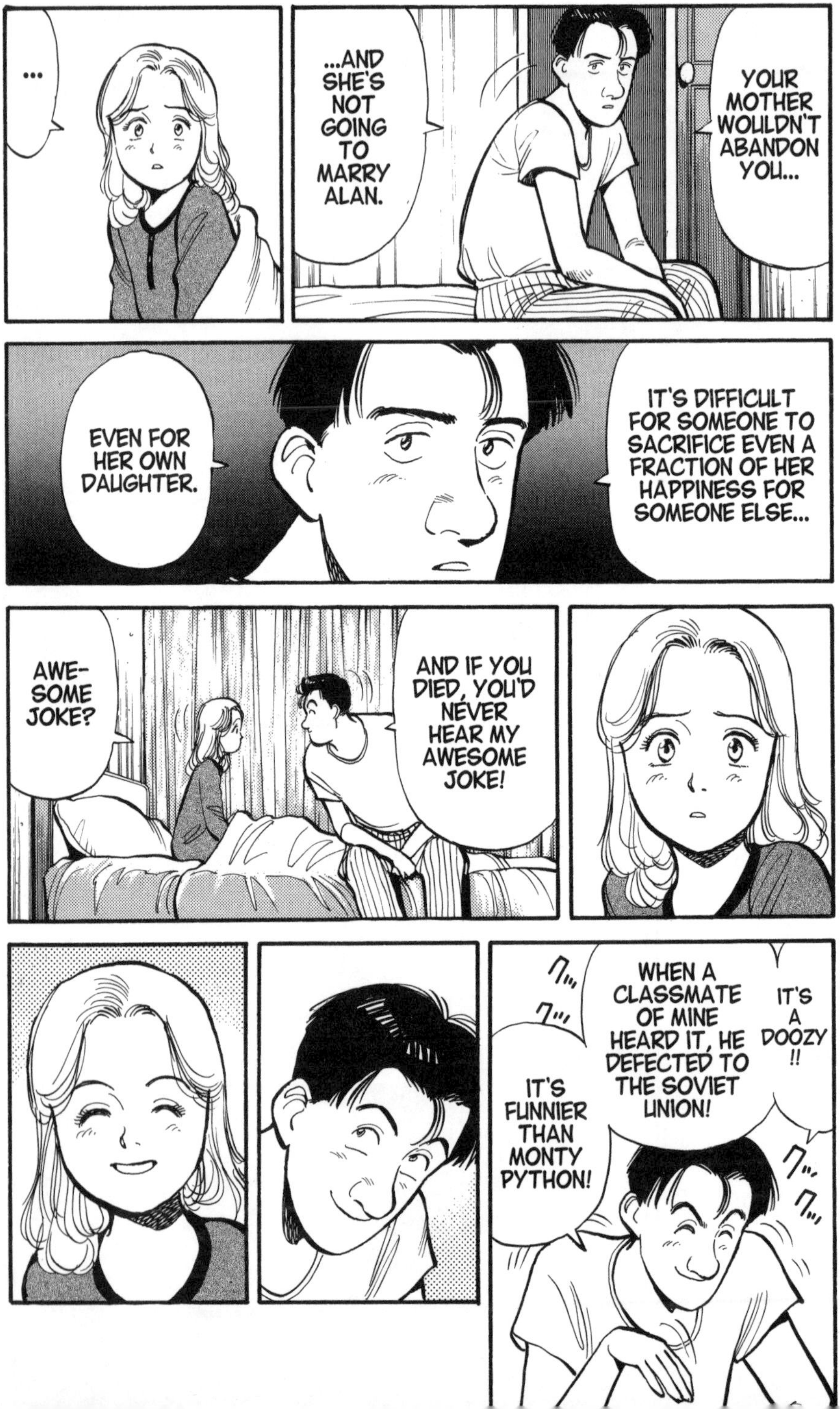
YOUR MOTHER WOULDN'T ABANDON YOU...
...AND SHE'S NOT GOING TO MARRY ALAN.
...
IT'S DIFFICULT FOR SOMEONE TO SACRIFICE EVEN A FRACTION OF HER HAPPINESS FOR SOMEONE ELSE...
EVEN FOR HER OWN DAUGHTER.
AND IF YOU DIED, YOU'D NEVER HEAR MY AWESOME JOKE!
AWE-SOME JOKE?
IT'S A DOOZY!!
WHEN A CLASSMATE OF MINE HEARD IT, HE DEFECTED TO THE SOVIET UNION!
IT'S FUNNIER THAN MONTY PYTHON!

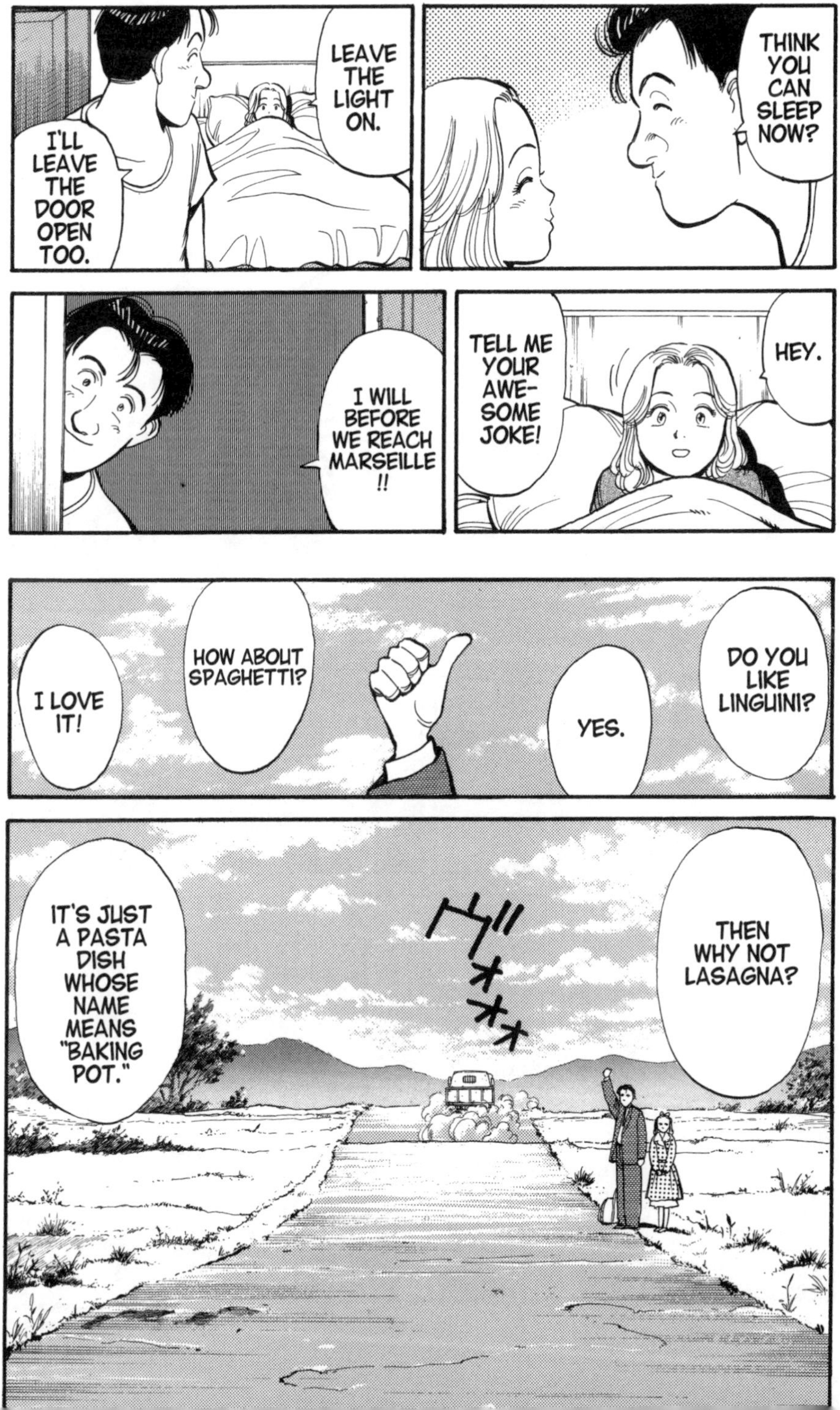
THINK YOU CAN SLEEP NOW?
LEAVE THE LIGHT ON.
I'LL LEAVE THE DOOR OPEN TOO.
HEY.
TELL ME YOUR AWE-SOME JOKE!
I WILL BEFORE WE REACH MARSEILLE!!
DO YOU LIKE LINGUINI?
YES.
HOW ABOUT SPAGHETTI?
I LOVE IT!
THEN WHY NOT LASAGNA?
ヴォォォ
IT'S JUST A PASTA DISH WHOSE NAME MEANS "BAKING POT."

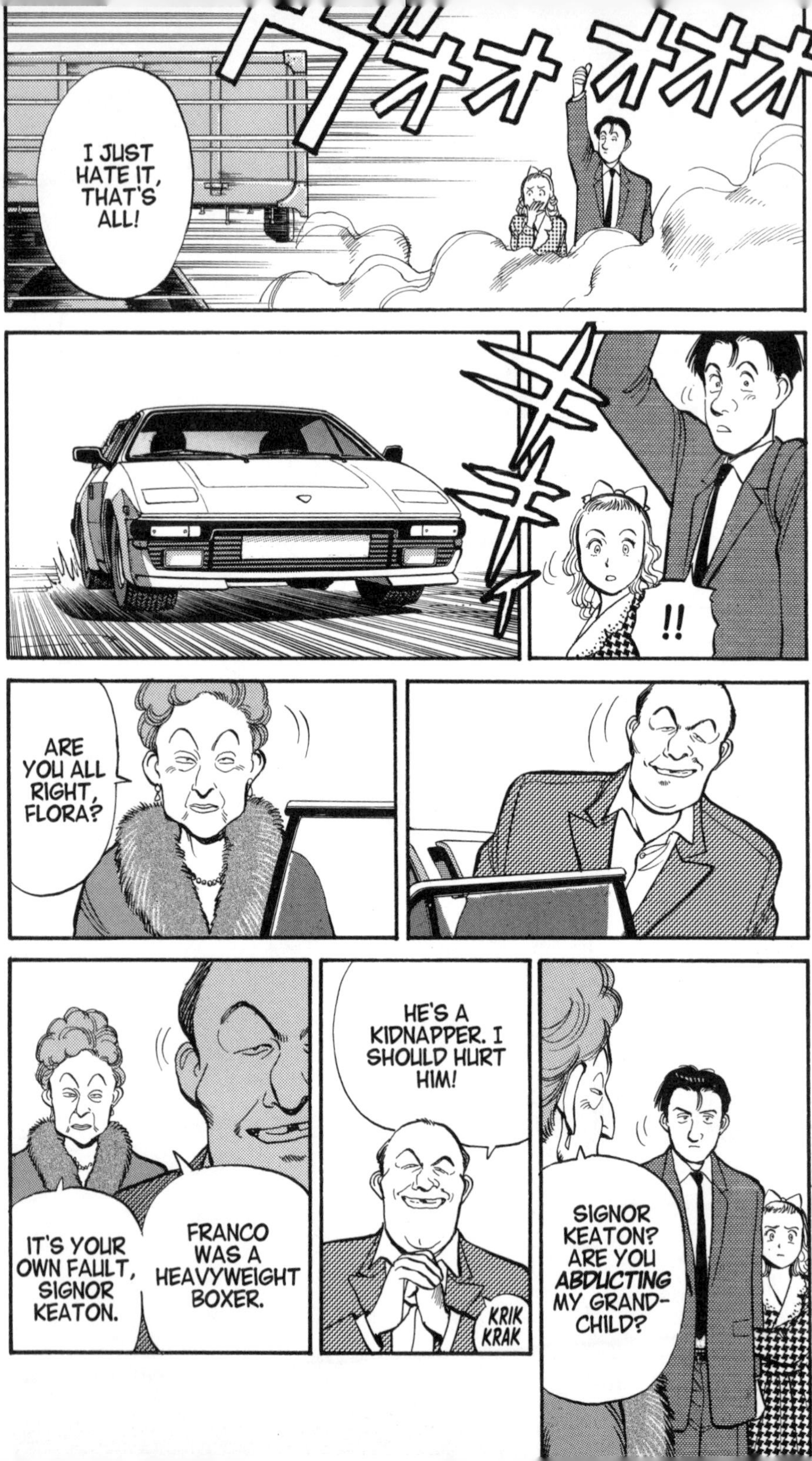
ヴオオ オオオオ
I JUST HATE IT, THAT'S ALL!
!!
キキキィ
ARE YOU ALL RIGHT, FLORA?
SIGNOR KEATON? ARE YOU ***ABDUCTING*** MY GRAND-CHILD?
HE'S A KIDNAPPER. I SHOULD HURT HIM!
KRIK KRAK
FRANCO WAS A HEAVYWEIGHT BOXER.
IT'S YOUR OWN FAULT, SIGNOR KEATON.

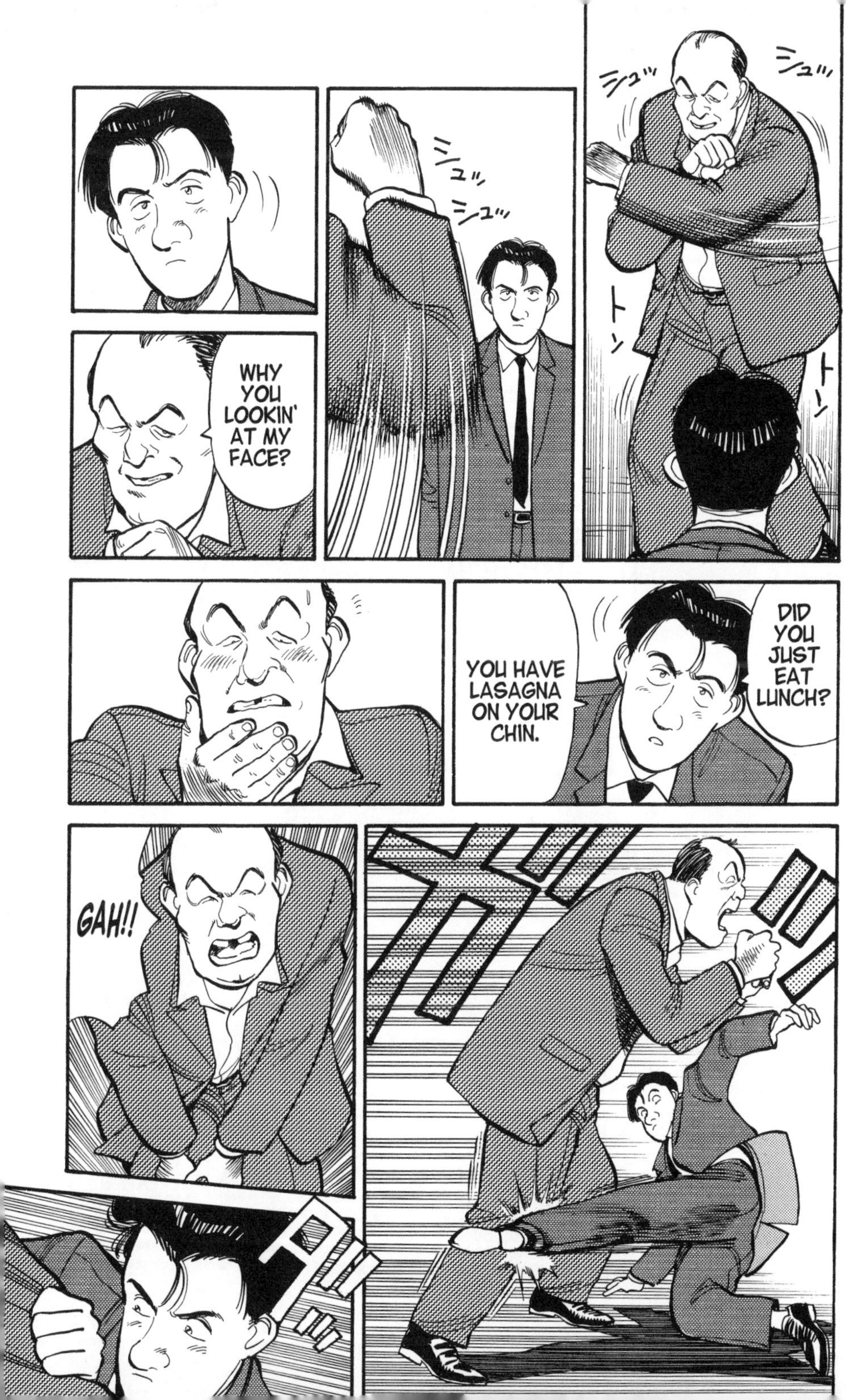
シュッ
シュッ
トン
トン
シュッ
シュッ
WHY YOU LOOKIN' AT MY FACE?
DID YOU JUST EAT LUNCH?
YOU HAVE LASAGNA ON YOUR CHIN.
GAH!!

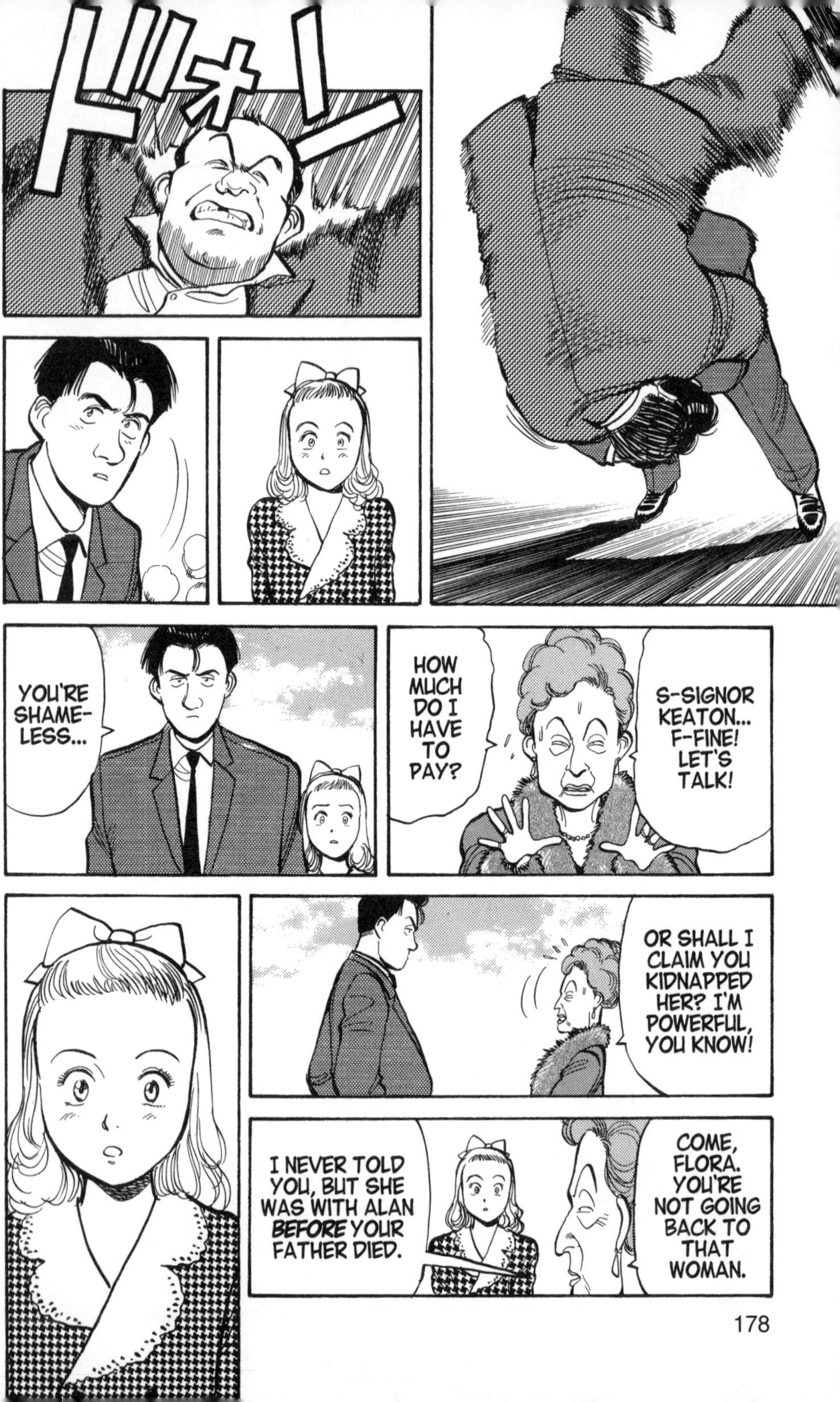
ドォーン
S-SIGNOR KEATON... F-FINE! LET'S TALK!
HOW MUCH DO I HAVE TO PAY?
YOU'RE SHAME-LESS...
OR SHALL I CLAIM YOU KIDNAPPED HER? I'M POWERFUL, YOU KNOW!
COME, FLORA. YOU'RE NOT GOING BACK TO THAT WOMAN.
I NEVER TOLD YOU, BUT SHE WAS WITH ALAN *BEFORE* YOUR FATHER DIED.

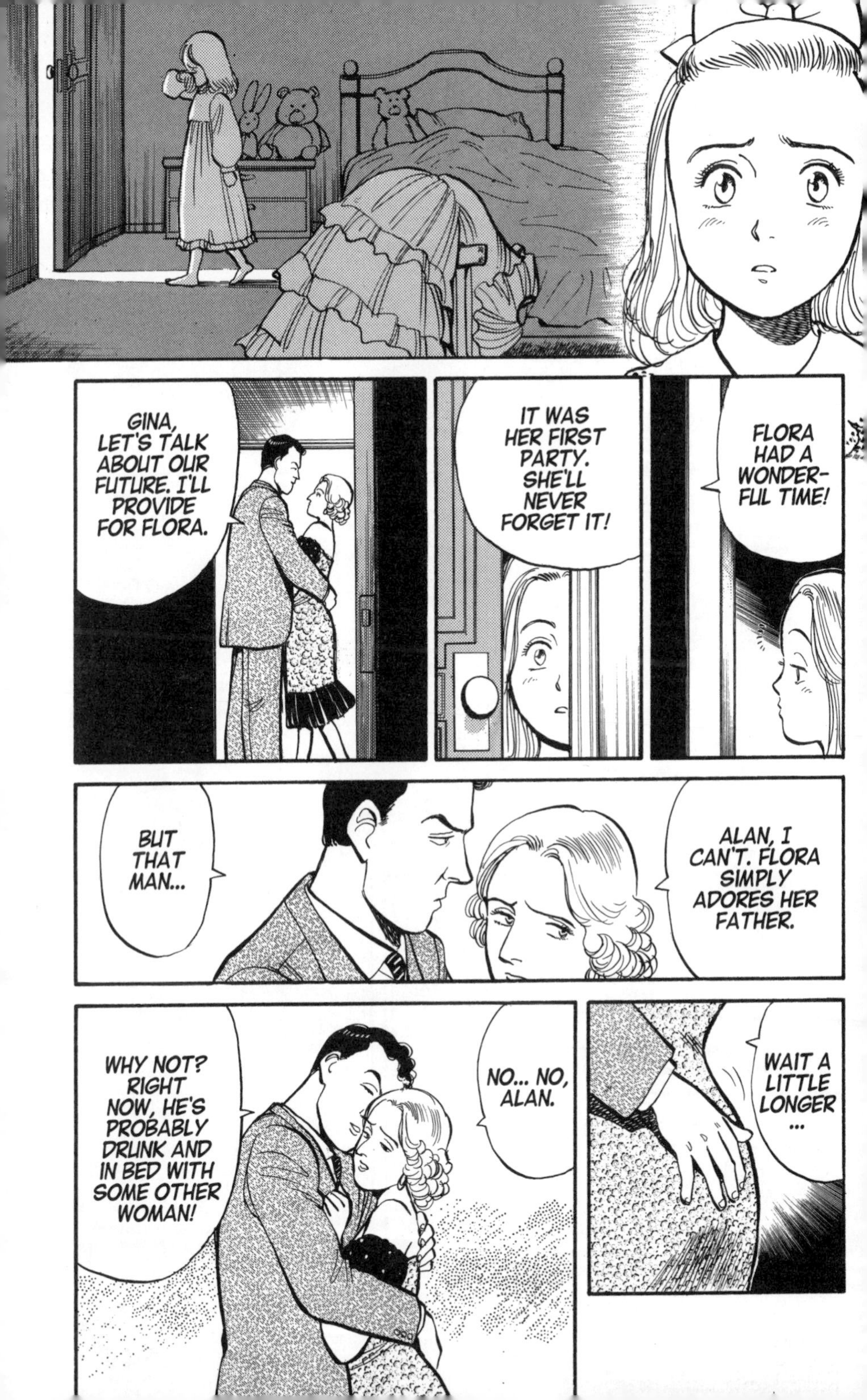
FLORA HAD A WONDERFUL TIME!
IT WAS HER FIRST PARTY. SHE'LL NEVER FORGET IT!
GINA, LET'S TALK ABOUT OUR FUTURE. I'LL PROVIDE FOR FLORA.
ALAN, I CAN'T. FLORA SIMPLY ADORES HER FATHER.
BUT THAT MAN...
WAIT A LITTLE LONGER ...
NO... NO, ALAN.
WHY NOT? RIGHT NOW, HE'S PROBABLY DRUNK AND IN BED WITH SOME OTHER WOMAN!

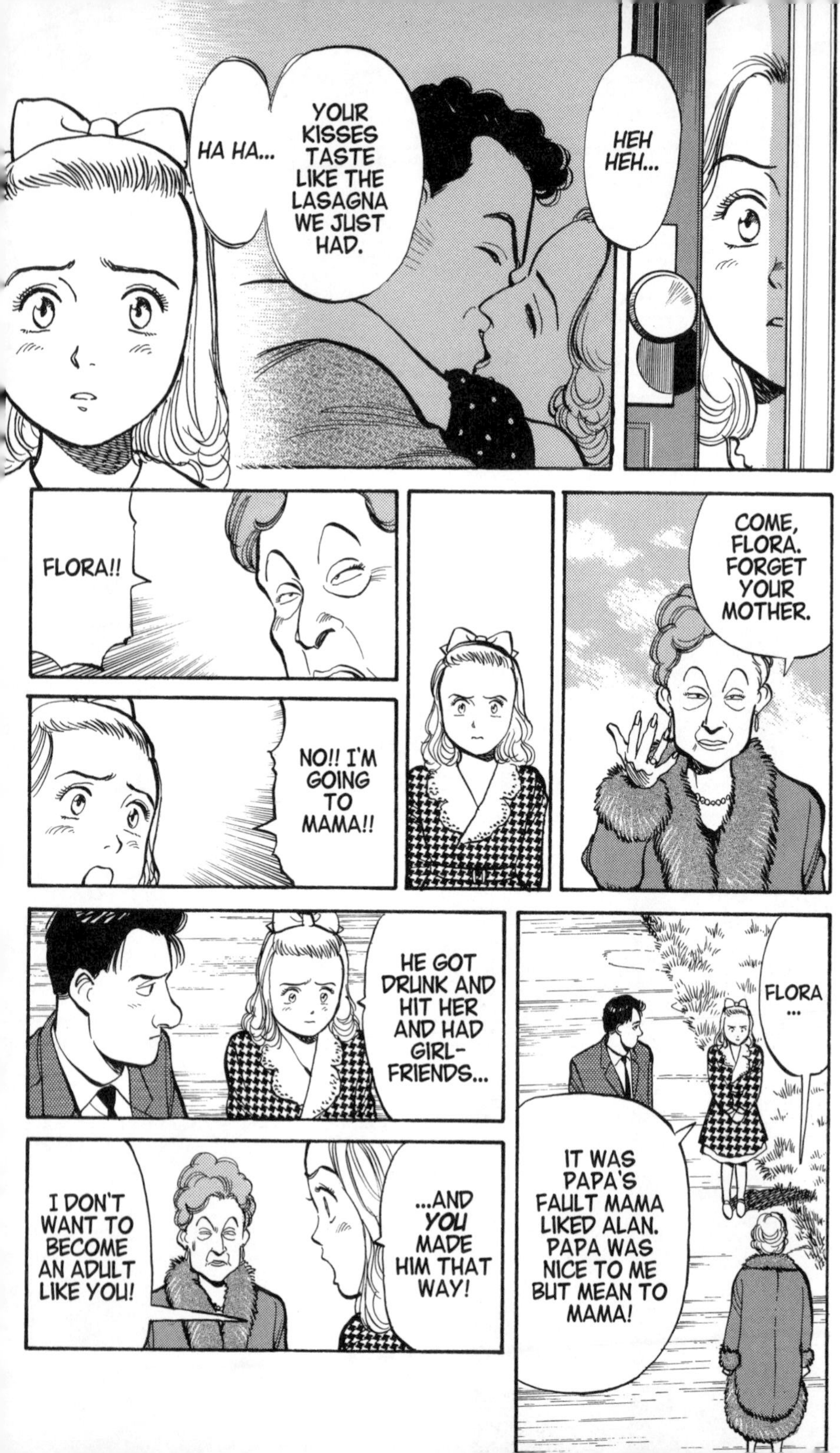
HEH HEH...
YOUR KISSES TASTE LIKE THE LASAGNA WE JUST HAD.
HA HA...
COME, FLORA. FORGET YOUR MOTHER.
FLORA!!
NO!! I'M GOING TO MAMA!!
FLORA ...
IT WAS PAPA'S FAULT MAMA LIKED ALAN. PAPA WAS NICE TO ME BUT MEAN TO MAMA!
HE GOT DRUNK AND HIT HER AND HAD GIRL-FRIENDS...
...AND *YOU* MADE HIM THAT WAY!
I DON'T WANT TO BECOME AN ADULT LIKE YOU!

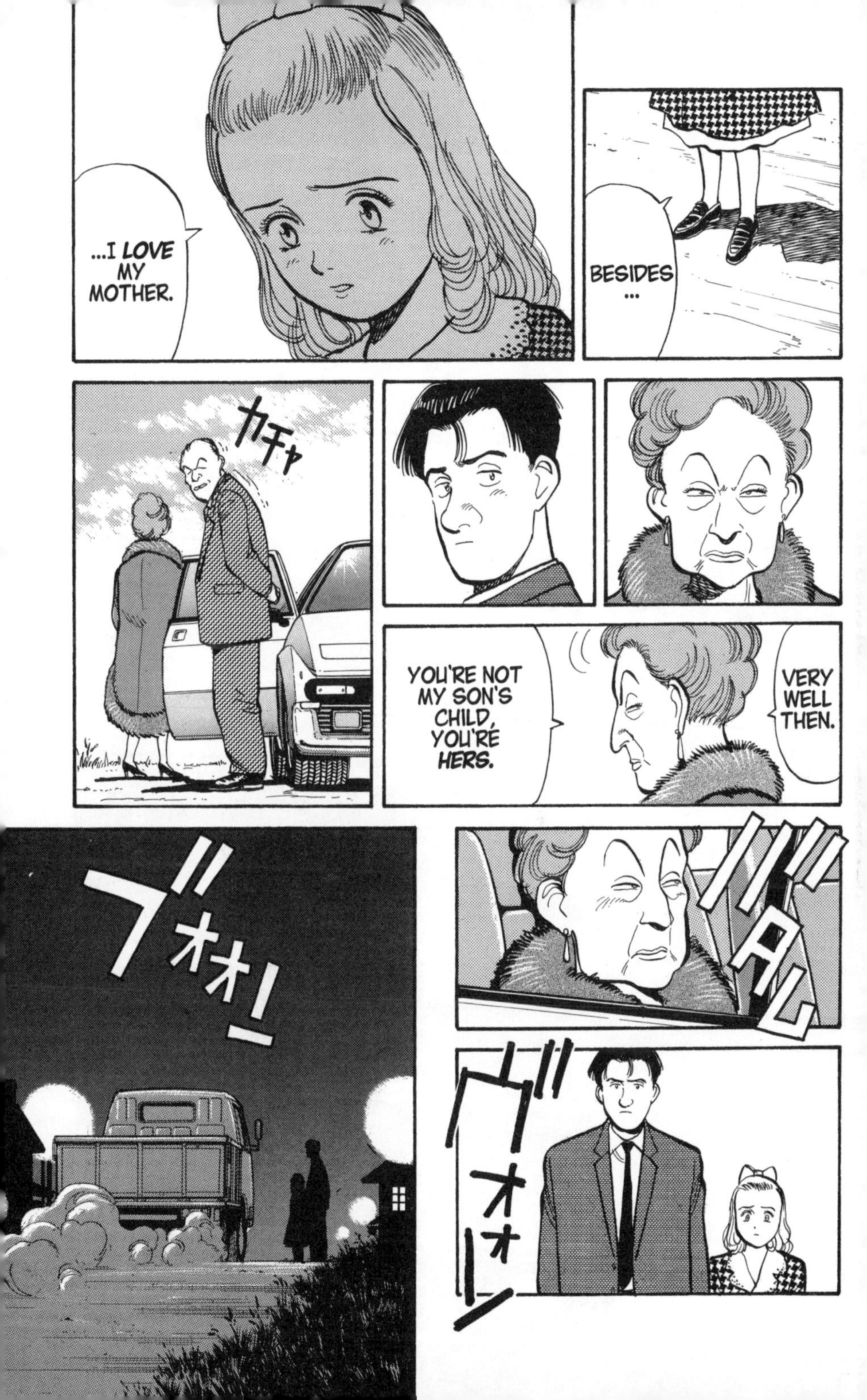
BESIDES...
...I LOVE MY MOTHER.
VERY WELL THEN.
YOU'RE NOT MY SON'S CHILD, YOU'RE HERS.
カチャ
バタム
ブォォーン
ブォォン!

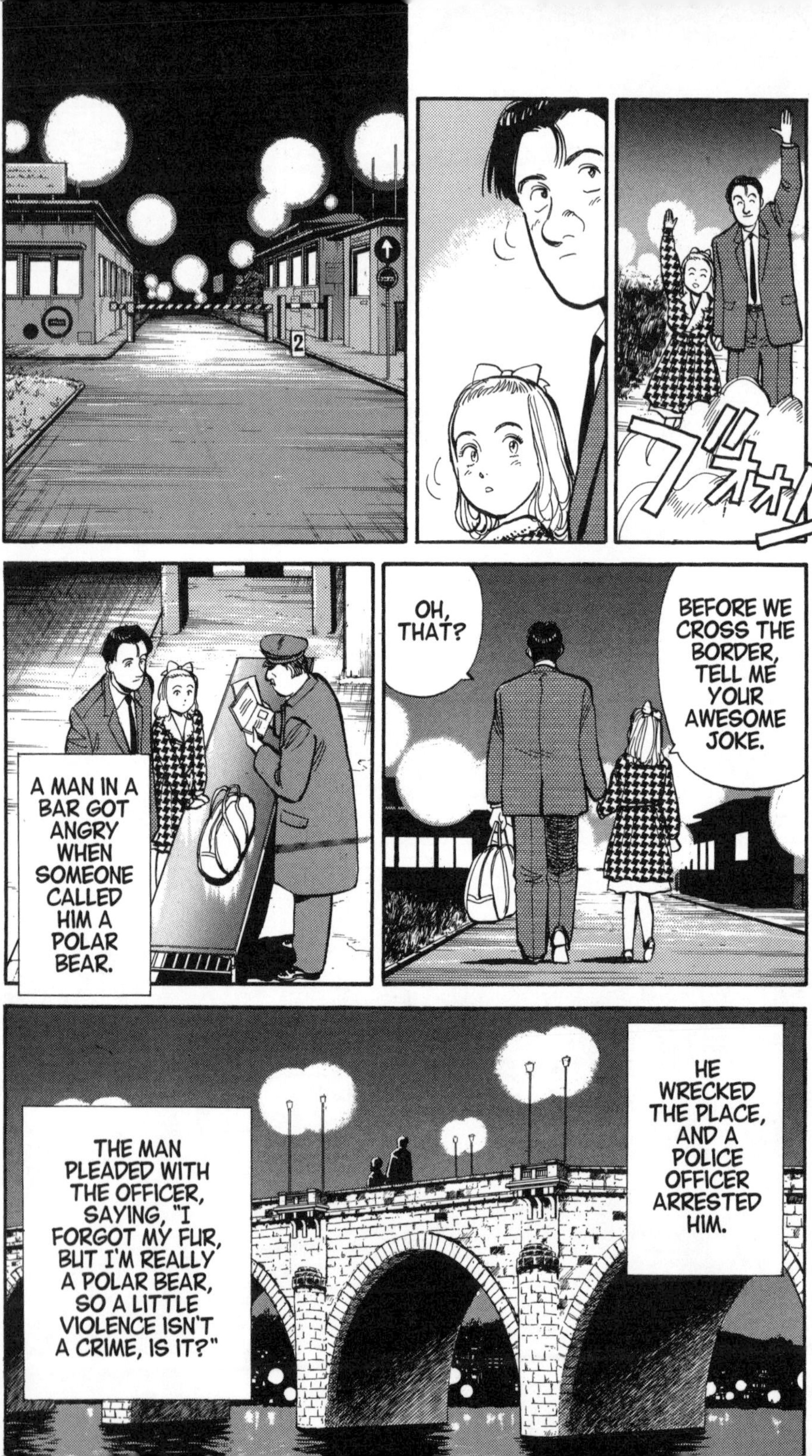
BEFORE WE CROSS THE BORDER, TELL ME YOUR AWESOME JOKE.
OH, THAT?
A MAN IN A BAR GOT ANGRY WHEN SOMEONE CALLED HIM A POLAR BEAR.
HE WRECKED THE PLACE, AND A POLICE OFFICER ARRESTED HIM.
THE MAN PLEADED WITH THE OFFICER, SAYING, "I FORGOT MY FUR, BUT I'M REALLY A POLAR BEAR, SO A LITTLE VIOLENCE ISN'T A CRIME, IS IT?"

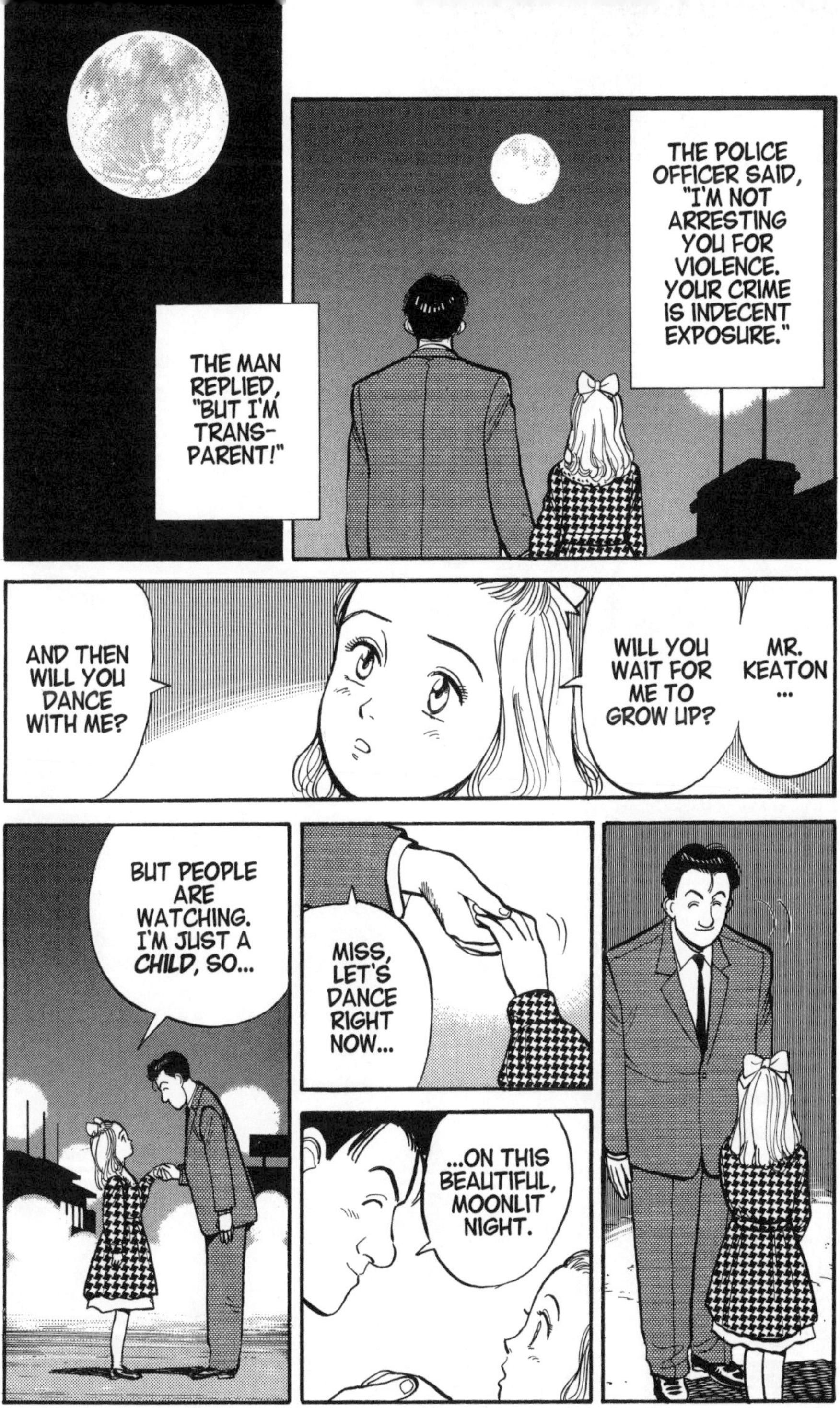
THE POLICE OFFICER SAID, "I'M NOT ARRESTING YOU FOR VIOLENCE. YOUR CRIME IS INDECENT EXPOSURE."
THE MAN REPLIED, "BUT I'M TRANS-PARENT!"
MR. KEATON ...
WILL YOU WAIT FOR ME TO GROW UP?
AND THEN WILL YOU DANCE WITH ME?
MISS, LET'S DANCE RIGHT NOW...
...ON THIS BEAUTIFUL, MOONLIT NIGHT.
BUT PEOPLE ARE WATCHING. I'M JUST A *CHILD*, SO...

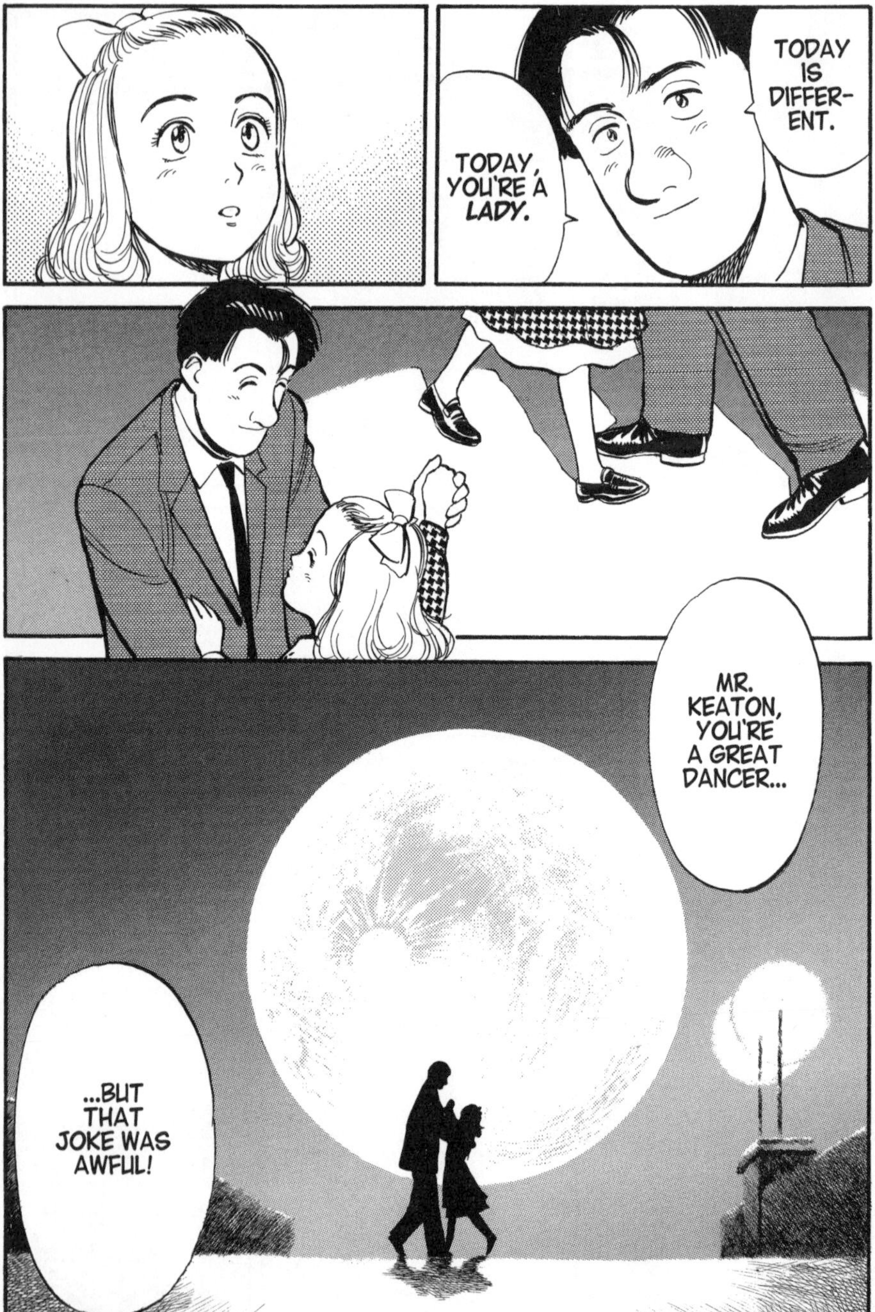
TODAY IS DIFFER-ENT.
TODAY, YOU'RE A *LADY*.
MR. KEATON, YOU'RE A GREAT DANCER...
...BUT THAT JOKE WAS AWFUL!

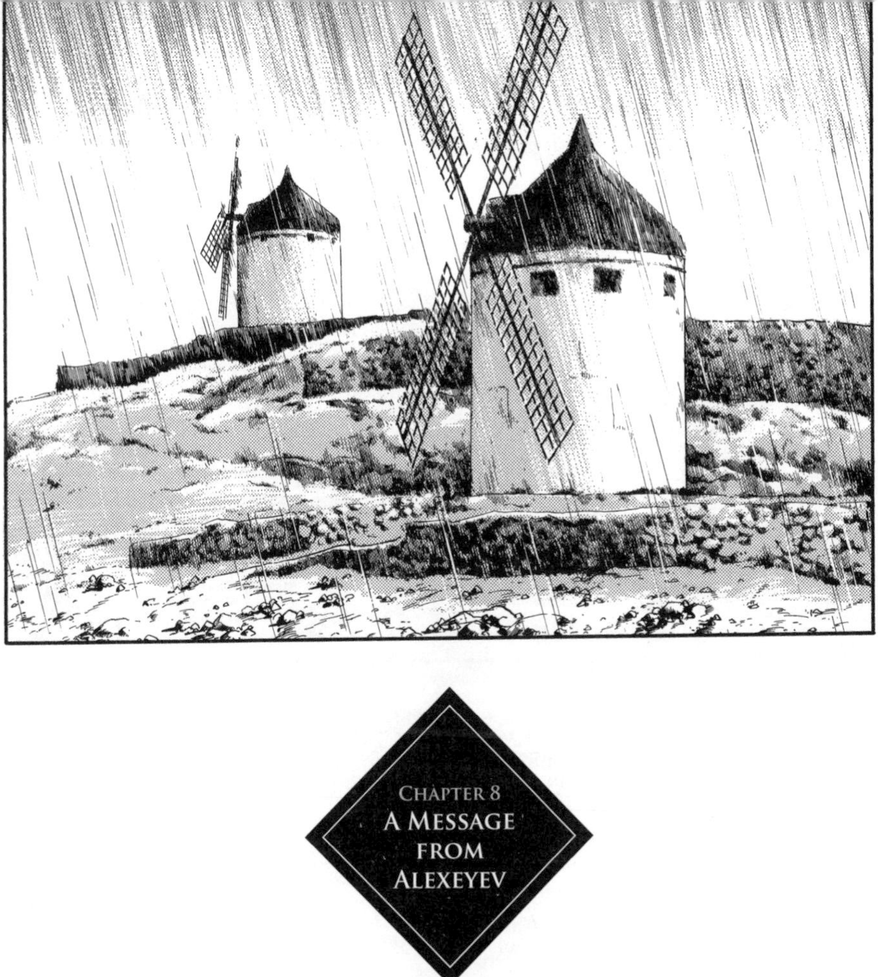

## Chapter 8
## A Message from Alexeyev

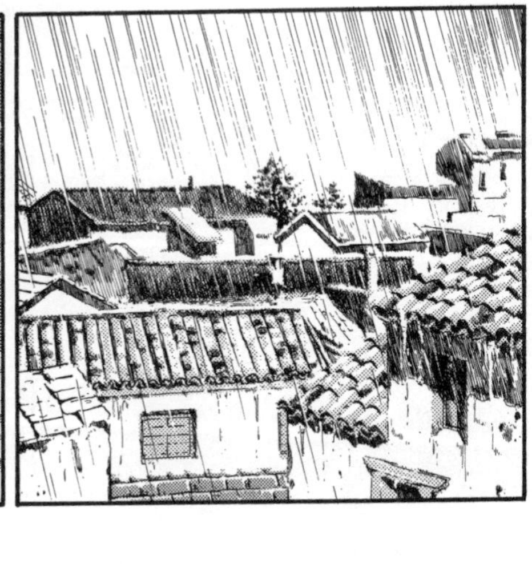

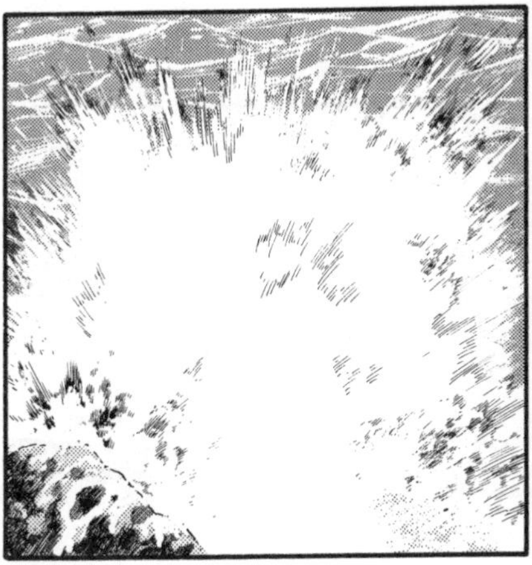

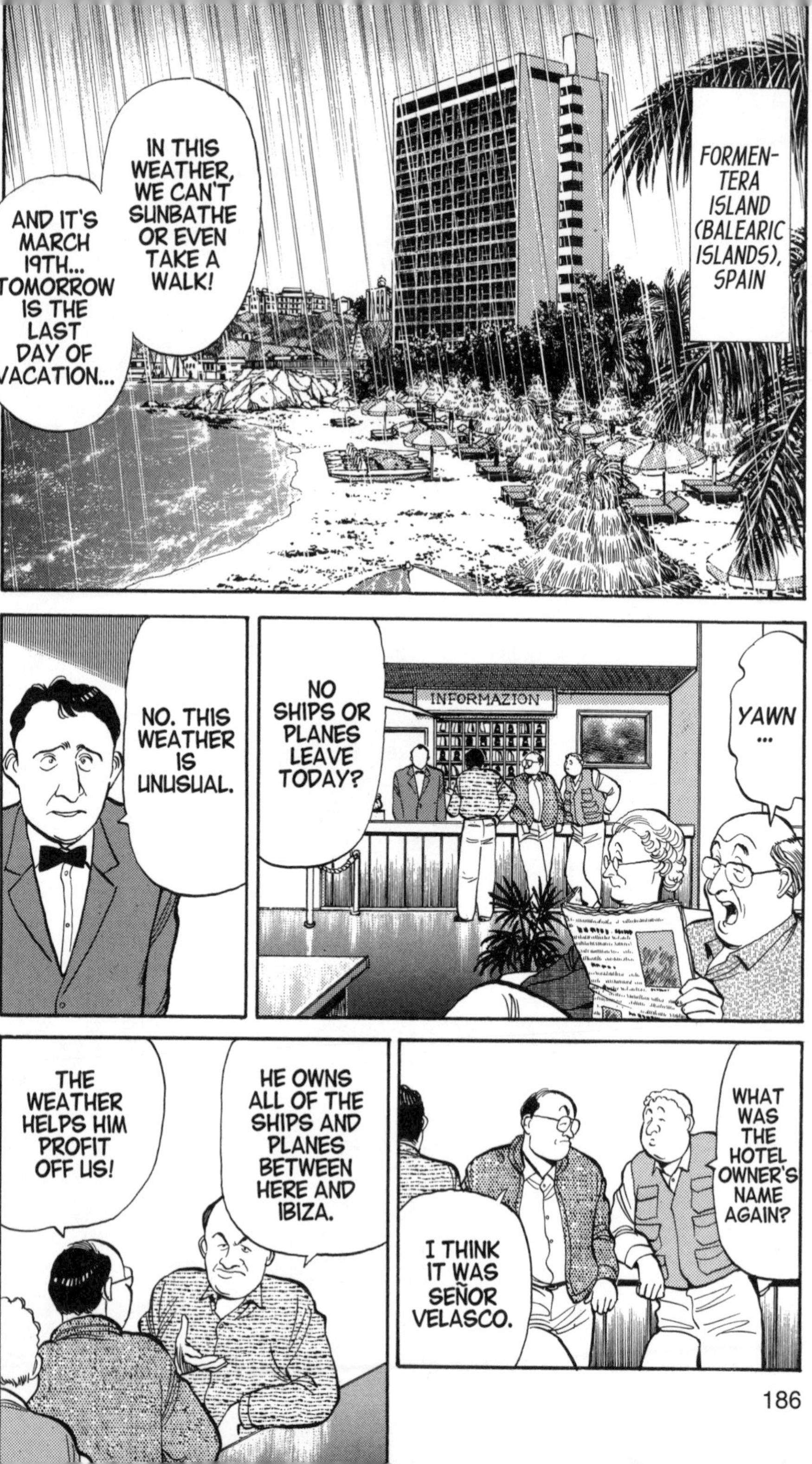
FORMENTERA ISLAND (BALEARIC ISLANDS), SPAIN
IN THIS WEATHER, WE CAN'T SUNBATHE OR EVEN TAKE A WALK!
AND IT'S MARCH 19TH... TOMORROW IS THE LAST DAY OF VACATION...
YAWN ...
INFORMAZION
NO SHIPS OR PLANES LEAVE TODAY?
NO. THIS WEATHER IS UNUSUAL.
WHAT WAS THE HOTEL OWNER'S NAME AGAIN?
I THINK IT WAS SEÑOR VELASCO.
HE OWNS ALL OF THE SHIPS AND PLANES BETWEEN HERE AND IBIZA.
THE WEATHER HELPS HIM PROFIT OFF US!

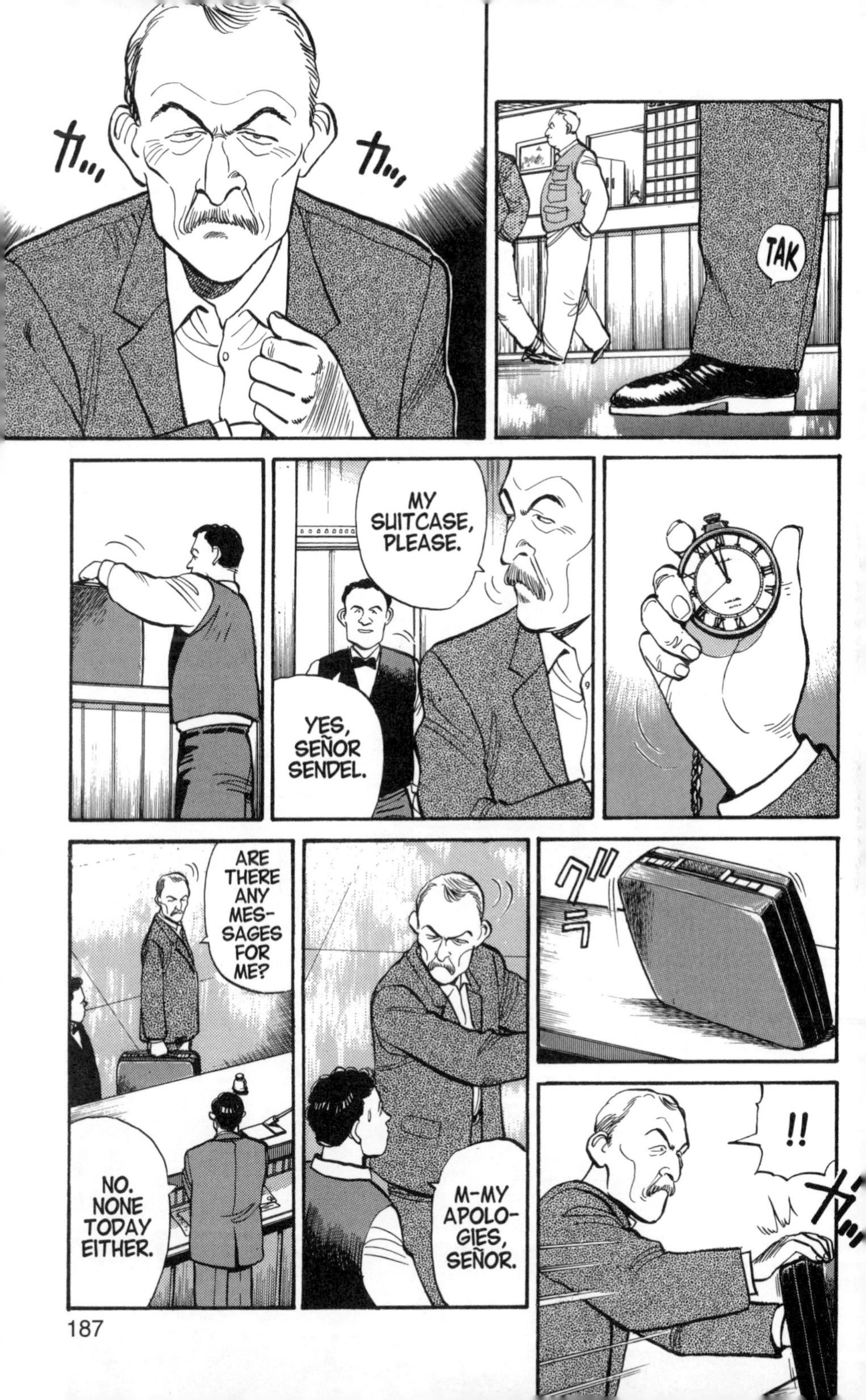
TAK
MY SUITCASE, PLEASE.
YES, SEÑOR SENDEL.
!!
M-MY APOLOGIES, SEÑOR.
ARE THERE ANY MES-SAGES FOR ME?
NO. NONE TODAY EITHER.

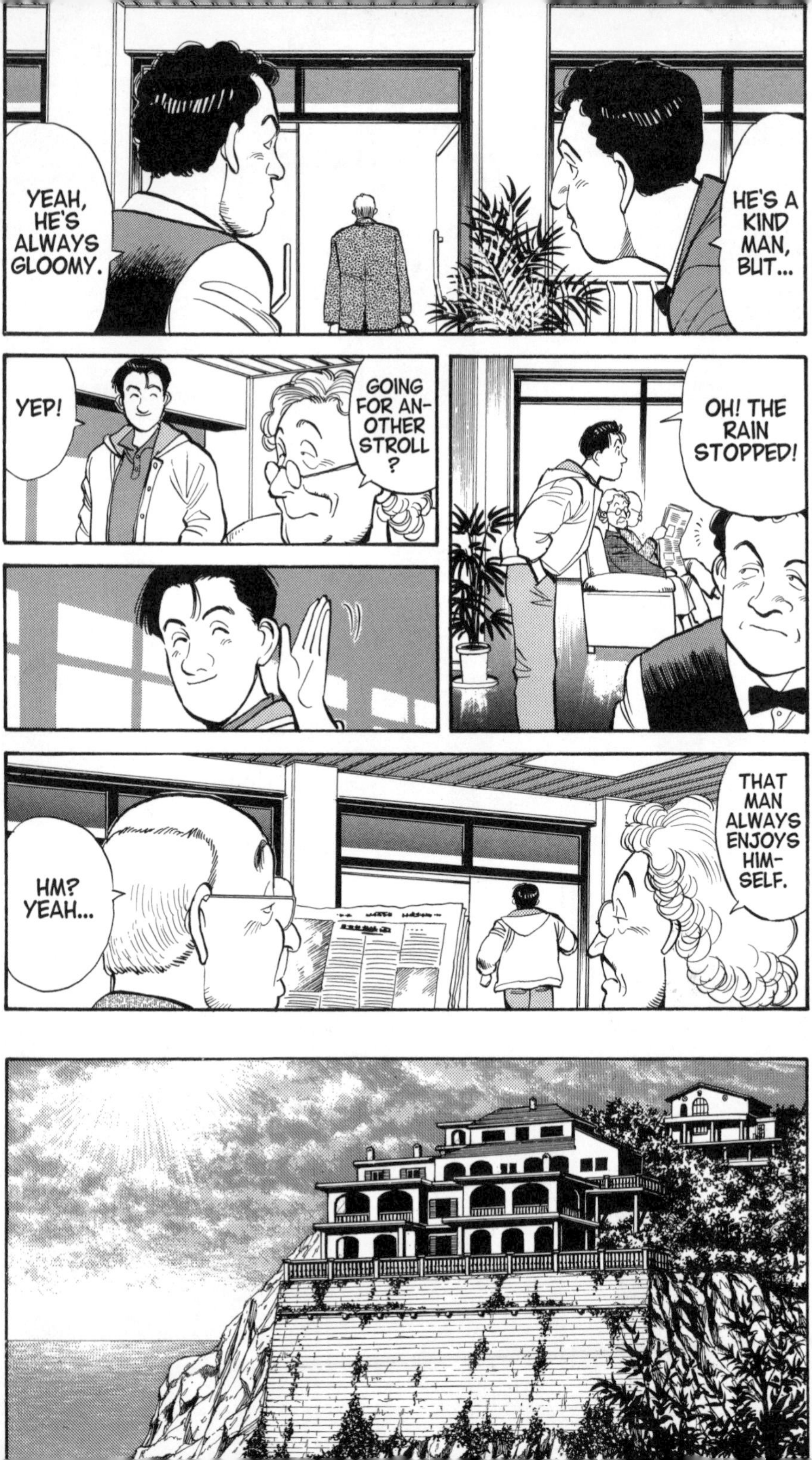
HE'S A KIND MAN, BUT...
YEAH, HE'S ALWAYS GLOOMY.
OH! THE RAIN STOPPED!
GOING FOR AN-OTHER STROLL?
YEP!
THAT MAN ALWAYS ENJOYS HIM-SELF.
HM? YEAH...

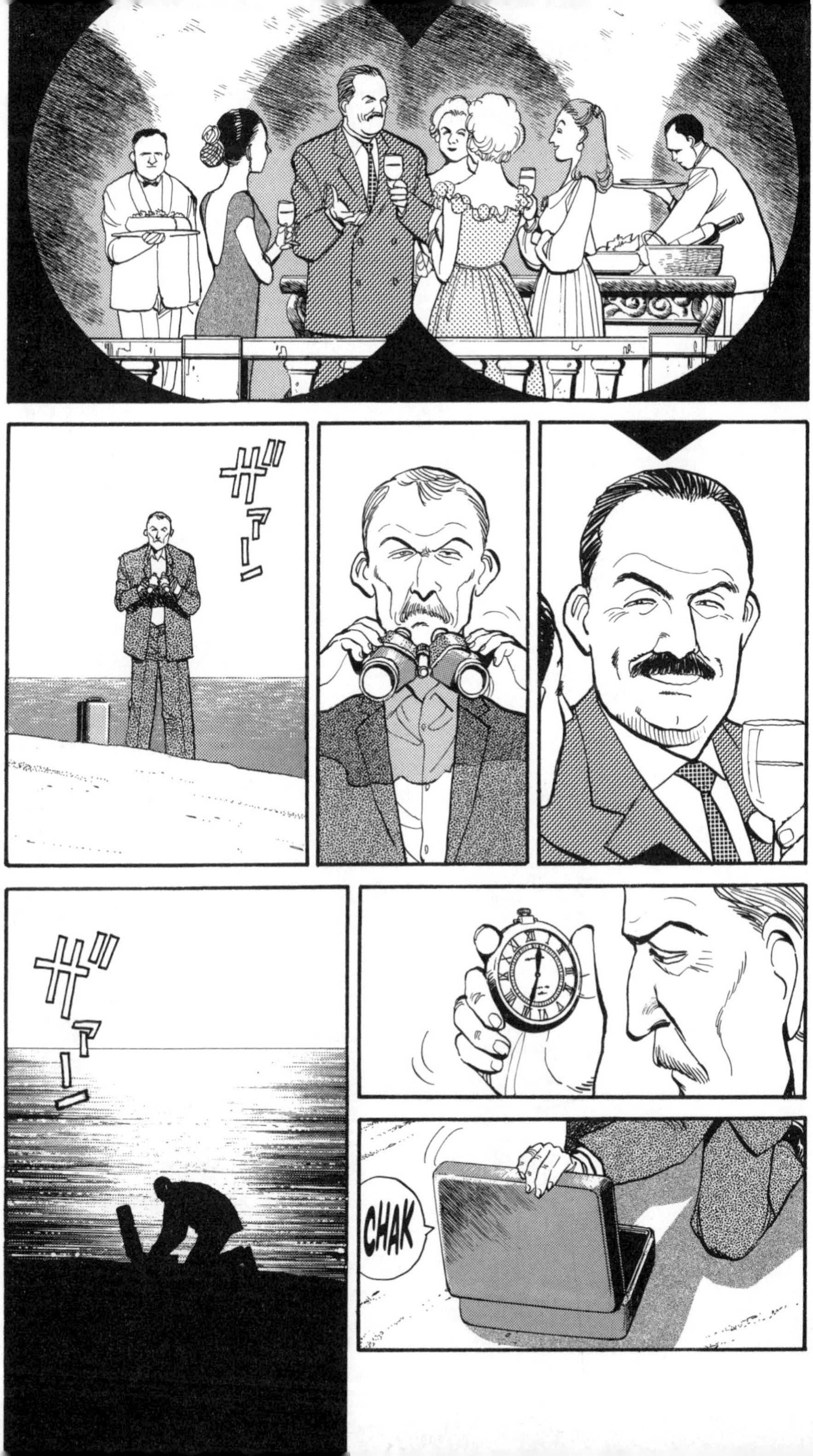
ザァーー
CHAK
ザァーー

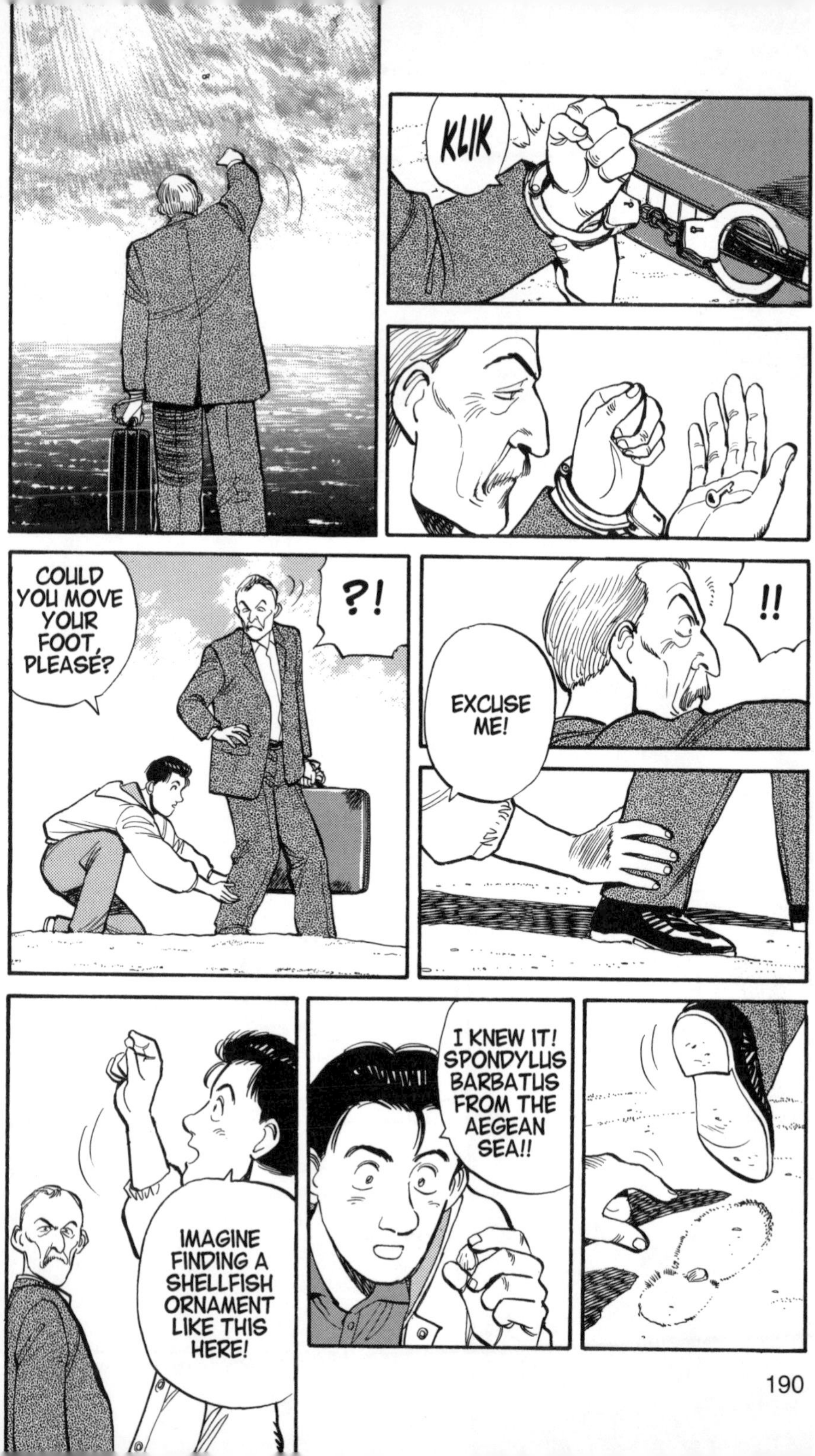

KLIK
!!
EXCUSE ME!
?!
COULD YOU MOVE YOUR FOOT, PLEASE?
I KNEW IT! SPONDYLUS BARBATUS FROM THE AEGEAN SEA!!
IMAGINE FINDING A SHELLFISH ORNAMENT LIKE THIS HERE!

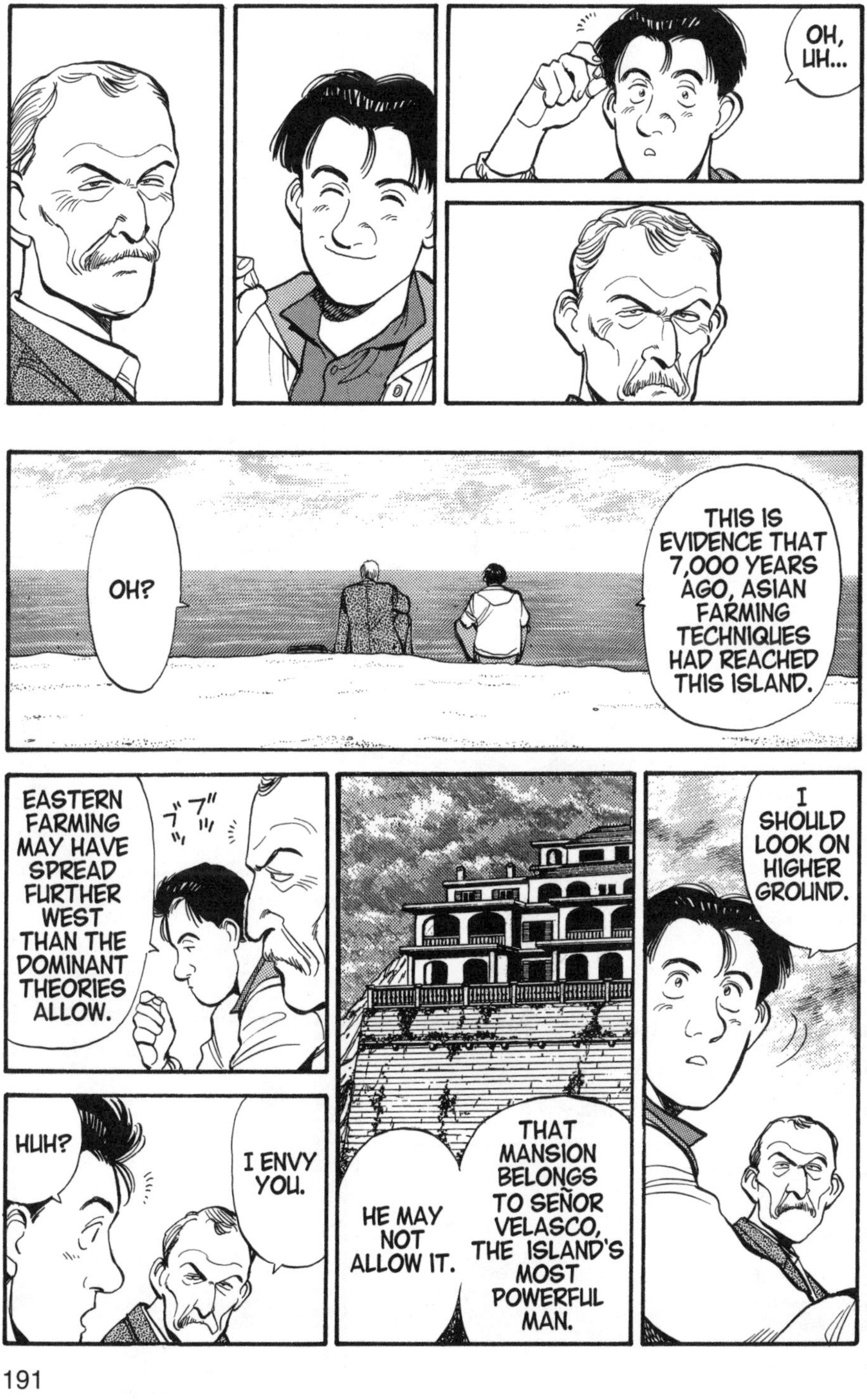
OH, UH...
THIS IS EVIDENCE THAT 7,000 YEARS AGO, ASIAN FARMING TECHNIQUES HAD REACHED THIS ISLAND.
OH?
I SHOULD LOOK ON HIGHER GROUND.
THAT MANSION BELONGS TO SEÑOR VELASCO, THE ISLAND'S MOST POWERFUL MAN.
HE MAY NOT ALLOW IT.
EASTERN FARMING MAY HAVE SPREAD FURTHER WEST THAN THE DOMINANT THEORIES ALLOW.
I ENVY YOU.
HUH?

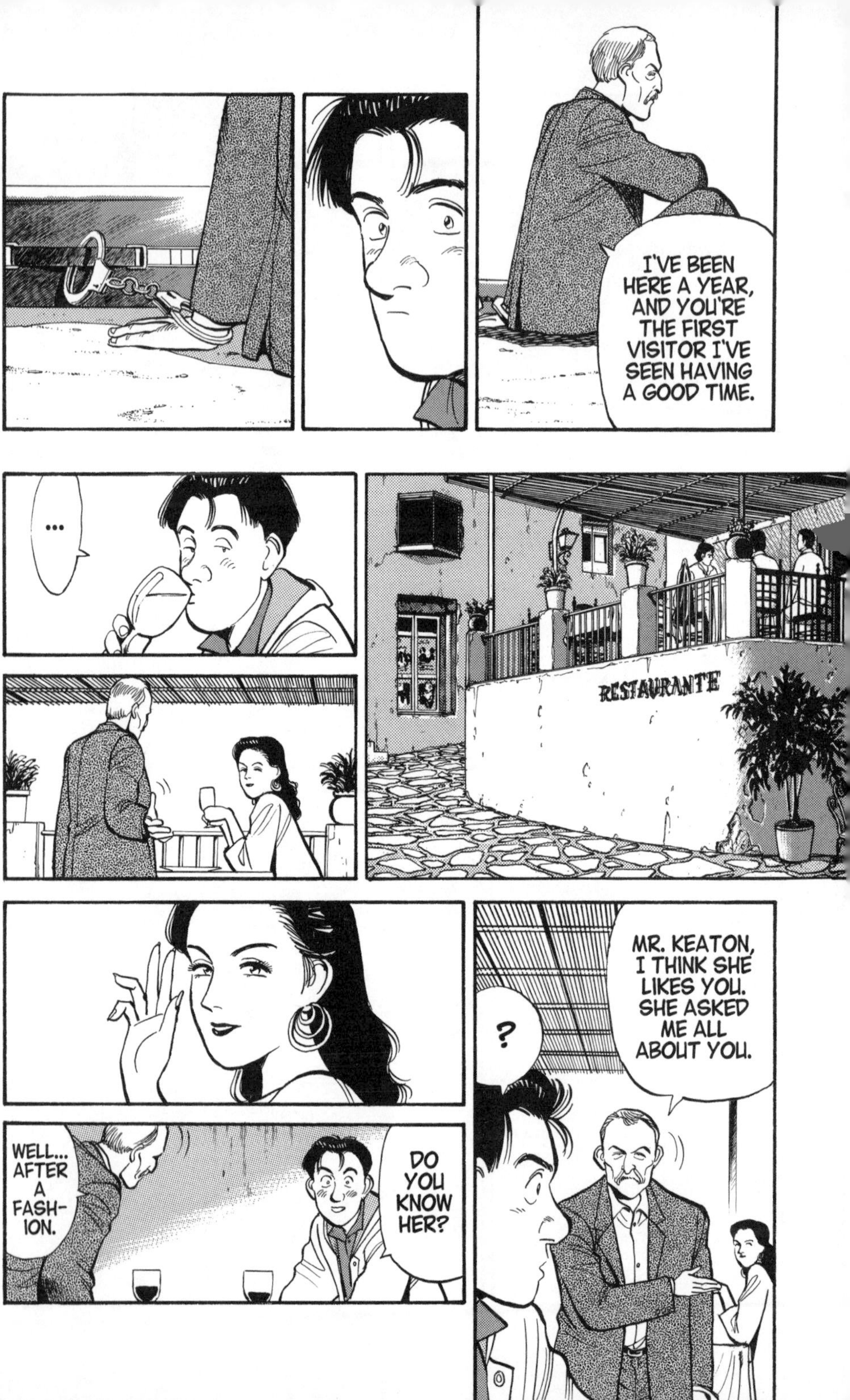
I'VE BEEN HERE A YEAR, AND YOU'RE THE FIRST VISITOR I'VE SEEN HAVING A GOOD TIME.
RESTAURANTE
...
MR. KEATON, I THINK SHE LIKES YOU. SHE ASKED ME ALL ABOUT YOU.
?
DO YOU KNOW HER?
WELL... AFTER A FASHION.

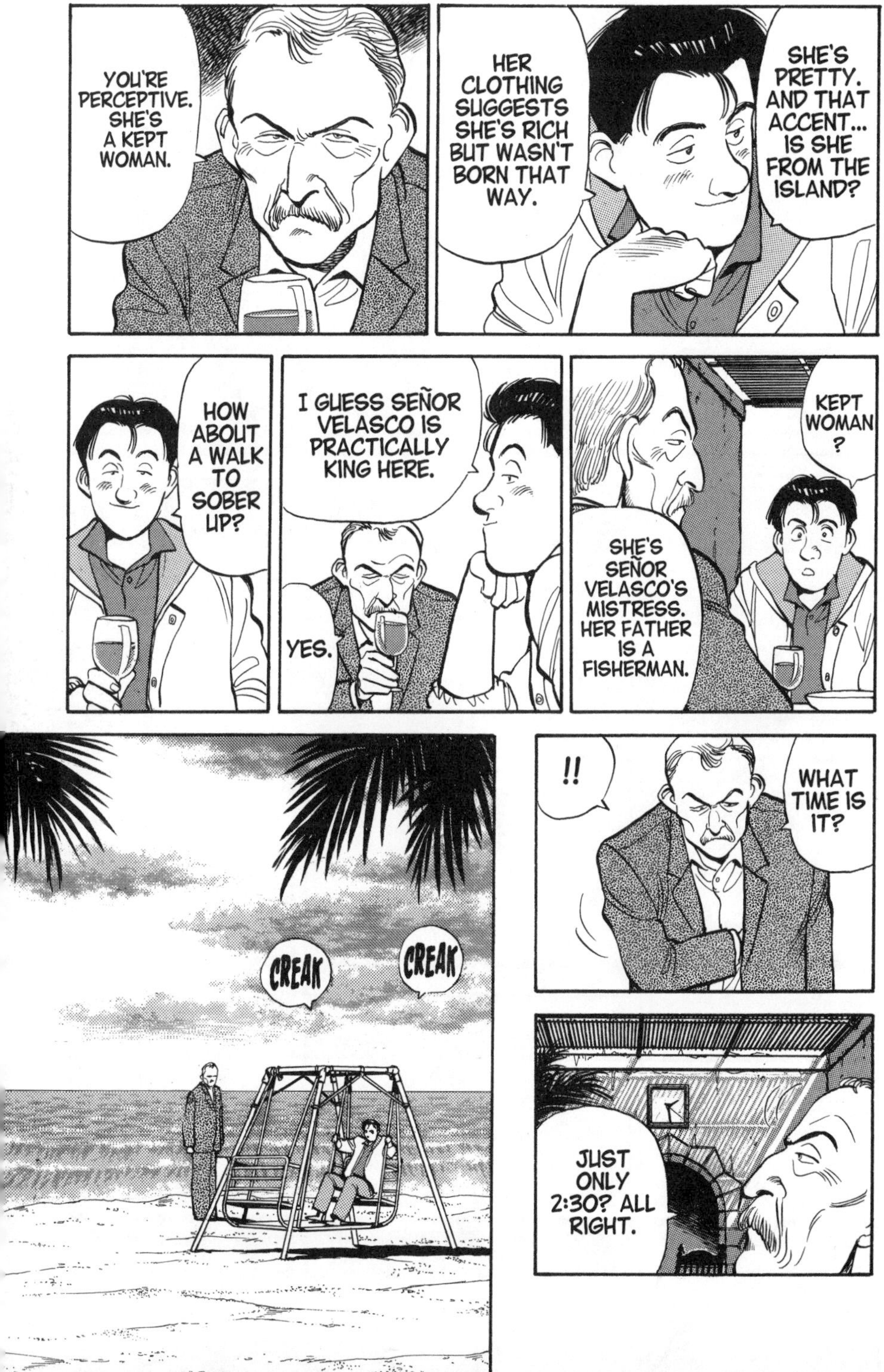
SHE'S PRETTY. AND THAT ACCENT... IS SHE FROM THE ISLAND?
HER CLOTHING SUGGESTS SHE'S RICH BUT WASN'T BORN THAT WAY.
YOU'RE PERCEPTIVE. SHE'S A KEPT WOMAN.
KEPT WOMAN?
SHE'S SEÑOR VELASCO'S MISTRESS. HER FATHER IS A FISHERMAN.
I GUESS SEÑOR VELASCO IS PRACTICALLY KING HERE.
YES.
HOW ABOUT A WALK TO SOBER UP?
WHAT TIME IS IT?
!!
JUST ONLY 2:30? ALL RIGHT.
CREAK
CREAK

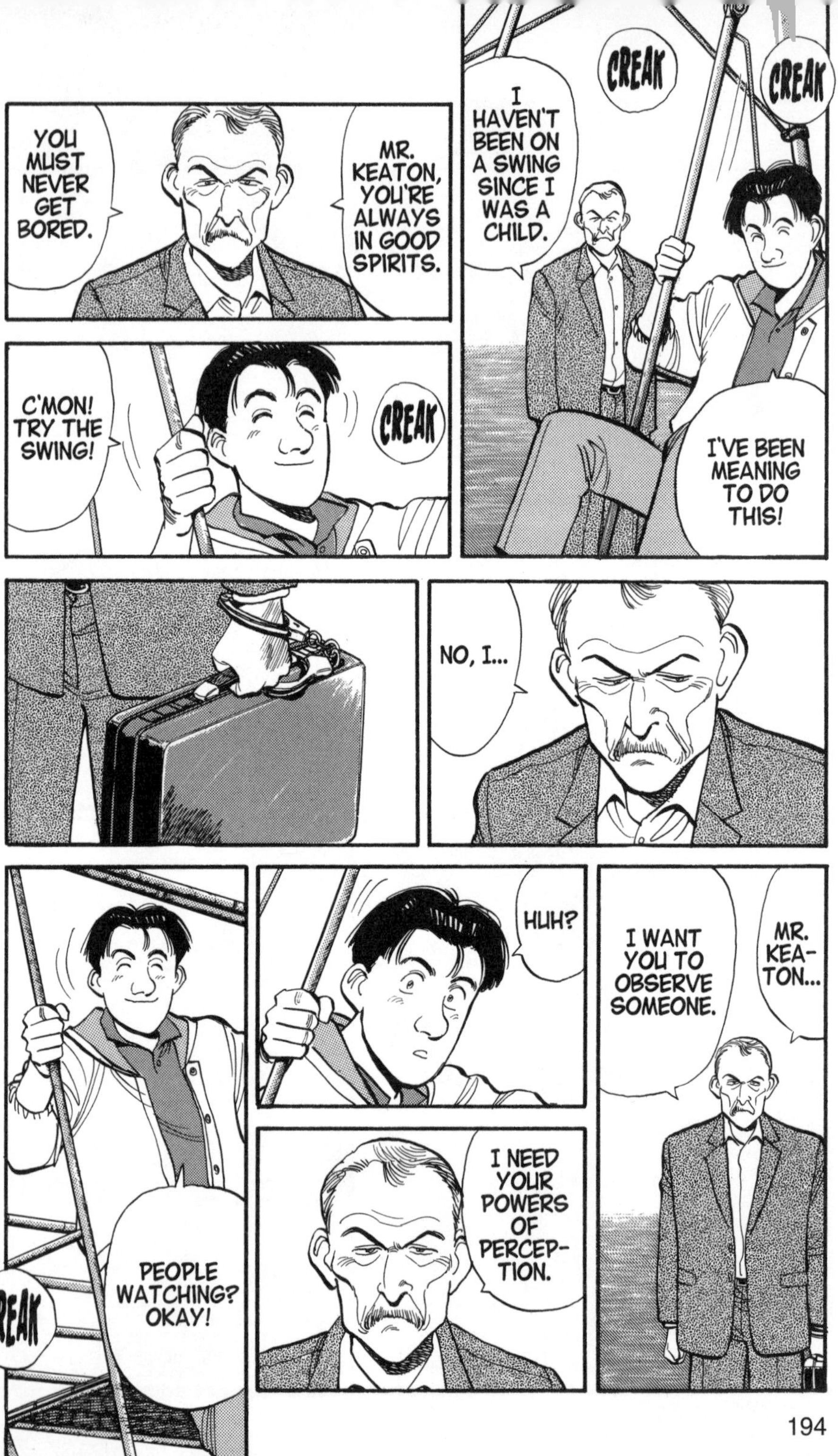
CREAK
CREAK
I HAVEN'T BEEN ON A SWING SINCE I WAS A CHILD.
I'VE BEEN MEANING TO DO THIS!
MR. KEATON, YOU'RE ALWAYS IN GOOD SPIRITS.
YOU MUST NEVER GET BORED.
CREAK
C'MON! TRY THE SWING!
NO, I...
MR. KEA-TON...
I WANT YOU TO OBSERVE SOMEONE.
HUH?
I NEED YOUR POWERS OF PERCEP-TION.
PEOPLE WATCHING? OKAY!
CREAK

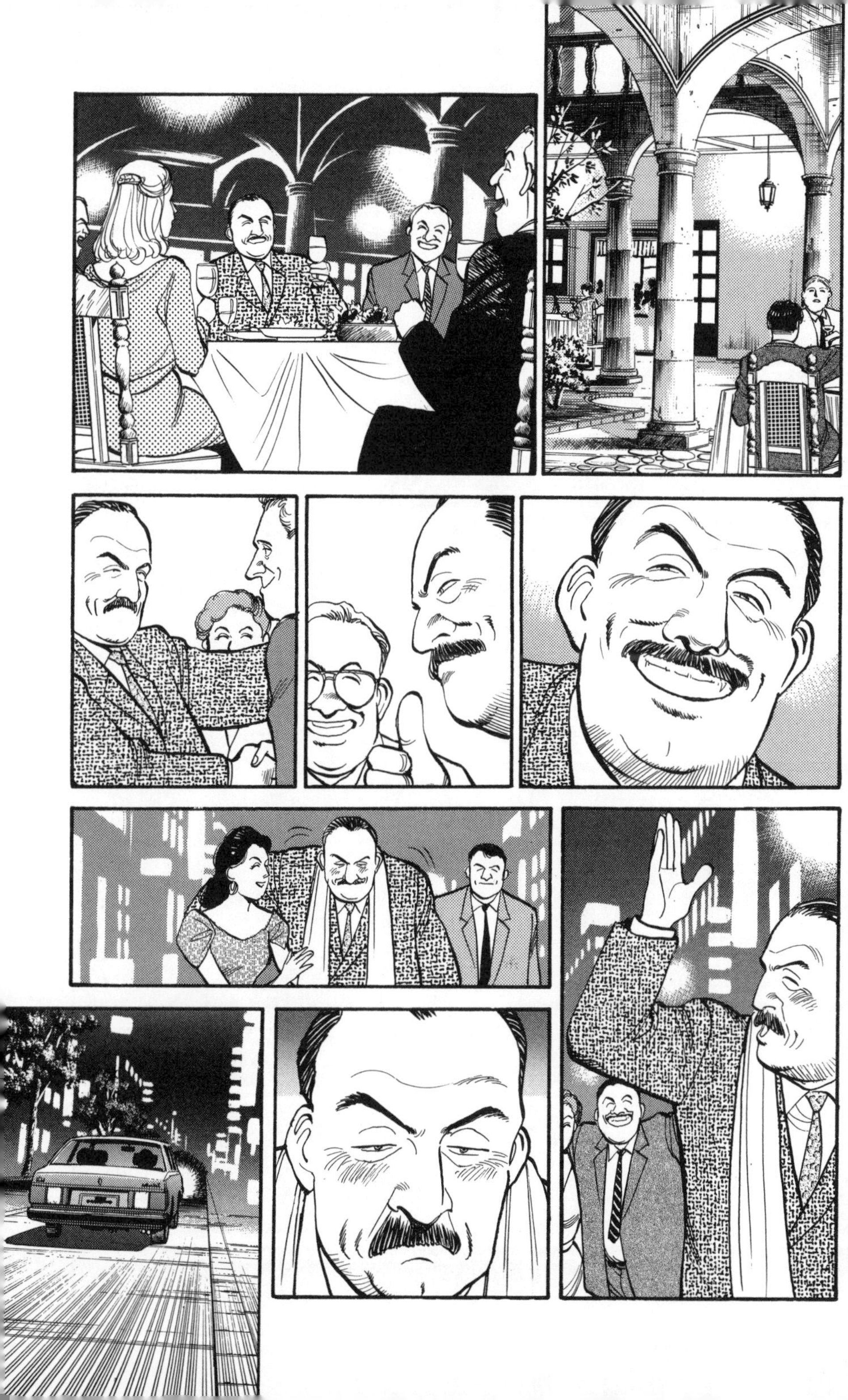

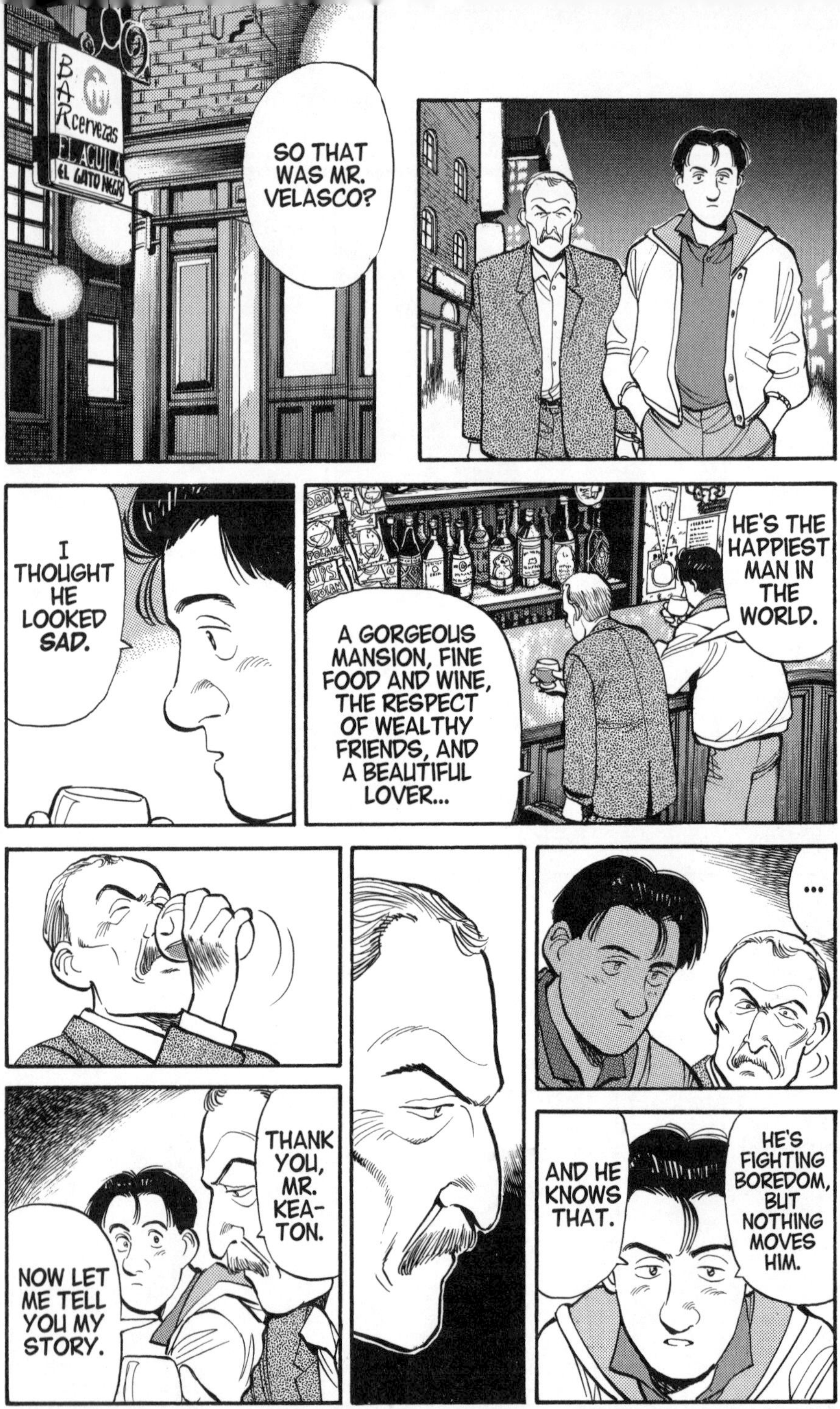
SO THAT WAS MR. VELASCO?
BAR
cervezas
EL AGUILA
HE'S THE HAPPIEST MAN IN THE WORLD.
A GORGEOUS MANSION, FINE FOOD AND WINE, THE RESPECT OF WEALTHY FRIENDS, AND A BEAUTIFUL LOVER...
I THOUGHT HE LOOKED SAD.
...
HE'S FIGHTING BOREDOM, BUT NOTHING MOVES HIM.
AND HE KNOWS THAT.
THANK YOU, MR. KEATON.
NOW LET ME TELL YOU MY STORY.

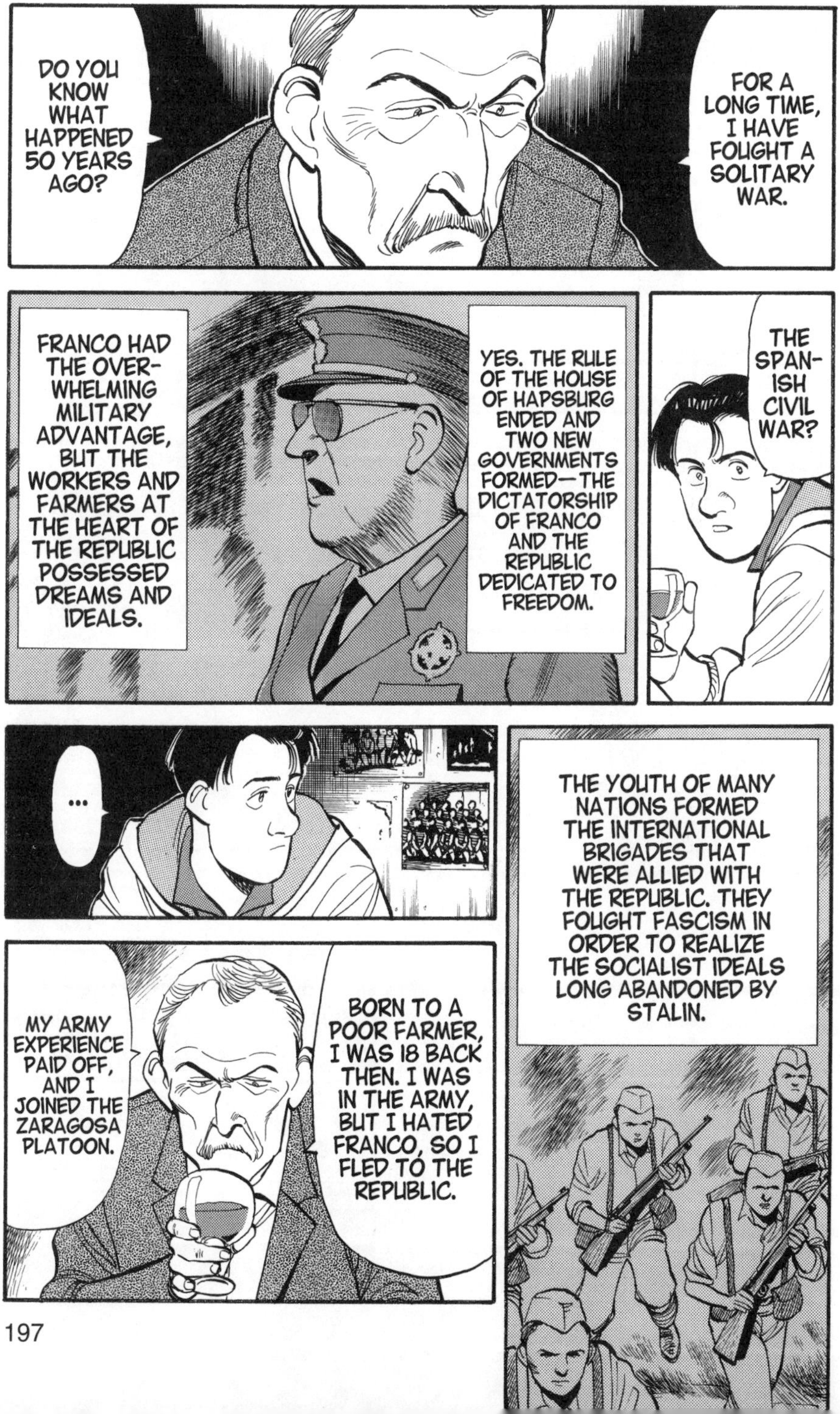
FOR A LONG TIME, I HAVE FOUGHT A SOLITARY WAR.
DO YOU KNOW WHAT HAPPENED 50 YEARS AGO?
THE SPANISH CIVIL WAR?
YES. THE RULE OF THE HOUSE OF HAPSBURG ENDED AND TWO NEW GOVERNMENTS FORMED—THE DICTATORSHIP OF FRANCO AND THE REPUBLIC DEDICATED TO FREEDOM.
FRANCO HAD THE OVERWHELMING MILITARY ADVANTAGE, BUT THE WORKERS AND FARMERS AT THE HEART OF THE REPUBLIC POSSESSED DREAMS AND IDEALS.
THE YOUTH OF MANY NATIONS FORMED THE INTERNATIONAL BRIGADES THAT WERE ALLIED WITH THE REPUBLIC. THEY FOUGHT FASCISM IN ORDER TO REALIZE THE SOCIALIST IDEALS LONG ABANDONED BY STALIN.
...
BORN TO A POOR FARMER, I WAS 18 BACK THEN. I WAS IN THE ARMY, BUT I HATED FRANCO, SO I FLED TO THE REPUBLIC.
MY ARMY EXPERIENCE PAID OFF, AND I JOINED THE ZARAGOSA PLATOON.

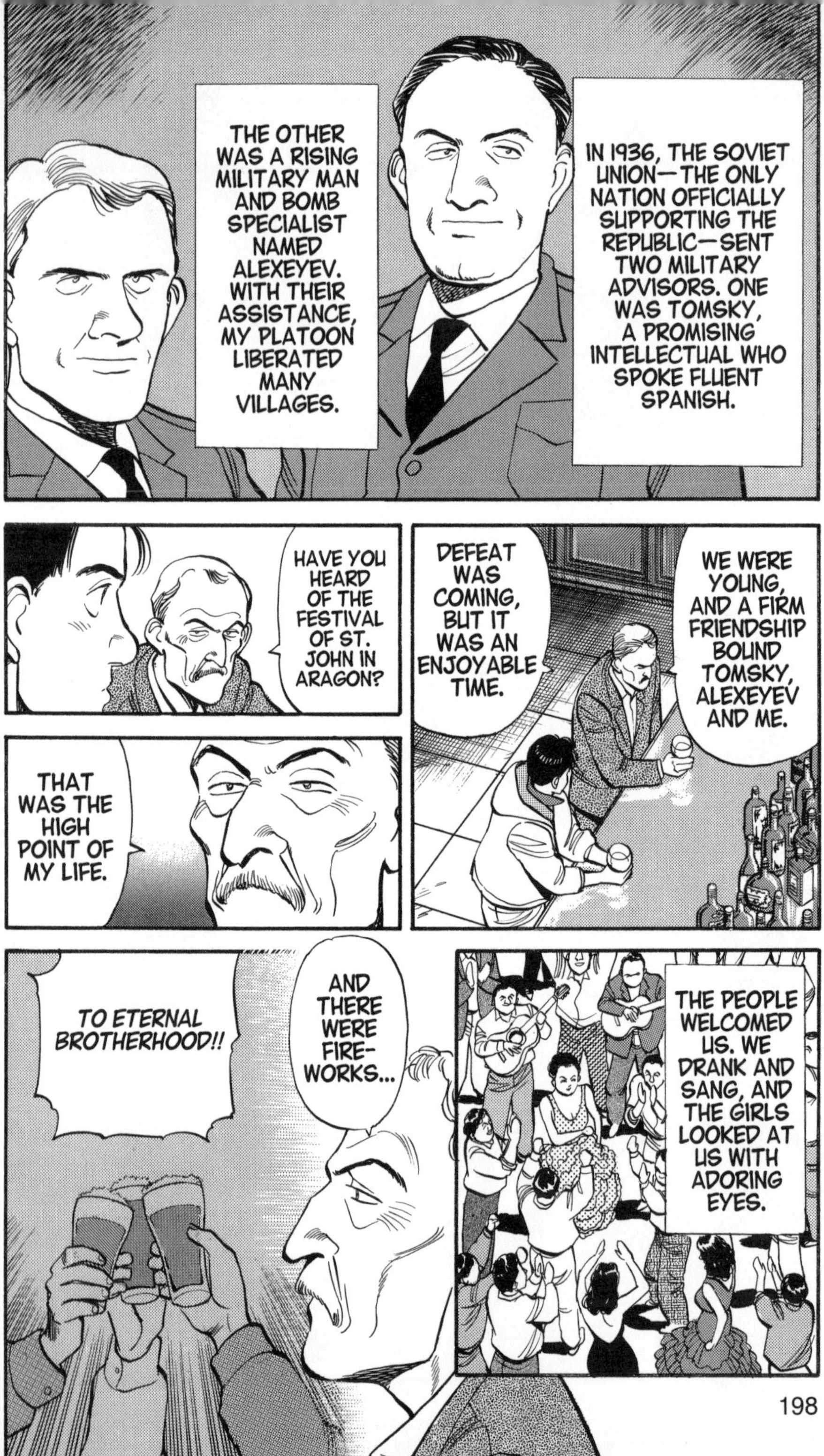
IN 1936, THE SOVIET UNION—THE ONLY NATION OFFICIALLY SUPPORTING THE REPUBLIC—SENT TWO MILITARY ADVISORS. ONE WAS TOMSKY, A PROMISING INTELLECTUAL WHO SPOKE FLUENT SPANISH.
THE OTHER WAS A RISING MILITARY MAN AND BOMB SPECIALIST NAMED ALEXEYEV. WITH THEIR ASSISTANCE, MY PLATOON LIBERATED MANY VILLAGES.
WE WERE YOUNG, AND A FIRM FRIENDSHIP BOUND TOMSKY, ALEXEYEV AND ME.
DEFEAT WAS COMING, BUT IT WAS AN ENJOYABLE TIME.
HAVE YOU HEARD OF THE FESTIVAL OF ST. JOHN IN ARAGON?
THAT WAS THE HIGH POINT OF MY LIFE.
THE PEOPLE WELCOMED US. WE DRANK AND SANG, AND THE GIRLS LOOKED AT US WITH ADORING EYES.
AND THERE WERE FIRE-WORKS...
TO ETERNAL BROTHERHOOD!!

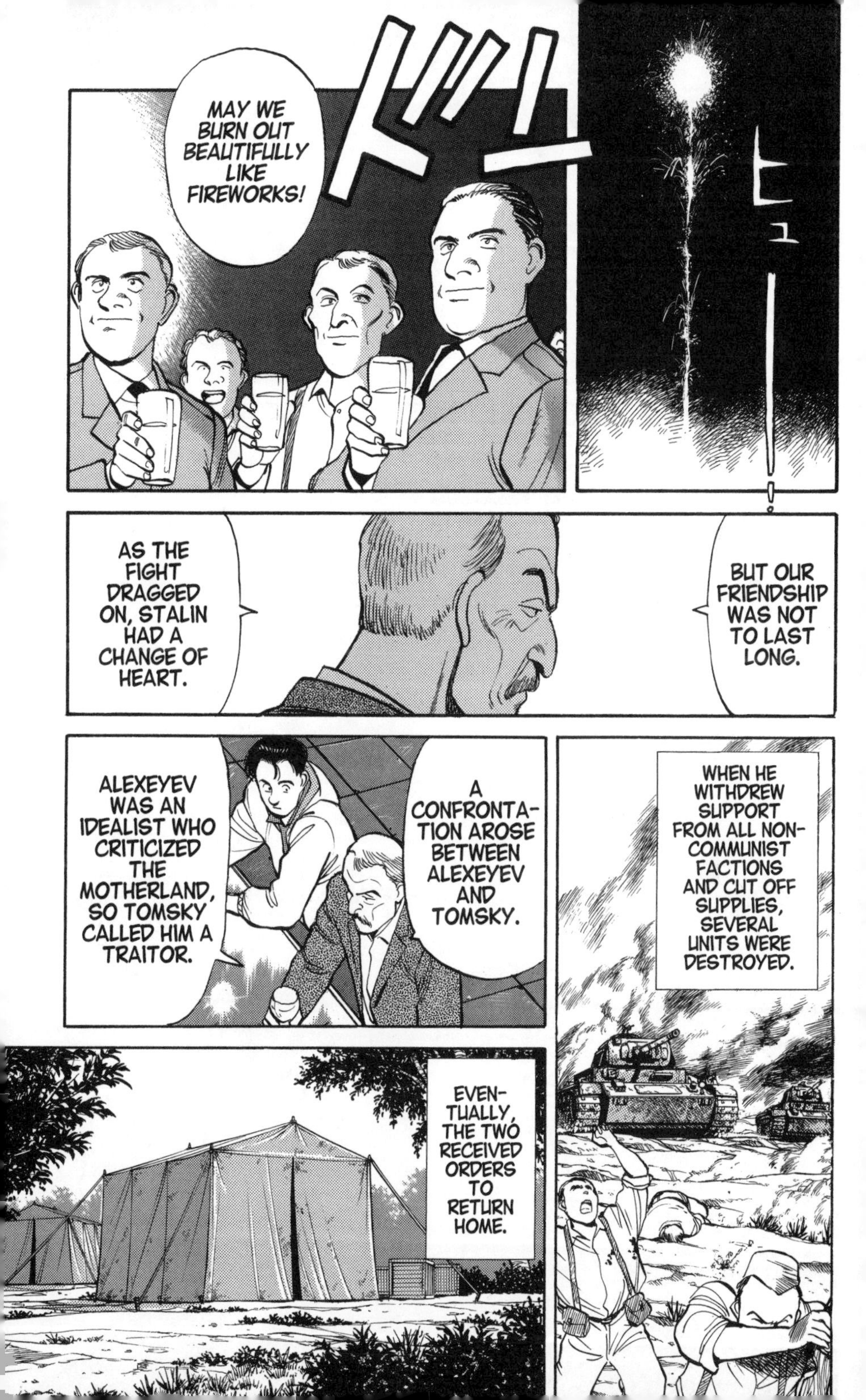
ヒュー!
ドン
MAY WE BURN OUT BEAUTIFULLY LIKE FIREWORKS!
BUT OUR FRIENDSHIP WAS NOT TO LAST LONG.
AS THE FIGHT DRAGGED ON, STALIN HAD A CHANGE OF HEART.
WHEN HE WITHDREW SUPPORT FROM ALL NON-COMMUNIST FACTIONS AND CUT OFF SUPPLIES, SEVERAL UNITS WERE DESTROYED.
A CONFRONTATION AROSE BETWEEN ALEXEYEV AND TOMSKY.
ALEXEYEV WAS AN IDEALIST WHO CRITICIZED THE MOTHERLAND, SO TOMSKY CALLED HIM A TRAITOR.
EVENTUALLY, THE TWO RECEIVED ORDERS TO RETURN HOME.

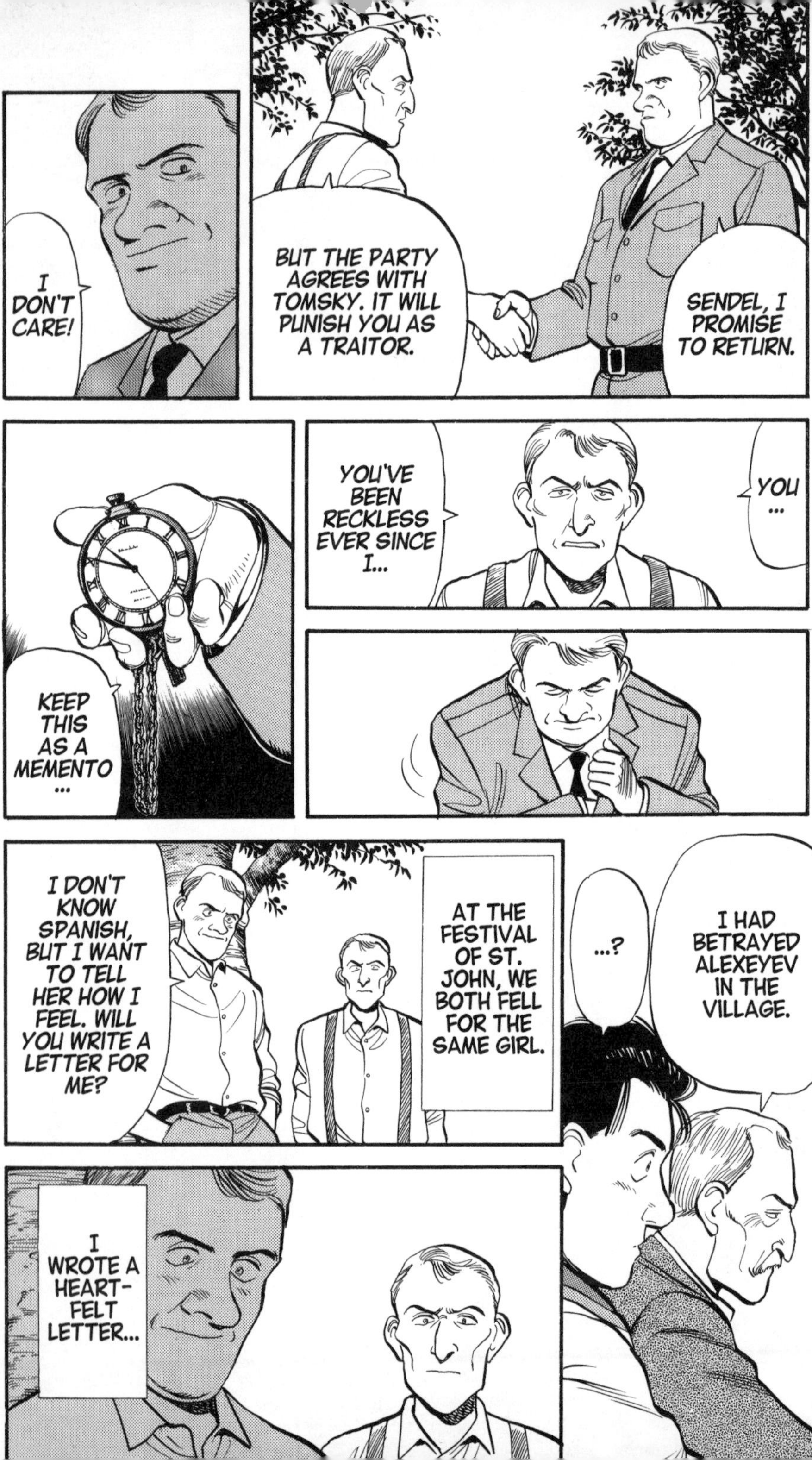
SENDEL, I PROMISE TO RETURN.
BUT THE PARTY AGREES WITH TOMSKY. IT WILL PUNISH YOU AS A TRAITOR.
I DON'T CARE!
YOU ...
YOU'VE BEEN RECKLESS EVER SINCE I...
KEEP THIS AS A MEMENTO ...
I HAD BETRAYED ALEXEYEV IN THE VILLAGE.
...?
AT THE FESTIVAL OF ST. JOHN, WE BOTH FELL FOR THE SAME GIRL.
I DON'T KNOW SPANISH, BUT I WANT TO TELL HER HOW I FEEL. WILL YOU WRITE A LETTER FOR ME?
I WROTE A HEART-FELT LETTER...

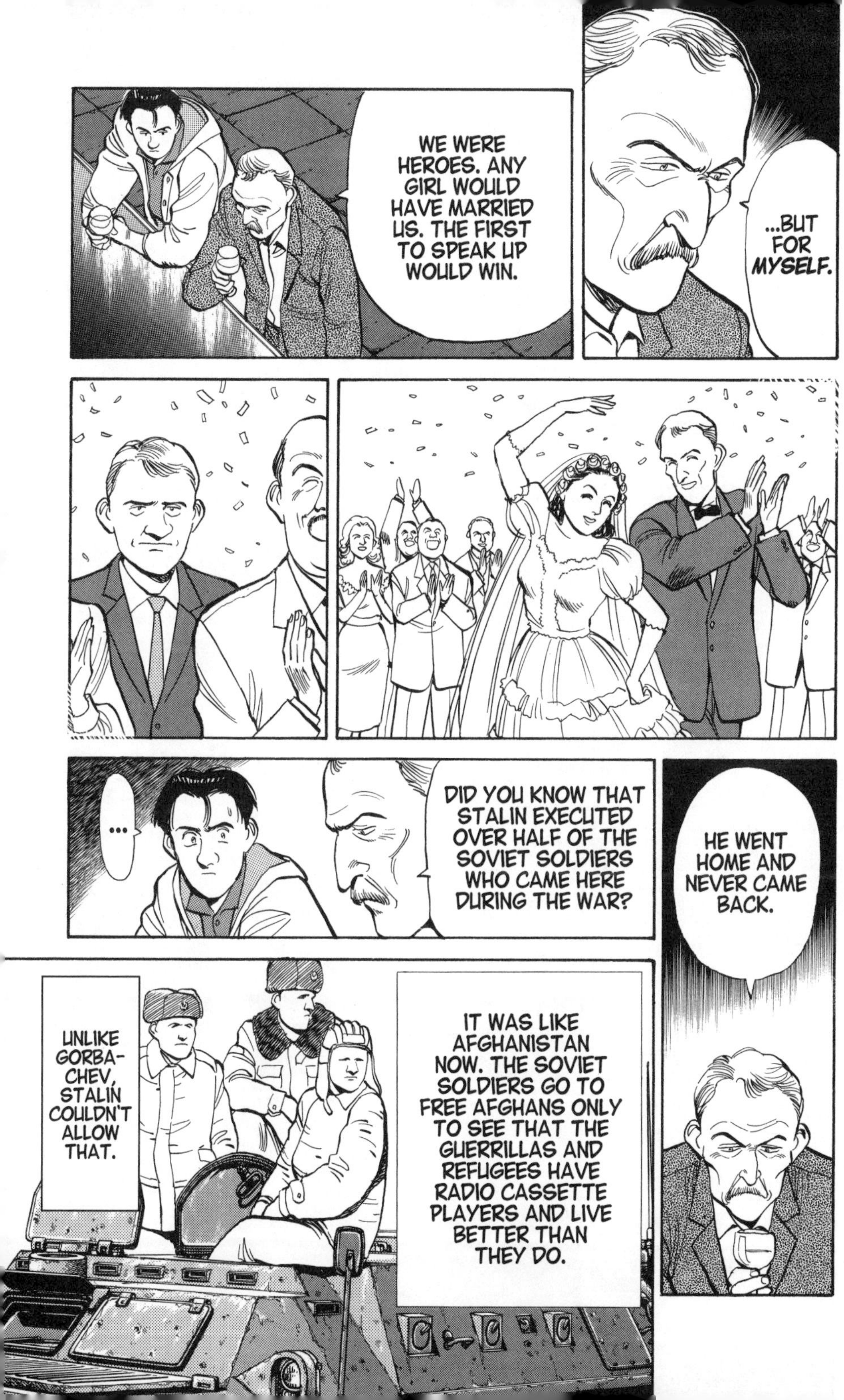
...BUT FOR MYSELF.
WE WERE HEROES. ANY GIRL WOULD HAVE MARRIED US. THE FIRST TO SPEAK UP WOULD WIN.
HE WENT HOME AND NEVER CAME BACK.
DID YOU KNOW THAT STALIN EXECUTED OVER HALF OF THE SOVIET SOLDIERS WHO CAME HERE DURING THE WAR?
...
IT WAS LIKE AFGHANISTAN NOW. THE SOVIET SOLDIERS GO TO FREE AFGHANS ONLY TO SEE THAT THE GUERRILLAS AND REFUGEES HAVE RADIO CASSETTE PLAYERS AND LIVE BETTER THAN THEY DO.
UNLIKE GORBA-CHEV, STALIN COULDN'T ALLOW THAT.

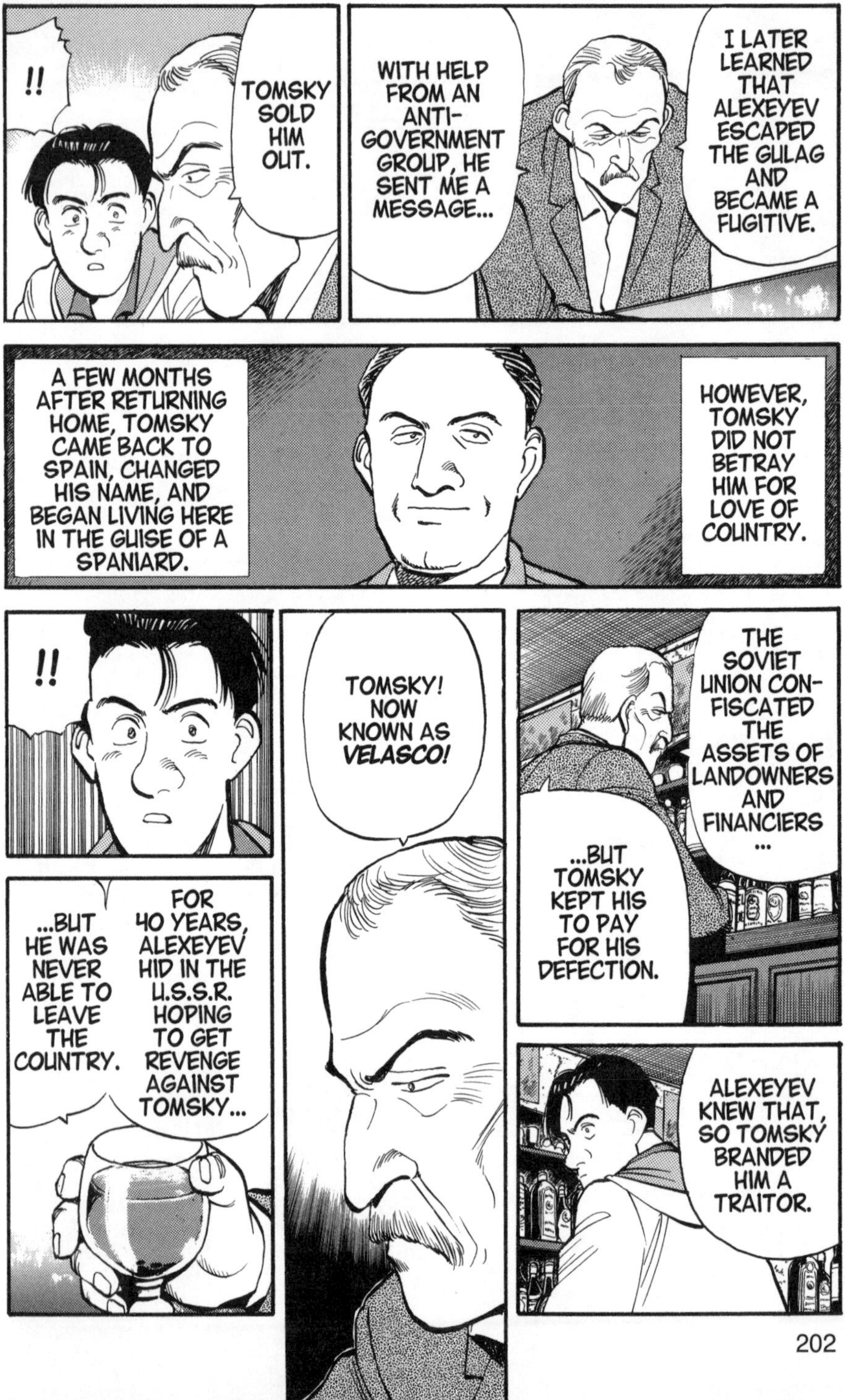
I LATER LEARNED THAT ALEXEYEV ESCAPED THE GULAG AND BECAME A FUGITIVE.
WITH HELP FROM AN ANTI-GOVERNMENT GROUP, HE SENT ME A MESSAGE...
TOMSKY SOLD HIM OUT.
!!
HOWEVER, TOMSKY DID NOT BETRAY HIM FOR LOVE OF COUNTRY.
A FEW MONTHS AFTER RETURNING HOME, TOMSKY CAME BACK TO SPAIN, CHANGED HIS NAME, AND BEGAN LIVING HERE IN THE GUISE OF A SPANIARD.
THE SOVIET UNION CONFISCATED THE ASSETS OF LANDOWNERS AND FINANCIERS...
...BUT TOMSKY KEPT HIS TO PAY FOR HIS DEFECTION.
ALEXEYEV KNEW THAT, SO TOMSKY BRANDED HIM A TRAITOR.
TOMSKY! NOW KNOWN AS *VELASCO!*
!!
FOR 40 YEARS, ALEXEYEV HID IN THE U.S.S.R. HOPING TO GET REVENGE AGAINST TOMSKY...
...BUT HE WAS NEVER ABLE TO LEAVE THE COUNTRY.

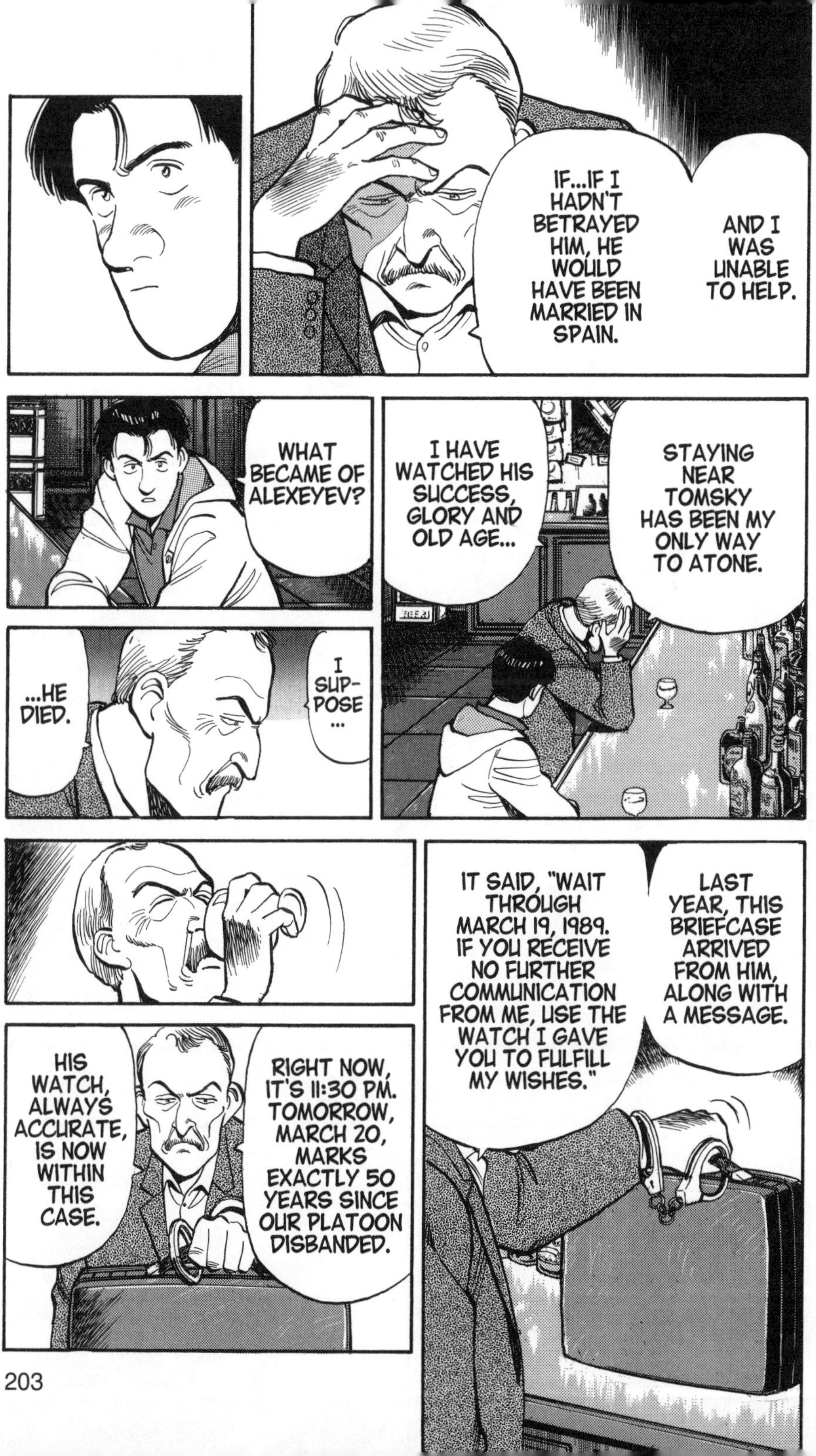
AND I WAS UNABLE TO HELP.
IF...IF I HADN'T BETRAYED HIM, HE WOULD HAVE BEEN MARRIED IN SPAIN.
STAYING NEAR TOMSKY HAS BEEN MY ONLY WAY TO ATONE.
I HAVE WATCHED HIS SUCCESS, GLORY AND OLD AGE...
WHAT BECAME OF ALEXEYEV?
I SUP-POSE...
...HE DIED.
LAST YEAR, THIS BRIEFCASE ARRIVED FROM HIM, ALONG WITH A MESSAGE.
IT SAID, "WAIT THROUGH MARCH 19, 1989. IF YOU RECEIVE NO FURTHER COMMUNICATION FROM ME, USE THE WATCH I GAVE YOU TO FULFILL MY WISHES."
RIGHT NOW, IT'S 11:30 PM. TOMORROW, MARCH 20, MARKS EXACTLY 50 YEARS SINCE OUR PLATOON DISBANDED.
HIS WATCH, ALWAYS ACCURATE, IS NOW WITHIN THIS CASE.

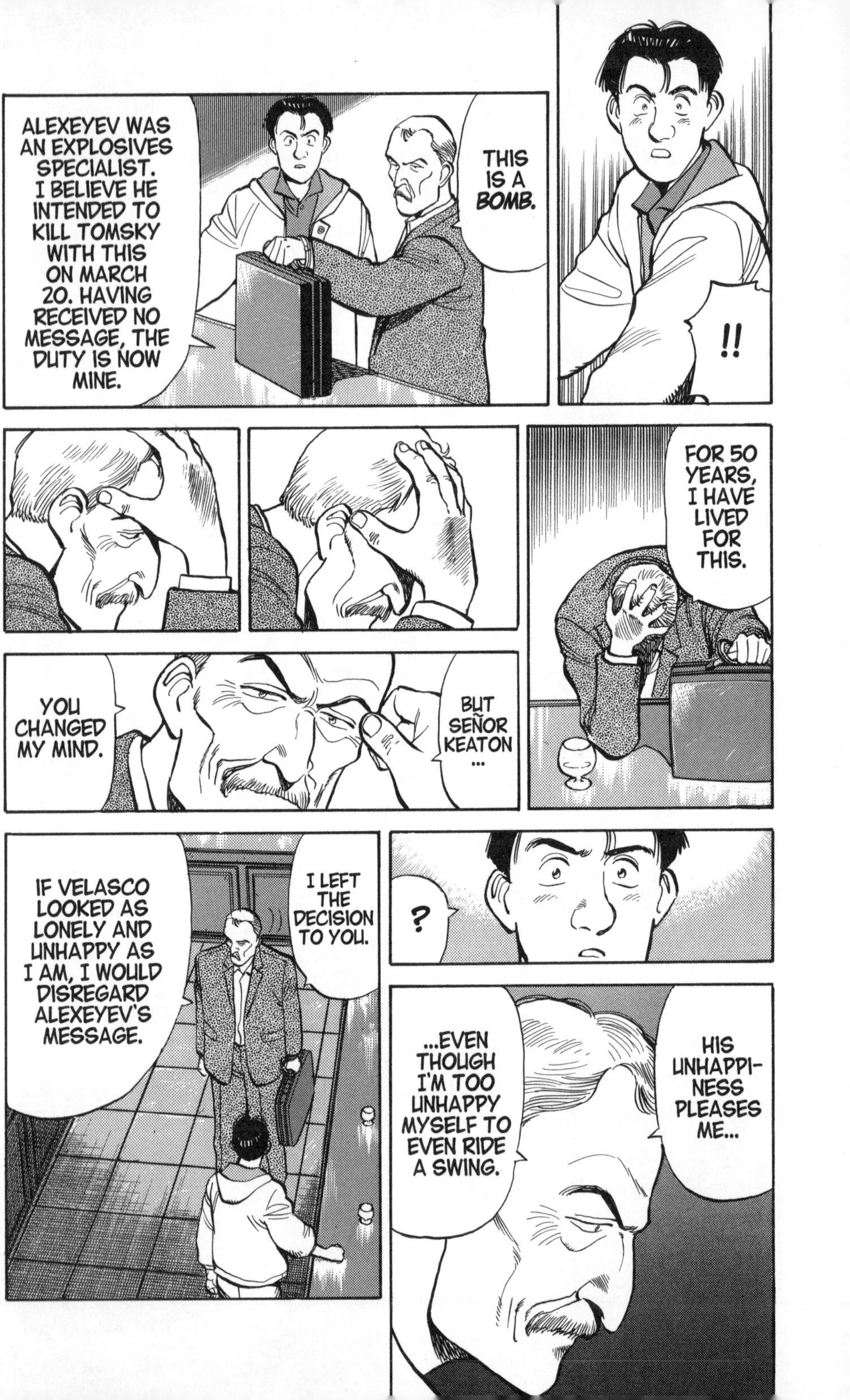
!!
THIS IS A BOMB.
ALEXEYEV WAS AN EXPLOSIVES SPECIALIST. I BELIEVE HE INTENDED TO KILL TOMSKY WITH THIS ON MARCH 20. HAVING RECEIVED NO MESSAGE, THE DUTY IS NOW MINE.
FOR 50 YEARS, I HAVE LIVED FOR THIS.
BUT SEÑOR KEATON...
YOU CHANGED MY MIND.
?
HIS UNHAPPI-NESS PLEASES ME...
...EVEN THOUGH I'M TOO UNHAPPY MYSELF TO EVEN RIDE A SWING.
I LEFT THE DECISION TO YOU.
IF VELASCO LOOKED AS LONELY AND UNHAPPY AS I AM, I WOULD DISREGARD ALEXEYEV'S MESSAGE.

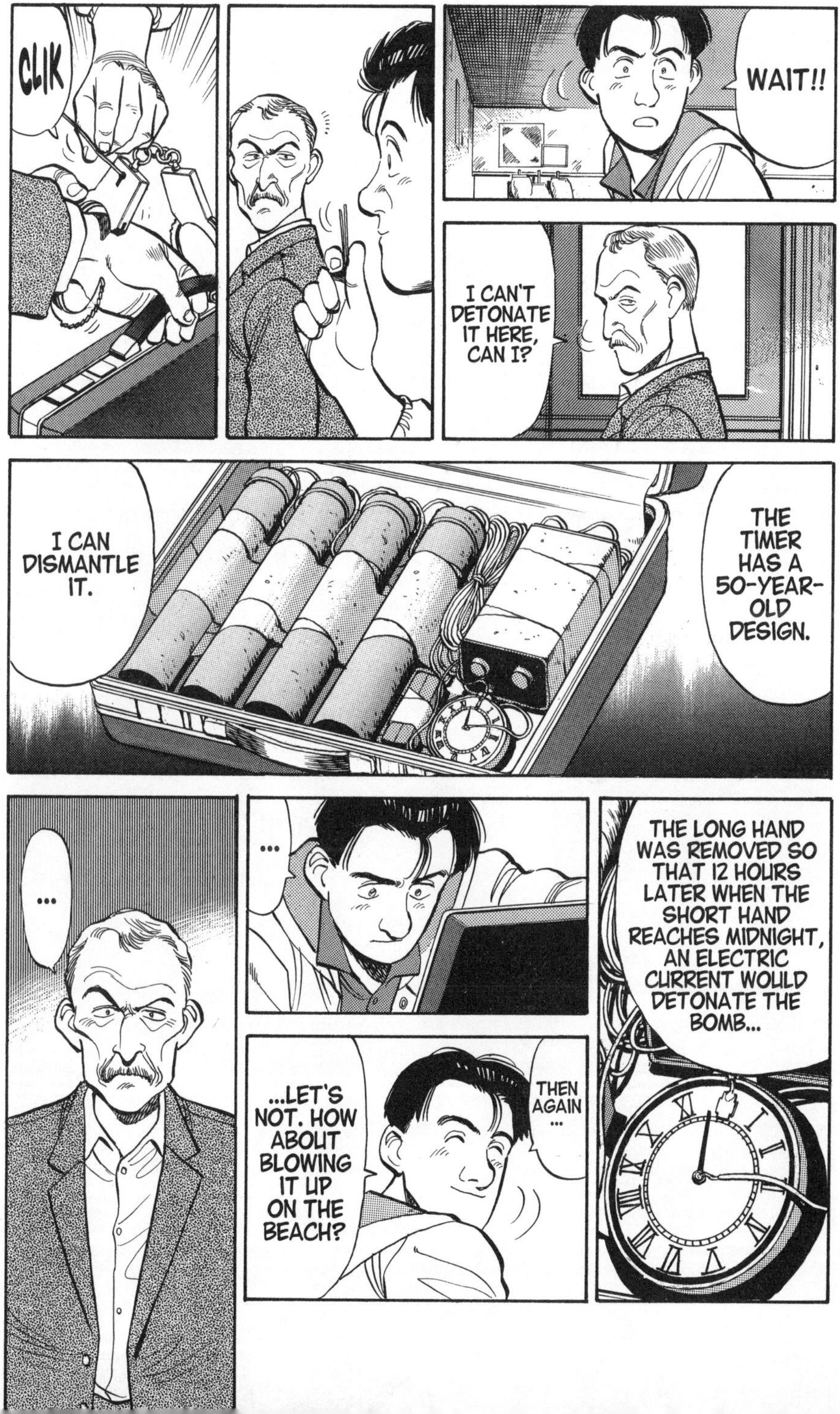
WAIT!!
I CAN'T DETONATE IT HERE, CAN I?
CLIK
THE TIMER HAS A 50-YEAR-OLD DESIGN.
I CAN DISMANTLE IT.
THE LONG HAND WAS REMOVED SO THAT 12 HOURS LATER WHEN THE SHORT HAND REACHES MIDNIGHT, AN ELECTRIC CURRENT WOULD DETONATE THE BOMB...
...
THEN AGAIN ...
...LET'S NOT. HOW ABOUT BLOWING IT UP ON THE BEACH?
...

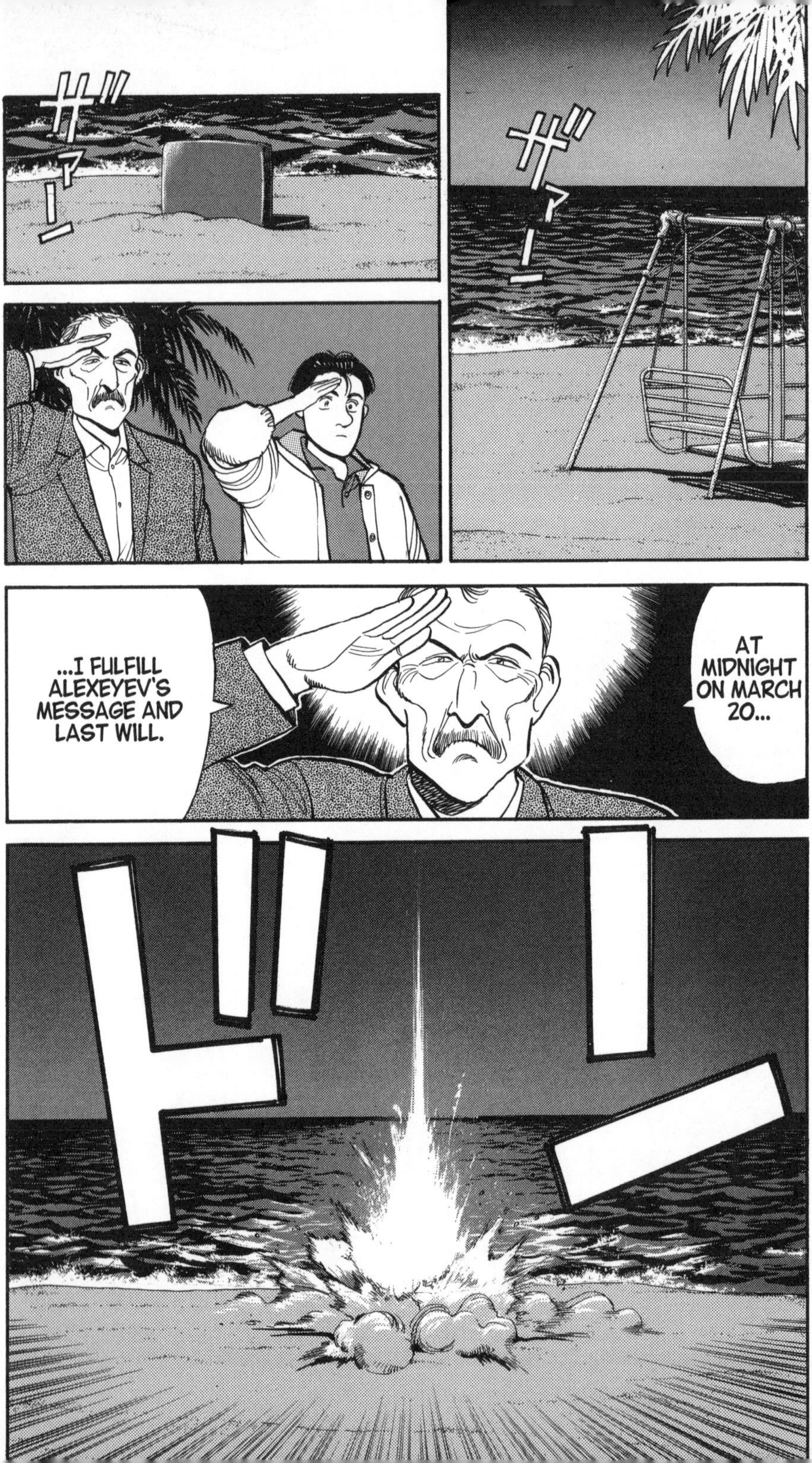
AT MIDNIGHT ON MARCH 20...
...I FULFILL ALEXEYEV'S MESSAGE AND LAST WILL.

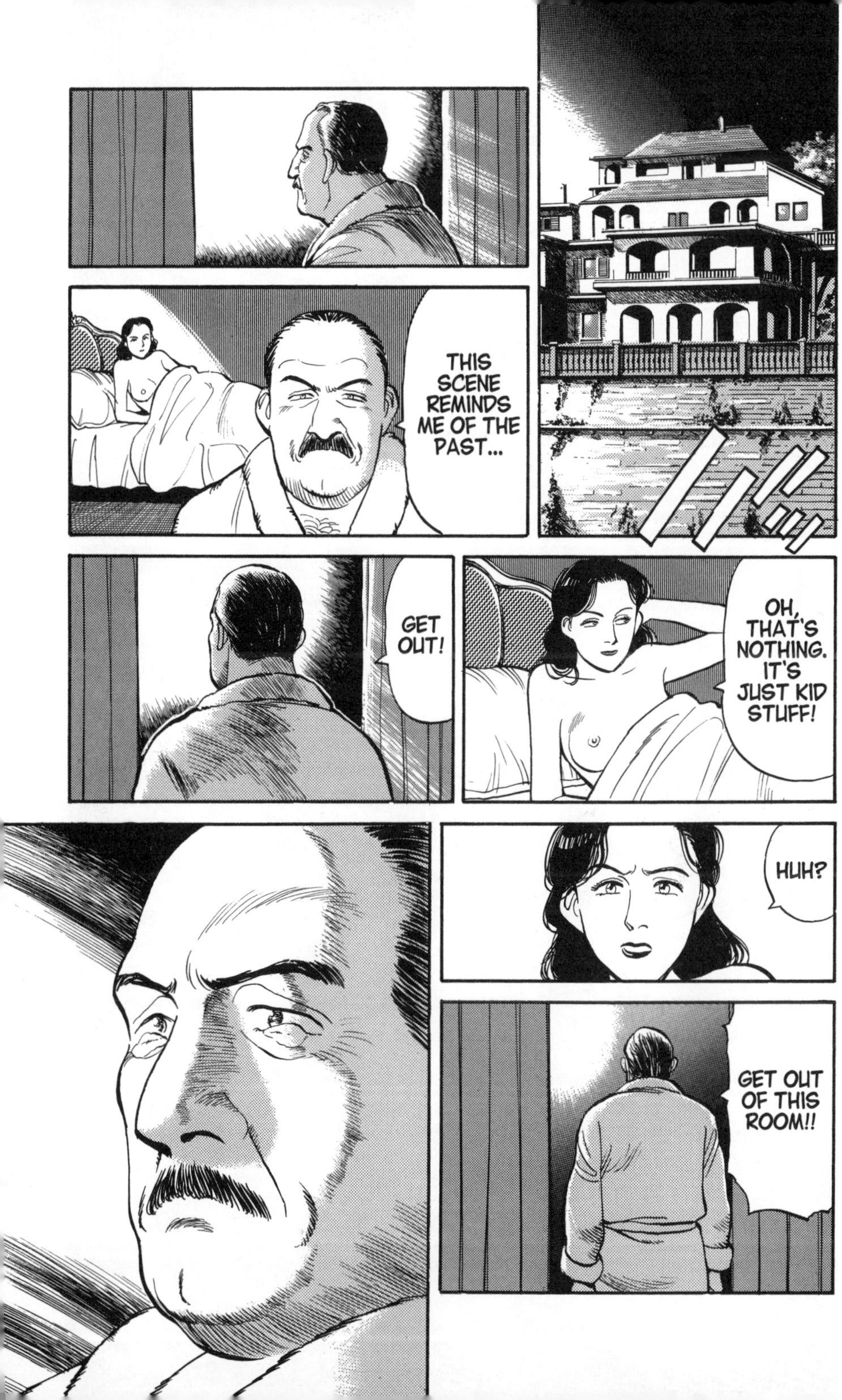
THIS SCENE REMINDS ME OF THE PAST...
OH, THAT'S NOTHING. IT'S JUST KID STUFF!
GET OUT!
HUH?
GET OUT OF THIS ROOM!!

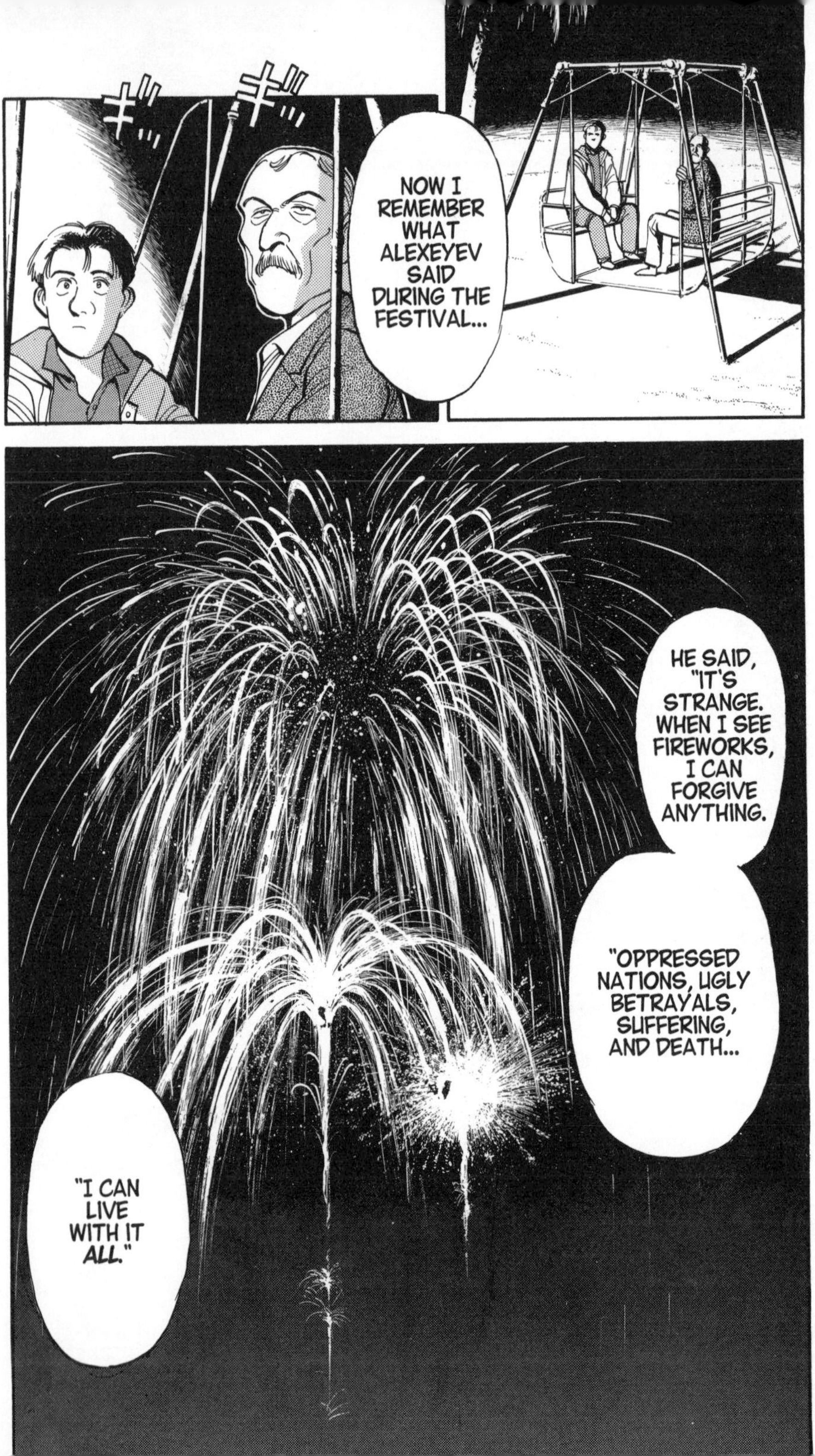
NOW I REMEMBER WHAT ALEXEYEV SAID DURING THE FESTIVAL...
HE SAID, "IT'S STRANGE. WHEN I SEE FIREWORKS, I CAN FORGIVE ANYTHING.
"OPPRESSED NATIONS, UGLY BETRAYALS, SUFFERING, AND DEATH...
"I CAN LIVE WITH IT ALL."

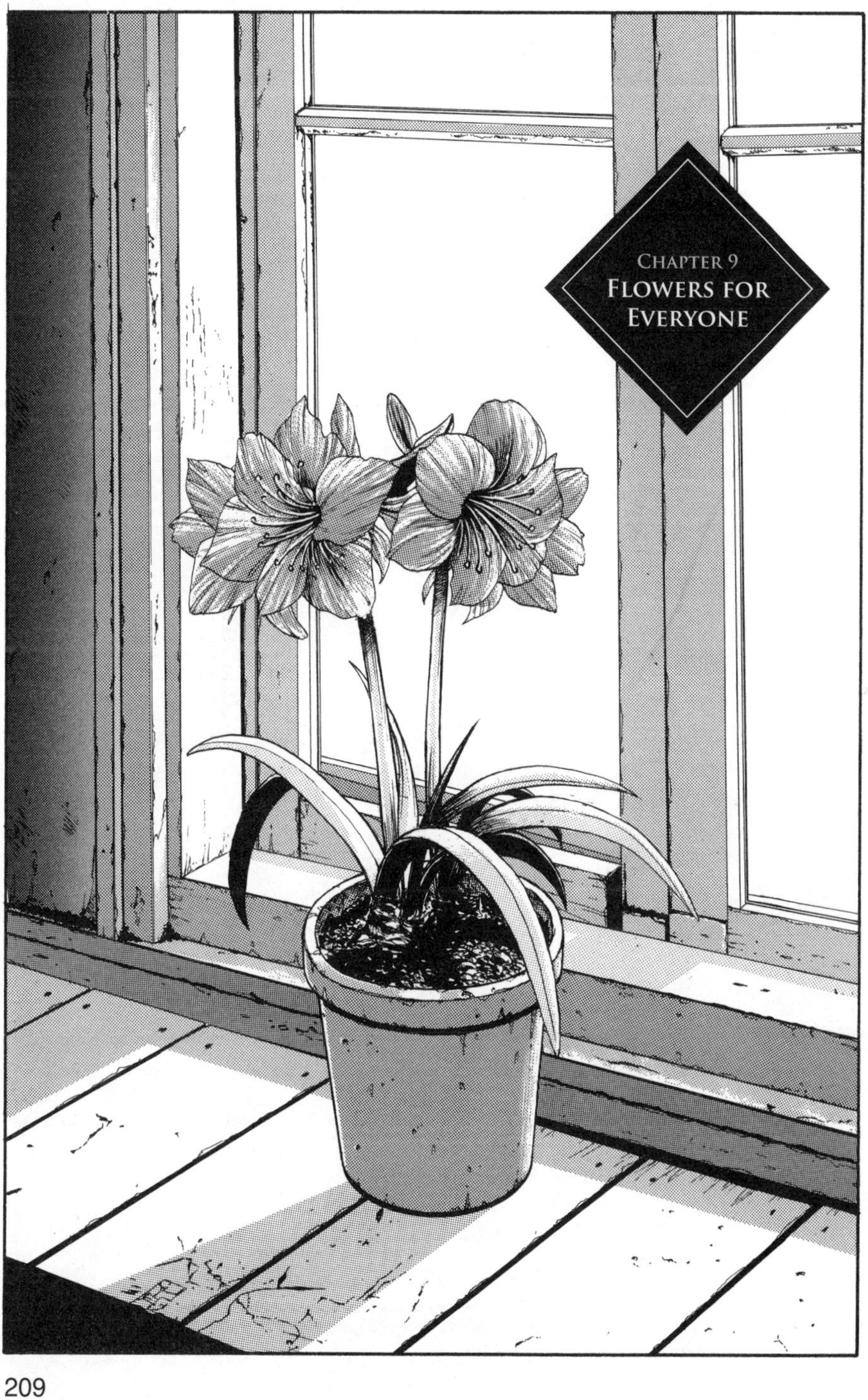
Chapter 9
Flowers for Everyone

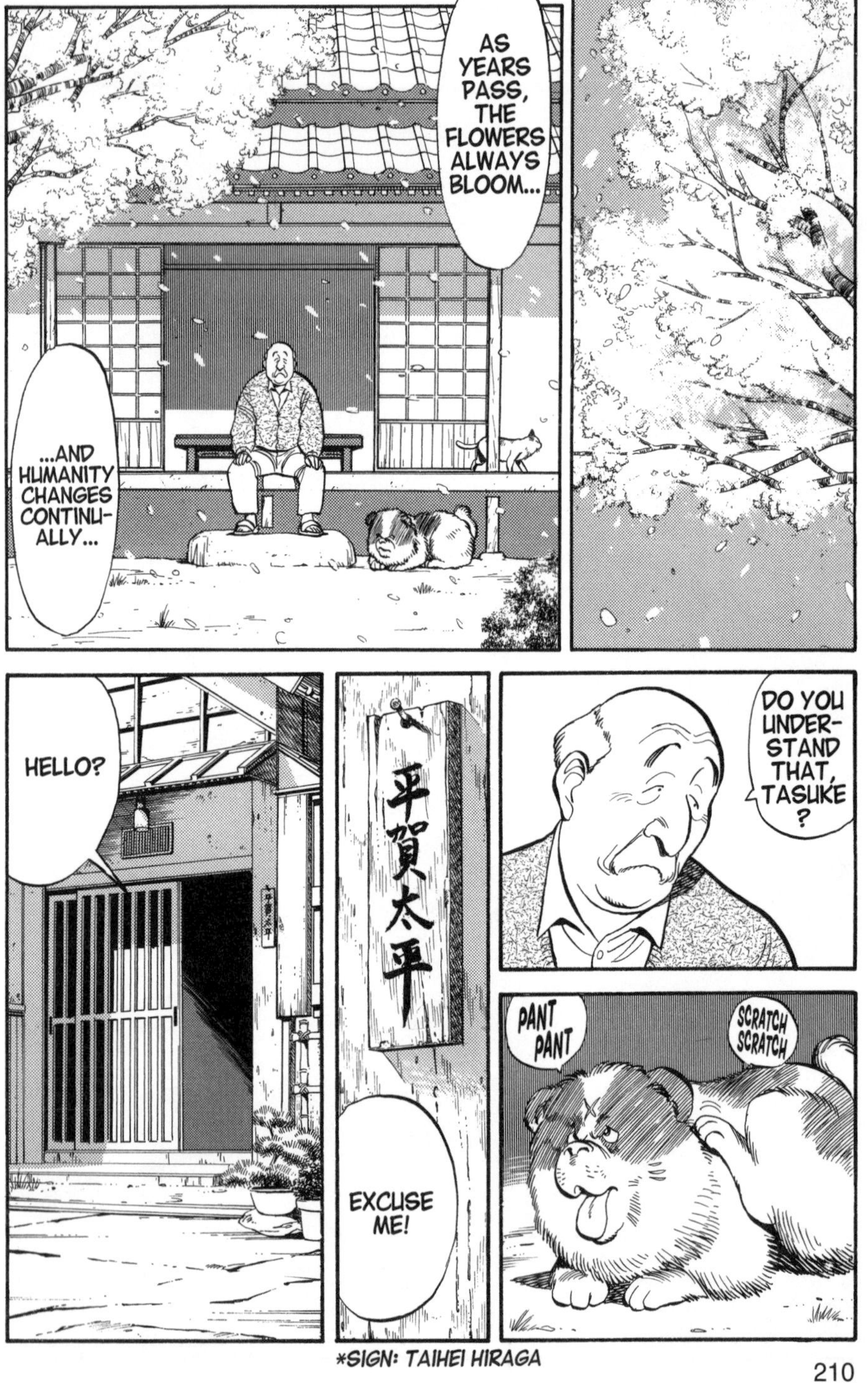
AS YEARS PASS, THE FLOWERS ALWAYS BLOOM...
...AND HUMANITY CHANGES CONTINU-ALLY...
DO YOU UNDER-STAND THAT, TASUKE?
PANT PANT
SCRATCH SCRATCH
平賀太平
EXCUSE ME!
HELLO?

*SIGN: TAIHEI HIRAGA

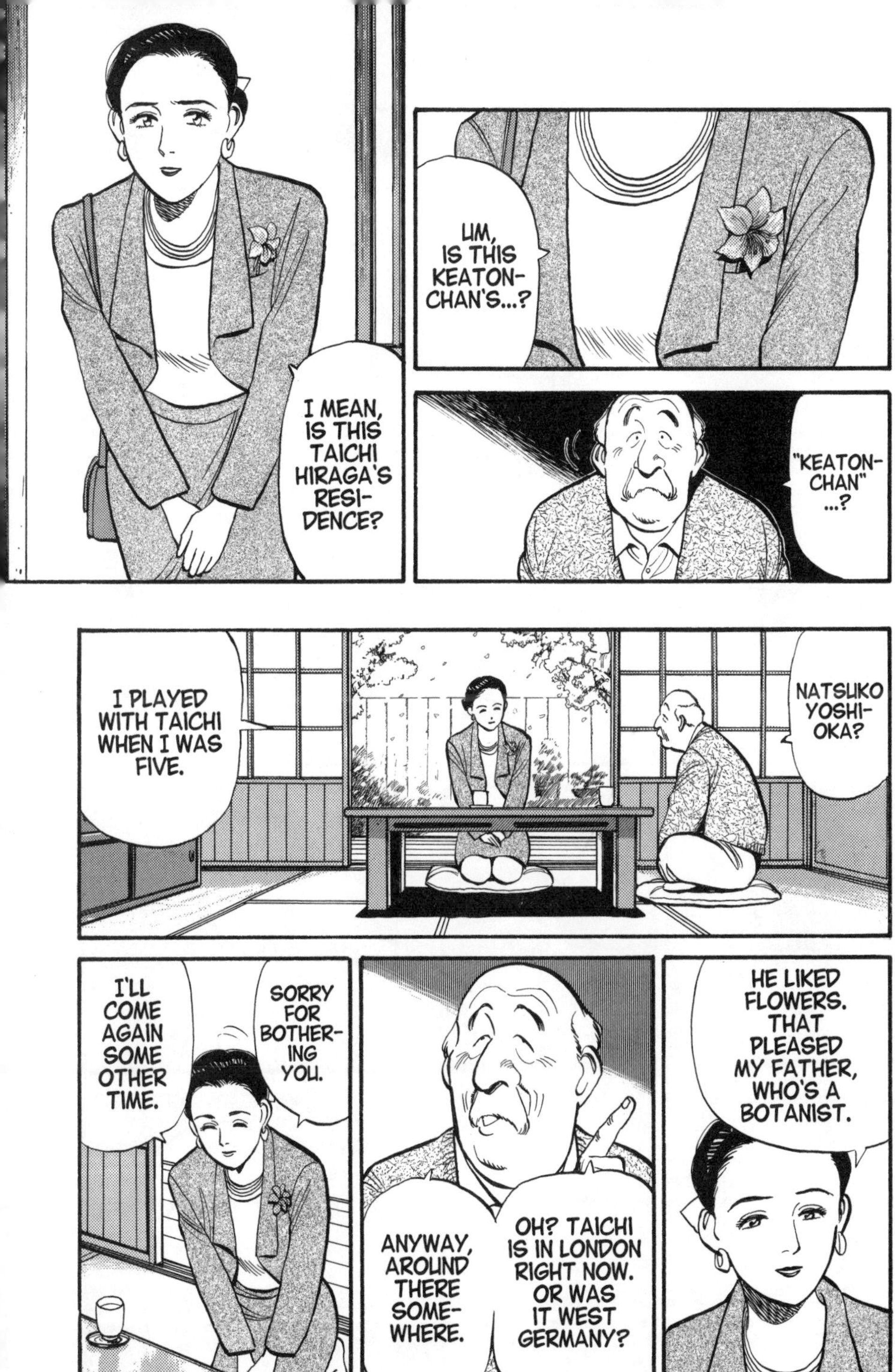
UM, IS THIS KEATON-CHAN'S...?
"KEATON-CHAN" ...?
I MEAN, IS THIS TAICHI HIRAGA'S RESIDENCE?
NATSUKO YOSHIOKA?
I PLAYED WITH TAICHI WHEN I WAS FIVE.
HE LIKED FLOWERS. THAT PLEASED MY FATHER, WHO'S A BOTANIST.
OH? TAICHI IS IN LONDON RIGHT NOW. OR WAS IT WEST GERMANY?
ANYWAY, AROUND THERE SOMEWHERE.
SORRY FOR BOTHERING YOU.
I'LL COME AGAIN SOME OTHER TIME.

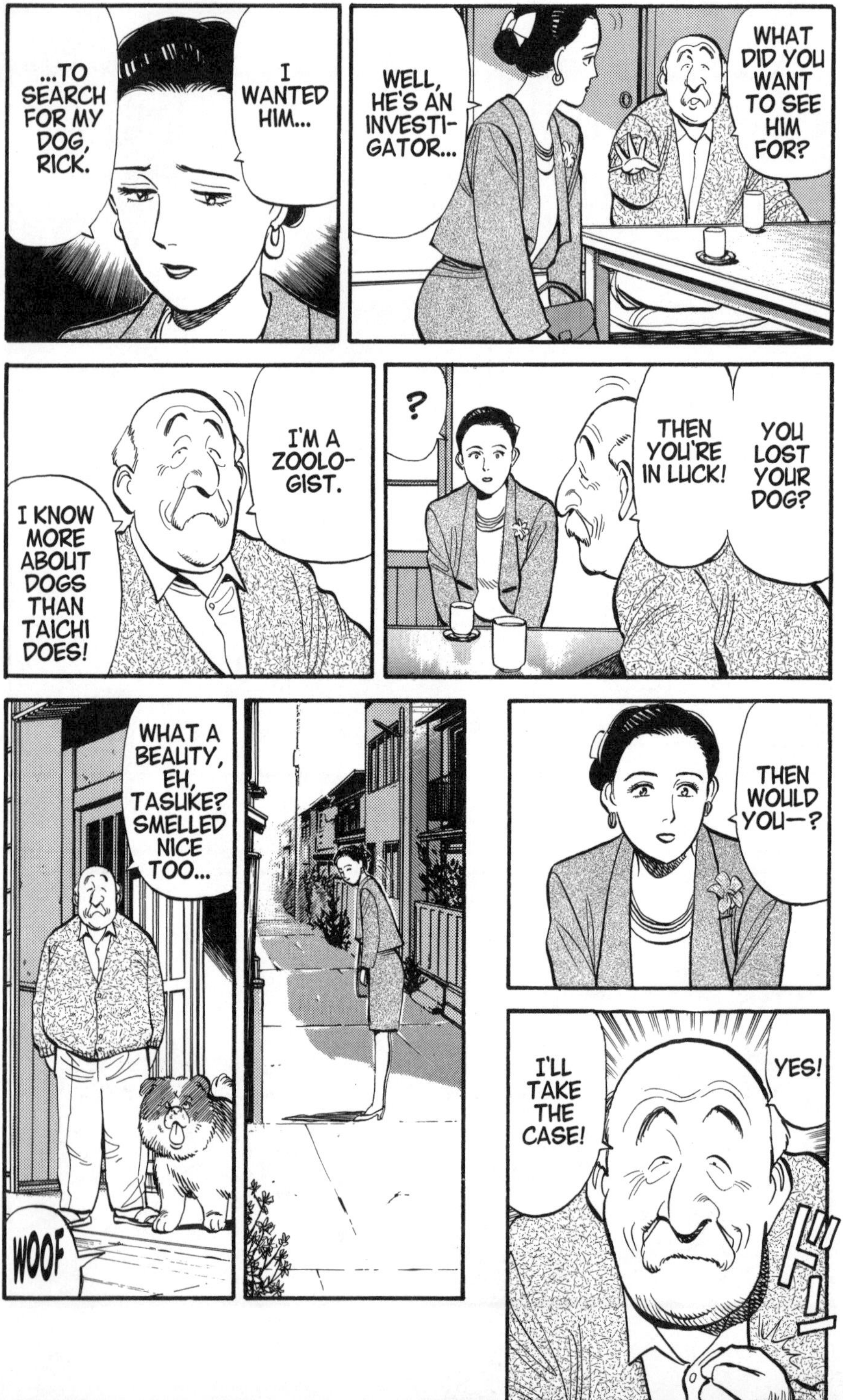
WHAT DID YOU WANT TO SEE HIM FOR?
WELL, HE'S AN INVESTIGATOR...
I WANTED HIM...
...TO SEARCH FOR MY DOG, RICK.
YOU LOST YOUR DOG?
THEN YOU'RE IN LUCK!
?
I'M A ZOOLOGIST.
I KNOW MORE ABOUT DOGS THAN TAICHI DOES!
THEN WOULD YOU—?
YES!
I'LL TAKE THE CASE!
WHAT A BEAUTY, EH, TASUKE? SMELLED NICE TOO...
WOOF

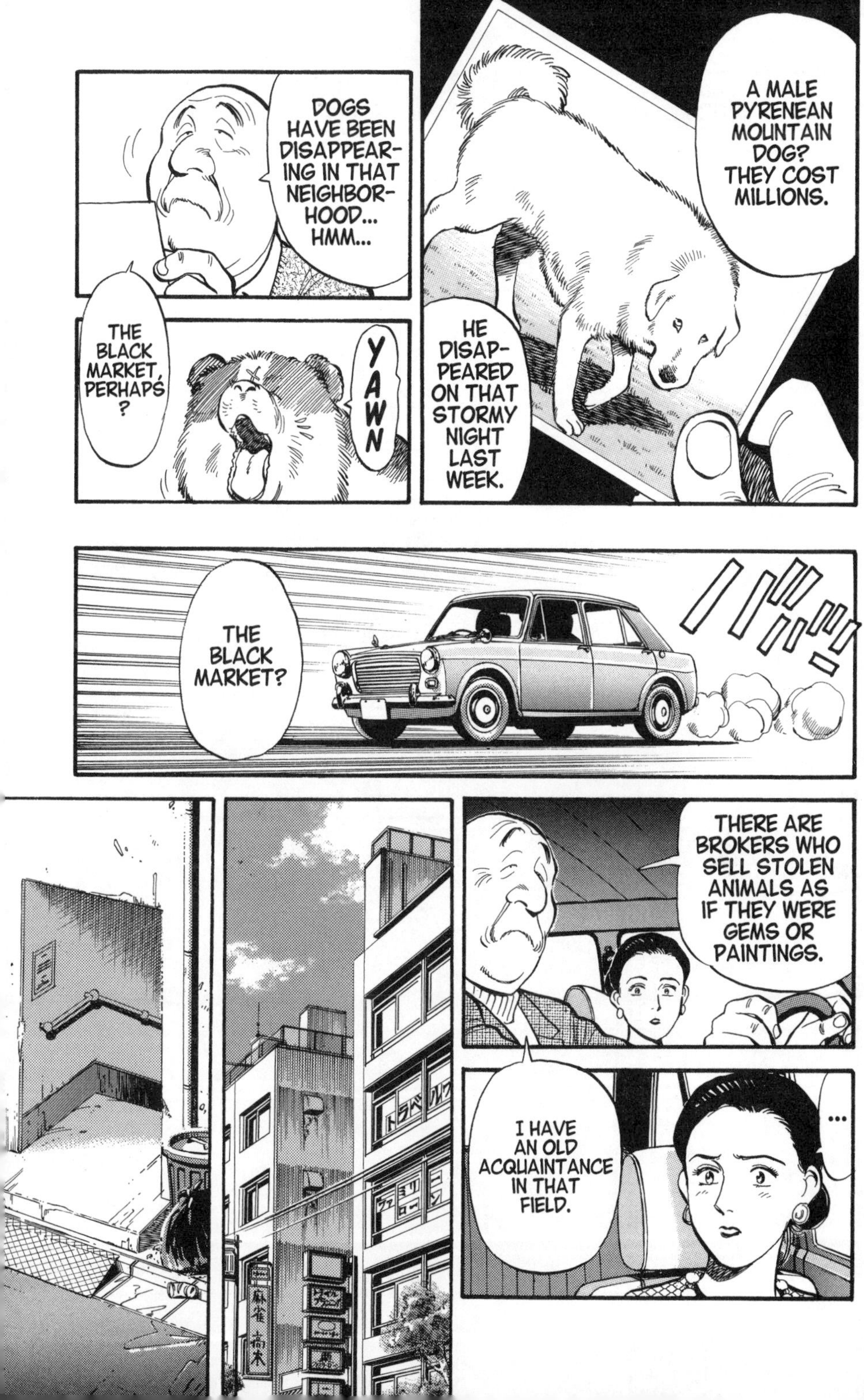
A MALE PYRENEAN MOUNTAIN DOG? THEY COST MILLIONS.
HE DISAPPEARED ON THAT STORMY NIGHT LAST WEEK.
DOGS HAVE BEEN DISAPPEARING IN THAT NEIGHBORHOOD... HMM...
YAWN
THE BLACK MARKET, PERHAPS?
THE BLACK MARKET?
THERE ARE BROKERS WHO SELL STOLEN ANIMALS AS IF THEY WERE GEMS OR PAINTINGS.
...
I HAVE AN OLD ACQUAINTANCE IN THAT FIELD.

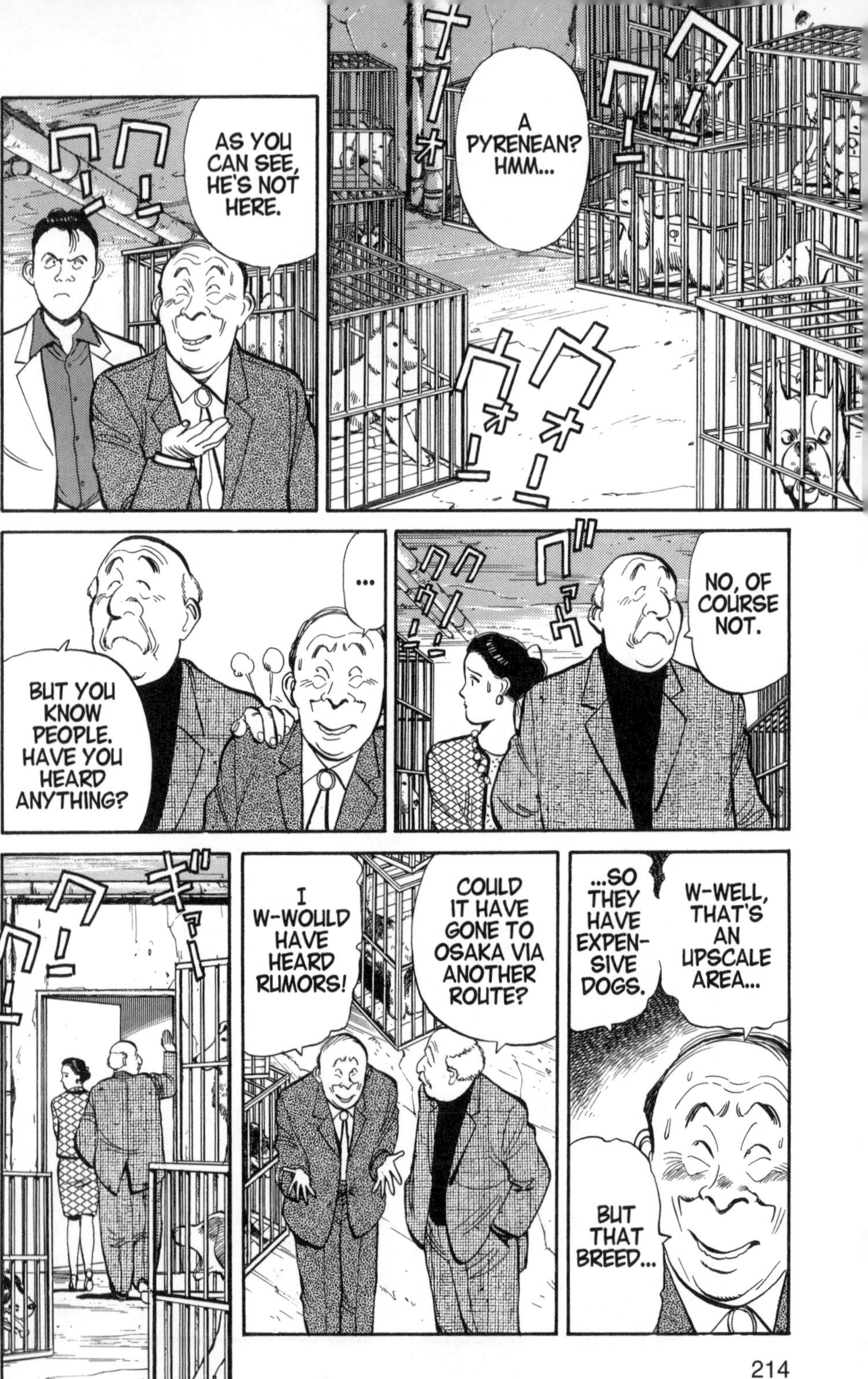
A PYRENEAN? HMM...
AS YOU CAN SEE, HE'S NOT HERE.
NO, OF COURSE NOT.
...
BUT YOU KNOW PEOPLE. HAVE YOU HEARD ANYTHING?
W-WELL, THAT'S AN UPSCALE AREA...
...SO THEY HAVE EXPEN-SIVE DOGS.
BUT THAT BREED...
COULD IT HAVE GONE TO OSAKA VIA ANOTHER ROUTE?
I W-WOULD HAVE HEARD RUMORS!

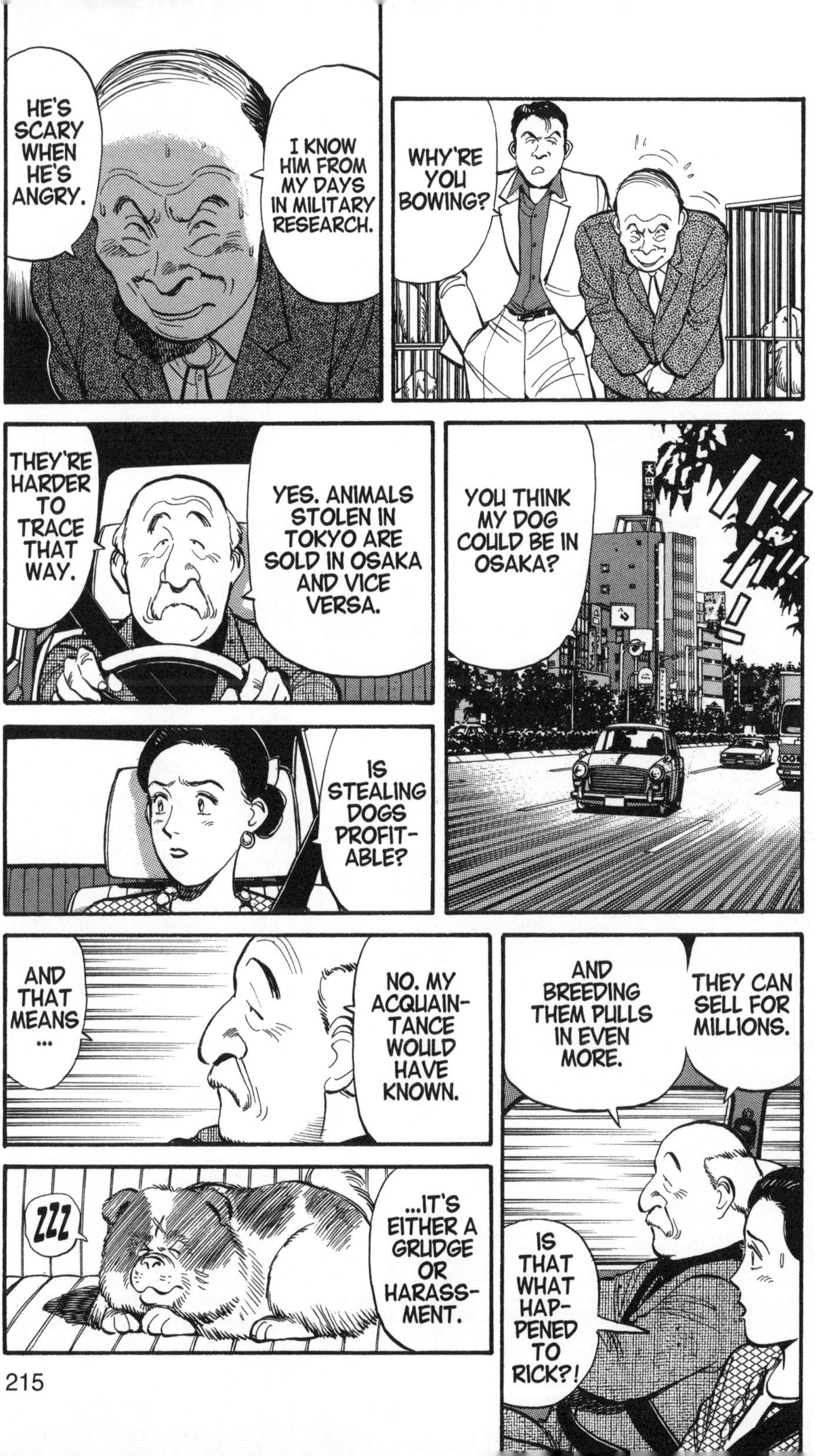
WHY'RE YOU BOWING?
I KNOW HIM FROM MY DAYS IN MILITARY RESEARCH.
HE'S SCARY WHEN HE'S ANGRY.
YOU THINK MY DOG COULD BE IN OSAKA?
YES. ANIMALS STOLEN IN TOKYO ARE SOLD IN OSAKA AND VICE VERSA.
THEY'RE HARDER TO TRACE THAT WAY.
IS STEALING DOGS PROFIT-ABLE?
THEY CAN SELL FOR MILLIONS.
AND BREEDING THEM PULLS IN EVEN MORE.
IS THAT WHAT HAP-PENED TO RICK?!
NO. MY ACQUAIN-TANCE WOULD HAVE KNOWN.
AND THAT MEANS...
...IT'S EITHER A GRUDGE OR HARASS-MENT.
ZZZ

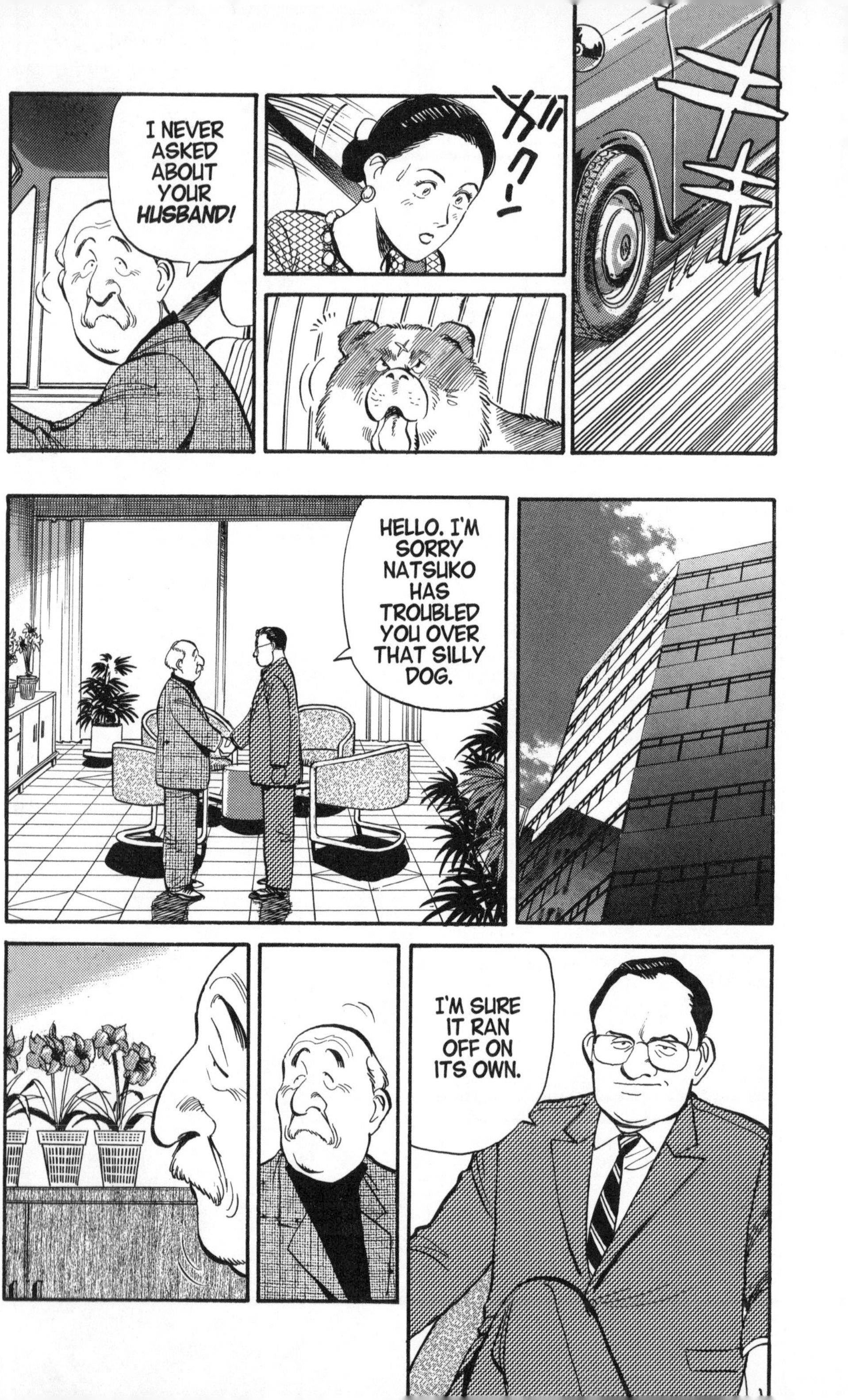
I NEVER ASKED ABOUT YOUR HUSBAND!
HELLO. I'M SORRY NATSUKO HAS TROUBLED YOU OVER THAT SILLY DOG.
I'M SURE IT RAN OFF ON ITS OWN.

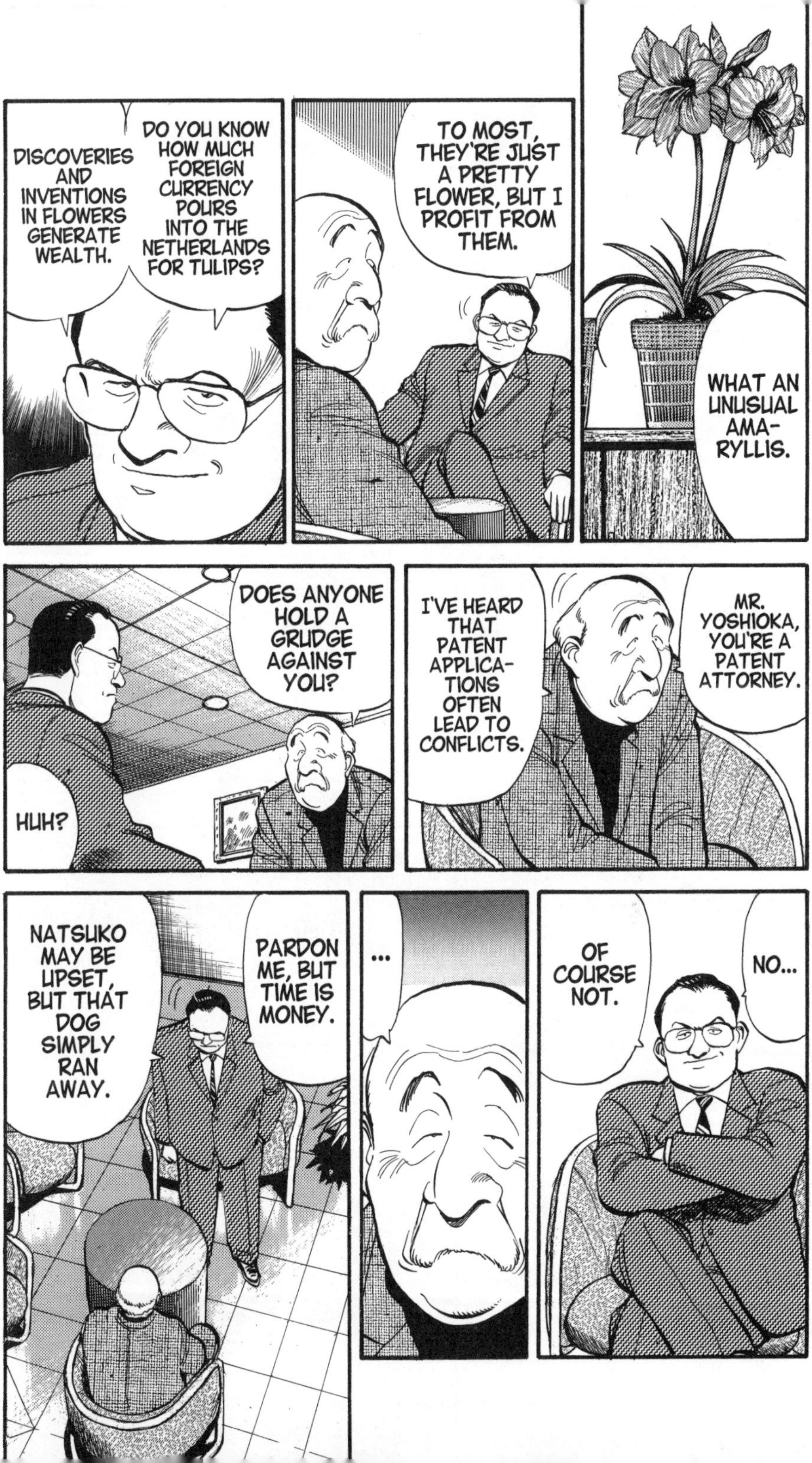
WHAT AN UNUSUAL AMA-RYLLIS.
TO MOST, THEY'RE JUST A PRETTY FLOWER, BUT I PROFIT FROM THEM.
DO YOU KNOW HOW MUCH FOREIGN CURRENCY POURS INTO THE NETHERLANDS FOR TULIPS?
DISCOVERIES AND INVENTIONS IN FLOWERS GENERATE WEALTH.
MR. YOSHIOKA, YOU'RE A PATENT ATTORNEY.
I'VE HEARD THAT PATENT APPLICA-TIONS OFTEN LEAD TO CONFLICTS.
DOES ANYONE HOLD A GRUDGE AGAINST YOU?
HUH?
NO...
OF COURSE NOT.
...
PARDON ME, BUT TIME IS MONEY.
NATSUKO MAY BE UPSET, BUT THAT DOG SIMPLY RAN AWAY.

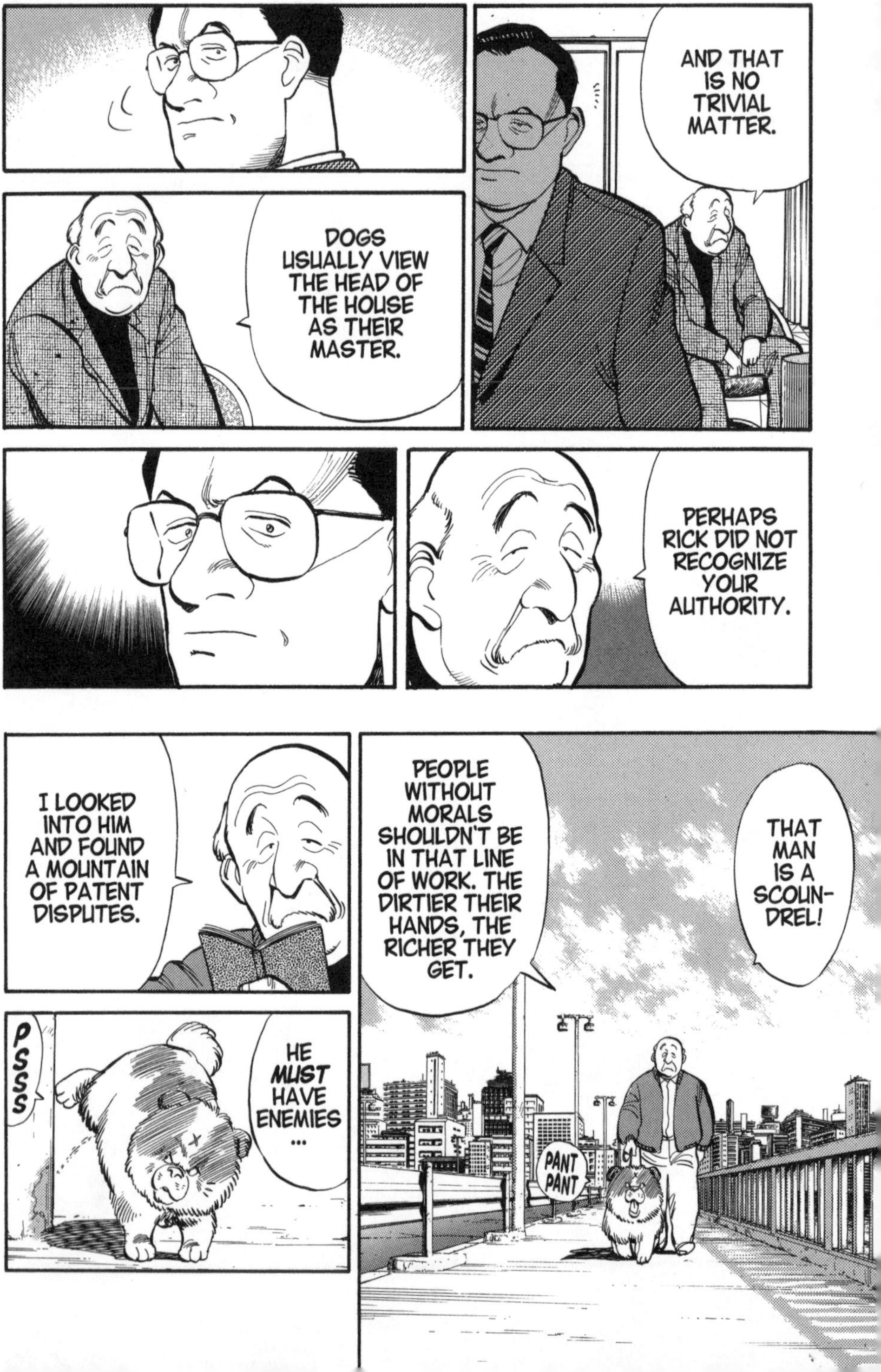
AND THAT IS NO TRIVIAL MATTER.
DOGS USUALLY VIEW THE HEAD OF THE HOUSE AS THEIR MASTER.
PERHAPS RICK DID NOT RECOGNIZE YOUR AUTHORITY.
THAT MAN IS A SCOUN-DREL!
PEOPLE WITHOUT MORALS SHOULDN'T BE IN THAT LINE OF WORK. THE DIRTIER THEIR HANDS, THE RICHER THEY GET.
PANT PANT
I LOOKED INTO HIM AND FOUND A MOUNTAIN OF PATENT DISPUTES.
HE *MUST* HAVE ENEMIES...
PSSS

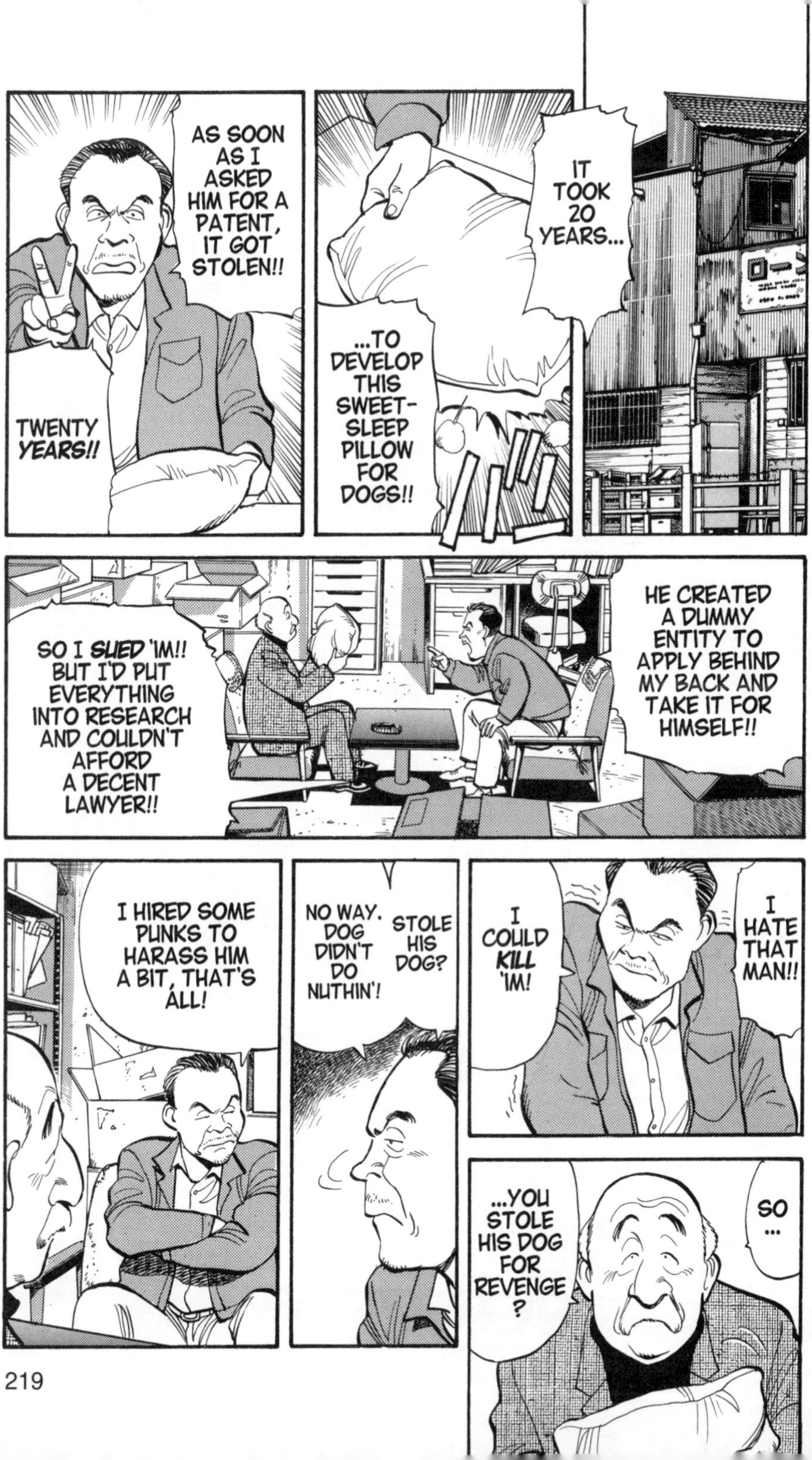
IT TOOK 20 YEARS...
...TO DEVELOP THIS SWEET-SLEEP PILLOW FOR DOGS!!
AS SOON AS I ASKED HIM FOR A PATENT, IT GOT STOLEN!!
TWENTY YEARS!!
HE CREATED A DUMMY ENTITY TO APPLY BEHIND MY BACK AND TAKE IT FOR HIMSELF!!
SO I SUED 'IM!! BUT I'D PUT EVERYTHING INTO RESEARCH AND COULDN'T AFFORD A DECENT LAWYER!!
I HATE THAT MAN!!
I COULD KILL 'IM!
SO ...
...YOU STOLE HIS DOG FOR REVENGE?
STOLE HIS DOG?
NO WAY. DOG DIDN'T DO NUTHIN'!
I HIRED SOME PUNKS TO HARASS HIM A BIT, THAT'S ALL!

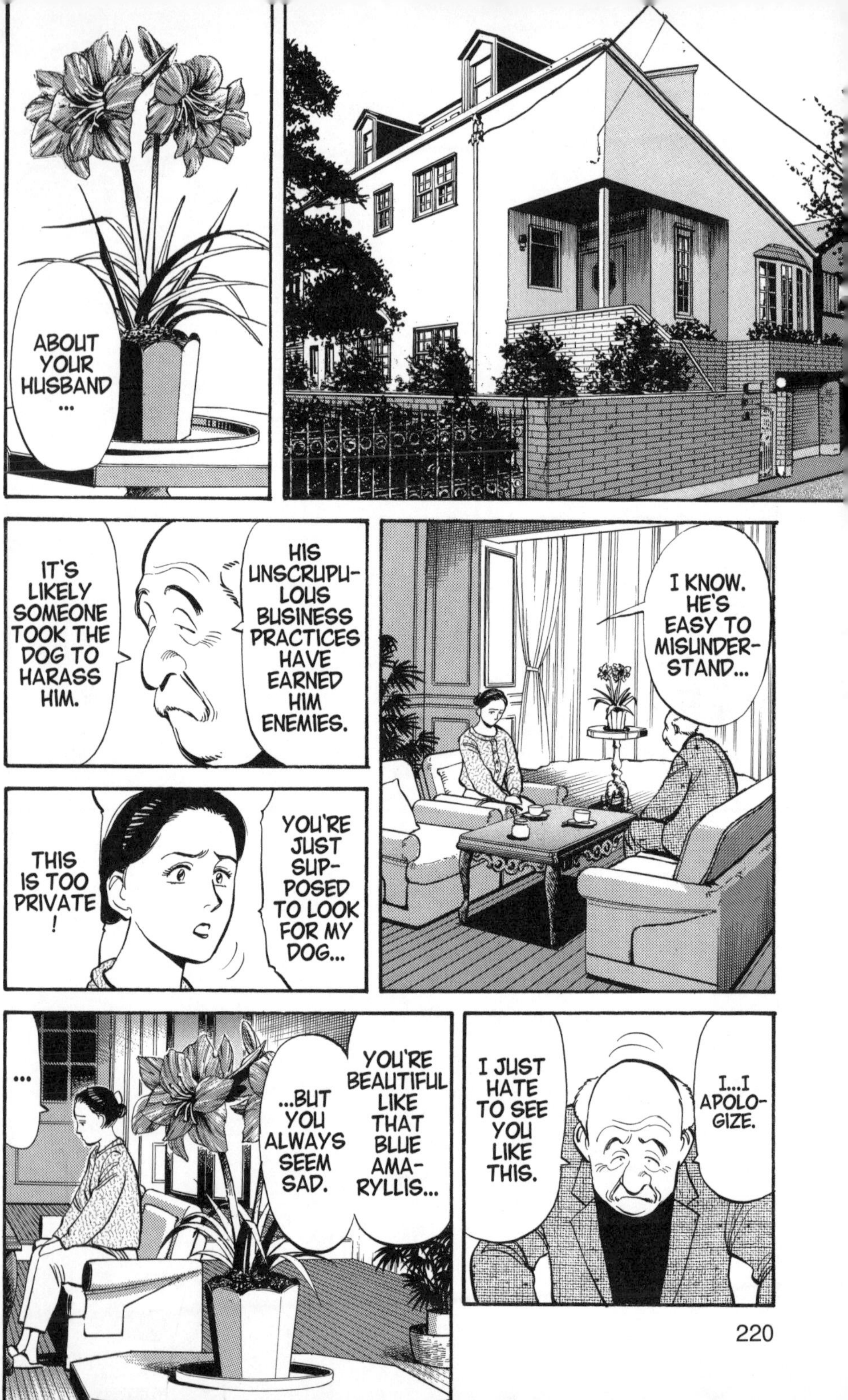
ABOUT YOUR HUSBAND ...
I KNOW. HE'S EASY TO MISUNDERSTAND...
HIS UNSCRUPULOUS BUSINESS PRACTICES HAVE EARNED HIM ENEMIES.
IT'S LIKELY SOMEONE TOOK THE DOG TO HARASS HIM.
YOU'RE JUST SUPPOSED TO LOOK FOR MY DOG...
THIS IS TOO PRIVATE!
I...I APOLOGIZE.
I JUST HATE TO SEE YOU LIKE THIS.
YOU'RE BEAUTIFUL LIKE THAT BLUE AMARYLLIS...
...BUT YOU ALWAYS SEEM SAD.
...

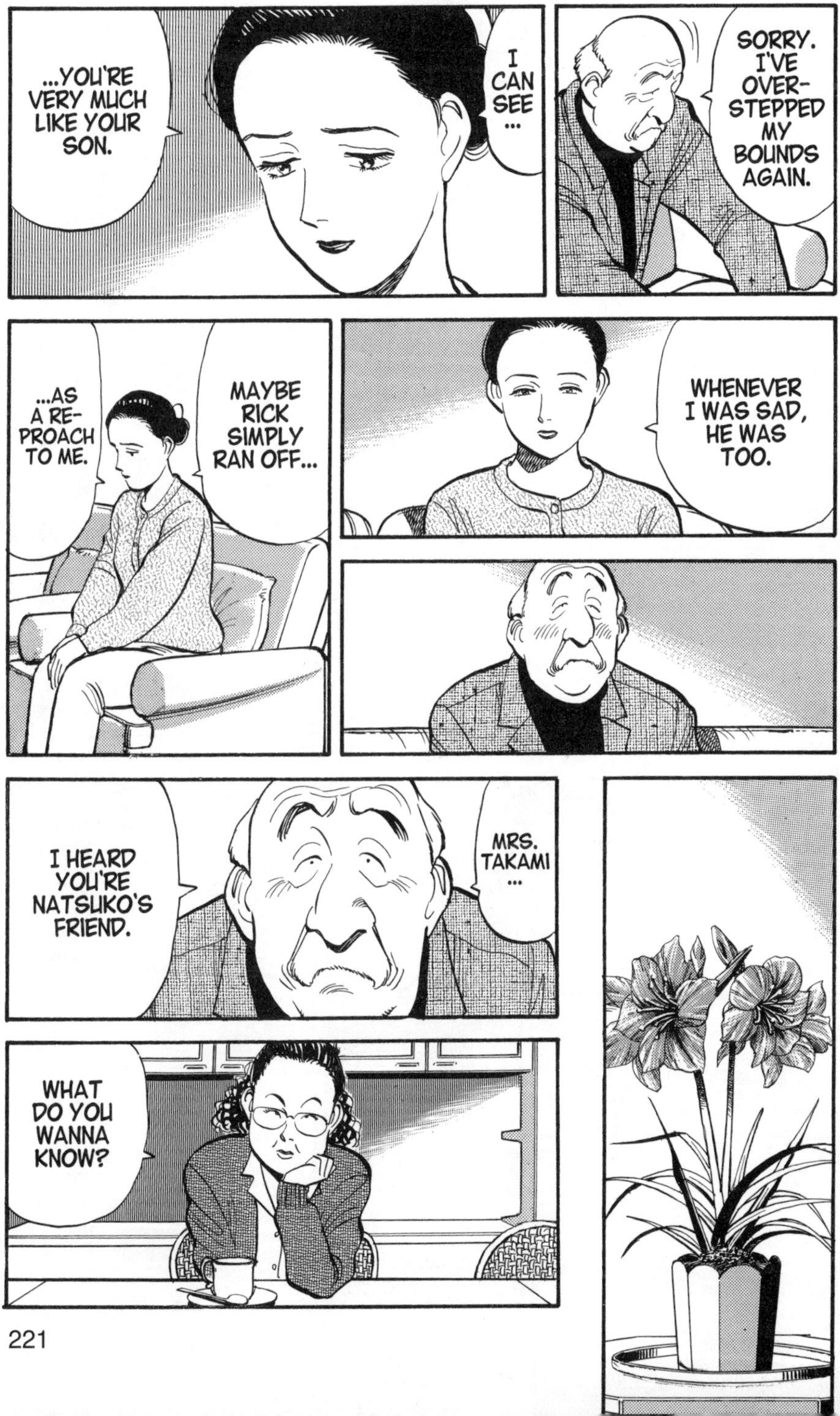
SORRY. I'VE OVER-STEPPED MY BOUNDS AGAIN.
I CAN SEE...
...YOU'RE VERY MUCH LIKE YOUR SON.
WHENEVER I WAS SAD, HE WAS TOO.
MAYBE RICK SIMPLY RAN OFF...
...AS A RE-PROACH TO ME.
MRS. TAKAMI...
I HEARD YOU'RE NATSUKO'S FRIEND.
WHAT DO YOU WANNA KNOW?

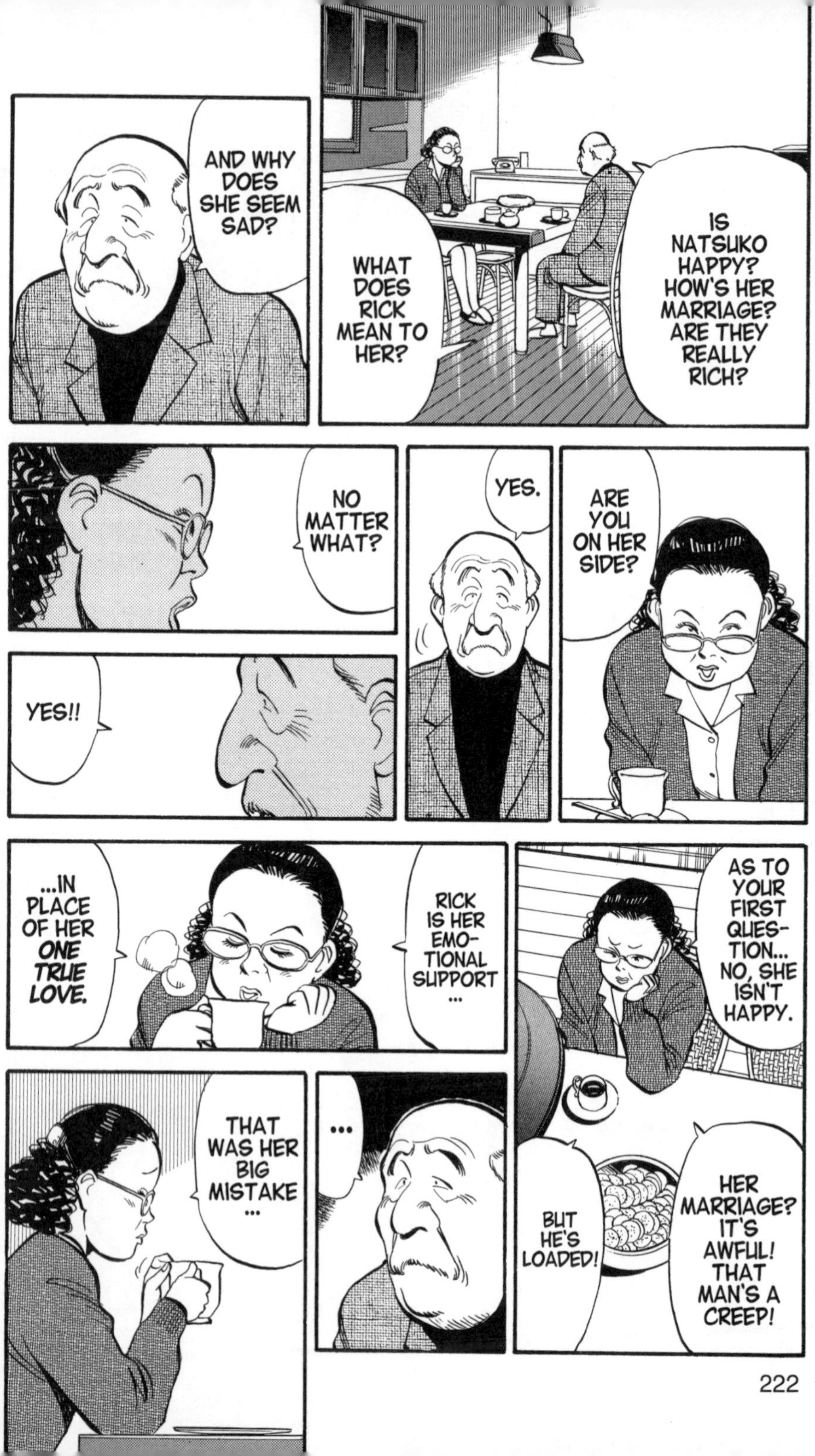
IS NATSUKO HAPPY? HOW'S HER MARRIAGE? ARE THEY REALLY RICH?
WHAT DOES RICK MEAN TO HER?
AND WHY DOES SHE SEEM SAD?
ARE YOU ON HER SIDE?
YES.
NO MATTER WHAT?
YES!!
AS TO YOUR FIRST QUESTION... NO, SHE ISN'T HAPPY.
HER MARRIAGE? IT'S AWFUL! THAT MAN'S A CREEP!
BUT HE'S LOADED!
RICK IS HER EMOTIONAL SUPPORT...
...IN PLACE OF HER ONE TRUE LOVE.
...
THAT WAS HER BIG MISTAKE...

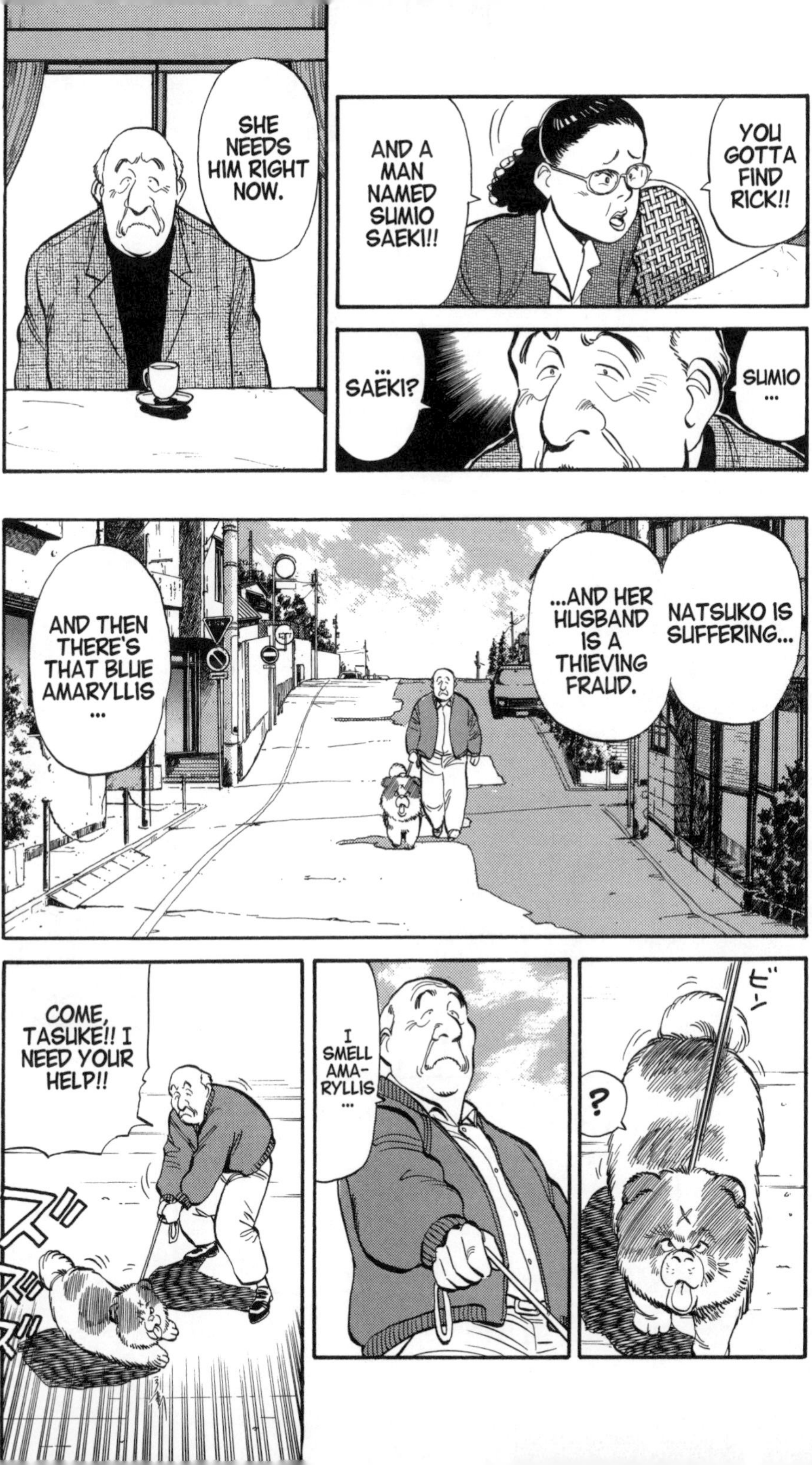
YOU GOTTA FIND RICK!!
AND A MAN NAMED SUMIO SAEKI!!
SUMIO ...
... SAËKI?
SHE NEEDS HIM RIGHT NOW.
NATSUKO IS SUFFERING...
...AND HER HUSBAND IS A THIEVING FRAUD.
AND THEN THERE'S THAT BLUE AMARYLLIS ...
ビーン
?
I SMELL AMA-RYLLIS ...
COME, TASUKE!! I NEED YOUR HELP!!
ズズズ

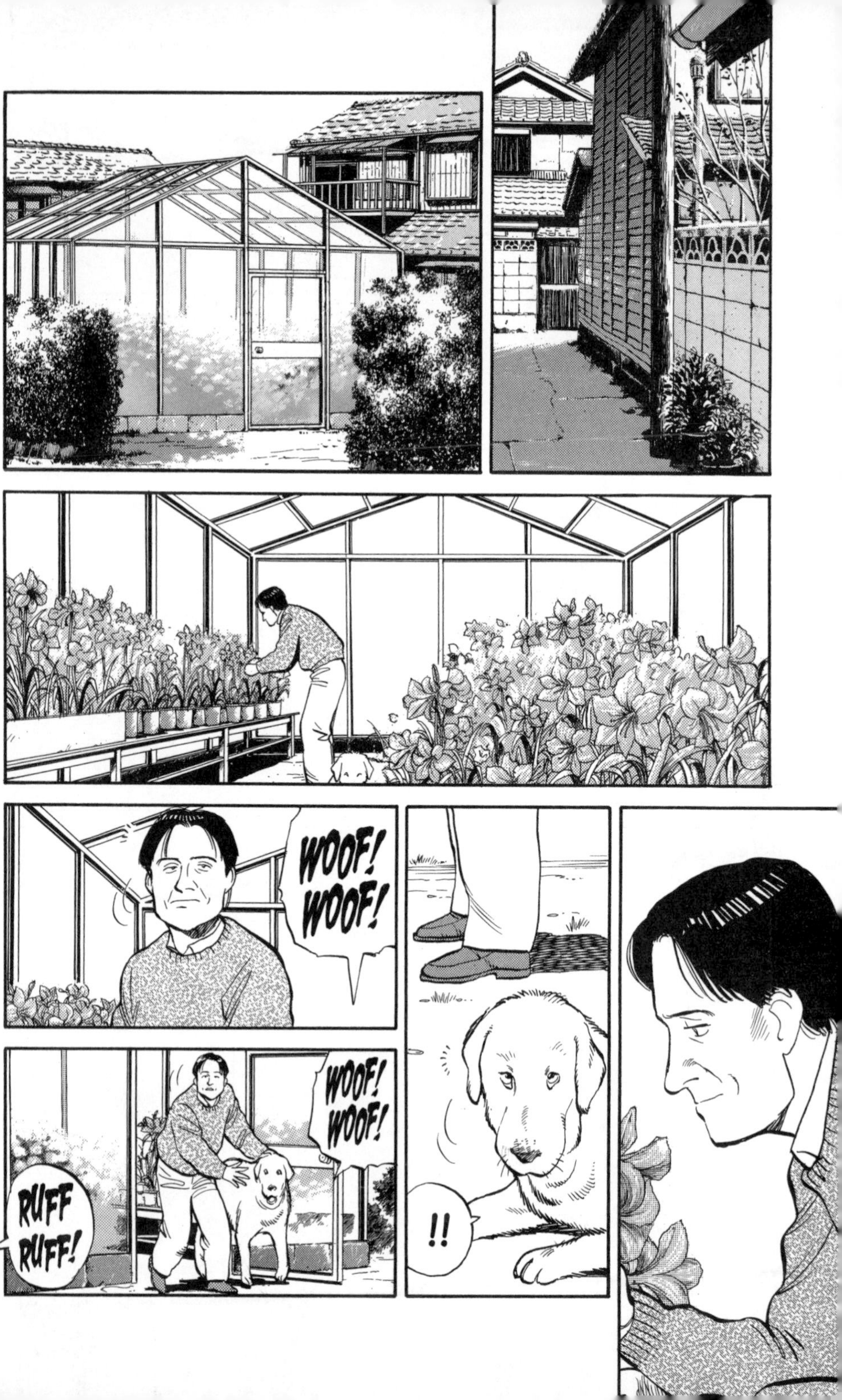
!!
WOOF! WOOF!
WOOF! WOOF!
RUFF RUFF!

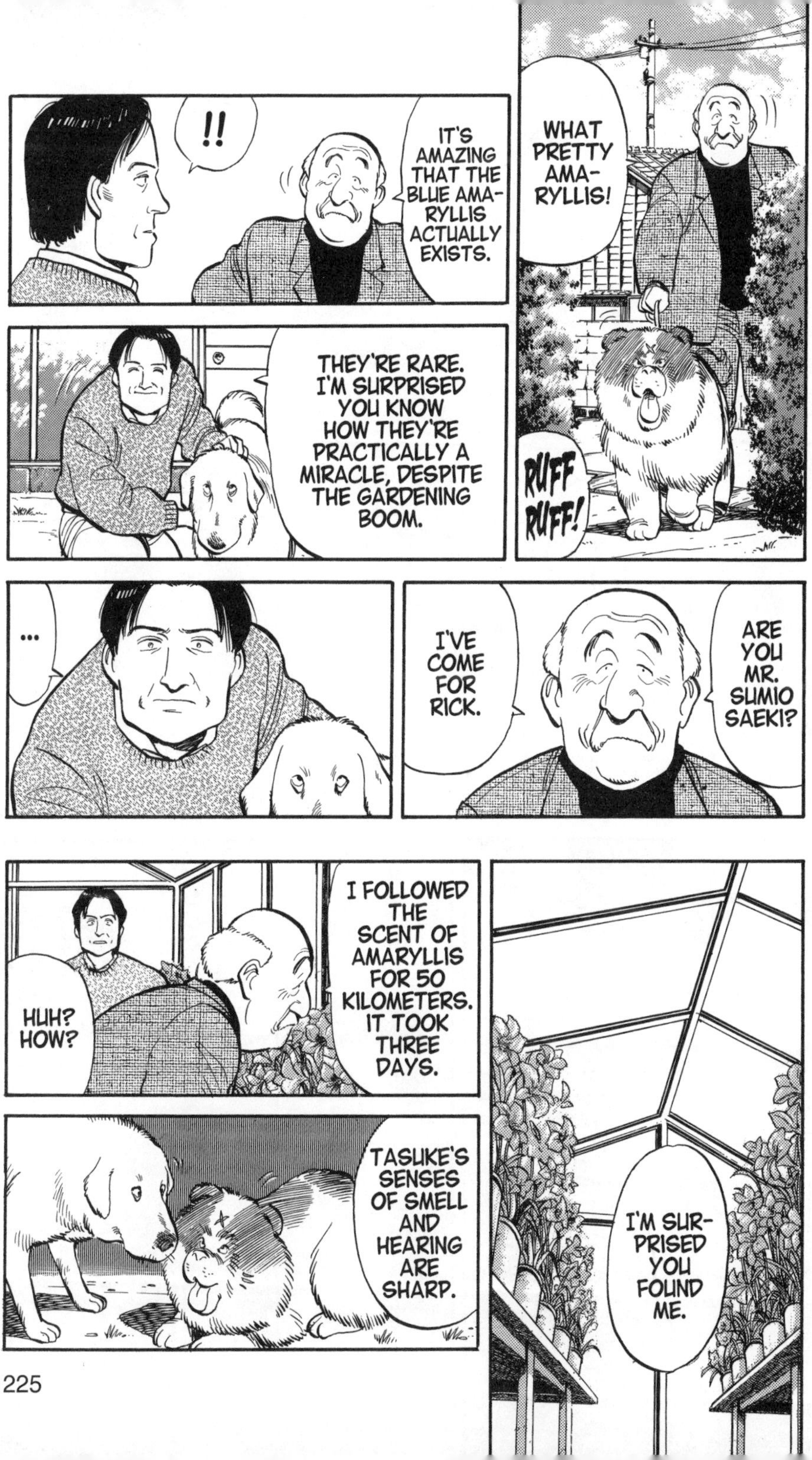
WHAT PRETTY AMARYLLIS!
RUFF RUFF!
IT'S AMAZING THAT THE BLUE AMARYLLIS ACTUALLY EXISTS.
!!
THEY'RE RARE. I'M SURPRISED YOU KNOW HOW THEY'RE PRACTICALLY A MIRACLE, DESPITE THE GARDENING BOOM.
ARE YOU MR. SUMIO SAEKI?
I'VE COME FOR RICK.
...
I'M SURPRISED YOU FOUND ME.
I FOLLOWED THE SCENT OF AMARYLLIS FOR 50 KILOMETERS. IT TOOK THREE DAYS.
HUH? HOW?
TASUKE'S SENSES OF SMELL AND HEARING ARE SHARP.

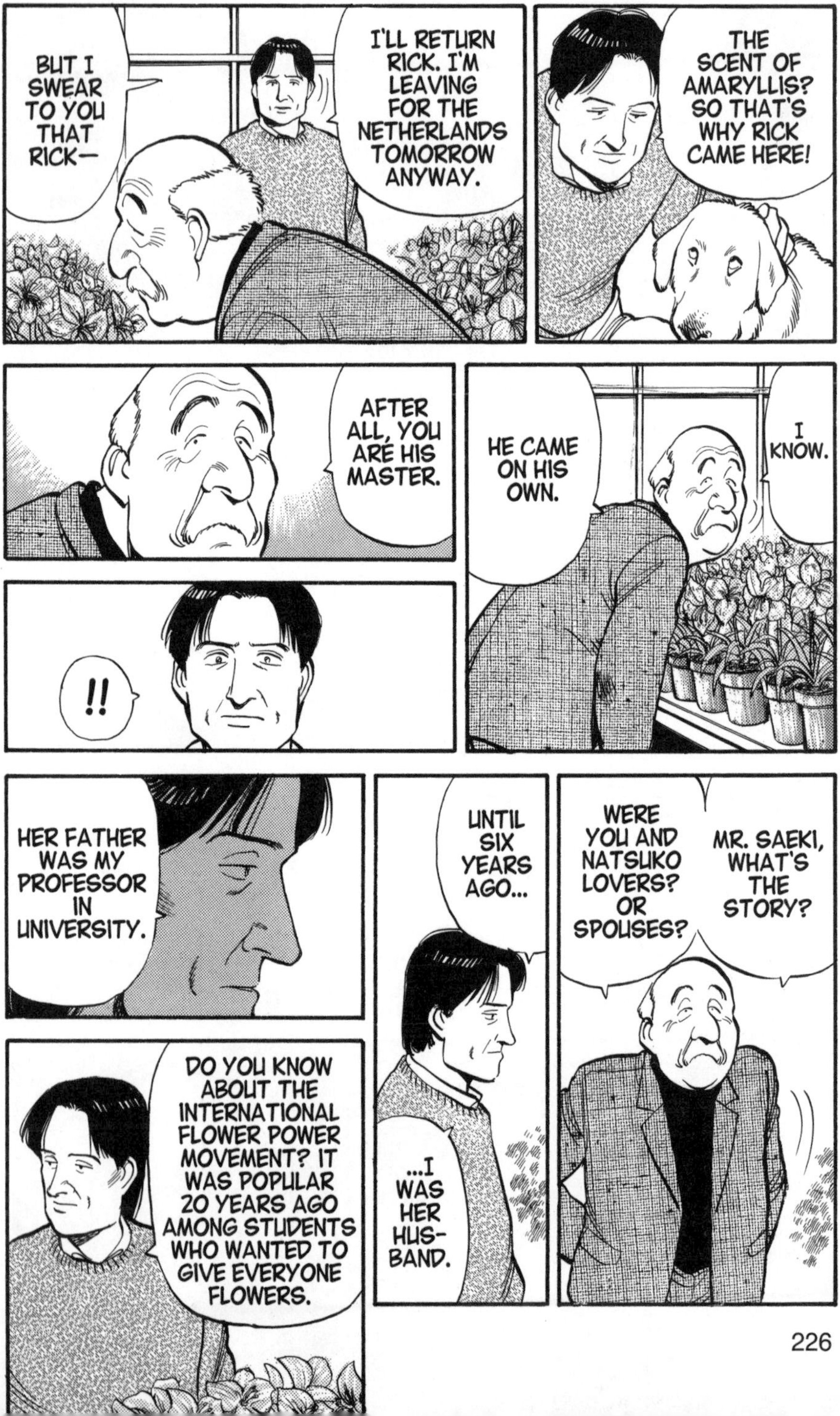
THE SCENT OF AMARYLLIS? SO THAT'S WHY RICK CAME HERE!
I'LL RETURN RICK. I'M LEAVING FOR THE NETHERLANDS TOMORROW ANYWAY.
BUT I SWEAR TO YOU THAT RICK—
I KNOW.
HE CAME ON HIS OWN.
AFTER ALL, YOU ARE HIS MASTER.
!!
MR. SAEKI, WHAT'S THE STORY?
WERE YOU AND NATSUKO LOVERS? OR SPOUSES?
UNTIL SIX YEARS AGO...
...I WAS HER HUS-BAND.
HER FATHER WAS MY PROFESSOR IN UNIVERSITY.
DO YOU KNOW ABOUT THE INTERNATIONAL FLOWER POWER MOVEMENT? IT WAS POPULAR 20 YEARS AGO AMONG STUDENTS WHO WANTED TO GIVE EVERYONE FLOWERS.

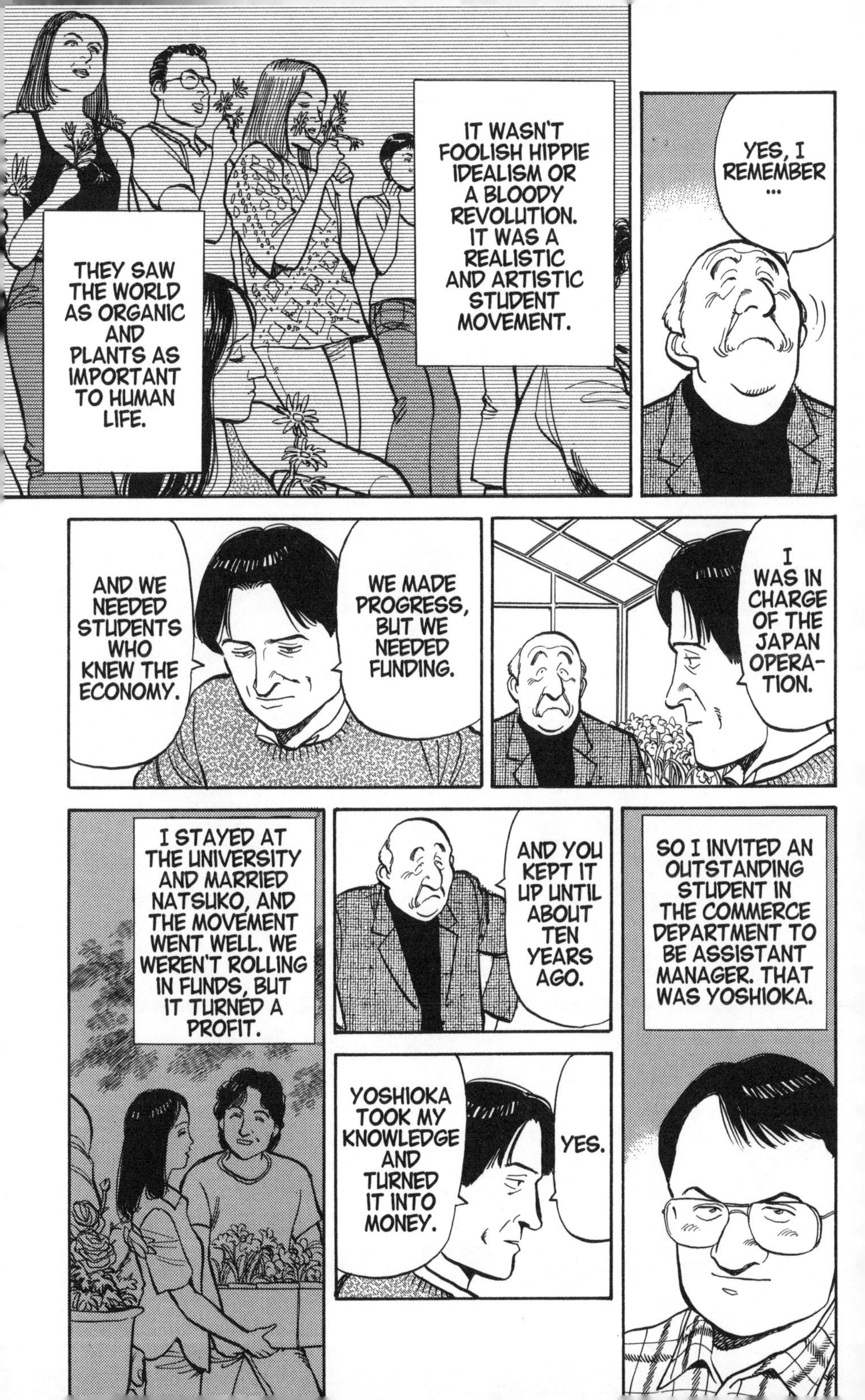
YES, I REMEMBER ...
IT WASN'T FOOLISH HIPPIE IDEALISM OR A BLOODY REVOLUTION. IT WAS A REALISTIC AND ARTISTIC STUDENT MOVEMENT.
THEY SAW THE WORLD AS ORGANIC AND PLANTS AS IMPORTANT TO HUMAN LIFE.
I WAS IN CHARGE OF THE JAPAN OPERA-TION.
WE MADE PROGRESS, BUT WE NEEDED FUNDING.
AND WE NEEDED STUDENTS WHO KNEW THE ECONOMY.
SO I INVITED AN OUTSTANDING STUDENT IN THE COMMERCE DEPARTMENT TO BE ASSISTANT MANAGER. THAT WAS YOSHIOKA.
AND YOU KEPT IT UP UNTIL ABOUT TEN YEARS AGO.
YES.
YOSHIOKA TOOK MY KNOWLEDGE AND TURNED IT INTO MONEY.
I STAYED AT THE UNIVERSITY AND MARRIED NATSUKO, AND THE MOVEMENT WENT WELL. WE WEREN'T ROLLING IN FUNDS, BUT IT TURNED A PROFIT.

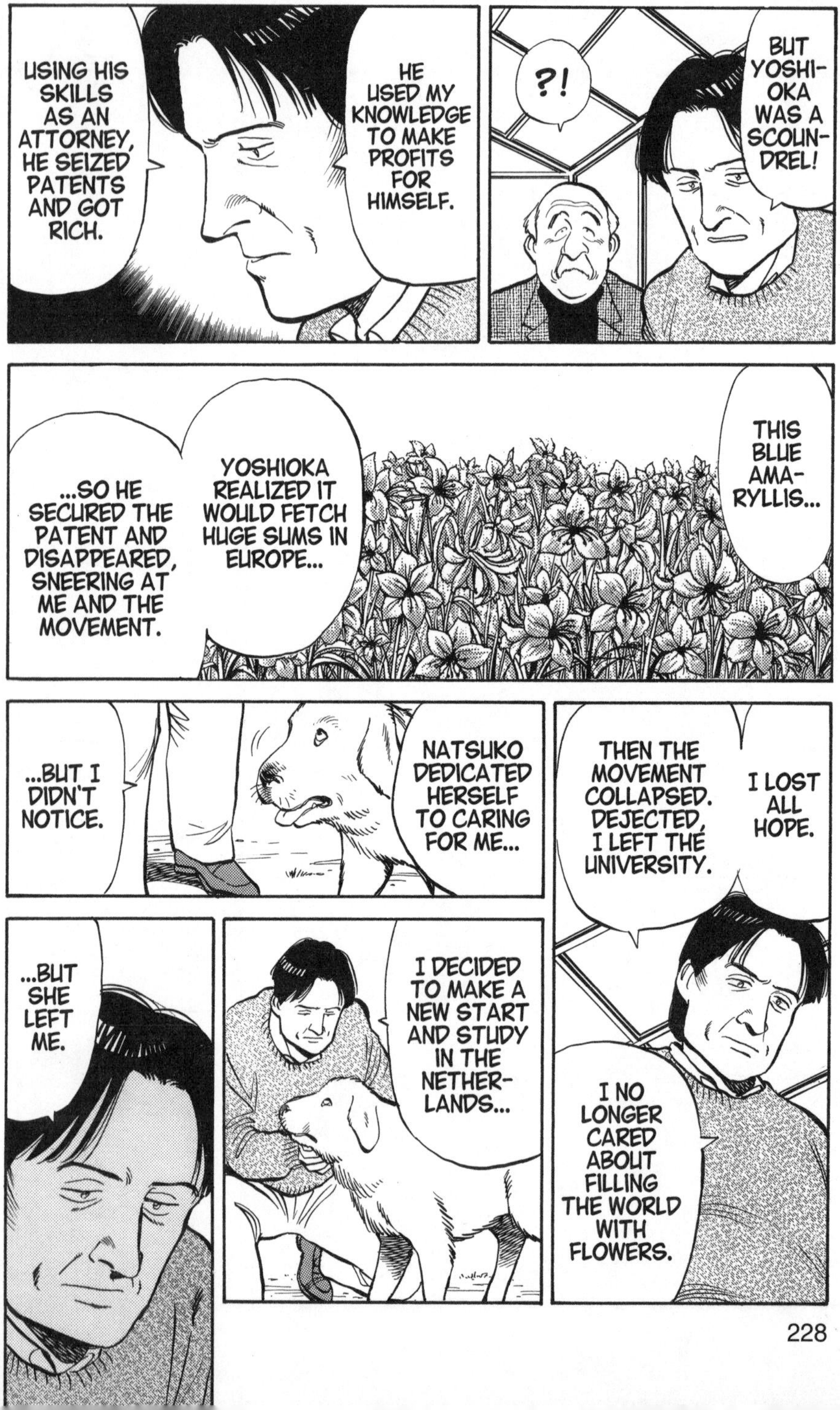
BUT YOSHIOKA WAS A SCOUNDREL!
?!
HE USED MY KNOWLEDGE TO MAKE PROFITS FOR HIMSELF.
USING HIS SKILLS AS AN ATTORNEY, HE SEIZED PATENTS AND GOT RICH.
THIS BLUE AMARYLLIS...
YOSHIOKA REALIZED IT WOULD FETCH HUGE SUMS IN EUROPE...
...SO HE SECURED THE PATENT AND DISAPPEARED, SNEERING AT ME AND THE MOVEMENT.
I LOST ALL HOPE.
THEN THE MOVEMENT COLLAPSED. DEJECTED, I LEFT THE UNIVERSITY.
I NO LONGER CARED ABOUT FILLING THE WORLD WITH FLOWERS.
NATSUKO DEDICATED HERSELF TO CARING FOR ME...
...BUT I DIDN'T NOTICE.
I DECIDED TO MAKE A NEW START AND STUDY IN THE NETHERLANDS...
...BUT SHE LEFT ME.

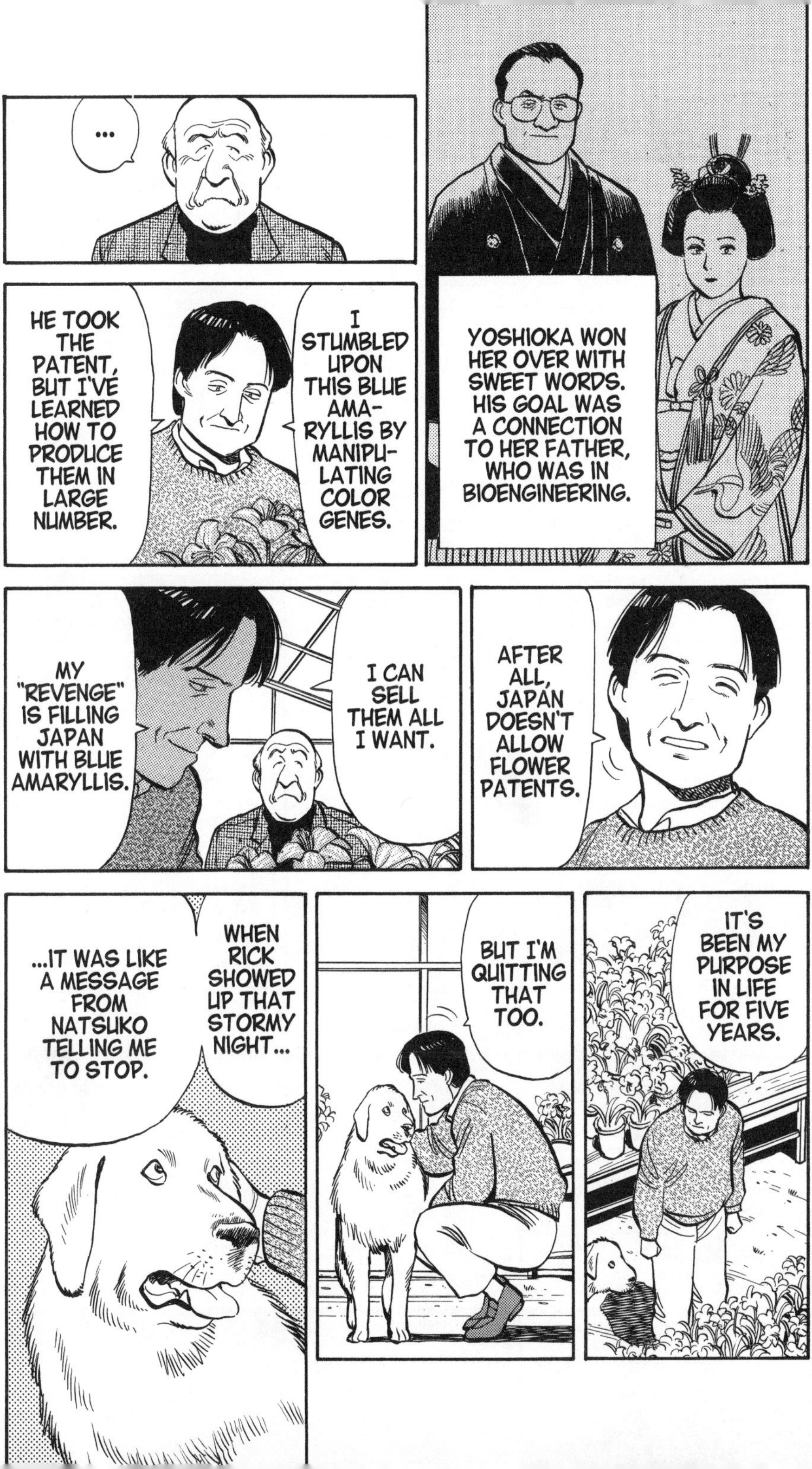

YOSHIOKA WON HER OVER WITH SWEET WORDS. HIS GOAL WAS A CONNECTION TO HER FATHER, WHO WAS IN BIOENGINEERING.
...
I STUMBLED UPON THIS BLUE AMA-RYLLIS BY MANIPU-LATING COLOR GENES.
HE TOOK THE PATENT, BUT I'VE LEARNED HOW TO PRODUCE THEM IN LARGE NUMBER.
AFTER ALL, JAPAN DOESN'T ALLOW FLOWER PATENTS.
I CAN SELL THEM ALL I WANT.
MY "REVENGE" IS FILLING JAPAN WITH BLUE AMARYLLIS.
IT'S BEEN MY PURPOSE IN LIFE FOR FIVE YEARS.
BUT I'M QUITTING THAT TOO.
WHEN RICK SHOWED UP THAT STORMY NIGHT...
...IT WAS LIKE A MESSAGE FROM NATSUKO TELLING ME TO STOP.

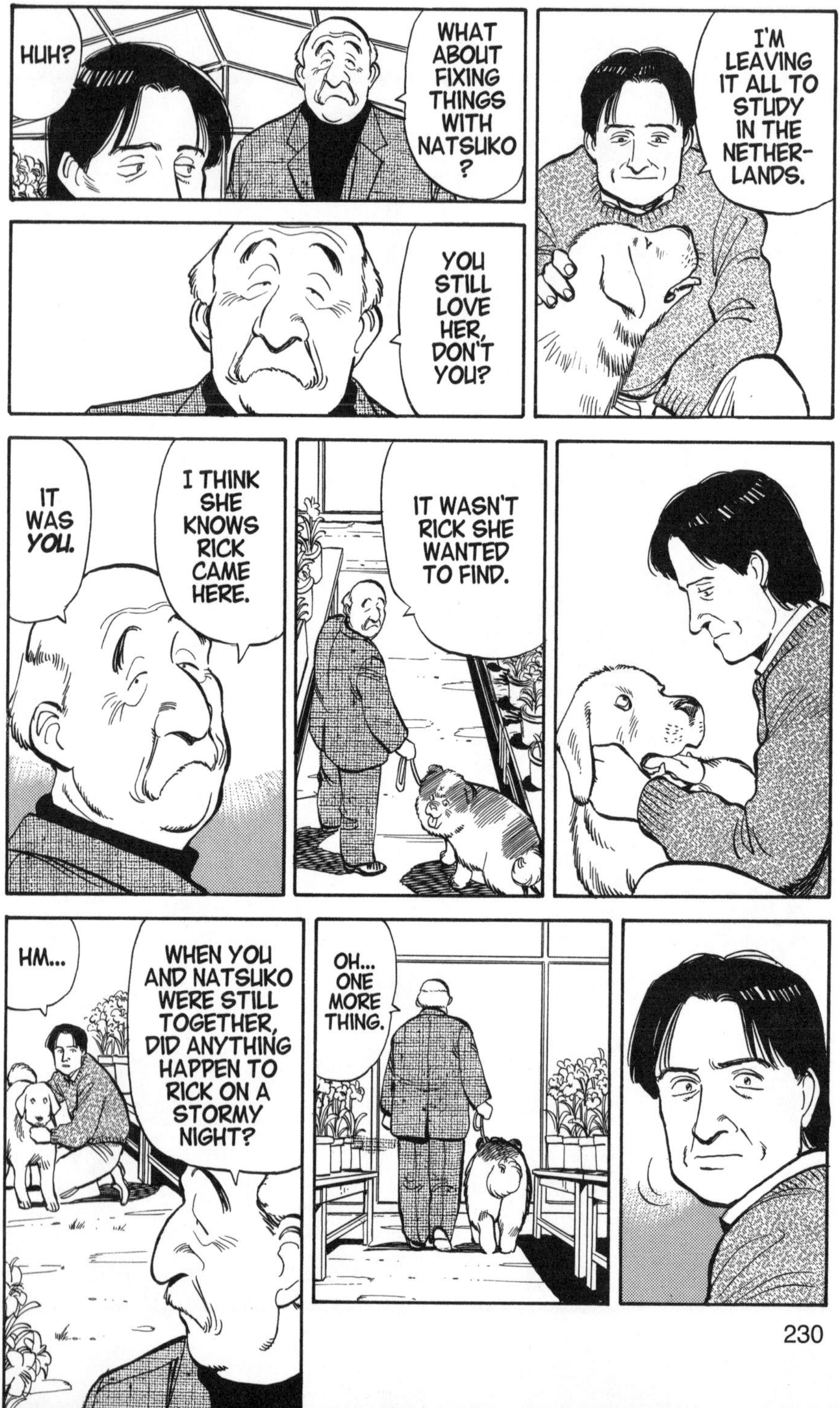
I'M LEAVING IT ALL TO STUDY IN THE NETHERLANDS.
WHAT ABOUT FIXING THINGS WITH NATSUKO?
HUH?
YOU STILL LOVE HER, DON'T YOU?
IT WASN'T RICK SHE WANTED TO FIND.
I THINK SHE KNOWS RICK CAME HERE.
IT WAS *YOU*.
OH... ONE MORE THING.
WHEN YOU AND NATSUKO WERE STILL TOGETHER, DID ANYTHING HAPPEN TO RICK ON A STORMY NIGHT?
HM...

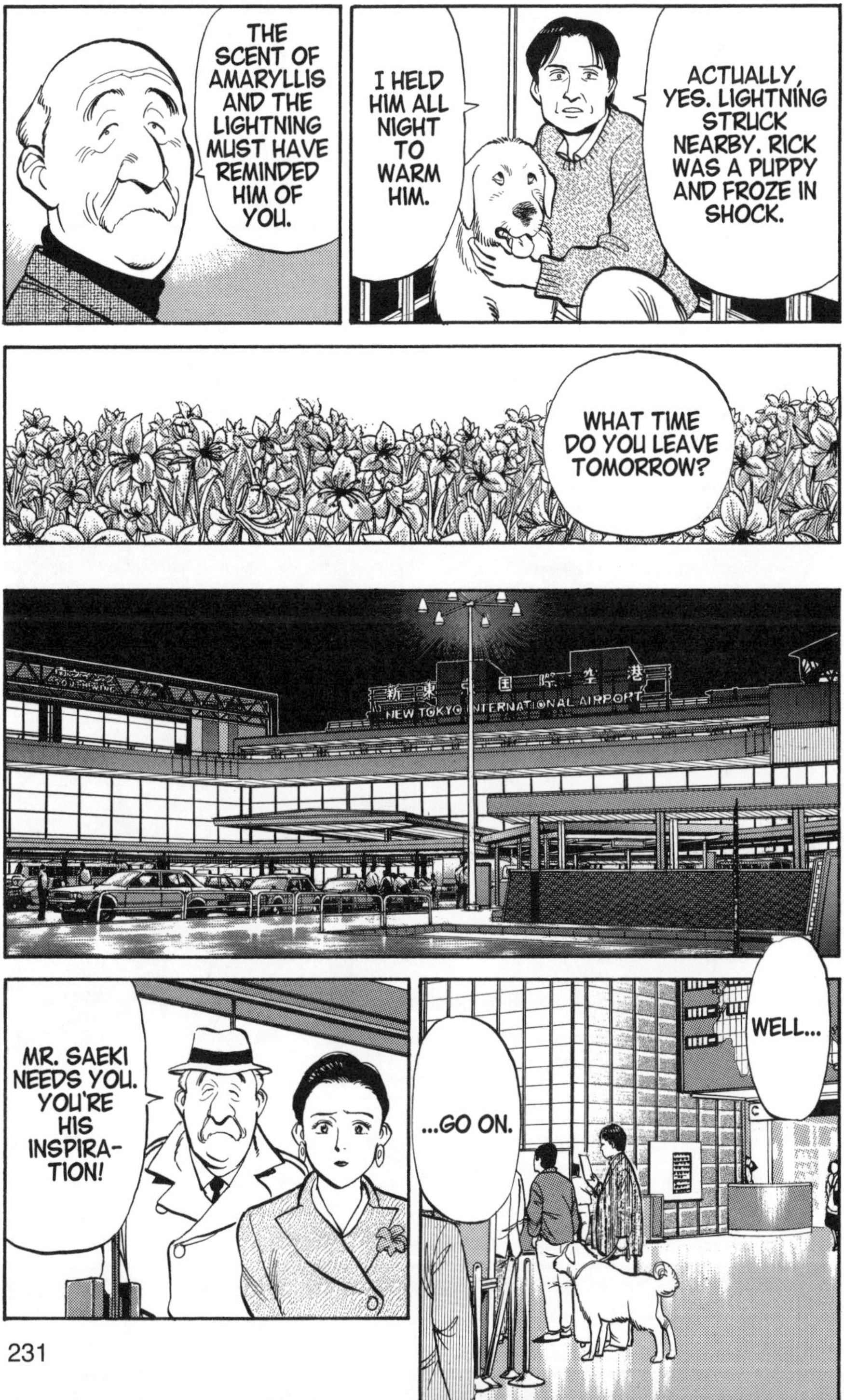
ACTUALLY, YES. LIGHTNING STRUCK NEARBY. RICK WAS A PUPPY AND FROZE IN SHOCK.
I HELD HIM ALL NIGHT TO WARM HIM.
THE SCENT OF AMARYLLIS AND THE LIGHTNING MUST HAVE REMINDED HIM OF YOU.
WHAT TIME DO YOU LEAVE TOMORROW?
新東京国際空港
NEW TOKYO INTERNATIONAL AIRPORT
WELL...
...GO ON.
MR. SAEKI NEEDS YOU. YOU'RE HIS INSPIRATION!

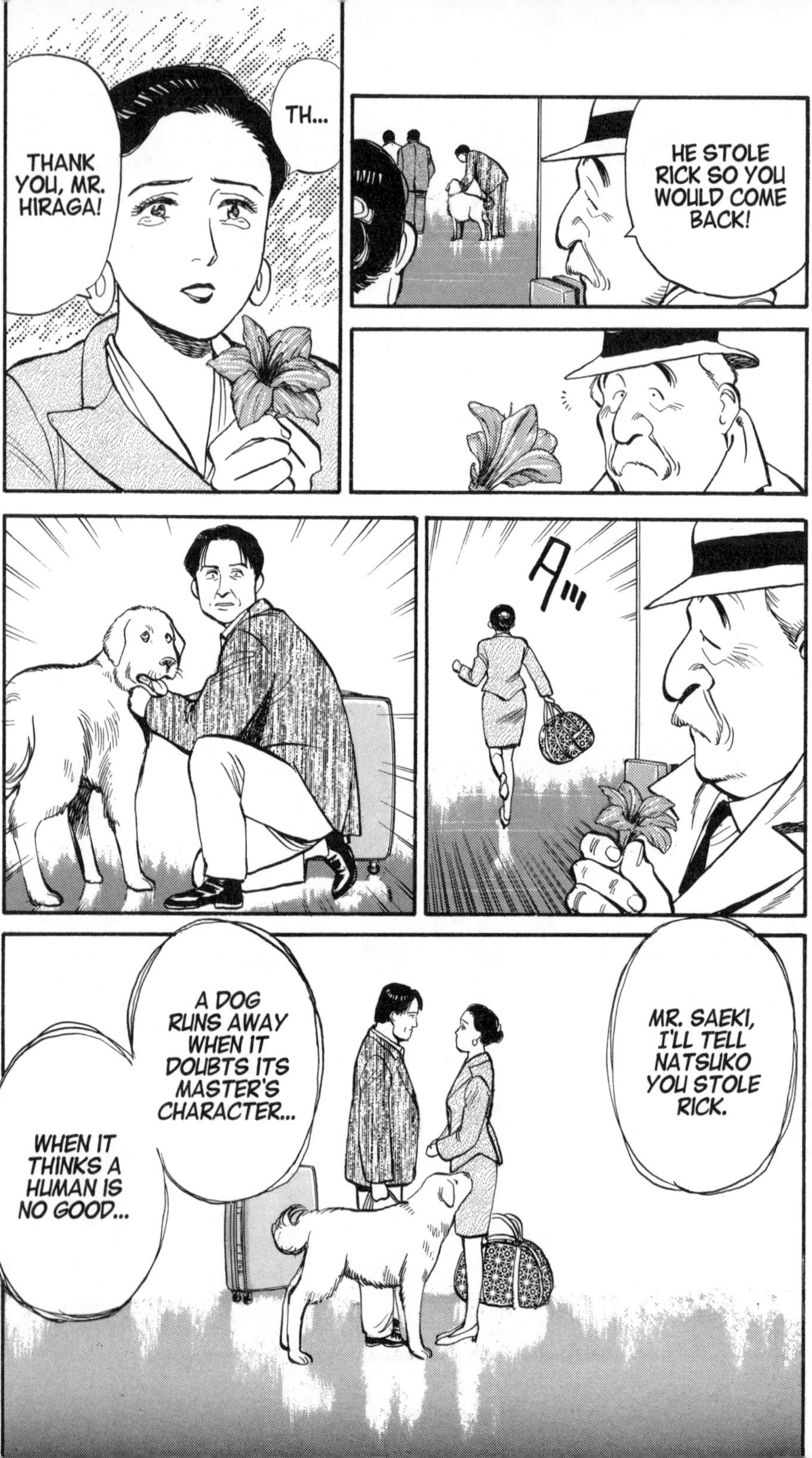
HE STOLE RICK SO YOU WOULD COME BACK!
TH...
THANK YOU, MR. HIRAGA!
A
MR. SAEKI, I'LL TELL NATSUKO YOU STOLE RICK.
A DOG RUNS AWAY WHEN IT DOUBTS ITS MASTER'S CHARACTER...
WHEN IT THINKS A HUMAN IS NO GOOD...

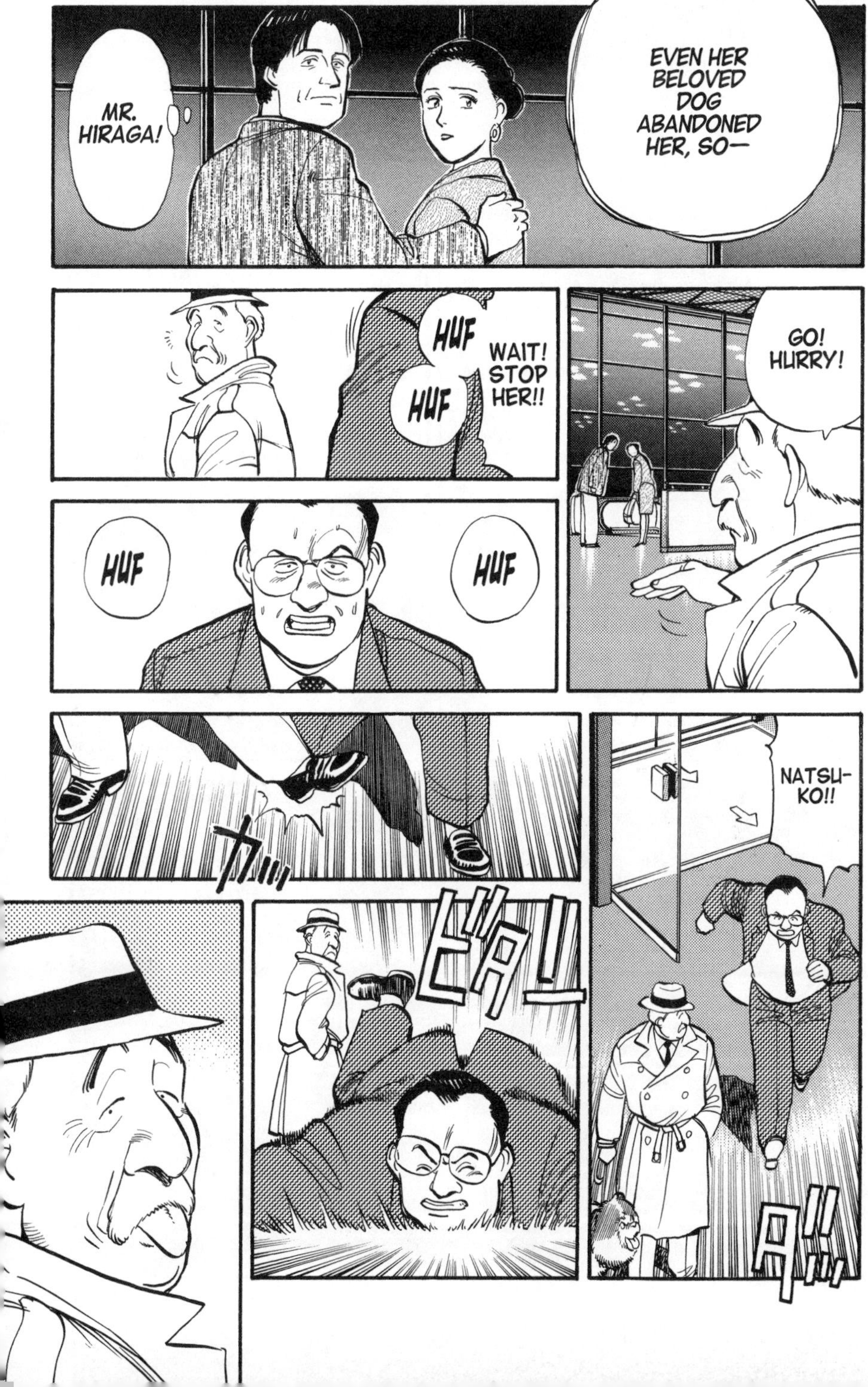
EVEN HER BELOVED DOG ABANDONED HER, SO—
MR. HIRAGA!
GO! HURRY!
HUF
HUF
WAIT! STOP HER!!
HUF
HUF
NATSU-KO!!
ア!!
カッ

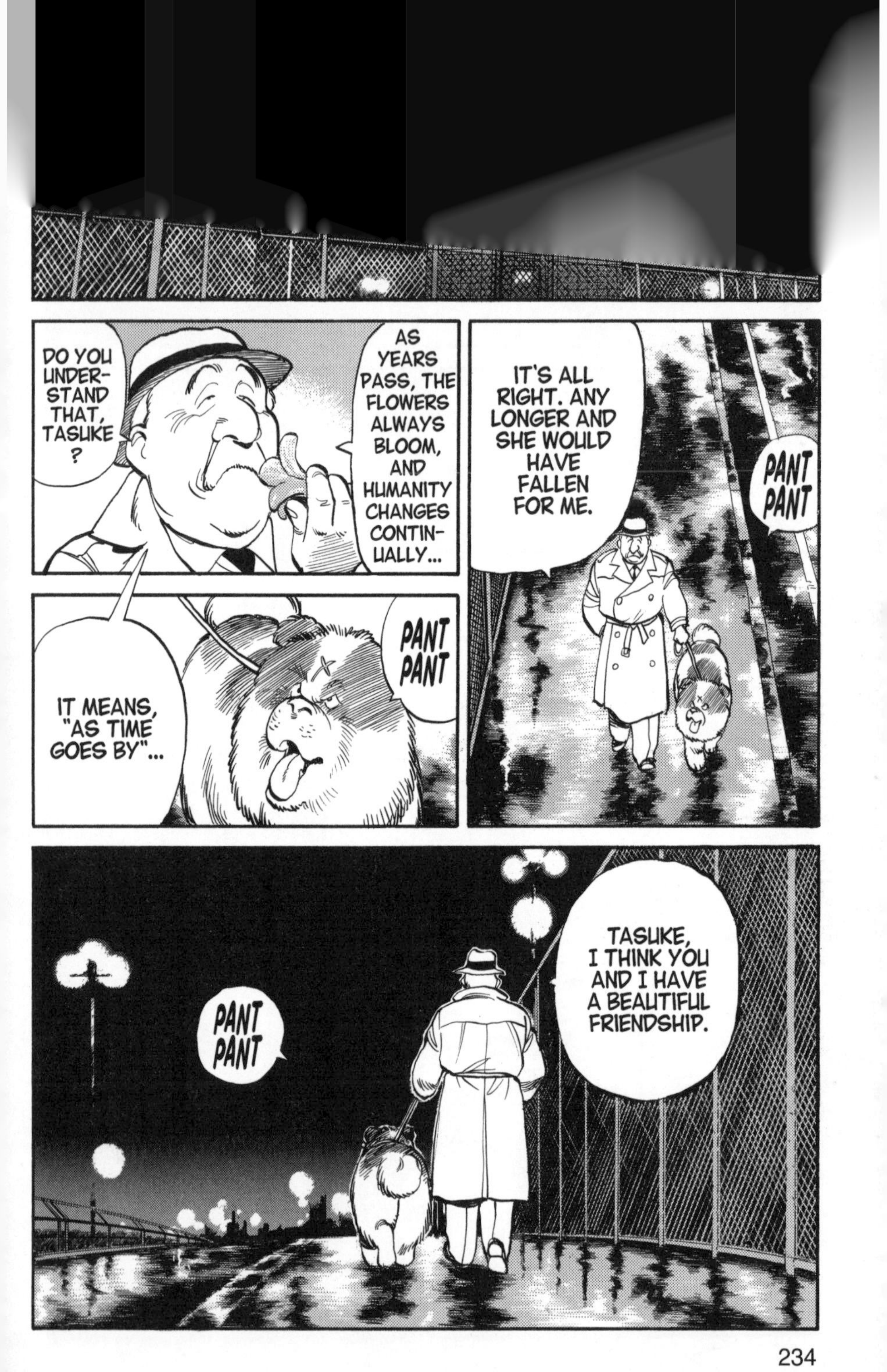
IT'S ALL RIGHT. ANY LONGER AND SHE WOULD HAVE FALLEN FOR ME.
PANT PANT
AS YEARS PASS, THE FLOWERS ALWAYS BLOOM, AND HUMANITY CHANGES CONTIN-UALLY...
DO YOU UNDER-STAND THAT, TASUKE?
PANT PANT
IT MEANS, "AS TIME GOES BY"...
TASUKE, I THINK YOU AND I HAVE A BEAUTIFUL FRIENDSHIP.
PANT PANT

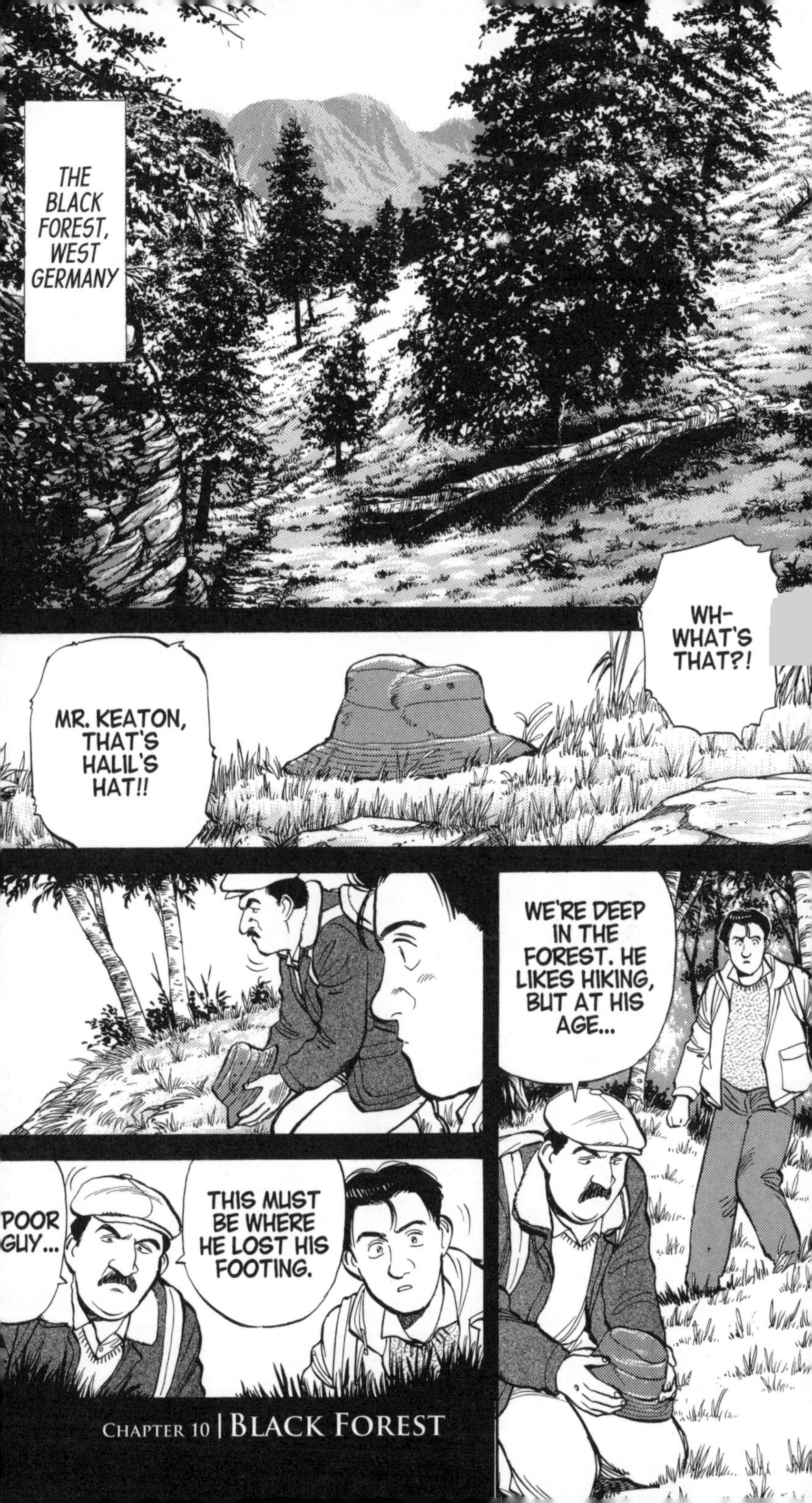
THE BLACK FOREST, WEST GERMANY
WH- WHAT'S THAT?!
MR. KEATON, THAT'S HALIL'S HAT!!
WE'RE DEEP IN THE FOREST. HE LIKES HIKING, BUT AT HIS AGE...
THIS MUST BE WHERE HE LOST HIS FOOTING.
POOR GUY...

# Chapter 10 | Black Forest

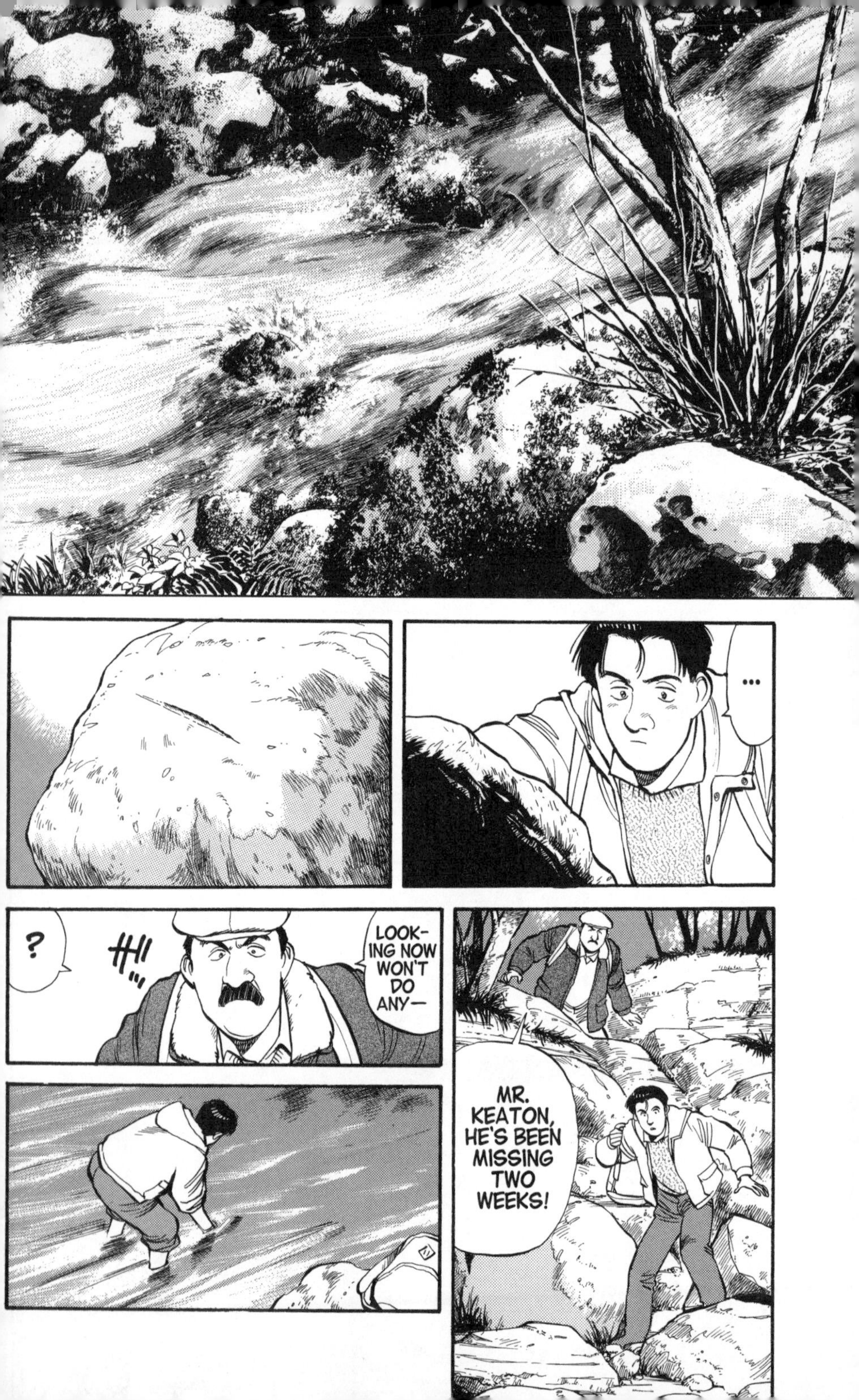
...
MR. KEATON, HE'S BEEN MISSING TWO WEEKS!
LOOKING NOW WON'T DO ANY—
?

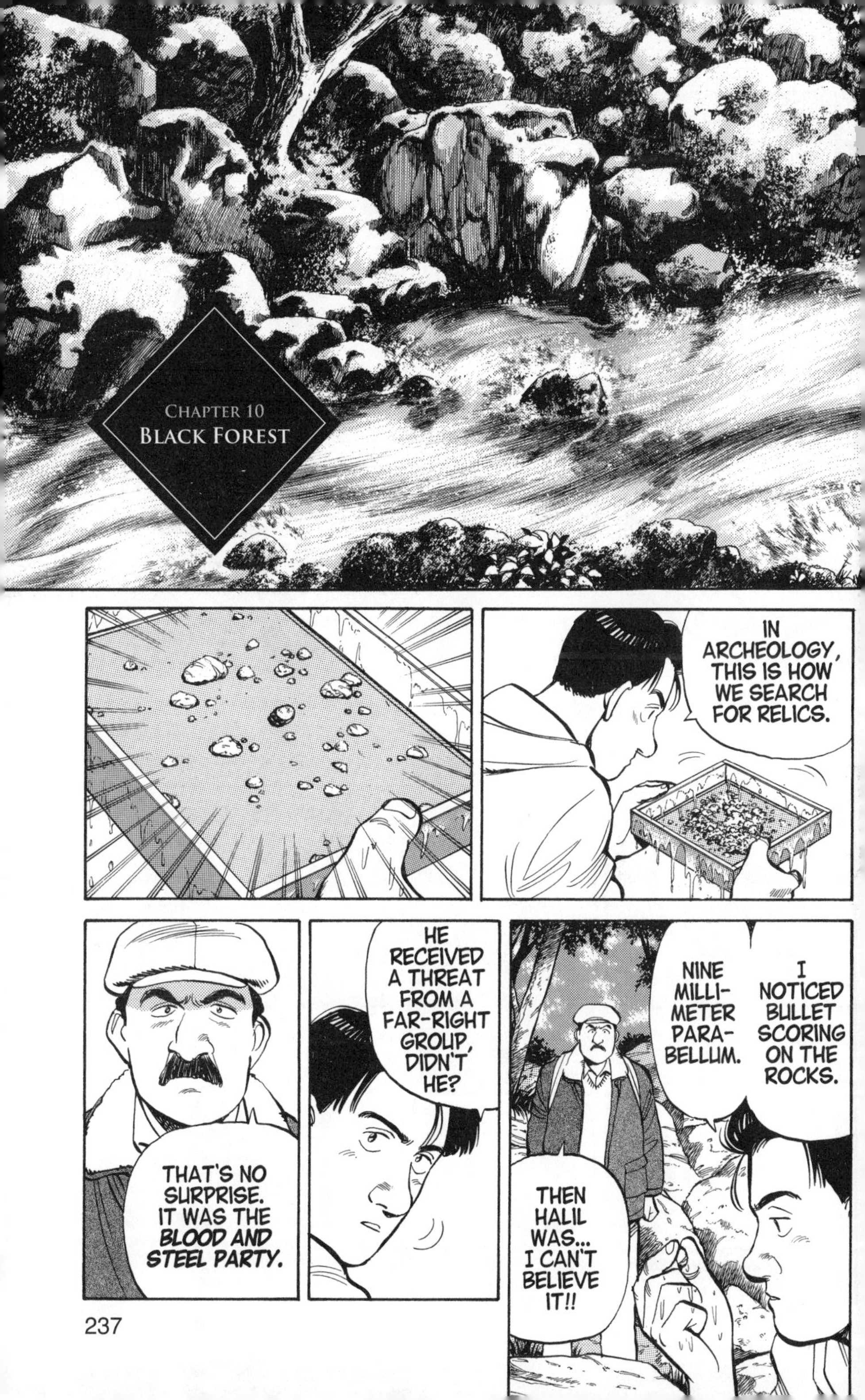
CHAPTER 10
BLACK FOREST
IN ARCHEOLOGY, THIS IS HOW WE SEARCH FOR RELICS.
I NOTICED BULLET SCORING ON THE ROCKS.
NINE MILLI-METER PARA-BELLUM.
THEN HALIL WAS... I CAN'T BELIEVE IT!!
HE RECEIVED A THREAT FROM A FAR-RIGHT GROUP, DIDN'T HE?
THAT'S NO SURPRISE. IT WAS THE BLOOD AND STEEL PARTY.

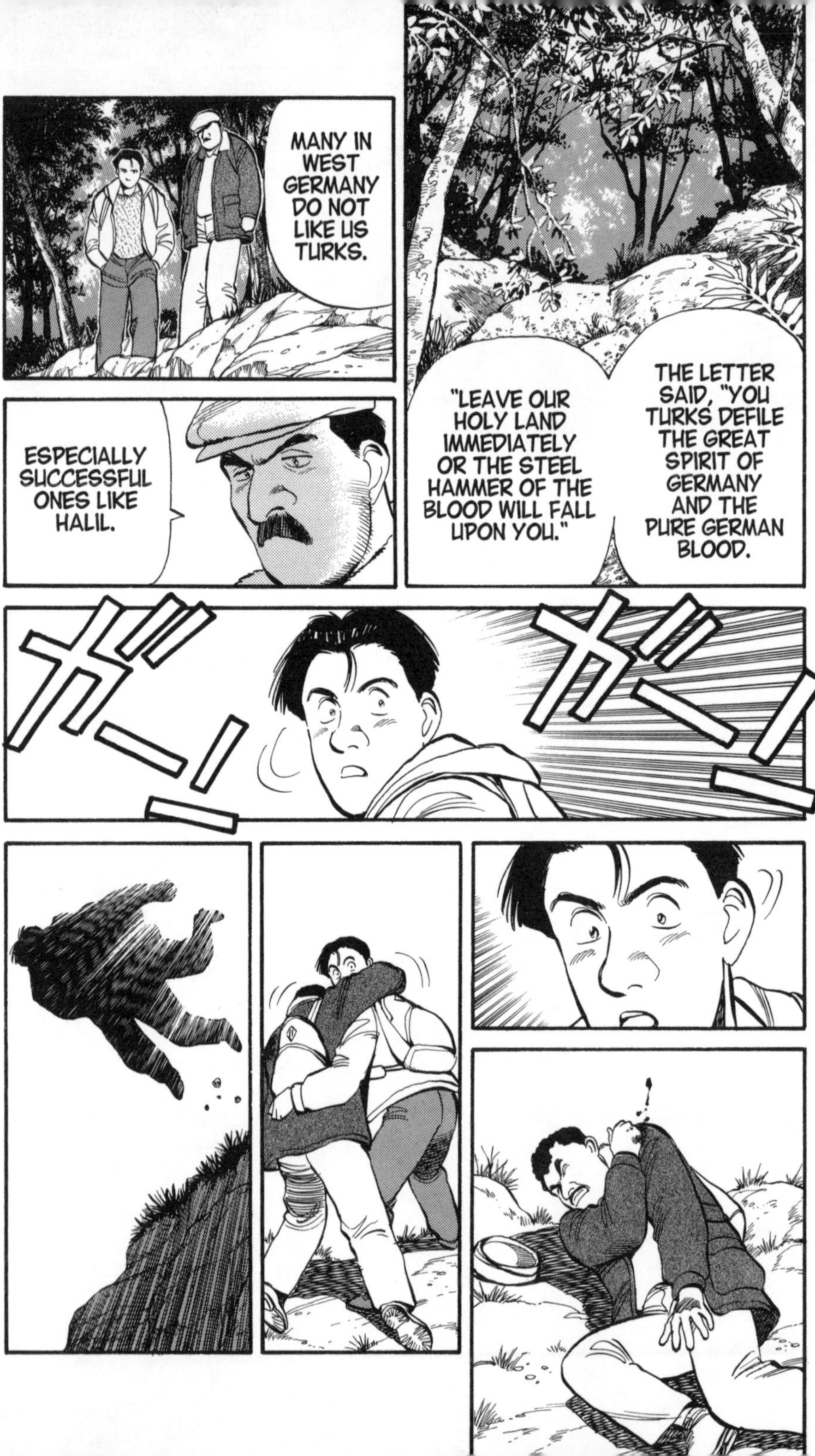
THE LETTER SAID, "YOU TURKS DEFILE THE GREAT SPIRIT OF GERMANY AND THE PURE GERMAN BLOOD.
"LEAVE OUR HOLY LAND IMMEDIATELY OR THE STEEL HAMMER OF THE BLOOD WILL FALL UPON YOU."
MANY IN WEST GERMANY DO NOT LIKE US TURKS.
ESPECIALLY SUCCESSFUL ONES LIKE HALIL.

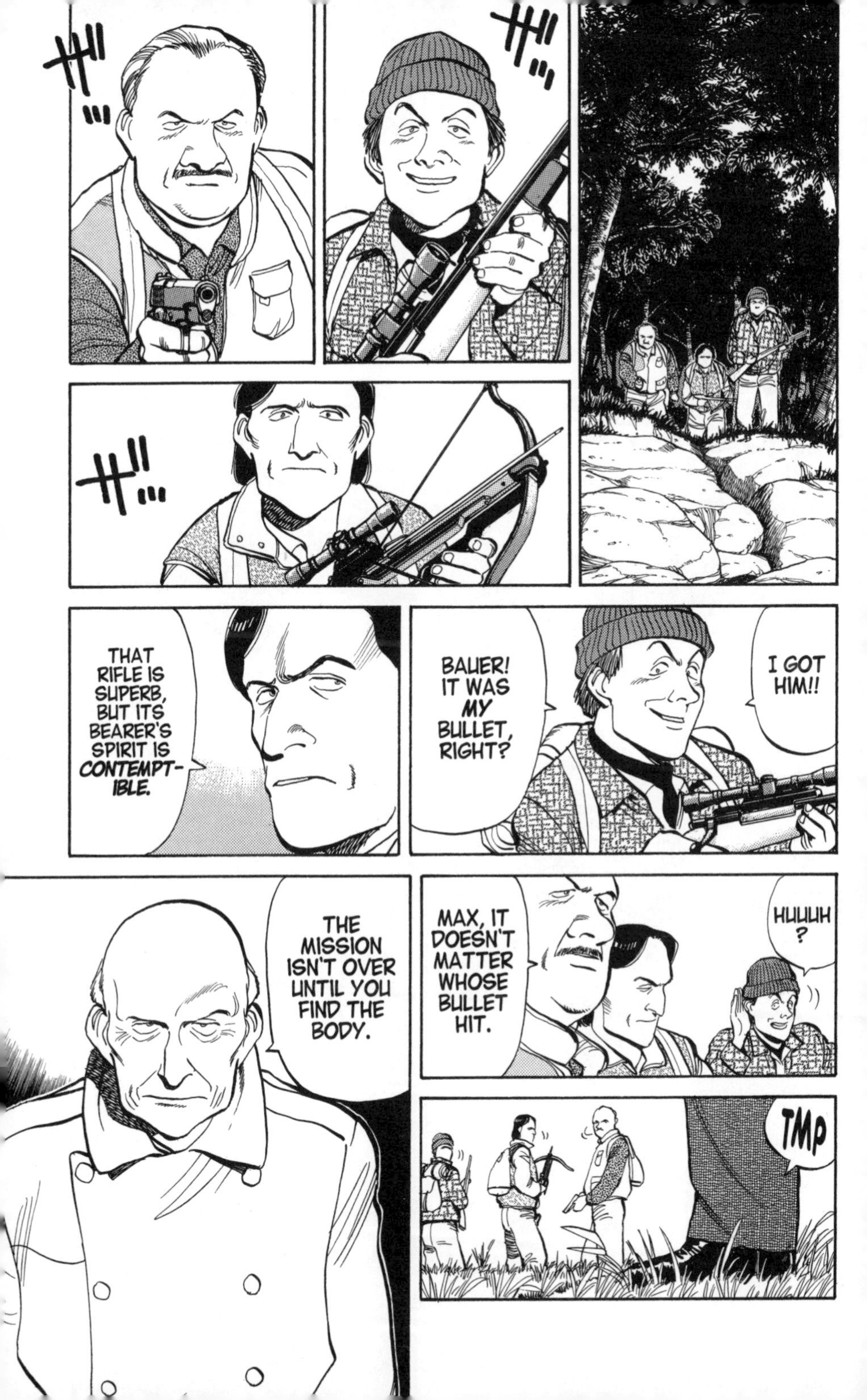
I GOT HIM!!
BAUER! IT WAS MY BULLET, RIGHT?
THAT RIFLE IS SUPERB, BUT ITS BEARER'S SPIRIT IS CONTEMPTIBLE.
HUUUH?
MAX, IT DOESN'T MATTER WHOSE BULLET HIT.
TMP
THE MISSION ISN'T OVER UNTIL YOU FIND THE BODY.

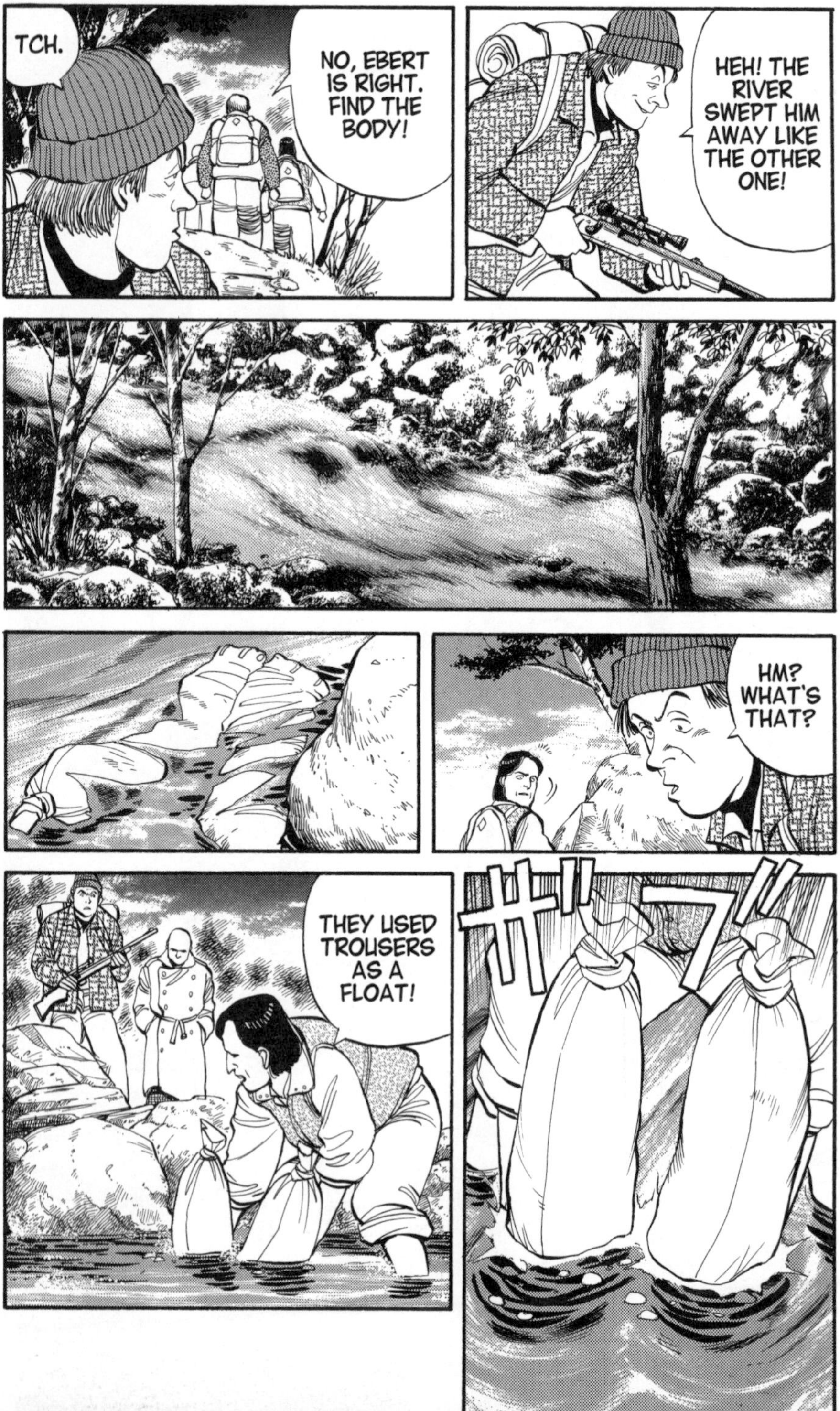
HEH! THE RIVER SWEPT HIM AWAY LIKE THE OTHER ONE!
NO, EBERT IS RIGHT. FIND THE BODY!
TCH.
HM? WHAT'S THAT?
ザブ
THEY USED TROUSERS AS A FLOAT!

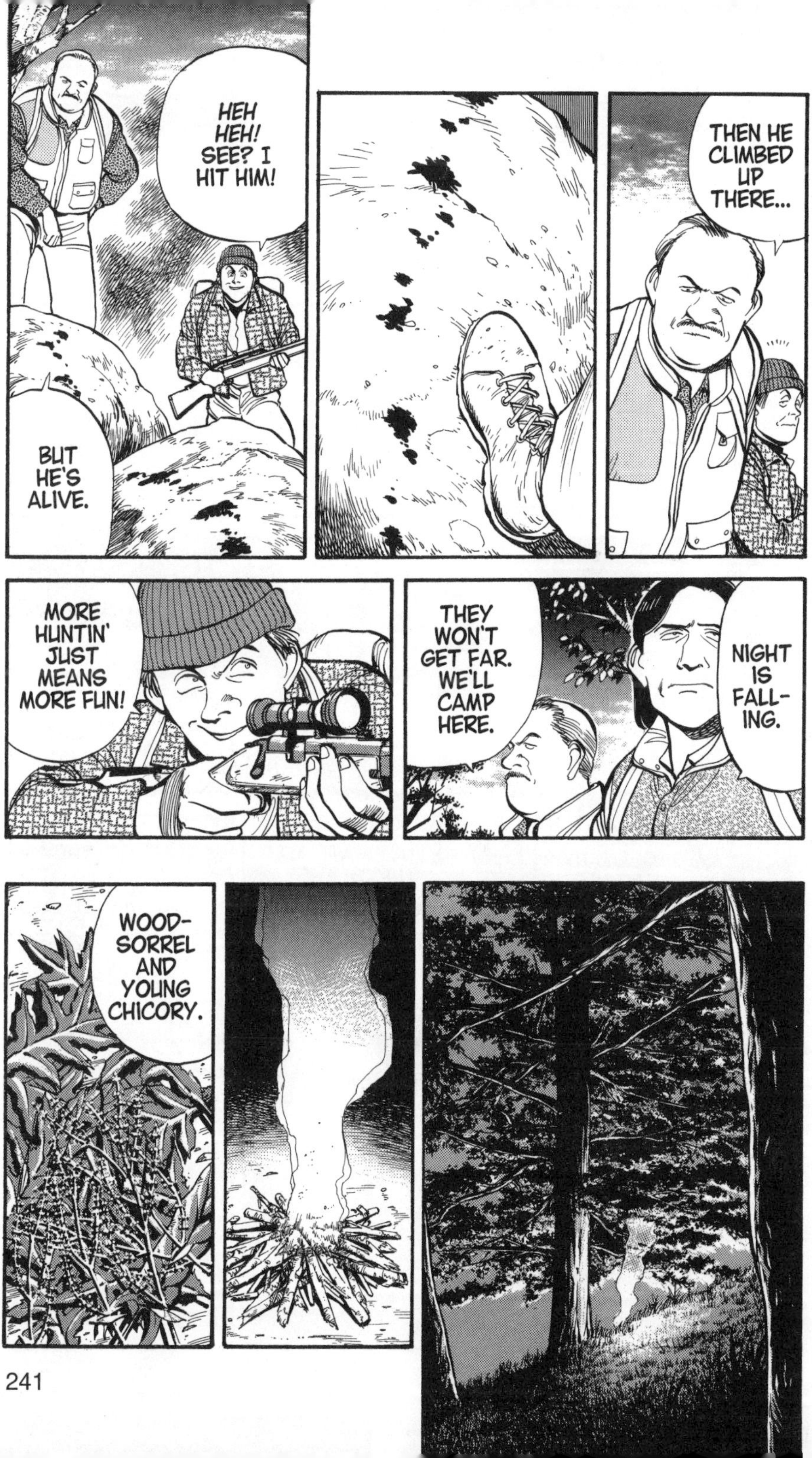
THEN HE CLIMBED UP THERE...
HEH HEH! SEE? I HIT HIM!
BUT HE'S ALIVE.
NIGHT IS FALLING.
THEY WON'T GET FAR. WE'LL CAMP HERE.
MORE HUNTIN' JUST MEANS MORE FUN!
WOOD-SORREL AND YOUNG CHICORY.

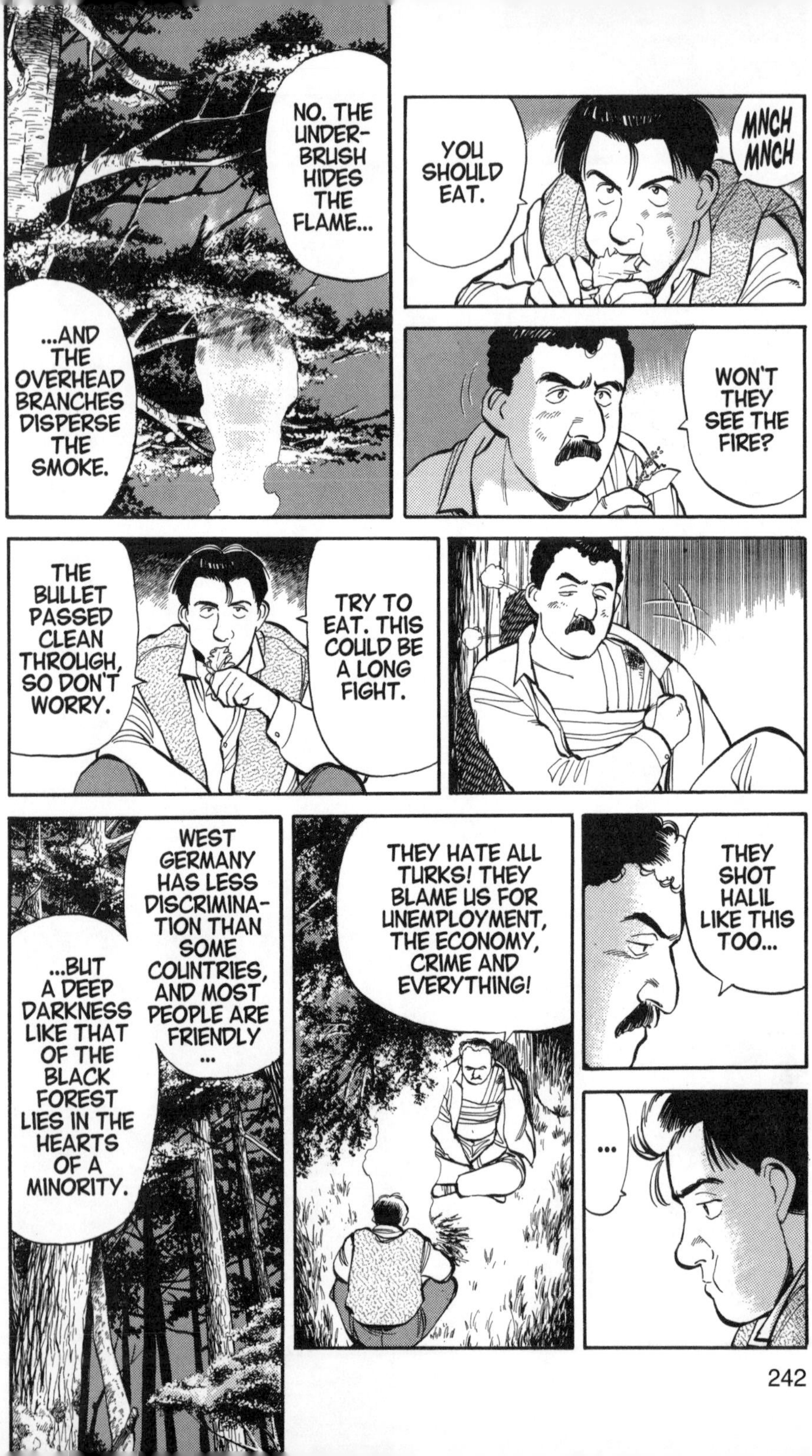
MNCH MNCH
YOU SHOULD EAT.
WON'T THEY SEE THE FIRE?
NO. THE UNDER-BRUSH HIDES THE FLAME...
...AND THE OVERHEAD BRANCHES DISPERSE THE SMOKE.
TRY TO EAT. THIS COULD BE A LONG FIGHT.
THE BULLET PASSED CLEAN THROUGH, SO DON'T WORRY.
THEY SHOT HALIL LIKE THIS TOO...
...
THEY HATE ALL TURKS! THEY BLAME US FOR UNEMPLOYMENT, THE ECONOMY, CRIME AND EVERYTHING!
WEST GERMANY HAS LESS DISCRIMINA-TION THAN SOME COUNTRIES, AND MOST PEOPLE ARE FRIENDLY...
...BUT A DEEP DARKNESS LIKE THAT OF THE BLACK FOREST LIES IN THE HEARTS OF A MINORITY.

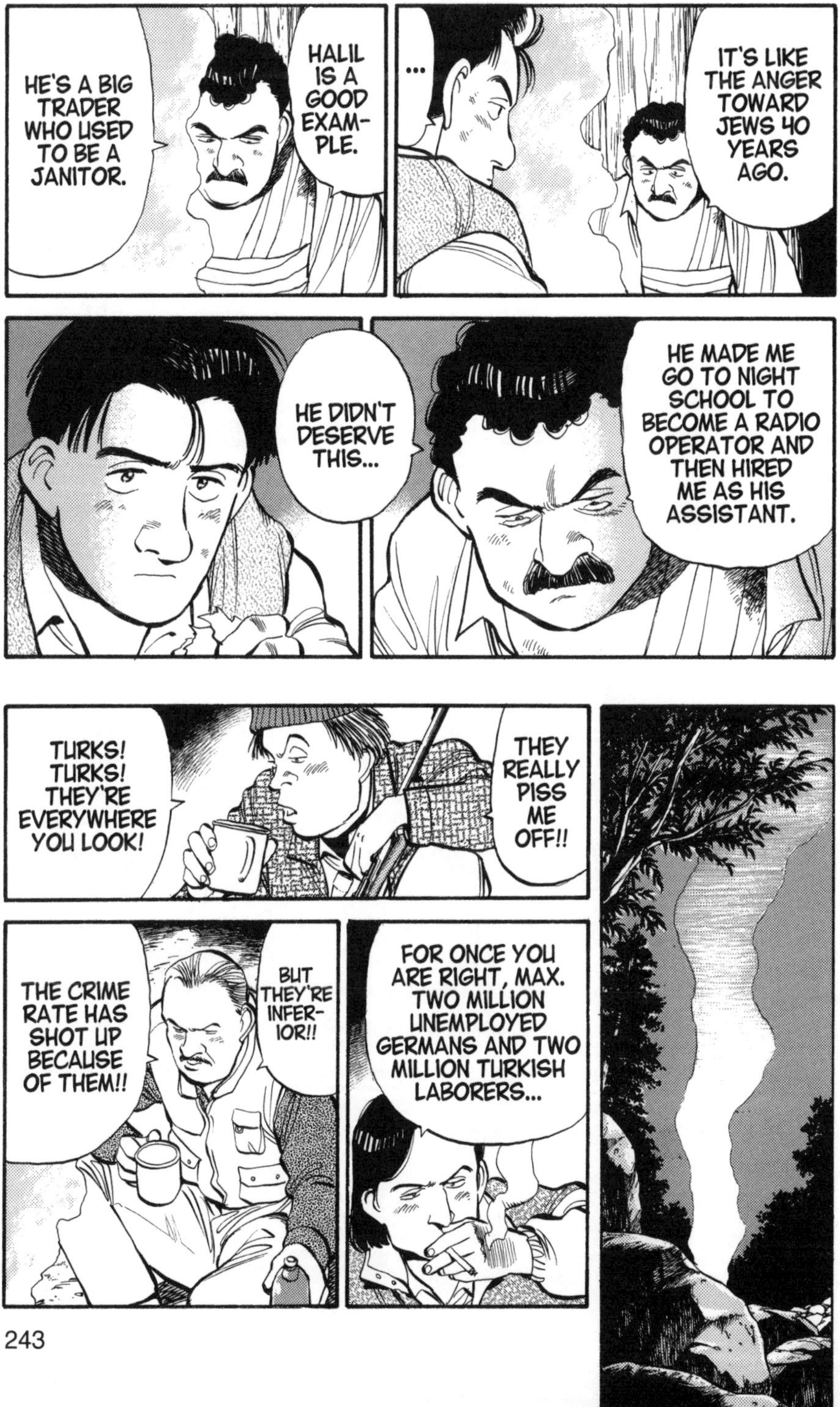
IT'S LIKE THE ANGER TOWARD JEWS 40 YEARS AGO.
...
HALIL IS A GOOD EXAM-PLE.
HE'S A BIG TRADER WHO USED TO BE A JANITOR.
HE MADE ME GO TO NIGHT SCHOOL TO BECOME A RADIO OPERATOR AND THEN HIRED ME AS HIS ASSISTANT.
HE DIDN'T DESERVE THIS...
THEY REALLY PISS ME OFF!!
TURKS! TURKS! THEY'RE EVERYWHERE YOU LOOK!
FOR ONCE YOU ARE RIGHT, MAX. TWO MILLION UNEMPLOYED GERMANS AND TWO MILLION TURKISH LABORERS...
BUT THEY'RE INFER-IOR!!
THE CRIME RATE HAS SHOT UP BECAUSE OF THEM!!

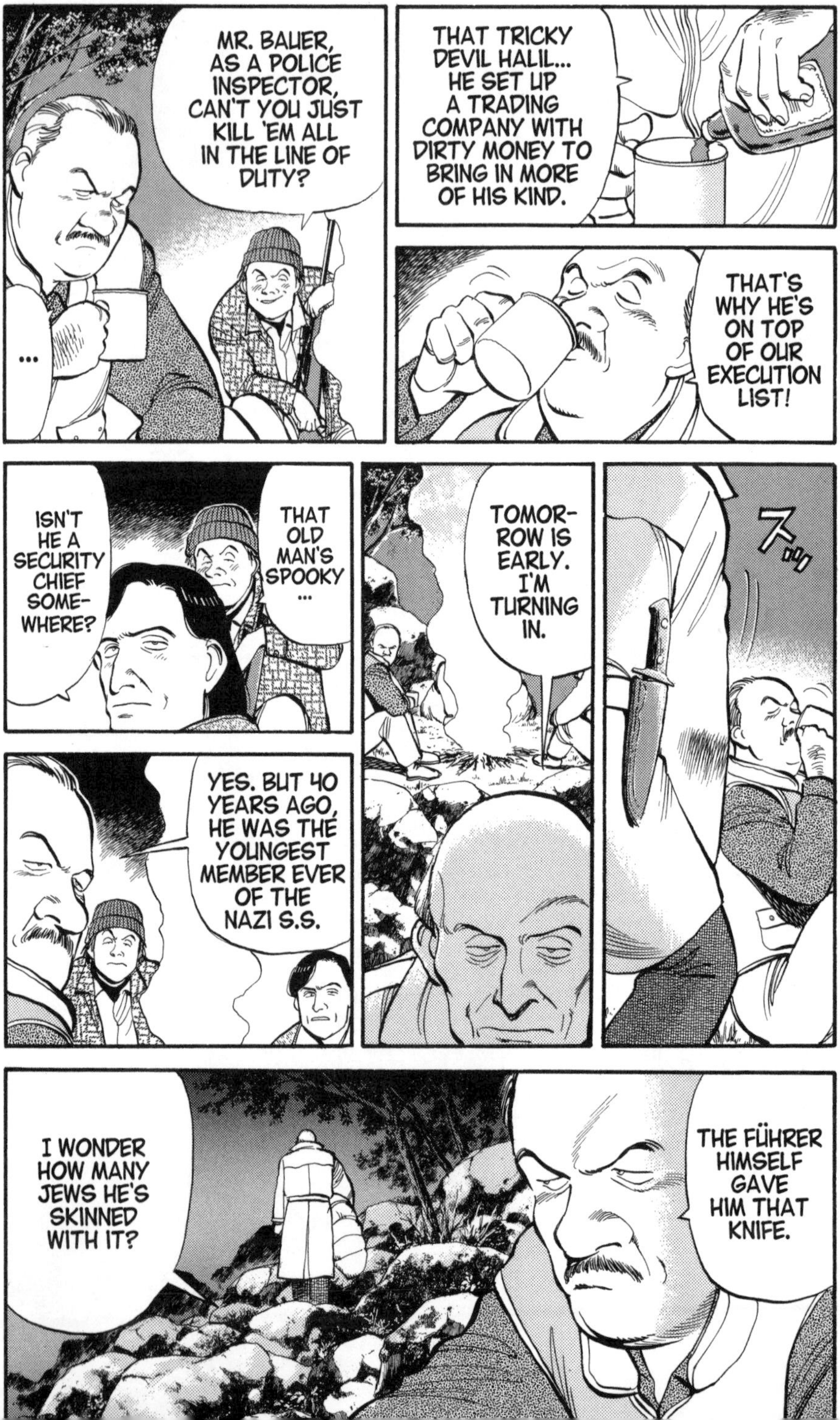
THAT TRICKY DEVIL HALIL... HE SET UP A TRADING COMPANY WITH DIRTY MONEY TO BRING IN MORE OF HIS KIND.
THAT'S WHY HE'S ON TOP OF OUR EXECUTION LIST!
MR. BAUER, AS A POLICE INSPECTOR, CAN'T YOU JUST KILL 'EM ALL IN THE LINE OF DUTY?
...
スッ
TOMOR-ROW IS EARLY. I'M TURNING IN.
THAT OLD MAN'S SPOOKY ...
ISN'T HE A SECURITY CHIEF SOME-WHERE?
YES. BUT 40 YEARS AGO, HE WAS THE YOUNGEST MEMBER EVER OF THE NAZI S.S.
THE FÜHRER HIMSELF GAVE HIM THAT KNIFE.
I WONDER HOW MANY JEWS HE'S SKINNED WITH IT?

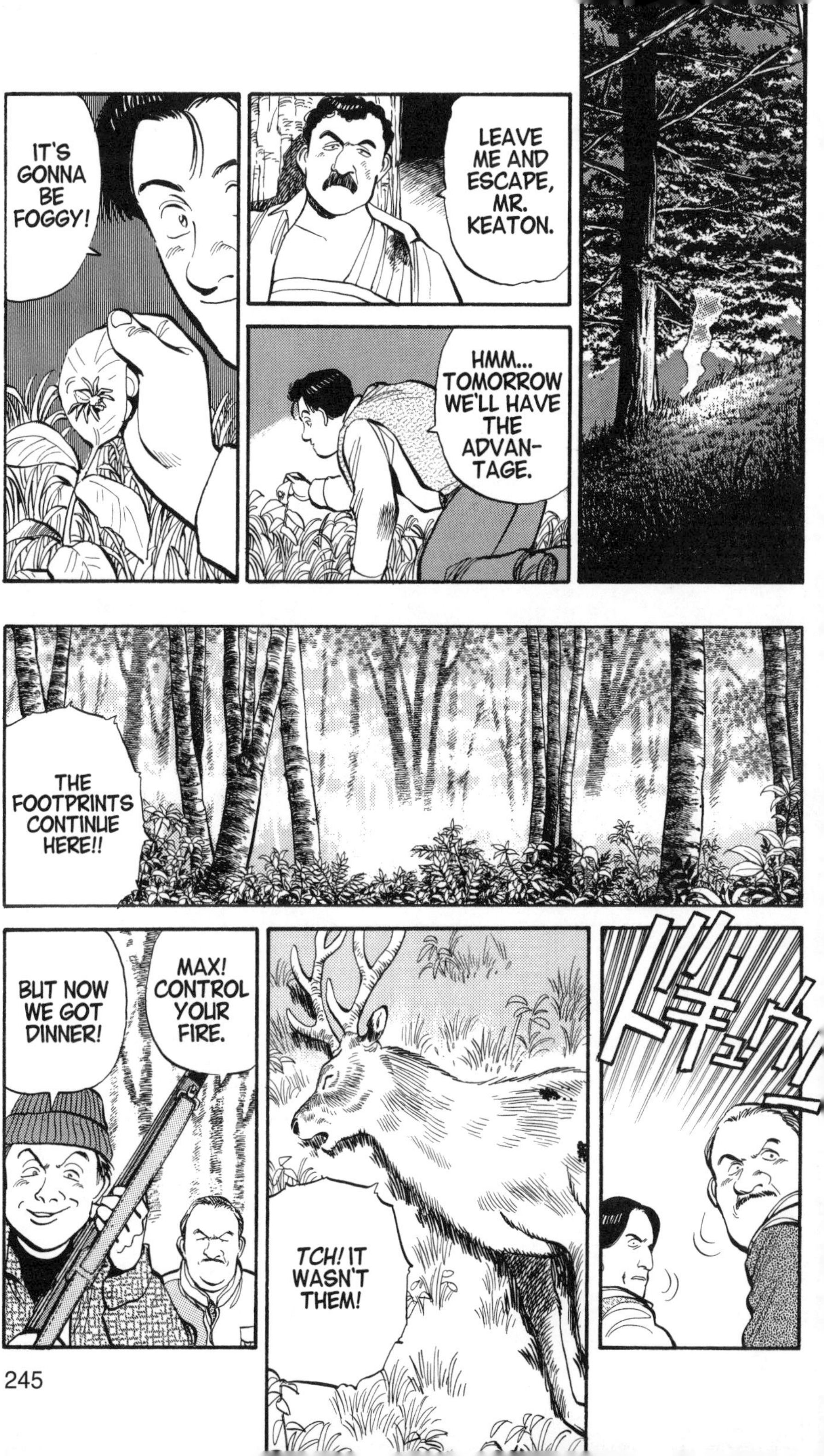
LEAVE ME AND ESCAPE, MR. KEATON.
HMM... TOMORROW WE'LL HAVE THE ADVANTAGE.
IT'S GONNA BE FOGGY!
THE FOOTPRINTS CONTINUE HERE!!
TCH! IT WASN'T THEM!
MAX! CONTROL YOUR FIRE.
BUT NOW WE GOT DINNER!

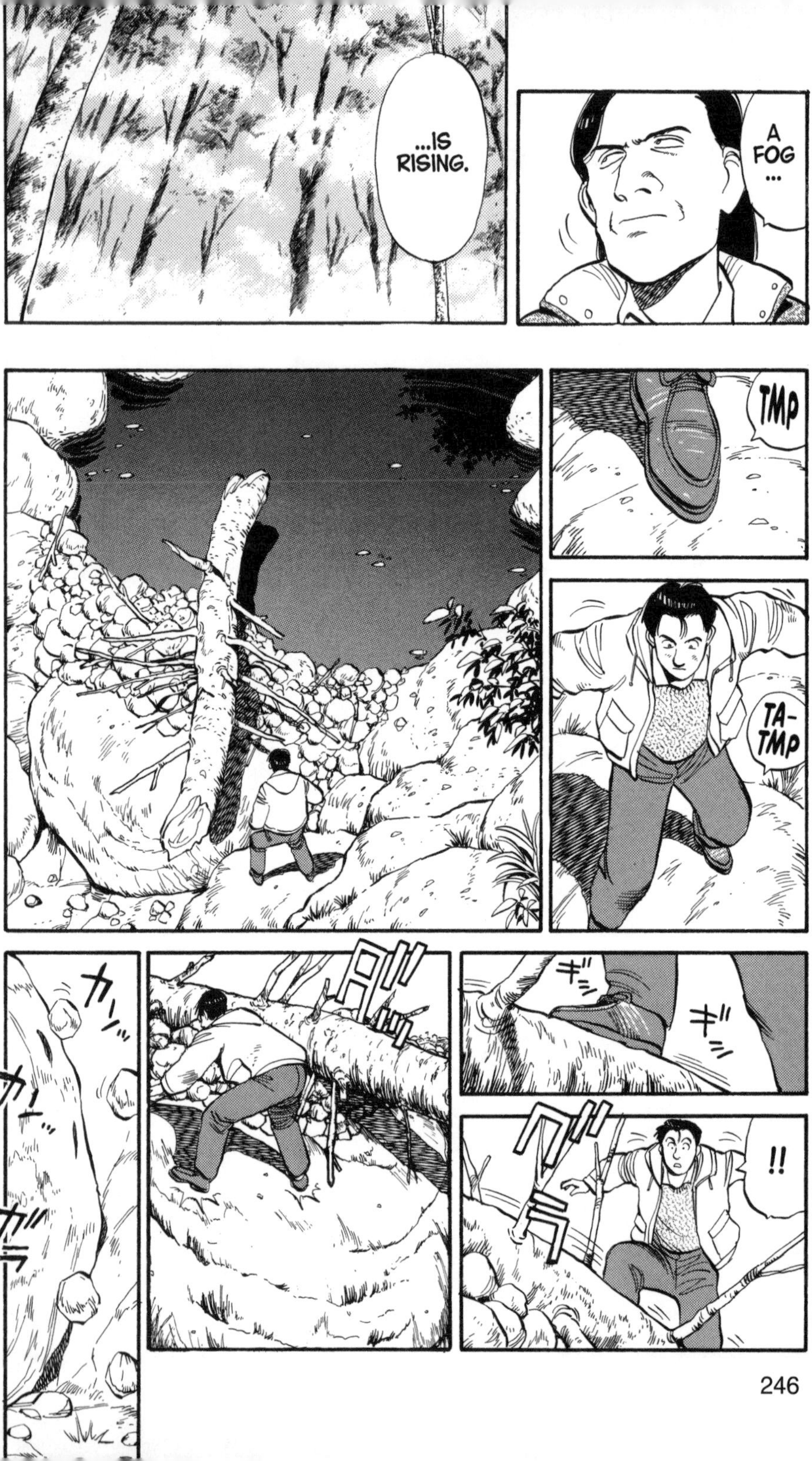
A FOG ...
...IS RISING.
TMP
TA-TMP
ギシ
ギシ
ガラ
!!
ガッ
カン
カン
ガラ

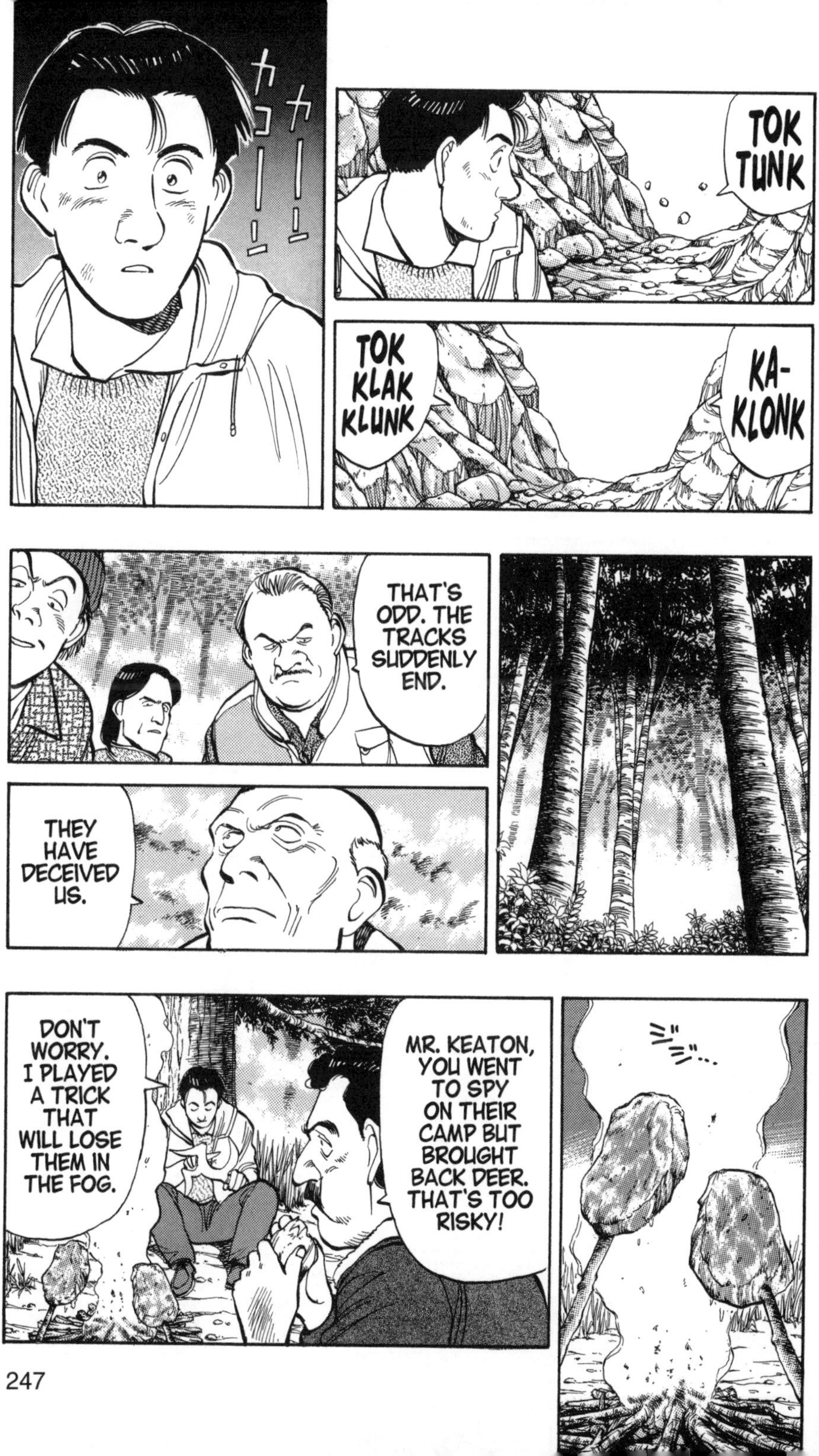
TOK TUNK
KA-KLONK
TOK KLAK KLUNK
カーーン
カコーーン
THAT'S ODD. THE TRACKS SUDDENLY END.
THEY HAVE DECEIVED US.
ジジ…
MR. KEATON, YOU WENT TO SPY ON THEIR CAMP BUT BROUGHT BACK DEER. THAT'S TOO RISKY!
DON'T WORRY. I PLAYED A TRICK THAT WILL LOSE THEM IN THE FOG.

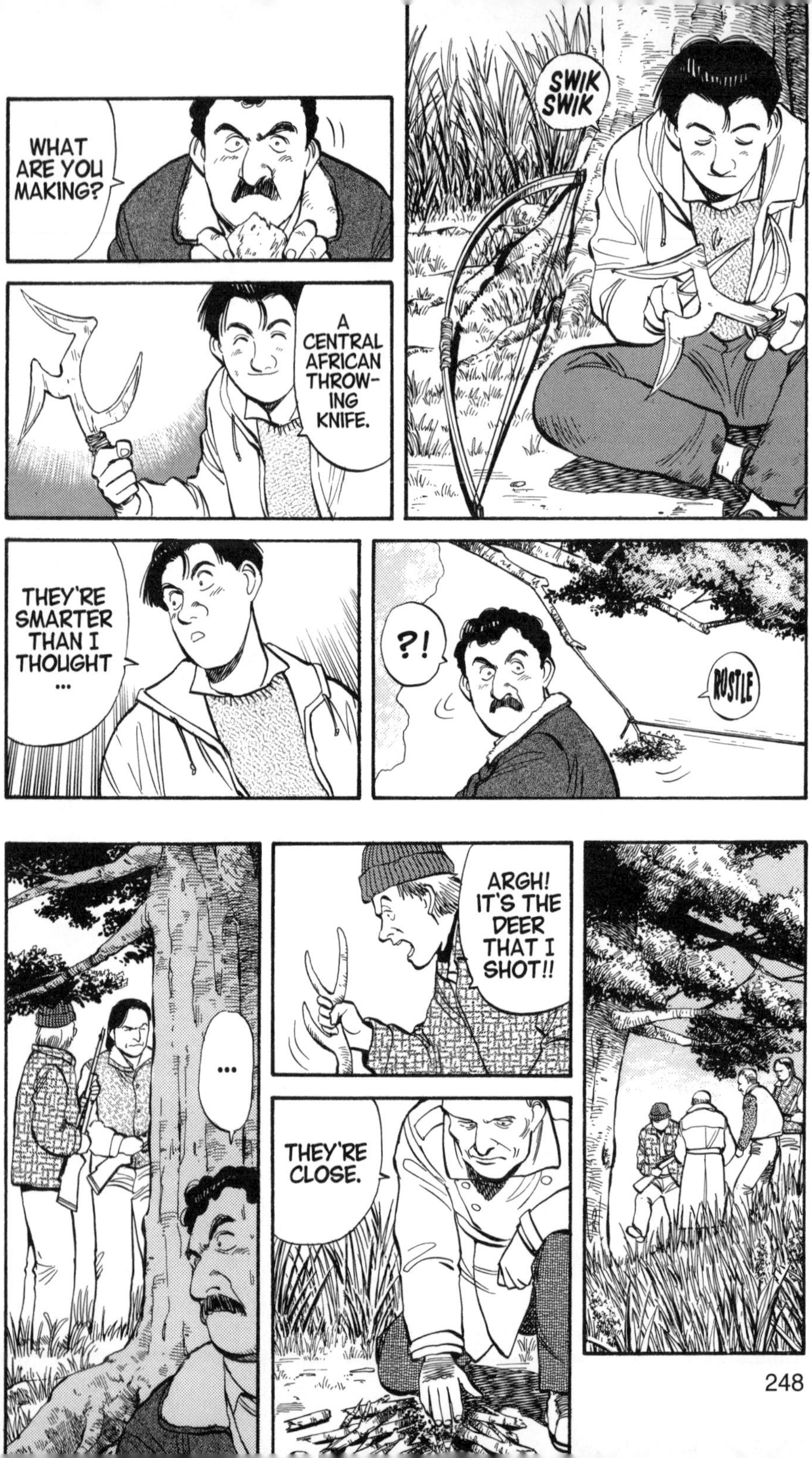
SWIK SWIK
WHAT ARE YOU MAKING?
A CENTRAL AFRICAN THROWING KNIFE.
?!
RUSTLE
THEY'RE SMARTER THAN I THOUGHT...
ARGH! IT'S THE DEER THAT I SHOT!!
THEY'RE CLOSE.
...

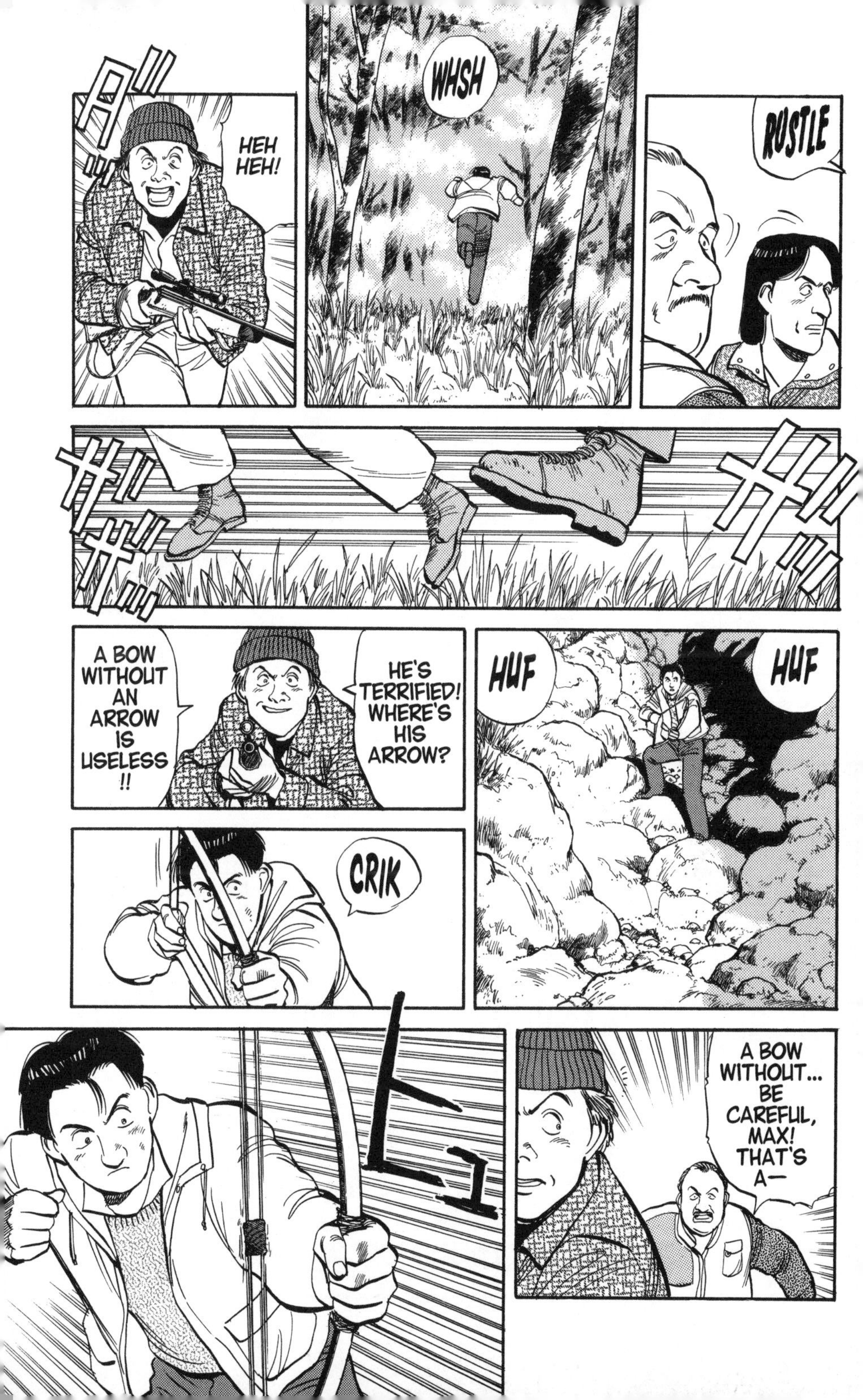
RUSTLE
WHSH
HEH HEH!
HUF
HUF
HE'S TERRIFIED! WHERE'S HIS ARROW?
A BOW WITHOUT AN ARROW IS USELESS !!
CRIK
A BOW WITHOUT... BE CAREFUL, MAX! THAT'S A—

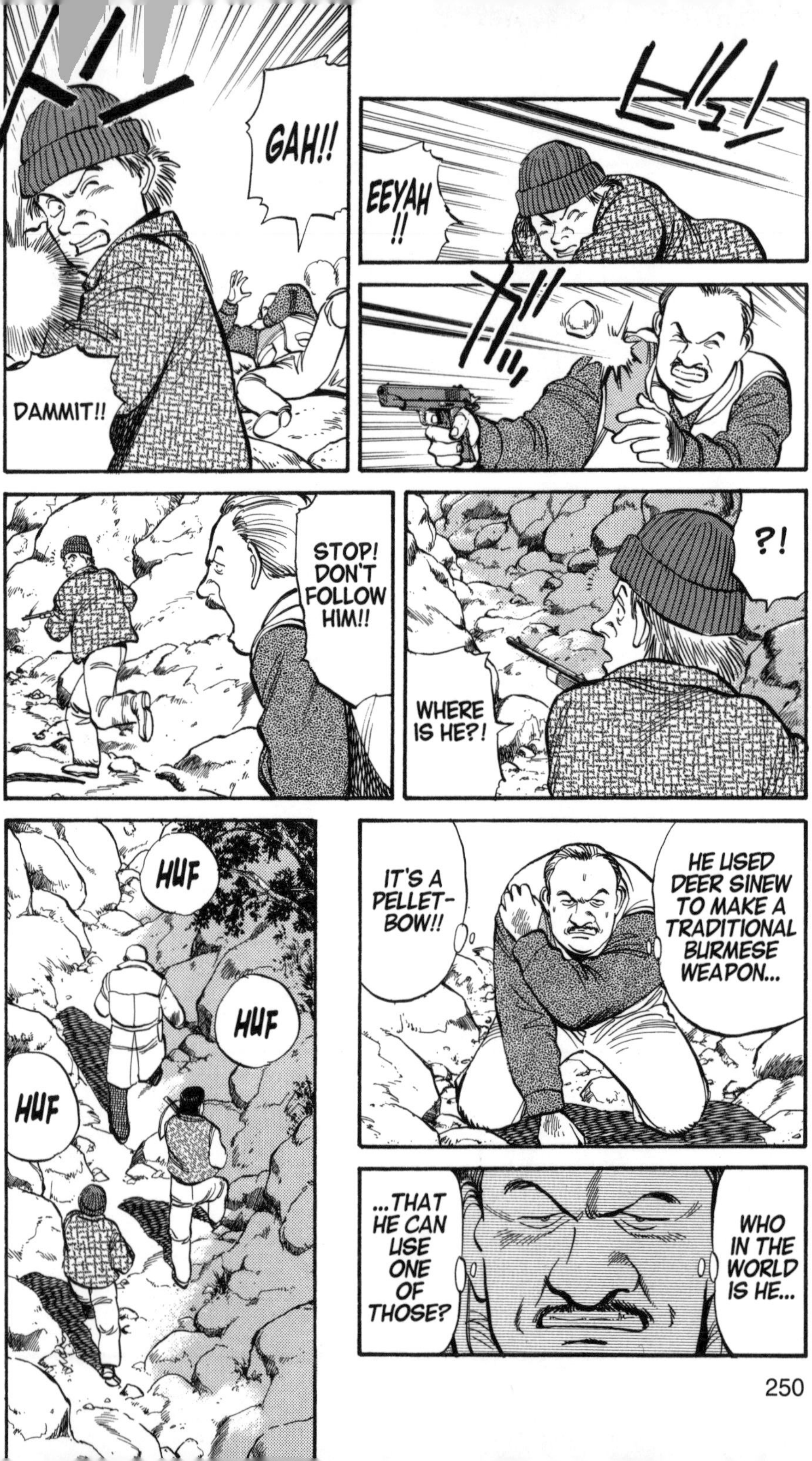
EEYAH!!
GAH!!
DAMMIT!!
?!
WHERE IS HE?!
STOP! DON'T FOLLOW HIM!!
HE USED DEER SINEW TO MAKE A TRADITIONAL BURMESE WEAPON...
IT'S A PELLET-BOW!!
WHO IN THE WORLD IS HE...
...THAT HE CAN USE ONE OF THOSE?
HUF
HUF
HUF

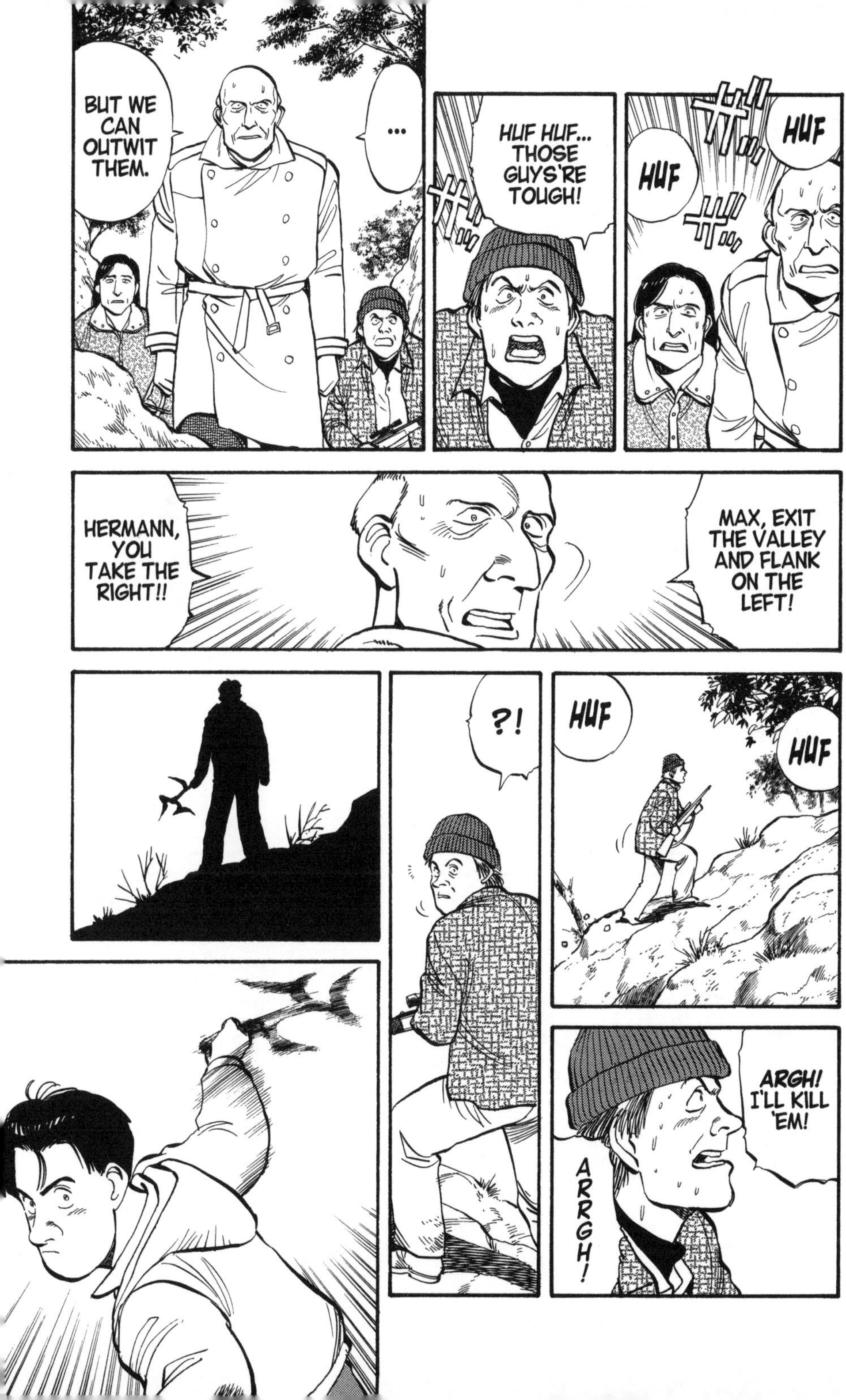
HUF
HUF
HUF HUF... THOSE GUYS'RE TOUGH!
...
BUT WE CAN OUTWIT THEM.
MAX, EXIT THE VALLEY AND FLANK ON THE LEFT!
HERMANN, YOU TAKE THE RIGHT!!
HUF
HUF
ARGH! I'LL KILL 'EM!
ARRGH!
?!

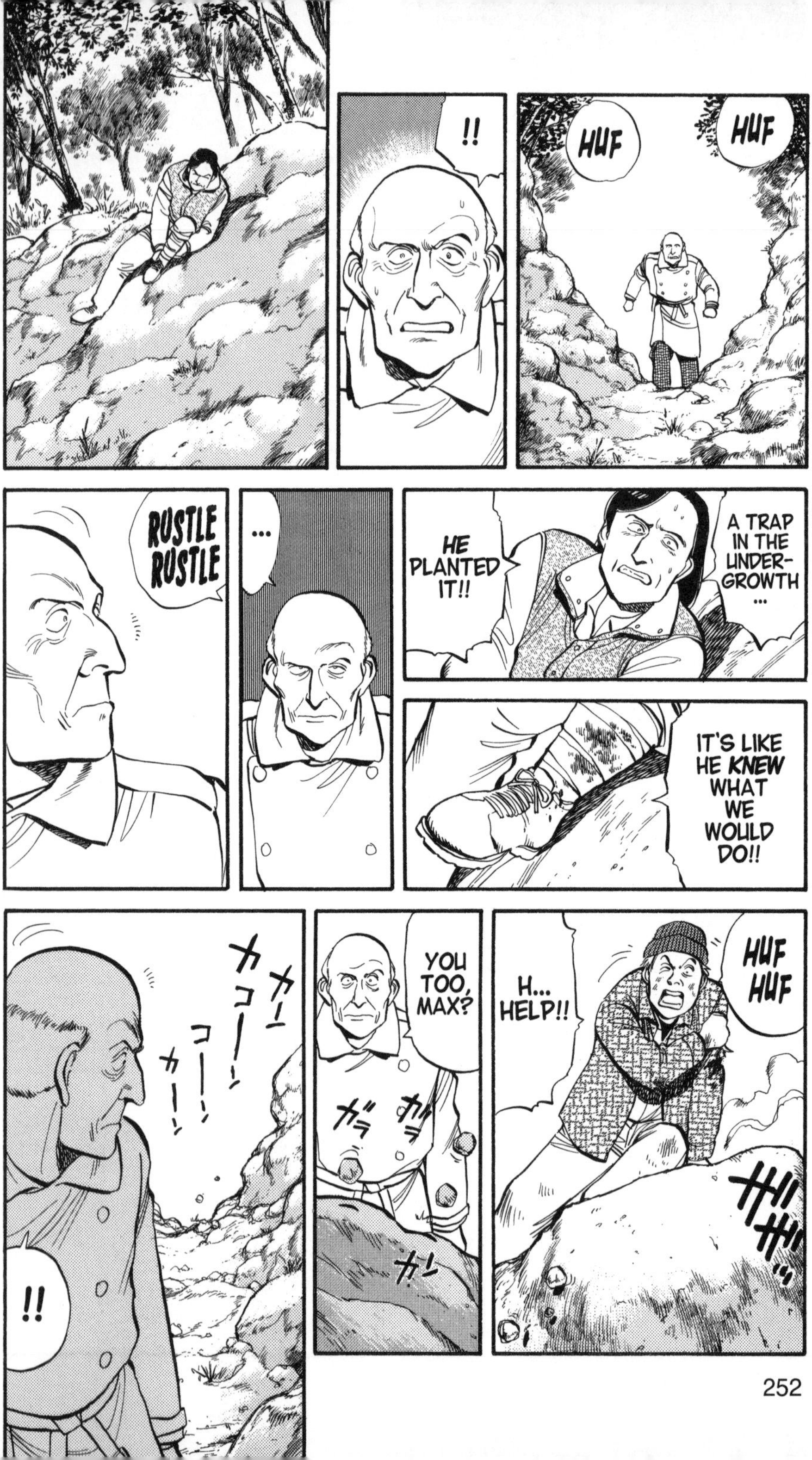
HUF
HUF
!!
A TRAP IN THE UNDERGROWTH...
HE PLANTED IT!!
IT'S LIKE HE KNEW WHAT WE WOULD DO!!
...
RUSTLE RUSTLE
HUF HUF
H... HELP!!
YOU TOO, MAX?
ガラ
ガラ
カン
カーン
カコーン
コーン
カーン
!!

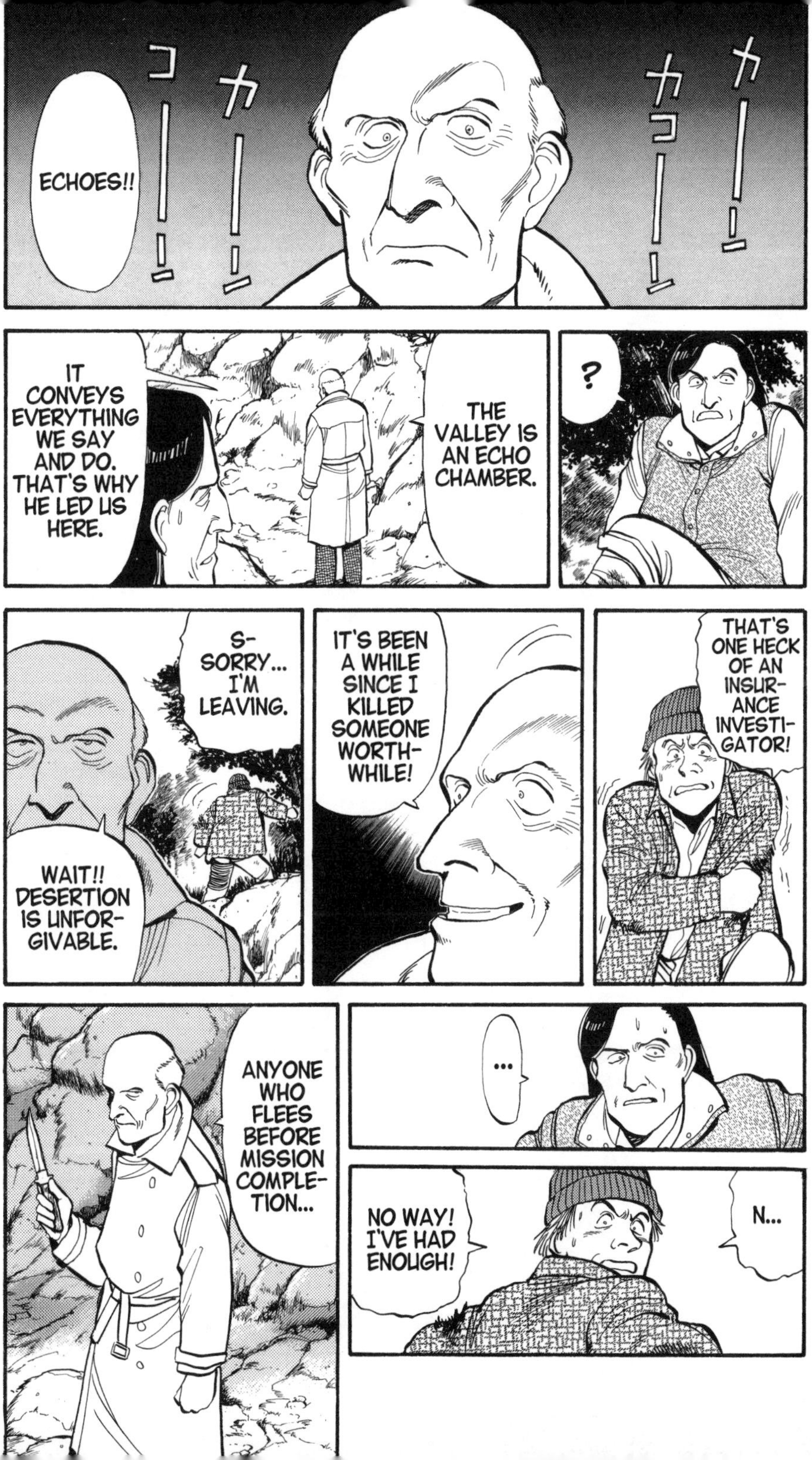

カーーン
カコーーン
カーーン
コーーン
ECHOES!!
?
THE VALLEY IS AN ECHO CHAMBER.
IT CONVEYS EVERYTHING WE SAY AND DO. THAT'S WHY HE LED US HERE.
THAT'S ONE HECK OF AN INSURANCE INVESTIGATOR!
IT'S BEEN A WHILE SINCE I KILLED SOMEONE WORTHWHILE!
S-SORRY... I'M LEAVING.
WAIT!! DESERTION IS UNFORGIVABLE.
...
N...
NO WAY! I'VE HAD ENOUGH!
ANYONE WHO FLEES BEFORE MISSION COMPLETION...

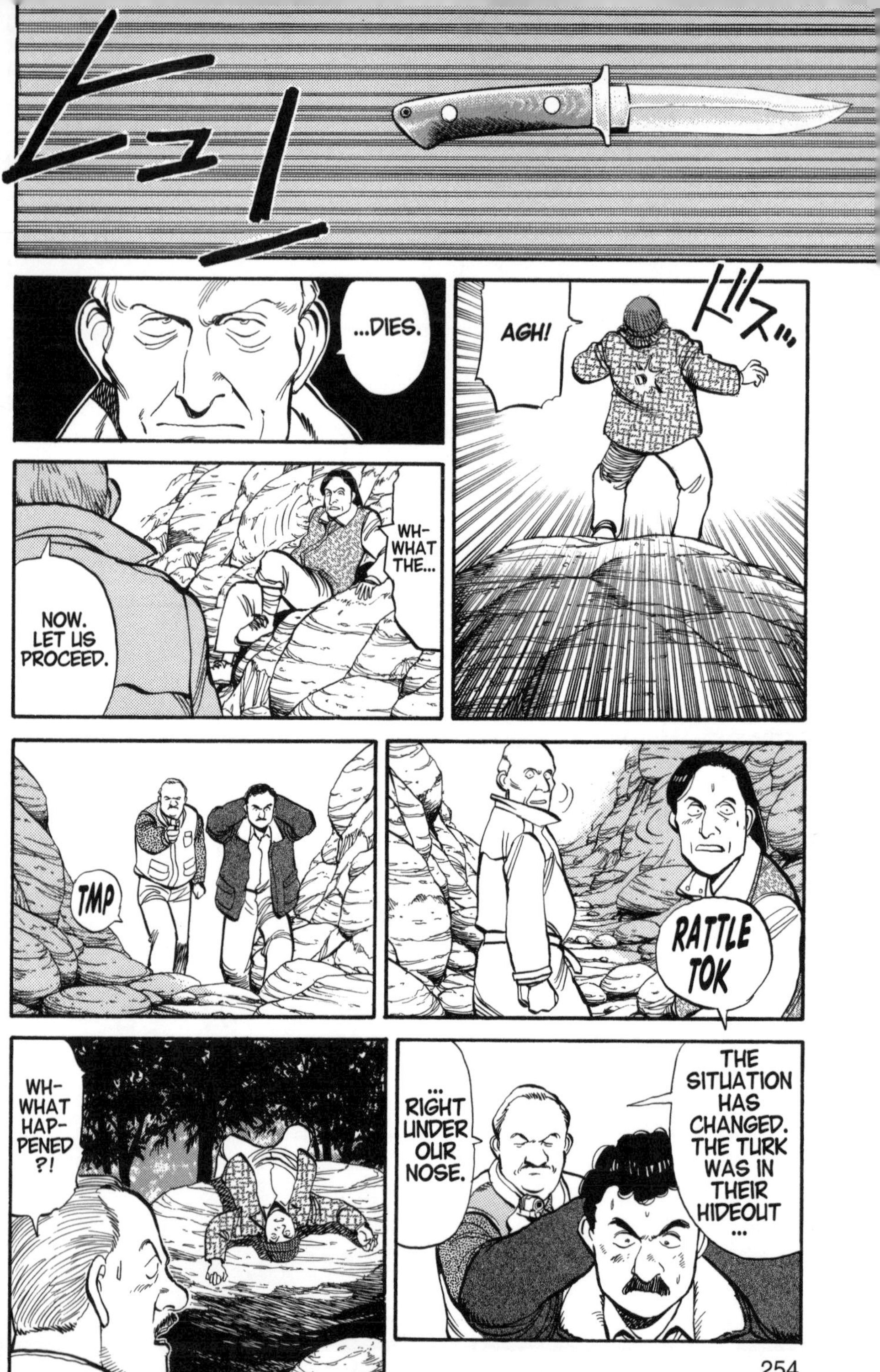

ヒュー
ドスッ
AGH!
...DIES.
WH- WHAT THE...
NOW. LET US PROCEED.
RATTLE TOK
TMP
THE SITUATION HAS CHANGED. THE TURK WAS IN THEIR HIDEOUT ...
... RIGHT UNDER OUR NOSE.
WH- WHAT HAP- PENED ?!

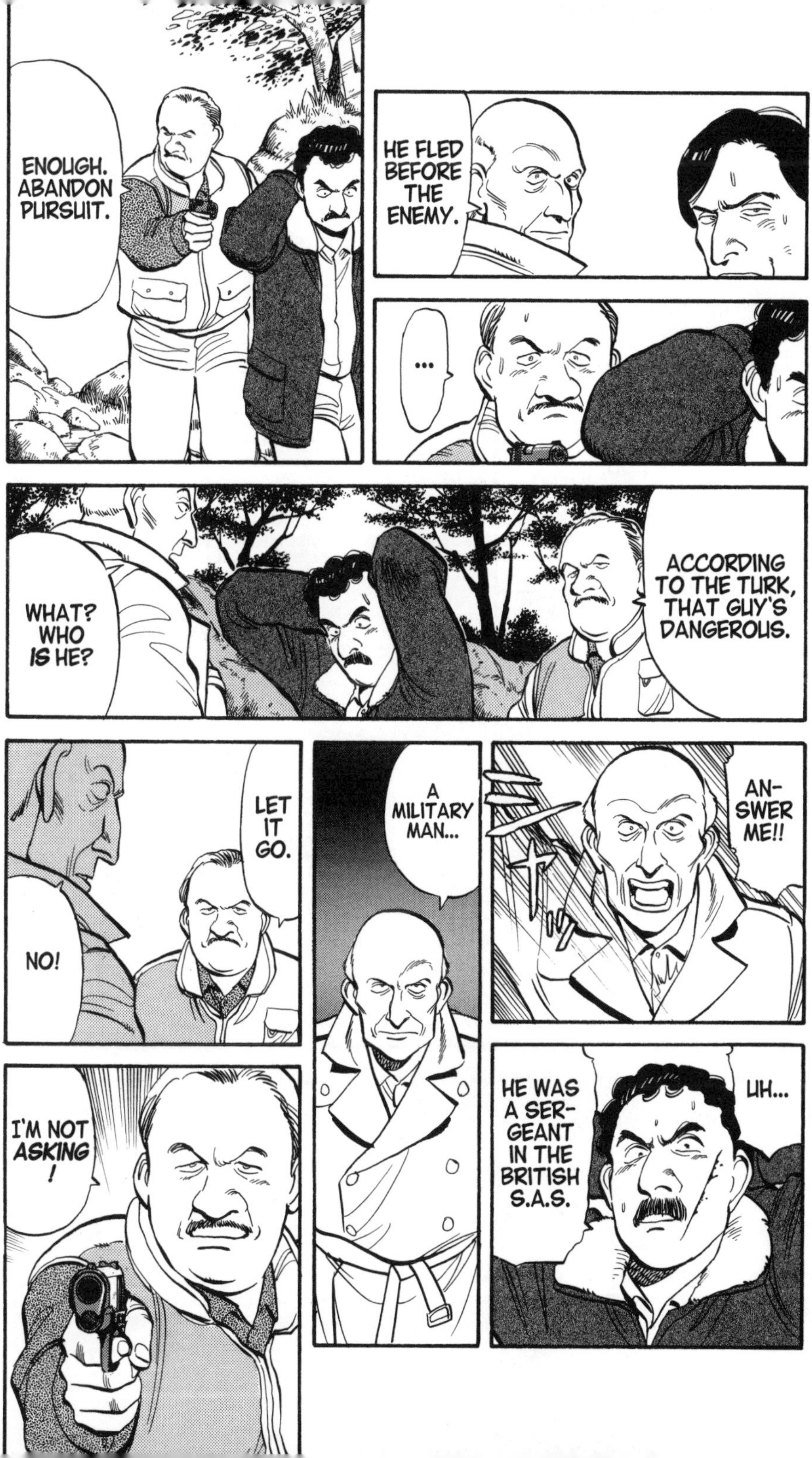
HE FLED BEFORE THE ENEMY.
...
ENOUGH. ABANDON PURSUIT.
ACCORDING TO THE TURK, THAT GUY'S DANGEROUS.
WHAT? WHO IS HE?
AN-SWER ME!!
UH...
HE WAS A SER-GEANT IN THE BRITISH S.A.S.
A MILITARY MAN...
LET IT GO.
NO!
I'M NOT ASKING!

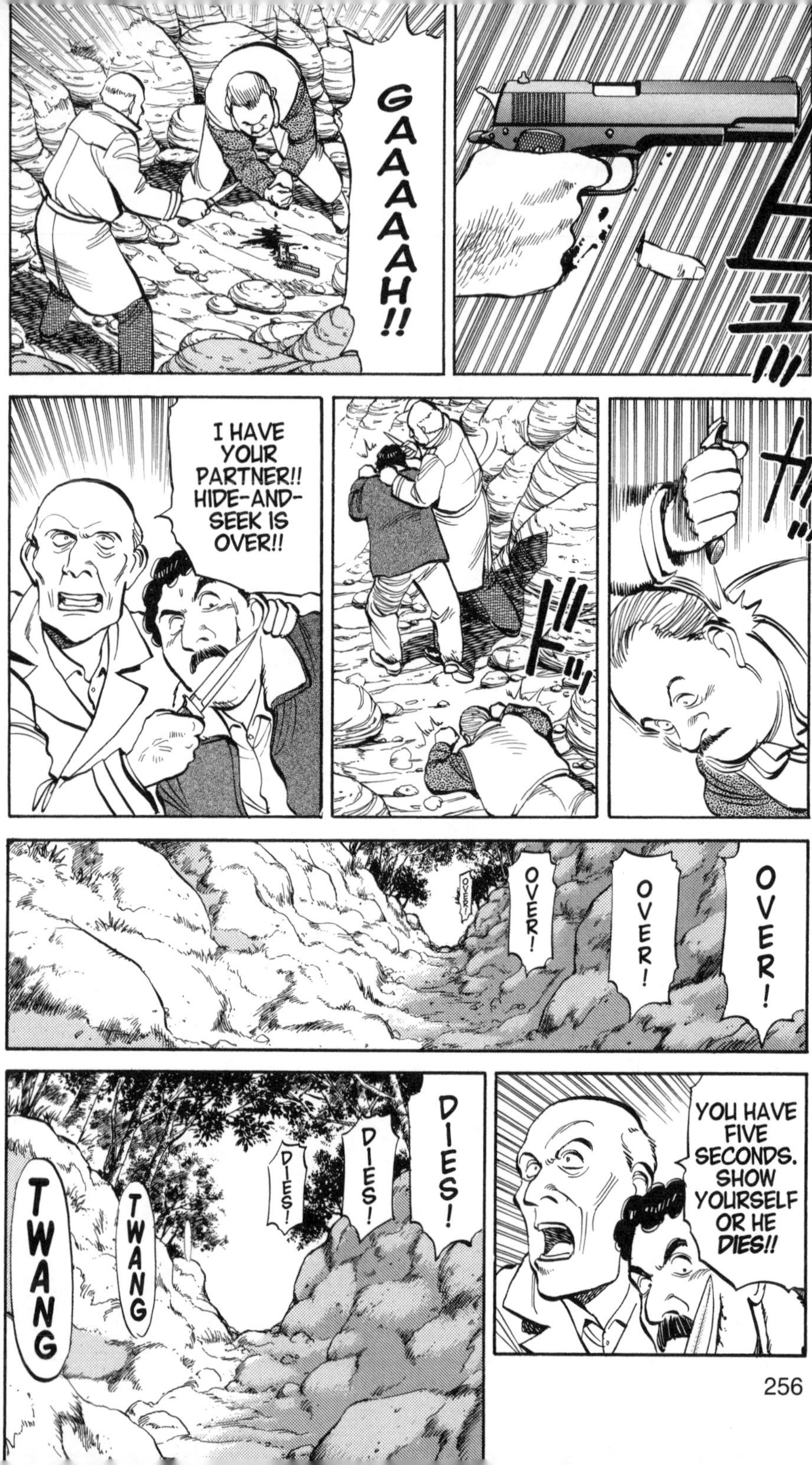

ヒュ
GAAAAAAH!!
I HAVE YOUR PARTNER!! HIDE-AND-SEEK IS OVER!!
OVER!
OVER!
OVER!
OVER!
YOU HAVE FIVE SECONDS. SHOW YOURSELF OR HE DIES!!
DIES!
DIES!
DIES!
TWANG
TWANG

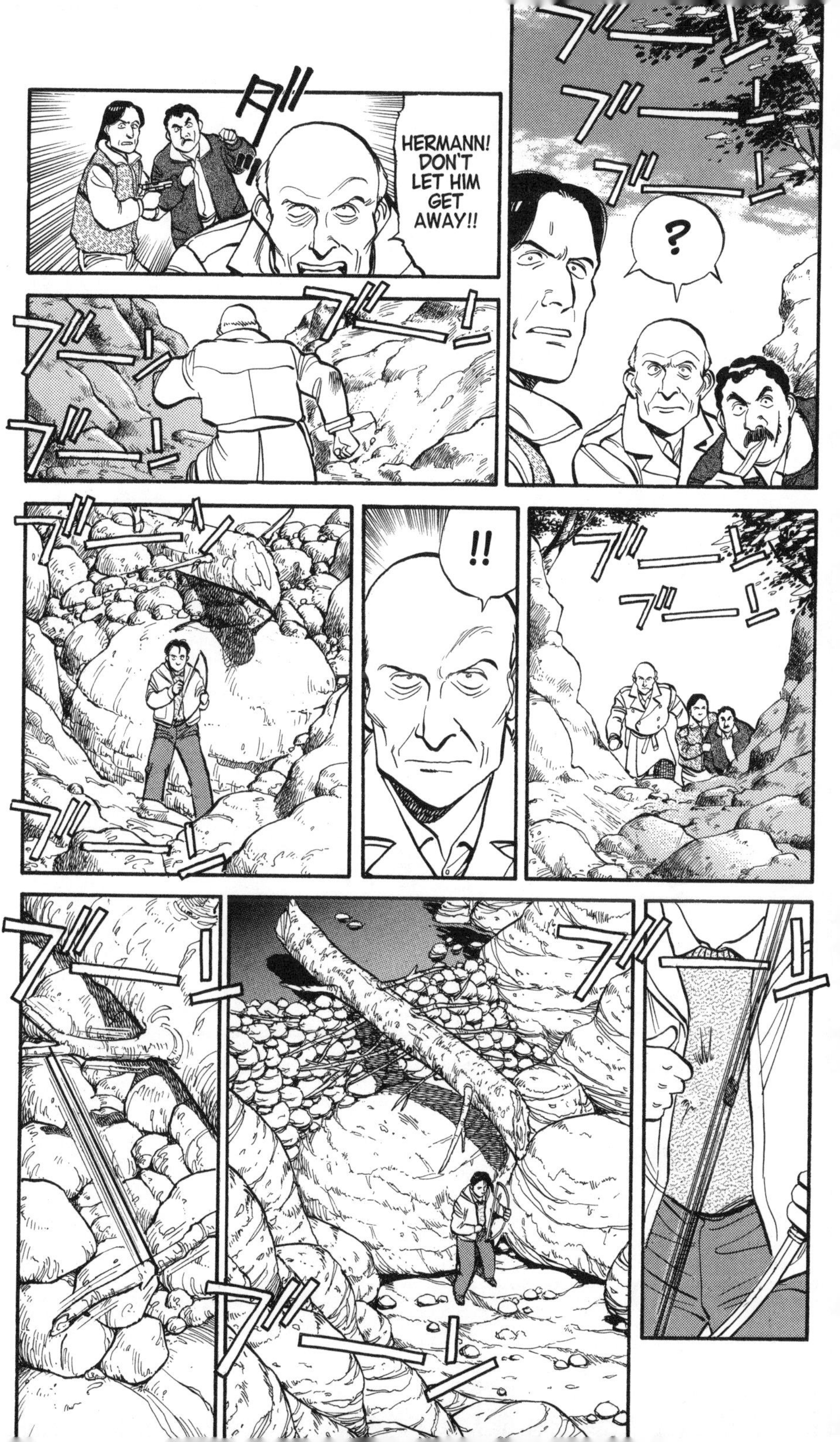
?
HERMANN! DON'T LET HIM GET AWAY!!
!!

KEEP WALK-ING!

SHTMP

WH...WHAT?

UNLESS YOU WANT TO DIE, DON'T GO ANY CLOSER.

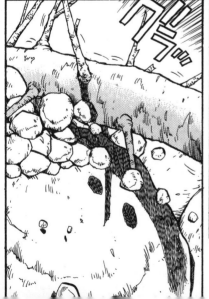

HUNH?!

THAT'S MORSE CODE! AND THE MESSAGE IS BAD NEWS!!

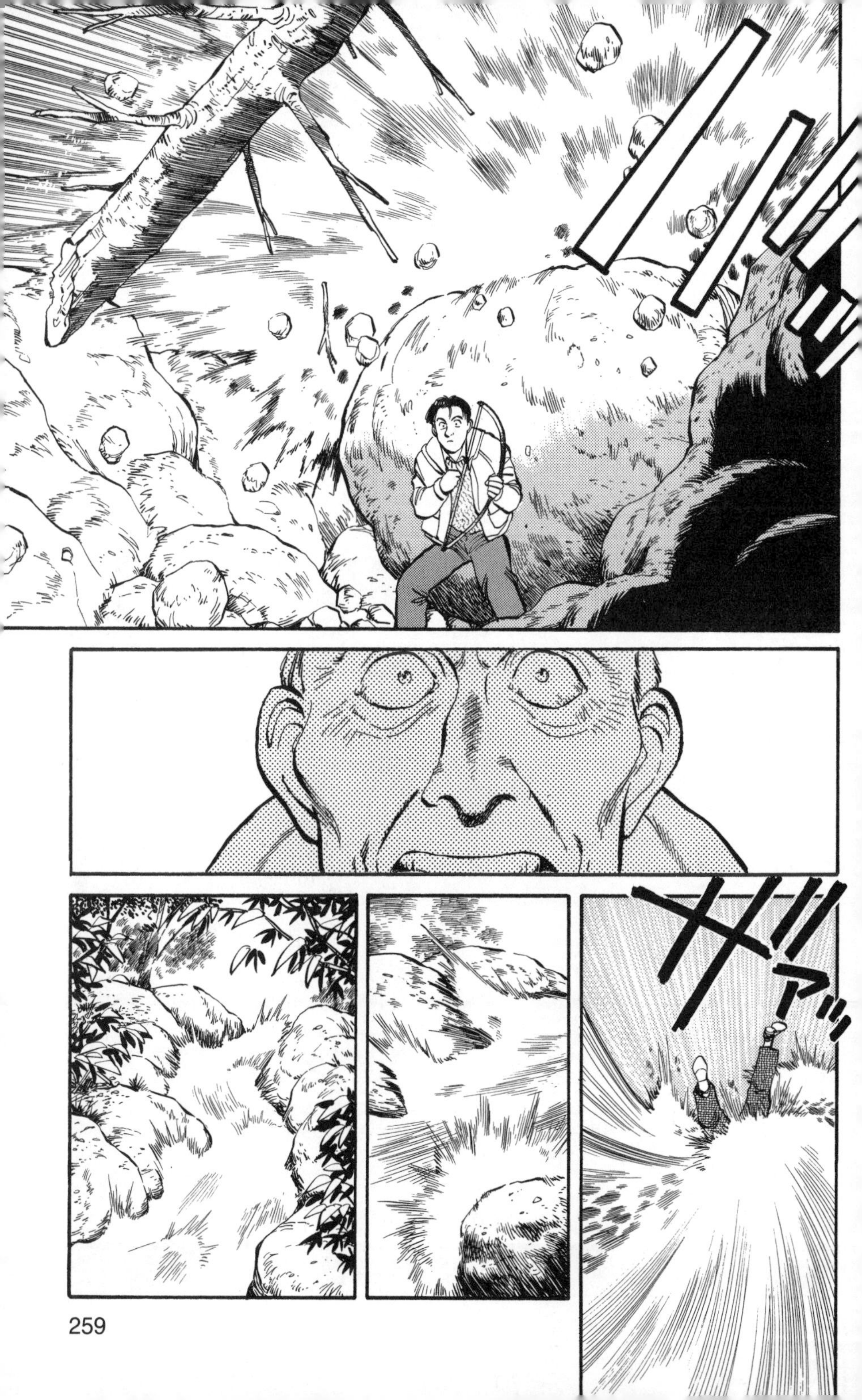
ザアッ

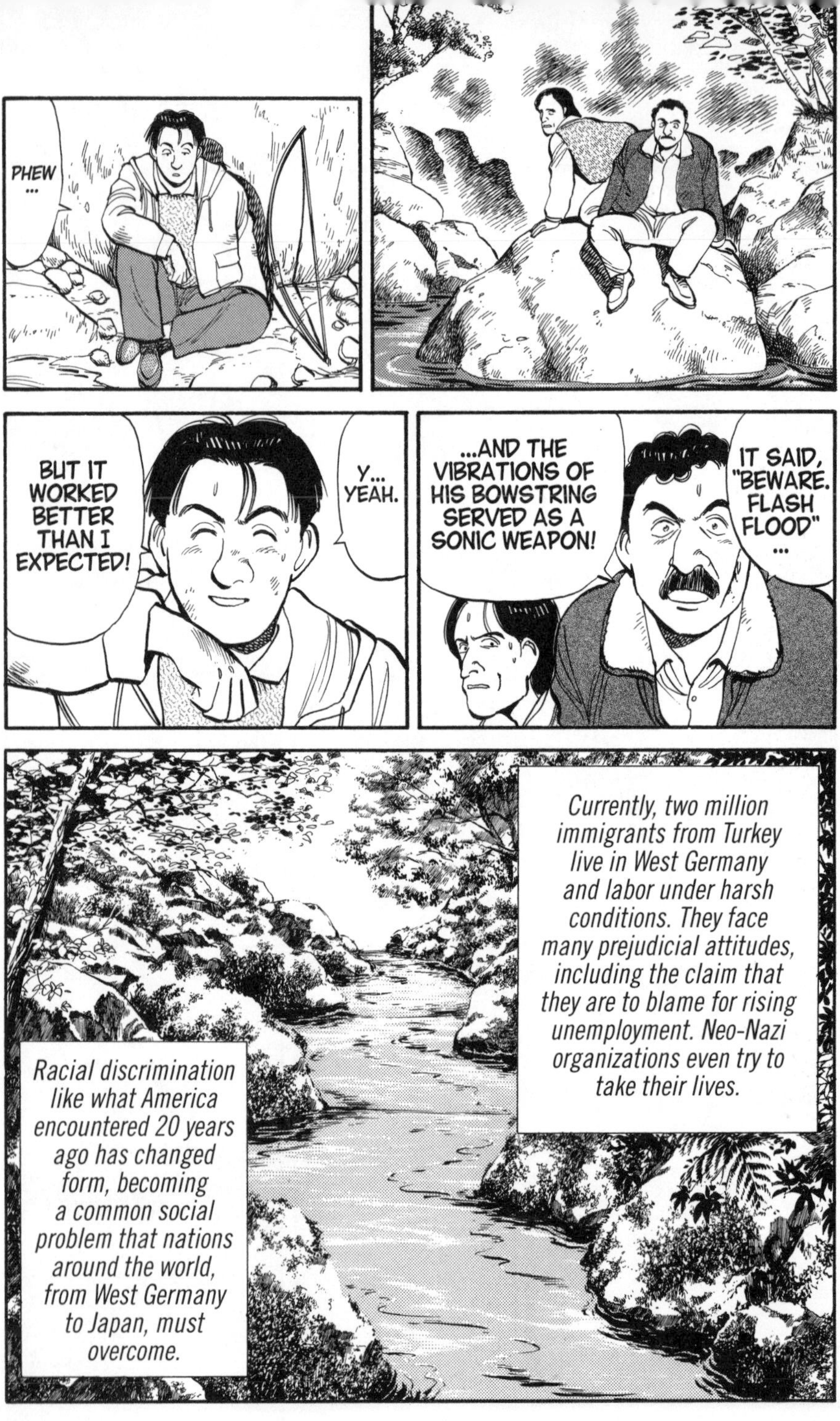
PHEW ...
IT SAID, "BEWARE. FLASH FLOOD" ...
...AND THE VIBRATIONS OF HIS BOWSTRING SERVED AS A SONIC WEAPON!
Y... YEAH.
BUT IT WORKED BETTER THAN I EXPECTED!
Currently, two million immigrants from Turkey live in West Germany and labor under harsh conditions. They face many prejudicial attitudes, including the claim that they are to blame for rising unemployment. Neo-Nazi organizations even try to take their lives.
Racial discrimination like what America encountered 20 years ago has changed form, becoming a common social problem that nations around the world, from West Germany to Japan, must overcome.

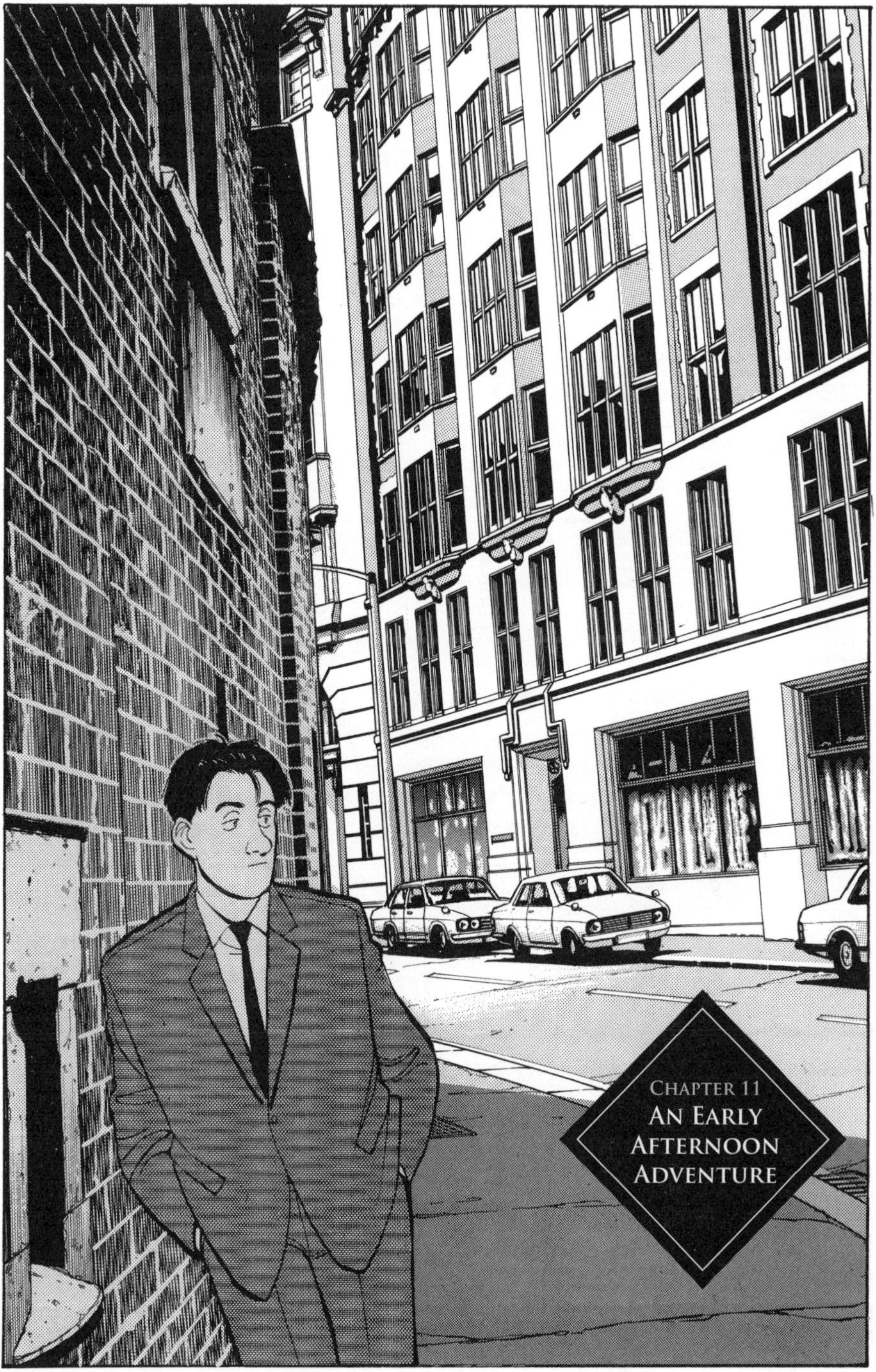
Chapter 11
An Early Afternoon Adventure

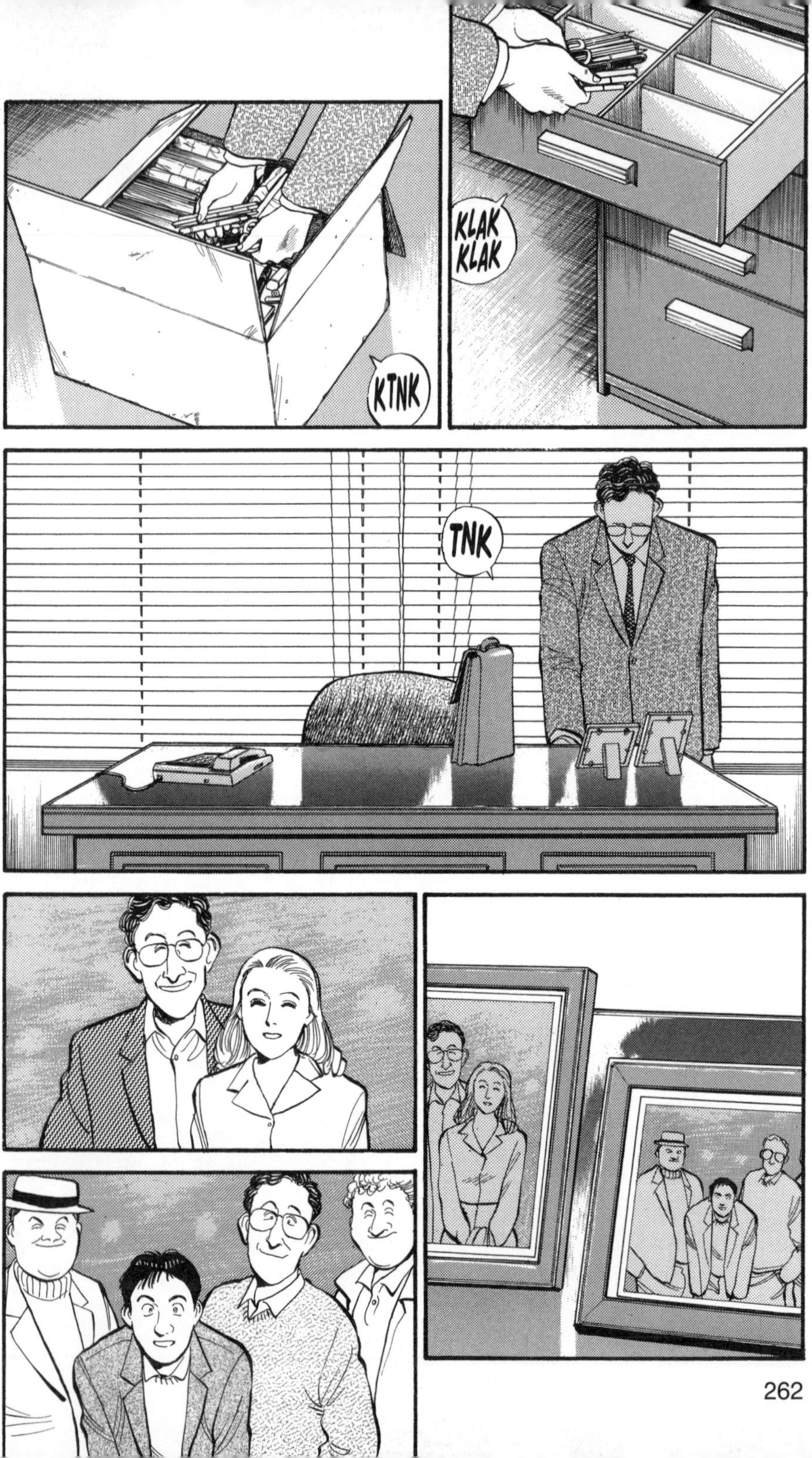
KLAK
KLAK
KTNK
TNK

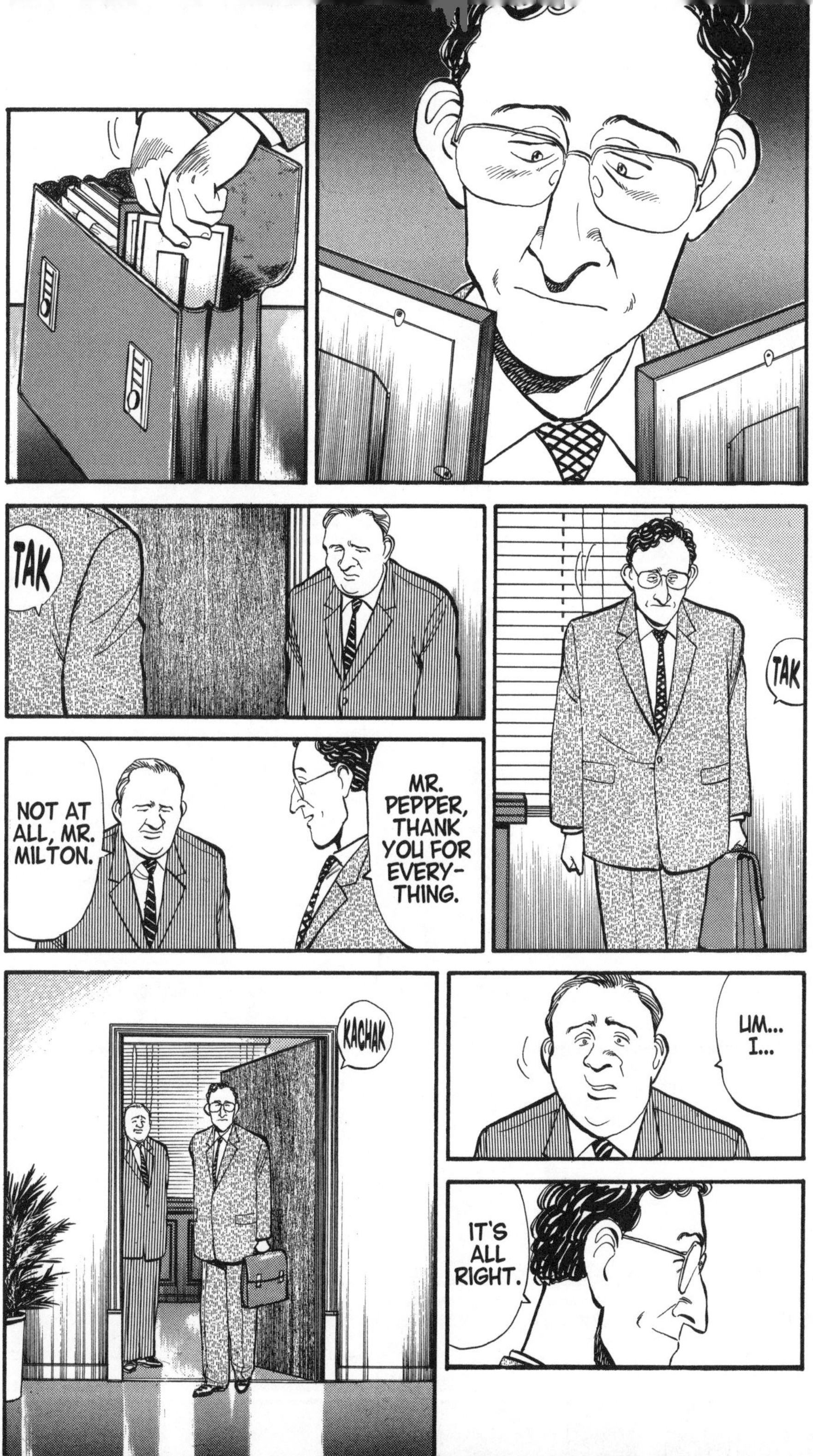
TAK
TAK
MR. PEPPER, THANK YOU FOR EVERYTHING.
NOT AT ALL, MR. MILTON.
UM... I...
IT'S ALL RIGHT.
KACHAK

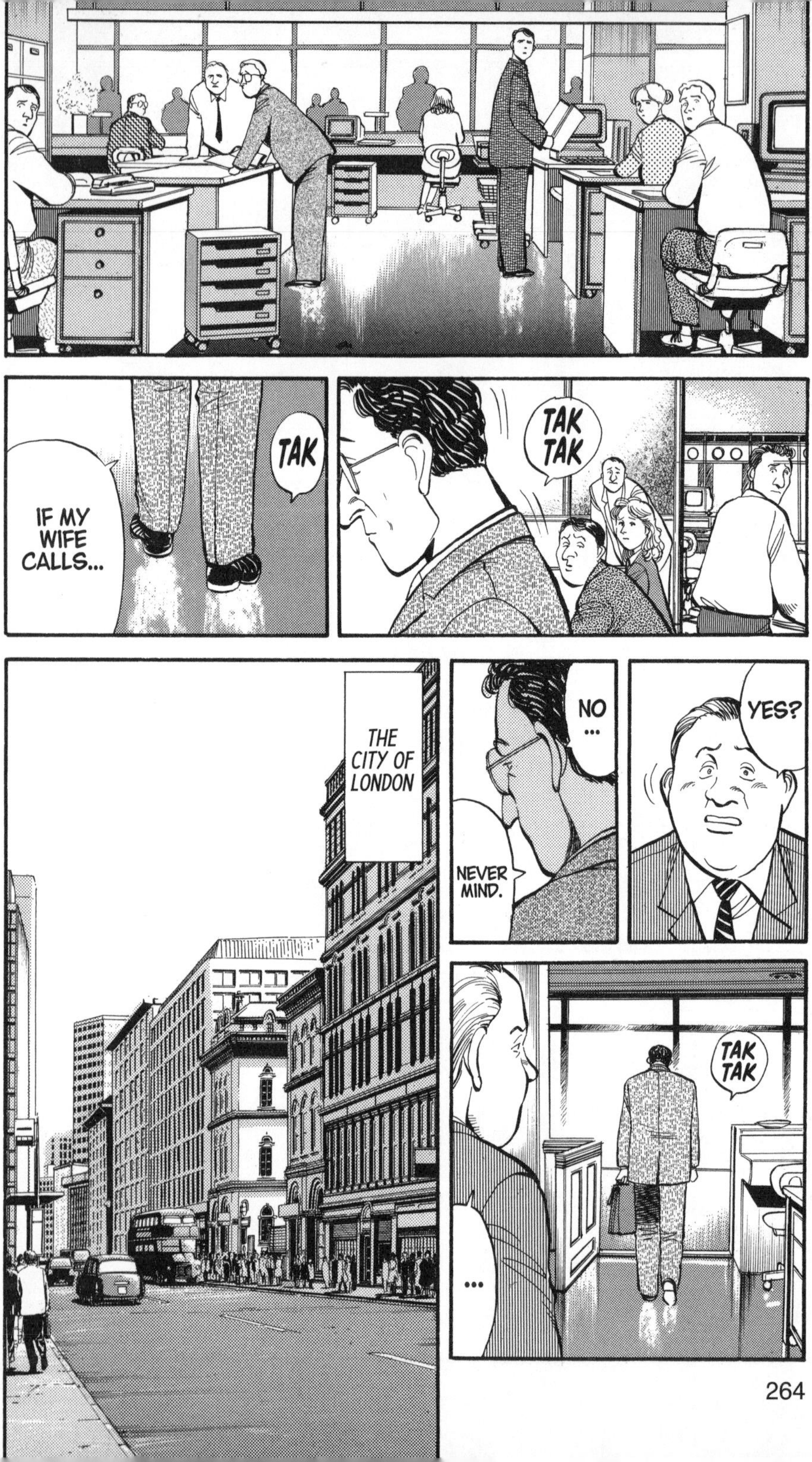
TAK TAK
TAK
IF MY WIFE CALLS...
YES?
NO ...
NEVER MIND.
TAK TAK
...
THE CITY OF LONDON

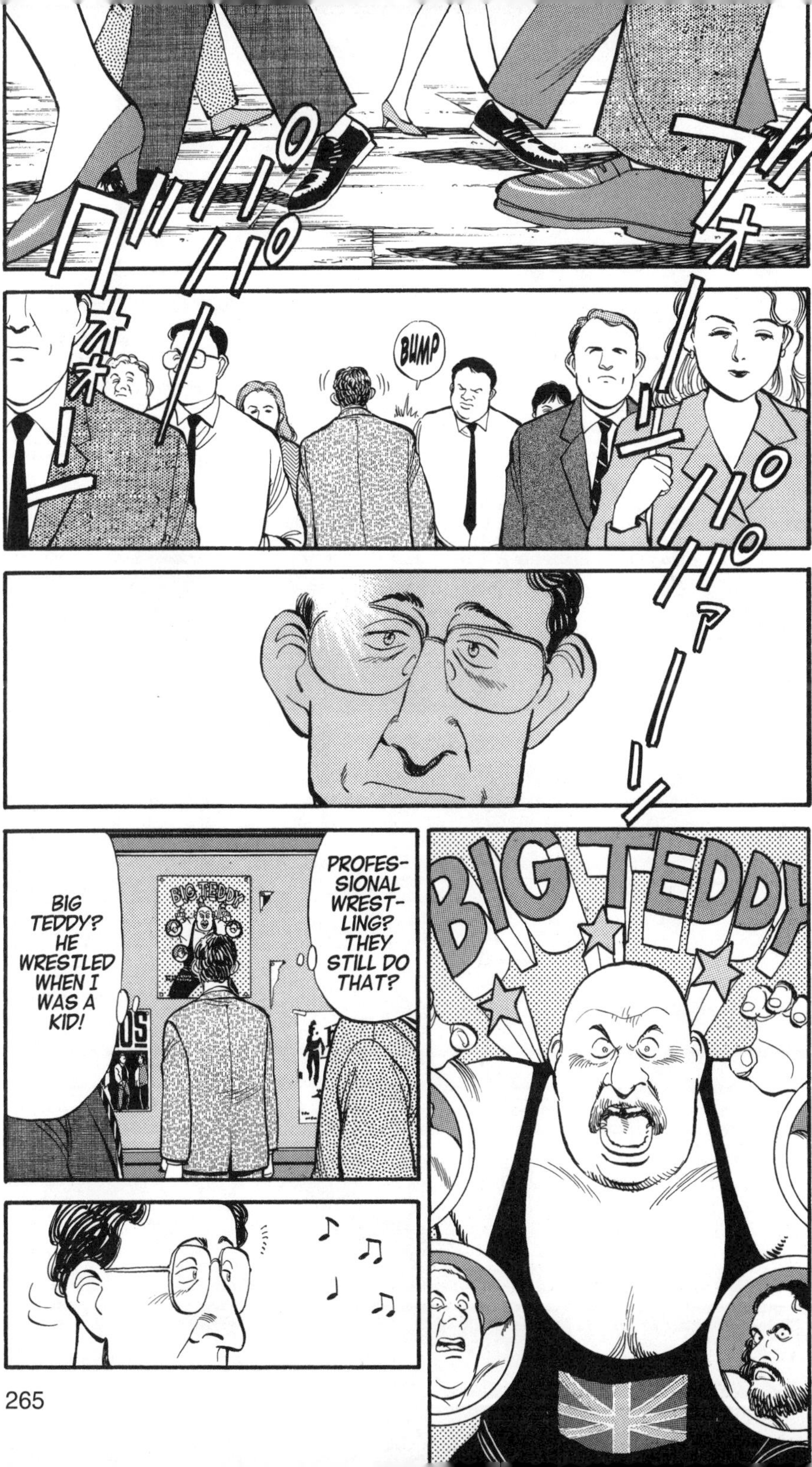
BUMP
BIG TEDDY
PROFESSIONAL WRESTLING? THEY STILL DO THAT?
BIG TEDDY? HE WRESTLED WHEN I WAS A KID!

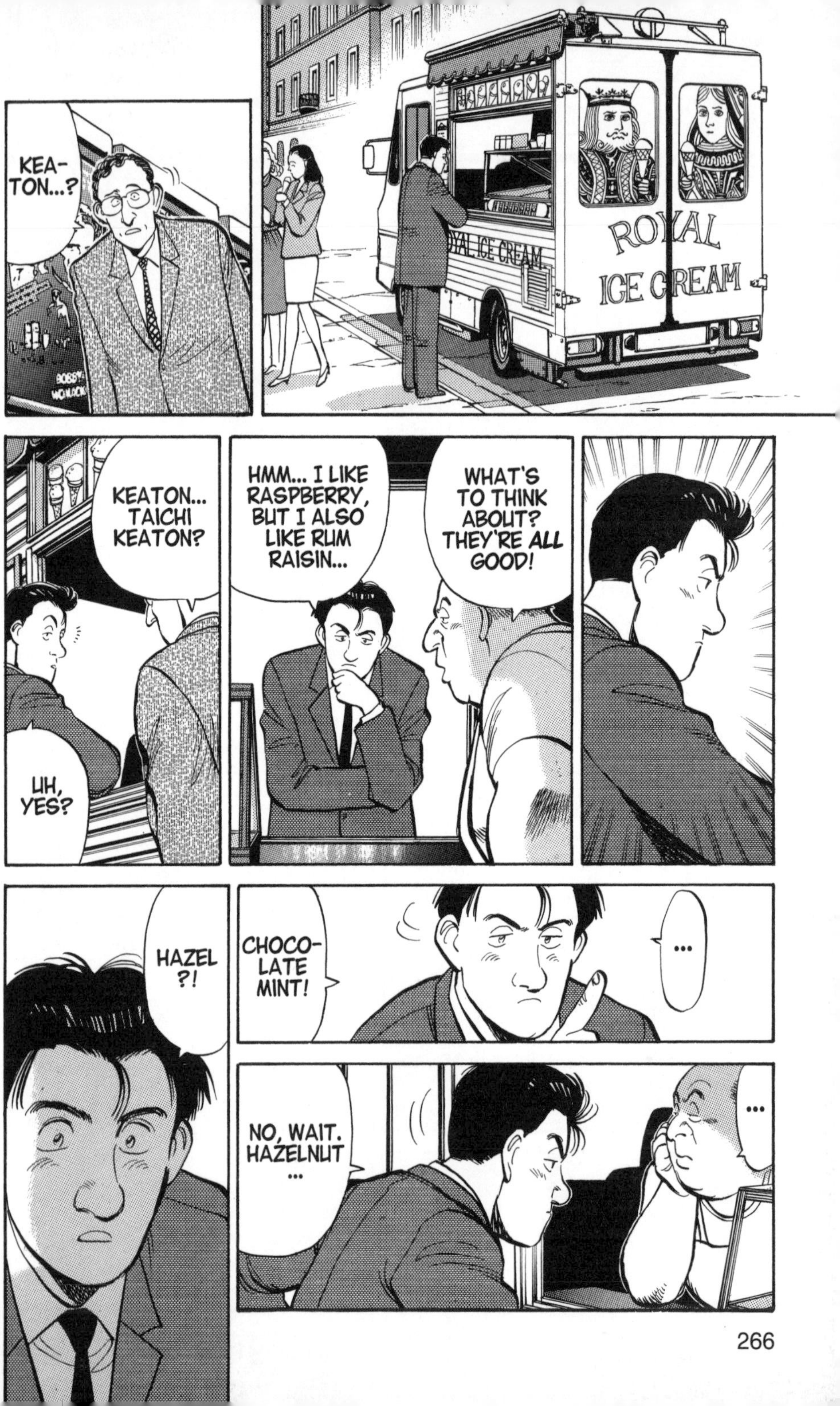
ROYAL ICE CREAM
ROYAL ICE CREAM
KEA-TON...?
WHAT'S TO THINK ABOUT? THEY'RE ALL GOOD!
HMM... I LIKE RASPBERRY, BUT I ALSO LIKE RUM RAISIN...
KEATON... TAICHI KEATON?
UH, YES?
...
CHOCO-LATE MINT!
...
NO, WAIT. HAZELNUT ...
HAZEL ?!

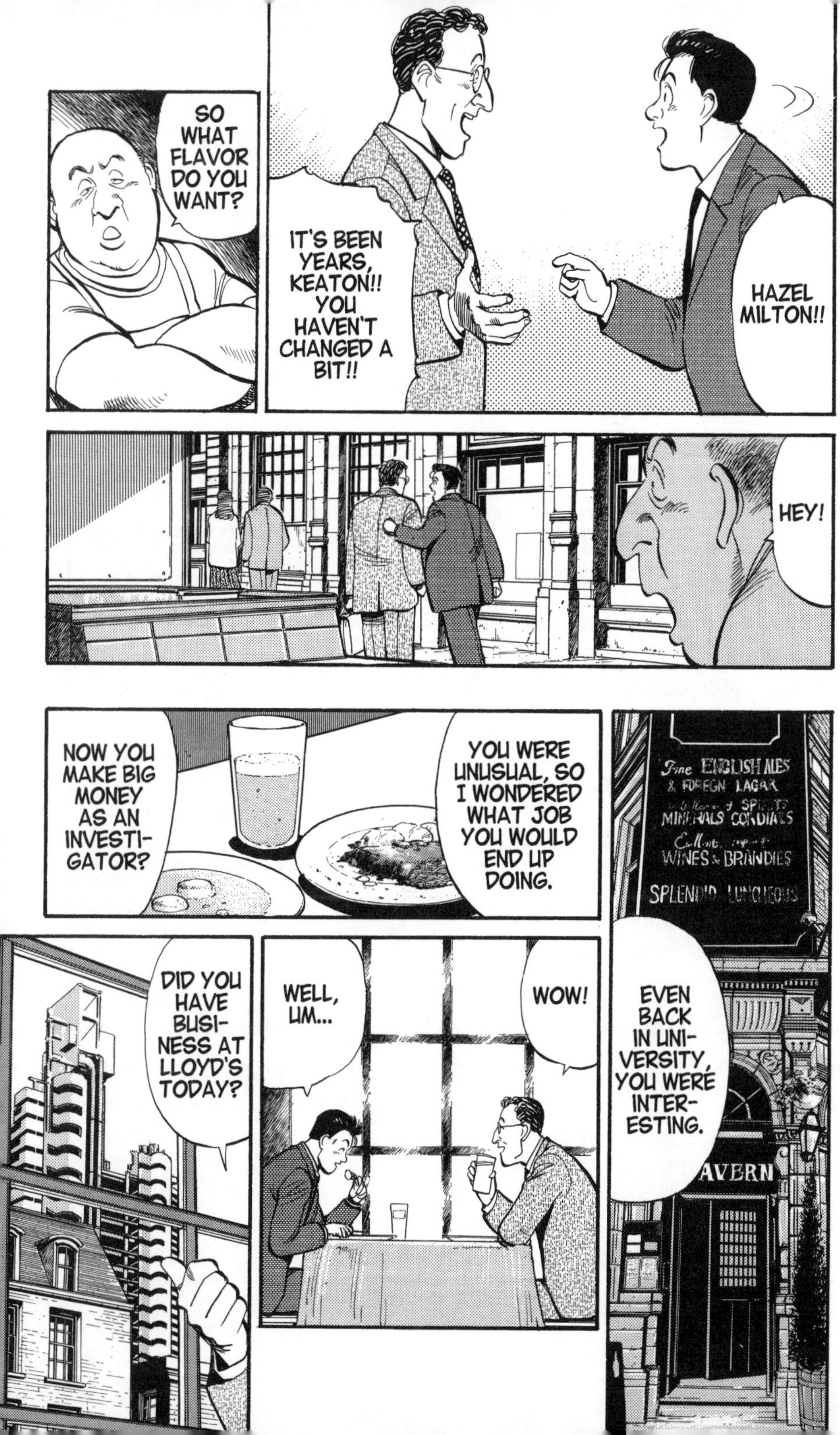
HAZEL MILTON!!
IT'S BEEN YEARS, KEATON!! YOU HAVEN'T CHANGED A BIT!!
SO WHAT FLAVOR DO YOU WANT?
HEY!
ENGLISH ALES
MINERALS CORDIALS
WINES & BRANDIES
EVEN BACK IN UNIVERSITY, YOU WERE INTERESTING.
YOU WERE UNUSUAL, SO I WONDERED WHAT JOB YOU WOULD END UP DOING.
NOW YOU MAKE BIG MONEY AS AN INVESTIGATOR?
WOW!
WELL, UM...
DID YOU HAVE BUSINESS AT LLOYD'S TODAY?

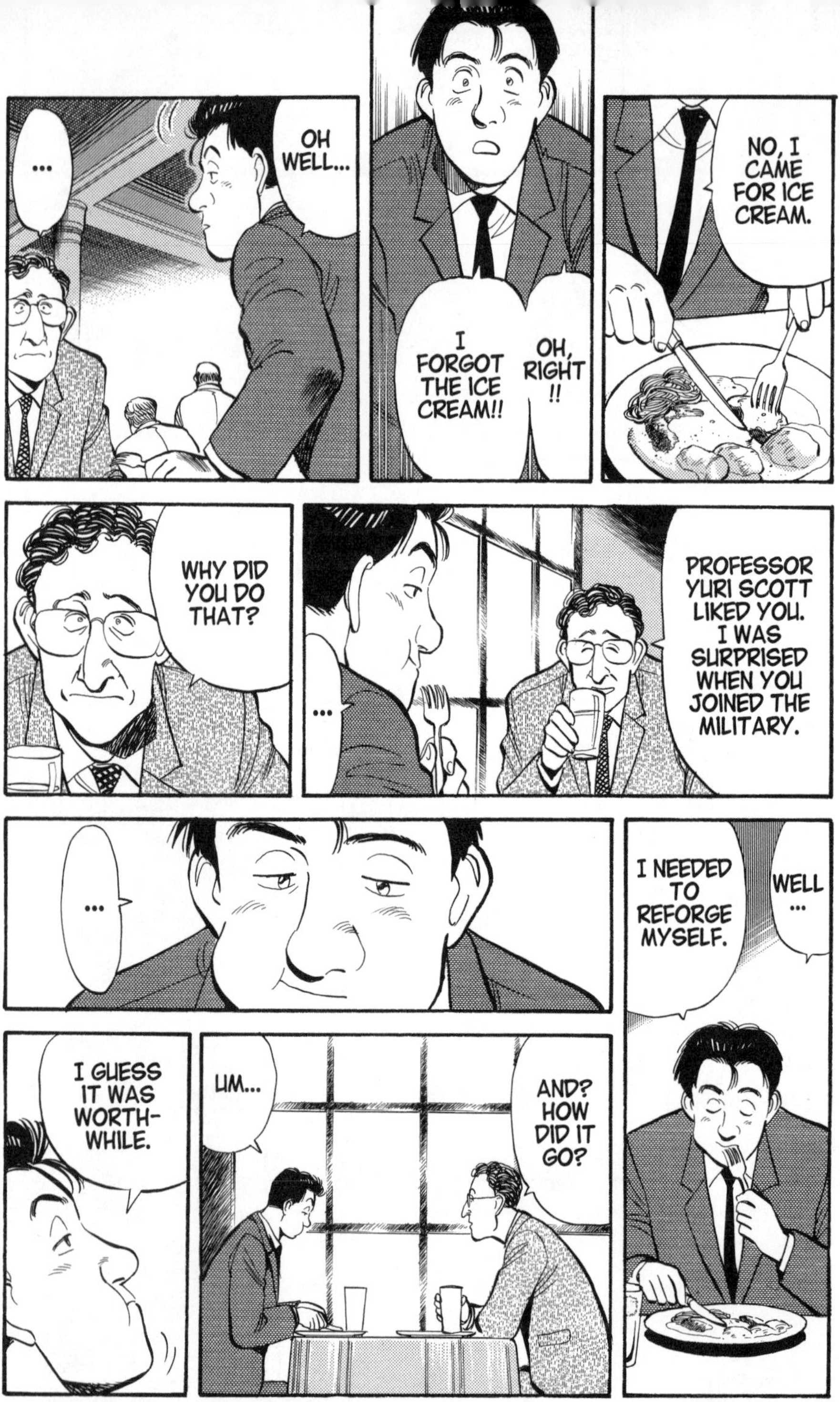
NO, I CAME FOR ICE CREAM.
OH, RIGHT!!
I FORGOT THE ICE CREAM!!
OH WELL...
...
PROFESSOR YURI SCOTT LIKED YOU. I WAS SURPRISED WHEN YOU JOINED THE MILITARY.
...
WHY DID YOU DO THAT?
WELL...
I NEEDED TO REFORGE MYSELF.
...
AND? HOW DID IT GO?
UM...
I GUESS IT WAS WORTH-WHILE.

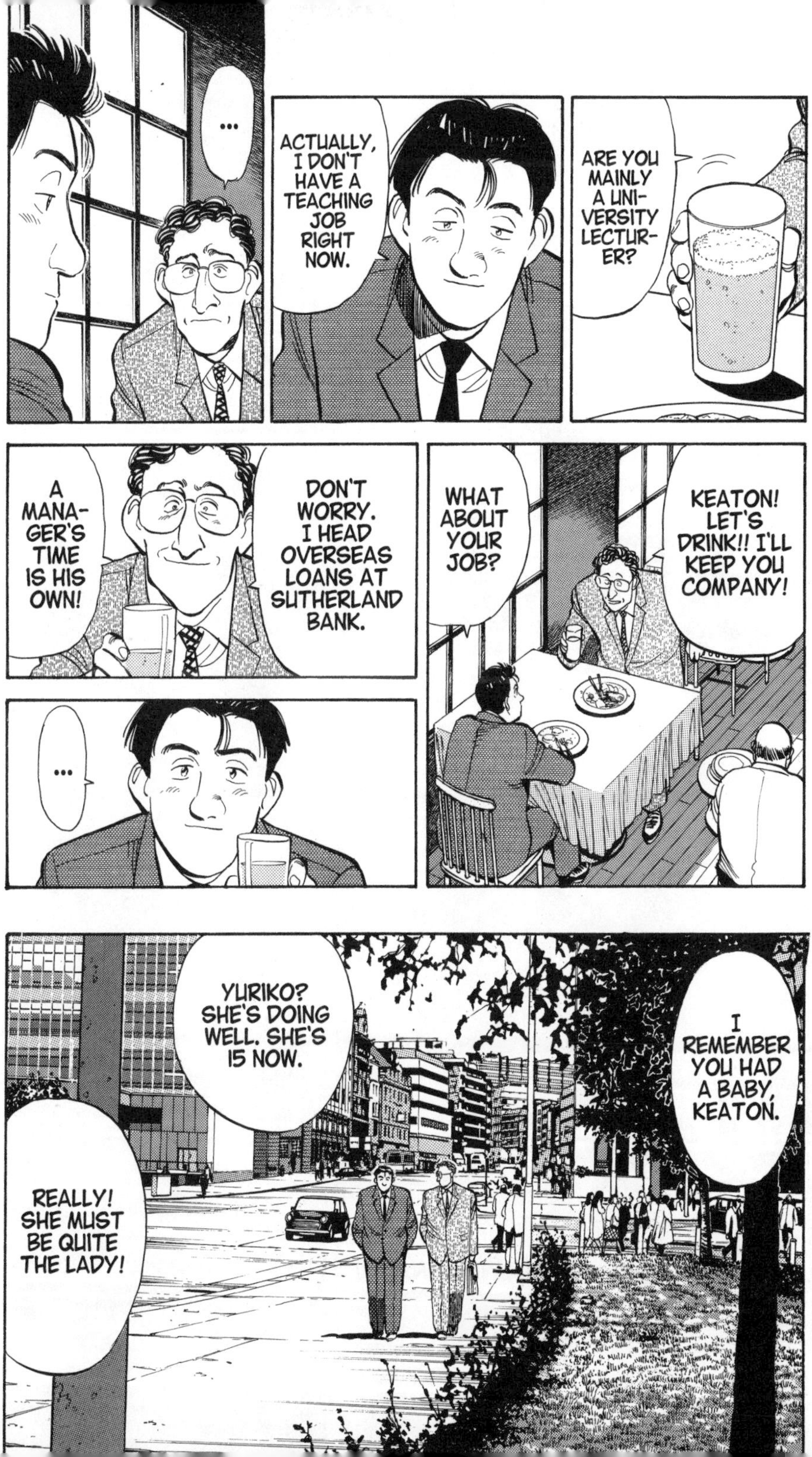
ARE YOU MAINLY A UNI-VERSITY LECTUR-ER?
ACTUALLY, I DON'T HAVE A TEACHING JOB RIGHT NOW.
...
KEATON! LET'S DRINK!! I'LL KEEP YOU COMPANY!
WHAT ABOUT YOUR JOB?
DON'T WORRY. I HEAD OVERSEAS LOANS AT SUTHERLAND BANK.
A MANA-GER'S TIME IS HIS OWN!
...
I REMEMBER YOU HAD A BABY, KEATON.
YURIKO? SHE'S DOING WELL. SHE'S 15 NOW.
REALLY! SHE MUST BE QUITE THE LADY!

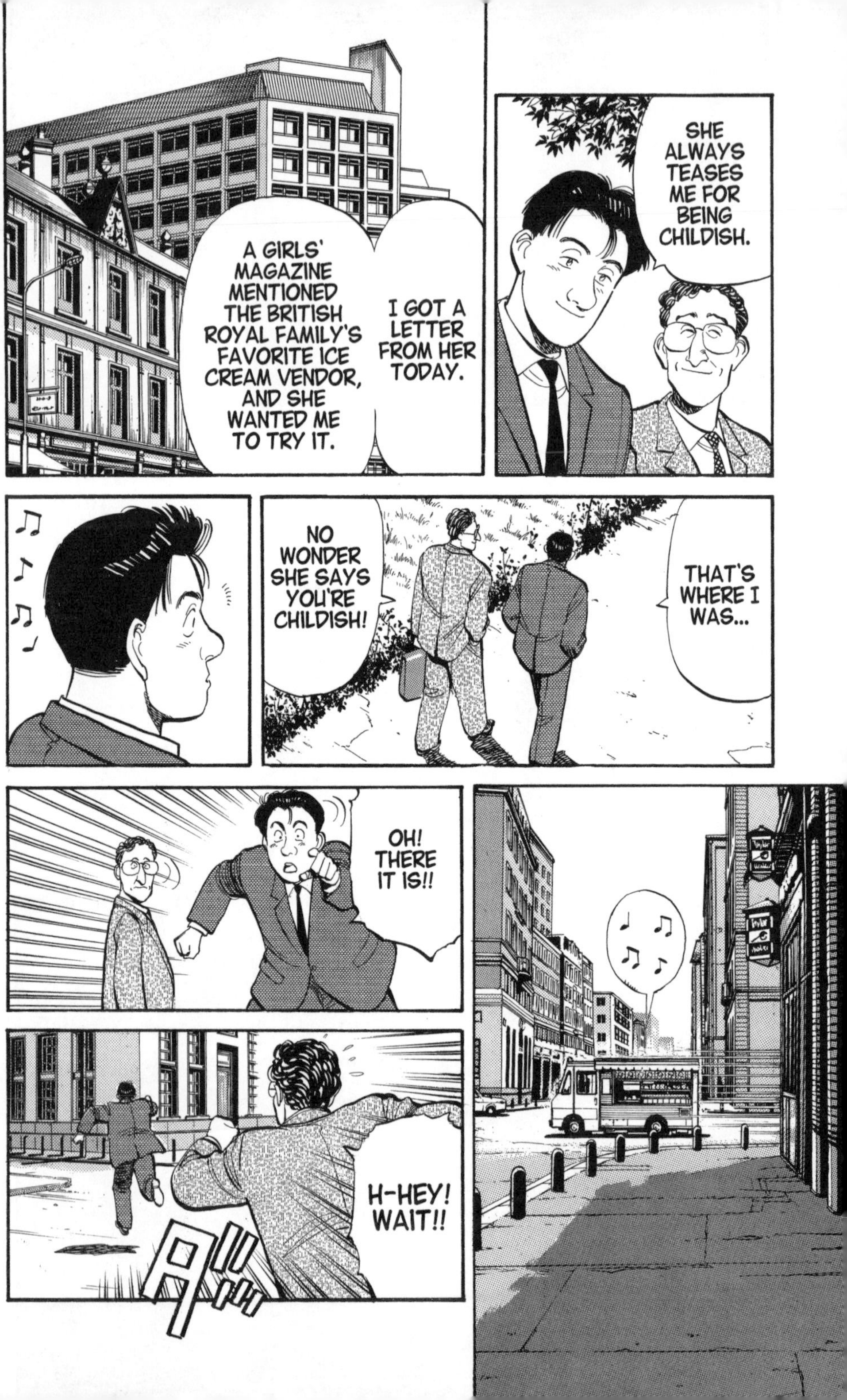
SHE ALWAYS TEASES ME FOR BEING CHILDISH.
I GOT A LETTER FROM HER TODAY.
A GIRLS' MAGAZINE MENTIONED THE BRITISH ROYAL FAMILY'S FAVORITE ICE CREAM VENDOR, AND SHE WANTED ME TO TRY IT.
THAT'S WHERE I WAS...
NO WONDER SHE SAYS YOU'RE CHILDISH!
OH! THERE IT IS!!
H-HEY! WAIT!!

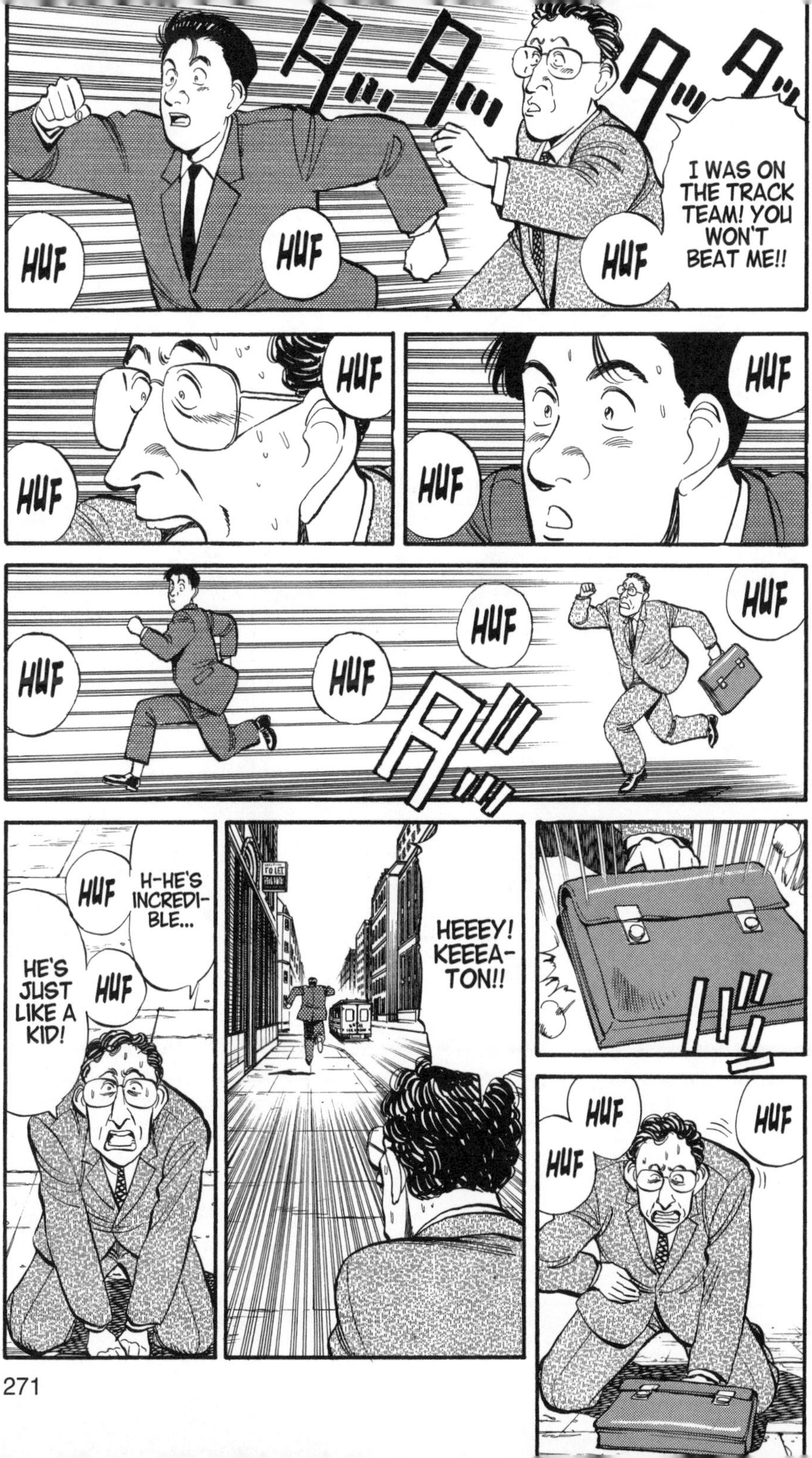
I WAS ON THE TRACK TEAM! YOU WON'T BEAT ME!!
HUF
HUF
HUF
HUF
HUF
HUF
HUF
HUF
HUF
HUF
HUF
HUF
HUF
HUF
HUF
HEEEY! KEEEA-TON!!
TO LET
H-HE'S INCREDIBLE...
HUF
HE'S JUST LIKE A KID!
HUF

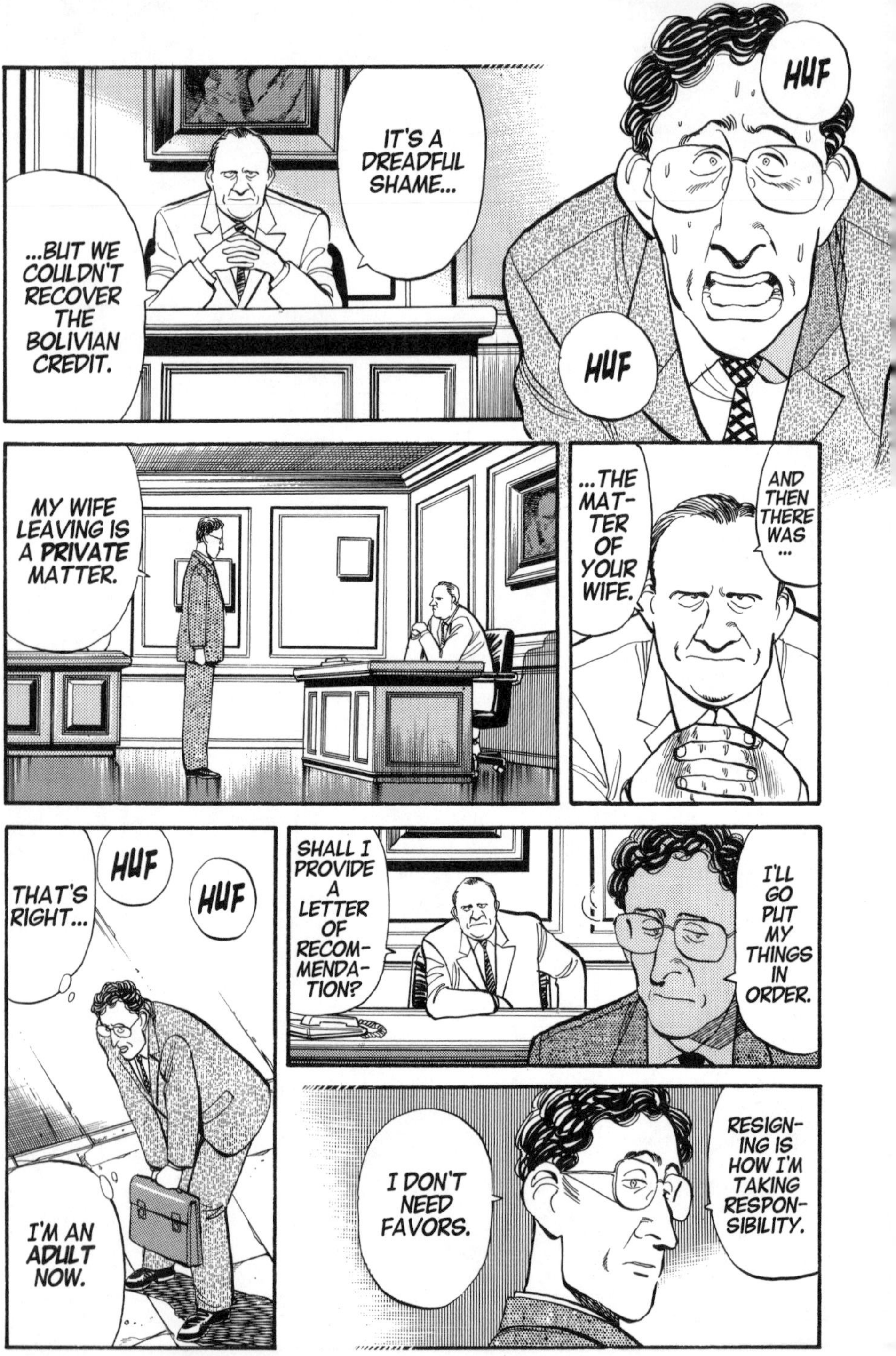
HUF
HUF
IT'S A DREADFUL SHAME...
...BUT WE COULDN'T RECOVER THE BOLIVIAN CREDIT.
AND THEN THERE WAS...
...THE MATTER OF YOUR WIFE.
MY WIFE LEAVING IS A **PRIVATE** MATTER.
I'LL GO PUT MY THINGS IN ORDER.
SHALL I PROVIDE A LETTER OF RECOMMENDATION?
RESIGNING IS HOW I'M TAKING RESPONSIBILITY.
I DON'T NEED FAVORS.
HUF
HUF
THAT'S RIGHT...
I'M AN **ADULT** NOW.

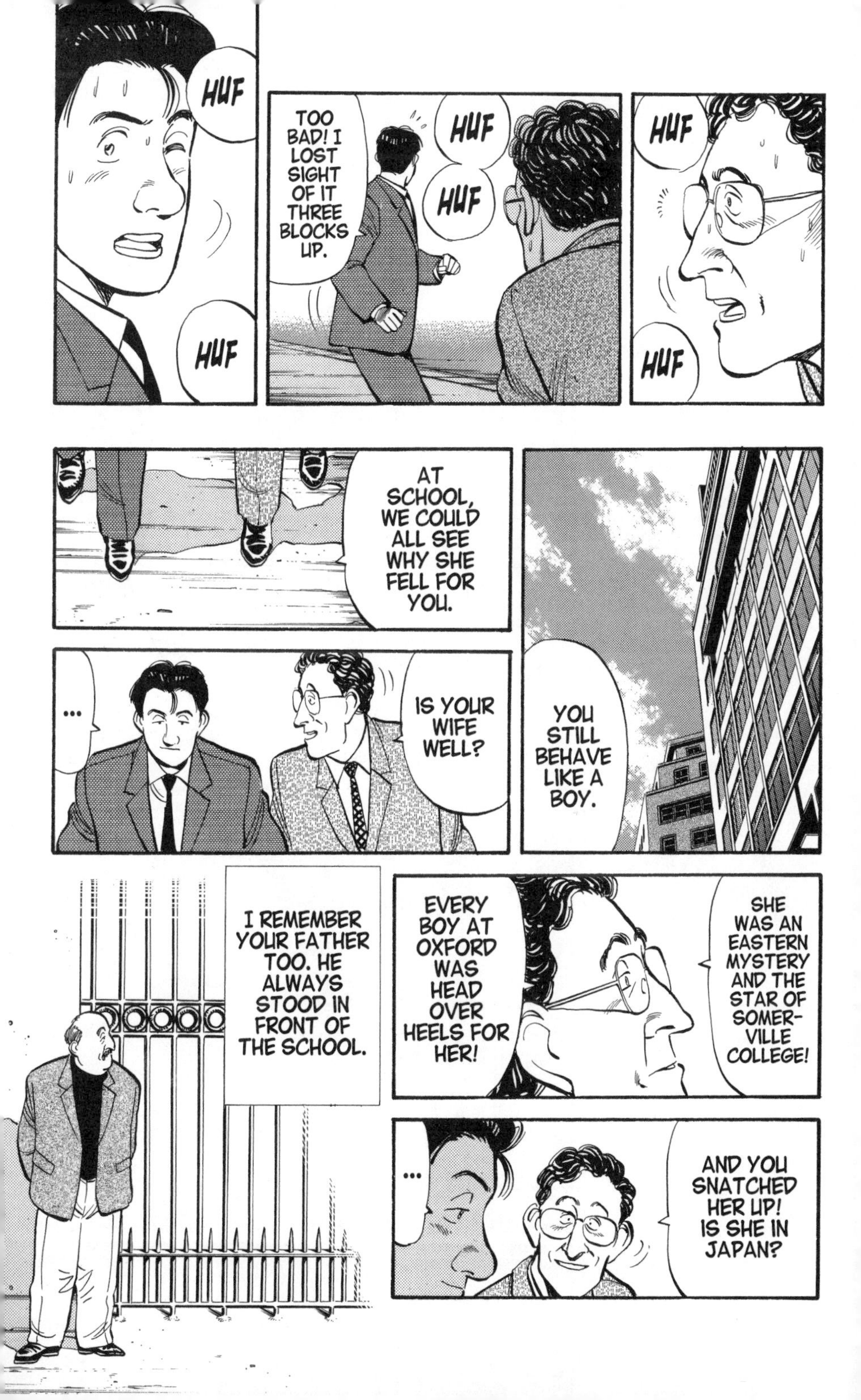
HUF
HUF
HUF
HUF
TOO BAD! I LOST SIGHT OF IT THREE BLOCKS UP.
HUF
HUF
YOU STILL BEHAVE LIKE A BOY.
AT SCHOOL, WE COULD ALL SEE WHY SHE FELL FOR YOU.
IS YOUR WIFE WELL?
...
SHE WAS AN EASTERN MYSTERY AND THE STAR OF SOMER-VILLE COLLEGE!
EVERY BOY AT OXFORD WAS HEAD OVER HEELS FOR HER!
AND YOU SNATCHED HER UP! IS SHE IN JAPAN?
...
I REMEMBER YOUR FATHER TOO. HE ALWAYS STOOD IN FRONT OF THE SCHOOL.

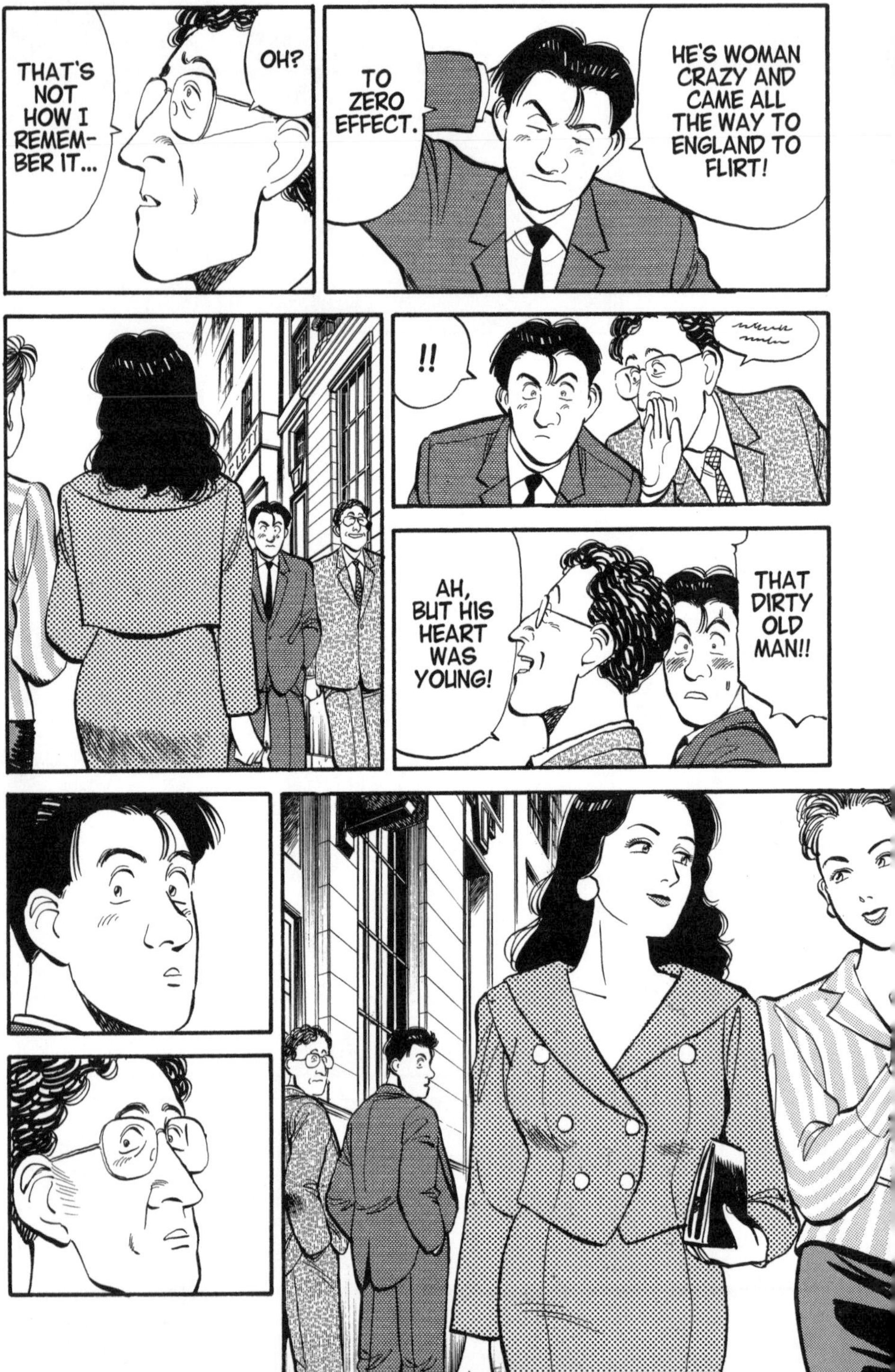
HE'S WOMAN CRAZY AND CAME ALL THE WAY TO ENGLAND TO FLIRT!
TO ZERO EFFECT.
OH?
THAT'S NOT HOW I REMEM-BER IT...
!!
THAT DIRTY OLD MAN!!
AH, BUT HIS HEART WAS YOUNG!

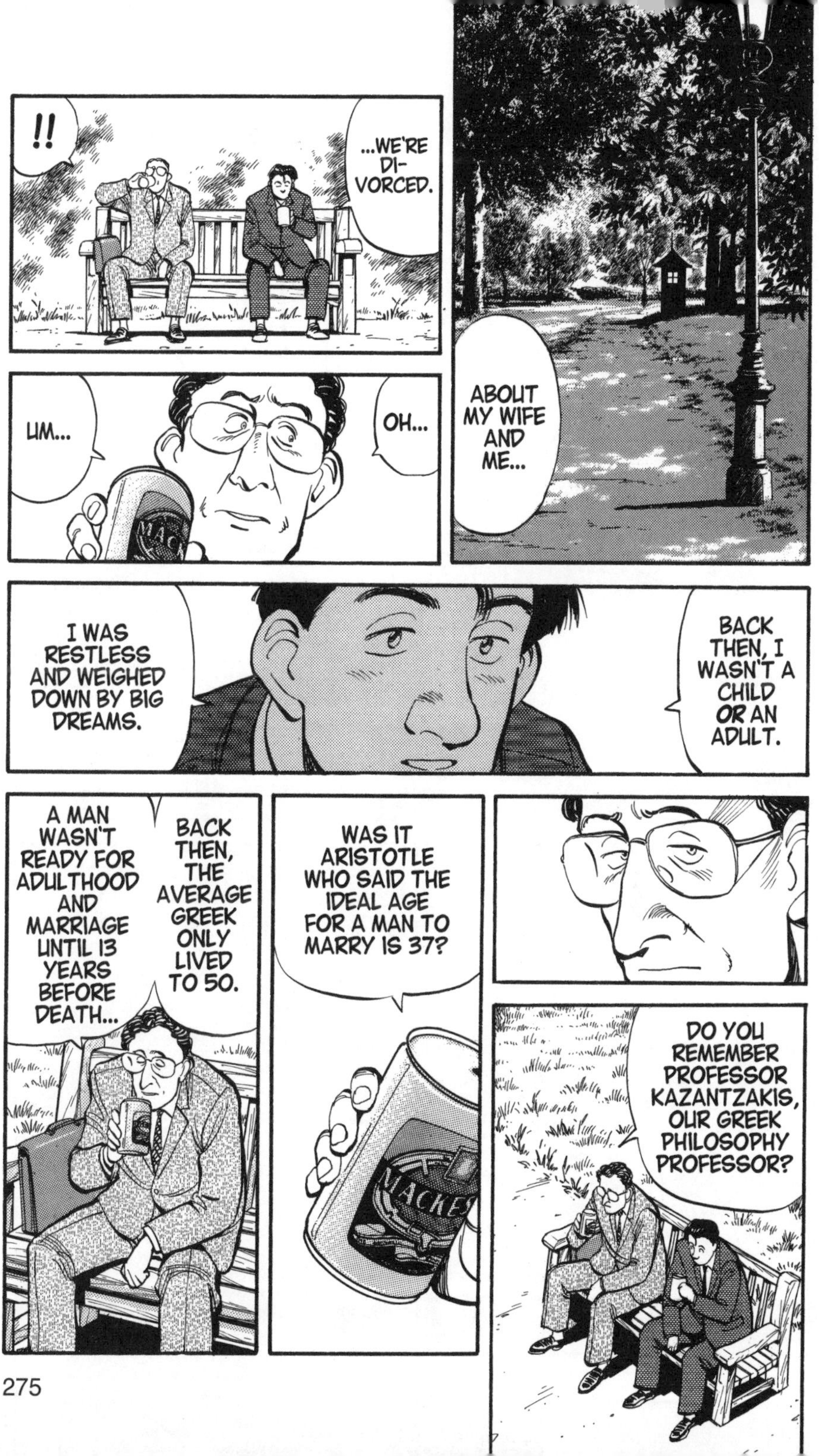
ABOUT MY WIFE AND ME...
...WE'RE DI-VORCED.
!!
OH...
UM...
BACK THEN, I WASN'T A CHILD OR AN ADULT.
I WAS RESTLESS AND WEIGHED DOWN BY BIG DREAMS.
WAS IT ARISTOTLE WHO SAID THE IDEAL AGE FOR A MAN TO MARRY IS 37?
BACK THEN, THE AVERAGE GREEK ONLY LIVED TO 50.
A MAN WASN'T READY FOR ADULTHOOD AND MARRIAGE UNTIL 13 YEARS BEFORE DEATH...
DO YOU REMEMBER PROFESSOR KAZANTZAKIS, OUR GREEK PHILOSOPHY PROFESSOR?

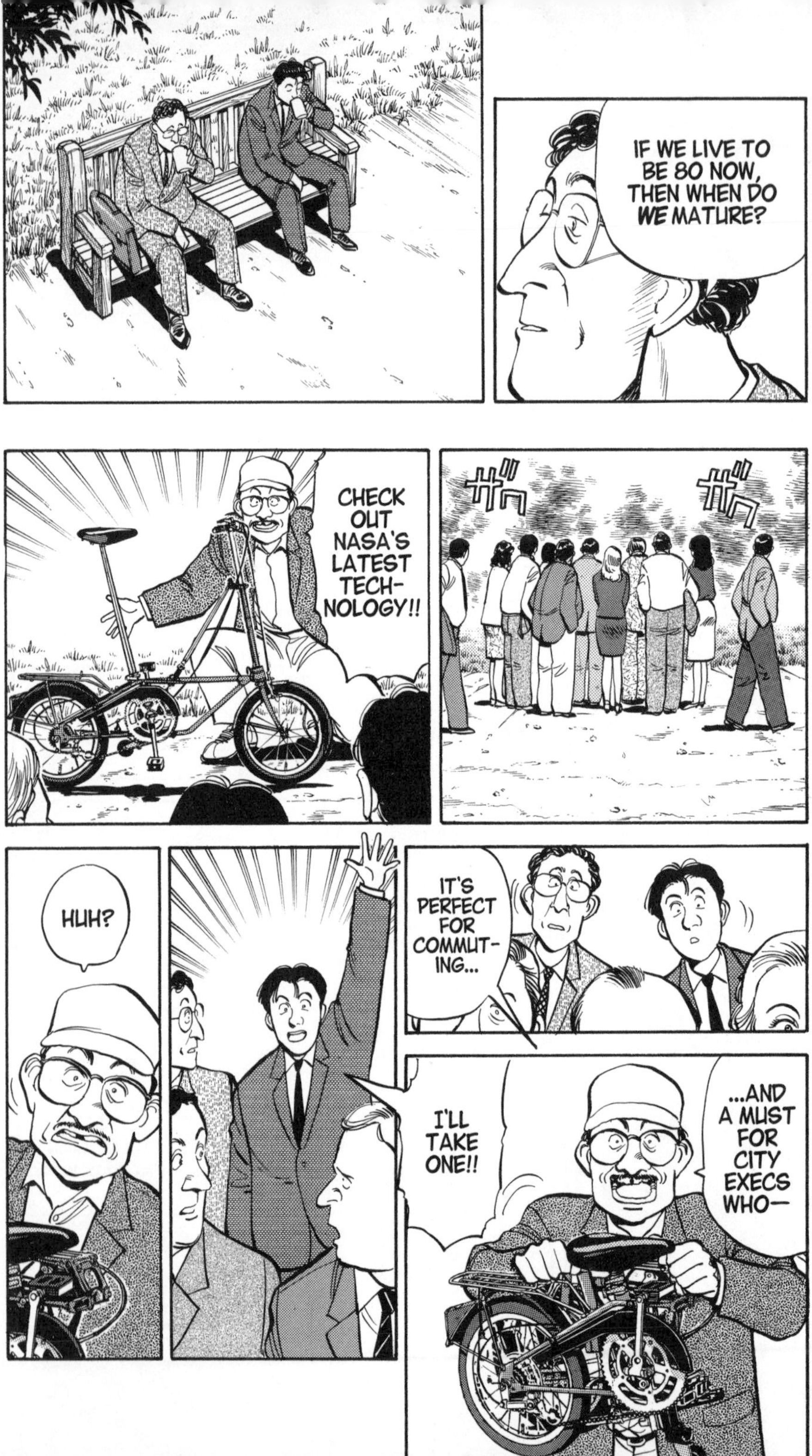
IF WE LIVE TO BE 80 NOW, THEN WHEN DO WE MATURE?
ガヤ
ガヤ
CHECK OUT NASA'S LATEST TECH-NOLOGY!!
IT'S PERFECT FOR COMMUT-ING...
...AND A MUST FOR CITY EXECS WHO—
I'LL TAKE ONE!!
HUH?

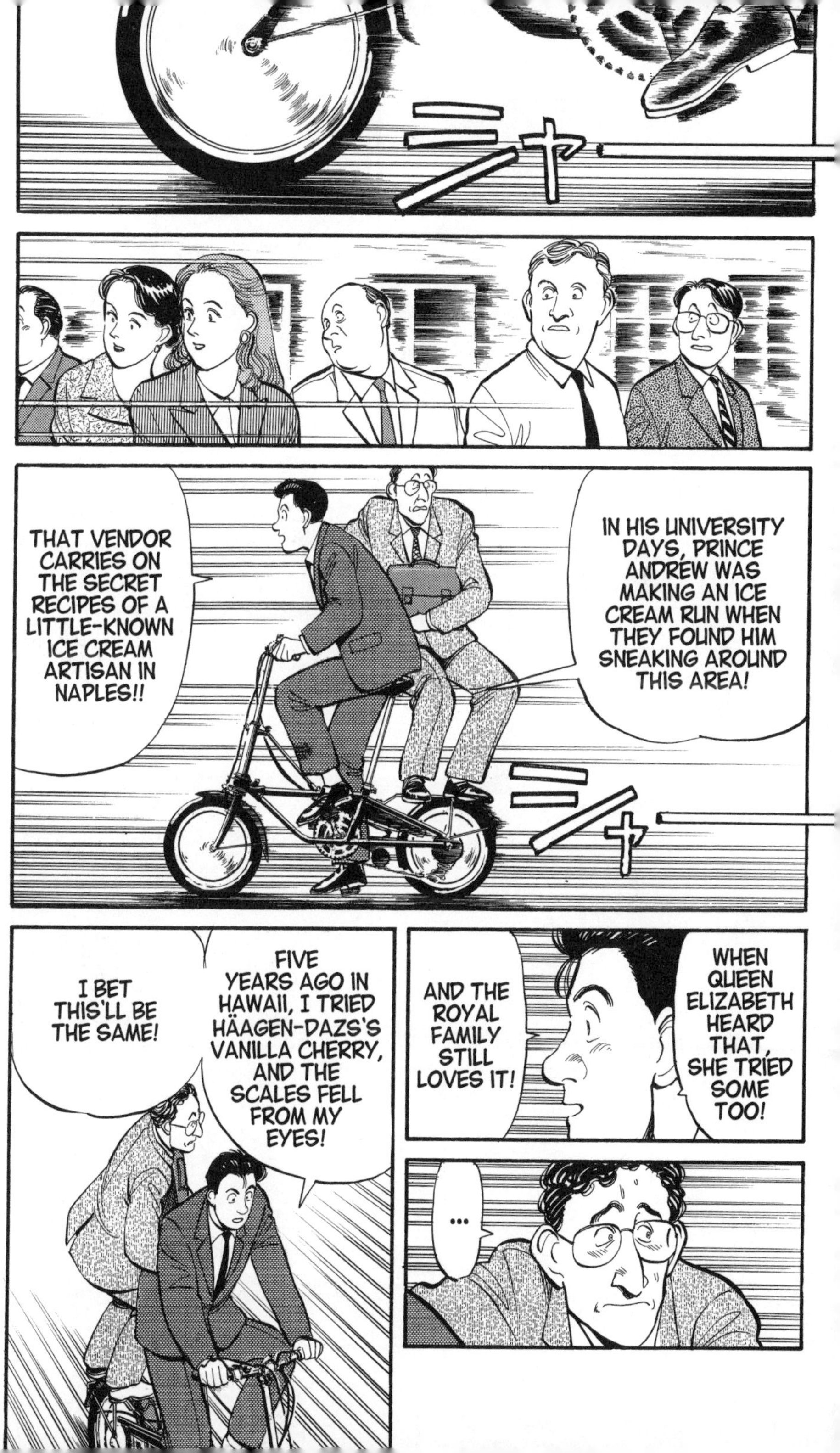

シャー
IN HIS UNIVERSITY DAYS, PRINCE ANDREW WAS MAKING AN ICE CREAM RUN WHEN THEY FOUND HIM SNEAKING AROUND THIS AREA!
THAT VENDOR CARRIES ON THE SECRET RECIPES OF A LITTLE-KNOWN ICE CREAM ARTISAN IN NAPLES!!
シャー
WHEN QUEEN ELIZABETH HEARD THAT, SHE TRIED SOME TOO!
AND THE ROYAL FAMILY STILL LOVES IT!
...
FIVE YEARS AGO IN HAWAII, I TRIED HÄAGEN-DAZS'S VANILLA CHERRY, AND THE SCALES FELL FROM MY EYES!
I BET THIS'LL BE THE SAME!

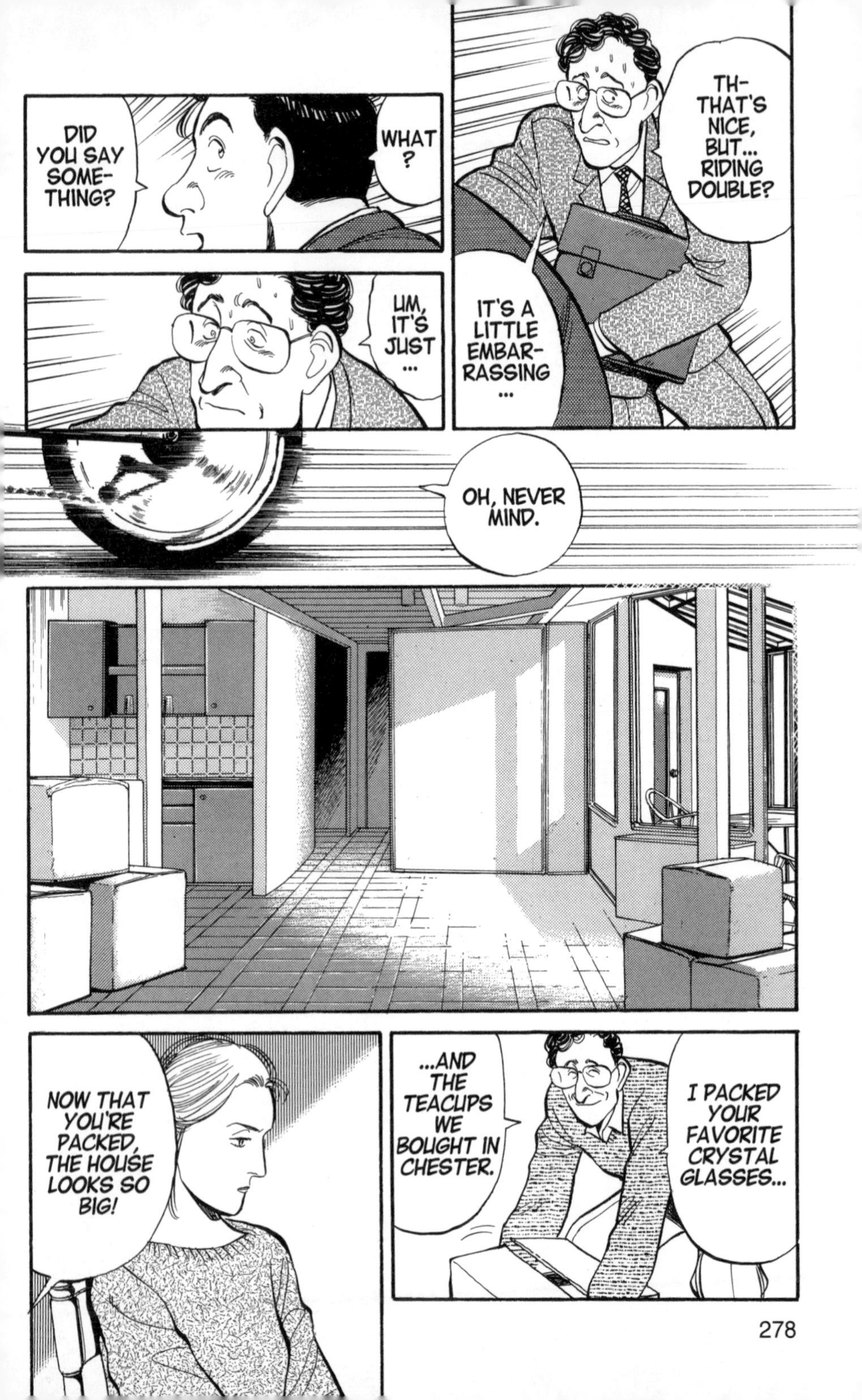
TH-THAT'S NICE, BUT... RIDING DOUBLE?
IT'S A LITTLE EMBARRASSING...
WHAT?
DID YOU SAY SOMETHING?
UM, IT'S JUST...
OH, NEVER MIND.
I PACKED YOUR FAVORITE CRYSTAL GLASSES...
...AND THE TEACUPS WE BOUGHT IN CHESTER.
NOW THAT YOU'RE PACKED, THE HOUSE LOOKS SO BIG!

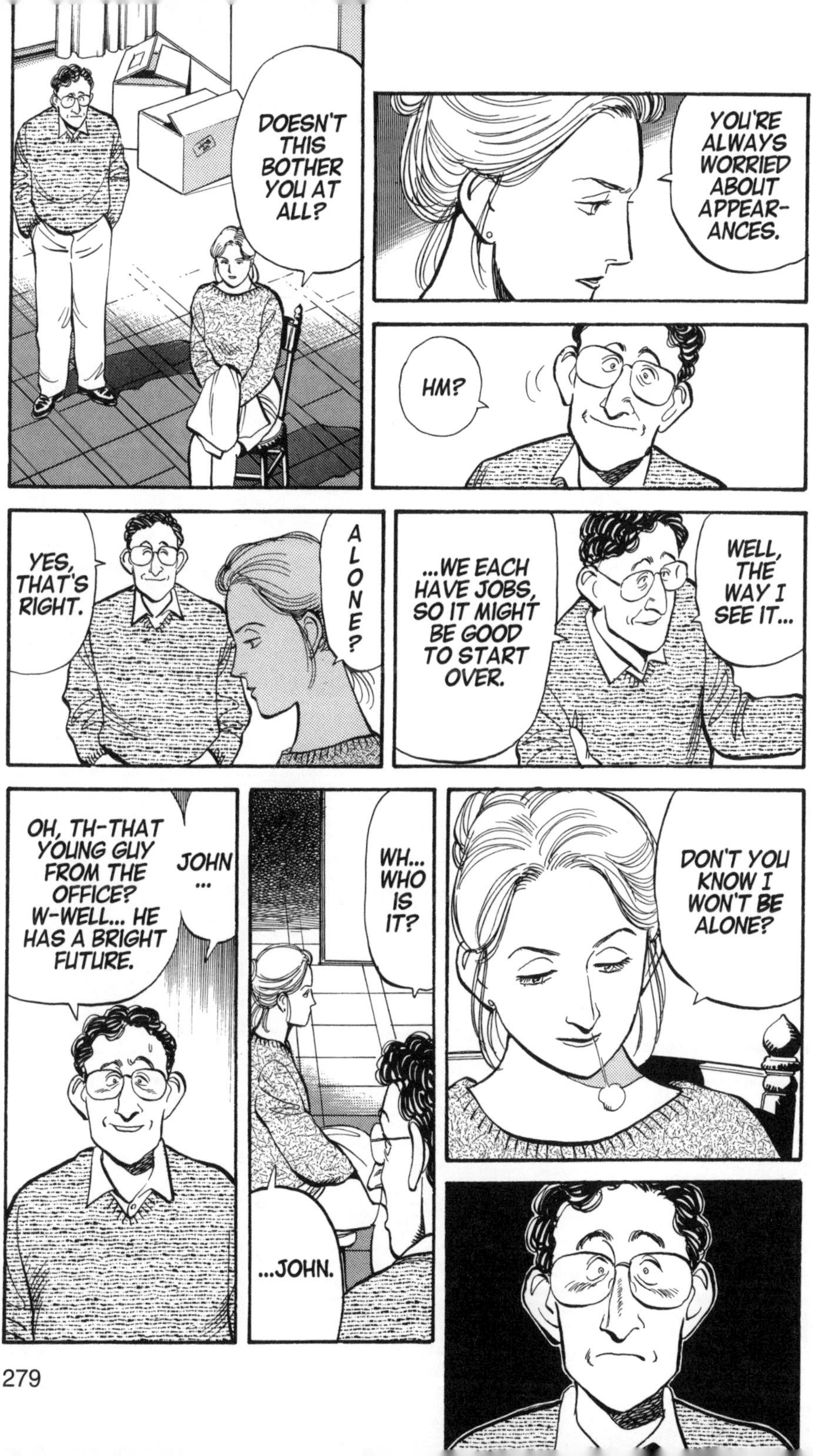
YOU'RE ALWAYS WORRIED ABOUT APPEAR-ANCES.
HM?
DOESN'T THIS BOTHER YOU AT ALL?
WELL, THE WAY I SEE IT...
...WE EACH HAVE JOBS, SO IT MIGHT BE GOOD TO START OVER.
ALONE?
YES, THAT'S RIGHT.
DON'T YOU KNOW I WON'T BE ALONE?
WH... WHO IS IT?
...JOHN.
JOHN ...
OH, TH-THAT YOUNG GUY FROM THE OFFICE? W-WELL... HE HAS A BRIGHT FUTURE.

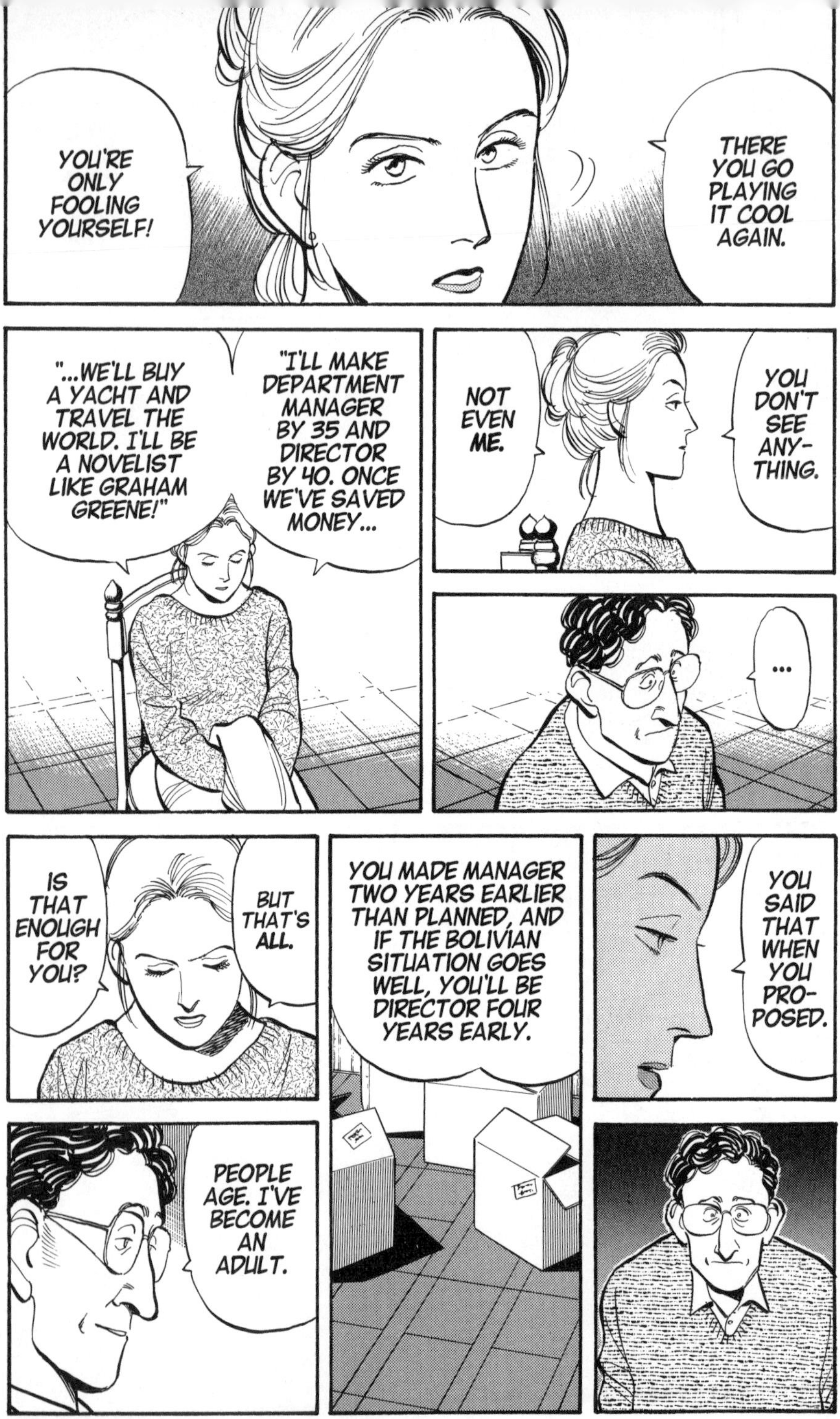
THERE YOU GO PLAYING IT COOL AGAIN.
YOU'RE ONLY FOOLING YOURSELF!
YOU DON'T SEE ANY-THING.
NOT EVEN ME.
...
"I'LL MAKE DEPARTMENT MANAGER BY 35 AND DIRECTOR BY 40. ONCE WE'VE SAVED MONEY...
"...WE'LL BUY A YACHT AND TRAVEL THE WORLD. I'LL BE A NOVELIST LIKE GRAHAM GREENE!"
YOU SAID THAT WHEN YOU PRO-POSED.
YOU MADE MANAGER TWO YEARS EARLIER THAN PLANNED, AND IF THE BOLIVIAN SITUATION GOES WELL, YOU'LL BE DIRECTOR FOUR YEARS EARLY.
BUT THAT'S ALL.
IS THAT ENOUGH FOR YOU?
PEOPLE AGE. I'VE BECOME AN ADULT.

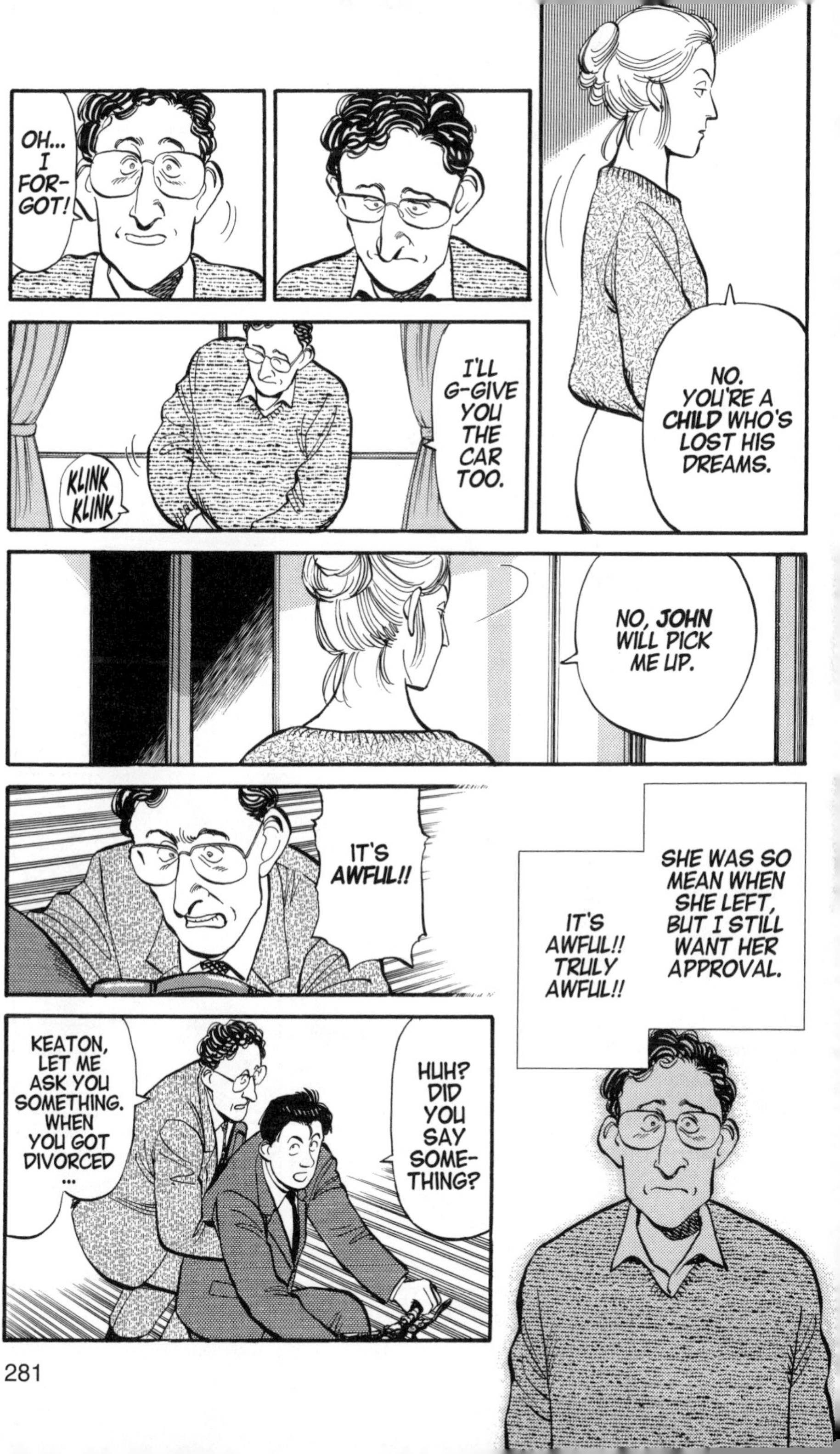
NO. YOU'RE A CHILD WHO'S LOST HIS DREAMS.
OH... I FORGOT!
I'LL G-GIVE YOU THE CAR TOO.
KLINK KLINK
NO, JOHN WILL PICK ME UP.
SHE WAS SO MEAN WHEN SHE LEFT, BUT I STILL WANT HER APPROVAL.
IT'S AWFUL!! TRULY AWFUL!!
IT'S AWFUL!!
HUH? DID YOU SAY SOME-THING?
KEATON, LET ME ASK YOU SOMETHING. WHEN YOU GOT DIVORCED ...

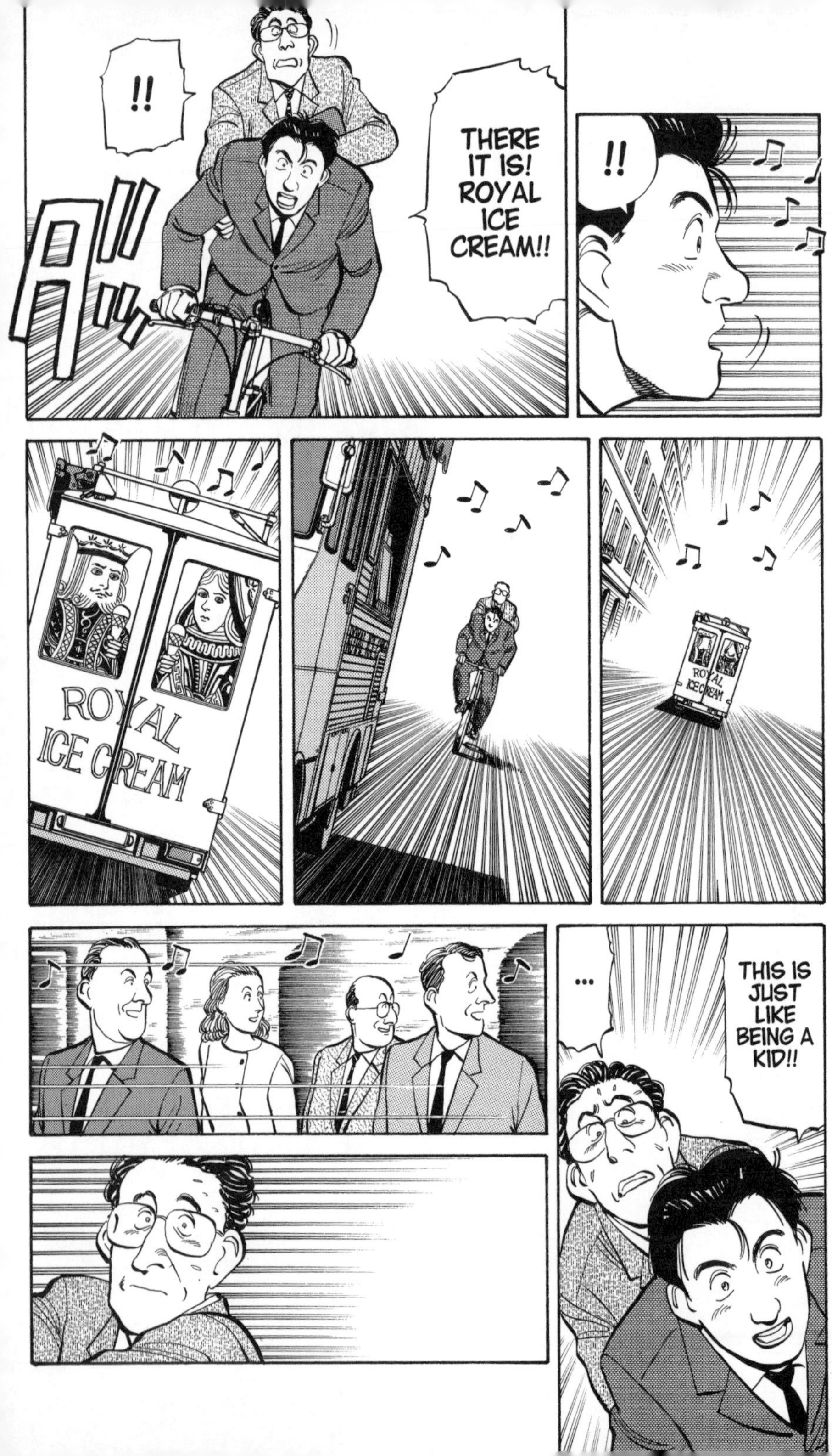
!!
THERE IT IS! ROYAL ICE CREAM!!
!!
ROYAL ICE CREAM
ROYAL ICE CREAM
THIS IS JUST LIKE BEING A KID!!
...

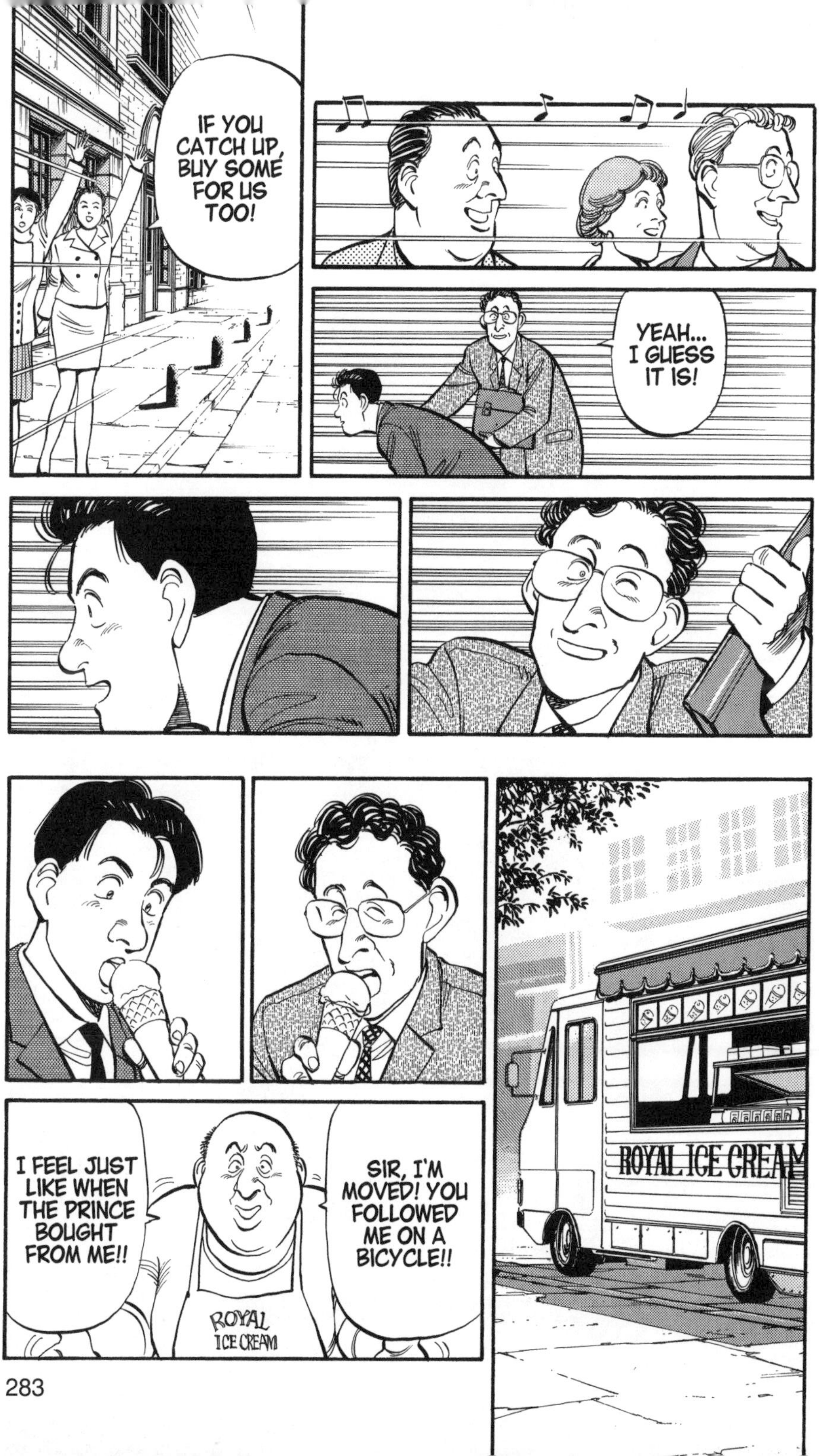
YEAH... I GUESS IT IS!
IF YOU CATCH UP, BUY SOME FOR US TOO!
ROYAL ICE CREAM
SIR, I'M MOVED! YOU FOLLOWED ME ON A BICYCLE!!
I FEEL JUST LIKE WHEN THE PRINCE BOUGHT FROM ME!!
ROYAL ICE CREAM

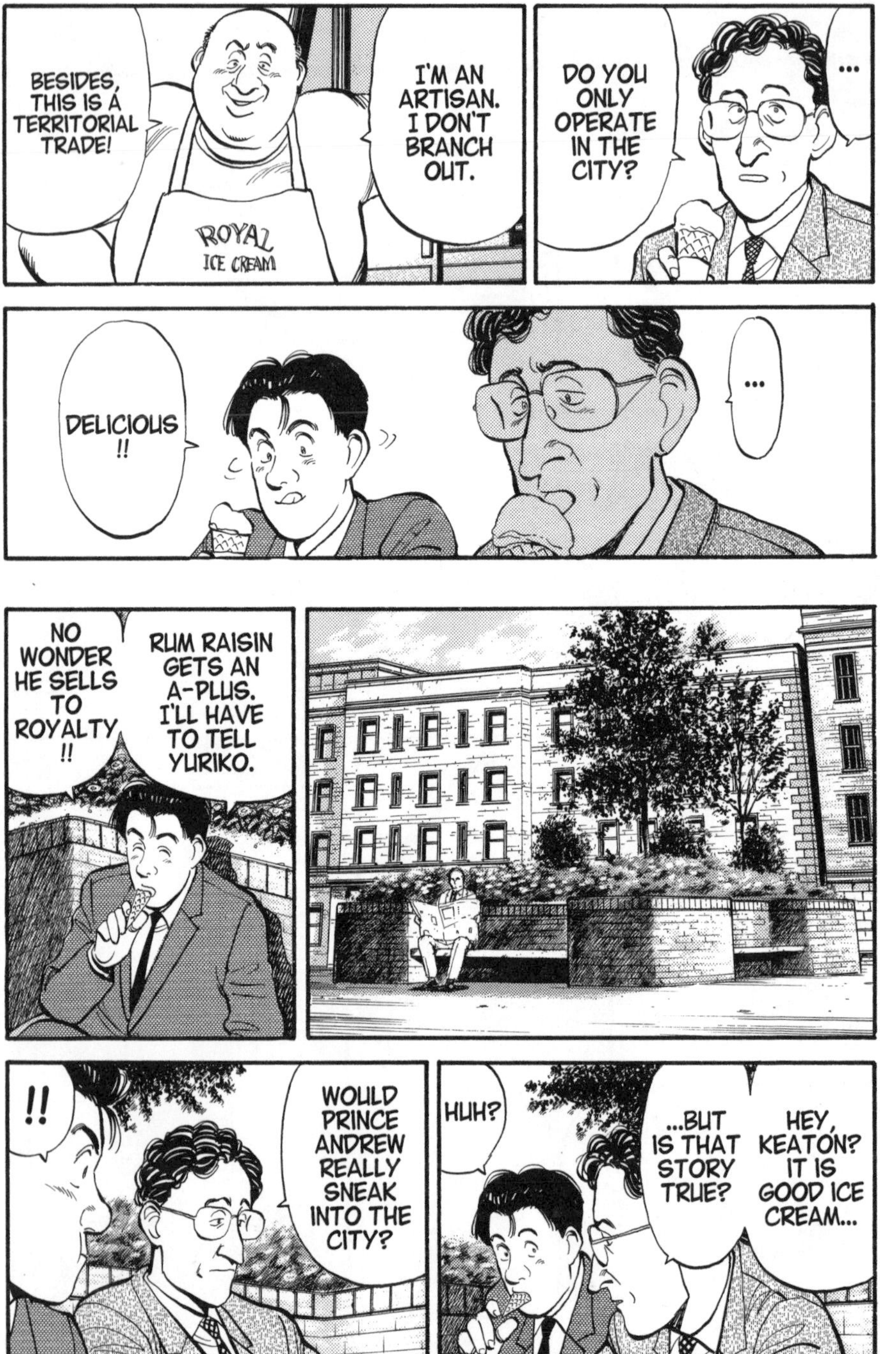
...
DO YOU ONLY OPERATE IN THE CITY?
I'M AN ARTISAN. I DON'T BRANCH OUT.
BESIDES, THIS IS A TERRITORIAL TRADE!
ROYAL ICE CREAM
...
DELICIOUS !!
RUM RAISIN GETS AN A-PLUS. I'LL HAVE TO TELL YURIKO.
NO WONDER HE SELLS TO ROYALTY !!
HEY, KEATON? IT IS GOOD ICE CREAM...
...BUT IS THAT STORY TRUE?
HUH?
WOULD PRINCE ANDREW REALLY SNEAK INTO THE CITY?
!!

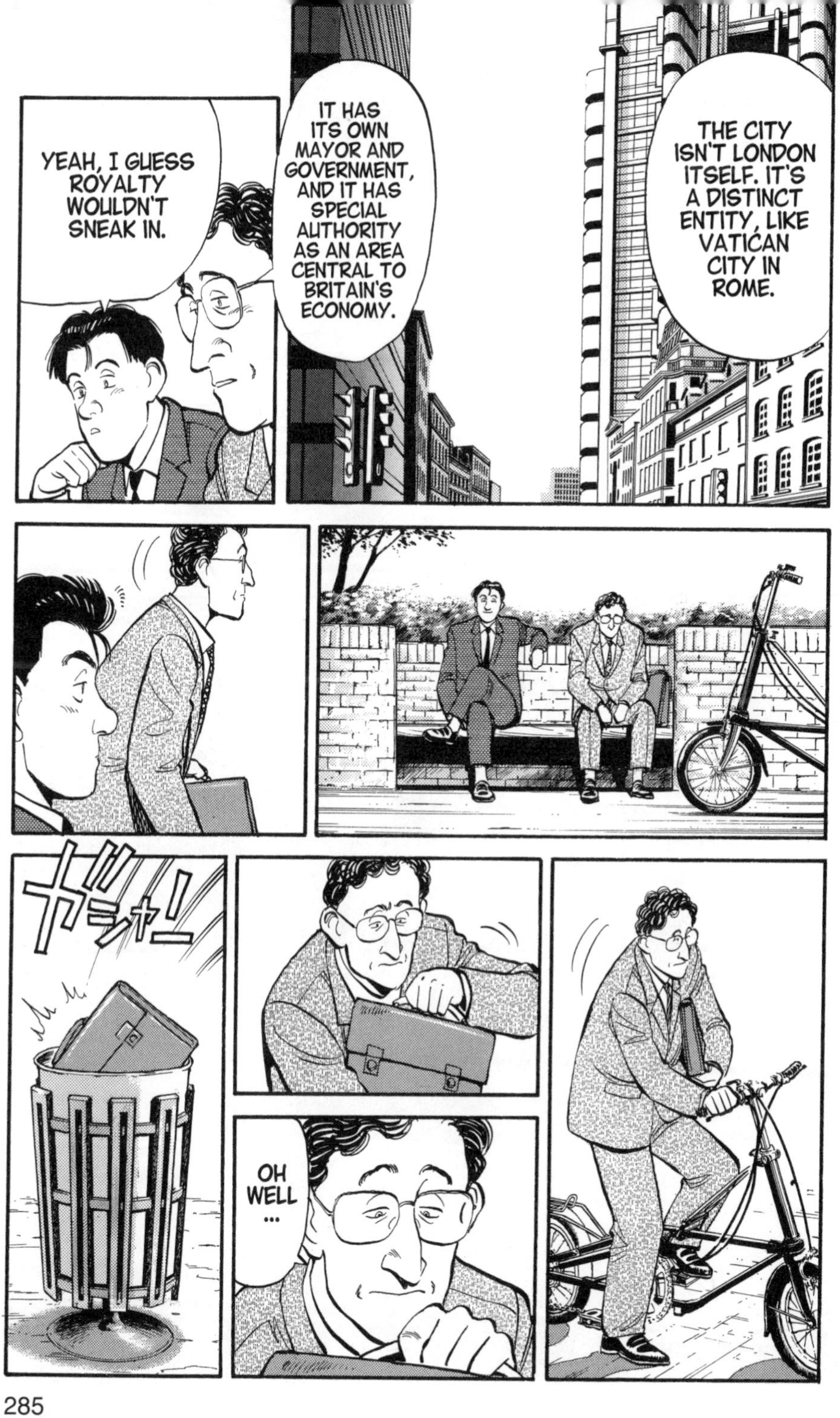
THE CITY ISN'T LONDON ITSELF. IT'S A DISTINCT ENTITY, LIKE VATICAN CITY IN ROME.
IT HAS ITS OWN MAYOR AND GOVERNMENT, AND IT HAS SPECIAL AUTHORITY AS AN AREA CENTRAL TO BRITAIN'S ECONOMY.
YEAH, I GUESS ROYALTY WOULDN'T SNEAK IN.
OH WELL ...

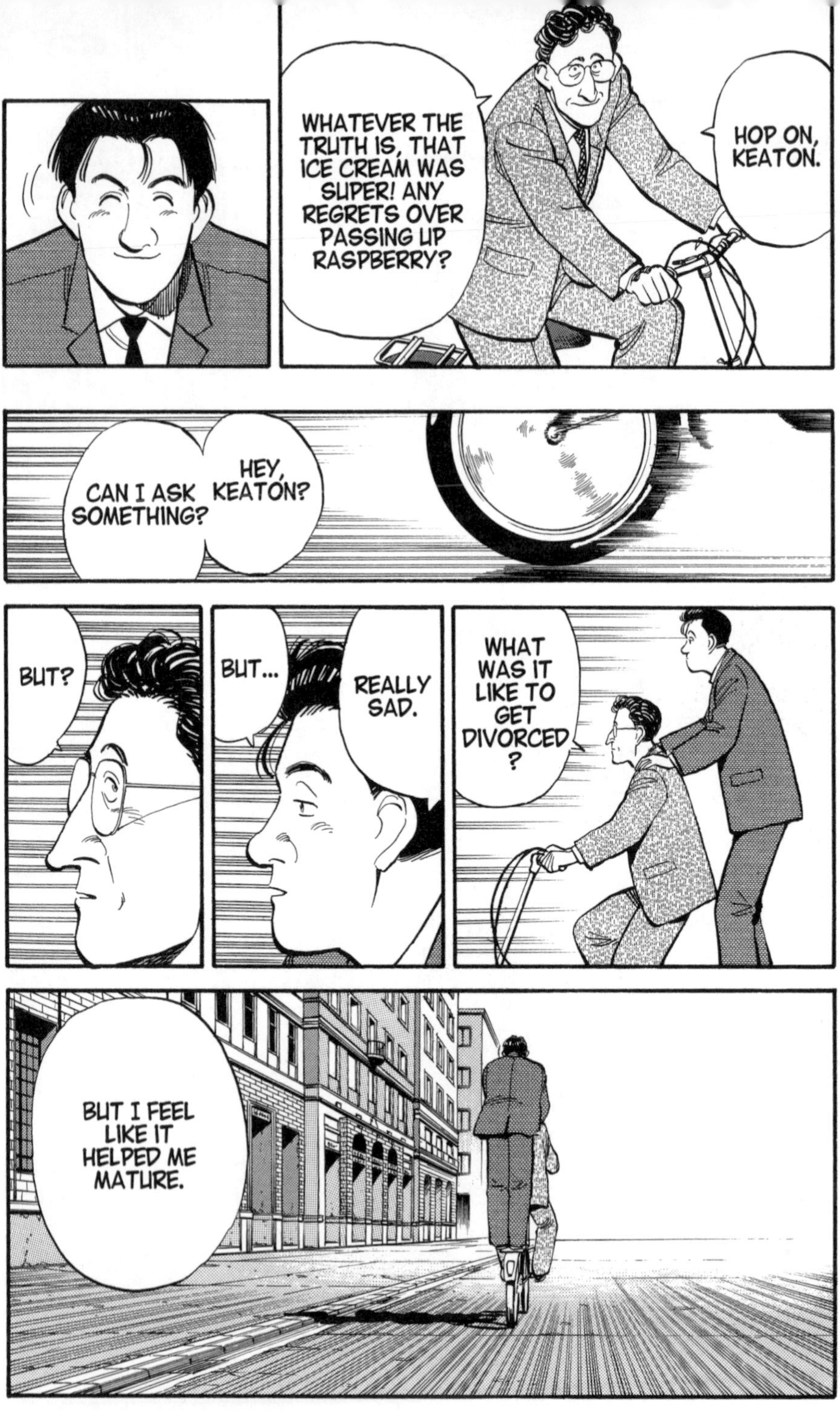
HOP ON, KEATON.
WHATEVER THE TRUTH IS, THAT ICE CREAM WAS SUPER! ANY REGRETS OVER PASSING UP RASPBERRY?
HEY, KEATON?
CAN I ASK SOMETHING?
WHAT WAS IT LIKE TO GET DIVORCED?
REALLY SAD.
BUT...
BUT?
BUT I FEEL LIKE IT HELPED ME MATURE.

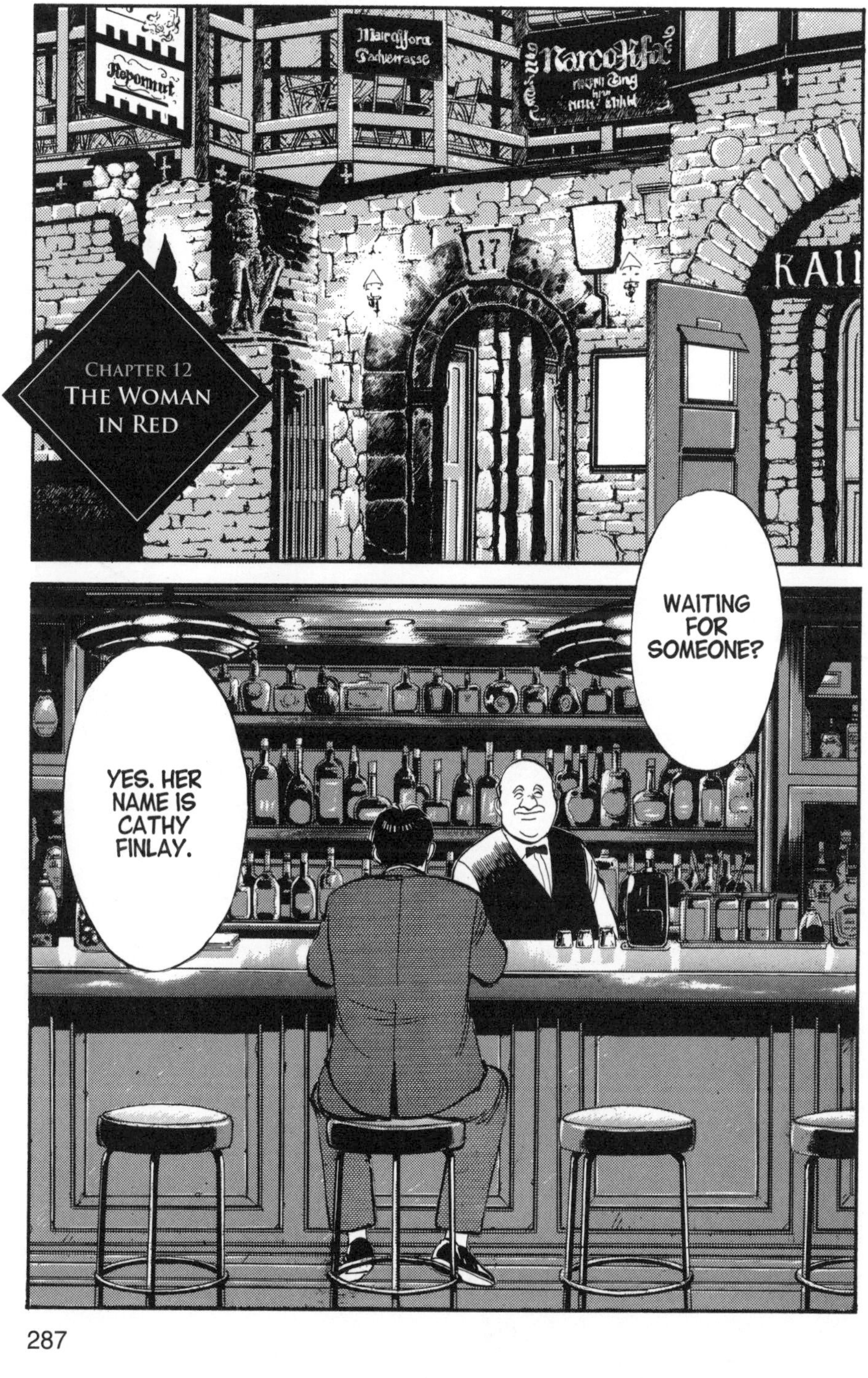
Chapter 12
The Woman in Red
WAITING FOR SOMEONE?
YES. HER NAME IS CATHY FINLAY.

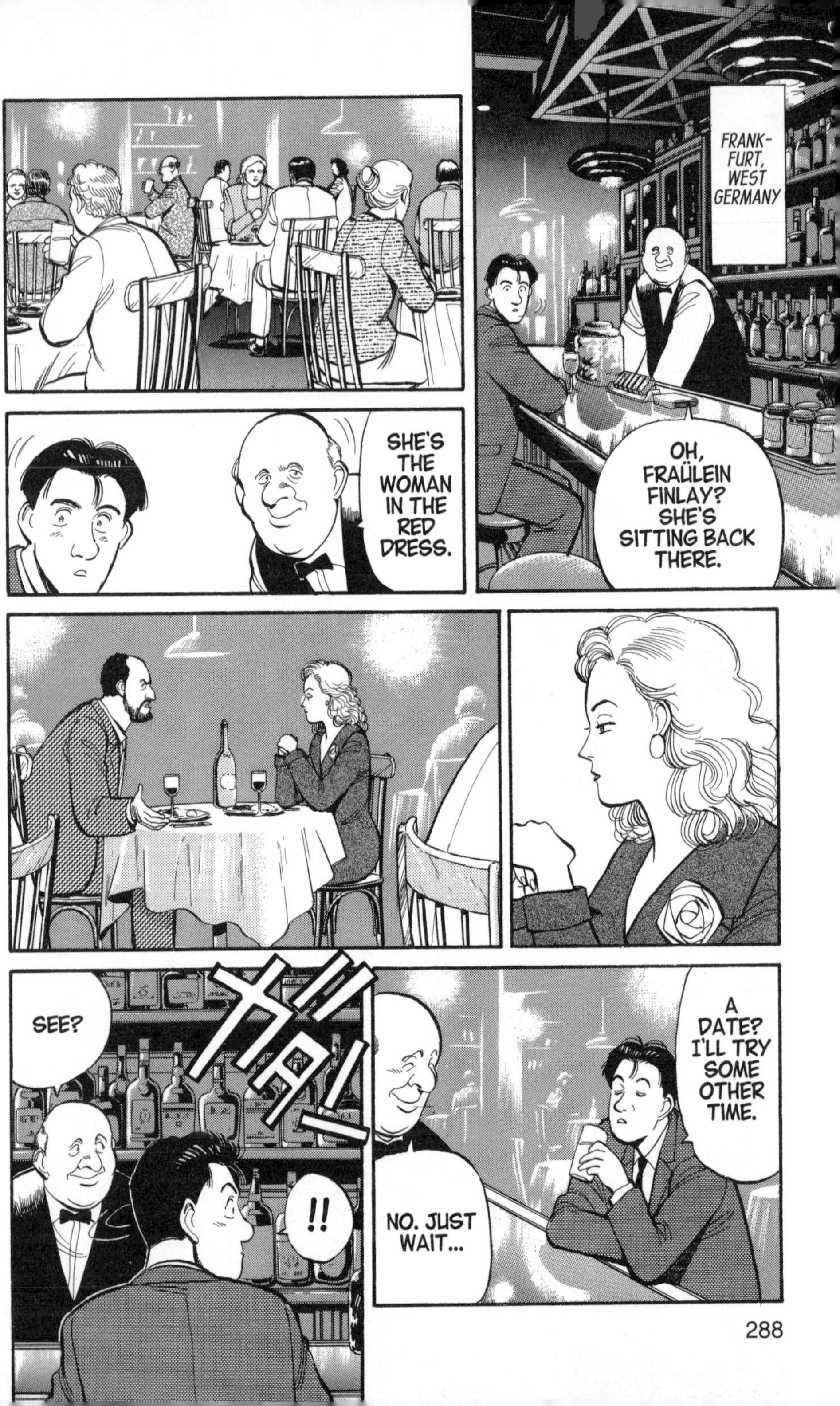
FRANK-FURT, WEST GERMANY
OH, FRAÜLEIN FINLAY? SHE'S SITTING BACK THERE.
SHE'S THE WOMAN IN THE RED DRESS.
A DATE? I'LL TRY SOME OTHER TIME.
NO. JUST WAIT...
SEE?
!!

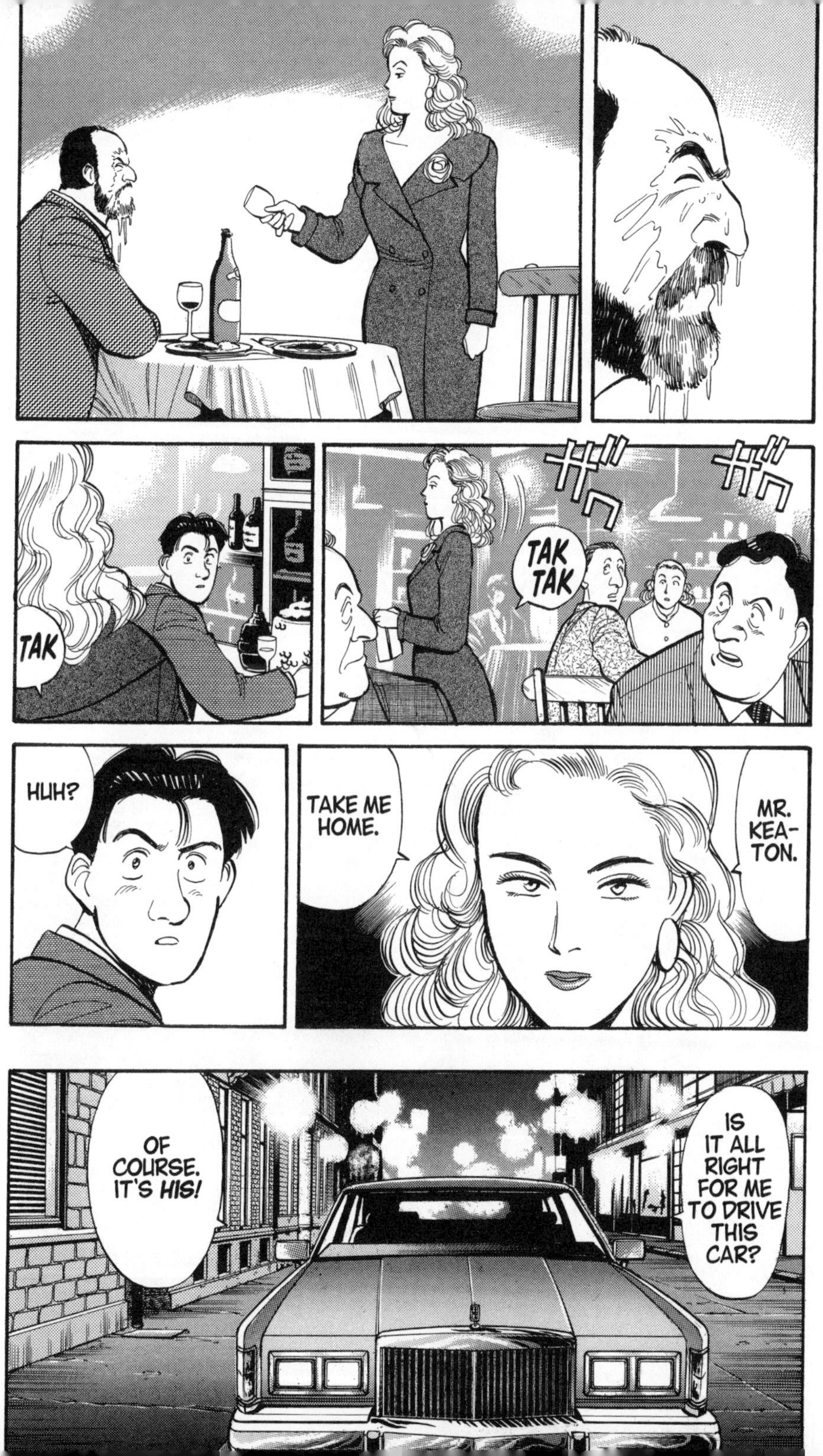
TAK TAK
TAK
MR. KEA-TON.
TAKE ME HOME.
HUH?
IS IT ALL RIGHT FOR ME TO DRIVE THIS CAR?
OF COURSE. IT'S HIS!

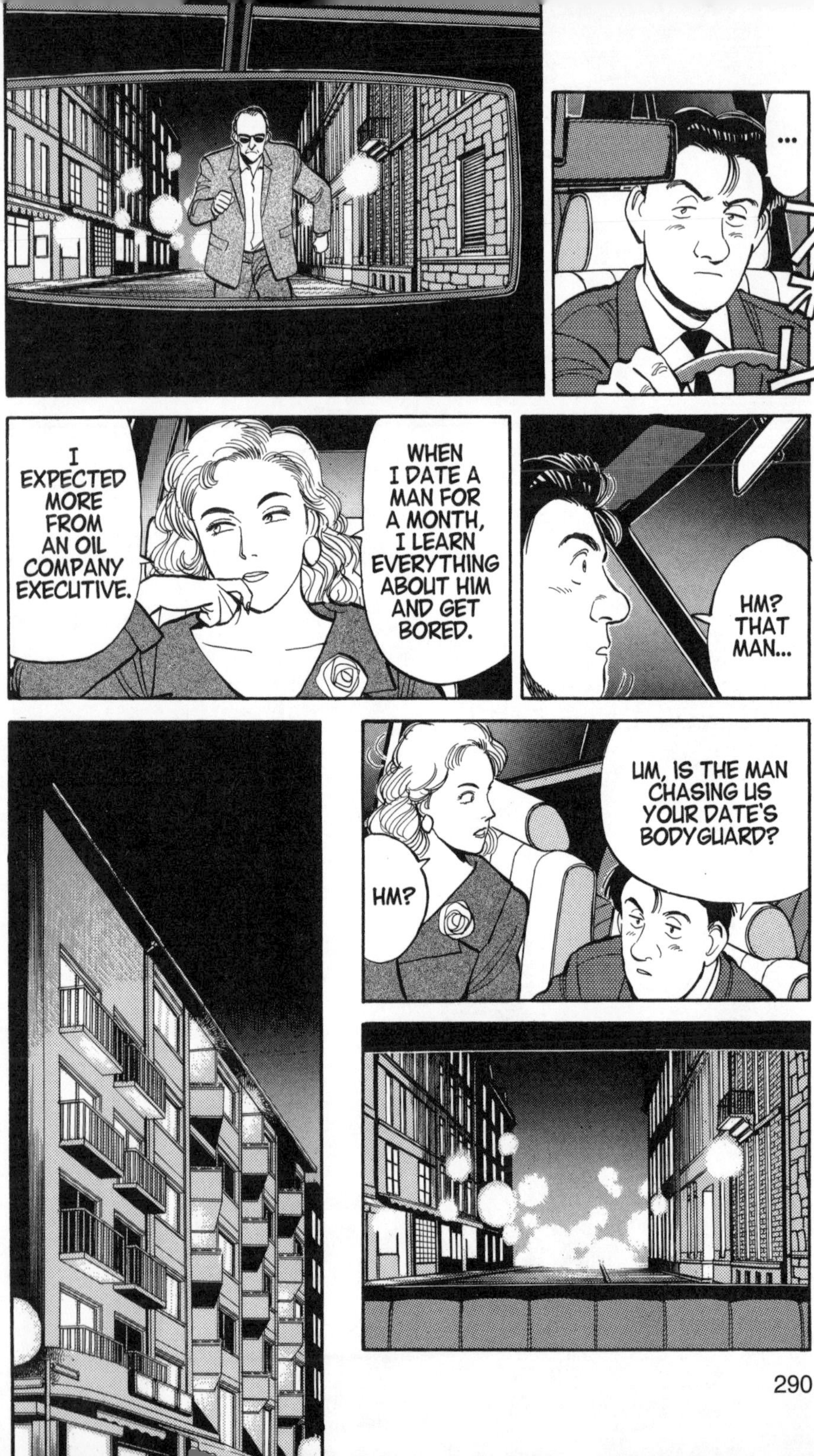
...
HM? THAT MAN...
WHEN I DATE A MAN FOR A MONTH, I LEARN EVERYTHING ABOUT HIM AND GET BORED.
I EXPECTED MORE FROM AN OIL COMPANY EXECUTIVE.
UM, IS THE MAN CHASING US YOUR DATE'S BODYGUARD?
HM?

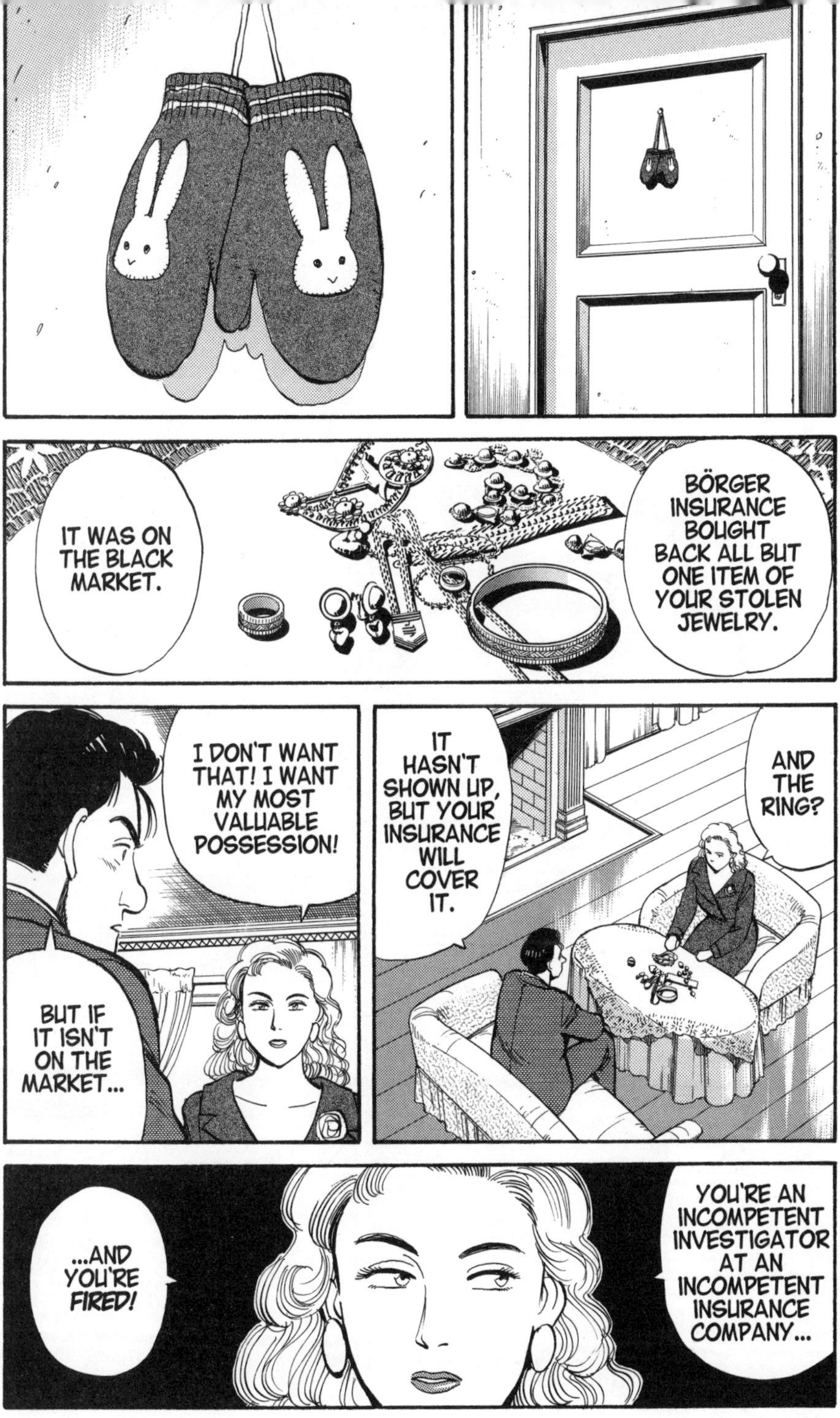

BÖRGER INSURANCE BOUGHT BACK ALL BUT ONE ITEM OF YOUR STOLEN JEWELRY.
IT WAS ON THE BLACK MARKET.
AND THE RING?
IT HASN'T SHOWN UP, BUT YOUR INSURANCE WILL COVER IT.
I DON'T WANT THAT! I WANT MY MOST VALUABLE POSSESSION!
BUT IF IT ISN'T ON THE MARKET...
YOU'RE AN INCOMPETENT INVESTIGATOR AT AN INCOMPETENT INSURANCE COMPANY...
...AND YOU'RE FIRED!

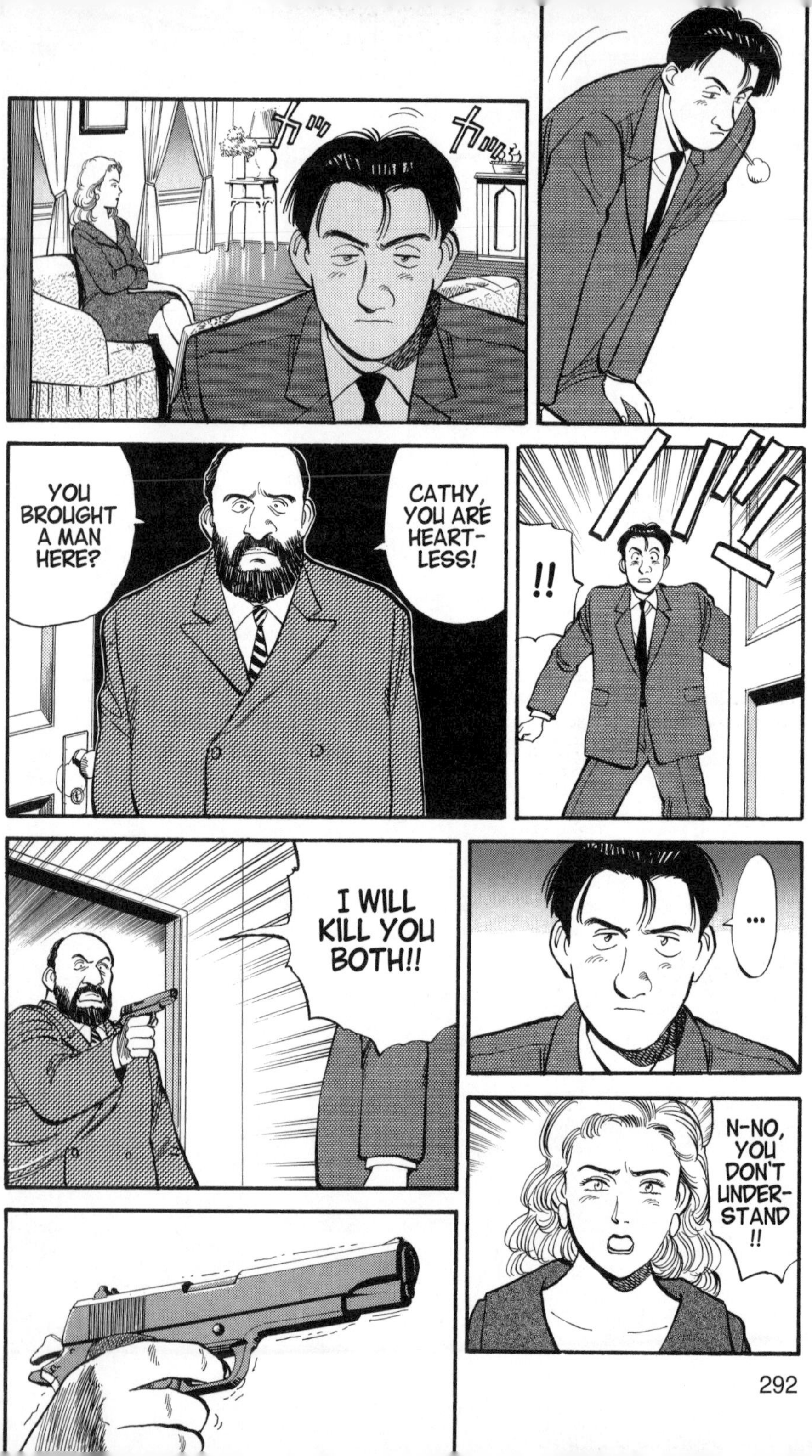
!!
CATHY, YOU ARE HEART-LESS!
YOU BROUGHT A MAN HERE?
...
I WILL KILL YOU BOTH!!
N-NO, YOU DON'T UNDER-STAND!!

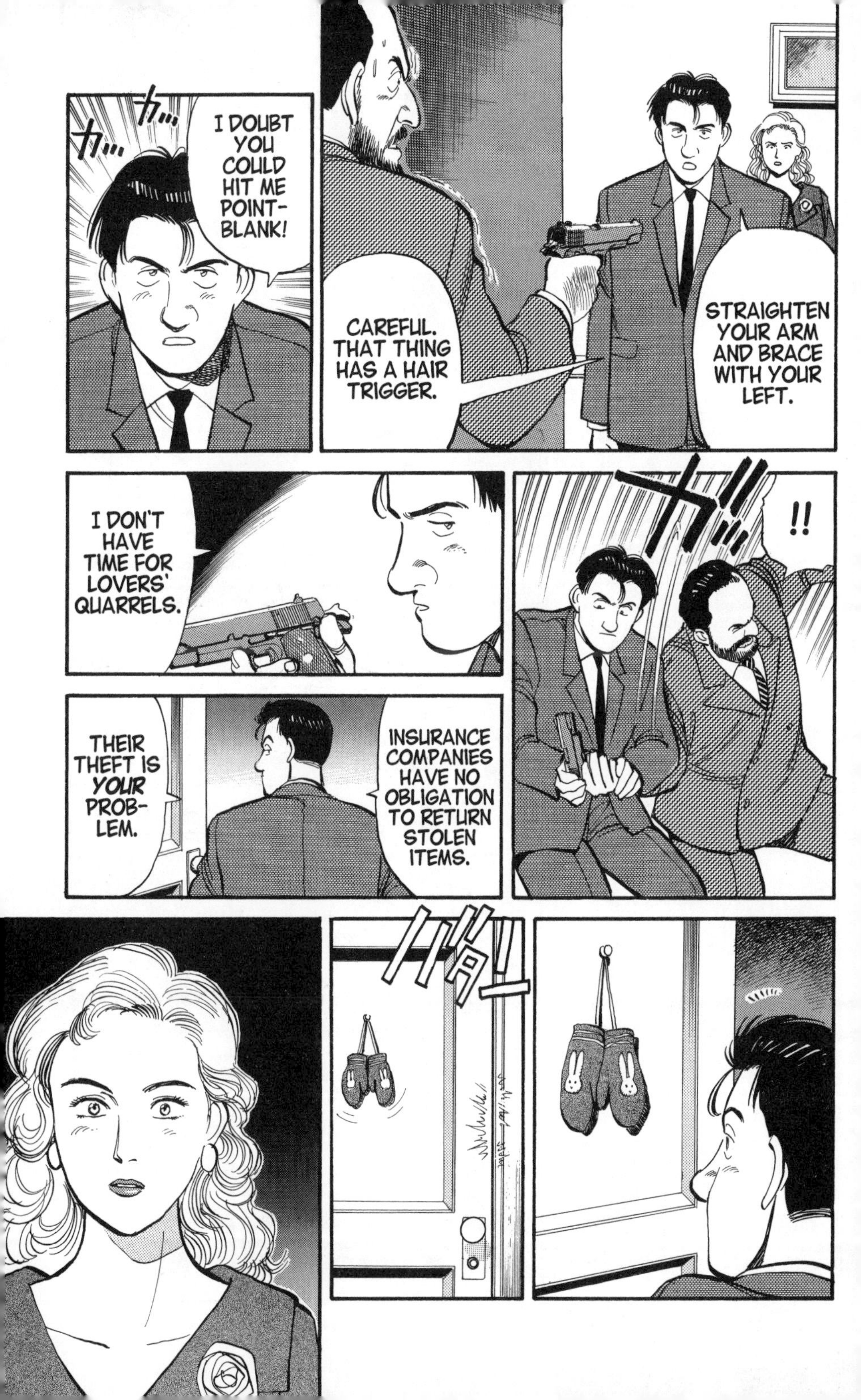
STRAIGHTEN YOUR ARM AND BRACE WITH YOUR LEFT.
CAREFUL. THAT THING HAS A HAIR TRIGGER.
I DOUBT YOU COULD HIT ME POINT-BLANK!
!!
I DON'T HAVE TIME FOR LOVERS' QUARRELS.
INSURANCE COMPANIES HAVE NO OBLIGATION TO RETURN STOLEN ITEMS.
THEIR THEFT IS *YOUR* PROBLEM.

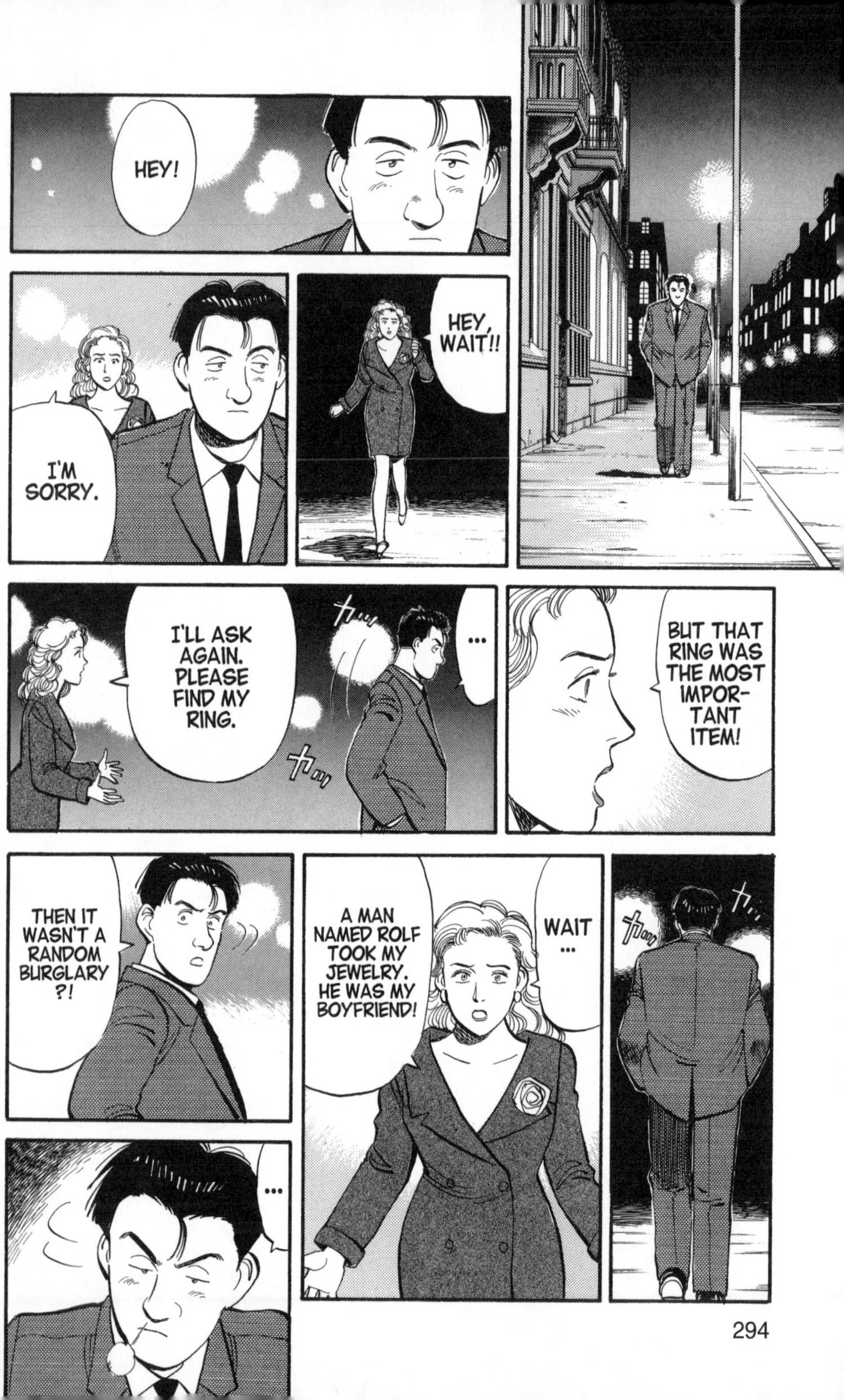
HEY!
HEY, WAIT!!
I'M SORRY.
BUT THAT RING WAS THE MOST IMPORTANT ITEM!
...
I'LL ASK AGAIN. PLEASE FIND MY RING.
WAIT ...
A MAN NAMED ROLF TOOK MY JEWELRY. HE WAS MY BOYFRIEND!
THEN IT WASN'T A RANDOM BURGLARY ?!
...

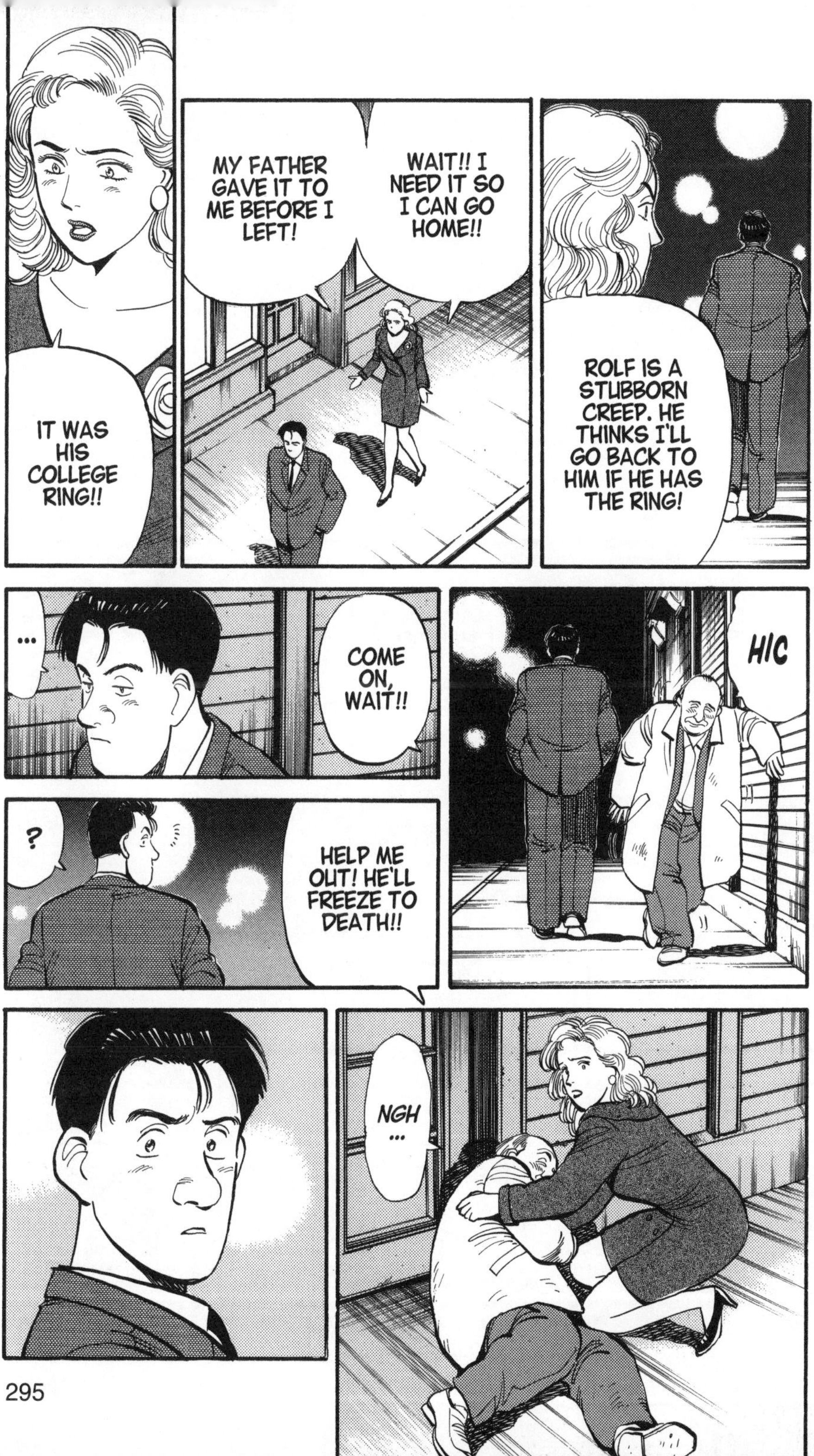
ROLF IS A STUBBORN CREEP. HE THINKS I'LL GO BACK TO HIM IF HE HAS THE RING!
WAIT!! I NEED IT SO I CAN GO HOME!!
MY FATHER GAVE IT TO ME BEFORE I LEFT!
IT WAS HIS COLLEGE RING!!
HIC
COME ON, WAIT!!
...
HELP ME OUT! HE'LL FREEZE TO DEATH!!
?
NGH...

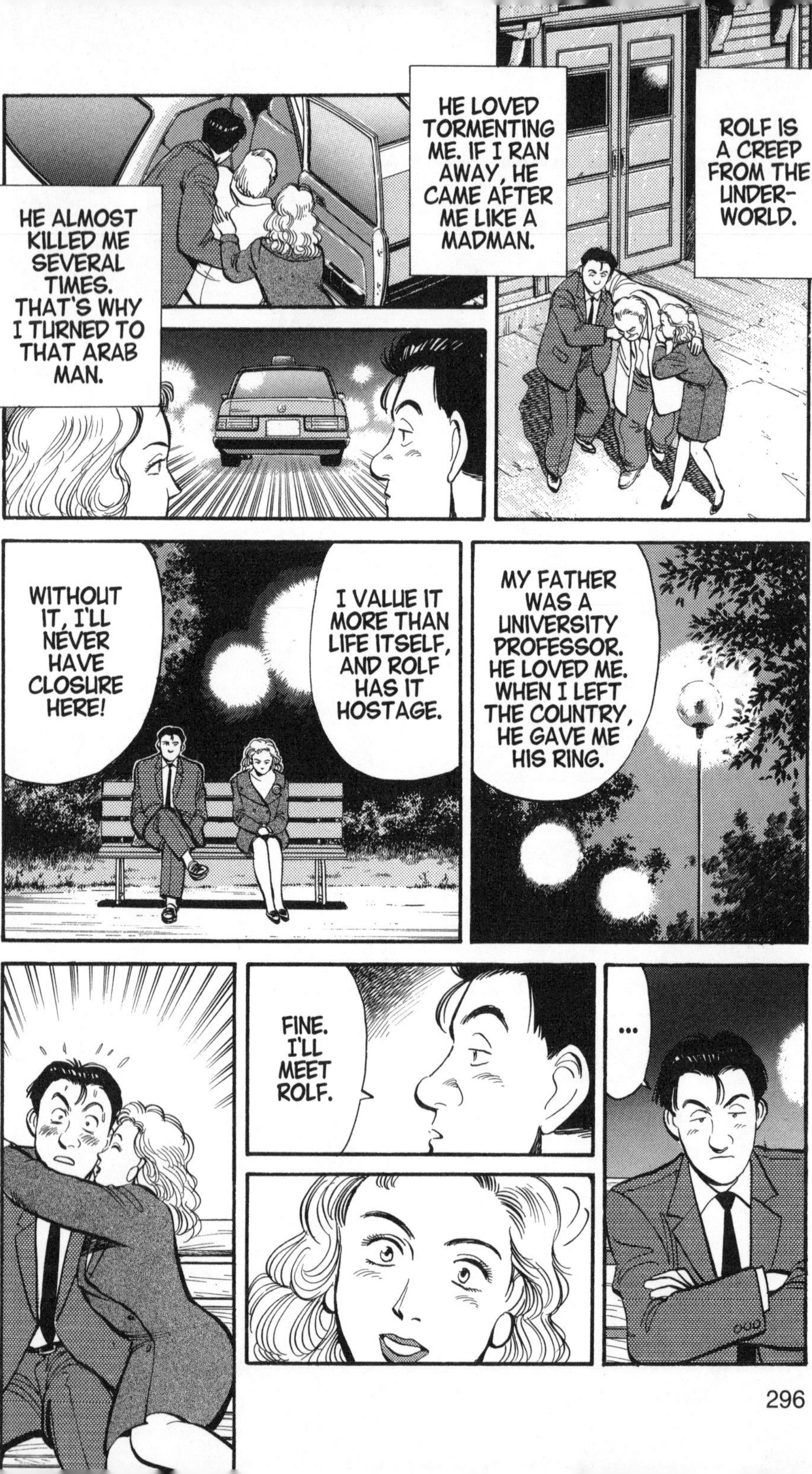
ROLF IS A CREEP FROM THE UNDER-WORLD.
HE LOVED TORMENTING ME. IF I RAN AWAY, HE CAME AFTER ME LIKE A MADMAN.
HE ALMOST KILLED ME SEVERAL TIMES. THAT'S WHY I TURNED TO THAT ARAB MAN.
MY FATHER WAS A UNIVERSITY PROFESSOR. HE LOVED ME. WHEN I LEFT THE COUNTRY, HE GAVE ME HIS RING.
I VALUE IT MORE THAN LIFE ITSELF, AND ROLF HAS IT HOSTAGE.
WITHOUT IT, I'LL NEVER HAVE CLOSURE HERE!
...
FINE. I'LL MEET ROLF.

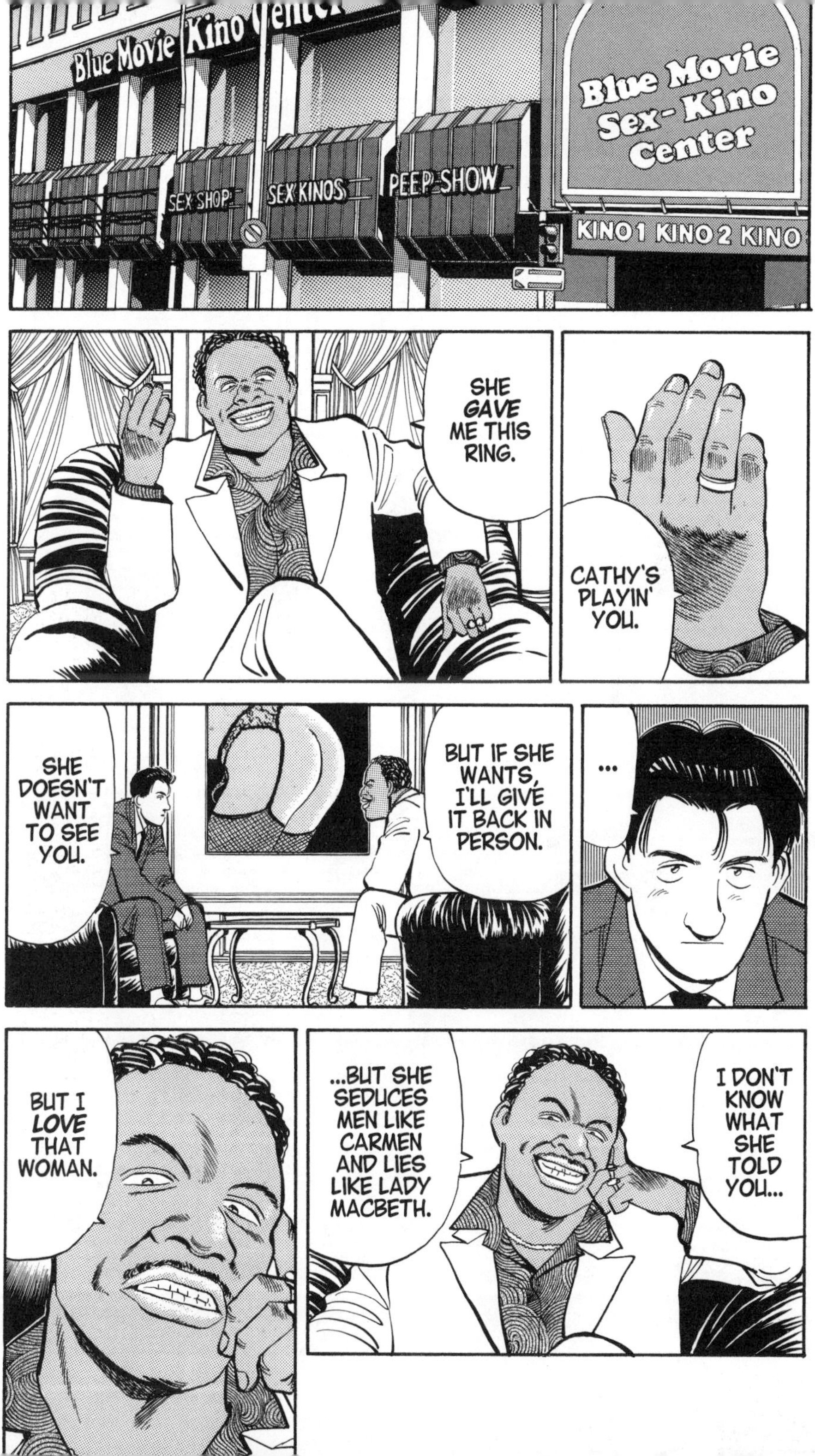
Blue Movie Sex-Kino Center
KINO 1 KINO 2 KINO
Blue Movie Kino Center
PEEP-SHOW
SEX KINOS
SEX SHOP
CATHY'S PLAYIN' YOU.
SHE *GAVE* ME THIS RING.
...
BUT IF SHE WANTS, I'LL GIVE IT BACK IN PERSON.
SHE DOESN'T WANT TO SEE YOU.
I DON'T KNOW WHAT SHE TOLD YOU...
...BUT SHE SEDUCES MEN LIKE CARMEN AND LIES LIKE LADY MACBETH.
BUT I *LOVE* THAT WOMAN.

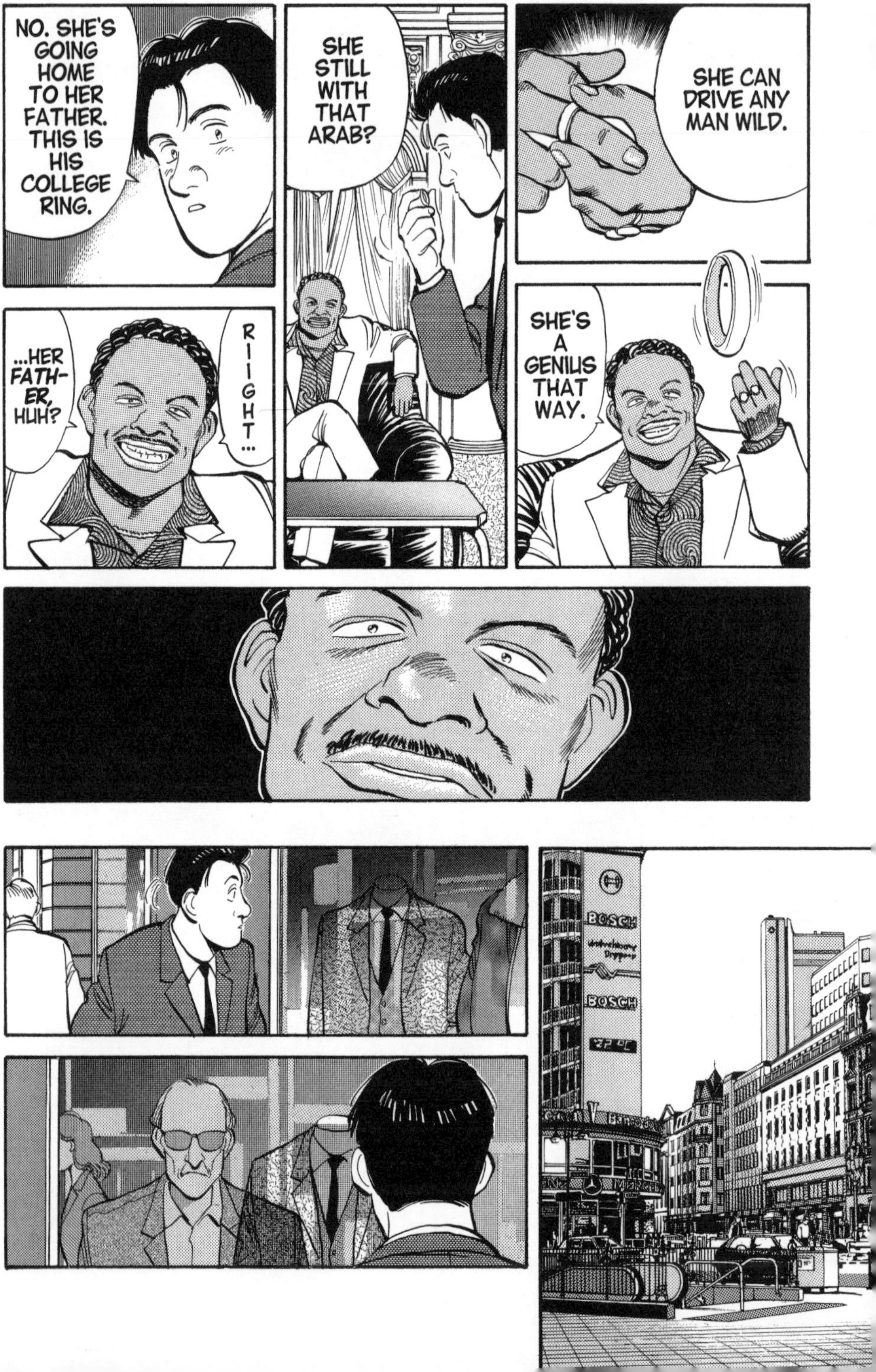
SHE STILL WITH THAT ARAB?
NO. SHE'S GOING HOME TO HER FATHER. THIS IS HIS COLLEGE RING.
...HER FATHER, HUH?
RIIGHT...
SHE CAN DRIVE ANY MAN WILD.
SHE'S A GENIUS THAT WAY.
BOSCH
BOSCH

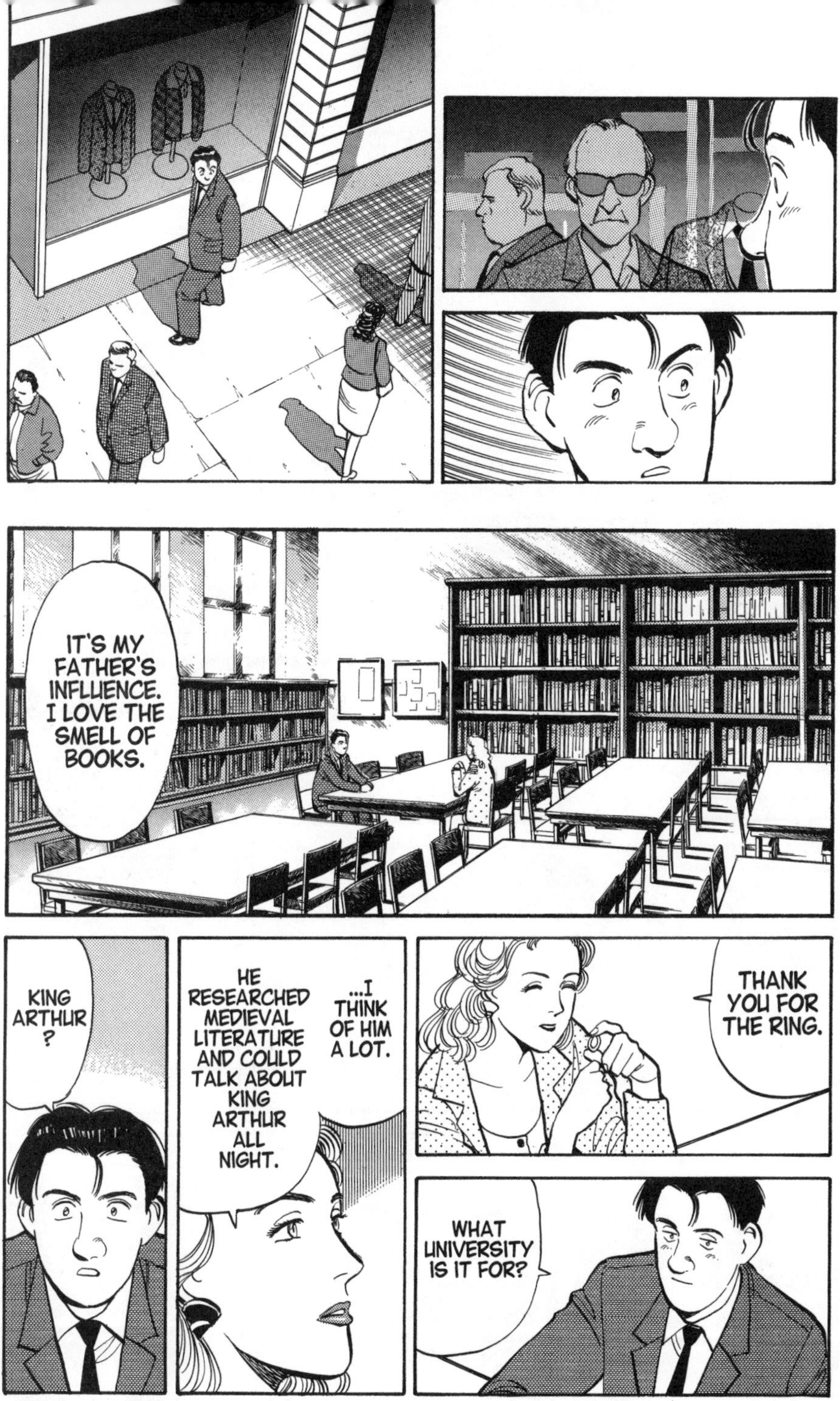
IT'S MY FATHER'S INFLUENCE. I LOVE THE SMELL OF BOOKS.
THANK YOU FOR THE RING.
WHAT UNIVERSITY IS IT FOR?
...I THINK OF HIM A LOT.
HE RESEARCHED MEDIEVAL LITERATURE AND COULD TALK ABOUT KING ARTHUR ALL NIGHT.
KING ARTHUR?

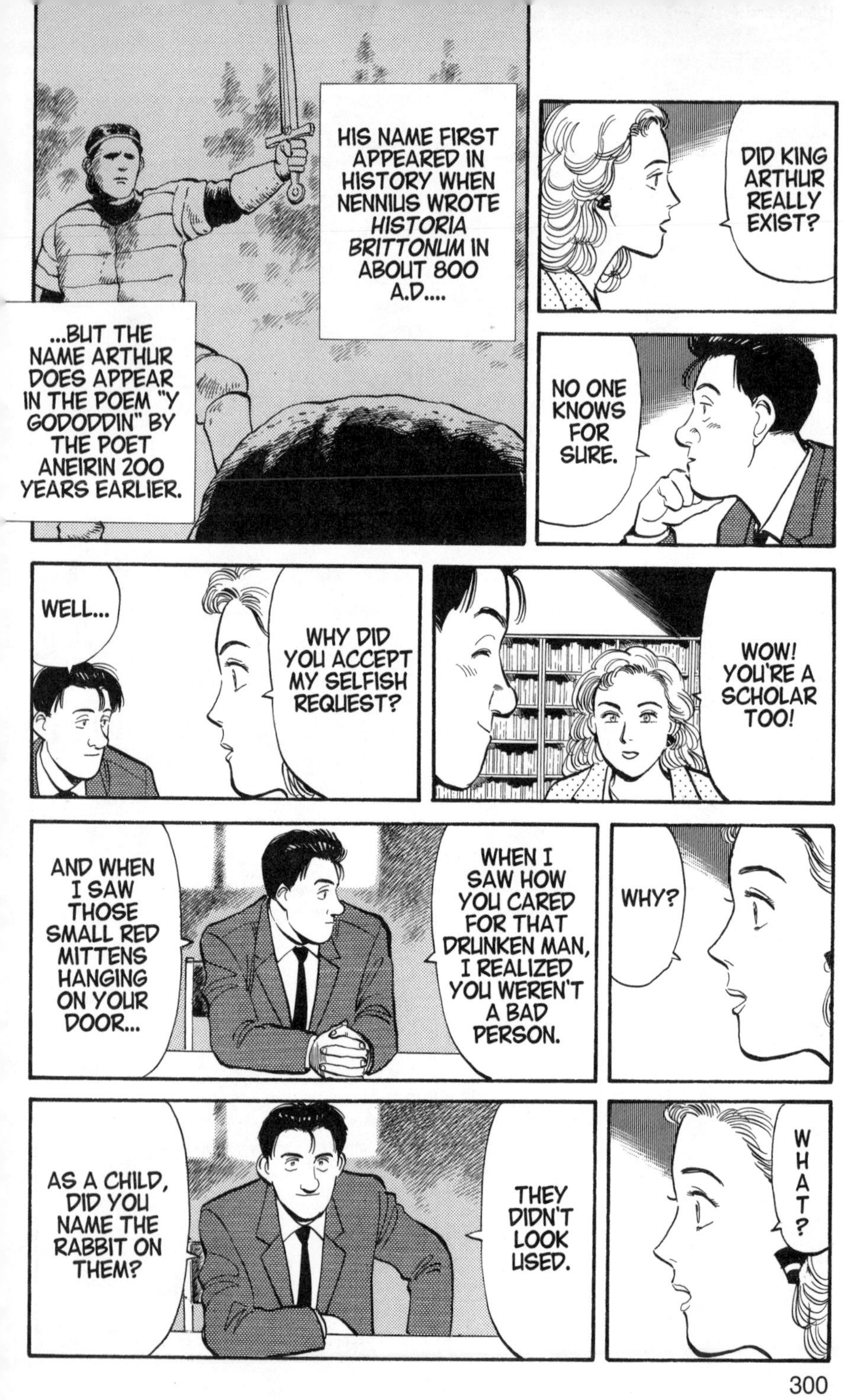
DID KING ARTHUR REALLY EXIST?
NO ONE KNOWS FOR SURE.
HIS NAME FIRST APPEARED IN HISTORY WHEN NENNIUS WROTE HISTORIA BRITTONUM IN ABOUT 800 A.D....
...BUT THE NAME ARTHUR DOES APPEAR IN THE POEM "Y GODODDIN" BY THE POET ANEIRIN 200 YEARS EARLIER.
WOW! YOU'RE A SCHOLAR TOO!
WHY DID YOU ACCEPT MY SELFISH REQUEST?
WELL...
WHY?
WHEN I SAW HOW YOU CARED FOR THAT DRUNKEN MAN, I REALIZED YOU WEREN'T A BAD PERSON.
AND WHEN I SAW THOSE SMALL RED MITTENS HANGING ON YOUR DOOR...
WHAT?
THEY DIDN'T LOOK USED.
AS A CHILD, DID YOU NAME THE RABBIT ON THEM?

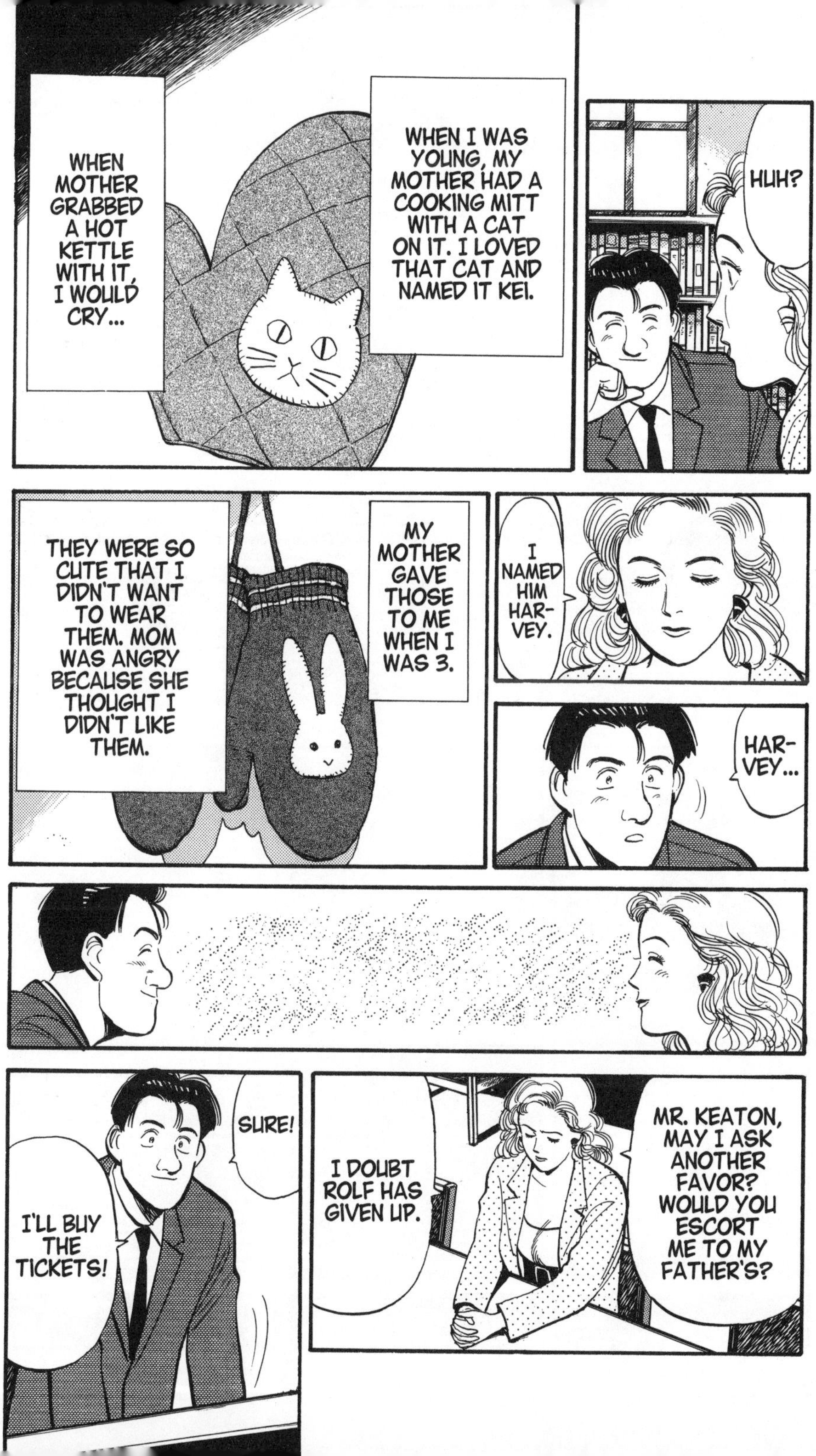
HUH?
WHEN I WAS YOUNG, MY MOTHER HAD A COOKING MITT WITH A CAT ON IT. I LOVED THAT CAT AND NAMED IT KEI.
WHEN MOTHER GRABBED A HOT KETTLE WITH IT, I WOULD CRY...
I NAMED HIM HARVEY.
HARVEY...
MY MOTHER GAVE THOSE TO ME WHEN I WAS 3.
THEY WERE SO CUTE THAT I DIDN'T WANT TO WEAR THEM. MOM WAS ANGRY BECAUSE SHE THOUGHT I DIDN'T LIKE THEM.
MR. KEATON, MAY I ASK ANOTHER FAVOR? WOULD YOU ESCORT ME TO MY FATHER'S?
I DOUBT ROLF HAS GIVEN UP.
SURE!
I'LL BUY THE TICKETS!

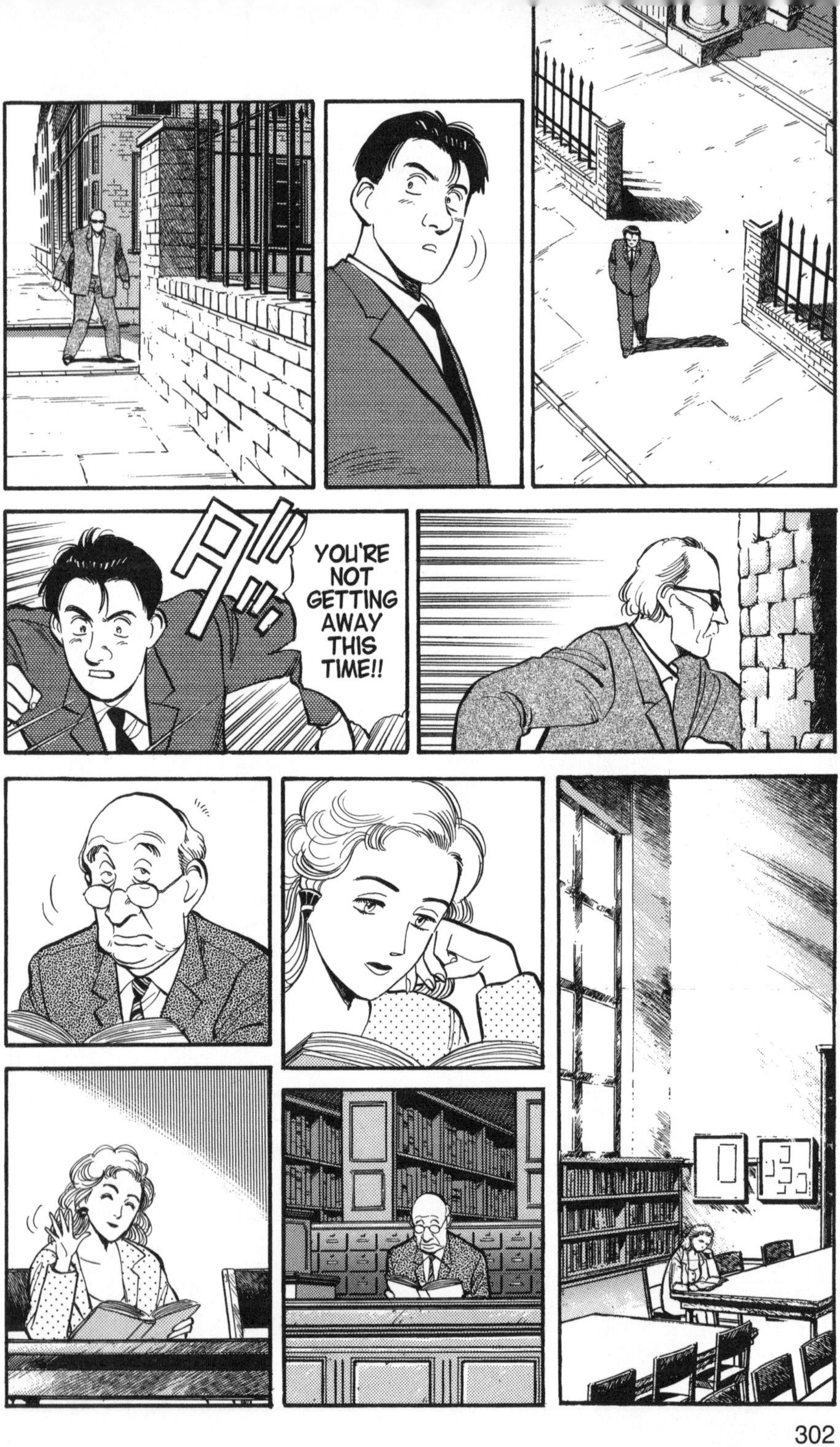
YOU'RE NOT GETTING AWAY THIS TIME!!

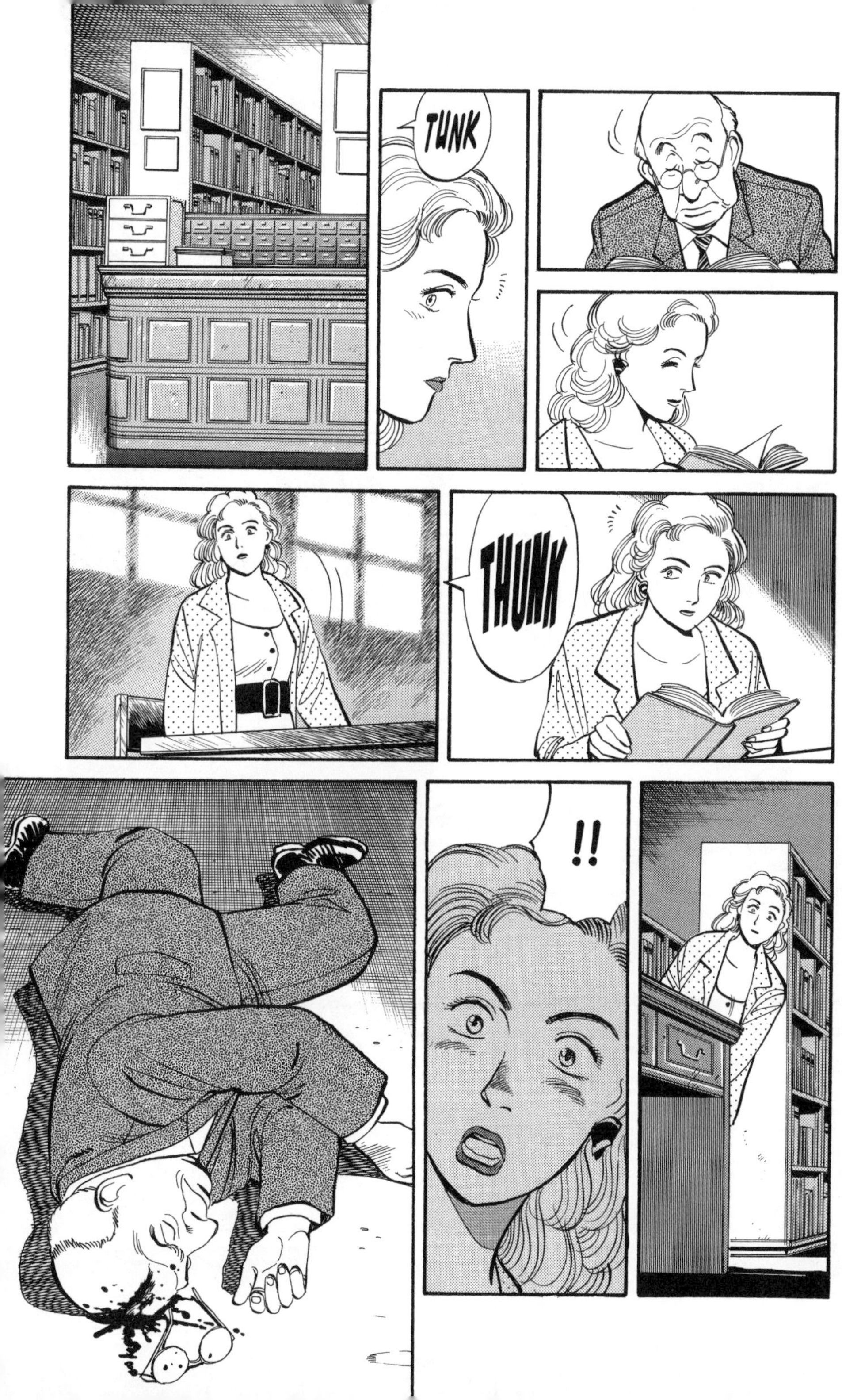
TUNK
THUNK
!!

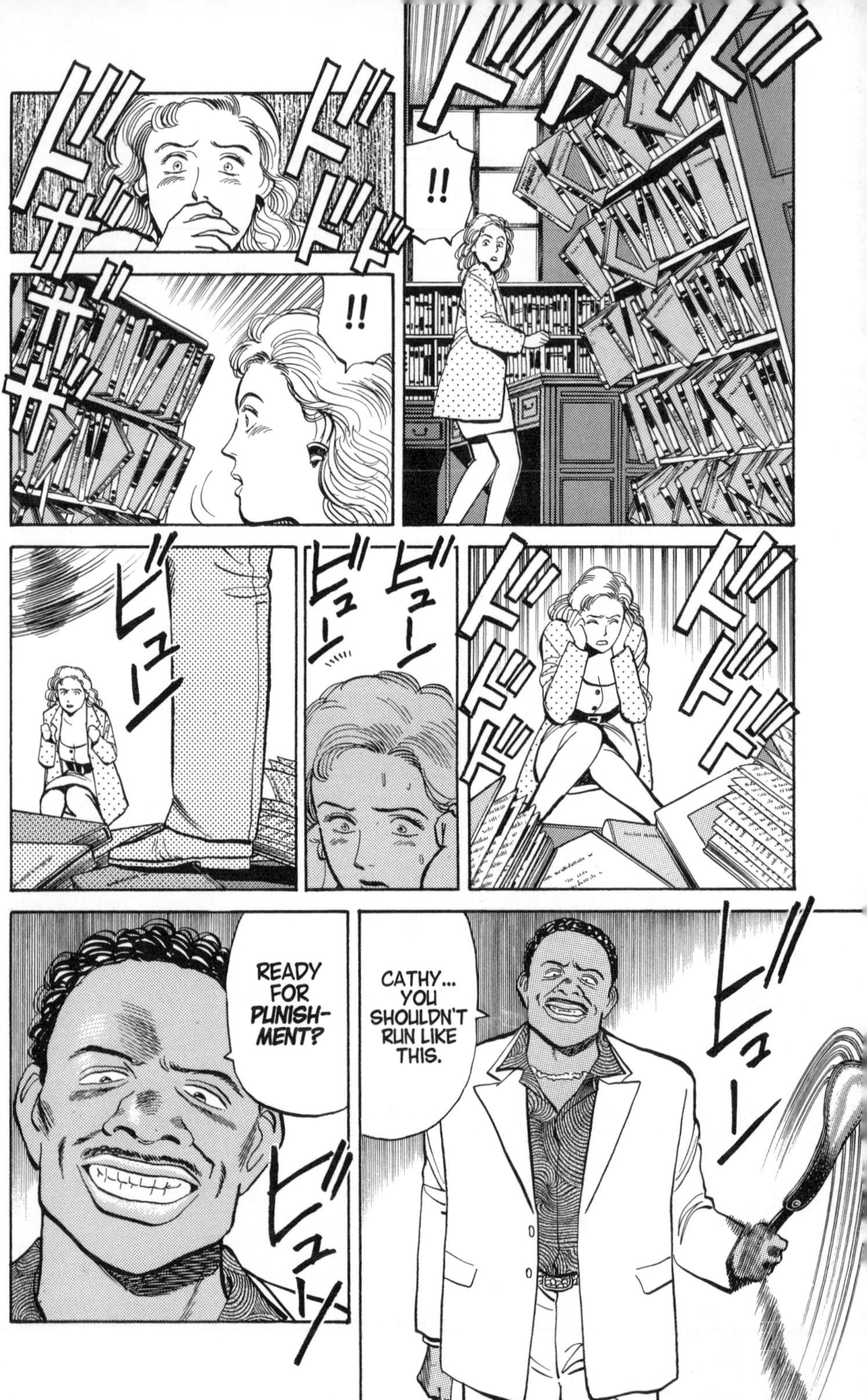

!!
!!
CATHY... YOU SHOULDN'T RUN LIKE THIS.
READY FOR PUNISH-MENT?

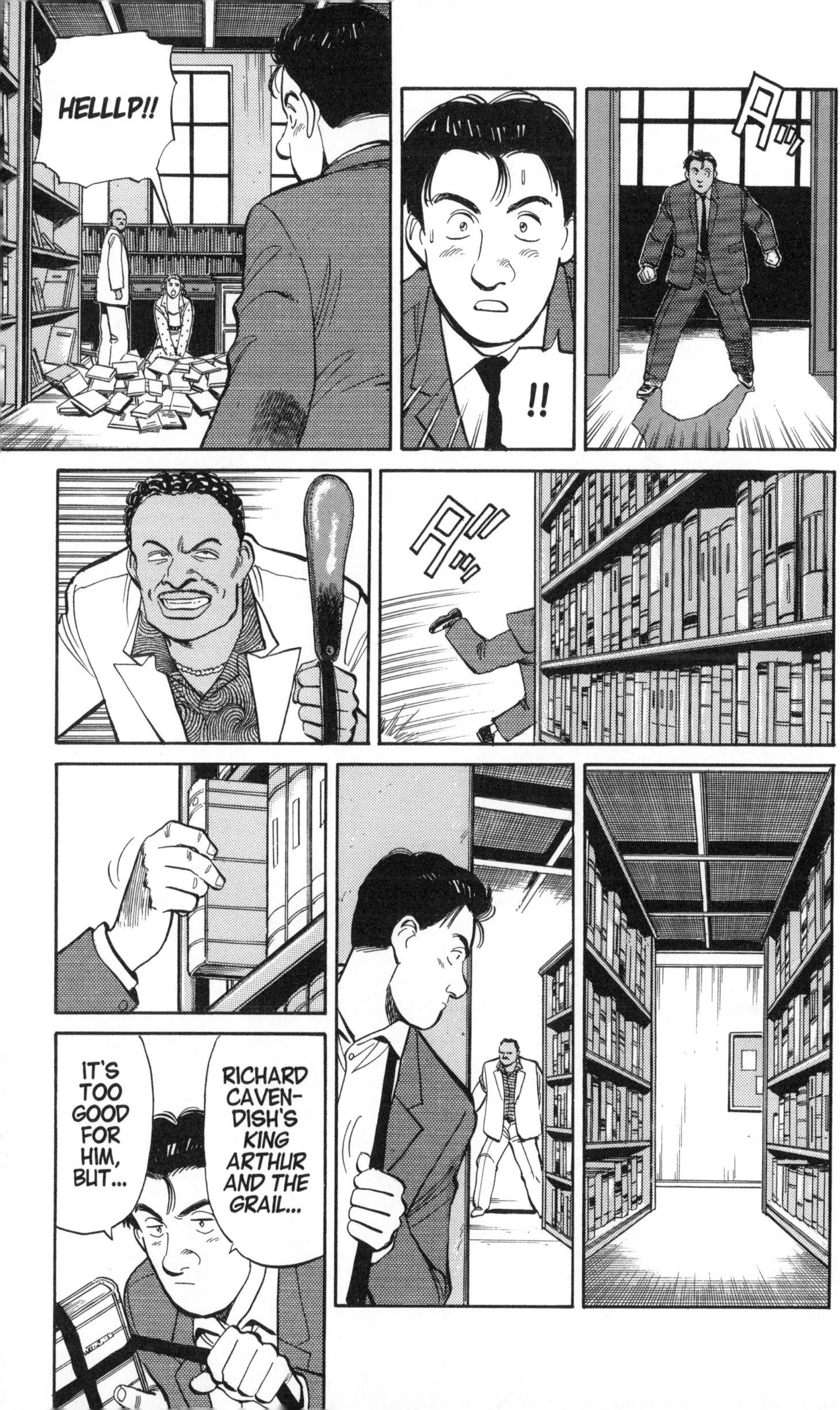
!!
HELLLP!!
RICHARD CAVEN-DISH'S KING ARTHUR AND THE GRAIL...
IT'S TOO GOOD FOR HIM, BUT...

...OH WELL.

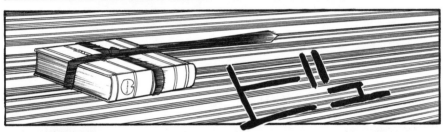

I WAS PURSUING A SUSPICIOUS MAN BUT GREW WORRIED ABOUT YOU AND CAME BACK.

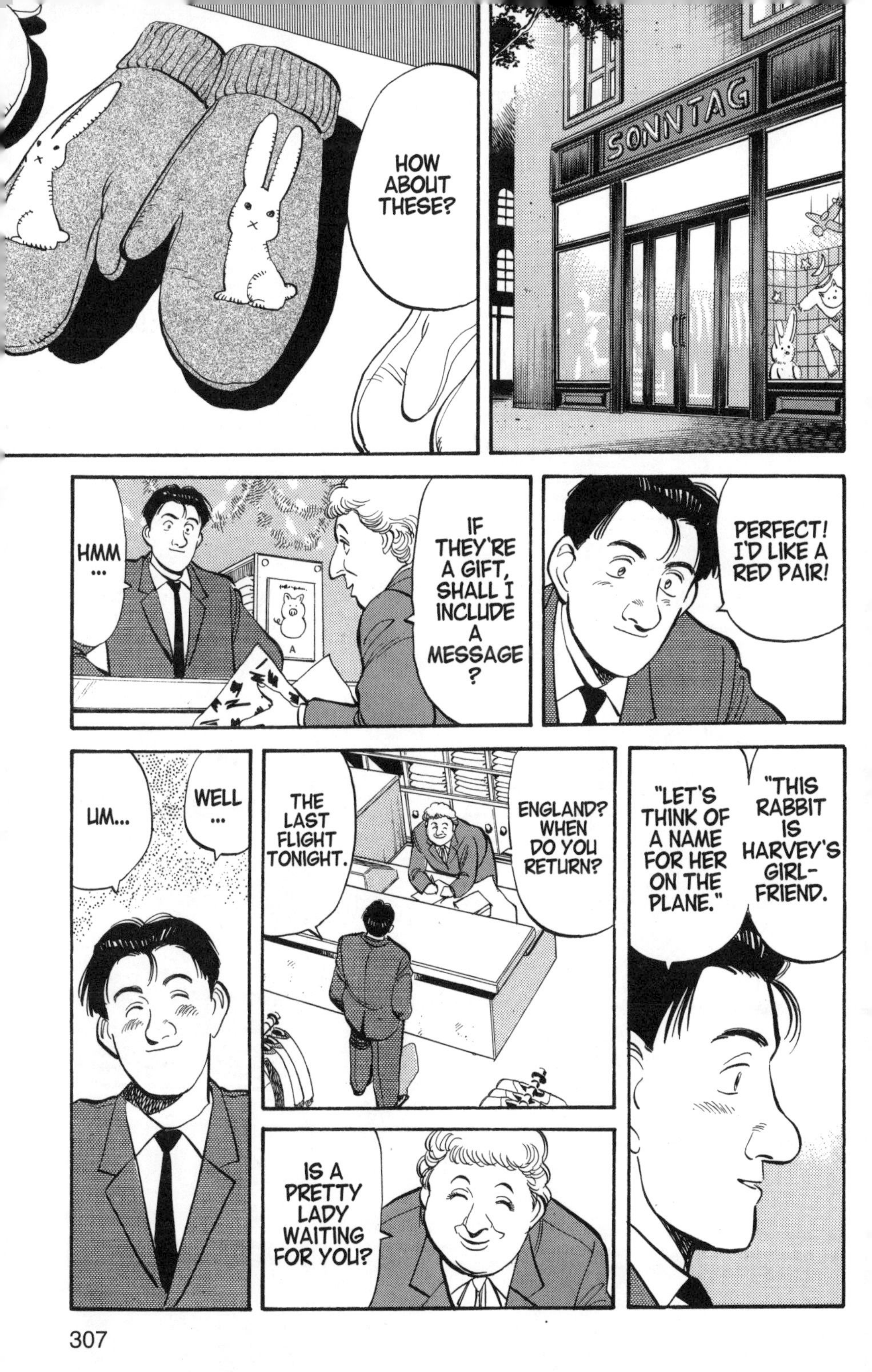
SONNTAG
HOW ABOUT THESE?
PERFECT! I'D LIKE A RED PAIR!
IF THEY'RE A GIFT, SHALL I INCLUDE A MESSAGE?
HMM...
"THIS RABBIT IS HARVEY'S GIRL-FRIEND.
"LET'S THINK OF A NAME FOR HER ON THE PLANE."
ENGLAND? WHEN DO YOU RETURN?
THE LAST FLIGHT TONIGHT.
IS A PRETTY LADY WAITING FOR YOU?
WELL...
UM...

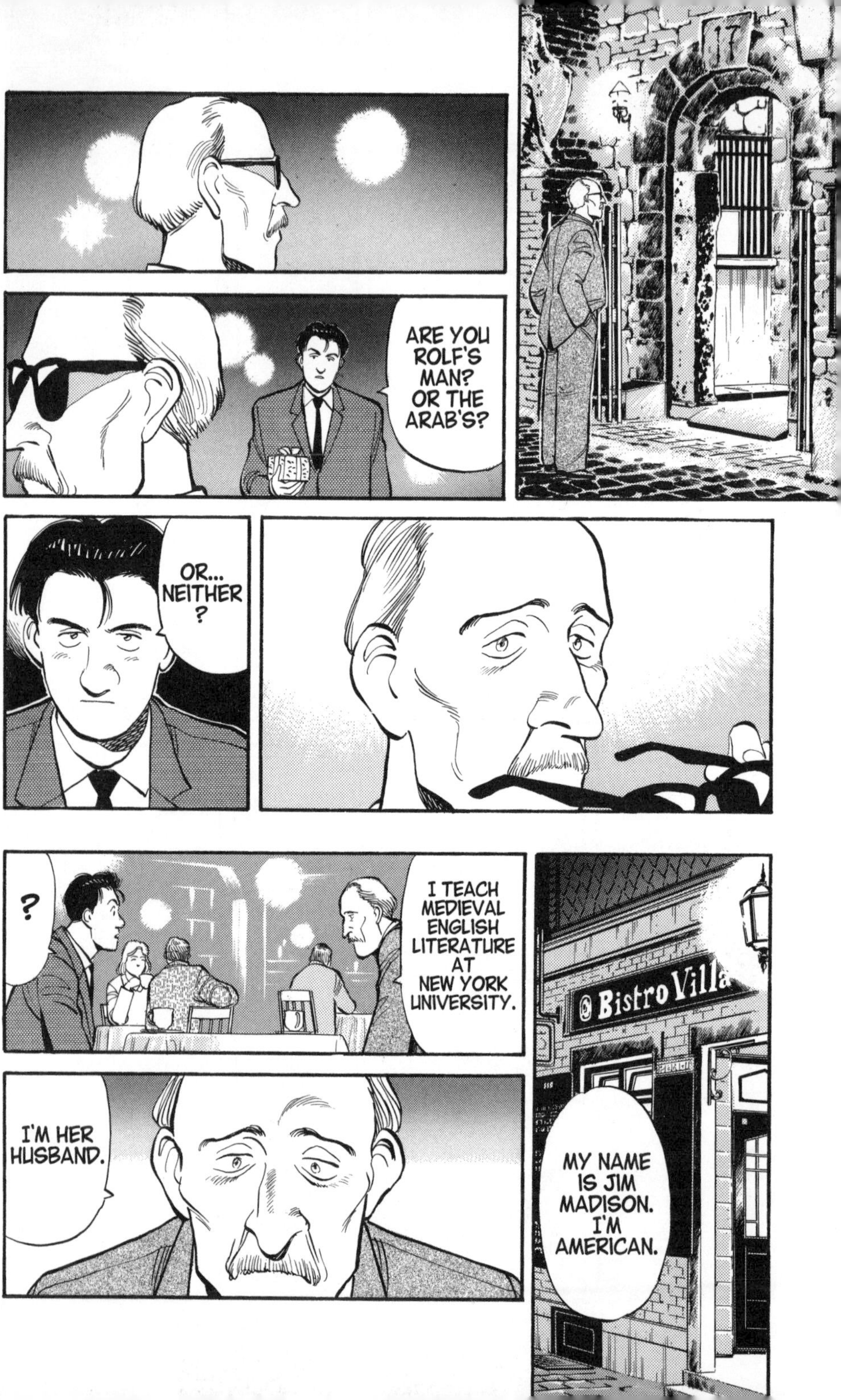
ARE YOU ROLF'S MAN? OR THE ARAB'S?
OR... NEITHER?
Bistro Villa
MY NAME IS JIM MADISON. I'M AMERICAN.
I TEACH MEDIEVAL ENGLISH LITERATURE AT NEW YORK UNIVERSITY.
?
I'M HER HUSBAND.

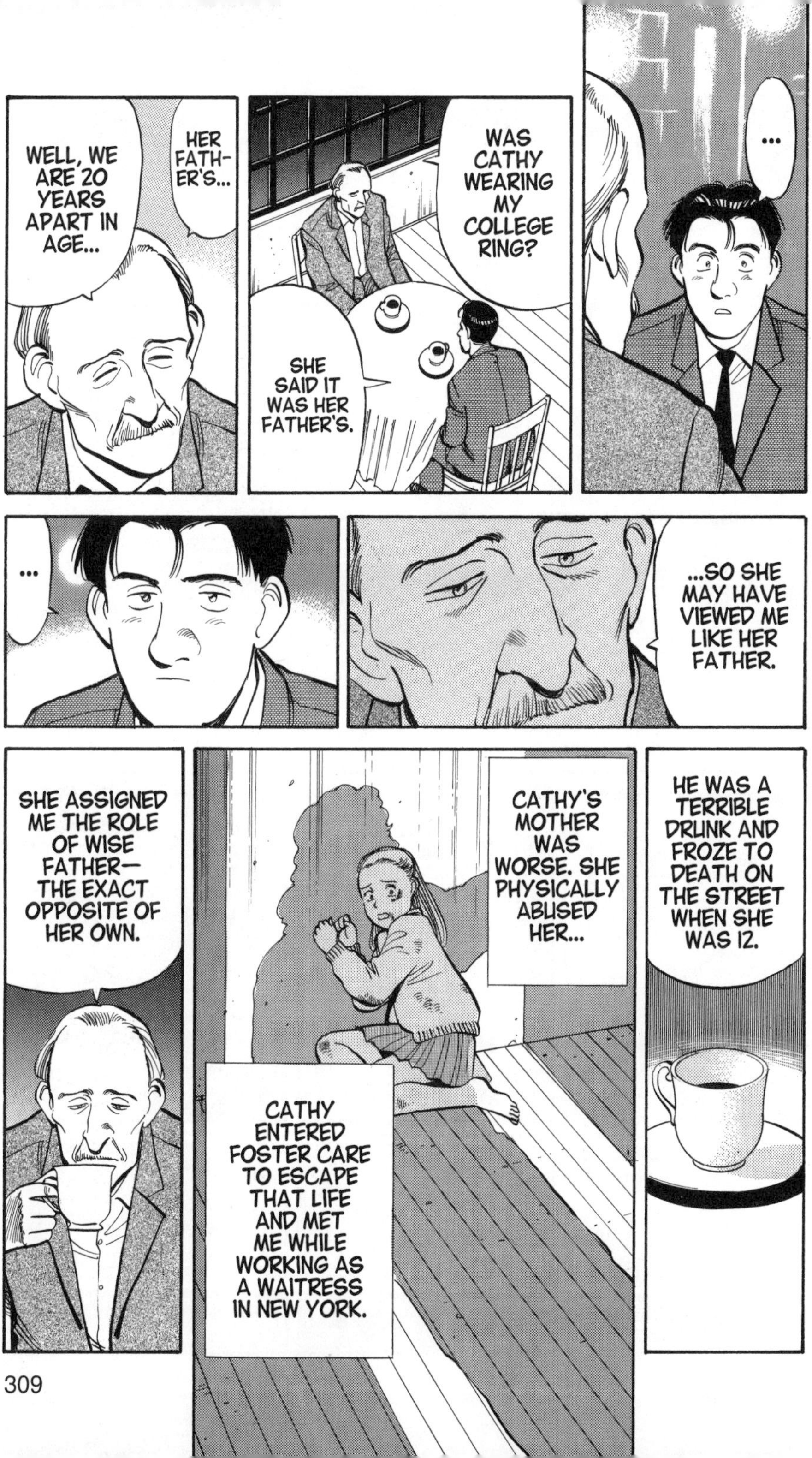
...
WAS CATHY WEARING MY COLLEGE RING?
SHE SAID IT WAS HER FATHER'S.
HER FATHER'S...
WELL, WE ARE 20 YEARS APART IN AGE...
...SO SHE MAY HAVE VIEWED ME LIKE HER FATHER.
...
HE WAS A TERRIBLE DRUNK AND FROZE TO DEATH ON THE STREET WHEN SHE WAS 12.
CATHY'S MOTHER WAS WORSE. SHE PHYSICALLY ABUSED HER...
CATHY ENTERED FOSTER CARE TO ESCAPE THAT LIFE AND MET ME WHILE WORKING AS A WAITRESS IN NEW YORK.
SHE ASSIGNED ME THE ROLE OF WISE FATHER—THE EXACT OPPOSITE OF HER OWN.

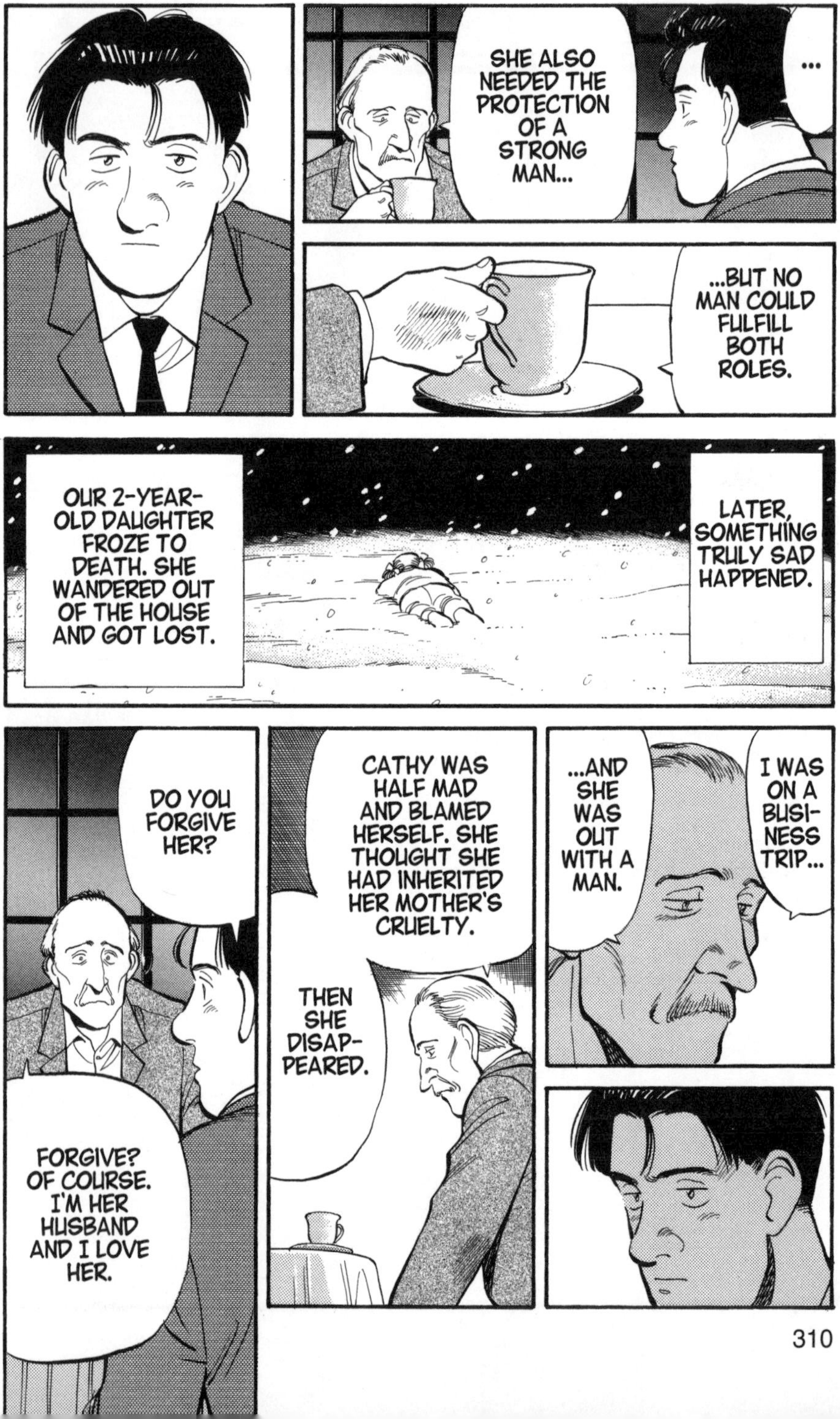
...
SHE ALSO NEEDED THE PROTECTION OF A STRONG MAN...
...BUT NO MAN COULD FULFILL BOTH ROLES.
LATER, SOMETHING TRULY SAD HAPPENED.
OUR 2-YEAR-OLD DAUGHTER FROZE TO DEATH. SHE WANDERED OUT OF THE HOUSE AND GOT LOST.
I WAS ON A BUSINESS TRIP...
...AND SHE WAS OUT WITH A MAN.
CATHY WAS HALF MAD AND BLAMED HERSELF. SHE THOUGHT SHE HAD INHERITED HER MOTHER'S CRUELTY.
THEN SHE DISAPPEARED.
DO YOU FORGIVE HER?
FORGIVE? OF COURSE. I'M HER HUSBAND AND I LOVE HER.

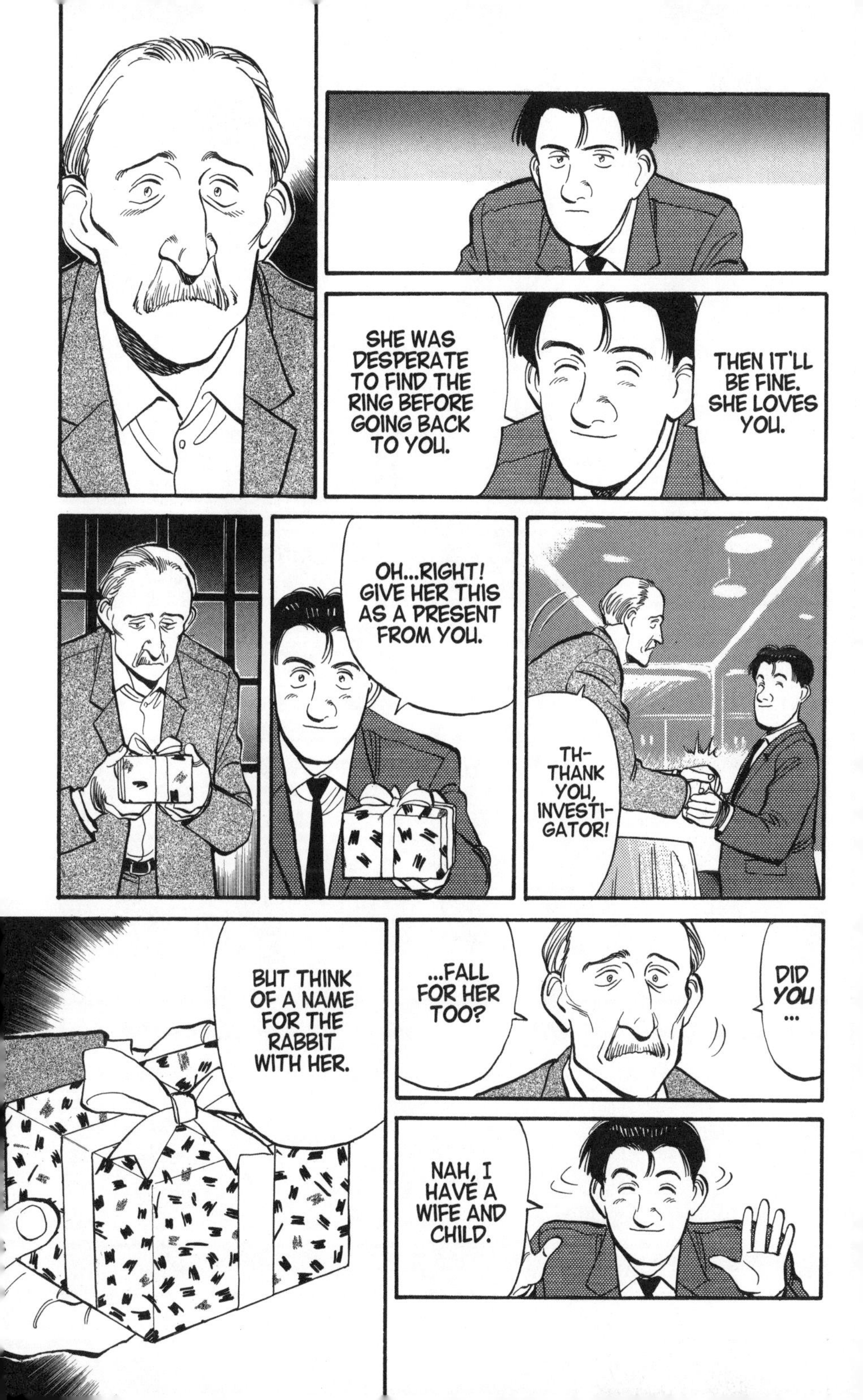
THEN IT'LL BE FINE. SHE LOVES YOU.
SHE WAS DESPERATE TO FIND THE RING BEFORE GOING BACK TO YOU.
TH-THANK YOU, INVESTIGATOR!
OH...RIGHT! GIVE HER THIS AS A PRESENT FROM YOU.
DID YOU ...
...FALL FOR HER TOO?
NAH, I HAVE A WIFE AND CHILD.
BUT THINK OF A NAME FOR THE RABBIT WITH HER.

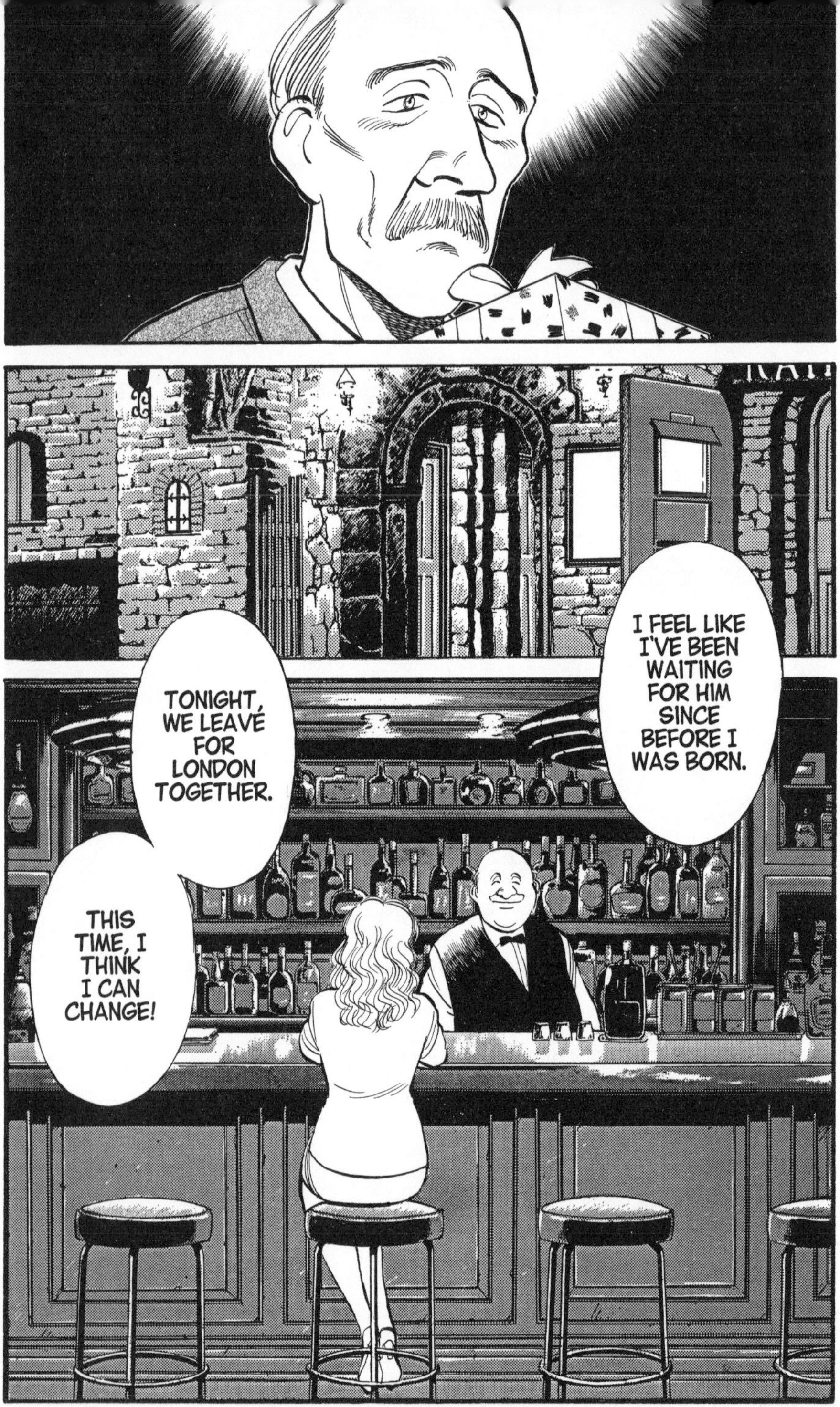
I FEEL LIKE I'VE BEEN WAITING FOR HIM SINCE BEFORE I WAS BORN.
TONIGHT, WE LEAVE FOR LONDON TOGETHER.
THIS TIME, I THINK I CAN CHANGE!

*Master Keaton 2 —The End—*

# Sound Effects Glossary

he sound effects in *Master Keaton* have been preserved in their original Japanese format. To avoid additional lettering cluttering up the panels, a list of the sound effects (FX) is provided here. Each FX is listed by page and panel number. For example, "5.5" means the FX is on page 5, panel 5.

---

7.5 – tmp tmp tmp (ka ka ka: footsteps)

9.1 – clap clap clap clap clap (pachi pachi pachi pachi: clapping)

9.2 – clap clap clap clap clap clap clap clap clap clap clap clap clap clap clap clap clap clap clap clap clap (pachi pachi pachi pachi pachi pachi pachi pachi pachi pachi pachi pachi pachi pachi pachi pachi pachi pachi pachi: clapping)

9.3 – clap clap clap (pachi pachi pachi: clapping)

9.4 – clap clap clap clap clap (pachi pachi pachi pachi pachi: clapping)

9.9 – clap clap clap clap clap clap clap clap clap clap clap clap clap clap (pachi pachi pachi pachi pachi pachi pachi pachi pachi pachi pachi: clapping)

?.3 – kchak (gacha: door opening)

?.1 – fwap (basa: slapping papers)

?.7 – slam (batan: door closing)

?.4 – vrrr vrr (guon guon: machinery)

?.5 – vrr vrr vrr (guon guon guon: machinery)

?.1 – vrrr vrr (guon guon: machinery)

?.2 – fwip (basa: raising newspaper)

?.4 – vrrr vrr (guon guon: machinery)

?.6 – clomp (da: leaving)

?.1 – boom (don: explosion)

?.2 – bang (dan: bullet striking)

?.4 – poom (bon: grenade detonating)

?.5 – tromp (da: storming in)

?.6 – tik tok tik tok tik (chi chi chi chi chi: watch)

?.7 – boom blam wham (bon don dodon: simulation folding)

?.4-5 – vrr vrr vrr (guon guon guon: machinery)

?.2 – clomp clomp (za za: footsteps)

?.3 – clomp (da: footstep)

?.4 – ta tmp (dada: footsteps)

?.8-9 – krash (gashaan: wall breaking)

?.4 – blam (don: shooting)

?.5 – bang bang (ban gan: bullets striking)

?.6 – hwip (hyun: tossing grenade)

?.7 – poom (bon: grenade detonating)

5.1 – baboom wham bang (dodon bon don: raid folding)

5.4 – kchak (gacha: door opening)

?.1 – fwup (basa: tossing newspaper)

?.2 – yank (gi: pulling door)

?.3 – tonk (ga: blocking door)

?.4 – rattle rattle (gacha gacha: trying to open door)

?.8 – slam (ban: doors closing)

?.7 – revvv (garyuryuryu: starting engine)

?.8 – vroom (baon: car)

?.9 – whsh (da: running)

?.4 – klak klak (gakon gakon: train)

?.9 – klak klak (gakon gakon: train)

?.6 – heh heh heh heh (ku ku ku ku: laughter)

5.6 – vroom (vuooo: car)

?.1 – vrooosh (vuooooo: driving past)

?.2-3 – screech (kikii: car stopping)

7.1 – swf swf (shu shu: air boxing)

7.1 – tmp tmp (ton ton: moving legs)

7.2 – swf swf (shu shu: air boxing)

7.7 – whok (ga: kicking)

5.5 – tmp tmp tmp tmp (ta ta ta ta: footsteps)

6.1 – clomp (da: stepping out)

6.5 – grab (ga: grabbing)

6.6 – whsh (da: running away)

7.2 – whsh (da: running)

7.8 – wham (ban: bag hitting)

7.9 – hwsh (byun: running away)

13.3 – kchak (batan: door closing)

19.6 – whsh (da: running)

20.8 – whsh (da: running)

21.2 – fwsh (bun: flying)

21.3 – whup (ga: wrapping)

21.4 – fwud (zudaan: falling)

21.5 – whsh (da: running out)

21.6 – grab (ga: apprehending)

36.4 – clomp clomp (ka ka: footsteps)

36.5 – clomp clomp (ka ka: footsteps)

43.6 – gulp (gui: drinking)

45.5 – hwsh (da: ducking back)

47.5 – wham (doka: kicking)

47.6 – wham wham (doka doka: kicking)

47.7 – bwam (baan: kicking open)

48.6 – tmp tmp (ka ka: footsteps)

49.4 – fwsh (hyun: flying)

52.2 – clasp (ga: taking Keaton's hand)

54.1 – bzzz (buun: fly buzzing)

55.2 – bzzz bzzz (buun buun: fly buzzing)

55.6 – twitch twitch (buru burun: twitching)

61.1 – fwip (basa: turning page)

62.1 – blam (don: shooting)

62.2 – zinnng (kyuuuun: bullet flying)

62.3 – zinnng (dogyuuuun: bullet flying)

62.6 – hawooooo (uoooooon: a wolf-like howl)

65.6 – slash (za: scratching)

66.2 – shut (batan: door closing)

69.8 – snatch (basa: taking the newspaper)

70.1 – whsh (da: rushing to leave)

70.2 – slam (batan: door closing)

71.4 – gasp gasp gasp (hiku hiku hiku: choking)

71.5 – whak (ga: hitting)

71.6 – crash (gashan: breaking)

78.1 – kchak (batamu: door closing)

80.4 – fwash (pasha: camera)

81.1 – clik (pasha: camera)

88.2 – tak (ka: footstep)

95.6 – kchak (batamu: door closing)

96.3 – tmp tmp (za za: footsteps)

97.4 – kchak (gacha: door opening)

105.8 – chonk (dan: cutting)

106.1 – grawr grawr (guwau guwau: growling)

108.1 – pat pat (ban ban: dusting off)

110.1 – chak chak (gata gata: taking seats)

116.5 – kchak (gacha: door opening)

116.6 – clomp clomp clomp clomp (ka ka ka ka: footsteps)

116.7 – shluf shluf (zoro zoro: filing in)

117.2, 117.3 – nok nok (kon kon: knocking)

117.4-5 – zwip (shaa: extending measure)

120.4 – rrring (jiriririririririri: bell ringing)

127.2 – murmur murmur murmur murmur (zawa zawa zawa: talking)

254.1 – hwip (hyun: throwing knife)
254.2 – shnk (dosu: stabbing)
255.5 – shwip (sha: raising arm)
256.1 – hwuk (hyu: lopping off a finger)
256.3 – thonk (ga: hitting)
256.4 – fwud (do: falling)
257.1 – twang twang twang (buun buun buun: string vibrating)
257.2 – whsh (da: running)
257.3 – twang twang twang (buun buun buun: string vibrating)
257.4 – twang twang (buun buun: string vibrating)
257.6 – twang twang (buun buun: string vibrating)
257.7-9 – twang twang twang (buun buun buun: string vibrating)
258.1 – twang (buun: string vibrating)
258.1 – tok tok tok tok (gara gara kan kon: rocks falling)
258.1-3 – twang twang (buun buun: string vibrating)
258.6 – tok tok tok tok (gara gara kan kara: rocks falling)
258.6-7 – twang (buun: string vibrating)
258.9 – whsh (da: rushing forward)
258.10 – krunk (gura: breaking free)
259.1 – boosh (ba: water rushing)
259.3 – slosh (zaa: flood)
265.1-2 – vroom honk vroom (buoon papaa guoon: traffic)
265.2-3 – honnnk (papaaan: car horn)
270.7 – whsh (da: running)
271.1 – tmp tmp tmp tmp (ta ta ta ta: footsteps)
271.4 – whoosh (da: fast movement)
271.5 – bwap (ban: slamming down briefcase)
276.3 – chatter chatter (zawa zawa: talking)
277.1 – zwoosh (shaa: bicycle)
277.3 – zwoosh (shaa: bicycle)
282.2 – whoosh (da: fast movement)
285.8 – tunk (gashan: throwing away briefcase)
288.7 – klatter (gatan: standing suddenly)
289.3 – murmur murmur (zawa zawa: talking)
290.1 – vroom (buon: car)
292.2 – stomp stomp (ka ka: footsteps)
292.3 – bam (ban: door flying open)
293.2 – stomp stomp (ka ka: footsteps)
293.3 – whunk (ga: taking gun)
293.7 – slam (batan: slamming door)
294.6 – stomp stomp (ka ka: footsteps)
294.7 – stomp stomp (ka ka: footsteps)
302.5 – dash (da: running)
304.1 – thruk thruk (dododo: bookshelf falling)
304.2 – thud (dododo: books falling)
304.2-3 – thrrunk (dozazaza: bookshelf falling)
304.4 – thud thud (dodododo: books falling)
304.5 – thwsh thwsh (byun byun: swinging blackjack)
304.6 – thwsh (byun: swinging blackjack)
304.7 – thwsh (byun: swinging blackjack)
304.8 – thwsh (byun: swinging blackjack)
305.1 – tmp (ta: appearing)
305.4 – hwsh (da: hiding)
306.3 – bwsh (byu: flying)
306.5 – thonk (gan: hitting)

177.9 – whsh (da: quick movement)
178.2 – fwam (doon: falling)
181.6 – kchak (kacha: door opening)
181.7 – shmp (kacha: door closing)
181.8 – vroom (vuoon: car)
181.9 – vroom (buoon: car)
182.1 – vroosh (buoon: car leaving)
187.2 – tmp tmp (ka ka: footsteps)
187.6 – wobble (gura: briefcase falling)
187.7 – kch (ga: catching)
189.4 – zshh (zaan: waves)
189.7 – zshh (zaan: waves)
191.8 – mumble mumble (butsu butsu: talking softly)
199.1 – fweee (hyuu: firework rising)
199.2 – poom (don: firework exploding)
206.1 – zshh (zaan: waves)
206.2 – zshh (zaan: waves)
206.5 – boom (don: bomb exploding)
207.1 – vup (ba: waking up)
208.2 – crik crik (gi gi: swing creaking)
212.6 – whmp (don: pounding fist)
213.4 – vroom (baban: car)
214.1 – woof woof (wan wan: dogs barking)
214.1 – meeeow (naao: cat meowing)
214.1 – woof woof (uon uon: dogs barking)
214.2 – woof woof (wan wan: dogs barking)
214.3 – grr (guau: dog growling)
214.3 – whimper whimper (kuun kuun: dogs whining)
214.7 – yowl (gyaa: cat yowling)
214.7 – woof woof (wan wan: dogs barking)
215.3 – vroom (baban: car)
216.1 – screech (kikii: stopping suddenly)
216.2 – whup (gakun: leaning forward)
219.2 – pumf (ban: slamming down pillow)
223.5 – bing (bin: leash tightening)
223.7 – tug (zuzuzu: pulling at leash)
232.4 – fwsh (ta: hurrying)
233.5 – whsh (da: running)
233.6 – thnk (ka: tripping)
233.7 – fwud (bitan: falling)
236.5 – tmp (za: footstep)
238.4 – blam blam (gaan gaan: gunshots)
239.2 – clomp (za: footstep)
239.3 – clomp (za: footstep)
239.4 – clomp (za: footstep)
240.6 – splosh (zabu: splashing)
244.4 – swip (su: moving)
245.6 – blam (dokyuun: gunshot)
246.6 – crik crik (gishi gishi: branch creaking)
246.7 – wobble (gura: wobbling)
246.8 – tomp (da: jumping off)
246.9 – tok tok tok (kan kan gara: rocks falling)
247.3 – tok tatok (kaan kakoon: rock echoes)
247.7 – szzz (jiji: sizzling)
249.3 – whsh (da: chasing)
249.4 – tromp tromp (za zaza: running)
249.9 – thwip (hyu: shooting)
250.1 – zing (byun: flying past)
250.2 – whok (ga: rock striking)
250.3 – blam (don: gunshot)
251.1 – tmp tmp (za za: footsteps)
251.2 – tmp (za: footstep)
252.8 – shump (zaza: dragging himself)
252.9 – tok tok tok (gara gara kan: rocks falling)
252.10 – tok tatok tok tok (kan kakoon koon kaan: ro[ck] falling)
253.1 – tok tatok tok tok (kaan kakoon kaan koon: r[ock] echoes)

# MASTER KEATON: THE PERFECT EDITION
## Volume 2
### VIZ Signature Edition

by NAOKI URASAWA
Story by HOKUSEI KATSUSHIKA, TAKASHI NAGASAKI

Translation & English Adaptation/John Werry
Lettering/Steve Dutro
Cover & Interior Design/Yukiko Whitley
Editor/Amy Yu

MASTER KEATON Vol.2
by Naoki URASAWA, Hokusei KATSUSHIKA, Takashi NAGASAKI
© 1989 Naoki URASAWA/Studio Nuts, Hokusei KATSUSHIKA, Takashi NAGASAKI
All rights reserved.
Original Japanese edition published by SHOGAKUKAN.
English translation rights in the United States of America, Canada, United Kingdom,
Ireland, Australia and New Zealand arranged with SHOGAKUKAN.
Original Art Direction by Kazuo UMINO
Original cover design by Mikiyo KOBAYASHI + Bay Bridge Studio

Published by VIZ Media, LLC
P.O. Box 77010
San Francisco, CA 94107

10 9 8 7 6 5 4 3 2 1
First printing, March 2015

PARENTAL ADVISORY
MASTER KEATON is rated T+ and is
recommended for ages 16 and up. This volume
contains brief nudity and scenes of violence.
ratings.viz.com

www.viz.com

VIZ SIGNATURE

JUL 10/24